T0304708

ROUTLEDGE HANDBOOK OF MACROECONOMIC METHODOLOGY

The present macroeconomic crisis has demonstrated that a deeper understanding of the importance of relevant macroeconomic theories and methods is wanting. Additionally, lack of methodological awareness is behind much of the disagreement within macroeconomics which, looked upon from outside, often appears incomprehensible.

The Handbook gives a structured presentation of the study of principles and procedures by which macroeconomics is researched, taught and communicated both within academia and to a wider audience, and why specific theories, research strategies and teaching are preferred. The principles of selecting theory relevant to real-world problems are the core of methodology. This book contains a broad range of arguments behind theory construction and appraisal and the consequences of these choices within the field of macroeconomics.

An international range of experts provide clear analysis of key concepts, ideas and principles to give academics, students and others a better understanding of the macroeconomics behind policy conclusions which are put forward at different levels.

Jesper Jespersen is professor emeritus at Roskilde University, Denmark. His research interests include the economics of Keynes and macroeconomic methodology.

Victoria Chick is professor emeritus at University College London, UK. She has written extensively on macroeconomics and the economics of Keynes.

Bert Tieben is researcher at SEO Amsterdam Economics, the Netherlands. He also teaches history of economic thought at Amsterdam University College. His research focuses on economic methodology and the history of economic thought.

ROUTLEDGE HANDBOOK OF MACROECONOMIC METHODOLOGY

Edited by
Jesper Jespersen, Victoria Chick and Bert Tieben

LONDON AND NEW YORK

Designed cover image: © Gremlin / Getty Images

First published 2023
by Routledge
4 Park Square, Milton Park, Abingdon, Oxon OX14 4RN

and by Routledge
605 Third Avenue, New York, NY 10158

Routledge is an imprint of the Taylor & Francis Group, an informa business

British Library Cataloguing-in-Publication Data
A catalogue record for this book is available from the British Library

ISBN: 978-1-138-81662-6 (hbk)
ISBN: 978-1-032-46349-0 (pbk)
ISBN: 978-1-315-74599-2 (ebk)

DOI: 10.4324/9781315745992

Typeset in Times New Roman
by codeMantra

In memoriam, Victoria Chick, 1936–2023

CONTENTS

Contents

ILLUSTRATIONS

Figures

Tables

CONTRIBUTORS

Alan Freeman is researcher attached to the University of Manitoba, Canada. He is a retired but research-active cultural economist. His has published many books and articles on economics and politics.

Alessandro Vercelli is professor (em), University of Siena, Italy. He writes on sustainability, finance and macroeconomics.

Andy Denis, PhD, FRSA, is fellow emeritus in the Department of Economics at City, University of London. His research interests are in the history and philosophy of economics, in particular, collective and individual rationality in the history of economic thought.

Arjo Klamer is professor(em) at Vrije Universiteit, the Netherlands. His research interests include cultural economics and the value-based approach to economics.

Bert Tieben is researcher at SEO Amsterdam Economics, the Netherlands. He also teaches history of economic thought at Amsterdam University College. His research focuses on economic methodology and the history of economic thought.

Claude Gnos is emeritus professor at the Université de Bourgogne in France. His research areas are monetary macroeconomics, circuit theory and the history of economic thought.

J. Daniel Hammond is Hultquist Family Professor of Economics, Emeritus, at Wake Forest University, USA. He has written extensively on Milton Friedman and the history of the Chicago School of Economics, and various other topics in the history of economic thought.

Finn Olesen is professor in macroeconomics at Aalborg University, Business School in Denmark. He is the Head of Research of the Macroeconomic Group. He has done research within the fields of macroeconomics, Post-Keynesianism, history of economic thought and methodology.

Frank A. G. den Butter is professor (em), Vrije Universiteit, the Netherlands. He writes on macroeconomic policy, the history of macroeconomic thought and the use of macroeconomic models in economics.

Geoff Tily, PhD is an economist at the Trades Union Congress, UK. His research interests include economic policy and Economic and labour market analysis.

Henning Bunzel is retired associate professor at the Department of Economics and Business Economics, Aarhus University, Denmark. His research interests include statistical computation and nonlinear optimisation and applied and theoretical econometrics.

Ioana Negru, PhD, was previously lecturer of Cambridge University, UK. Her research interests lie in the Philosophy of Economics and are especially related to Ethics in Economics.

Jan Holm Ingemann is an associate professor and head of Study, Aalborg University, Denmark. He has a PhD in agricultural economics and policy. His research is primarily related to interdisciplinary studies of interaction between agricultural economics and social frames in postindustrial society.

Jesper Jespersen is professor emeritus at Roskilde University, Denmark. His research interests include the economics of Keynes and macroeconomic methodology.

John Hart retired as an associate professor of economics, University of KwaZulu-Natal, in 2014, before joining the Department of Economics, University of South Africa, from 2015 to 2019, with which he is currently affiliated for research purposes. His interests include the methodology of economics.

John King is at La Trobe University and Honorary Professor, Federation University Australia. His interests include the history of Marxian and Post-Keynesian economics.

Katarina Juselius is professor emerita at the Department of Economics, University of Copenhagen. She has written extensively on the econometric analysis of macroeconomic problems.

Lars Josephsen is an independent senior adviser on sustainable development issues, affiliated with some Danish civil society organisations. He has 25 years of experience in Danish Ministries, concerning public planning and strategy development within energy and environment.

Lars Syll, PhD, is professor of social science at Malmö University, Sweden. His primary research areas are the philosophy, history and methodology of economics.

As a social scientist and economist, he is strongly influenced by John Maynard Keynes, and an avowed critic of neoliberalism and market fundamentalism.

Marcel Boumans is professor at Utrecht University, the Netherlands. His research interests include economic methodology and the history of economic thought.

Mark Setterfield is professor of economics in the Department of Economics at The New School for Social Research, New York, USA. He is also a member of the faculty at Eugene Lang College at The New School. His research interests focus on macroeconomics, growth and distribution and Post-Keynesian economics.

Mogens Ove Madsen, PhD, is associated professor of economics and Head of Study at Aalborg University, Denmark. His research interests include economic methodology and the economics of Keynes.

Nuno Ornelas Martins is professor at the School of Economics and Management of the Catholic University of Portugal, Catholic Porto Business School and CEGE. He writes on classical political economy and the Cambridge tradition in economics. Other scholarly interests include sustainable development and the philosophy of social sciences.

Scott Scheall, PhD, is an assistant professor at Arizona State University. His research interests focus on F.A. Hayek and the history of the Austrian school in economics.

Sheila Dow is professor (em) at the Division of Economics, Stirling Management School, University of Stirling, UK, and the Department of Economics, University of Victoria, Canada. She has written extensively on macroeconomic methodology and the economics of Keynes.

Victoria Chick is professor emeritus at University College London, UK. She has written extensively on macroeconomics and the economics of Keynes.

PREFACE

How to use this handbook and acknowledgments

This Handbook discusses 'how economists analyse *the economy as a whole* (i.e. macroeconomics)'. What sparked our initiative was the genuine surprise when we realised that there was hardly any monograph or recent textbook specifically on *mac-ro*economic methodology available in the market. How could it be that macroeconomists do not write and discuss the choice and relevance of the methods they employ? Of course, we found a number of books and the *Journal of Economic Methodology* which focus on economic methods at large, but these sources seldom took up *mac-ro*economics as a separate issue. The reason for this deficit may be explained by the fact that the discussion of principles behind the different methods in economics is often left to scholars within the philosophy of sciences. They are for good reasons not really concerned with the separate subdisciplines within economics. Another explanation might be that economists are more concerned with theory and empirical practices than refined methodological considerations. We have often heard the claim: 'let's do economics, why bother with methodology?' Macroeconomists are like the carpenter who ponders over the question whether to use a hammer or a screwdriver, but forgets to check if his construction is solid enough to carry the weight of the roof. In macroeconomics, the focus exclusively lies on choosing the right econometric tool for the job at hand to the detriment of the question if the method employed – i.e. the interaction between theory and empirical research – will further our knowledge of how the macroeconomy works.

The purpose of this Handbook is to make a start in filling this gap and to contribute to the neglected methodological discourse in macroeconomics. In some way the study of macroeconomic methodology is rather new. It is difficult to dispute that macroeconomics was not considered a topic in its own right before 1936, the year of publication of Keynes's *General Theory*. In this book, Keynes claimed that the economy as a whole is different from the sum of its parts. This means that macro-economics is in need of a specific methodological approach – a view which was not only challenged by his contemporary colleagues but, as we shall see in this hand-book, still is challenged by several dominant schools of thought, where trend-setting economists strive for a methodological unification of economics, and do not regard macroeconomics as a separate discipline. The point of the handbook is to focus on these divided opinions and see if the differences can be understood in terms of the methods employed by these schools. This debate has taken momentum after the more recent macroeconomic crises, which the mainstream macroeconomic models were unable to handle. Even the British queen asked, when she visited the London School of Economics in 2009: 'why did you not warn us?' The global financial crisis of 2008 came as a surprise to many mainstream macroeconomic models. It appeared that global disruptions emanating from the financial sector are difficult to predict and even afterwards to explain. In contrast, several other economists warned about the danger of debt-financed speculation and the risk of a global downturn several years before the financial crisis of 2008. Some of them explicitly referred to the work of non-mainstream macroeconomists like Hyman Minsky and his financial instability hypothesis.

The preparation and writing of the contributions to the Handbook have been underway for quite some time, but the relevance seems to have been increasing. The delay was partly caused by the difficulty to set up a balanced panel of contributors. In the end, we managed to secure a collection of entries to match the ambition of the Handbook which covers broad views on macroeconomic methods employed by different schools in theory and practice.

Our intention has been that each entry could be read as a balanced presentation of a topic in macroeconomic methodology in its own right. Of course, reading all the way through the Handbook will give a much richer view on macroeconomic methodology and its different dimensions, which will contribute to a better understanding of the methodological barriers between the different schools of thought in macroeconomics. By this the editors hope to establish a higher degree of mutual respect and pluralism within the macroeconomic discipline.

To our great regret Victoria Chick lost her eyesight in the final stages of the preparation of this Handbook. She apologises that she could not review the end result with the level of care that characterises her work. The other two editors are grateful for her contribution to the Handbook. Without her drive and vigour, the process of drafting this Handbook would not have started in the first place.

Finally, we would like to thank Andy Humphries at Routledge for his never failing and constructive support (and patience) to the project.

London, Copenhagen and
Amsterdam, July 2022
Victoria Chick
Jesper Jespersen
Bert Tieben

INTRODUCTION

The scope and content of the handbook

Victoria Chick, Jesper Jespersen and Bert Tieben

Introduction

This Handbook intends to contribute to the understanding of how macroeconomists work. Macroeconomists use different methods. They are not just 'doing' economics, but quite often they use a specific method (theory and practice) without really contemplating or discussing its specific relevance. The pivot argument of this Handbook is that one method does not fit unequivocally to all macroeconomic problems. By method we mean the systemic combination of theory, empirical practice and communication (i.e. how research is presented to the public and in teaching). One of the editors' shared views is that macroeconomists employ different, we nearly said very different, methods.

The Handbook is planned to give an overview of these different methods. In other words: what we by using an overarching concept have called Macroeconomic Methodology.

Accordingly, the aim of the Handbook is to cover major aspects of macroeconomic methodology, as they are represented in a wide range of academic works with regard to undertaking systematic analysis of macroeconomic issues. By macroeconomics we mean the economy as a whole as a relevant analytical entity. A view, we have to confess, which is contested in the economic literature, see, for instance, Lucas (1987).

We have the conviction that the choice of method plays an important role in the message derived from macroeconomic analysis and therefore is indispensable to get the correct interpretation, but also limitation of, the presented outcome.

Unfortunately, teaching in macroeconomic methodology is underdeveloped in most economic studies even at the university level. There are several possible explanations for this unfortunate situation, which demonstrates that methodology is not considered important. It mirrors the often met position that, according to the dominant mainstream paradigm, there is only one way to do macroeconomics. This view has contributed to the present deplorable state of the art that relevant textbooks in **macro**economic methodology are lacking. Although, in fairness, it has to be mentioned that a number of (text)books carrying the title *economic method* (or methodology) have a section on macroeconomic methods, but as an addendum rather than as

DOI: 10.4324/9781315745992-1

a main dish, see for instance, Blaug (1992 [1980]), Hausman (1992) and Dow (2002). When the importance of macroeconomic methodology, as different from just economic methodology, has been recognised, you will be surprised with how scanty the number of books, even journal articles, there are in this specific field. Below we have listed a few relevant reference books on method carrying the word macroeconomics in its title.[1]

It is our sincere belief that the understanding and usefulness of research into macroeconomic topics could be improved, if the methodological fundamentals were presented thoroughly (and even better, also discussed) before any macroeconomic investigation – let it be in theory, in empirical work or even in teaching – is initiated. Obviously, theories and models in macroeconomics cannot be plucked out of thin air. They will always be anchored by the employed method. Methodological analysis could be helpful to secure consistency between scientific practice and the theoretical and empirical intentions. When scholars present their macroeconomic findings to colleagues and/or to the wider public the limitations of the employed method ought to be mentioned. If, for instance, the goal of a macroeconomic analysis is to provide policy recommendations to actually change the macroeconomic development, then the theory must be anchored within a realistic methodology. If, on the contrary, the goal is to investigate the existence of equilibrium in a theoretical model, then, obviously, another method should be chosen to fit this very different area of research. Thus, it is important that the goal of the analysis is recognised when the employed models are developed and selected, whether it is for policy recommendations or theoretical abstractions.

The Handbook is intended to represent a useful collection of entries on a variety of issues. Each issue covers one important (partly) self-contained aspect of macroeconomic methodology. Accordingly, the scope of the Handbook should be relevant for researchers, teachers and academics in high schools and universities dealing with macroeconomics. To facilitate the use of the Handbook we have divided the entries into five sections. Each of them has a specific theme to make it easier for the user to select the relevant entries depending on what kind of macroeconomic study one is undertaking, because no one is expected to be a specialist in all methodological themes.

In sum: This Handbook sets out to demonstrate that methodology is an indispensable part of macroeconomic understanding regardless of whether one is engaged in theorising, modelling, teaching and/or policy advice. The entries cover crucial knowledge for academics doing macroeconomic research but are equally important for professionals using macroeconomic output while being high school/university teachers, civil servants involved in policy advice, public communicators or CEOs in large public or private companies.

Defining macroeconomic methodology

Macroeconomic methodology is a vast topic. It investigates how economists approach research questions related to the economy as a whole, where economic activity cannot be analysed in isolation. In other words, it is the interdependence of parts of the economic system that really separates macroeconomic from (micro) economic analysis. In our view, this characteristic supports the need of specific methodology.

To give just one example: The often used assumption in microeconomics, *ceteris paribus* (all other things being equal), hardly makes any sense in macroeconomic analysis. Other things do not remain equal when we investigate changes affecting the operation of the economy as a whole. So, it is seldom meaningful to employ uncritically the same method or use the same type of models in economics. It is a trade mark of macroeconomic analysis to include all relevant aspects of the economy as a whole and to consider the feedback loops between the different parts of the system.[2]

Unfortunately, a methodological discussion of the appropriateness of the choice of method is seldom practised within the different macroeconomic schools. These schools can (at least partly) be identified by their preferred method, as Dow (1996 [1985]) has argued for macroeconomics. This is a combination of theory, modelling and empirical work, which has become the standard within the school or paradigm. Using Thomas Kuhn's (1970 [1962]) terminology, one can speak of a paradigmatic dividing line within macroeconomics set by the preferred methods of the different schools of thought. Kuhn also described paradigms as incomparable: the methodology that characterises one paradigm is often not accepted by a rival paradigm. Consequently, the members of different schools of thought are often, quite literally, not on speaking terms. Paradigms are generally unwilling to ferret out the methodological differences with their rivals. This colours the methodological debate in macroeconomics, but also in other parts of science.

Examples of deep methodological differences abound in macroeconomics. Take the methodological difference between the Austrian School's denial of macroeconomics as a separate discipline and the Keynesian analysis in terms of aggregate variables. The Keynesians see market failure as the inescapable outcome of the operation of the economy as a whole, while the Austrians believe that markets always tend towards equilibrium, as long as governments do not meddle with the economy. These two schools could hardly be more divided on their view or the employed method.

The Austrians also claim that human action is the basis of economic analysis. In their view, the essence of human decision making can never be penetrated in a mathematical model, which puts them in direct opposition to the neoclassicals, a school which also prefers methodological individualism but strongly relies on the mathematical exploration of general equilibrium models as the main method of macroeconomic analysis.

There is definitely no agreement on what the correct method is for explaining macroeconomic development and/or how to make projections. This is one of the important conclusions of the Handbook.

Macroeconomic methodology: A brief history of the field

When we take a look at the history of economic methodology, it is a characteristic that has changed somewhat drastically through time. There are, of course, many reasons for these changes. Economics is partly a cumulative science. Take, for instance, the separation of economics into micro and macro (although still contested). But society is also a moving target as a result of changes in structures and political ideologies.

The importance of changes in structures is obvious from a historical point of view. The "economy as a whole" has been a variable research object through time. Going back 200 years, the economy was dominated by agriculture, later came the industrialisation and within the last 50 years the growth of (private, public and financial) services took over. This transformation required new analytical models and tools, which made some of the old ones obsolete. Take, for instance, the break-down of the neoclassical model in the 1930s, the Keynesian model in the 1970s, the Marxist model in the 1980s and the present challenges to the general equilibrium model. What counts as standard practice or the mainstream is generally a sequence of analytical models, one replacing the other as economic insight or political preferences develop over time.

For macroeconomic methodology, it is therefore of interest to investigate the causes of the shifts in the dominant macro-theoretical paradigms: what forces and ideas determine the dominating (so-called mainstream) models?

Let's start with the obvious reason. It unquestionably seems that the above-mentioned break-downs were caused by the lack of predicting power of the dominant economic models in use when severe macroeconomic crises hit. As a consequence of this failure to predict and prevent, there was a call for new government policies joined to a search for new (and hopefully better) understanding of how the macroeconomic system works. As a consequence, the re-modelling strategies were often to build a new and different model, which also corresponded with the world-view of the new government and its policies. It is no coincidence that Keynes's macroeconomics met open doors in the US with Franklin D. Roosevelt as the newly elected president and in Europe just after the war with the socialist-democratic governments in power in many places.

Something similar happened as a consequence of the crisis in the 1970s but with reversed political sign, where the dominant ideology swung from left to right. A development which took extra momentum by the fall of the Berlin Wall in 1989, which supported the revival of neoclassical free market theory and its general equilibrium method, although in a renewed form with the application of rational expectations.

More recently it became a disadvantage that financial markets, which grew immensely during the early years of the 21st century, were not adopted into the mainstream macroeconomic models. This lack of inclusion was (partly) justified with reference to the *Hypothesis of Efficient Financial Markets*, see Fama (1970). This hypothesis argued that financialisation has no direct impact on the real part of the economy (GDP). The rate of interest became the only financial variable to impact macroeconomic outcomes. It was treated as an exogenous variable set by the Central Bank with a view on expected inflation. But, the financial crisis which emerged in 2008/2009 demonstrated that these macroeconomic models were not prepared for a global economic downturn of this magnitude. The financial turmoil had a vast impact on the real part of the economy nationally and internationally, which quickly spread into public debt crises. Like the 1970s the mainstream profession was in disarray and lacked a relevant theory of integrating financial markets and the real part of the macroeconomic system.

Today, a similar story can be told with regard to the consequences of the COVID-19 pandemic. This time it has been the disruption of international supply chains, which caused production bottlenecks and unexpected inflation. This development came as a surprise to the mainstream macroeconomic models. Accordingly, some changes in methodology have to be established. The world economic system has one more time given evidence that it is an illusion to assume that the international or national macroeconomic system works like a well-oiled clockwork, which is one of the basic assumptions behind the general equilibrium model.

But as long as an alternative macroeconomic methodology is lacking, it is difficult to judge where or when a change in macromodelling will emerge. This is worrying, because behind the recurring production crises, there looms the much larger climate crisis. Each summer it seems to come as a surprise to politicians and their economic advisers that erratic and unstable weather conditions cause damages on an increasing economic scale. But, there is no macroeconomic methodology available that combines real production, the financial sector and the environment and climate convincingly. In our view, the closure of this gap is the major challenge to the macroeconomic profession – the sooner the better. This is a challenge and a call which will be stronger year by year, as the consequences of the rising temperatures and sea levels become more and more visible, undeniably and costly.

Organisation of the handbook

The 29 contributions to this Handbook are independent and self-contained entry of a specific but, as described in the introduction, often highly contested topics. We have structured the Handbook into five subsections to secure a shared topical focus by the contributors. The intention has been to give a wide range of relevant views and opinions within each section. Together the entries cover the main aspects of macroeconomic methodology:

  I   Philosophy of Science Perspectives
  II Concepts
  III Schools of Thought
  IV Modelling, Econometrics and the Real World
  V Teaching and Communication of Macroeconomics

It has been our deliberate intention to articulate different ways of seeing macroeconomic methodology within each section. After this Introduction the Handbook starts with a discussion of the fundamental principles of method relevant for undertaking macroeconomic analysis.

In Section I a number of basic ideas and principles from *Philosophy of Science* are presented.

Andy Denis starts with an entry on *Methodological Individualism* (I.1) which is basic to dynamic stochastic general equilibrium (DSGE) models. This method fulfils the neoclassical claim of giving macroeconomic models a solid microfoundation. Lars Syll's entry on *Deduction, Induction and Abduction* (I.2) goes beyond the well-known debate between methodologists: whether to start the analysis from a few axioms or from observations of reality. This entry present abduction as a possible middle way with inspiration from critical realism. There cannot be only one right way to conduct macroeconomic analysis. The choice of method must depend on context and circumstances.

Daniel Hammond takes up in his entry on *Instrumentalism* (I.3) an equally important debate about the fundamental question related to the theoretical part of a macroeconomic analysis: Is the employed theory just an instrument as claimed by, e.g., Milton Friedman (1953) or should relevant theory have an indisputable realistic anchor as argued strongly by, e.g., Karl Popper (1983)?

John Hart's entry *From Positivism to Naturalism in Macroeconomics* (I.4) discusses the realist methodological approach to macroeconomic analysis. He gives a historical account of the development from (naïve) positivism to more refined naturalism, which has followed the trend within the practice of natural science. But naturalists in social sciences have to go further in their critique and discussion of how to interpret the output of (partly unobservable) macroeconomic analysis.

Victoria Chick and Jesper Jespersen emphasise in their entry *Holism and Fallacy of Composition* (I.5) the *macro*-perspective of economic methodology. Here, the focus point is the economic system as a whole, where the sum of the parts differs from the outcome of an integrated whole. This methodological challenge is summarised under the label 'Fallacy of Composition' and is relevant in all social sciences. In macroeconomics this discussion refers to Keynes's methodological turn around during the early 1930 and presented in *The General Theory* (1936), where we find his warning of committing a fallacy of composition and how to avoid it.

Finally, within the section on Philosophy of Science Finn Olesen points in his entry on *Macroeconomics and Ethics* (I.6) at two ethical challenges, which macroeconomists should confront. One is related to economic theory as an analytical abstraction: The employed theory does not (fully) correspond to reality, but is, anyhow, used to legitimise an economic counselling for obtaining specific macroeconomic outcomes. The financial crisis and the following period of stagnation are used as a point in case, where the dominant macroeconomic models gave misleading projections. The second ethical challenge is related to the prioritising within macroeconomic analysis: how to evaluate and value a projection and the impact of economic policies on the outcome of, for instance, growth, distribution and the environment?

Section II is a collection of eight entries, presenting often used analytical concepts by (macro)economists. Mogens Ove Madsen initiates this section with an essay on *Time in Macroeconomics* (II.1). His methodological starting point is: The economic system is a moving target. It evolves through time. But macroeconomic reasoning has always been divided between scholars who mainly focus on the one side on dynamic forces. Take, for instance, some of the high-profile classical economists (Smith, Malthus and Marx, see Nuno Martins' entry) as a showcase. On the other side are economists mainly using a stationary state or comparative static analysis (see Negru and Vercelli's entry on pluralism). This essay concludes on a methodological account demonstrating that a middle way between static and dynamic analysis as developed by Keynes within *A Treatise on Money* (*CW* V & VI) and especially in *The General Theory* (*CW* VII) can be traced back to two of his (older) colleagues in Cambridge: (1) John M.E. McTaggart (1866–1925) suggested an ordering and combination of events structured as dynamic A- and a static B-series respectively, and (2) Alfred Marshall (1842–1924) who combined a sequence of short period analyses leading up to a long period equilibrium.

Sheila Dow discusses *Uncertainty and Macroeconomic Methodology* (II.2). The purpose of the entry is to explore how uncertainty is understood and analysed within macroeconomics. She argues that the different understandings of uncertainty are foundational to the choice of methodological approach, which then determines how this social phenomenon is treated in macroeconomic theory.

Mark Setterfield takes up in his entry on *Path Dependency* (II.3) the dynamic dimension of macroeconomic analysis. Hence, path dependency is defined, and three different specific concepts of path dependency – cumulative causation, lock in and hysteresis – are analysed. The relationships between path dependency and equilibrium, and path dependency and fundamental uncertainty are also discussed. Finally, a typology of dynamic systems is developed to clarify these relationships. Bert Tieben takes in his entry on *Equilibrium* (II.4) a closer look at this concept. He demonstrates that nearly all schools of macroeconomics have adopted some form of equilibrium concept as a tool to decrease the complexity of finding relevant answer to the analytical question (see also Tieben 2012). In this sense equilibrium has become indispensable. In his view, it is the task of methodology to investigate and delimitate the relevant use of equilibrium in macroeconomic analyses. He provides an example by demonstrating the change in the use of the general equilibrium model in neoclassical macroeconomics. General equilibrium theory was once seen as the pinnacle of scientific achievement in economics. Today, the aim of general equilibrium theory is more modest and applications are generally seen as problem solvers.

Alessandro Vercelli gives in his entry on *Causality and Macroeconomics* (II.5) a partly theoretical and partly historical presentation of how causality has been an instrumental concept in (macro)economics for more than 200 years. Causality has to do with the fundamental relationships of our knowledge of the real world. The empirically detected and/or theoretically postulated causal structures have a vast impact on policy decisions. Therefore, we need a thorough analysis of the meaning and implications of alternative notions of causality to improve the critical awareness of macroeconomic arguments in a pluralist perspective, see also the entry on *Methodological Pluralism* (III.7). The importance of the analytical treatment of causality is also given a number of historical accounts to underline the crucial features of this concept.

Nuno Martins argues in his entry on *Microeconomic Foundation of Macroeconomics* (II.6) that in contemporary methodological debates, it is not whether macroeconomics must possess a microeconomic foundation or not, but rather which type of microeconomic foundation is presupposed by each macroeconomic school. To this point, he addresses two competing approaches to the microeconomic foundation of macroeconomics, which can be traced back to Frank Ramsey and John Maynard Keynes, respectively. Many subsequent controversies within macroeconomics can be understood in terms of a greater adherence either to Ramsey's approach to microeconomic foundations, or Keynes's approach, where the treatment of especially uncertainty plays a determining role. He also warns that the meaning of terms such as classical and Keynesian has changed significantly through this period.

Victoria Chick presents arguments for choosing between *Open and Closed Macroeconomic Systems* (II.7). Two different concepts of open and closed systems are current in today's economics. One is concerned with the structure of economic theory, which follows the definitions of open and closed systems in other fields; the other focuses on the predictability of analytical outcomes: whether there is causal regularity (closed) or only a loose connection between events (open). Though these concepts are related, there is no one-to-one mapping between them. The applicability of the two concepts and their relationship to ontology is explored together with different sources of openness in the first concept, which allows the nesting of closed systems (models) within open-system theories.

This section is closed by Claude Gnos's entry on *Money and Macroeconomic Methodology* (II.8). The conventional view that is still predominant in economics is that money analytically only is a medium of exchange with the related notion that monetary changes have no real impact. This view is represented by the *quantity theory of money and prices* and grounded in aggregated microeconomic arguments. The second part of the entry examines how Keynes expanded the concept of money into a store of value connecting the present with the future. Finally, the entry shows how *circuit theory* has attempted to enlarge both views by exploring the role of banking and accounting in macroeconomic models.

Section III is devoted to the presentation of the macroeconomic method employed within different *Schools of Thought*. The section demonstrates that each school, up to a point, can be identified by its methodological approach.

Nuno Martins opens the section with *Classical Political Economy* (III.1). This entry provides an historical perspective on the philosophical and methodological underpinnings of the classical perspective on economics. The neoclassical challenge of the classical method is highlighted with a view on the modern debate on the use of mathematics and the explanation of value in different macroeconomic schools.

Bert Tieben concludes in his entry *The Methodology of Neoclassical Macroeconomics* (III.2) that the unifying element of neoclassical macroeconomics is methodological individualism in combination with an axiomatic approach to the study of the economy as a whole, such as applied by general equilibrium theory. This approach is historically represented among others by the Solow-Swan growth model developed in the 1950s. This approach has increasingly been challenged by empirical models, which no longer fit the mould of neoclassical methodology with its rigorous focus on logical deduction. Accordingly, orthodoxy no longer fully describes how neoclassical-inspired macroeconomists, like for instance New-Keynesians and Neo-Walrasians, actually work.

Victoria Chick and Jesper Jespersen present the fundamental shift described in *Keynes's Macroeconomic Method* (III.3). They argue that Keynes made a sea change in macroeconomic methodology when he published *The General Theory of Employment, Interest and Money* (*GT*) in 1936. His method of analysing the economy as a whole deviated substantially from the neoclassical convention of accepting Say's Law and full employment equilibrium. His fellowship dissertation published in 1921 as *A Treatise on Probability* was an important building block for his new macroeconomic theory integrating individual behaviour in a realm of uncertainty. Equally important was his challenge to the market economic system considered as a self-adjusting system which moves towards full employment. The combination of these two methodological novelties made it possible for him to develop his new macro theory labelled the principle of effective demand. Within *GT* Keynes redefined the concept of equilibrium as a point of rest, where there is no inducement for employers as a whole to change employment. To achieve this conclusion, he developed an open-system method, where even a well-functioning market system could get stuck in high unemployment equilibrium due to lack of demand. Furthermore, he demonstrated that a more flexible wage level or rate of interest would not solve the problem with persistent unemployment. It would rather have the opposite effect by making the system more unstable and thereby increase uncertainty. So, in the longer run the macroeconomic development is open, determined partly by institutional path dependency and partly by economic policy.

John E. King points out in his entry on *Post-Keynesian Methodology* (III.4) that today there are many schools with the prefix Keynesian (old-, new- and post-Keynesian). But it is only the Post-Keynesians who carry the torch of Keynes's macro method, building on uncertainty and open-system analysis with particular reference to the role of realism in macroeconomics. In addition, arguments for and against formalism, microeconomic foundation and pluralism in macroeconomics theory are presented.

Scott Scheall presents in *Complexity, Policymaking, and The Austrian Denial of Macroeconomics* (III.5) the opposite view to the Post-Keynesian represented by the Austrian School's rejection of macroeconomics as a meaningful concept. In the view of this school, economics can only be analysed as the outcome of the activities of individuals. Human acts are not grounded in facts but in subjective beliefs. Hence, the economist's task is to trace the emergence of economic phenomena from interactions among individuals. This approach leads to a rejection of macroeconomics, which is best summarised by Hayek (2012). On this account, it may come as a surprise that Austrians are engaged in theorising about business cycle. This (macro)phenomenon is theoretically partly explained by individuals' subjective, but mistaken, views on economic prospects, and partly explained due to complexity, which causes the market system only to be semi self-correcting.

Alan Freeman brings us in his entry on *What Was Marx's Method, Actually* (III.6) to a rather similar debate as the one we found within the Keynesian camp: the mainstream economists' (mis)representation of Marx's texts confronted with a direct interpretation of the original contributions. The dominant Western view of Marx, termed 'Marxism without Marx' by scholars of the Temporal Single System Interpretation (TSSI), argues that Marx's method is a variant of the General Equilibrium method that has prevailed in post-war economic theory. Accordingly, the present dominant Marxist school deduces its theory from the assumption of Market Perfection and reduces hereby its potential for describing the realities of the capitalist market system, above all its crises. This dominant view can be understood as a theory in its own right, but quite distinct from Marx's. Then we are confronted with the difficult question: What was Marx's method? His writings suggest it was radically different from what is commonly thought of as a macroeconomic method among mainstream economists, being rooted – as Marx himself stated in his descriptions of his method – in philosophy. It was used not to interpret history but to change it.

Finally, within this section Alessandro Vercelli and Ioana Negru establish in their entry on *Methodological Pluralism in Macroeconomics* (III.7) a kind of synthesis of how the choice of method identifies the different macroeconomic schools. In this entry they use methodological criteria to investigate some fundamental differences in the foundations and implications of competing macroeconomic schools. Rather than considering alternative research programmes to be incommensurable due to their differences at various levels (Kuhn 1970 [1962]), schools of thought are interpreted as open entities that may be compared. The intention is to investigate the use of method through a cross-paradigm discussion in an attempt to extend the dialogue between macroeconomic schools, which may give inspiration for a fruitful dialogue of advancing new ideas, concepts or theories (see e.g. Dow 1996 [1985]).

Section IV deals with *Models, Econometrics and Measurement* within macroeconomics. Focus is on the different methodologies used in modelling, empirical research and forecasting.

Lars Josephsen asks in his entry on *Use of Mathematics and Modelling* (IV.1): What are the potentials and limitations associated with the use of mathematics in relation to macroeconomic analysis? Arguments in favour of formalisation are: rigorously defined relations between variables and internal consistency. The limitations are concerned with non-known relationships, inconclusive parameters and behavioural uncertainties. The entry discusses the implication, but also disadvantages, of mathematics for modelbuilding and macroeconomic analysis especially in the perspective of the requirements of investigating the economy as a whole which also comprehend social and environmental aspects.

Marcel Boumans emphasises in his entry on *Explanation and Forecasting* (IV.2) that models are built for explanatory, predictive and/or policy evaluation purposes. The success of such models depends on the degree of invariance through time. The invariance domain depends on the potential model stability with regard to internal parameters and external events. Models are built on past observations; but forecasting has to integrate expectations about the future development and policies. Between macroeconomic schools it is discussed intensively how to delimitate the domain of invariance. On this matter, opinions are divided.

Frank den Butter gives in his entry *Using Macroeconomic Models in Policy Practice* (IV.3) an historical account from the Netherlands on the use of macroeconomic models in practical policy analysis. He concludes that the design of models and the employed method is much influenced by the actual need for policy analysis and of the specific economic circumstances. The practical use of macroeconomic models as an integrated part of policy advising and evaluation has demonstrated that economists, the model and the political purpose cannot be separated. To make the model a useful (but also accepted) tool for governmental planning a number of requirements have to be fulfilled: using mainstream macroeconomic theory, making the model fit for policy analysis and combining model outcomes with tacit knowledge. Therefore, the entry concludes that economic policy analysis based on macro models will always require a combination of Model *and* Man, or more pretentiously of Science *and* Art.

The following three entries within Section IV are devoted to specific empirical methods of macroeconomic modelbuilding and statistical measurement.

Henning Bunzel gives us in his entry *Traditional Methods of Macroeconometrics* (IV.4) an historical account of the development of macroeconometric models and the employed methods. The Keynes-Tinbergen debate on the stability of empirically estimated relations using time series is a classic case. This debate caused a number of innovative methods of estimation to be suggested – but is still not settled. Haavelmo (1944) advocated a search for and selection of theoretically derived structural equations, which were invariant through time and he suggested furthermore one joint distribution for all relevant variables. In the 1970s the large "Keynesian" econometric models were challenged by the so-called Lucas critique that macro-equations estimated on the basis of timeseries could not be invariant to changes in policy. But the proposed requirement of a microeconomic foundation based on deep (i.e. policy-independent) parameters did not solve the problem of unstable parameters. The entry ends with a call for a return to the approach suggested by Haavelmo to elaborate on an encompassing, congruent model-structure.

In some way Katarina Juselius takes the opposite view in her entry *Macroeconometrics: The Cointegrated VAR (CVAR) Method* (IV.5) on how to construct and estimate a macroeconometric simulation model. The CVAR method does not start with the imposition of untested (structural) restrictions on the data-set and, therefore, can represent a larger number of possible economic models. The usefulness of the method comes from the possibility to test relevant hypotheses on the exogenous forces and structural changes that have pushed the economic system out of equilibrium and the equilibrating forces that have driven the macroeconomic system forward. The scientific problem is how to associate the statistically based CVAR model to a theoretically grounded macroeconomic model. A so-called theory-consistent CVAR scenario offers such a bridging principle. In practice, few models have passed this test. Reasons for this failure are discussed at the end of the entry.

Finally, Geoff Tily presents in his entry *National Accounts and Macroeconomic Methodology* (IV.6) the statistical foundation of empirical macroeconometric models. Initially, he gives an historical account of the theory and practice of national accounting systems. Keynes's role as inspirator is emphasised and his sceptical attitude of converting nominal (GDP) figures into real (growth) numbers is presented. Keynes's view was that any transformation of observed data may infuse a bias. Another risk is that due to the dominant position of GDP in the National Accounts, growth of GDP has also become the dominant success criterion in the economic policy discourse. To give growth in GDP the highest priority and to build macroeconomic models mainly on figures from the national accounting system implies that social and environmental consequences become less visible in the economic political discourse. This bias of focusing on monetary transactions only has motivated an increasing call for a green national accounting system, where environmental costs are registered and become an integrated part of the policy evaluation. How to achieve this objective is not yet settled.

The final section (Section V) *Communicating Macroeconomics* focusses on how to select strategies for better communication with a wider public audience and for conveying the importance of methodology in macroeconomic teaching.[3]

Arjo Klamer asks in his entry *The Rhetorical Perspective on Macroeconomics* (V.1): 'What is macroeconomics good for?', and he gives himself the answer, 'for making sense of the macroeconomy'. In his view, it is the philosophical notion of sense-making that imputes macroeconomics with meaning. To arrive at this conclusion, he discusses the opposition between the view of idealists and cynics on the meaning of macroeconomics. Idealists in academia think that the goal of macroeconomics is to give policy advice in the best possible and objective way. The cynics use macroeconomics as an instrument to present their preferred policy as a necessity: there is no alternative![4] Klamer claims that both viewpoints are mistaken, misguided by an outdated philosophy of science. Within the rhetorical perspective macroeconomists help in different ways to make sense of understanding an abstract and complex system and thereby giving guidance. Accordingly, the message of the macroeconomic discourse should be to generate meaningful explanations to the public rather than pretend to give exact predictions. In this role, it facilitates communication with the media and a wider public audience.

Finally, Jan Holm Ingemann gives an account on *Teaching Macroeconomic Methodology* (V.2). His claim is that economic method has to be integrated into the teaching of economics and should not be a separate course. In his view, Problem-Based Learning (PBL) is a very useful pedagogical strategy for this purpose. How can it be that economists recommend different policies to the same problem? The explanation can be that they have different preferences, prefer different theories, but also different analytical methods. This diversity forms the challenge of teaching economics, where PBL can be very useful. Teaching according to PBL often requires students to write a prolonged essay as part of a project. For this project, they are asked to be specific on their choice of method as to why they have made that choice. The entry ends by discussing how insights from critical realism provide directions for both understanding and teaching methodology and how they can assist research into macroeconomic problems in their social and environmental context.

Notes

1 To our knowledge very few books have been published specifically on **macro**economic methodology. Sheila Dow, *The Methodology of Macroeconomic Thought* (1996 [1985]); Kevin Hoover, *The Methodology of Empirical Macroeconomics* (2001); and Jespersen, *Macroeconomic Methodology* (2009) are some of the few examples. See also Sims (1996).
2 *Ceteris paribus non est.*
3 We recall the late Frank Hahn at a seminar in the Critical Realist Workshop in Cambridge back in the 1990s asking: 'why bother with methodology, let's do economics'. Personal recollection.
4 Attributed among others to Margaret Thatcher, British prime minister (1979–1990).

References

Blaug, M. (1992 [1980]) *Methodology of Economics – Or, How Economists Explain*, Second edition, Cambridge, UK: Cambridge University Press.

Chick, V. (1983) *Macroeconomics after Keynes: A Reconsideration of The General Theory*, Cambridge, MA: MIT Press.

Dow, S. C. (1996 [1985]) *The Methodology of Macroeconomic Thought*, Cheltenham: Edward Elgar.

Dow, S. C. (2002) *Economic Methodology: An Inquiry*, Oxford: Oxford University Press.

Fama, E. F. (1970) 'Efficient capital markets: A review of theory and empirical work', *Journal of Finance* 25 (2), 383–417.

Friedman, M. (1953) *Essays in Positive Economics*, Chicago, IL: University of Chicago Press.

Haavelmo, T. (1944) 'The probability approach in econometrics', *Econometrica* 12, 12–17.

Hausman, D. (1992) *The Inexact and Separate Science of Economics*, Cambridge, UK: Cambridge University Press.

Hayek, F. A. (2012) 'Business cycles', in H. Klausinger, ed., *The Collected Works of F. A. Hayek*, volume VIII, Chicago, IL: Chicago University Press.

Hoover, K. (2001) *The Methodology of Empirical Macroeconomics*, Cambridge, UK: Cambridge University Press.

Jespersen, J. (2009) *Macroeconomic Methodology*, Cheltenham: Edward Elgar.

Kuhn (1970 [1962]) *The Structure of Scientific Revolutions*, Chicago, IL: University of Chicago Press.

Lucas, R. E. Jr. (1987) *Studies in Business-Cycle Theory*, Massachusetts: MIT Press.

Popper, K. (1983) *Realism and the Aim of Science*, Totowa, NJ: Rowman and Littlefield.

Sims, C. A. (1996) 'Macroeconomics and methodology', *Journal of Economic Perspectives* 10 (1), 105–20.

Tieben, B. (2012) *The Concept of Equilibrium in Different Economic Traditions*, Cheltenham: Edward Elgar.

PART I

Philosophy of science perspectives

1

METHODOLOGICAL INDIVIDUALISM AND MACROECONOMICS

Andy Denis

Introduction

Macroeconomics is easily defined as the study of the economy as a whole, in distinction from microeconomics, the study of activity in individual markets. Methodological individualism (MI) is less easily identified. It is often invoked as a fundamental description of the methodology of both neoclassical and some alternative paradigms within economics. However, the methodologies of those to whom the theoretical practice of MI is ascribed vary widely (Hodgson 2007) and, indeed, differ profoundly on the status of the individual economic agent, some adopting a more holistic and some a more reductionist standpoint. MI is generally stated to be the requirement that social phenomena be explained by reference to the actions of individual agents (see, for example, Heath 2015). But as we shall see, what this implies is highly ambiguous. On one interpretation the principle of MI has been said to be extremely destructive for macroeconomics:

> methodological individualism strictly interpreted ... would rule out all macroeconomic propositions that cannot be reduced to microeconomic ones, and since few have yet been so reduced, this amounts in turn to saying goodbye to almost the whole of received macroeconomics.
>
> *(Blaug 1992, p. 46)*

Blaug adds that 'There must be something wrong with a methodological principle that has such devastating implications'. But many macroeconomists today might be tempted to riposte that there must be something wrong with received macroeconomics if it fares so badly when put to the test of methodological individualism. On the contrary, they would argue, it is precisely the microfoundations which lie at the heart of New Neoclassical Synthesis Economics – embodying the principle of methodological individualism – which distinguish it from 'received macroeconomics', and which provide it with its scientific status.

MI thus requires the explanation of social phenomena by reference to the behaviour of individual agents. But this can be interpreted in two ways, depending on

DOI: 10.4324/9781315745992-3

the underlying ontology assumed by the economist or stream of thought in question. It might be said that the proposed explanation of macro-level phenomena should ultimately be capable of being shown to be consistent with plausible behaviour on the part of individuals. For example, if a paradigm holds that individual agents are rational and act in their own interests, a macroeconomic theory would be anomalous within that paradigm if it were shown that it contradicted the assumption of self-seeking agents. A much stronger version of MI, however, says that the explanation of macro phenomena must not only be *consistent* with micro behaviour, but must be *reducible* to it. In other words, it must be possible to *derive* the proposed macro-level theory purely from what is held by the paradigm to be true at the micro-level.

These two versions of MI are associated with two opposed ontologies. To require macro theories to be derived from micro theories implies a conception about the way the world is – in particular, that phenomena can be reduced to congeries of lower level, substrate entities: aggregates of atoms, each taken in isolation. Were the substrate atoms permitted to have relations with each other, we would no longer be founding the explanation at the level of the individual atom. This reductionist ontology is absent when we invoke the looser requirement of *consistency* between the micro and the macro, as organic interrelations between the substrate entities are now permitted – they are no longer atoms. To illustrate from the natural sciences, biological theory must be consistent with what we know about atoms and molecules – no élan vital is permitted, for example – but it cannot be derived from them. Rather, biological theory depends on the nature of the interrelationships between those atomic-level entities, such as those in the double helix of DNA. In a world in which not all macro-level phenomena are congeries of lower-, substrate-level entities, the assertion that wholes are merely the sums of their parts, and hence that we can derive the macro from the micro by aggregation, commits the mereological fallacies of composition and division.

This chapter contends that the bulk of modern, mainstream macroeconomics is founded in the hard, reductionist version of MI noted above, and is vitiated thereby. Others who claim to have adopted an MI approach, such as for example Friedrich Hayek (Denis 2014), adopt the weaker, holistic version. It seems a recipe for confusion for such approaches to be described as methodologically individualist at all.

Before proceeding we should note a third possibility: the attempt to explain the world without adopting methodological individualism in either sense. Posited macro-level entities within this explanatory strategy are not intended to be consistent with any micro-level behaviour. Schopenhauer's concept of a world driven by a noumenal *Wille*, and Bergson's explanation of self-organisation by reference to an élan vital, are instances of this approach. More often such notions are *ad hoc*, in the sense that they are not adopted in the belief that they embody any ultimate truth, but on pragmatic grounds, to fill an explanatory need perhaps imperfectly, perhaps even incorrectly, but to the best of our current ability. Much of Old Neoclassical Keynesian econometrics was of this character, and this is what Lucas – rightly – objected to, though the alternative of a reductionist MI which he advocated was no improvement. As we shall see, New Keynesian (or New Neoclassical Synthesis) models are not free of these methodologically individualistic constructs.

MI was first named by Schumpeter in 1908, in German, in a chapter entitled 'Methodological Individualism' (Schumpeter 1980), and the term was introduced into the English language, again by Schumpeter, the following year (Schumpeter 1909, p. 231).

Without going into a lengthy analysis of Schumpeter's views here, it is evident that he endorses the reductionist version of MI indicated above. This has remained true of the discipline, by and large, ever since, though Hayek, as noted above, constitutes an interesting exception. In particular, reductionist MI explicitly or implicitly forms the heart of modern *microfounded* macroeconomics: the dynamic stochastic general equilibrium (DSGE) approach. We can see this by exploring a modern graduate-level textbook in macroeconomics, *Macroeconomic Theory: A Dynamic General Equilibrium Approach* by Michael Wickens (2011), and a popular DSGE model much used by academics and practitioners alike, the Smets-Wouters model (Smets and Wouters 2003, 2007). A final section discusses alternatives to the reductionist version of MI underlying the 'microfoundations' approach.

Michael Wickens's textbook: Methodological individualism and macroeconomics

Wickens (2011) is a mainstream graduate textbook setting out the DSGE approach to macroeconomics (where possible the stochastic element is suppressed for pedagogical purposes, and the model is then referred to as a dynamic general equilibrium (DGE) model, as the title suggests). The book is worth studying to see exactly where individualism enters into the modelling strategy. Chapter 1 is an introduction and Chapter 2 is on 'the centralised economy'. Chapter 1 explains in the very first sentences that '[m]odern macroeconomics seeks to explain the aggregate economy using theories based on strong microeconomic foundations. This is in contrast to the traditional Keynesian approach to macroeconomics, which is based on ad hoc theorising about the relations between macroeconomic aggregates' (Wickens 2011, p. 1).

The account in Chapter 2 is based on the Ramsey model of optimal saving (Ramsey 1928). It attempts to explain 'how the optimal level of output is determined in the economy and how this is allocated between consumption and capital accumulation or, put another way, between consumption today and consumption in the future' (Wickens 2011, p. 15). The model described forms the substance of the rest of the book: 'The rest of the book builds on this first pass through this highly simplified preliminary account of the macroeconomy' (Wickens 2011, pp. 15, 41). The model described has multiple interpretations:

1 as a central planning model 'in which the decisions are taken centrally', and in which either

    a those decisions are made 'in the light of individual preferences, which are identical', or

    b 'the social planner's preferences [are] ... imposed on everyone';

2 as 'a representative agent model when all economic agents are identical and act as both a household and a firm'; and, finally,

3 as a model which refers 'to a single individual ... a Robinson Crusoe economy' (Wickens 2011, p. 15).

Despite its simplicity, this model, according to Wickens, 'captures most of the essential features of the macroeconomy' (Wickens 2011, p. 15). Indeed, even when we decentralise the economy so that we have individual firms and households meeting in markets, according to Wickens, 'the behaviour of the decentralized economy when in general equilibrium is remarkably similar to that of the basic representative-agent model discussed previously' – i.e. the Ramsey model (Wickens 2011, p. 60).

The 'decentralised economy' is introduced in Chapter 4. It is decentralised in the sense of interpretation (1) above. Now it is no longer assumed that a single agent makes all the decisions: the economy is divided into households and firms. Households make consumption decisions, supply labour to firms, and save by accumulating capital assets; they also own firms, and receive dividend income from them. Firms make decisions about output, employment of labour, and investment; they pay wages, dividends, and interest payments to households, and decide how much to borrow to finance investment. Although Wickens speaks of 'firms' and 'households' in the plural, there is in fact only one of each: in terms of interpretation (2) the model is still a representative agent model, now with a representative firm and a representative household. In terms of interpretation (3), the model no longer refers to a single individual, but to two individuals. Although there is continual reference to the need for markets, in which the agents meet, there is no discussion of market structure: nevertheless, internal evidence shows that markets are considered to be perfectly competitive – the wage rate is constant and not a function of the firm's employment decision, for example – rather than the bilateral monopoly that one might perhaps have expected.

Chapter 5 decentralises the economy one step further by introducing the state ('government') as an agent. Beyond that, if further detail in a particular sector is required, this tends to be achieved by reconfiguring the sectors of the economy so that they are not increased in number. For example, to examine the macro consequences of banking, a model with three sectors is used – a combined household-firm sector (i.e. the non-bank private sector), a banking sector, and a consolidated government-central bank (Wickens 2011, p. 491) – where each sector is embodied in the corresponding representative agent.

The reductionist version of individualism is evident here in that in each case we have either a single agent, or a small number of agents, *each acting in isolation*. So it is assumed that there are no interdependencies, other than those mediated by the price system, that is, no externalities. It should not be thought that the fact that methodologically individualist approaches allow agents to interact via prices exculpates those approaches from the charge of reductionism. It is indeed difficult to propose and defend a consistently reductionist outlook – the world simply isn't like that, and compromises with reality have to be made. On the physical plane, atoms have at the very least the relationship of contiguity with other atoms. Similarly in economics, agents cannot be utterly isolated, but the reductionist strategy minimises interrelationships by assuming that all relationship with others is via prices. Prices impound and transmit to other agents the information required for agents to act in their own interests, given what everyone else is doing, that is, to achieve Nash equilibrium. Hence it cannot be a defence to the charge of reductionism that agents are not isolated but are related to each other via prices. It may be noted that the assumption that the price system can be assumed to have this effect is self-defeating. The price system itself and the vector of prices we actually end up with are themselves public goods: they are the unintended consequences of the actions of many self-seeking agents. Their provision is *not mediated by prices* – no dollar votes are cast for a price system, or for this or that vector of prices. Simple economics suggests that the level of an activity which confers beneficial or harmful effects on others, effects which are not mediated by prices, will diverge from the socially desirable level of that activity.

Like many other papers, Bianchi (2009) seems to contradict what has been said about externalities in DSGE models. The full title is 'Overborrowing and Systemic Externalities in the Business Cycle', and the paper sets up a two-sector DSGE model of a small open economy in which '[c]redit constraints that link a private agent's debt to market-determined prices embody a credit externality that drives a wedge between competitive and constrained socially optimal equilibria' (Bianchi 2009, p. ii). However, these credit constraints are not derived from microfoundations, but imposed in an *ad hoc* manner for the sake of the macro effects they induce:

> Although this constraint is not derived from an optimal contract, our results are robust to any framework where the private agent's borrowing ability depends on the real exchange rate. Moreover, the empirical evidence widely supports the use of borrowing constraints of this form.
>
> *(Bianchi 2009, p. 6)*

This raises an important issue. It is not in principle impossible to set out a model of the individual agent in which behaviour is impacted by influences not transmitted by prices. If this were done systematically, it would violate the reductionist version of MI – we would no longer be dealing with a congeries of isolated agents. But it would require some method of modelling the influences which the individual agents were assumed to respond to, and that would go well beyond the DSGE model. Solving models with this sort of interdependence would present challenges.

The reductionist version of MI discussed above is evident right from the start in the Ramsey model set out in Chapter 2 of Wickens (2011), on the centralised economy. The single agent, the economy, has preferences, faces a constraint, and must optimise. The solution to the optimisation problem is set out. The capital stock must remain constant as, if it were to decline in equilibrium, then it would go to zero and the agent would starve, and if it were to expand, then in each period the agent would be consuming less than he could have been. What is assumed therefore is that we are dealing with a Walrasian, well-functioning economy. A small increase or decrease in the accumulation of capital would have no effect on utility. In an earlier and simpler presentation of the model, the 'Golden Rule Solution', equation (2.7) imposes the assumption, as a first-order condition, that the marginal effect on consumption of an increment in capital, $\partial c / \partial k = 0$ (Wickens 2011, p. 18). In the later, more sophisticated, 'Optimal Solution', solving the model leads to an Euler equation, 'the fundamental dynamic equation in intertemporal optimization problems in which there are dynamic constraints' (Wickens 2011, p. 22). The Euler equation is shown to imply that in the long run, 'in the absence of shocks to the macroeconomic system, consumption and the capital stock will be constant through time' (Wickens 2011, p. 24). Again, at the margin, V_t, the present value of current and future utility from consumption is unchanged by small changes in the capital stock in either direction.

The investment multiplier in representative agent models of this kind is thus always zero: there are no macroeconomic consequences to investment. That must mean that there is always full employment. The agent's decision-making is carried out in a vacuum as the agent can assume he is an isolated atom: his actions have no consequences for others beyond those mediated by price. The model is not *wrong* per se: it is rather a description of an economy in a happy state where most of the issues that macroeconomists are concerned about are already resolved. If we treat it as a Robinson Crusoe economy, a depiction of the whole economy as a unity, in its interaction with the natural world, then its findings can be interpreted as correct *normative* statements as to how the economy should behave in order to maximise social welfare. This was indeed the way Ramsey himself treated the model, as an examination of his framing of the problem in Ramsey (1928) will quickly confirm. To regard it as a *positive* description of the economy we actually have, however, is an egregious error – because it assumes that the individual representative agent, the Robinson Crusoe, is in fact *able* to optimise: that there are no *coordination* problems, and that the spontaneous macroeconomic outcomes of individual self-seeking behaviour can be assumed to be socially desirable. This is Panglossian.

The Smets-Wouters model: MI and macroeconomics in practice

We have seen that Wickens claims that the simple, centralised model underpins DSGE modelling. We can see this by examining what is perhaps currently the most popular model used in DSGE modelling, the Smets-Wouters model, set out in two papers (Smets and Wouters 2003, 2007) applying the model to the euro area and to the US respectively. Frank Smets is Director General, Economics, at the European Central Bank (ECB), and has been Counsellor to the President of the ECB, and Co-ordinator of the Counsel to the Executive Board of the bank. The Smets-Wouters model is used by the ECB and other central banks for policy analysis. For Smets and Wouters, the model, which they characterise as a 'New Keynesian or New Neoclassical Synthesis' model (Smets and Wouters 2007, p. 586), features 'a sound, microfounded structure suitable for policy analysis' (Smets and Wouters 2007, p. 587). The claim that microfoundations confer scientific status, or 'soundness', on DSGE models is an expression of MI. The model is regarded as suitable for policy analysis in two senses. By deriving the laws of motion of the economy from the preferences of individual agents and the constraints facing them, it is thought that such models can avoid the 'Lucas critique' of *ad hoc* econometrics. In other words, analysis of macroeconomic aggregates *without* microeconomic foundations will suggest parameter values which might change with a change in government economic policy – hence rendering them inappropriate for policy analysis. Microfounded studies, on the other hand, should suggest parameter values based on household preferences and constraints: these – often referred to as 'deep' or 'structural' parameters – should be relatively robust to changes in government policy. The other sense in which they are suited to policy evaluation is that they are based on agent preferences and hence it should be possible to use the model to make comparisons of the welfare properties of different possible states of the world.

The Smets-Wouters model is a curious mix of the extreme, reductionist, version of MI, and elements that are not methodologically individualist at all, but *ad hoc*.

The basic models of the household and the firm retain all the reductionism of Wickens's version of the Ramsey model. But the mass of frictions and shocks to which they are subject to is entirely *ad hoc* – included to ensure the model displays desirable macroeconomic features: there is no suggestion that they are built on any individual behaviour likely to be found plausible by macroeconomists. In order to satisfy space constraints most of the detail of the model will not be discussed here, and neither will the relatively minor differences between the US and euro-area papers.

Instead of the single household of Wickens's Ramsey model, we now have a continuum of households, which might seem as if it goes to the opposite extreme, but in fact makes no difference to the question of the individualist methodology the model embodies. The continuum of households allows the authors to assume that each is identical, except that they supply differentiated labour with monopolistic competition in the labour market. Each household maximises a utility function with two arguments, consumption and leisure. Households also hold bonds and they own the firms and make decisions on capital accumulation. Their income therefore is the sum of wage income, coupons on the bonds they hold, and net capital income from owning firms. We can see that the household is a representative agent in the sense of Wickens (2011) when Smets and Wouters (2003, p. 1128) argue that, since the households insure against household-specific variations in labour income, 'the first component in the household's income [i.e. wage income] will be equal to aggregate labour income'. Clearly, if every household receives aggregate labour income then there can only be one household. In the technical appendix to the US paper the authors initially index the households by the subscript j, but once they have established that '[i]n equilibrium households will make the same choices for consumption, hours worked, bonds, investment and capital utilisation' (Smets and Wouters 2006, p. 4), the index is dropped: the household stands for all households and the quantities of consumption, labour supplied, etc., are all directly aggregates for the economy. So we are in effect back to the Ramsey model. By modelling the economy as a household, the analysis logically rules out all the coordination issues which arise in economies which consist of many households, each with decentralised decision-making capacity.

But wait. Consumption in the model 'appears in the utility function relative to a time-varying external habit variable' (Smets and Wouters 2007, p. 588). External habit refers to the history of previous aggregate consumption, rather than the history of the agent's own consumption (or 'internal habit'). It is frequently referred to as 'catching up with the Joneses'. But if households derive satisfaction from emulating others, it means that when those others – i.e. everyone – choose to consume, they are themselves imposing an externality on others. Households are responding to an influence not mediated by price. Does this not contradict what was said above? In a sense it does, but it does so by contradicting the Ramsey model itself. If the representative household in its consumption decision is setting itself a threshold for the future, then, given rational expectations, it should include in today's objective function the discounted expected future damage or pleasure its current actions will yield it in the future. It should internalise the externality. Simply imposing this feature is, precisely, *ad hoc*. No attempt is made to refer the assumption of the external habit variable to the household's attempt to optimise. Rather, it is introduced in order for the model to display desirable macro features: 'external habit formation in consumption is used to introduce the necessary empirical persistence in the consumption process' (Smets and Wouters 2003, p. 1124). Exactly the same can be said of many of the aspects of the model, in particular the various constraints and frictions facing agents, and the shocks which drive the dynamics, including sticky nominal prices and wages, investment adjustment costs, and variable capital utilisation with fixed production costs, total factor productivity shocks, risk premium shocks, investment-specific technology shocks, wage and price mark-up shocks, and shocks to exogenous spending and monetary policy. These features are not derived from microfoundations, and this is indeed recognised by the authors, bearing in mind the freight of meaning borne by the terms 'deep' and 'structural' as signalling 'microfounded':

> a *deeper* understanding of the various nominal and real frictions that have been introduced would increase the confidence in using this type of model for welfare analysis. Our analysis also raises questions about the *deeper* determinants of the various *"structural"* shocks, such as productivity and wage mark-up shocks.
>
> *(Smets and Wouters 2007, p. 604)*

Alternatives to methodological individualism

What are the alternatives to MI and today's DSGE models? Usually the alternative is said to be the kind of Old Keynesian econometrics criticised by Lucas. In the papers mentioned above by Smets and Wouters, the alternative is presented as Vector Autoregression (VAR) models, a statistical technique without microfoundations: the authors claim that their DSGE model performs well against VAR models, 'indicating that the theory embedded in the structural model is helpful' (Smets and Wouters, 2007, p. 604). In the face of criticism of DSGE models, those who use them are apt, not unreasonably perhaps, to ask what else they should do. Christopher Sims took this view in his lecture to the inaugural INET conference (Sims 2010), arguing that DSGE models are at least as good as the next best alternative methods. But in fact, there *are* promising alternatives.

What MI misses is the possibility that there may be causally efficacious macroeconomic entities which are not derivable from any description of the activity of micro-level agents taken in isolation. The very same people can constitute a feudal society or a capitalist economy, the catholic church or the mafia – it is not possible to derive the market economy or an organised religion from a consideration of the individual people composing it at the substrate level. Just so, the proposed macroeconomic entities of heterodox thinkers such as Keynes, Marx and Hayek, to mention just some of the most salient, are consistent with, but not reducible to, micro-level behaviours, and consequently offer hope of a more profound understanding of the working of economies. For Marx, for example, states and capitals are hypostatisations of an aspect of human activity, parasitic on their human substrate. Again, for Hayek, the networks of social relations which constitute the proper subject matter of social science are filtered through an evolutionary process and guide individuals to behave in a way which ensures the survival of those networks of relations, whatever the individuals concerned may think they are doing. Two entries in this volume, by Freeman and by King, discuss post-Keynesian and Marxian alternatives.

It certainly is the case that these alternatives will not generate the apparent precision of the parameter estimates and so on issuing from DSGE models, but this may be due either (a) to neglect of the paradigm within which they are embedded by mainstream economics, leaving heterodox approaches far less technically developed, or (b) to simply the sheer impossibility of generating such precision with any reliability in economics considered as a human science. It may be that, as Hayek insists, 'pattern prediction' is the best we can get.

Conclusion

This chapter has argued that the methodological individualism of modern, mainstream macroeconomics, embodied in the dynamic stochastic general equilibrium approach (DSGE), is individualist in an extreme, reductionist sense. Individual agents are assumed to form a congeries without mutual interaction, except via prices. Externalities and coordination problems are assumed away. An examination of a key text in the postgraduate teaching of DSGE (*Macroeconomic Theory. A Dynamic General Equilibrium Approach* by Michael Wickens), and of a key model used by central banks in applying it (the Smets-Wouters model), shows both the deficiency of this approach, and the continual need to add on frictions and shocks in a wholly *ad hoc* way, in order to make it more empirically relevant. The chapter concludes by suggesting that alternatives to the methodologically individualist microfoundations approach be sought in heterodox trends emphasising not isolated individuals but individual agents embedded in networks of social relations.

Bibliography

Bianchi, J. (2009) 'Overborrowing and systemic externalities in the business cycle', Working Paper No. 2009–24, Federal Reserve Bank of Atlanta; a revised version is published in *American Economic Review*, 101 (December 2011), 3400–26, without the passages cited here.

Blaug, M. (1992 [1980]) *The Methodology of Economics or How Economists Explain* (second edition), Cambridge, UK: Cambridge University Press.

Denis, A. (2014) 'Methodological individualism and society: Hayek's evolving view', in G. L. Nell, ed., *Austrian Economic Perspectives on Individualism and Society: Moving Beyond Methodological Individualism*, Ch 1, pp. 7–20, New York: Palgrave Macmillan.

Heath, J. (2015) 'Methodological individualism', *The Stanford Encyclopedia of Philosophy*, plato.stanford.edu/entries/methodological-individualism, accessed 21 September 2021.

Hodgson, G. M. (2007) 'Meanings of methodological individualism' *Journal of Economic Methodology* 14 (2) (June), 211–26.

Ramsey, F.P. (1928) 'A mathematical theory of saving', *The Economic Journal* 38 (152), 543–59.

Schumpeter, J. (1909) 'On the concept of social value', *The Quarterly Journal of Economics* 23 (2) (February), 213–32.

Schumpeter, J. (1980) *Methodological Individualism*, Brussels: Institutum Europæum. English translation by Michiel van Notten of the corresponding chapter of Joseph Schumpeter (1908) *Das Wesen und der Hauptinhalt der theoretischen Nationalökonomie*, with a preface by FA Hayek, and a Summary by Frank van Dun.

Sims, C. (2010) 'How empirical evidence does or does not influence economic thinking and theory: calibration, statistical inference, and structural change'. Institute for New Economic Thinking, Inaugural Conference, 8–11 April 2010, Kings College Cambridge, www.youtube.com/watch?v=TH6QexRT0Fg, accessed 21 September 2021.

Smets, F., and R. Wouters (2003) 'An estimated dynamic stochastic general equilibrium model of the euro area', *Journal of the European Economic Association* 1 (5) (September), 1123–75.

Smets, F., and R. Wouters (2006) 'Model appendix', appendix to Smets and Wouters (2007), assets.aeaweb.org/asset-server/articles-attachments/aer/data/june07/20041254_app.pdf, accessed 21 September 2021.

Smets, F., and R. Wouters (2007) 'Shocks and frictions in US business cycles: A Bayesian DSGE approach', *The American Economic Review* 97 (3), 586–606.

Wickens, M. (2011 [2008]) *Macroeconomic Theory: A Dynamic General Equilibrium Approach*, Second edition, Princeton, and Oxford: Princeton University Press.

2

DEDUCTION, INDUCTION AND ABDUCTION

Lars Syll

Introduction

In the mainstream macroeconomic modelling strategy there has for long been an insisting on formalistic (mathematical) modelling, and to some economic methodologists (e.g. Lawson 2015; Syll 2016) this has forced economists to give up on realism and substitute axiomatics for real-world relevance. According to the critique, the deductivist orientation has been the main reason behind the difficulty that mainstream economics has had in terms of understanding, explaining and predicting what takes place in modern economies. But it has also given mainstream economics much of its discursive power – at least as long as no one starts asking tough questions on the veracity of and justification for the assumptions on which the deductivist foundation is erected.

The kind of formal-analytical and axiomatic-deductive mathematical modelling that makes up the core of mainstream economics is hard to make compatible with a real-world ontology. It is also the reason why so many critics find mainstream economic analysis patently and utterly unrealistic and irrelevant.

Although there has been a clearly discernible increase and focus on 'empirical' economics in recent decades, the results in these research fields have not fundamentally challenged the main deductivist direction of mainstream economics. They are still mainly framed and interpreted within the core 'axiomatic' assumptions of individualism, instrumentalism and equilibrium (cf. Arnsperger and Varoufakis 2006) that make up even the 'new' mainstream economics. Although, perhaps, a sign of an increasing – but highly path-dependent – theoretical pluralism, mainstream economics is still, from a methodological point of view, mainly a deductive project erected on a formalist foundation.

If macroeconomic theories and models are to confront reality there are obvious limits to what can be said 'rigorously' in economics. For although it is generally a good aspiration to search for scientific claims that are both rigorous and precise, the chosen level of precision and rigour must be relative to the subject matter studied. An economics that is relevant to the world in which we live can never achieve the same degree of rigour and precision as in logic, mathematics or the natural sciences.

DOI: 10.4324/9781315745992-4

But in science at large deduction is not the only method available for doing proper research. One could argue that there basically are three kinds of argumentation methods available: deduction, induction and abduction. We start by having a look at deduction.

Deduction

An example of *a logically* valid deductive inference (and whenever 'logic' is used in this entry, 'logic' refers to deductive/analytical logic) may look like this:

> Premise 1: All Chicago economists believe in REH
> Premise 2: Bob is a Chicago economist
> _____
> Conclusion: Bob believes in REH

In a hypothetico-deductive reasoning – hypothetico-deductive *confirmation* in this case – we would use the conclusion to test the law-like hypothesis in premise 1 (according to the hypothetico-deductive model, a hypothesis is confirmed by evidence if the evidence is deducible from the hypothesis). If Bob does not believe in REH we have gained some warranted reason for non-acceptance of the hypothesis (an obvious shortcoming here being that further information beyond that given in the explicit premises might have given another conclusion).

The hypothetico-deductive method (in case we treat the hypothesis as absolutely sure/true, we rather talk of an *axiomatic-deductive* method) basically means that we

- Posit a hypothesis
- Infer empirically testable propositions (consequences) from it
- Test the propositions through observation or experiment
- Depending on the testing results find the hypothesis either corroborated or falsified

However, in science we regularly use a kind of 'practical' argumentation where there is little room for applying the restricted logical 'formal transformations' view of validity and inference. Most people would probably accept the following argument as a 'valid' reasoning even though from a strictly logical point of view it is non-valid:

> Premise 1: Bob is a Chicago economist
> Premise 2: The recorded proportion of Keynesian Chicago economists is zero
> _____
> Conclusion: So, certainly, Bob is not a Keynesian economist

How come? One reason is that in science, contrary to what you find in most logic textbooks, not very many argumentations are settled by showing that 'All Xs are Ys.' In scientific practice we instead present other-than-analytical explicit warrants and backings – data, experience, evidence, theories, models – for our inferences. As long as we can show that our 'deductions' or 'inferences' are justifiable and have well-backed warrants, other scientists will listen to us. That our scientific 'deductions' or 'inferences' are logical non-entailments simply is not a problem. To think otherwise is committing the fallacy of misapplying formal-analytical logic categories to areas where they are irrelevant or simply beside the point.

Scientific arguments are not analytical arguments, where validity is solely a question of formal properties. Scientific arguments are *substantial* arguments. If Bob is a Keynesian or not is not something we can decide on formal properties of statements/propositions. We have to check out what he has actually been writing and saying to check if the hypothesis that he is a Keynesian is true or not.

In a *deductive-nomological* explanation – also known as a *covering law explanation* – we would try to explain why Bob believes in REH with the help of the two premises (in this case actually giving an explanation with only little explanatory value). These kinds of explanations – both in their *deterministic* and *statistic/probabilistic* versions – rely heavily on deductive entailment from assumed to be true premises. But they have preciously little to say on where these assumed to be true premises come from.

Deductive logic of confirmation and explanation may work well – given that they are used in deterministic closed models. In mathematics, the deductive-axiomatic method has worked just fine. But science is not mathematics. Conflating those two domains of knowledge has been one of the most fundamental mistakes made in the science of economics. Applying the deductive-axiomatic method to real-world systems immediately proves it to be excessively narrow and irrelevant. Both the confirmatory and explanatory ilk of hypothetico-deductive reasoning fail since there is no way you can relevantly analyse confirmation or explanation as a purely logical relation between hypothesis and evidence, or between law-like rules and explananda. In science we argue and try to substantiate our beliefs and hypotheses with reliable evidence – propositional and predicate deductive logic, on the other hand, is not about *reliability*, but the *validity* of the conclusions *given* that the premises are true.

Deduction – and the inferences that go with it – is an example of 'explicative reasoning', where the conclusions we make are already included in the premises. Deductive inferences are purely *analytical* and it is this truth-preserving nature of deduction that makes it different from all other kinds of reasoning. But it is also its limitation, since truth in the deductive context does not refer to a real-world ontology (only relating propositions as true or false within a formal-logic system), and as an argument scheme, deduction is totally non-ampliative – the output of the analysis is nothing else than the input.

Just to give an economics example, consider the following rather typical, but also uninformative and tautological, deductive inference:

Premise 1: The firm seeks to maximise its profits
Premise 2: The firm maximises its profits when marginal cost equals marginal income

---

Conclusion: The firm will operate its business at the equilibrium where marginal cost equals marginal income

This is as empty as deductive-nomological explanations of singular facts building on simple generalisations:

Premise 1: All humans are less than 20 feet tall
Premise 2: Bob is a human

Conclusion: Bob is less than 20 feet tall

Although a logically valid inference, this is not much of an explanation (since we would still probably want to know why *all* humans are less than 20 feet tall).

Deductive-nomological explanations also often suffer from a kind of emptiness that emanates from a lack of real (causal) connection between premises and conclusions:

Premise 1: All humans that take birth control pills do not get pregnant
Premise 2: Bob took birth control pills

Conclusion: Bob did not get pregnant

Most people would probably not consider this much of a real explanation.

Learning new things about reality demands something else than a reasoning where the knowledge is already embedded in the premises. These other kinds of reasoning may give *good* – but not *conclusive* – reasons. That is the price we have to pay if we want to have something substantial and interesting to say about the real world.

Induction

An example of an *inductive* inference may look like this:

Premise 1: This is a randomly selected large set of economists from Chicago
Premise 2: These randomly selected economists all believe in REH

Conclusion: All Chicago economists believe in REH

Induction is a kind of inference that is logically non-valid inference, and to really warrant it we have to supply strong empirical evidence. And that is no simple matter at all, as Keynes (1973 [1921], p. 468f) noticed:

In my judgment, the practical usefulness of those modes of inference, here termed Universal and Statistical Induction, on the validity of which the boasted knowledge of modern science depends, can only exist—and I do not now pause to inquire again whether such an argument must be circular—if the universe of phenomena does in fact present those peculiar characteristics of atomism and limited variety which appear more and more clearly as the ultimate result to which material science is tending...

But even though induction is more demanding in terms of justification than deduction, we should not draw the conclusion that it is no inference at all:

> Now it might be charged that moving from such facts as that F's have always been followed by C's, to the claim that F's obtaining is a good reason for expecting C, – that this is not an inference at all … Entailment it may not be, granted. But inference it certainly is, as must be every case of drawing reasonable conclusions from evidence.
>
> *Hanson (1971, p. 242)*

Justified inductions presuppose a *resemblance* of sort between what we have experienced and know, and what we have not yet experienced and do not yet know. Two examples may exemplify this problem of induction.

Assume you're a Bayesian turkey and hold a nonzero probability belief in the hypothesis H that 'people are nice vegetarians that do not eat turkeys and that every day I see the sun rise confirms my belief'. For every day you survive, you update your belief according to Bayes' Rule

$$P(H|e) = [P(e|H)P(H)]/PI,$$

where evidence e stands for 'not being eaten' and $P(e|H) = 1$. Given that there do exist other hypotheses than HI(e) is less than 1 and a fortiori $P(H|e)$ is greater than $P(H)$. Every day you survive increases your probability belief that you will not be eaten. This is totally rational according to the Bayesian definition of rationality. Unfortunately – as Bertrand Russell famously noticed – for every day that goes by, the traditional Christmas dinner also gets closer and closer …

Or take the case of macroeconomic forecasting, which perhaps better than anything else illustrates the problem of induction in economics. As a rule, macroeconomic forecasts arguably tend to be little better than intelligent guesswork. Or in other words – macroeconomic mathematical-statistical forecasting models, and the inductive logic upon which they ultimately build, are as a rule far from successful. The empirical and theoretical evidence is clear. Predictions and forecasts are inherently difficult to make in a socio-economic domain where genuine uncertainty and unknown unknowns often rule the roost. The real processes underlying the time series that economists use to make their predictions and forecasts do not confirm with the inductive assumptions made in the applied statistical and econometric models. The forecasting models fail to a large extent because the kind of uncertainty that faces humans and societies actually makes the models strictly seem inapplicable. The future is inherently unknowable – and using statistics and econometrics does not in the least overcome this ontological fact. The economic future is not something that we normally can predict in advance. Better than perhaps to accept that as a rule 'we simply do not know'.

Induction is sometimes a good guide for evaluating hypotheses. But for the creative generation of plausible and relevant hypotheses it is conspicuously silent. For that we need, as noted already by Peirce (1931, §145), another – non-algorithmic and ampliative – kind of reasoning.

Abduction

Premise 1: All Chicago economists believe in REH
Premise 2: These economists believe in REH

Conclusion: These economists are from Chicago

In this case, again, we have an example of a logically non-valid inference – *the fallacy of affirming the consequent*:

p => q
q
----
p

or, in instantiated form

∀x (Gx => Px)
Pa

Ga

But it is nonetheless an inference that may be a strongly warranted and *truth-producing* – in contradistinction to *truth-preserving* deductions – reasoning, following the general pattern

Evidence => Explanation => Inference.

Here we infer something based on what would be the best explanation given the law-like rule (premise 1) and an observation (premise 2). The truth of the conclusion (explanation) is nothing that is *logically* given, but something we have to justify, argue for and test in different ways to possibly establish with any certainty or degree. And as always when we deal with explanations, what is considered best is relative to what we know of the world. In the real world all evidence has an irreducible holistic aspect. We never conclude that evidence follows from hypothesis *simpliciter*, but always given some more or less explicitly stated contextual background assumptions. All non-deductive inferences and explanations are *a fortiori* context-dependent.

If extending the abductive scheme to incorporate the demand that the explanation has to be the *best* among a set of *plausible* competing/rival/contrasting potential and satisfactory explanations, we have what is nowadays usually referred to as *inference to the best explanation* (IBE). In this way IBE is a refinement of the original (Peircean) concept of abduction by making the background knowledge requirement more explicit.

In abduction we start with a body of (purported) data/facts/evidence and search for explanations that can account for these data/facts/evidence. Having the best explanation means that you, given the context-dependent background assumptions, have a satisfactory explanation that can explain the fact/evidence better than any other competing explanation – and so it is *reasonable* to consider/believe the hypothesis to be true. Even if we do not (inevitably) have deductive certainty, our abductive reasoning gives us a licence to consider our belief in the hypothesis as reasonable. The model of inference to the best explanation is, as Peter Lipton (2000, p. 184) writes,

> designed to give a partial account of many inductive inferences, both in science and in ordinary life... Its governing idea is that explanatory considerations are a guide to inference, that scientists infer from the available evidence to the hypothesis which would, if correct, best explain that evidence. Many inferences are naturally described in this way...
>
> Inference to the Best Explanation can be seen as an extension of the idea of 'self-evidencing' explanations, where the phenomenon that is explained in turn provides an essential part of the reason for believing the explanation is correct... According to Inference to the Best Explanation, this is a common situation in science: hypotheses are supported by the very observations they are supposed to explain. Moreover, on this model, the observations support the hypothesis precisely because it would explain them.

Accepting a hypothesis means that you consider it to explain the available evidence better than any other competing hypothesis. The acceptability warrant comes from the explanatory power of the hypothesis, and the conscious act of trying to rule out the possible competing potential explanations in itself increases the plausibility of the preferred explanation. Knowing that we – after having earnestly considered and analysed the other available potential explanations – have been able to *eliminate* the competing potential explanations warrants and enhances the confidence we have that our preferred explanation is the best – 'loveliest' – explanation, i.e., the explanation that provides us with the greatest understanding (given it is correct). As Sherlock Holmes had it in *The Sign of Four*: 'Eliminate the impossible, and whatever remains, however improbable, must be the truth.' Subsequent confirmation of our hypothesis – by observations, experiments or other future evidence – makes it even more well-confirmed (and underlines that all explanations are incomplete, and that the models and theories that we as scientists use cannot only be assessed by the extent of their fit with experimental or observational data, but also need to take into account their explanatory power).

This, of course, does not in any way mean that we cannot be wrong. But as Alan Musgrave (2010, p. 94) writes:

> People object that being the best available explanation of a fact does not prove something to be true or even probable. Quite so – and again, so what? The explanationist principle – 'It is reasonable to believe that the best available explanation of any fact is true' – means that it is reasonable to believe or think true things that have not been shown to be true or probable, more likely true than not.

Abductions are *fallible* inferences – since the premises do not logically entail the conclusion – so from a *logical* point of view, abduction is a weak mode of inference. But if the abductive arguments put forward are strong enough, they can be warranted and give us justified true belief, and hence, knowledge, even though they are fallible inferences. As scientists we sometimes – much like Sherlock Holmes and other detectives that use abductive reasoning – experience disillusion. We thought that we had reached a strong abductive conclusion by ruling out the alternatives in the set of contrasting explanations. But what we thought was true turned out to be false. But that does not necessarily mean that we had no good reasons for believing what we believed. If we cannot live with that contingency and uncertainty, well, then we're in the wrong business.

What makes the works of people like Galileo, Newton or Keynes truly interesting is not that they describe new empirical facts. The truly seminal and pioneering aspects of their works are that they managed to find out and analyse what makes empirical phenomena possible. What are the fundamental physical forces that make heavy objects fall the way they do? Why do people get unemployed? Why are market societies haunted by economic crises? Starting from well-known facts these scientists discovered the mechanisms and structures that made these empirical facts possible.

The works of these scientists are good illustrations of the fact that in science we are usually not only interested in observable facts and phenomena. Since structures, powers, institutions, relations, etc., are not *directly* observable, we need to use theories and models to *indirectly* obtain knowledge of them (and to be able to *recontextualise* and *redescribe* observables to discover new and (perhaps) hitherto unknown dimensions of the world around us). Deduction and induction do not give us access to these kinds of entities. They are things that to a large extent have to be *discovered*. Discovery processes presuppose creativity and imagination, virtues that are not very prominent in inductive analysis (statistics and econometrics) or deductive-logical reasoning. We need another mode of inference. We need inference to the best explanation.

Inference to the best explanation is a (non-demonstrative) ampliative method of reasoning that makes it possible for us to gain new insights and come up with – and evaluate – theories and hypotheses that – in contradistinction to the entailments that deduction provides us with – *transcend* the epistemological content of the evidence that brought about them. And instead of only delivering inductive generalisations from the evidence at hand – as the inductive scheme – it typically opens up for conceptual novelties and *retroduction*, where we from analysis of empirical data and observation reconstruct the ontological conditions for their being what they are. As scientists we do not only want to be able to deal with observables. We try to make the world more intelligible by finding ways to understand the fundamental processes and structures that rule the world we live in. Science should help us penetrate to these processes and structures behind facts and events we observe. We should look out for causal relations, processes and structures, but models can never be more than a starting point in that endeavour. There is always the possibility that there are other (non-quantifiable) variables – of vital importance and although perhaps unobservable and non-additive not necessarily epistemologically inaccessible – that were not considered for the formalised mathematical model. The content-enhancing aspect of inference to the best explanation gives us the possibility of acquiring new and warranted knowledge and understanding of things beyond empirical sense data.

Outside mathematics and logic, scientific methods do not deliver absolute certainty or prove things. However, many economists are still in pursuit of absolute certainty. But there will always be a great number of theories and models that are compatible/consistent with facts, and no logic makes it possible to select one as the right one. The search for absolute certainty can never be anything else but disappointing since all scientific knowledge is more or less uncertain. That is a fact of the way the world is, and we just have to learn to live with that inescapable limitation of scientific knowledge.

> Traditionally, philosophers have focused mostly on the logical template of inference. The paradigm-case has been deductive inference, which is topic-neutral and context-insensitive. The study of deductive rules has engendered the search for the Holy Grail: syntactic and topic-neutral accounts of all prima facie reasonable inferential rules. The search has hoped to find rules that are transparent and algorithmic, and whose following will just be a matter of grasping their logical form. Part of the search for the Holy Grail has been to show that the so-called scientific method can be formalised in a topic-neutral way ...
> There is no Holy Grail to be found.
>
> *(Psillos 2007, p. 441)*

Explanations are *per se* not deductive proofs. And deductive proofs often do not explain at all, since validly deducing X from Y does not *per se* explain *why* X is a fact, because it does not say anything at all about *how* being Y is connected to being X. Explanations do not necessarily have to *entail* the things they explain. But they can nevertheless confer warrants for the conclusions we reach using inference to the best explanation. The evidential force of inference to the best explanation is consistent with having less than certain belief.

As economists we entertain different hypotheses on inflation, unemployment, growth, wealth inequality and so on. From the available evidence and our context-dependent background knowledge we evaluate how well the different hypotheses would explain these evidences and which of them qualifies for being the best accepted hypothesis. Given the information available, we base our inferences on explanatory considerations.

Where did economics go wrong?

Although – under specific and restrictive assumptions – deductive methods may be usable tools, insisting that economic theories and models ultimately have to be built on a deductive-axiomatic foundation to count as being economic theories and models will only make economics irrelevant for solving real-world economic problems. Modern deductive-axiomatic mainstream economics is sure very rigorous – but if it's rigorously wrong, who cares?

Instead of making formal logical argumentation based on deductive-axiomatic models of the message, we are arguably better served by economists who more than anything else try to contribute to solving real problems – and in that endeavour inference to the best explanation is much more relevant than formal logic.

> Despite their reference to reality, the laws stated by pure economics have little, if any, information content. To the extent that theories of rational choice lay claim to empirical-analytic knowledge, they are open to the charge of Platonism ...
> The central point is the confusion of logical presuppositions with empirical conditions. The maxims of action introduced are treated not as verifiable hypotheses

but as assumptions about actions by economic subjects that are in principle possible. The theorist limits himself to formal deductions of implications in the unfounded expectation that he will nevertheless arrive at propositions with empirical content.

(Habermas 1988, p. 48)

Science is made possible by the fact that there are structures that are durable and partly independent of our knowledge or beliefs about them. There exists a reality beyond our theories and concepts of it. It is this independent reality that our theories in some way deal with. From that point of view, it could be argued that the generalisations we look for in economics (often with statistical and econometric methods) when using inductive methods (to say anything about a population based on a given sample) are abductions. From the premise 'All *observed* real-world markets are non-perfect' we conclude 'All real-world markets are non-perfect.' If we have tested all the other potential hypotheses and found that, e.g., there is no reason to believe that the sampling process has been biased and that we are dealing with a non-representative non-random sample, we could, given relevant background beliefs/assumptions, say that we have justified belief in treating our conclusion as warranted. Being able to eliminate/refute contesting/contrastive hypotheses – using both observational *and* non-observational evidence – confers an increased certainty in the hypothesis believed to be 'the loveliest'.

Instead of building models based on logic-axiomatic, topic-neutral, context-insensitive and non-ampliative deductive reasoning – as in mainstream economic theory – it would arguably be more fruitful and relevant to apply inference to the best explanation, given that what we are looking for is to be able to explain what's going on in the world we live in. Although inevitably defeasible, abduction is also our only source of scientific discovery.

One important rationale behind mainstream economic model building is the quest for rigour, and more precisely, *logical* rigour. Formalisation of economics has been going on for more than a century and with time it has become obvious that the preferred kind of formalisation is the one that rigorously follows the rules of formal logic. As in mathematics, this has gone hand in hand with a growing emphasis on axiomatics. Instead of basically trying to establish a connection between empirical data and assumptions, 'truth' has come to be reduced to a question of fulfilling internal consistency demands between conclusion and premises, instead of showing a 'congruence' between model assumptions and reality. This has severely restricted the applicability of economic theory and models, since unpacking premises and relationships within a consistent model is not enough in empirical sciences, where we do also have to be concerned with the truth-status of the premises and conclusions *re* the world in which we live.

When applying deductivist thinking – an idea maintaining the feasibility and relevance of describing an entire science as (more or less) a self-contained axiomatic-deductive system – to economics, mainstream economists usually set up 'as if' models based on a set of tight axiomatic assumptions from which consistent and precise inferences are made. The beauty of this procedure is of course that if the axiomatic premises are true, the conclusions *necessarily* follow. But if the models are to be relevant, we also have to argue that their precision and rigour still hold when they are applied to real-world situations.

The rather one-eyed focus on validity and consistency has made mainstream economics irrelevant, since its insistence on deductive-axiomatic foundations does not seem to earnestly consider the fact that its formal logical reasoning, inferences and arguments show an amazingly weak relationship to their everyday real-world equivalents. Searching in vain for absolute and deductive knowledge and 'truth', one forgoes the opportunity of getting more relevant and better (defeasible) knowledge. Rigour and precision have a devastatingly important trade-off: the higher the level of rigour and precision, the smaller the range of real-world applications.

To understand and explain relations between different entities in the real economy the predominant strategy is to build models and make things happen in these 'analogue-economy models' rather than engineering things happening in real economies. This formalistic-deductive modelling strategy may seem impressive, but the one-sided insistence on axiomatic-deductivist modelling as the only scientific activity worthy of pursuing in economics is of little value to simply make claims about models and lose sight of reality.

> In due course deductivism in economics, through morphing into mathematical deductivism on the back of developments within the discipline of mathematics, came to acquire a new lease of life, with practitioners (once more) potentially oblivious to any inconsistency between the ontological presuppositions of adopting a mathematical modelling emphasis and the nature of social reality. The consequent rise of mathematical deductivism has culminated in the situation we find today.
>
> *Lawson (2015, p. 84)*

Theories and models being 'coherent' or 'consistent' with data do not make the theories and models success stories. To have valid evidence is not enough. What economics needs is *sound* evidence. The premises of a valid argument do not have to be true, but a sound argument, on the other hand, is not only valid, but builds on premises that are true. Aiming only for validity, without soundness, is setting the economics aspirations level too low for developing a realist and relevant science.

Conclusion

Abduction and inference to the best explanation show the inherent limits of formal logical reasoning in science. No new ideas or hypotheses in science originate by deduction or induction. In order to come up with new ideas or hypotheses and explain what happens in our world, scientists *have to* use inference to the best explanation. All scientific explanations inescapably rely on a reasoning that is, from a *logical* point of view, fallacious. Thus in order to give macroeconomic explanations of what happens in real-world economies, we have to use a reasoning that *logically* is a fallacy. There is no way around this – unless one wants to follow the rather barren way that mainstream economics has been following for more than half a century now – retreating into the world of thought experimental 'as if' axiomatic-deductive-mathematical models.

The purported strength of modern mainstream economics is that it ultim–ely has a firm anchorage in 'rigorous' and 'precise' deductive reasoning in mathematical models. To some, however, this 'strength' has come at too high a price. Perhaps more than anywhere else can this be seen in macroeconomics, where an almost quasi-religious insistence that economics has to have microfoundations – without ever presenting neither ontological nor epistemological justifications for this patently invalid claim – has put a blind eye to the weakness of the whole enterprise of trying to depict a complex economy based on an all-embracing representative actor equipped with superhuman knowledge, forecasting abilities and forward-looking rational expectations. How can we be sure the lessons learned in these models have external validity, when based on a set of highly specific assumptions with an enormous descriptive deficit? To have a deductive warrant for things happening in a model is no guarantee for them being preserved when applied to the real world.

References

Arnsperger, C. and Y. Varoufakis (2006). 'What is neoclassical economics?' *Post-autistic Economics Review*, (38), 2–12.

Habermas, J. (1988). *On the Logic of the Social Sciences*, Cambridge, MA.: MIT Press.

Hanson, N. R. (1971). *What I Do Not Believe, and Other Essays*, Dordrecht: Reidel.

Keynes, J. M. (1973 [1921]). *The Collected Writings of John Maynard Keynes*. Vol. VIII, *A Treatise on Probability*. [New ed.], London: Macmillan.

Lawson, T. (2015). *Essays on the Nature and State of Modern Economics*, London: Routledge.

Lipton, P. (2000). 'Inference to the best explanation', in W. H. Newton-Smith, ed., *A Companion to the Philosophy of Science*, Oxford: Blackwell, 184–93.

Musgrave, A. (2010). 'Critical rationalism, explanation, and severe tests', in D. G. Mayo and A. Spanos, eds, *Error and Inference: Recent Exchanges on Experimental Reasoning, Reliability, and the Objectivity and Rationality of Science*. Cambridge, UK: Cambridge University Press, 88–112.

Peirce, C. S. (1934). *Collected Papers of Charles Sanders Peirce*. Vol. 5, Pragmatism and pragmaticism. Cambridge, MA: Belknap Press of Harvard University Press.

Psillos, S. (2007). 'The fine structure of inference to the best explanation', *Philosophy and Phenomenological Research* 74, 441–48.

Syll, L. (2016). *On the Use and Misuse of Theories and Models in Mainstream Economics*. Bristol: WEA Books.

3

INSTRUMENTALISM

J. Daniel Hammond

Introduction

Instrumentalism is a philosophy of science that developed in the 20th century but
has roots in the early modern period. A succinct definition of instrumentalism is the
belief that scientific theories are merely instruments, practical devices, for organising empirical (observational) data and drawing implications from empirical data for
other empirical data. The modifier merely is stressed, for according to instrumentalism, theories are not descriptions of the subject matter of the science. Theoretical
statements are in this sense meaningless and not subject to tests of any sort for their
truth or falsity. The only test of a theory therefore is whether it is useful for the scientist's purpose. It is presumed that the scientist's purpose is not to describe his or her
subject matter. This obviously raises questions about whether science is explanatory.

Philosophical Background

Although he was not an instrumentalist, instrumentalism as with much in the modern conception of science can be traced to Francis Bacon (1561–1626). Bacon argued
for the use of induction rather than the syllogistic method of the Scholastics for natural philosophy. In *Novum Organum* (1620) he set out a list of aphorisms on the logic
and practice of science. A selection of these aphorisms illustrates Bacon's advocacy
of the inductive method:

> I. Man, as the minister and interpreter of nature, does and understands as much
> as his observations on the order of nature, either with regard to things or the
> mind, permit him, and neither knows nor is capable of more.

> IX. The sole cause and root of almost every defect in the sciences is this, that
> while we falsely admire and extol the powers of the human mind, we do not
> search for its real helps.

> XIV. The syllogism consists of propositions; propositions of words; words are the
> signs of notions. If, therefore, the notions (which form the basis of the whole) be

DOI: 10.4324/9781315745992-5

confused and carelessly abstracted from things, there is no solidity in the super-structure. Our only hope, then, is in genuine induction.

XIX. There are and can exist but two ways of investigating and discovering truth. The one hurries on rapidly from the senses and particulars to the most general axioms, and from them, as principles and their supposed indisputable truth, de-rives and discovers the intermediate axioms. This is the way now in use. The other constructs its axioms from the senses and particulars, but ascending con-tinually and gradually, till it finally arrives at the most general axioms, which is the true but unattempted way.

(Quoted from Novum Organum, Bacon 1902[1620])

Subsequent steps on the way to instrumentalism are the idealism of George Berkeley (1685–1753) and Immanuel Kant (1724–1804) and the scepticism of David Hume (1711–1776). They identified problems with what Bacon considered 'the true but unattempted way'. Bacon expected that a move from the interior of the mind with syllogism to the external world with induction would foster scientific progress. In contrast the idealists drew attention to the limits of inferences from observational data. In effect they located the 'external world' that scientists sought to penetrate in the scientist's mind. So the ob-jects of knowledge are not materials of nature but ideas of the mind. Hume's scepticism cast doubt on the possibility of using the inductive method to access the causal connec-tions in the material world. He asked what grounds are there to infer 'that instances, of which we have had no experience, must resemble those, of which we have had experi-ence, and that the course of nature continues always uniformly the same?' (Hume 1896, p. 89). His answer was, none. This is the 'problem of induction'. No matter how close the correlation between variables in observational data, there is no guarantee that the correlation will hold in the future, i.e., in data not yet observed. Moreover, correlation does not establish causation, even with lagged data – *post hoc non ergo propter hoc.*

Instrumentalism versus realism

The philosophy of instrumentalism was developed as a way to reconcile this 'problem of induction' with the empirical methods that are the hallmark of modern scientific prac-tice. The doctrine was developed most fully by logical empiricists such as Rudolf Carnap and Carl Hempel in the early 20th century. According to the philosopher Ernest Nagel,

the central claim of the instrumentalist view is that a theory is neither a summary description nor a generalised statement of relations between observable data. On the contrary, a theory is held to be a rule or a principle for analysing and symbolically representing certain materials of gross experience, and at the same time an instru-ment in a technique for inferring observation statements from other such statements.

(1961, p. 129)

Nagel refers to the instrumentalist conception of theories as 'inference tickets' rather than as premises about the world.

Scientific realism is the alternative to instrumentalism and its progenitors, the idealism of Berkeley and the scepticism of Hume. The realist critique is made on different levels. Ontological realism claims that the objects of a theory are real.

Semantic realism claims that the terms and statements of theories are descriptions of reality, and therefore are either true or false. Epistemological realism claims that we can learn of the secrets of nature. Karl Popper was a prominent realist critic of instrumentalism. In *Realism and the Aim of Science* (1983) Popper replaced Nagel's 'inference tickets' with the more pejorative 'gadgets' as a summary term for the instrumentalist view of theories. He suggested that instrumentalism reduced the scientist to nothing more than a 'glorified plumber'. For instrumentalism 'there is no truth in science: there is only utility. Science is unable to enlighten our minds: it can only fill our bellies' (ibid., p. 123).

Popper acknowledged the weight of concerns that motivated Berkeley and Hume – that science depends on metaphysical entities such as causality not subject to observation and verification. But he dismissed the inference that science is either 'all in the head', which would make it subject to Francis Bacon's criticism of the syllogistic method, or that it is merely instrumental. Popper appealed to the aims of working scientists over and above the aims which philosophers could justify by their philosophical standards. He claimed that scientific language, i.e., language used by scientists, is explanatory language. Scientific language shares this quality with ordinary language. Scientific explanations are indeed fallible, as are ordinary explanations, and in many cases they have instrumental value. But they are nonetheless explanations rather than mere instruments.

Popper's way of reconciling realistic scientific theories with the problem of induction was to propose that what scientists do is to begin their work with problems for which an explanation is sought. This is in contradistinction to sifting data in search of patterns. Scientific problems emerge when there are gaps between the accepted theory and that which the theory is intended to explain. These anomalies prompt scientists to make theoretical conjectures, which they compare to the existing theory. If the new theory explains that which the existing theory explains plus the anomaly, the new theory is tested for its conformity with empirical evidence. Then if the theory conforms with empirical evidence it is accepted as the working theory. It is through this process of conjecture and refutation in iteration that scientific progress occurs.[1]

Milton Friedman and instrumentalism

Milton Friedman's 'The methodology of positive economics' (1953) was a touchstone for discussions of scientific methodology in economics in the second half of the 20th century. As such, it is instructive to consider how the essay was interpreted in regard to instrumentalism. One of the lessons we can draw from discussion of the essay is that it is much easier to define instrumentalism than to identify it in a methodological statement by someone who is a working scientist rather than a philosopher, or in the scientist's practice. We will elaborate on this lesson after examining ties between Friedman's essay and discussions of instrumentalism. Friedman wrote the essay over a number of years and in response to criticisms and developments during the time he was writing it. He also wrote it as a practising economist in dialogue with other economists rather from the perspective of the philosophy of science. Thus, the essay does not fit neatly into philosophical or methodological boxes. But one of the persistent interpretative themes in commentary about the essay is that the perspective it presents is instrumentalism. This interpretation is traced to Friedman's critique of the claim that economic theory should be tested by the realism or, more precisely, the realisticness of its assumptions. Friedman responded to the proposed test of theories by their assumptions:

> In so far as a theory can be said to have 'assumptions' at all, and in so far as their 'realism' can be judged independently of the validity of predictions, the relation between the significance of a theory and the 'realism' of its 'assumptions' is almost the opposite of that suggested by the view under criticism. Truly important and significant hypotheses will be found to have 'assumptions' that are wildly inaccurate descriptive representations of reality, and, in general, the more significant the theory, the more unrealistic the assumptions (in this sense).
>
> *(ibid., p. 14)*

The first identifications of Friedman's essay as advocacy of instrumentalism highlighted this idea. These are Stanley Wong's 'The F-twist and the Methodology of Paul Samuelson' (1973) and Lawrence Boland's 'A Critique of Friedman's Critics' (1979). Wong wrote:

> That Friedman is an instrumentalist is quite evident. The apparent ambiguities and inconsistencies in his essay can best be sorted out by considering his view as instrumentalist. All methodological prescriptions that Friedman makes are subsidiary to the one overriding methodological maxim – that of successful prediction.
>
> *(1973, p. 314)*

With support of a letter from Friedman endorsing his interpretation, Boland wrote that 'his methodological position is both logically sound and unambiguously based on a coherent philosophy of science – Instrumentalism' (1979, p. 503).

However, other commentators (Hoover 2009; Mäki 2009) interpret Friedman's essay as, perhaps confused, an argument for realism. Mäki reads Friedman's example of hypothesising that a body falls 'as if' it were in a vacuum as analogous to hypothesising that firms behave 'as if' they were maximising profit as being in the spirit of realism. Theorists working with 'as if' idealisations of real forces are consistent with realism, whereas 'as if' fictions of forces that do not exist are not. According to Mäki, Friedman's 'as if' refers to idealisations of real forces that affect decisions made in business firms. Hoover argues that one cannot sustain the conclusion that Friedman's methodology is instrumentalism if the essay is read in the context of his work in monetary economics. Hoover points, for example, to the passage in 'Money and business cycles' (1963) where Friedman and Anna J. Schwartz contrast a dressmakers' pins theory of the business cycle with a monetary theory of the cycle. Friedman and Schwartz suggest hypothetically that if one found compelling evidence that production of dressmakers' pins displayed a regular cyclical pattern of reaching a peak well before the business cycle peak and a trough well before the business cycle trough, and higher correlation of amplitudes of business activity with pins than with (Keynesian) autonomous expenditures, this evidence 'would persuade neither us nor our readers to adopt a pin theory of the cycle' (ibid., p. 49).

The purpose of this comparison for Friedman and Schwartz is to show that their monetary theory of the business cycle is based on more than statistical correlation. If it were not, with equal correlation the pins theory would be as acceptable as the monetary theory. The monetary theory is preferred because there is other evidence in support of it, evidence bearing on the causal role of money. With this and other examples of causal realism from Friedman's monetary economics, Hoover concludes that despite statements in the 1953 essay which in isolation look like instrumentalism, Friedman was a realist.

It seems indeed that in examining the context in which Friedman wrote on methodology and his work as an economist the label instrumentalist does not fit either his ideas on methodology or his practice. The core commitment from which he wrote on methodology is captured by his quotation of Alfred Marshall, that economic theory is 'an engine for the discovery of concrete truth' (1949, p. 90). However, the discussion of instrumentalism in economics continues. We conclude by visiting a recasting and defence of instrumentalism by Julian Reiss (2012).

Causal structure in economic models

Much of the philosophical debate about realism in relation to economics has been about theories that have unobservable variables, such as preferences, expectations, GDP or inflation.[2] These are unobservable in the sense that any empirical data are proxies rather than direct observations of the theoretical entity. Reiss however shifts attention away from unobservable variables in economic theory to causal relations in economic models. By their nature, models are not wholly realistic. Geographical maps, for instance, are used as commonplace models. No map is wholly realistic. Economic models can be either causal or non-causal. Reiss's test of whether economists working with models are instrumentalists or not is to ask if they require that models be causal. Do economists require that models represent true causal structures of the economic system being modelled? A realist economist would claim that they do need to be causal. An instrumentalist would claim that they do not. Reiss's argument is that in light of economists' purposes in building models, representation of true causal structures has no incremental value. Economists do not desire knowledge of how economic systems function, i.e., their causal structures, for the sake of knowing. They want to know causal structure in order to forecast and affect patterns of economic activity. They want to know in order to control inflation, maintain full employment and avoid or mitigate recessions. Thus, Reiss argues, knowledge of causal structure is only of instrumental value in economic models. Furthermore, this incremental instrumental value of causal structure is nil in a model that otherwise allows successful forecasting and control. So, for example, suppose an economist has two alternative models to forecast inflation. One is a causal structural model and the other a non-causal reduced form model. If the models perform equally for forecasting and policy design, according to Reiss an economist would be indifferent between them. Otherwise, the economist would choose the model that performed better with no concern for whether it isolated the structural causal linkages. Thus, Reiss argues that economists are instrumentalists. He closes his article with 'three cheers' for instrumentalism based on his understanding of the purpose of economic analysis, which is forecasting and control, and economists' pessimistic perceptions of the prospects for identifying causal structure.

We can see from the foregoing that placing an individual economist into the instrumentalist box is problematic because of the exclusive nature of the box. Reiss's argument for instrumentalism depends on the accuracy of his claim that prediction and control are the sole ends of economists in their economic analysis. To be an instrumentalist is to not be a realist; to be an instrumentalist is to be concerned exclusively with prediction, forecasting and control. To be an instrumentalist is to not want to know for the sake of knowing. Popper's derisive comment that instrumentalism presumes that scientists are glorified plumbers captures well the instrumentalist vision of science, but it may unfairly disparage plumbers. I suspect that many plumbers appreciate the beauty of a well-designed and properly functioning plumbing system. Instrumentalism leaves no room for such appreciation.

Conclusion

We have seen with Milton Friedman the difficulty of applying the mutually exclusive categories realism and instrumentalism. Economic methodologists have more often than not read 'The Methodology of Positive Economics' as an instrumentalist tract. Yet this same Milton Friedman fondly recalled in an autobiographical essay his high school civics teacher who had a love for geometry and quoted Keats's *Ode to a Grecian Urn* – 'Beauty is truth, truth beauty – that is all / Ye know on earth, / and all ye need to know' (1986, p. 80). Friedman's first intellectual love was mathematics, not economics. Curiously, it may then seem, his methodology essay was the culmination of a series of publications in which he criticised the push in the 1940s to mathematise economics.[3] His grounds for the critique were two: that mathematical technique tended to replace careful and extensive empirical and institutional analysis and that it tended to turn economics into mathematics, which he said 'was fascinating to explore, but you mustn't draw any conclusions from it. It wasn't going to enable you to solve any problems' (Hammond, 1992a, p. 110).

Friedman certainly did think of economics as an applied science for the purpose of prediction and public policy. In this regard, his approach was conventional among 20th-century economists. Economic scientists are few and far between whose motivation is wholly knowledge for the sake of knowing. The modern conception of economic science, like physics and chemistry, is heavily instrumental. But this does not make economic scientists instrumentalists.

Notes

1 See Popper (1963).
2 See Hoover (2009).
3 See Hammond (1992b).

Bibliography

Bacon, F. (1902 [1620]) *Novum Organum*, J. Devey, ed., New York: P.F. Collier. http://oll. libertyfund.org/titles/bacon-novum-organum.

Boland, L. (1979) 'A Critique of Friedman's Critics', *Journal of Economic Literature* 17, 503–22.

Friedman, M. (1953) [1949] 'The Marshallian demand curve', in *Essays in Positive Economics*, Chicago, IL: University of Chicago Press, pp. 47–99.

Friedman, M. (1953) 'The methodology of positive economics', in *Essays in Positive Economics*, Chicago, IL: University of Chicago Press, pp. 3–46.

Friedman, M. (1963) 'Money and Business Cycles', *Review of Economics and Statistics* 45 Supplement, 32–64.

Friedman, M. (1986) 'My evolution as an economist', in W. Breit and R. Spencer, eds, *Lives of the Laureates: Seven Nobel Economists*, Cambridge, MA: MIT Press, pp. 77–92.

Hammond, J. D. (1992a) 'An interview with Milton Friedman on methodology', *Research in the History of Economic Thought and Methodology* 10, 91–118.

Hammond, J. D. (1992b) 'The problem of context for Friedman's methodology', *Research in the History of Economic Thought and Methodology* 10, 129–47.

Hoover, K. D. (2009) 'Milton Friedman's stance: The methodology of causal realism', in U. Mäki, ed., *The Methodology of Positive Economics: Reflections on the Milton Friedman Legacy*, Cambridge, UK and New York: Cambridge University Press.

Hume, D. (1896) *A Treatise of Human Nature*, L. A. Selby Bigge, ed., Oxford: Clarendon Press. http://oll.libertyfund.org/titles/hume-a-treatise-of-human-nature.

Mäki, U. (2009) 'Unrealistic assumptions and unnecessary confusions: Rereading and rewriting F53 as a realist statement', in U. Mäki, ed., *The Methodology of Positive Economics: Reflections on the Milton Friedman Legacy*, Cambridge, UK and New York: Cambridge University Press, pp. 90–116.

Nagel, E. (1961) *The Structure of Science*, New York: Harcourt, Brace, and World.

Popper, K. (1963) *Conjectures and Refutations: The Growth of Scientific Knowledge*, London: Routledge,

Popper, K. (1983) *Realism and the Aim of Science*, Totowa: Rowman and Littlefield.

Reiss, J. (2012) 'Idealization and the aims of economics: Three cheers for instrumentalism', *Economics and Philosophy* 28, 363–83.

Wong, S. (1973) 'The 'F-twist' and the methodology of Paul Samuelson', *American Economic Review* 63, 312–25.

4

FROM POSITIVISM TO NATURALISM IN MACROECONOMICS

John Hart

Introduction

Back in the 1970s, positivism was widely regarded amongst heterodox economists as supporting mainstream economics. Amongst its well-known claims was that 'positive economics is, or can be, an "objective" science, in precisely the same sense as any of the physical sciences' (Friedman 1953, p. 4). Consequently, heterodox economists welcomed the criticisms directed against positivism, initially by Popper and later by Kuhn, Lakatos and Feyerabend. Yet in the 21st century mainstream orthodoxy *continues* to dominate economics. For most economists today, 'economics is a positive, value-free science with no place for value judgments of any kind' (Boumans and Davis 2010, p. 169).

I argue that this state of affairs exists partly because it was the reformist influence of Quine, rather than Kuhn, that prevailed in post-positivist philosophy of science. According to Dupré (2003, p. 534), 'Hands [2001] exaggerates the rift in the philosophy of science constituted by the collapse of logical positivism'. While Kuhn *et alia* criticised positivism in order to displace it, Quine's criticism sought to reform it in terms of a new form of the naturalistic approach to the philosophy of science. The result has been the perpetuation (amongst orthodox economists) of Friedman's view of positive economics as apolitical.

Historically, the central dispute as to how the social sciences should proceed has been viewed as arising from two 'vastly different "paradigms"': naturalism and interpretation (Rosenberg 2016, p. 25). Naturalists claim that, for progress in the social sciences, one should look to the approach of the natural sciences. By contrast, for interpretivist social scientists, 'human life can be understood only by means of categories which do not apply to knowledge of the physical world like "purpose", "value", "development" and "ideal" – aspects of "meaning"' (Hollis 2002, p. 17).

Braybrooke (1998) also distinguishes between naturalistic (concerned with regularities and causal explanations) and interpretive (concerned with rules and interpretations) 'schools', but adds a critical school. While this draws on the approaches of both of the other schools, it makes a distinctive claim, inherited from Marx, that 'so-called social science is in fact an ideological … defense of an oppressive social system' (Braybrooke 1987, pp. 17–19). It is thus committed to the project of social emancipation.

DOI: 10.4324/9781315745992-6

The three-schools distinction addresses the fact that the inquiries of social scientists themselves respond to the differences between these schools. Furthermore, it facilitates (a) criticism of their claims to exclusive truth, (b) questioning of whether any one school should predominate, and (c) exploration of their interrelations.

For present purposes, Braybrooke's classification highlights the fact that naturalism constitutes but one of three viewpoints about social science. Nevertheless, given its rapidly increasing influence in social studies (particularly economics), the focus hereafter is on the naturalist, rather than interpretivist and critical, schools. Indeed, the contemporary philosophical debate has been cast as that between two different types of naturalism: 'scientific' versus 'liberal' (De Caro and Macarthur 2004). 'Scientific naturalism' today appears to be the dominant and seemingly insuperable type. Part of its appeal is that it involves a totalising worldview in which the only reality is 'nature', where what is 'natural' is determined by the natural sciences. This means that, for scientific naturalism, the social world is part and parcel of the mindless, purposeless universe of natural science. Consequently, for scientific progress in the social world, its normative features such as free will, moral and political values, consciousness and the intentionality of mental states *must* be 'naturalised', that is, made describable in the vocabulary of the exact natural sciences. Hands (2001) details this necessary naturalisation project in the social sciences as well as aspects of naturalism that fall outside the position of 'scientific naturalism'. According to Andler (2015, p. 329), the aim of scientific naturalists 'is to redeploy all or most of the corpus of social science in a proper naturalistic framework' so as to produce a fully naturalistic social science. By contrast, for liberal or pluralistic naturalism, science is not restricted by such a naturalisation requirement. For example, the traditional practice in economics of explaining action as the result of goals or intentions does not necessitate naturalisation.

Given the dominance of scientific naturalism, and that already for many years social scientists have 'unwittingly been going down the [scientific] naturalist's path' (p. 329), the focus will be on scientific, rather than liberal, naturalism. Consequently, subsequent reference to 'naturalism' should be understood as scientific naturalism. The chapter aims to provide a basic understanding of this new post-Quinean form of naturalism as reflected in the new 'philosophy of economics' (Reiss 2013; Ross 2014) so as to clarify its consequences for macroeconomic methodology. Empiricism and positivism are discussed only as necessary background.

Nineteenth-century empiricism and positivism

There are two long-standing epistemological theories about how we acquire knowledge. For rationalists such as Descartes, Copernicus's achievements in his *De Revolutionibus* (that heralded the scientific revolution) were due to his rational insight unaided by religious revelation or sense experience. For empiricists the scientific revolution was rather due to the careful observations of the 'great experimenters' such as Bacon and Newton. The classical empiricism of Locke, Berkeley and Hume arose as a reaction to rationalism. Hume took issue with the claims of Descartes. For Descartes knowledge required certainty. The questioning of what makes intuitions certain, amongst other things, led to the demise of rationalism in the 20th century. Yet, as Markie (1998, p. 79) points out, 'so long as we find we have knowledge of the external world which appears to go beyond what experience can provide', some form of rationalism will continue to be attractive.

The new spirit of inquiry also helped catalyse the French Revolution of 1789. Around 1820 Auguste Comte was secretary to Saint-Simon who had been active in the Revolution. Comte (1974, p. 20) distinguished three main stages through which human thought and society developed. In the first, phenomena were explained in terms of supernatural or divine powers. The second, although marked by the scientific revolution, unsatisfactorily explained phenomena in metaphysical terms of causes which lay 'behind' phenomena. The final, positivist stage, which began with the French Revolution, marked the completion of the scientific revolution. In terms of this stage, the search for underlying causes was abandoned in favour of establishing laws that described relations amongst phenomena. To attempt to go 'beyond' observable phenomena was to slip back into negativism or the metaphysical stage. By the mid-19th century, positivism was triumphant. Its influence was reflected in medicine, biology (Charles Darwin), ethics (John Stuart Mill) and sociology (Comte's [1974, p. 162] 'social dynamics') (Beed 1991, p. 461). In terms of economics, it lay behind Alfred Marshall's decision to entitle his famous work in 1890 the principles of 'economics' rather than 'political economy'.

Early/mid-20th-century positivism

Logical positivism had its origins in the *Wiener Kreis*, or Vienna Circle, which met regularly in Vienna between the years 1925 and 1936. From the late 1930s through to the early 1960s a more sophisticated positivism developed known as logical empiricism. The Vienna Circle's 1929 manifesto and declaration of independence from traditional philosophy boldly stated:

> We have characterized the *scientific world-conception* essentially by *two features*. *First* it is *empiricist and positivist*: there is knowledge only from experience, which rests on what is immediately given. This sets the limits for legitimate science. *Second*, the scientific world-conception is marked by the application of a certain method, namely *logical analysis*. The aim of scientific effort is to reach the goal, unified science, by applying logical analysis to the empirical material.
>
> *(Hahn et al. 1973, p. 309, emphasis in original)*

I turn to examine these two features. The first implies that philosophy is to be knocked off its pedestal as the head of a hierarchy concerning knowledge claims about the world. Its place is to be taken instead by science which is viewed as *empiricist* and *positivist*. 'Science describes ... the only world there is ... the world of things around us ... All [philosophy] can do is analyse and criticize the theories, the concepts, of science ... [philosophy is] to be the handmaiden of science' (Ayer 1978, p. 97).

By using the term 'positivist', the Vienna Circle affirmed Comte's rejection of metaphysics, or what they saw as speculative claims to knowledge about the nature of reality that could not be supported or refuted by any possible evidence.

By the term 'empiricist', they (at least Schlick and Carnap) had in mind phenomenalism. This is the notion that individuals have access to the external world via their mental states that interpret the sense data of experience. Like Hume, they were concerned with 'quantity or number', with 'matter of fact and existence'. They probably also had in mind Lord Kelvin's famous 1895 dictum. A version engraved above the entrance to the 1930s Chicago social sciences building reads: 'When you cannot measure, your knowledge is meager and unsatisfactory' (Merton et al. 1984, p. 329).

Let us now turn to the second feature. Whereas Wittgenstein had applied the newly discovered symbolic logic to philosophy, the positivists applied *logical analysis* to the propositions of science. They argued that not only is knowledge derived from experience, but so is the very meaning of a proposition. That is, its meaning is cast in physical terms as its method of empirical verification. That metaphysical statements are incapable of verification thus demonstrated their meaninglessness. As such, they are excluded from the domain of science. Only two types of statements are deemed meaningful. The first are synthetic or empirical statements (since they are verifiable). The second are analytic. While these are not verifiable, they are admitted as meaningful at the price of being tautological.

Finally, the Vienna Circle's declaration sets out the goal of scientific effort: a unified science. 'There are not different sciences with fundamentally different methods or different sources of knowledge, but only *one* science' (Carnap 1959, p. 144).

A major problem confronting the positivists was that the revolutionary science of the early 20th century involved theoretical terms such as atoms, electrons, magnetic fields and bacteria – none of which had been observed. However, according to the verifiability principle, each individual meaningful statement must be capable of confrontation with sense experience. It was soon realised that this made theorising very difficult, if not impossible, in science. Carnap (1955 [1938]) dropped this requirement (Putnam 2002, p. 23). Instead, so long as the 'system' as a whole (science reconstructed in terms of a formalised language) enables more successful predictions of phenomena, its predicates are 'cognitively meaningful' (Putnam 2012, p. 114). During the 1940s and 1950s Carnap and Hempel clarified the role of theoretical terms in their hypothetico-deductive (H-D) model, in which the structure of a theory is simply a mechanical calculus or a hypothetico-deductive system. This may be thought of as hierarchical with high-level premises often referring to theoretical terms (e.g. atoms) and low-level conclusions (deduced implications of the theory) to observable entities (e.g. an atomic explosion). In terms of the indirect testability hypothesis, these theoretical terms gain meaning indirectly once the theory as a whole is confirmed.

Putnam (2002) argues that this development had fatal consequences for the positivists. First, a fact no longer corresponded to an individual observation statement: it was only the system of scientific statements as a whole that had 'factual content' (p. 24). Second, the system became 'empirically meaningful' only through its predictions. But to predict means to deduce observation sentences from a theory (p. 29). And, deduction involves both analytic (factually empty) and synthetic (factual) statements. Therefore, defining the factual (system) now depended, following Carnap, crucially on the analytic-synthetic distinction. However, Quine is widely regarded as having demolished the positivist notion of the analytic (p. 29).

I turn briefly to two well-known criticisms of positivism. The positivist notion that science proceeds from observation and careful measurement to theory was criticised early on by Popper (1959, p. 107n) who pointed to the theory-ladenness of observations: observations 'are always interpretations of the facts observed; they are interpretations in the light of theories'. Another criticism concerns the underdetermination of theories by data. The so-called Duhem-Quine problem is that no conclusive or decisive empirical test of a theory can ever be performed. This is because a theory is never verified (or falsified) in isolation but always in conjunction with a number of auxiliary hypotheses. Thus, if it fails the test, it is not clear if this is due to the theory under examination or to one of the many auxiliary hypotheses.

Mid-20th-century Quinean naturalism

Already before Quine there had begun a resurgence of 'naturalism in its 20th century American incarnation' (Roth 2013, p. 646). Documenting this 'return', Kitcher (1992, p. 56) argues that contemporary naturalists might view positivism as 'a desertion of philosophy's proper task and proper roots'. Positivists mistakenly embarked on the conceptual analysis of language. They became too concerned with how we should acquire knowledge if we were logically consistent, rather than with how in fact fallible human beings actually *acquire* their beliefs. Instead of integrating philosophy with the actual practice of science, they emphasised that the logic of science was 'independent of any inferences actual scientists might in fact make' (Giere 1998, p. 729).

While the positivists regarded themselves as rejecting metaphysics, Quine made explicit metaphysical commitments. His physicalism conflates 'the world', or everything that exists, with the subject matter of the physical sciences: 'there is nothing more' to the mental and physical realms 'than arrangements of physical entities' (Papineau 2016, p. 4). Physicalism involves a thesis about the 'causal completeness' of the physical realm: 'every physical effect is fixed by a fully physical prior history'. This implies that 'any mental or biological causes must themselves be physically constituted if they are to produce physical effects' i.e. that 'anything that makes a difference to the physical realm must itself be physical' (p. 8). In line with this, Quine adopts a radical view that dispenses with any role whatsoever for philosophy to pronounce on what constitutes knowledge. Instead, he views philosophy as 'continuous with science' (Quine 1969, p. 126). That is, philosophy 'collapses' completely into a Skinnerian-type behaviourist psychology.

Quine is perhaps best seen as 'an empiricist reforming empiricism' (Orenstein 1998, p. 6). Apart from physicalism, his perspective in reforming empiricism is one of holism. Holists, in opposition to individualists or atomists, argue that wholes are more than the sums of their parts: they have characteristics that cannot be explained solely in terms of the parts, i.e. by analysis. For Quine, 'science is not an assemblage of isolable bits of belief but an interconnected system which is adjusted as a whole to the deliverances of experience' (Quinton 1999, p. 400). Quine's holism had two consequences. First, the positivists' empiricism was deemed too individualist: its stance was that of how the individual gained knowledge. In addition, given his physicalism, Quine rejected talk about mentalistic notions such as 'experience' or 'observation' in favour of talk about natural entities (Orenstein 1998, p. 5).

Second, his holism lay behind his criticism of the 'dogmas' of empiricism (Quine 1951). Concerning that of the positivist analytic-synthetic dichotomy, Quine showed that the system of scientific knowledge depends on both conventions and empirical descriptions without there being a single scientific sentence that is true *simply* by convention or *simply* in terms of experience (Putnam 2012, p. 114). For Putnam (2002, pp. 12–13), Quine's insight is that there are large ranges of statements that are statements neither of analytic truths nor of observable facts. Putnam explains that this leads to Quine arguing, in a famous metaphor, that the lore of our fathers (inherited knowledge) is a pale grey fabric of sentences black with fact and white with convention but with no quite black or white threads in it. In other words, the positivist analytic-synthetic distinction is no dichotomy. Consequently, for Quine, there are no purely analytic statements. Instead all statements are empirical (and hence revisable) to some degree. The radical consequence is that 'since conceptual matters are not entirely distinct from empirical ones, philosophy of science can no longer be a purely conceptual enterprise' (Kincaid 1996, p. 20).

Late-20th-/early-21st-century post-Quinean naturalism

Many, if not most, post-Quinean naturalists have found Quine's epistemological stance too extreme, not least because it dismisses any possibility of a naturalised social science. As against Quine's 'replacement' naturalism, Kitcher (1992) argues that 'traditional' naturalists are concerned with trying to preserve the possibility of a normative epistemology: philosophy is not completely continuous with science. Likewise, they have found his physicalism too extreme. Early versions of physicalism required a one-to-one relationship between mental and brain states. To attempt to circumvent this kind of problem, many post-Quineans have used the concept of supervenience to formulate a non-reductive physicalism, i.e. although mental properties supervene on physical properties, they are not reducible to them. Supervenience supports 'a kind of dependence of the mental on the physical without having to defend the implausible assumption that mental terms can be defined in or reduced to physical terms' (Kincaid 1998b, p. 487).

While the adoption of a non-reductive formulation of physicalism helps post-Quineans in their move away from Quine, it is by no means necessary. Some post-Quineans make no ontological commitments regarding nature, deferring such issues to science: 'those things exist which science finds it fruitful to employ in its explanations' (Jarvie 2011, p. 24). However, like Quine, for post-Quineans it is to science that we must look to find out how knowledge is acquired. Given the dramatic mid-20th-century advances in psychology and biology, naturalists looked to these two fields.

Concerning psychology, the cognitive revolution led to the development of cognitive science (e.g. artificial intelligence, cognitive neuroscience and cognitive psychology). In contrast to positivism, it now allowed psychologists to legitimately refer to mental entities (such as desires) as causes provided these were appropriately naturalised. In terms of the widely accepted causal closure argument for physicalism, such mental causes are not regarded as 'genuinely additional to the physical cause' (Papineau 2016, p. 13). This was one of the ways by which naturalists introduced new findings about preferences and expectations into economics, thereby encouraging the rapidly expanding fields of applied microeconomics, behavioural economics and neuroeconomics.

Developments in biology have challenged the conception of physics as the paradigmatic science. In line with Quine's suggestion that there is 'encouragement in Darwin', many naturalists have turned towards biological explanations viewed as not reducible to those of physics. As Rosenberg (2009, p. 65) points out, 'developments in biology began rapidly to add predictive content and considerable testability to the theory of natural selection in the years after 1953'. These encouraged the growth of today's evolutionary economics and evolutionary game theory.

Naturalism and macroeconomic methodology

For naturalists, there exists no philosophically derived methodology to be set out for macroeconomists in advance to guide their (scientific) practice. Works in today's 'philosophy of economics' are simply exercises in a naturalist approach to the philosophy of science (Reiss 2013; Ross 2014). In a similar vein, Kincaid (2012) argues that *a priori* methodological problems thought up by philosophers do not present real problems for scientists. For example, Popper's problem of theory-ladenness 'does not mean that every piece of data is laden with whole theories' (Kincaid 2012, p. 6). Likewise, concerning the Duhem-Quine problem, evidence does not only bear on theories as a whole. Instead, it is possible to test individual theories. Indeed, 'the relationships between theories, applications, and tests propagated by Quine, Kuhn, and Lakatos look like philosophers' fantasies' (p. 6).

A problem naturalism presents for macroeconomists is that, while it rejects major tenets of positivism, it retains key positivist conclusions inimical to macroeconomics. Take two examples. First, like positivism, it continues to view economics as an objective science. Ethical (scientific) naturalists accept the fact that values intrude into the very heart of science. However, they argue that, since these supervene 'on the basic physical natures of things', this has no consequences for the objectivity of science (Copp 2006, p. 8). Consequently, heterodox criticisms of mainstream economics are dismissed as resulting from the political ideology of 'anti-economists' (Ross 2012). Second, like positivism, naturalism is prescriptivist. It sets out the way to undertake research in economics for it to be regarded as scientific: 'good social science embodies the scientific method common to the natural sciences' (Kincaid 1998a, p. 559). For positivists, this prescript followed from their view that there is one general *a priori* method for all sciences. For naturalists, it arises from their metaphysical and/or epistemological commitments.

Besides perpetuating positivist beliefs, the increasing influence of naturalism raises specific problems in three areas of macroeconomic methodology. These result from the rejection, in some degree or other, of the long-standing concerns of the interpretive and critical schools in the philosophy of social science.

The first area concerns the role in macroeconomics of conceptual, or armchair, theorising. This role is disputed by naturalists. Yet such theorising plays an important part in Keynes's writings. In contrast to applied microeconomics, which deals with problems specific to time and place, macroeconomics deals with problems of general, rather than partial, equilibrium (e.g. the aggregate level of unemployment or rate of inflation that concerns entire economies). In his *General Theory* Keynes (1936) pointed to the hurdle of having to overcome powerful established ideas in arguing that the classical theory was only a special case of his more general theory of employment. Besides dismissing any such power of ideas, naturalists regard many of the important issues raised by Keynes as defying formulation in terms of the vocabulary of the natural sciences. Instead, they argue, research should be limited to specific problems concerning unemployment by looking for causal patterns in the empirical data. In like manner, they regard discussion of competing schools of macroeconomic thought as futile.

The second area under attack by naturalists concerns subjectivism. Yet this is central to those who stress the core role of subjectivist features in Keynes's writings. In letters to Harrod dated 4th and 16th July, Keynes wrote:

> It seems to me... that you do not repel sufficiently firmly attempts à la Schultz to turn [economics] into a pseudo-natural-science... economics is essentially a moral science and not a natural science. That is to say, it employs introspection

and judgments of value. [Later he complained that] the pseudo-analogy with the physical sciences leads directly counter to the habit of mind which is most important for an economist proper to acquire.

(Keynes 1938, CW XIV, pp. 296–7, 300)

The key component of aggregate expenditure involved in Keynes's principle of effective demand is investment. Here uncertainty (as opposed to probability) plays a fundamental role. Investment crucially depends on the subjective expectations of market players, particularly those of entrepreneurs. Unlike rational expectations, if these expectations are disappointed the economic system is affected. By contrast, the disappointed expectations of astronomers do not affect the appearance of a lunar eclipse (Torr 1988, p. 41).

The third refers to the bias of naturalism in favour of the *status quo*. By virtue of its philosophical commitments naturalism necessarily excludes the concerns of the critical school. To the extent that naturalists adopt scientism (e.g. Ross 2005, p. 16), this problem is exacerbated. Fortunately, there are some naturalists who acknowledge Kuhn's stance that 'there is no basis for concluding that the actual evolution of science is self-correcting' (Kitcher, 1992, p. 93). Kitcher goes on to list Kuhnian-influenced claims such as that 'heterodox views have only a small chance of acceptance or transmission because of the importance of reliance on authority within scientific communities' (p. 95). In this respect, Feyerabend (2011) has warned of the problem of the abuse of the authority of science on society.

Has there been methodological progress in macroeconomics? If one accepts Braybrooke's three-schools approach to the philosophy of social science, the short answer is 'no'. Naturalism's dominance in the philosophy of social science today threatens to overwhelm the interpretivist and critical schools to which it stands opposed. Yet these schools have been a fundamental philosophical influence in the development of both mainstream and non-mainstream economics since Adam Smith.

Bibliography

Andler, D. (2015) 'Naturalism', in J. D. Wright, ed., *International Encyclopedia of the Social and Behavioral Sciences*, vol. 16, 2nd edition, Amsterdam: Elsevier, pp. 325–33.

Ayer, A. J. (1978) 'Logical positivism and its legacy', in B. Magee, ed., *Men of Ideas*, Oxford: Oxford University Press, pp. 95–109.

Beed, C. (1991) 'Philosophy of science and contemporary economics: An overview', *Journal of Post Keynesian Economics* 13, 459–94.

Boumans, M. and J. B. Davis (2010) *Economic Methodology*, Basingstoke: Palgrave Macmillan.

Braybrooke, D. (1987) *Philosophy of Social Science*, New York: Prentice Hall.

Braybrooke, D. (1998) 'Contemporary philosophy of social science', in E. Craig, ed., *The Routledge Encyclopedia of Philosophy*, vol. 8, London: Routledge, pp. 838–47.

Carnap, R. (1955 [1938]) 'The Foundations of logic and mathematics', in O. Neurath, R. Carnap and C.W. Morris, eds, *International Encyclopedia of Unified Science*, vol. 1(3), Chicago, IL: Chicago University Press, Combined edition, Part 1, pp. 139–214.

Carnap, R. (1959) 'The old and the new logic', (trans. I. Levi) in A. J. Ayer, ed., *Logical Positivism*, Glencoe: The Free Press, pp. 133–46.

Comte, A. (1974) *The Essential Comte*, S. Andreski ed., London: Croom Helm.

Copp, D. (2006) 'Introduction: Metaethics and normative ethics', in D. Copp, ed., *The Oxford Handbook of Ethical Theory*, pp. 3–34. Oxford Scholarship Online. DOI: 10.1093/0195147790.001.0001

CW: see Keynes (1971–89)

De Caro, M. and D. Macarthur (2004) 'Introduction', in M. de Caro and D. Macarthur, eds, *Naturalism in Question*, Cambridge, MA: Harvard University Press, pp. 1–17.

Dupré, J. (2003) 'Horticultural diversity in the post-positivist garden' (book review of Hands 2001), *Journal of Economic Methodology* 10, 531–5.

Feyerabend, P. K. (2011) *The Tyranny of Science*, E. Oberheim ed., Cambridge, UK: Polity Press.

Friedman, M. (1953) 'The methodology of positive economics', in his *Essays in Positive Economics*, Chicago, IL: University of Chicago Press, pp. 3–43.

Giere, R. N. (1998) 'Naturalized philosophy of science', in E. Craig, ed., *The Routledge Encyclopedia of Philosophy*, vol. 6, London: Routledge, pp. 728–31.

Hahn, H., O. Neurath and R. Carnap, (1973) [1929] 'The scientific conception of the world: The Vienna circle', in M. Neurath and R. Cohen, eds, (trans. P. Foulkes and M. Neurath) *Otto Neurath: Empiricism and Sociology*, Dordrecht, Holland: D. Reidel, pp. 299–318.

Hands, D. W. (2001) *Reflection without Rules: Economic Methodology and Contemporary Science Theory*, Cambridge, UK: Cambridge University Press.

Hollis, M. (2002) *The Philosophy of Social Science*, Revised and updated version, Cambridge, UK: Cambridge University Press.

Jarvie, I. C. (2011) 'Introduction', in I. C. Jarvie and J. Zamora-Bonilla, eds, *The Sage Handbook of the Philosophy of Social Sciences*, London: Sage Publications, pp. 1–36.

Keynes, J. M. (1936) *The General Theory of Employment, Interest and Money*, London: Macmillan.

Keynes, J. M. (1971–89) *Collected Writings*, (*CW*), D. E. Moggridge, ed., 30 vols, London: Macmillan and New York: St Martin's Press.

Kincaid, H. (1996) *Philosophical Foundations of the Social Sciences*, New York: Cambridge University Press.

Kincaid, H. (1998a) 'Positivism in the social sciences', in E. Craig, ed., *The Routledge Encyclopedia of Philosophy*, vol. 7, London: Routledge, pp. 558–61.

Kincaid, H. (1998b) 'Supervenience', in J. B. Davis, D. W. Hands and U. Mäki, U., eds, *The Handbook of Economic Methodology*. Cheltenham: Edward Elgar, pp. 487–8.

Kincaid, H. (2012) 'Introduction', in H. Kincaid, ed., *The Oxford Handbook of Philosophy of Social Science*. Oxford: Oxford University Press, pp. 3–17.

Kitcher, P. (1992) 'The naturalists return', *Philosophical Review* 101, 53–114.

Markie, P. (1998) 'Rationalism', in E. Craig, ed. *The Routledge Encyclopedia of Philosophy*, vol. 8, pp. 75–80.

Merton, R. K., D. L. Sills and S. M. Stigler (1984) 'The Kelvin dictum and social science: An excursion into the history of an idea', *Journal of the History of the Behavioral Sciences* 20, 319–31.

Orenstein, A. (1998) 'Willard van Orman Quine', in E. Craig, ed., *The Routledge Encyclopedia of Philosophy*, vol. 8, London: Routledge, pp. 3–14.

Papineau, D. (2016) 'Naturalism', in E. N. Zalta, ed., *The Stanford Encyclopedia of Philosophy* (Winter 2016 edn PDF), URL = http://plato.stanford.edu/archives/win2016/entries/naturalism

Popper, K. R. (1959) *The Logic of Scientific Discovery*, London: Hutchinson.

Putnam, H. (2002) *The Collapse of the Fact/Value Dichotomy*, Cambridge, MA: Harvard University Press.

Putnam, H. (2012) 'For ethics and economics without the dichotomies', in H. Putnam and V. Walsh, eds, *The End of Value-Free Economics*, London: Routledge, pp. 111–29.

Quine, W. V. O. (1951) 'Two dogmas of empiricism', *Philosophical Review* 60, 20–43.

Quine, W. V. O. (1969) *Ontological Relativity and Other Essays*, New York: Columbia University Press.

Quinton, A. (1999) 'Holism', in A. Bullock and S. Trombley, eds, *The New Fontana Dictionary of Modern Thought*, Third edition, London: HarperCollinsPublishers, p. 400.

Reiss, J. (2013) *Philosophy of Economics: A Contemporary Introduction*, Abingdon: Routledge.

Rosenberg, A. (2009) 'If economics is a science, what kind of a science is it?', in H. Kincaid and D. Ross, eds, *The Oxford Handbook of Philosophy of Economics*, Oxford: Oxford University Press, pp. 55–67.

Rosenberg, A. (2016) *Philosophy of Social Science*, Fifth edition, Boulder: Westview Press.

Ross, D. (2005) *Economic Theory and Cognitive Science: Microexplanation*, Cambridge, MA: The MIT Press.

Ross, D. (2012) 'Economic theory, anti-economics and political ideology', in U. Mäki, ed., *Philosophy of Economics, Handbook of the Philosophy of Science,* vol. 13, Amsterdam: Elsevier, pp. 241–85.

Ross, D. (2014) *Philosophy of Economics*, Basingstoke: Palgrave Macmillan.

Roth, P. A. (2013) 'Naturalized epistemology', in B. Kaldis, ed., *Encyclopedia of Philosophy and the Social Sciences*, vol. 2, London: Sage Reference, pp. 646–9.

Torr, C. S. W. (1988) *Equilibrium, Expectations and Information: A Study of the General Theory and Modern Classical Economics*, Cambridge, UK: Polity Press.

5

HOLISM AND THE FALLACY OF COMPOSITION IN MACROECONOMICS

Victoria Chick and Jesper Jespersen

Introduction: from parts to the whole

The word 'holism' comes, remarkably, from Jan Smuts.[1] His book *Holism and Evolution* (1926) was written in a period when he was leader of the opposition in South Africa, when we suppose he felt the duties left time for such an undertaking. The book is an exercise in natural history, a passion of his from his time in the University of Cambridge. He defines 'holism' as 'the fundamental factor operative towards the creation of wholes in the universe'. It lays out a plan for nature's actions at several different levels, which, it is openly acknowledged, is only ever partly realised – hence the need for evolution. The forward press of evolution is forever, he argues, making good the imperfections of the Whole that nature is trying to forge. Evolution should be thought of as continuing growth towards this goal.

He begins this work at the level of atoms and molecules, describing the behaviour of atoms and molecules as active agents whizzing through space-time. They and their 'fields'-areas of influence are around them. In space-time they carry time with them as they change in response to stimuli, while trying, as their equilibrium is disturbed, to form new 'Wholes; to incorporate the new stimulus and form a new configuration'. This part of the book is founded strongly on fact. As the argument goes forward, the book becomes more of a visionary undertaking.

This vision is carried forward to encompass the formation of cells: first Life, then the Mind and human Personality. At each level there is some sort of ideal Whole towards which, at each level, they are striving. At each stage the stakes are higher but so are the rewards. Cells play their role as specialised units, taking the role they are to play from the plant or animal of which they are a part and thus aiming to produce a whole object.

The human mind then enters as the directing element, choosing to accept some modifications to the structures and elements of connection with the purpose of creating a more complete whole. The operation of mind in shaping progress is the step that leads to Personality.

When raised to Personality, the direction becomes even more evident: the mind selects its role in relation to stimuli according to the type of personality, in order to

DOI: 10.4324/9781315745992-7

keep the person's belief system on an even keel. Any failure of these governing principles (and there are many) results in a personality, which is confused and dis-unified. This sort of person is criticised by others as morally or ethically confused. They are not (yet) the Whole that they deserve to be. An integrated personality is one in sight of or near the Whole that his/her personality is supposed to be. At the highest level the Whole personality holds the values of, for example, Truth and Beauty. At each step of the pruning and shaping that leads to a Whole, there is recourse to the lower levels, to discover whether there is a need for reorganisation at those levels too. All nature's wholes are bound together.

Holism as used in economics

The idea of looking at the economy as a whole has been used by economists as a counterweight to individualism (see Andy Denis on 'Methodological Individualism' in this volume). This idea comes into economics (by some means, whether direct from Smuts or some secondary source) to form a view of the larger framework. A non-reductive stance against viewing a collection (of animals, people, etc.) as understandable only as a whole, where the system in question is known by the connections between elements as much as by the elements themselves, forms a unique whole. This view is opposed to methodological individualism, which believes that the system can only be understood by examining the parts. The differences in structure determine, in the theory of parts, that all decisions are taken by individuals. These connections are deemed absent in the individualist view. In economics these two ideas are typically used dualistically: the two attitudes have no area of overlap or common ground. In the holistic view, some decisions are taken by committees or groups representing the organisations of which they are a part. Exactly how this is done is not clear.

This dichotomy of views gives rise to two views of the economy: the one sees all decisions being taken by individuals, where those individuals are regarded as 'atoms', independent of each other. The other, non-reductive view, is that understanding the system as a whole requires looking not only at the elements of the system but also at the connections, and only when the connections are made clear is it possible to discover feedback relations and other intra-system repercussions that result from an event that impinges on the system.

The trap of the fallacy of composition

[I]ndividual actions, if common to a large number of individuals, will generate an outcome different from what was intended by each (Dow 1996, p. 85).

The fallacy of composition consists in treating individual behaviour as if it were representative for a collective of people. It occurs when one makes the mistake of attributing to a group (or a whole) some characteristic that is true only of its individual members (or its parts), and then draws conclusions based on that mistaken assumption. In macroeconomics this fallacy is likely to occur either because of the use of methodological individualism or when a general equilibrium analytical framework is presumed. Accordingly, there are within modern macroeconomics two likely possibilities of committing the fallacy of composition (Jespersen 2009, chapters 3 and 7).

Firstly, a single behavioural equation is often used to represent an aggregate of individuals who have a (partly) interrelated activity. However, when the group's individuals are not fully homogenous, the 'representative agent' is not truly representative. In this case, a 'fallacy of composition' will easily occur. The trivial example is the so-called 'lemming effect', where people do not act independently of one another due to lack of full information. New classical economic theory overcomes this hurdle by assuming that the representative agent knows the general equilibrium solution of the entire market system, the so-called 'perfect information' assumption (see, for instance, Mankiw 2016).

Secondly, a fallacy of composition will also occur at the analytical level of the economy as a whole (the market system), if a macroeconomic conclusion is drawn on the basis of a single market analysis and eventually extrapolated to the entire macroeconomic system without taking relevant feedback effects and interdependence between the macro-markets into consideration. This fallacy might be committed when partial and general market equilibrium analyses are assumed to lead to identical outcomes. This is caused when the assumption of *ceteris paribus* is imposed on the analysis of a macro-market, for instance, if the labour market by this assumption is analysed in isolation from the other macro-markets within the system as a whole.

In sum: The fallacy of composition occurs when an economic argument is attempted incorrectly to be generalised from a relationship that is true for an individual or a single market, but is not true for the system as a whole.

Modern neoclassical theory: the fallacy of composition ruled out by assumption[2]

It is the ambition of the neoclassical school that the methodological point of departure should be methodological individualism. This assumes that the fundamentally stable analytical building blocks for the economic system are the individual preference structures. The individual has integrity in relation to his/her own economic dispositions. Rational choices and rational expectations are assumed to be relevant initial assumptions to make a macroeconomic analysis of optimising individual utility within a market system. With this methodological point of departure, the goal of the analysis is to detect important structural elements at the individual level which could improve the macroeconomic outcome (see, for example, Andersen 2000).

This call for a microeconomic foundation was explicitly formulated after the failed attempt to explain economic development throughout the 1970s with the large, so-called Keynesian, macro-econometric models (Harcourt 1977). This model tradition had been internationally represented by, among others, Klein's Link model (Klein 1985 [1976]).

The new neoclassical critique of this macroeconomic/macro-econometric tradition was summed up by Lucas and Sargent (1978) among others at the end of the 1970s.[3] At that time it had become evident that the Keynesian models were unable to describe, among other things, the 'stagflation process' that had characterised the macroeconomic development throughout the 1970s.

The 'new' methodological requirement was formulated in such a way that consistent macroeconomic theory should be built up 'from below' to avoid *ad hoc* assumptions about economic behaviour on the macroeconomic level. It is the individual's preferences which are *assumed* to be invariant with respect to external macroeconomic events and political initiatives. According to this argumentation, one important reason for the original macro-econometric models to break down was the fact that macroeconomic behavioural relations were specified in an *ad hoc* way, and that parameters were not rooted in rational economic behaviour, but only determined as detected from historical evidence. These statistically estimated parameters used by the "Keynesian' macro-models would therefore not be invariant with respect to changes in, among other things, economic policy and/or changed institutions. In the 1970s the collapse of the explanatory power of these models was attributed to this lack of invariation.

The macroeconomic slate had to be washed clean, for which purpose a new neo-classical, macroeconomic model tradition was developed, in which microeconomic-based behavioural relations formed the model structures. The 1995 Nobel Prize winner Robert Lucas was one of the main architects behind this research strategy. This strategy is widely used by neoclassical economists today and also forms the basis of, for instance, the Danish Rational Economic Agent Macromodel (DREAM), used by the Danish Council of Economic Advisors. As early as 1987 Lucas wrote a programmatic declaration for his continued research within economic theory:

> The most interesting recent developments in macroeconomic theory seem to me describable as the reincorporation of aggregative problems such as inflation and the business cycle within the general framework of 'microeconomic' theory. If these developments succeed, *the term 'macroeconomics' will simply disappear* from use and the modifier 'micro' will become superfluous. We will simply speak, as did Smith, Ricardo, Marshall and Walras, of economic theory.
> *(Lucas 1987, pp. 107–8, italics added).*

It is certainly an exclusive company of former economics scholars that the new clas-sical macroeconomists have selected as their role models. But it is still worth ac-knowledging that Lucas had to look more than one hundred years back in economic thinking to find his icons. Missing are the economists of the 20th century – the period when macroeconomic theory as a distinct field of study was established.

Why did Lucas skip the economic thinking of the 20th century, represented by John Maynard Keynes and others? He did this with reference to the failures, among others, of the Klein tradition of modelling mentioned above, which he identified with Keynes and *The General Theory.* But here he made a mistake by equating Keynes's macroeconomic theory with the neoclassical synthesis that lies behind the large (so-called Keynesian) macro-econometric models. If Lucas had taken a sincere interest into, for instance, Keynes's critique of Tinbergen's early econometric work (the orig-inal contributions are all printed in *CW*, XIV), then it would have been apparent to him that it was not Keynes's macroeconomic theory that was under attack for meth-odological inconsistency but rather the macroeconomic theory that had the 'neoclas-sical synthesis' as its point of departure.

The microeconomic basis for general equilibrium theory

Lucas could, with considerable accuracy, claim that there was no congruence be-tween individual optimising behaviour and these 'Keynesian' macro-econometric models. The ambition was to construct a model building on the 'rational' individu-als' expectation-formation which could be assumed to be invariant with respect to changing external conditions, including government policy. If it were possible suc-cessfully to formulate these representative agents' 'true' expectation-formation, then the model would be cleansed of systematic errors, since the rational agents would learn from their previous mistakes. The expectation-formation should therefore be forward-looking, not backward-looking at random mistakes. In the 1970s this forward-looking procedure was not in use, in either the macro-econometric models or the monetarist models.

The new classicals rejected these models, because they felt that they were based on *ad hoc* expectations formation or wrongly ignored information about future events. But they did, of course, not criticise that the neoclassical synthesis as well as the monetarist models were all framed within the general equilibrium method.

The new classical school presented an apparent methodological brainwave when in the 1970s they launched the hypothesis about rational expectation-formation. This hypothesis was based on the assumption that agents are rational, know the future and learn quickly from their random mistakes. So, why not as a consequence take, as the point of departure, the assumption that the agents do not make any systematic mistakes and that they optimise their economic behaviour on this basis? For, as Lucas argued, if the agents actually had this knowledge and did not use it fully, then it would be a case of irrational behaviour. At this point in the theoretical presentation, it is often added (with a deprecating gesture) that agents may not have full knowledge of the future, but they are assumed to learn from their randomly made forecasting errors, which will eventually give them the required knowledge to behave in accordance with the assumed full-employment equilibrium. Therefore, the outcome of the introduction of rational expectations into macroeconomics was that the individuals are assumed to know the (model-based) future. This has the logical implication that the theoretically most relevant part of the analytical model will be the position of general equilibrium, since here agents have realised their rational expectations.

Furthermore, there might be some institutional obstacles to the 'rational' learning and smooth adjustment process. These may delay even rational agents on their way towards the general equilibrium. Agents might know that, due to transaction costs, insufficient information and the like, there will be a kind of rational inertia in the adjustment process which takes some time to be overcome, but as long as the preference structures are invariant to this inertia, agents will learn. So the general equilibrium is still a highly relevant analytical point of reference for policy advice. This argument is also accepted by new-Keynesians economists.

In this new classical analytical practice, 'rational expectation-formation' is an indispensable, model-based precondition for ensuring consistency between the sum of the rational, individually decided actions, of the representative agent and the general equilibrium solution. In this case there is a logical consistent coincidence between the micro level and the macro level, which was also, as mentioned above, Lucas's research ambition.

New classical macroeconomics put the assumption of market clearing centre stage. Market failures – like fixed prices – were no longer required to derive meaningful macroeconomic results from new classical models. But the assumption of market clearing also alters a number of the key Keynesian conclusions.

So, within this stylised new classical macroeconomics, based on the neoclassical general equilibrium we will by a *priory* assumptions conclude, that:

1 An exogenous change in the individual preference structure, such as an increased propensity to save, increases the equilibrium macroeconomic growth rate. The representative agent will save more and, due to the perfect market-clearing

mechanism, society will end up having increased its total saving and, accordingly, total real investment.

2 A reduced social benefit will increase the representative agent's supply of labour and, due to the perfect market-clearing assumption where 'supply creates its own demand', employment will have increased.

Within this kind of micro-founded neoclassical macroeconomic model where uncertainty is abandoned and a general equilibrium solution is axiomatically imposed, it will hardly make any sense to discuss whether the fallacy of composition can happen. It is ruled out by assumption.

Keynes's macroeconomics: an attempt to overcome the fallacy of composition

Though an individual whose transactions are small in relation to the market can safely neglect the fact that demand is not a one-sided transaction, it makes nonsense to neglect it when we come to aggregate demand. This is the vital difference between the theory of the economic behaviour of the aggregate and the theory of the behaviour of the individual unit...

(Keynes 1936, CW VII, p. 85)

The microeconomic foundation developed by new classical economics is not relevant for Keynes's and Post-Keynesian macroeconomic analysis. The question is what sort of *empirically relevant* microeconomic foundation can be formulated and whether it can be incorporated into an analytical macroeconomic model that describes an open and structured landscape mirroring reality.

According to chapter 1 in *The General Theory*, it is obvious that Keynes considered the persistent full-employment macroeconomic model as a very special case, since it is based on so many, and empirically very unrealistic, assumptions. Keynes's macroeconomic 'landscape' has a dynamic structure without a clearly defined gravitation centre and without any rigid expectation-formation. The macroeconomic system was therefore evolving into an increasingly unknowable future, which methodologically could point towards a path-dependent analysis. Within the framework of a realistic macroeconomic model there would seldom, if ever, be a coincidence between what the individual expected, even with a forward-looking view, and the macroeconomic outcome, because of uncertainty about the actual situation in the present moment and about what the future might bring.

It is therefore no accident that Keynes has come to stand as an exponent of realistic, *macro*economic analysis. Keynes's contribution to macro-theory had the diametrically opposite analytical point of departure compared to neoclassical theory. Macroeconomic reality could not be understood, let alone explained, by a simple aggregation of identical, individual, economic actions based on secure knowledge and perfect market clearing. Macroeconomic analysis had, on the contrary, to start 'from above', based on what could be observed of *'the economy as a whole'*.

In *The General Theory*, persistent, involuntary unemployment was the current problem to be understood. It could not be explained within the framework of the neoclassical macro-theory that existed at his time. Keynes's colleague in Cambridge, Professor Arthur C. Pigou, had clearly demonstrated this in his book *The Theory of Unemployment* (1933).

Keynes's closest colleagues in Cambridge had the same experience at the presentation of 'the neoclassical synthesis' during the 1940s and 1950s with inspiration from Hicks (1937), see Kahn (1982). Here, involuntary unemployment was explained by wage inflexibility within the framework of a neoclassical model, in accordance with, for example, Modigliani (1944) and Patinkin (1960 [1956]). The theoretical paradox was that this neoclassical synthesis was presented as an interpretation of Keynes's macro-theory, despite the fact that Keynes had clearly demonstrated in *The General Theory* that his macroeconomic model could explain persistent unemployment independently of whether the wage formation was assumed to be inflexible or fully flexible! (See *CW* VII, Ch. 19.)

Post-Keynesian macroeconomic theory is therefore in methodological opposition to both the old-Keynesian neoclassical synthesis that dominated the 1950s and 1960s and the general equilibrium model of the new-Keynesians that is dominant today. In fact, the new-Keynesian macroeconomic model comes close to a Walrasian system with semi-rigid market prices and money wage levels (see Mankiw and Romer 1991). One of the overriding differences between these two schools is how uncertainty is handled analytically. If uncertainty is only identified by stochastic risk, then the law of large numbers applies, whereby individual, randomly determined mistakes disappear at the macro level and can be treated as calculable risk. If, on the other hand, uncertainty is not quantifiable and neither random nor stochastically independent, then the phenomenon of uncertainty will make a significant impact on macroeconomic behaviour. Furthermore, it has to be taken into account that the model will be notoriously dominated by uncertainty the longer one tries to draw the analytical path into the unknown future (Jespersen 2009, chapter 4). Keynes's and the Post-Keynesians' most important methodological conclusion is, therefore, that even at the idealised analytical level, the 'whole', that is, the macroeconomic reality, could not be described by a simple summation of the individual economic agents' rational behaviour within a perfect market system. The whole is different from the sum of its parts, where 'parts' might be human beings or (separate) markets. Therefore Keynes, as mentioned, concluded chapter 1 in *the General Theory* by calling the classical theory a very special case, and argued that its teaching would be disastrous. Or, phrased differently, the challenge of macroeconomic methodology is to understand that *the outcome of a macroeconomic analysis is different from the sum of the individual agents' intended economic actions.*

A solution: a non-dualistic view on the analysis of parts and the whole

In economics neither side is in the habit of giving quarter to the other. But it does not have to be like that. In other fields that have responded to the holism-individualism debate, some individualists have accepted the role of individuals in the larger groups of society and allowed decisions to be formed by them, in committees or otherwise on behalf of those groups. We are thinking of philosophy and political science, in particular. Holism, by contrast, is not so flexibly formulated. It tends to concentrate on the connections between the entities of the system. It concentrates on these as the distinctive features of holism, each one unique to every whole. So you find Lucas (1987) arguing for individualism while Keynes, for example, is clearly a holist in his *General Theory*. He states plainly that he wants to examine the macroeconomics of 'the system as a whole'. There the matter chiefly rests for economics, at the moment.

But that leaves much to do: How do members of a company, a club, a democratic nation, etc. take decisions? How are the aggregates of economics formed? We have the example of *The General Theory*, where aggregates were formed depending on the role those groups take in the system – as consumers, investors, holders of assets and so on. What relation do these aggregates have to individual decisions? We have in economics the example of Alfred Marshall, who understood industry equilibrium as pertaining to the industry as a whole but not to individual firms. This must have been the model for Keynes's aggregates.

The decision taken in representative organisations does not bind each member of that aggregate. This is the sort of decision-making that Jespersen (2009) has in mind when he speaks of the aggregate (of consumers, say) making a decision concerning how much to consume – a decision to which few individual consumers would agree. That just allows for the diversity of human beings playing their part in an aggregate. He calls such an aggregate a 'macro-actor'.

The two fundamentally different methodologies have resolved the macroeconomic models into a simple pair of duals: either all decisions are made by individuals who are regarded as separate decision units, or the system cannot be understood by looking only at the parts. The first gives rise to the requirement for microfoundations of macroeconomics – a scheme devised by individualists to make the modifier 'macro' superfluous. The second says that the macro system will never be understood only by looking at its individual parts. (This is now a far cry from Smuts's system, which gives rise to internally directed evolution towards hitherto unrealised wholes.)

There are scholars in all fields who find this dichotomy far too simple. First, they point to the fact that some philosophers have modified individualism to take into account the fact that people do participate in some collective decisions (List and Spiekermann 2003). Others have distinguished between description and explanation. One in particular has looked at Marx in this way, arguing that at the level of description he was a holist but at the level of explanation an individualist (Shell 1997). Still another has disputed the idea of different levels of analysis at all (Zahle 2019), demonstrating to her satisfaction that the division into levels of analysis does not help to alleviate the dichotomy between the two ideas. Perhaps the most far-reaching is Burge (2000), who takes issue with the whole idea of holism, regarding it as unnecessary and substituting partial systems analysis for it. We confess to a preference for systems analysis over these potentially divisive terms ourselves, as it cannot be used dualistically as can holism and individualism. None of this has been taken up by economists, who go on their merry way. But surely, there is more to the story of these two ideas than an irreconcilable opposition.

Above, we remarked that on the theoretical level it was the individualists who had made some compromises, rather than the holists. But when it comes to practical applications, the holists compromise also. Most systems are too complex to be analysed as a whole, at least the first time-round. Much of the success of a system-theoretic approach to the macroeconomy depends on decisions about how to parcel the system up into parts for analysis. In a system-theoretic approach, perhaps the first element following a description of the problem is to describe a system of cuts through the whole, while recognising the holistic nature of the thing under study. This follows Keynes's remarks about not losing track of the shape of the system as a whole. His recommended method would therefore be to make an initial overview of the macro system as a whole, then cut it into sub-systems (parts) which can only be analysed separately, if the outcome in a second round can be fitted back into an analysis of the economy as a whole – what we today would call an open system analysis of the macroeconomy. This follows Keynes's remarks about not losing track of the shape of the system as a whole, while analysing the parts (Chick 1993).

These partial analyses can also lead to false conclusions if done in a way that falsifies the natural whole of the system. Consider, for instance, the separation of money from the rest of the economy in neoclassical macroeconomics. The general price level is explained in terms of the quantity theory of money. The rest of the macroeconomy is analysed in terms of relative prices. Money only serves to determine the absolute price level, which seems like an afterthought, something which can be done after the analysis of real economic activity has been concluded. But this means that the macroeconomic system has been analysed as if all market activity took place without money, while money in our view is inherently a social good. The separation of money from the real economy, which constitutes the 'classical dichotomy', gives a fundamentally distorted view of the economy of the whole. So, establishing some sort of holistic vision using the method of semi-closures (see the entry on open/closed systems, this volume) is not without its pitfalls either.

Notes

1 Jan Smuts (24 May 1870–11 September 1950) was a South African statesman, military leader and philosopher. In addition to holding various military and cabinet posts, he served as prime minister of the Union of South Africa from 1919 to 1924 and 1939 to 1948.
2 This section is an edited and revised part of Chapter 7 in Jespersen (2009).
3 A contemporary theoretical reaction to the break-down of the Keynesian models was the application of non-Walrasian general equilibrium theory to the problem of involuntary unemployment, see also Weintraub (1977).

References

Andersen, T. M. (2000) *Makroteori*, in Chr. Hjorth-Andersen, ed., *Udviklingslinjer i økonomisk teori*, København: DJØFs Forlag, pp. 18–42.

Burge, M. (2000) 'Systematism: An alternative to individualism and holism', *Journal of Socio-Economics* 29 (2), 147–57.

Chick, V. (1993) 'Keynes's monetary theory: A partial survey', *Brazilian Journal of Political Economy* 13 (4), 125–34.

CW: see Keynes (1971–89).

Harcourt, G. ed. (1977) *The Microeconomic Foundations of Macroeconomics*, London: Macmillan.

Hicks, J. (1937) 'Mr. Keynes and the "Classics": A suggested interpretation', *Econometrica* 5 (2), 147–59.

Jespersen, J. (2009) *Macroeconomic Methodology: A Post-Keynesian Perspective*, Cheltenham and Brookfield: Edward Elgar.

Kahn, R. F. (1982) *The Making of Keynes' General Theory*, Cambridge, UK: Cambridge University Press.

Kahneman, D. 1. (2003) Maps of bounded rationality: Psychology for behavioral economics. *American Economic Review* 93 (5), 1449–57.

Keynes, J. M. (1971–89) *Collected Writings*, *(CW)*, D. E. Moggridge, ed., 30 vols, London: Macmillan and New York: St Martin's Press.

Keynes, J. M. (1933) 'A monetary theory of production', *CW* XIII, 408–11.

Keynes, J. M. (1936) *The General Theory of Employment, Interest and Money*, *CW* VII.

Klein, L. (1985) [1976]) Five-Year Experience of Linking National Econometric Models and of Forecasting International Trade in *Economic Theory and Econometrics of Lawrence Klein*, J. Marquez, ed., Oxford: Basil Blackwell.

Layard, R. (2005) *Happiness – Lessons from a New Science*. London: Allan Lane.

List, C. and K. Spiekermann (2003) 'Methodological individualism and holism: A reconciliation', *American Political Science Review* 107 (4), 29–43.

Lucas, R. E. Jr. (1976). 'Econometric policy evaluation: A critique', in K. Brunner, and A. Meltzer, eds., *The Phillips Curve and Labor Markets*. Carnegie-Rochester Conference Series on Public Policy. Vol. 1. New York: American Elsevier, pp. 19–46.

Lucas, R. E. Jr. (1987) *Models of Business Cycles*, Oxford: Basil Blackwell.

Lucas, R. E. Jr. and T. J. Sargent (1978) After Keynesian macroeconomics, in *After the Phillips Curve: Persistence of High Inflation and High Unemployment*, Boston: Federal Reserve Bank of Boston, Conference series No. 19, pp. 49–72.

Mankiw, N. G. (2016) *Macroeconomics*, Ninth edition. New York: Worth Publishers.

Mankiw, N. G., and D. Romer, eds, (1991) *New Keynesian Economics*, 2 vols. Cambridge, MA: MIT Press.

Marshall, A. (1890) *Principles of Economics*, London: Macmillan.

Modigliani, F. (1944) 'Liquidity preference and the theory of interest and money', *Econometrica* 12 (1), 45–88.

Patinkin, D. (1960 [1956]) *Money, Interest, and Prices: An Integration of Monetary and Value Theory*, Second edition. New York: Harbour and Row.

Pigou, A. C. (1933) *The Theory of Unemployment*, London: Macmillan.

Shell, T. (1997) 'On Marx's holism', *History of Philosophy* 4 (2), 235–46.

Smuts, J. (1926) *Holism and Evolution*, New York: The Macmillan Company.

Weintraub, R. (1977) 'Micro-foundations of macroeconomics – Critical survey', *Journal of Economic Literature* 15 (1) (January), 1–23.

Zahle, J. (2019) 'Limits to levels in the methodological', *Synthese* 198 (7), 6435–54.

6

MACROECONOMICS AND ETHICS

Finn Olesen[1]

Introduction

The lessons learnt from the years of the Great Recession became somewhat of a revelation to many economists. Criticism arose theoretically as well as methodologically, not only by most members of heterodox schools of thought, but also by some former mainstream macroeconomists.[2] You need to be more pluralistic than just to accept that the framework of *The New Neoclassical Synthesis* (NNS) and their DSGE models can unfold everything of macroeconomic importance. Modern internationally and financially linked economies are not performing to perfection. They hardly ever follow an intertemporal equilibrium path of full employment in the longer run nor, of course, in the short run. Modern economies may operate at disequilibrium positions for longer periods than just temporarily in the very short run. As such, involuntary unemployment may be seriously present at times.

However, the modern macroeconomic mainstream may be exposed to a different kind of criticism. What about ethical aspects? Ought macroeconomics not concern itself with questions of morality?[3] Can theory be value-free? And when economists give advices to the politicians in charge is the counselling free of normative aspects? The answer to both questions is of course a 'no'.

As known from the history of economic thought, classical economics was early on somehow coloured by moral aspects due to the writings of Adam Smith. Later on, however, when the political economy of the classical era evolved to become the neoclassical paradigm, and much later in modern times, after the Keynesian paradigm was pushed aside for good, when the NNS completely overtook the scene of macroeconomics, ethical and moral aspects became downplayed more and more in macroeconomics. Somehow, macroeconomics became somewhat synonymous with the (love of) market fetishism: more market was supposed with certainty to be better than less market and so was efforts to deregulate (especially in the financial sector and the labour market). Letting politicians pursue such a strategy, high levels of prosperity were guaranteed by the economists to be the outcome for citizens of modern societies. However, as shown by the events of the Great Recession, this prophesy of prosperity for the many lacked empirical support.

DOI: 10.4324/9781315745992-8

In the present chapter some important aspects concerning the moral dimension (or lack of) in macroeconomics are presented and discussed, highlighting the imperfection of the present mainstream practice in this respect.

The history of economics

Back in ancient times, discussion of economic matters always included aspects of the *quality* and *justice* of life. Therefore, as stated by Stapleford (2000, p. 79), in general: 'economic issues were always contextualised within an ethical framework. The ethical issues encompassed wealth *and* welfare, poverty *and* charity, growth *and* justice, individualism *and* community.' However important that ancient Greek connection in economics may be, a thorough focus on the economic processes of a market economy had to await the publication of Adam Smith's *Wealth of Nations* (WN) in 1776.

Studying the seminal work of Adam Smith, scholars have in general tried to figure out the connection between his *Theory of Moral Sentiments* (TMS) published in 1759, and his *Wealth of Nations*. Recently, Montes (2019) has addressed this famous 'Adam Smith Problem' in more detail. As a main result, Montes argues that we should probably interpret Smith's crucial concept of self-interest from the WN less narrowly than what is normally understood by the term selfishness. The concept of self-interest must be interpreted in a TMS context. As such, Smiths' use of the entrepreneurs' aim of pursuing self-interest as the key element in explaining why society is to become prosperous for all citizens due to the process of capital accumulation is not without moral implications.[4] And then of course as pointed out by Friedman (2011, p. 166), in both books Smith had as his guiding principle the aim of analysing 'individuals' motivations and psychological states, and the ways in which what we now call "economic" activity, carried out in inherently social settings, enables them to lead satisfying lives or not'.

In sum, Montes (2019, p. 3) finds that:

> In Smith's moral system, there is no room for Robinson Crusoe or the *homo economicus* of neoclassical economics ... Smith considers ethics to be a social phenomenon simply because a man without society cannot have a sense of good or bad.

And this is in good accordance with the statement of Robinson (1978, p. 63) as she points out; that Smith 'relied very much upon morality. He took it for granted that there is an ethical foundation for society, and it was against this background that he opened up his economic doctrine.' Therefore, Malek et al. (2016, p. 16) rightly conclude that Adam Smith viewed economics 'as a moral science'.

More so, the moral dimension is economics was also present in the writings of other classical economists. As pointed out by Alvey (2000), there were traces of ethical statements in the writings of Thomas Malthus and John Stuart Mill. However, later the neoclassical paradigm seems more or less to have abandoned moral aspects when it adopted a methodology of positivism and made mathematic formalism the prime engine of inquiry. As argued by Hodgson (2014), this further narrowed down the scope of economics as it was accepted that our altruistic and moral tendencies could and should be ignored when studying economics.

Therefore, to some economists, Adam Smith is seen more as the founding father of the social sciences than that of economics; to these economists, the credit should rather be given to David Ricardo. To others – including many of today's non-mainstreamers – Adam Smith is the true father of economics as he pointed to the fact that societies change over time. In doing so, such processes of transformation are determined by more than just economic factors alone. It includes a variety of political, historical, cultural and other relevant aspects to understand the true nature of such transformations. Society changes over time by the act of the people – and the way people act as human beings is coloured to a certain degree by ethical and moral aspects.

Modern mainstream macroeconomics

Modern mainstream macroeconomics is heavily reliant on the equilibrium-generating properties of the market mechanism. As such, the mainstream is firmly grounded on a kind of market fetishism as pointed out above. Letting the market forces act freely, efficiency and optimality is bound to be ensured as the outcome of every single market that works to perfection. And seen from a mainstream macroeconomic perspective, we know as documented by history that Western societies have benefitted from economic growth ever since the early days of the industrial revolution and onwards up to the present modern time, thereby improving economic conditions in general substantially. Therefore, to many mainstream economists, there is no relevant alternative to a free market economy.[5] This is the only route by which to gain prosperity to society with certainty.

This view on macroeconomics, however, has (perhaps) a kind of built-in moral dimension. As argued by Lee and Schug (2011, p. 75), we could probably talk about a kind of mundane morality. Such a kind of morality is perhaps best described 'as obeying the generally accepted rules and norms of engaging in impersonal exchange, such as being honest, keeping our promises and contractual obligations, respecting the property rights of others, and not intentionally harming others'. Although such a description might be correct in many normal situations, we know as a fact that at times it is certainly not. This was documented for instance during the process that led to the outbreak of the Great Recession.[6]

Furthermore, seen from the mainstream macroeconomic perspective, the rational economic man[7] transformed in modern macroeconomics to become the representative agent.[8] A such, he takes up a key position in mainstream macroeconomic theory as it is he, with his quest for gaining optimality through the design of a perfect intertemporal consumption plan, that makes every market clear and ensures a macroeconomic output of full employment. Therefore, '*homo economicus* is the god who is to be served' (Fikkert and Rhodes 2017, p. 110).[9] *Homo economicus* acting as the representative agent in modern mainstream macroeconomics has such superpowers that he knows everything of interest. To him, situations of bounded rationality are not a matter to consider seriously.[10]

Accepting the above, modern macroeconomics tries in principle to become a positive/deductive science that suppresses normative aspects. Therefore, besides the discussion of mundane morality mentioned earlier on, modern mainstream macroeconomics in general skips ostensibly any moral dimension. The macroeconomic analysis should be 'clean', making economics more of a natural science-like rather than a normal social science discipline. As Boulding (1969, p. 1) stated long time ago:

> We are strongly imbued today with the view that science should be *wertfrei* and we believe that science has achieved its triumph precisely because it has escaped the swaddling clothes of moral judgement and has only been able to take off into the vast universe of the 'is' by escaping from the treacherous launching pad of the 'ought'.[11]

However, we know for certain that normative aspects are important for real-life humans that inhabit our modern societies; see, e.g. Stapleford (2000) and Tatum (2017)[12] among others. Norms and values are determinants of actual human behaviour.

As such, with Fikkert and Rhodes (2017, p. 104) we know that: 'Human beings shape culture, and culture shapes human beings'. This fact has for long characterised the process of transformation of societies throughout history. Moreover, as society changes so does the institutional framework of the economic system. Therefore, macroeconomic theory is contextual in its nature. Finally, as Slade-Caffarel (2019, p. 532) points out:

> social reality is ... brought into existence by, and depends on, human beings. It emerges from, and is reproduced and transformed by, our interactions. Social structures are the ... results of socio-historically specific social relations ... these structures have a power of conditioning over the actions of human beings who, in turn, transform and reproduce them. It is a never-ending dynamic back and forth.

This is a fact of life which is perfectly evident to most people. More so, it should also be a straightforward statement even for modern macroeconomists.

John Maynard Keynes: economics is a moral science

Above it was argued partly that economics historically has had its roots in ethics as moral aspects were included in economic reasoning from the very beginning, and partly that this should also be the case concerning modern macroeconomics if the aim is to gain relevance in trying to cope with the economic behaviour of real human beings who inhabit modern economies. To those who have read their Keynes, this comes as no surprise. To Keynes, economics had to be a moral science.

In 1938, in a correspondence with Roy Harrod when Keynes was reviewing the pioneering econometric work of Jan Tinbergen, he argued that:

> Economics is a science of thinking in terms of models joined to the art of choosing models which are relevant to the contemporary world. It is compelled to be this, because, unlike the typical natural science, the material to which it is applied is, in too many respects, not homogeneous through time ... Progress in economics consists almost entirely in a progressive improvement in the choice of models ... I also want to emphasize strongly the point about economics being a moral science. I mentioned before that it deals with introspection and with

values. I might have added that it deals with motives, expectations, psychological uncertainties. One has to be constantly on guard against treating the material as constant and homogeneous.

(CW XIV, p. 296 & p. 300)

This view on economics was not new to Keynes as he in 1922 wrote the following statement in his Introduction to *Cambridge Economic Handbooks*:

The theory of economics does not furnish a body of settled conclusions immediately applicable to policy. It is a method rather than a doctrine, an apparatus of the mind, a technique of thinking, which helps its possessor to draw correct conclusions. It is not difficult in the sense in which mathematical and scientific techniques are difficult; but the fact that its modes of expression are much less precise than these, renders decidedly difficult the task of conveying it correctly to the minds of learners.

(CW XII, p. 859)[13]

To a Post-Keynesian, the above-mentioned view made by Keynes on economics as a social science discipline still seems to apply to modern macroeconomics. To a modern mainstream macroeconomist, however, such a view might be more problematic as it questions many of the core elements of modern mainstream macroeconomics. As such, Post-Keynesians and mainstreamers hold different views on how they see and interpret the outcome of the macroeconomic system. To a Post-Keynesian, the economic system is one of non-ergodicity as the system is an open, social dependent and changeable system characterised by various path dependencies; see Chick and Dow (2005). To a mainstream macroeconomist, the economic system is seen as one of ergodicity, thereby arguing that the system is a closed system and to a certain degree deterministic in its nature, as explained by, e.g. Dow (1996) and Jespersen (2009).

Concluding remarks

Fundamentally, economics is about human behaviour. We try to understand how households and firms plan and act based on expectations when they decide what to do in the future. And, the future is, at least to some degree, unforeseeable in some respect due to various aspects of uncertainty (epistemologically as well as ontologically); see, e.g. Dow (2016). Therefore, expectations are often based on knowledge about future matters about which neither households nor firms (or governments or other institutions for that matter) know for certainty. In addition, we know that when people plan and act, they go beyond the motives of gaining efficiency and optimality by aiming to maximise both utility and profit – the strategy that is used by *homo economicus* as the representative agent in much of modern mainstream macroeconomics. They act as humans not as robots. As human beings, they include other aspects when planning and acting economically. These may cover a wide variety of motives of which some include moral and ethical considerations. In real life, normative aspects are of importance to most people (at least some of the time). As for instance pointed out by Rider (1999, p. 269): 'Focusing on responsibility and accountability makes it clear that economics is a moral science'.

Unfortunately, modern macroeconomists in general do not put great emphasise on these matters. To them, economics is not a moral science. To a huge degree they follow the strategy advocated by Friedman (1953). Therefore, it hardly comes as any surprise when the modern macroeconomic understanding is mistaken at times as recently documented by the Great Recession. More market is not always better than less market – and deregulation actions could have devastating effects as shown by the behaviour of the financial sectors in our modern economies up to the outbreak of the global financial crisis.

With Hodgson (2014, p. 84), we as macroeconomists have to acknowledge the fact that neither our modern societies nor the economy can function proper without some moral thumb-of-rules: 'Our understanding of social institutions and organisations is inadequate unless we appreciate the moral motivations of individuals within them, and how those institutions help to sustain and replicate these moral sentiments'.

So back to basics. Old-timers got it right the first time. Economics really *is* (and *ought* to be) a moral science. That we need to tell our students when we teach macroeconomics. The field of macroeconomics is in general much more complex than what could be captured by the NNS storytelling and their DSGE models alone. There is plenty of room for alternatives for a more comprehensive understanding of the economy as a whole.

Notes

1 I have benefitted from useful comments from Jesper Jespersen. The usual caveats apply.
2 To name just a few; see the contributions of Solow (2010), Romer (2016) and Stiglitz (2018).
3 'An ethic of a particular kind is an idea or moral belief that influences the behaviour, attitudes, and philosophy of life of a group of people … Ethics are moral beliefs and rules about right and wrong' whereas

> Morals are principles and values based on what a person or society believes are the right, proper, or acceptable ways of behaving … A morality is a system of principles and values concerning people's behaviour, which is generally accepted by a society or by a particular group of people.
> (Collins Cobuild English Language Dictionary 1992, p. 480 & p. 937)

That is, both concepts have to do with how to distinguish between what is good or bad (or right and wrong). Perhaps many would argue that aspects of morality should be seen as something that is both personal and normative whereas aspects of ethics have more to do with the standards of good or bad accepted by a certain community (or social group). Despite this, to many the two concepts are probably most often used interchangeably.
4 See Montes (2019, p. 12) note 17 for more details. For a discussion in general of the cardinal virtues of Adam Smith see Raphael (2007, Chapter 9).
5 However, you must remember that all modern economies include a lot of economic activity that is not dependent on the operation of Adam Smith's invisible hands. Suffice in this respect just to mention the important part played by public sector activities in every modern economy. These and other economic activities are not supplied and demanded at the marketplace. And furthermore, in modern economies the market is also constrained in many ways by various social and political institutions.
6 Just to give one example:

> The general model of bank-financed, credit market-financed activity in the run-up to the Great Crisis was suffused with criminal behaviour. When it became clear that all of the major institutions with which one has to deal – the commercial banks; the investment banks; the rating agencies; the regulators – are part of, complicit in, or accessories to a vast criminal conspiracy, then there is a tendency to lose trust in such people and the system as a whole.
> (Galbraith 2016, p. 16)

7 Morgan (2006) gives a thoroughly and very enlightening presentation and discussion on the changing meaning of the concept 'rational economic man' from Adam Smith to today's contemporary economics.
8 A thorough critique of the representative agent is given by Kirman (1992).
9 However, within the field of microeconomics the case is somewhat different. In general, the understanding of the concept of the economic agent is much broader – take behavioural economics as just one example – in this respect, microeconomics has developed to become a game of economics that is in better accordance with the facts of real life compared to that of modern mainstream macroeconomics; see, e.g. Atkinson (2009).
10 On the importance of bounded rationality and its consequences for macroeconomics, see, e.g. Olesen (2010).
11 Having said that, later on, however, Boulding stresses that

> as science develops it no longer merely investigates the world; it creates the world which it is investigating ... what it creates becomes a problem of ethical choice, and will depend upon the common values of the societies in which the scientific subculture is embedded ... [and when] ... knowledge changes the world the question of the content of the common values, both of the subculture which is producing knowledge and of the total society in which that subculture is embedded, becomes of acute importance. Under these circumstances the concept of a value-free science is absurd.
>
> (Boulding 1969, p. 3 & p. 4)

12 Taking inspiration from theology, Tatum (2017, p. 135 & p. 138) points to the possibility 'that the utilization of a broader set of norms could contribute not only to better normative analysis in economics but also to better positive analysis ... [making economists become aware of the] ... blind spots in our worldviews and deficiencies in our empirical evidence'.
13 Probably the core elements of Keynes's view on the nature of economics had been formed when he as a youngster was under the influence of the philosophy of G.E. Moore as indicated in his autobiographical essay 'My Early Beliefs' from 1938 (*CW* X, pp. 433–50).

Bibliography

Alvey, J. (2000) 'An introduction to economics as a moral science', *International Journal of Social Economics* 27 (12), 1231–51.
Atkinson, A.B. (2009) 'Economics as a moral science', *Economica* 76 (issue s1), 791–804.
Boulding, K. (1969) 'Economics as a moral science', *The American Economic Review* 59 (1), 1–12.
Chick, V. and S. Dow (2005) 'The meaning of open system', *Journal of Economic Methodology* 12 (3), 363–81.
Collins Cobuild English Language Dictionary (1992), London: HarperCollins Publishers.
CW: see Keynes (1971–89).
CW (X), *The Collected Writings of John Maynard Keynes, Vol. X, Essays in Biography*, D. Moggridge, ed., London: Macmillan and New York: St Martin's Press.
CW (XII), *The Collected Writings of John Maynard Keynes, Vol. XII, Economic Articles and Correspondence – Investment and Editorial*, D. Moggridge, ed., London: Macmillan and New York: St Martin's Press.
CW (XIV), *The Collected Writings of John Maynard Keynes, Vol. XIV, The General Theory and After, Part II: Defence and Development*, D. Moggridge, ed., London: Macmillan and New York: St Martin's Press.
Dow, S. (1996) *The Methodology of Macroeconomic Thought*, Cheltenham: Edward Elgar.
Dow, S. (2016) 'Uncertainty: A diagrammatic treatment', *Economics – The Open-Access, Open Assessment E-Journal*, No. 2016-3, 1–25, http://www.economics-ejournal.org/economics/journalarticles/2016-3
Fikkert, B. and M. Rhodes (2017) '*Homo Economicus* Versus *Homo Imago Dei*', *Journal of Markets & Morality* 20(1), 101–26.
Friedman, B. (2011) 'Economics: A moral inquiry with religious origins', *The American Economic Review* 101 (3), 166–70.

Friedman, M. (1953) 'The methodology of positive economics', in *Essays in Positive Economics*, Chicago, IL: The University of Chicago Press, pp. 3–43.

Galbraith, J. (2016) 'Keynes 'in the twenty-first century': Tradition, circumstance, fad and pretence in the wake of the great crisis', in M. O. Madsen & F. Olesen, eds., *Macroeconomics After the Financial Crisis – A Post-Keynesian Perspective*, London: Routledge, pp. 10–19.

Hodgson, G. (2014) 'The evolution of morality and the end of economic man', *Journal of Evolutionary Economics* 24 (1), 83–106.

Jespersen, J. (2009), *Macroeconomic Methodology: A Post-Keynesian Perspective*, Cheltenham: Edward Elgar.

Keynes, J. M. (1971–89) *Collected Writings, (CW)*, D. E. Moggridge, ed., 30 vols, London: Macmillan and New York: St Martin's Press.

Kirman, A. P. (1992) 'Whom or what does the representative individual represent?', *The Journal of Economic Perspectives* 6 (2), 117–36.

Lee, D. and M. Schug (2011) 'The political economy of economic education: The moral dimensions', *Journal of Markets & Morality* 14 (1), 71–84.

Malek, N. et al. (2016) 'The relationship between economics and ethics and the effectiveness of normative economics on students' attitudes and learning', *Journal of Economics and Economic Education Research* 17 (1), 16–24.

Montes, L. (2019) 'Adam Smith's foundational idea of sympathetic persuasion', *Cambridge Journal of Economics* 43 (1), 1–15.

Morgan, M. (2006) 'Economic man as model man: ideal types, idealization and caricatures', *Journal of the History of Economic Thought* 28 (1), 1–27.

Olesen, Finn (2010) 'Uncertainty, bounded rationality and post Keynesian macroeconomics', *INTERVENTION: European Journal of Economics and Economic Policies* 7 (1), 109–24.

Raphael, D. D. (2007), *The Impartial Spectator: Adam Smith's Moral Philosophy*, Oxford University Press.

Rider, C. R. (1999) 'Art, ethics, and economics', *Review of Social Economy* 57 (3), 263–77.

Robinson, J. (1978) 'Morality and economics', *Challenge*, March-April 1978, 21 (1), 62–4.

Romer, P. (2016) 'The trouble with macroeconomics', 14th September 2016, https://paulromer.net/wp-content/uploads/2016/09/WP-Trouble.pdf.

Slade-Caffarel, Y. (2019) 'The nature of heterodox economics revisited', *Cambridge Journal of Economics* 43 (3), 527–40.

Solow, R. (2010) *Building a Science of Economics for the Real World*, Hearings before the Subcommittee on Investigations and Oversight Committee on Science and Technology, House of Representatives, 111th Congress, second session, July 20, 2010, Serial No. 111–106, Washington, DC, Printed for the use of the Committee on Science and Technology, pp.12–14.

Stapleford, J. (2000) 'Christian ethics and the teaching of introductory economics', *Journal of Markets & Morality* 3 (1), 67–87.

Stiglitz, J. E. (2018) 'Where modern macroeconomics went wrong', *Oxford Review of Economic Policy* 34 (1–2), 70–106.

Tatum, R. (2017) '*Homo Economicus* as fallen man: The need for theological economics', *Journal of Markets & Morality* 20 (1), 127–40.

PART II

Concepts

7

TIME IN MACROECONOMICS

Mogens Ove Madsen

Introduction

What is time? Let us start by asking the philosophers. Most philosophers agree that time exists, but disagree on what it is. Not surprisingly, the ancient Greek philosophers were preoccupied with the question: A moving image of eternity, says Plato. No, time is the number of motion in respect of before and after, says Aristotle. Nonsense, says Philon, time expresses only something about a number of days and nights, or Cicero, invoking the divine: Time is the god who put into place the years and days.

Just this small selection of statements about time illustrates that time is not easy to define or handle at all – it is not possible to refer to a more basic concept. We have knowledge of this basic concept, but not more than that. Therefore, it becomes more a matter of properties of time and studies of temporal argumentations.

The famous time-philosopher Augustin (354–430 c.e.) has a subjective perception of time, arguing that time is not something real, but exists only in the mind of man, but Augustin is also known for his work in creating a bridge between Aristotle's physics and the religious approach to time.

The societal attitude to time has had major implications for the development of art and science. If you have assumed a theologically oriented vision of the concept of time, there has been a tendency to downplay the measurement of time, because it is God given.

However, the secularisation of social relations, which for centuries had been governed by religious considerations, took hold in Europe in the 14th century. It happened with the Renaissance and then in the Enlightenment, which saw a shift in the development of mechanical methods for measuring time.

Science actively uses time measurement options to create new discoveries. In science, it was essential for the new understanding of astronomy and for experiments when controlling the motion of physical objects.

Different perceptions of time have also had an impact on economic thinking, but in several ways (Vickers 1994). The approach to time and sometimes the lack of it is essential to the analytical results. As stated by Currie and Steedman (1990, p. 241) it

DOI: 10.4324/9781315745992-10

is extremely healthy that more and more economists seem to be acknowledging that substantive progress in economic analysis can only come from confronting the formidable difficulties associated with time.

Before dealing with the concept of time specifically in economics, it would be appropriate to find inspiration for a firmer grasp of specific proportions of time. This implies a short introduction into temporal logic, which is a system of rules and symbolism for representing and reasoning about propositions qualified in terms of time. The awareness of time is of central importance, and it was further developed in J.M. Keynes's macroeconomic theory. This also establishes an agenda for what the basic conditions are that must be met to conduct economic analysis, taking due account of time. That might include the choice of a time unit and whether events that are studied are repetitive or unique, but also how the analyst places himself in and out of time and, not least, to what extent the approach applies to the concepts of past, present and future.

The properties of time

As described above, time is a fundamental concept. Therefore, we must make a few philosophical considerations about the concept. Can a concept of time from an older and more mature natural science readily be used in social science? Inspiration could be found in the study of mechanics and time, but this also provides some limitations for social sciences. This is related to the difference in objects that natural sciences and social sciences investigate. According to Boutellier et al. (2011) there is a huge difference between social and natural sciences and the difference lies in the object of knowledge. While the laws in natural sciences rule the world independently of the research results of scientists, this is not true for social sciences. The members of society are so to speak deeply influenced by theoretical models of the social sciences (Subrt 2001).

Initially it may be appropriate to look at time symbols. It is characteristic that those refer either to a static or to a dynamic picture of time (Dowden 2016).

A fixed line or an arrow of time is a classic representation of a static time. The timeline is a compact, continuous series of instants – like a row of numbers. The arrow of time, together with a single direction, adds the ability to determine before and after (or linearity). The arrow also introduces the concept of irreversibility.

In the dynamic concept of time, time is considered rather as a river, or Kronos. Events take place in the midst of endless change – the time river washes over everything and devours events, as Kronos devours his children. Events are constantly changing and can be arranged respectively as past, present and future.

This distinction can also be found in an approach using temporal logic and more precisely by an introduction of McTaggart's linear ordering of events in a dynamic *A-* and a static *B-series* (McTaggart 1908). The main point in McTaggart's position is that, without the *A-series*, there would be no change, and consequently the *B-series* by itself is not sufficient for time, since time involves change.

He states that the A- and *B-series* are equally essential to time, which must be distinguished as past, present and future, and must likewise be distinguished as earlier and later. But the two series are not equally fundamental. The distinctions of the *A-series* are ultimate. We cannot explain what is meant by past, present and future. We can, to some extent, describe them, but they cannot be defined. We can only show their meaning by examples (McTaggart 1908, p. 463).

There are two different approaches to the description of a temporal relationship. *A-series* is based on time – the time from the inside, so to speak. *B-series* is time seen from a perspective external to the progression of time – time from the outside.

This McTaggart division of life's temporal relation has since manifested itself in two schools – the dynamic conception of time based on the *A-series* and its tensed theory of time, and the static conception of time based on the *B-series* and a tenseless theory of time. If a language has tenses it is the same as positions in McTaggart's *A-series*. *B-series* gives a different analysis without tensed facts.

We use tense to locate events in the past, present or future. Even if this is possible, philosophers do not agree on the ontological questions that follow: is past, present and future real? However, it is possible to identify at least three approaches to this problem, namely presentism, growing-past theory and eternalism, which we will explain.

As the word presentism suggests, it is the present that is in scope and that neither past nor future exists. Only present objects exist. If it is so then McTaggart's *A-series* is fundamental because presentism requires tense to have a temporal discourse.

Growing-past theory argues that in addition to the present the past also is real, but the future is not real. If past is real, it is growing bigger when the now is moving forward but the future is indeterminate or merely potential.

Eternalists state that there are no ontological differences between past, present and future: all points in time are equally 'real'. In this context, it is not possible to pinpoint any moment in the dimension of time as a more real now. Objects from the past and future have equal ontological status and each spacetime moment exists in and of itself.

The fact that our perception of time is that we move from a known past towards an unknown future is, as already indicated, often called the arrow of time (Turk 2010). We can remember the past and do not attempt to change an already known past. Causality is also associated with the arrow of time. Cause precedes effect. If you crack the shell of an egg and beat out the yolk, there is no turning back. This phenomenon has a counterpart in physics, namely the second law of thermodynamics.

These key concepts can help structure the use of the concept of time and can be a baseline from which to assess how economic science should act to take due account of time. Further studies reveal, however, that economic thinking has made excellent attempts to define time. As an example, Shackle (1965) has done so especially in the chapter 'A Scheme of Economic Theory', where he defines four concepts of time. See also Carvalho (1983–84) for an interpretation of these four definitions of time, where mechanical time is the time of the external observer, who knows everything, the future as well as the past. In evolutionary time the observer is no longer omniscient – the object of study is a segment of real history. Timeless models are a special situation in which time does not flow – as in General Equilibrium models. In expectational time agents know that the past is immutable and the future is yet to be created. Termini (1981) has also worked to clarify the concepts of logical, mechanical and historical time in economics.

Maynard Keynes and awareness of time in macroeconomics

It is well known from Keynes's biographies that he was, especially in the early Cambridge years, a student of G.E. Moore and Alfred Marshall. This is evident in his attempts to break away from the Victorian social norms and conventions, and his firm contact with the Bloomsbury group for many years. But with regard to a number of more abstract philosophical issues, Keynes might have been influenced more than usually acknowledged by ideas put forward by J.M.E. McTaggart (Madsen 2012).

Particularly, the latter philosopher brought to Keynes a vital introduction to an ontological difference between the earlier mentioned theories of time. The same fundamental difference, from the above-mentioned philosophical discussions, is known and demonstrated in the work of Keynes, who presented the dynamic approach – according to which the essential notions are past, present and future. In this view, time is seen 'from the inside'. Secondly, there is also the static view of time according to which time is understood as a set of instants (or durations) ordered by the before-after relation.

In Keynes's (1903) paper, time is about the awareness of change and change requires that at least one aspect differs with respect to what is happening – i.e. whether the event is future, present or past – in McTaggart's theory, its A-characteristics. On the contrary, *B-series* alone cannot account for change, because 'earlier than' or 'later than' cannot be used to differentiate characteristics – a changeless state is a timeless state.

Keynes is explicit in his focus on time. For example, it appears early in a part of Keynes's writings that prediction is a very difficult matter. He notes, in an essay on Burke in 1904, that our power of prediction is so slight that it is seldom wise to sacrifice a present evil for a doubtful advantage in the future. This later becomes a recurring theme in a number of key writings.

His preoccupation with time has been the subject of several observations; see, e.g. Backhouse and Bateman (2006), where they point out that in a series of books Shackle argued that the Keynesian revolution concerned time. The essence of time is that it is irreversible and that we can know nothing about the future. The Keynesian revolution was about breaking with equilibrium, which can occur only in logical time, and creating a theory about how economic activity took place in historical time that was relevant to the real world. Similarly, Chick (1983) has argued that understanding Keynes lies in the concept of time and the General Theory is a static model of a dynamic process, the process of production.

Not least, Shackle's well-known 'de Vries Lectures', which were published under the title *Time in Economics* in 1958, marks a very significant breakthrough in thinking about time in a more complete Keynesian way.

Maynard Keynes in his 'My Early Beliefs' essay (1938) saw himself as an advocate of a principle of organic unity through time, as seen in his macroeconomic model. He got the inspiration from Moore that the whole has an intrinsic value different from the sum of its parts. It is important to notice that Keynes, in 1920, was inspired by this idea in his work on probability and he was well aware of the difference between laws connecting individual parts and laws for wholes of different degrees of complexity (Keynes, CW VIII, p. 277).

In 1938 Keynes CW XIV, p. 300) wrote a letter to Harrod explaining another aspect of organic complexes and where he emphasises the point about economics being a moral science and that it deals with motives, expectations, psychological uncertainties and, not least, that one has to be constantly on guard against treating the material as constant and homogeneous.

This means that intuitions and values always play a part in the art of forming an economic model – rather than induction – but they are not exclusive opposites. Behind this, it is important to determine the relatively constant (psychological) factors that allow one to make limited generalisations about the behaviours issuing from them (Jespersen, 2009).

In the light of chapter 18 of *The General Theory* (1936), Keynes's method was to take these factors as invariable basic assumptions, change some variable, such as the expectations governing investment, and trace the process of adjustment through the economic model to determine the fundamental *quaesitum*, which is the dependent variables of income and employment measured in wage-units.

The crucial independent psychological variables in his model are the propensity to consume, the schedule of the marginal efficiency of capital and the rate of interest.

This means that we end up with an interplay between changes in psychological factors and mechanical factors such as the multiplier. It also means that both the A- and the B-series of time logic are represented in Keynes's analysis in *The General Theory*. It provides the opportunity to pursue how the pattern of the marginal propensity to consume, the marginal efficiency of capital and liquidity preference specified in the beginning of a production period will unfold in the form of a mechanical law of motion that determines income and employment. The awareness of adequate incorporation of aspects of time as 'economic theory in time' in contrast to 'economic theory out of time' was later followed in the works of G.L.S. Shackle (1954, 1984), N. Kaldor (1972), J. Hicks (1976), J. Robinson (1980), V. Chick (1983, 2004) and John F. Henry (2012).

Implications of time for macroeconomics

A number of factors are important in order to identify how the concept of time is handled constructively. Winston (1988) has made clear the serious consequences of not handling it carefully and explains it simply that careless attention to time can mislead economic and social analysis when the temporal perspective to time can lead to the use of inappropriate methodology.

The crucial question is whether activities conducted by humans, the subject matter of economics, can be understood in relation to changes in real time and yet be analysed through abstract models that follow from a discrete set of general rules (Turk, 2012).

Many factors are directly linked to the phenomenon of time, which may also explain why Shackle (1965) left little room for a Walras-Pareto type of general static equilibrium, since its special characteristics derived from the lack of time.

We have theoretical systems that have little relation to reality, and little understanding of time, which despite these shortcomings must have a role that is fundamental and constructive. In reality, the future is uncertain and many developments are irreversible. This ultimately means that the connections we can form only list the options and not the certainties.

Conscious involvement of time requires the adoption of a number of well-informed choices. This will be explained in the following and relates to: the choice of a unit of time, whether the events studied are repetitive or unique and to what extent there is a need to be inside time or outside of it, and, finally, how to approach the trinity of past, present and future.

The time unit

Statistical agencies often bear the responsibility for the time units used in the registration or description of an economic phenomenon. Work on the application of economic theories, in turn, is often the responsibility of other economists, but is also a significant challenge. In some cases, however, there will be some forms of collaboration or joint projects between the producer and user of statistical material.

Measuring time is like a hunted hare. Economics has throughout time been subject to discrepancies in time perception and time measurement, but there is only one way forward: to aim to be as precise as possible in the choice of the size of the time unit in relation to the analysis to be made.

Winston (1988) has formulated this quite clearly by saying that more temporally meticulous analysis would self-consciously choose a time unit short enough to reveal the relevant social behaviour, a time unit that would suppress only that information deemed analytically uninteresting after an effort at explicit consideration.

The objective is to mitigate the risk that any time unit suppresses information about the timing of events within it. Otherwise, we cannot know when or in what order the events occurred.

Repetitive or unique behaviour

After determining the unit of time, the next area of focus is how it relates to the events that are explored. This is certainly not an easy exercise, and as indicated by Hicks (1979) at every stage in an economic process new things will be happening, things which have not happened before.

One way of dealing with this problem is to distinguish between what happens frequently and what happens more rarely. 'Frequently' can be said to reflect the patterns of repetition in which there may be an opportunity to build a degree of credible knowledge regarding such events. It will reflect what can be detected around the simple mechanical models. Unique events disturb this idea of repeated events, in which case there arises a situation of widespread ignorance. Hicks (1981), also in this context, developed an interesting point of the facts which we study. Our facts are not permanent. Or repeatable. Like the facts of the natural sciences, they change incessantly, and change without repetition.

As Hicks indicates, when the object of economics does not display repetitive movement, analysis has obvious limitations. There are many ideas regarding how non-repetitive events occur and how these do not fit into formal analyses. This unfortunately reduces the power analysis of a Cartesian-Euclidean approach (Levando, 2005). An alternative Babylonian approach (Dow, 1996) might be a better approach and comprises of a style thus conditioned by the problem at hand, employing a range of methods suited to the problem, and these methods cannot be combined into one formal deductive argument without drastically changing their nature.

Inside or outside time

If economics is treated from the perspective of an outside observer in the sense of Shackle (1954), its determinate behaviour will resemble a machine of limited design – and it will claim to be predictive. But theories which tell us what will happen are claiming too much.

Further to this, it is also important to acknowledge that one of the most striking changes in economic thinking comes primarily from J.M. Keynes, with his explicit focus on time. An anatomy of Keynes's concept of time can best be understood by studying his philosophical background, his understanding of society and his development of economic theory. It is possible to view his handling of the concept of time as both related to the *A*- and *B-series* of time logic. This dichotomy can be found in *The General Theory*, which both used a dynamic concept of time, which relates to a number of basic psychological mechanisms, and a static concept of time, related to the well-known spending multiplier. Despite numerous challenges to his perception of time, Keynes did not change his position, but rather became sharper in his view – not least when it comes to the concept of uncertainty.

We have an interplay between concretely assessed changes in psychological factors and mechanical factors such as the multiplier. It also means that both the *A*- and the *B-series* of time logic are represented in Keynes's analysis in *The General Theory*. This theory provides the opportunity to pursue how the pattern of the marginal propensity to consume, the marginal efficiency of capital and the liquidity preference specified at the beginning of a production period will unfold in the form of a mechanical law of motion that determines income and employment.

Keynes (1936) explained that life and history are made up of short periods, which might be the reason why he did not study the extent to which the value of the multiplier changed in historical time.

The division into *A* and *B time series* is also characterised in some contexts as perspective and analytical time respectively. Perspective time is characterised by the *now*, where the analyst has no knowledge of the future. In the analytical expression of time, it is possible to make a distant analysis in which it is an option to move back and forth in the analytical perspective. This is a challenging approach, and its analytical statements risk a departure from reality. In recent times, there have been efforts to address a number of assumptions more closely to reflect conditions in the real world:

'Bounded rationality' now more often replaces omniscience (Simon 1955; Williamson 1979); surprise replaces known lists of possible events (Knight 1921; Shackle 1959; Williamson 1979); search (Nelson and Winther 1982) and discovery (Schumpeter 1934; Kirzner 1973) replace maximisation. All of these notice the temporal perspective of the subjects of social analysis as being inherently different from the temporal perspective of their analysis.

Past, present and future

In his homage to Georgescu-Roegen, Hicks (1976) stated that the concept of time has always been present in much of his own work. And the vital and interesting principle in the concept of time is the irreversibility of time – time goes on, never goes back.

However, Hicks (1936) acknowledged, very early, that the method in Keynes's *General Theory* was the reintroduction of determinateness into a process of change, and in Hicks's view, from the standpoint of pure theory, the use of the method of expectations was the most revolutionary thing about the General Theory. Expectations of the future would affect what happened during the period. Expectations were strictly exogenous.

The method of expectations encapsulates very well the relationship between past, present and future. Choices made in the past can possibly affect present decisions and have consequences in the future. In its most simple form, the past can play an explicit role: Path dependence is an expression of the idea that history matters. It is a way of bringing history into economics. Normally a path-dependent process is one in which the outcome evolves as a consequence of the history of the process. The concept of path dependence is intended to capture the way in which small, historically contingent events can set off self-reinforcing mechanisms and processes that 'lock in' particular structures and pathways of development.

In New Institutional Economics there have been different and well-known studies of path dependence concerning technological 'lock-in' (Qwertynomics), dynamic increasing returns and institutional hysteresis. According to Setterfield (1995), the institutional structures of an economy may be best conceived in terms of a process of hysteresis. This exists when the long-term value of a variable depends on the value of the variable in the past, by virtue of the influence of this past value on the alleged exogenous variables that characterise the system that determines the variable.

Vahabi (1998) also states that the author/scientist of inertial dynamics is moving away from the role of prophet towards the task of scientific description. An alternative agenda should be set for the work of understanding the potential future development of an economy: It needs to move from single-line predictions to scenario.

From a Shackelian perspective, deterministic predictions in economics will be rejected, but it will not be denied that it is possible to provide insights on a range of things that could happen. This means that it should be possible to highlight areas of uncertainty and delimit the bounds of the unknown, but also to propose improvements to the design of a system and to discover ways of modifying or eliminating surprises that are in the environment (Madsen, 2016).

Concluding perspective

Economics has always been confronted with the formidable difficulties associated with time when time involves change. This implies the need for an awareness of adequately incorporating aspects of time as 'economic theory in time'.

Keynes and the Keynesian tradition develop a sense of time in which it is possible to combine the *A*- and *B-series*, that is, a dynamic and a static analysis of economic phenomena, which clearly offers new potential for analysis.

This also implies that it becomes more a matter of properties of time and studies of temporal argumentation. Conscious involvement of time requires the adoption of a number of well-informed choices of, for example, the choice of time unit, whether events are repetitive or unique, to what extent there is a need for the analyst to be placed inside or outside time and, finally, how to approach the trinity of past, present and future.

References

Backhouse, R. E. and B. W. Bateman (2006) 'John Maynard Keynes: Artist, philosopher, economist', *Atlantic Economic Journal* 34, 149–59.

Boutellier, R., O. Gassmann, and S. Raeder (2011) What is the difference between social and natural sciences? Doctoral Seminar "Forschungsmethodik I", ETH, Universität St. Gallen.

Carvalho, F. (1983–84) 'On the concept of time in Shacklian and Sraffian economics', *Journal of Post Keynesian Economics* 6 (Winter), 265–80.

Chick, V. (1983) *Macroeconomics after Keynes: A Reconsideration of the General Theory.* Oxford: Philip Allan.

Chick, V. (2004) 'On open systems', *Revista de Economia Politica (Brazilian Journal of Political Economy)* 24 (1), (January-March), 3–16.

Currie, M. and I. Steedman (1990) *Wrestling with Time: Problems in Economic Theory.* Manchester: Manchester University Press.

Dow, S. (1996) *The Methodology of Macroeconomic Thought*, Cheltenham: Edward Elgar.

Dowden, B. (2016) 'Time', Internet Encyclopedia of Philosophy. www.iep.utm.edu/time/, Accessed 9 May 2022.

Henry, J. F. (2012) 'Time in economic theory', in J. King, ed., *Post Keynesian Economics*, Cheltenham and Northampton: Edward Elgar, pp. 528–33.

Hicks, J. R. (1936) 'Keynes' theory of employment', *The Economic Journal*, 46 (182) (Jun., 1936), 238–53.

Hicks, J. R. (1976) 'Some questions of time in economics' in A. M. Tang, F. M. Westfield, and J. S. Worley, eds, *Evolution, Welfare and Time in Economics*, Toronto: Heath, pp. 135–51.

Hicks, J. R. (1979) *Causality in Economics*, London: Blackwell.

Hicks, J. (1981) 'IS-LM: An explanation', *Journal of Post Keynesian Economics* 3 (2) (Winther 1980–81), 139–45.

Jespersen, J. (2009) *Macroeconomic Methodology: A Post-Keynesian Perspective*, Cheltenham: Edward Elgar.

Kaldor, N. (1972) 'The irrelevance of equilibrium economics', *The Economic Journal* 82 (328) (December), 1237–55.

Keynes, J. M. (1903) *Essay on Time*, JMK/UA/17. Cambridge, UK: King's College Archive.

Keynes, J. M. (1904): *The Political Doctrines of Edmund Burke*. UA/20/315. Cambridge, UK: King's College Archive.

Keynes, J. M. (1936) *The General Theory of Employment, Interest and Money. CW* VII.

Keynes J. M. (1938) 'My early beliefs', *CW* XIV, 433–51.

Keynes, J. M. (1971–89) *Collected Writings* (CW), D.E. Moggridge, ed., 30 vols., London: Macmillan and New York: St Martin's Press.

Kirzner, I. M. (1973) 'Competition and entrepreneurship', University of Illinois at Urbana-Champaign's Academy for Entrepreneurial Leadership Historical Research Reference in Entrepreneurship.

Knight, F. H. (1921) *Risk, Uncertainty and Profit*, Boston: Houghton Mifflin Company.

Levando, D. (2005) 'Investigation into the structure of reasoning in economics', Electronic Publication of Pan-European Institute, 6/2005. Turku School of Economics and Business Administration.

Madsen, M. O. (2012) 'Keynes's early cognition of the concept of time', in J. Jespersen and M. O. Madsen, eds., *Keynes's General Theory for Today: Contemporary Perspectives.* Cheltenham and Northampton: Edward Elgar, 98–112.

Madsen, M. O. (2016) 'Shackle in time – time in Shackle: On challenging the art of making predictions', *Journal of Business and Economics* 7, 1000–08.

McTaggart, J. E. (1908) 'The unreality of time', *Mind* 17(October), 457–74.

Nelson, R. R. and S.G. Winter (1982) *An Evolutionary Theory of Economic Change*, Cambridge, MA: Harvard University Press.

Robinson, J. (1980) 'Time in economic theory', *Kyklos* 33, 219–29.

Schumpeter, J. A. (1934) *The Theory of Economic Development*, Harvard: Economic Studies.

Setterfield, M. (1995) 'Historical time and economic theory', *Review of Political Economy* 7 (1), 1–27.

Shackle, G. L. S (1954) 'The complex nature of time as a concept in economics', *Economica Internazionale* 7, 74–757.

Shackle, G. L. S (1959) 'Time and thought', *The British Journal for the Philosophy of Science* 9 (36), 285–98.

Shackle, G. L. S (1965) *A Scheme of Economic Theory*, Cambridge, UK: Cambridge University Press.

Shackle, G. L. S. (1984) 'To cope with time', in F. H. Stephen, ed., *Firms, Organization and Labour, Approaches to the Economics of Work Organization*, London: Macmillan, pp. 69–79.

Simon, H. A. (1955) 'A behavioral model of rational choice', *The Quarterly Journal of Economics* 69 (1), 99–118.

Subrt, J. (2001) 'The problem of time from the perspective of the social sciences', *Czech Sociological Review* IX (2), 211–24.

Termini, V. (1981) 'Logical, mechanical and historical time in economics', *Economic Notes* 10 (3). Faculty of Economics University of Roma Tre Italy, pp. 1–31

Turk, M. H. (2010) 'The arrow of time in economics: from Robinson's critique to the new historical economics', *The European Journal of the History of Economic Thought* 17 (3), 471–92.

Vahabi, M. (1998) 'The relevance of the Marshallian concept of normality in interior and inertial dynamics as revisited by Shackle and Kornai', *Cambridge Journal of Economics*, 22(5), 547–572.

Vickers, D. (1994) *Economics and the Antagonism of Time*, Ann Arbor and Michigan: The University of Michigan Press.

Williamson, O. E. (1979) 'Transaction-cost economics: The governance of contractual relations', *The Journal of Law and Economics* 22 (2), 233–61.

Winston, G. C. (1988) 'Three problems with the treatment of time in economics: perspectives, repetitiveness, and time units', in G. C. Winston and R. F. Teichgraeber III, eds, *The Boundaries of Economics*, Cambridge, UK: Cambridge University Press, pp. 30–52

8

UNCERTAINTY AND MACROECONOMIC METHODOLOGY

Sheila Dow

Introduction

The most direct way in which uncertainty features in macroeconomics relates to expectations; the greater the uncertainty about the reliability of expectations the less confidence in them, with consequences for the behaviour underpinning macroeconomic aggregates. But uncertainty is understood and represented differently according to macroeconomic approach, most notably according to whether or not it is judged that uncertainty can be represented by the variance of a frequency distribution. While conflating uncertainty with quantifiable risk in this way has been the traditional mainstream approach to uncertainty, it has been modified to encompass uncertainty variously as asymmetric information with respect to that variance, or as an exogenous shock.

This mainstream understanding contrasts with that in non-mainstream macroeconomics. In Post-Keynesian macroeconomics in particular, uncertainty refers to an inability to quantify risk as the general case for expectations-formation as well as to uncertainty as input into structural forces. Uncertainty of some degree is regarded as the norm rather than an aberration or an exogenous shock. Uncertainty has thus been the subject of much more in-depth analysis than in the mainstream. For example, following Keynes (1921), varying degrees of confidence in expectations are analysed in terms of weight of argument and are vulnerable to discrete shifts. As with the mainstream approach, uncertainty is attached to expectations, with consequences for market behaviour and outcomes. But within the Post-Keynesian approach it also plays a very different, active long-term role in the evolution of institutions. Thus, for example, the institutions of money and price stickiness are both understood as mechanisms to help society deal with uncertainty.

Uncertainty applies to economists as well as to the actors we study, a parallel made most explicit in rational expectations theory and in Post-Keynesian theory. Just as economic actors may regard their expectations variously as reliable or unreliable, so economists may have more or less confidence in their theories. Methodology is then designed to reflect confidence in reliability or else the sources of unreliability. Economists' own uncertainty therefore governs the way we build up theory, as well

DOI: 10.4324/9781315745992-11

as its content. In what follows we explore how the concept of uncertainty – how it is understood and applied – determines epistemology and methodology. This in turn determines the character of macroeconomics according to different approaches.

As ever, the meaning of concepts is different according to different approaches. We therefore start by considering the different meanings attached to the concept of uncertainty. We then consider the source of uncertainty according to different methodological approaches. The main differentiation at this stage is drawn between closed-system ontologies and epistemologies on the one hand and open-system ontologies and epistemologies on the other. We then explore what this implies for methodological approach, and then for macroeconomic theorising, in both mainstream economics and Post-Keynesian economics.

It should be emphasised that the discussion here inevitably draws only selectively on what is a vast literature on uncertainty.[1] We start with the definitions of uncertainty independently provided by the *Oxford Economic Dictionary*. But, consistent with the argument to be developed below about the methodologically foundational role of uncertainty, the discussion is inevitably coloured by my own methodological-pluralist stance as expressed in Post-Keynesian macroeconomics. With that caveat, the aim is to provide a way of approaching the subject which clarifies and explains the various ways in which uncertainty is currently approached within macroeconomics.

The meaning of uncertainty

We have already alluded to the fact that different meanings of uncertainty are employed by macroeconomists. Dictionary definitions illustrate the point by encompassing a range of meanings which we take as our starting point. The *Oxford Economic Dictionary* includes meanings which underpin different methodologies in macroeconomics. The following lists those meanings, excluding those particular to law and physics and also those which are circular by virtue of relying on a meaning of 'uncertain'.[2] All are relevant even though the last one is specifically ascribed to economics.

1 a. ... liability to chance or accident. Also, the quality of being indeterminate as to magnitude or value; the amount of variation in a numerical result that is consistent with observation.
    ...

2 a. The state of not being definitely known or perfectly clear; doubtfulness or vagueness.
    ...
    c. Something not definitely known or knowable; a doubtful point.

3 a. The state or character of being uncertain in mind; a state of doubt; want of assurance or confidence; hesitation, irresolution.
    ...

4 *Economics*. (The quality of) a business risk which cannot be measured and whose outcome cannot be predicted or insured against.
    ...

The fourth definition is what is often referred to as 'fundamental uncertainty', or 'radical uncertainty', to distinguish it from other meanings in economics. It is the meaning associated particularly with Knight (1921) and Keynes (1921) and applied more widely than business risk to all risks. It refers in part to the quantitative indeterminacy included in definition 1.a. Yet that definition also includes the possibility of measuring uncertainty by variance, which is the meaning of uncertainty most widely employed within mainstream economics: quantifiable risk. How the definition with respect to 'chance' is interpreted then depends on whether or not uncertainty is understood to be quantifiable. If uncertainty can be measured, then some knowledge of chance is implied, e.g. that it is the result of a random process. But if uncertainty is indeterminate, then the notion of chance implies no quantifiable knowledge, and therefore no demonstrable reason to expect any one outcome or another (Carabelli 1988, pp. 95–7).

But, while the quantifiability or otherwise of risk is a central distinction in the meaning of uncertainty in economics, it does not encompass the fullest possible meaning of uncertainty which is indicated in the notion of indeterminacy embodied in definitions 2.a. and 2.c. above. Keynes alludes to this broader definition when he opens the *Treatise on Probability* as follows:

> Part of our knowledge we obtain direct; and part by argument. The Theory of Probability is concerned with that part which we obtain by argument, and it treats of the different degrees in which the results so obtained are conclusive or inconclusive.
>
>   In most branches of academic logic, such as the theory of the syllogism or the geometry of ideal space, all the arguments aim at demonstrative certainty. They claim to be conclusive. But many other arguments are rational and claim some weight without pretending to be certain. In Metaphysics, in Science, and in Conduct, most of the arguments, upon which we habitually base our rational beliefs, are admitted to be inconclusive in a greater or less degree.
>
> *(Keynes 1921, p. 3)*

This passage contains key features of Keynes's understanding of uncertainty: that it concerns inconclusivity of argument, that it applies to knowledge in general (on the part of economists as well as economic actors) and that it is a matter of degree depending on weight of argument. This specific reference to degree of uncertainty further differentiates Keynes from Knight; determinacy and indeterminacy are not dualistic. For Keynes, certainty was the special case and uncertainty in different degrees was the general case, offering scope for detailed analysis of its cause, nature and consequences.

The final definition listed above, 3.a., is psychological, referring to uncertainty as a state of mind. How this features in economics depends on the underlying theory of mind: the extent to which uncertainty is objective or subjective, the role (if any) of emotion in cognition, and so on. If uncertainty is understood, as in traditional mainstream economics, as measurable by variance and if behaviour is strictly rational, then state of mind plays no part. Indeed the question of the meaning of uncertainty is irrelevant, being specified in terms of statistical variance. But, if uncertainty itself is a matter of cognition and inconclusive argument is the norm, then state of mind becomes critical and the range of meanings of uncertainty becomes important. We pick up the significance of this distinction when we explore different approaches to macroeconomics below.

Finally, there is an element of circularity in discussing the meaning of uncertainty: the very notion of ambiguity of meaning can be a feature of some understandings of uncertainty (see the second *Oxford Economic Dictionary* definition) but not others. Fixity of meaning is only associated with a dualistic mode of thought which in turn implies a particular, binary, understanding of uncertainty: the only possibilities are certainty with respect to known risk and ignorance. This has import particularly for empirical work. If uncertainty is identified purely with statistical variance, for example, then no issue of meaning arises. Given that the variance is known, this form of uncertainty is in fact a form of certainty. But if the meaning of uncertainty is itself open-ended then it is difficult to identify a general empirical counterpart; there is uncertainty about uncertainty (Dow 1995).

Sources of uncertainty

To understand these different meanings of uncertainty further we need to consider different views as to the source of uncertainty, including whether uncertainty arises at the ontological or epistemological level – or both. In other words, does uncertainty reflect the nature of the real world (i.e. is it aleatory), does it reflect cognitive limitations with respect to the real world, or is it some combination of the two (Lawson 1988, Dequech 2004)? The question can usefully be addressed with reference to closed and open systems, as defined by Chick and Dow (2005).

Closed systems

At the ontological level a closed system is characterised by immutable external and internal boundaries[3] within which atomistic elements interact in a pre-determined way. These interactions may be stochastic. Ontological uncertainty then refers to the possibility of chance outcomes, where these conform to some kind of stochastic structure. Uncertainty is then identified by that structure, but only accords with the last part of the first *Oxford English Dictionary* definition; uncertainty is the variance of a data series with respect to a closed real economic system. It only takes one of the multiple possibilities for openness in that system for the system not to be closed, and it is hard to imagine any economist insisting on ontological closure. Yet, as Lawson (1997) argues, the way in which mainstream economics is structured as a closed epistemological system logically requires the subject matter itself to be closed.

Epistemological uncertainty in traditional mainstream economics is represented by statistical variance, i.e. by what is seen as an objective measure of the real world. Knowledge is only uncertain because there is (known) randomness in nature. But a major strain within mainstream economics has followed Savage (1954, p. 4) in questioning, in effect, the closed-system ontology underpinning the frequentist approach. The real subject matter may well be a closed system but we lack sufficient knowledge to identify it. The resulting Bayesian approach focuses instead on the epistemological level and the subjective nature of expectations-formation in the absence of conclusive knowledge about the real nature of the economy. But subjective expected utility (SEU) theory depicts expectations-formation in terms of quantified probability distributions, albeit on the basis of beliefs and with a different understanding of probability. Since individual decision-makers establish their own (quantified) subjective probability distributions, the resulting expectations might be thought to be subject to the third category of uncertainty which refers to state of mind. Yet, being represented by quantified probability distributions, beliefs conform to a working assumption that the real system is closed.

Open systems

But like the different meanings of uncertainty, system openness and closure also need not be dualistic categories as they are in the mainstream approach. A system can be open in a multitude of ways (Chick and Dow 2005). Once the position is taken that a real economic system is open in any way, statistical variance becomes inadequate as a measure of ontological uncertainty. Creativity and the evolution of institutions, for example, alter the range of possible future outcomes in an indeterministic way so that, in the absence of stationary processes, frequency distributions are inadequate as a guide to expectations. More generally if, as Keynes (1921) argued, real systems are generally organic[4] rather than atomistic, then knowledge is uncertain in the non-frequentist sense that arguments are in general inconclusive. Thus the fourth *Oxford English Dictionary* definition of uncertainty actually explains the second.

It is this ontological openness which accounts for knowledge limitations and thus the need for an open theoretical system which in turn opens up the understanding of uncertainty beyond quantifiable probability. Some therefore put the emphasis on the aleatory source of uncertainty. Davidson (1996) puts it that the real world is non-ergodic, meaning that relations over time and space do not coincide (challenging the quantitative, frequentist approach to uncertainty). Only a closed-system reality is ergodic, allowing quantifiable measures of uncertainty based on frequency distributions, i.e. risk. Knight (1921) too identifies the nature of the real world as explaining the inability to quantify risk. Davidson and Knight therefore both provide an explanation for uncertainty in the fourth *Oxford Economic Dictionary* sense, where that uncertainty is aleatory. In principle the real system could be closed, but, following Hume, our experience justifies a working assumption as to its nature, that its underlying causal mechanisms are complex and inaccessible, i.e. that it is open (Hume 1739–40, Dow 2002).

For Keynes, given the indeterminacy of knowledge, yet the need for grounds for action, cognition and emotion are inextricably intertwined. Judgement about probability is objective in the sense that anyone in the same circumstances and with the same mindset would arrive at the same conclusion. But, not only do the circumstances differ for different actors (their ontologies differ), but so do their states of mind. Thus, for example, while more evidence in favour of a proposition normally increases the weight of argument, more evidence might instead reveal ignorance which had previously gone unrecognised (Runde 1990). Uncertainty is thereby increased. There is therefore scope for a wide range of reasonable judgements about the probability of particular outcomes. In particular, uncertainty is a matter of degree. State of mind not only reflects sentiment in the form of optimism and pessimism but also attitude to uncertainty; this approach thus encompasses also the second *Oxford Economic Dictionary* sense of uncertainty (see further Dow 1995).

Postmodern theorists take this argument furthest, that uncertainty is *only* a matter of state of mind (Park and Kayatekin 2002). In contrast, while the Bayesian approach is also purely subjectivist, it presumes a closed-system ontology. Individuals thus ignore the possibility of uncertainty other than quantifiable risk and are always prepared to take bets among what is presumed to be a known set of possible out-comes. In a Keynesian approach experience of an open-system reality, where the state space is not known and argument is inconclusive, uncertainty at times may be too high to ignore and bets not taken (see further Runde 1995).

Not only does an open-system ontology imply the need for an open-system episte-mology, but the results of that epistemology may in turn affect the nature of the real system. Interaction between ontological and epistemological open-system sources of uncertainty is thus possible in both directions. While for a closed system this cir-cularity simply ensures consistency, for an open system it influences the system's openness and thus experienced uncertainty. Not only does behaviour respond to un-certainty but also new institutions may emerge to address uncertainty. Uncertainty may thus be performative.

Uncertainty and methodological approach

Closed-system ontology and epistemology

We have seen that closed-system epistemology is a close reflection of a presumed closed-system ontology. In Lucas's (1980) terms, the former is designed as an ana-logue of the latter. Further the epistemology of the economist, i.e. methodological approach, parallels that of the economic agent.

Given the nature of closed systems, they can be fully represented by Classical logic, i.e. by deductivist formal mathematical models built on axiomatic foundations. In such a closed theoretical system all relevant variables are identified (with fixed meaning) and classified as endogenous or exogenous, and their immutable interre-lations specified within a known structure which may be stochastic or probabilis-tic. Epistemological uncertainty then only arises if knowledge of that structure is impeded, e.g. by cognitive limitations and/or information asymmetries. These lat-ter sources of epistemological uncertainty about a closed-system subject matter can have feedback effects on the subject matter. But, if the system is to remain closed, these feedbacks too need to be deterministic such that uncertainty remains limited to a quantified probability.

The mainstream methodological approach is therefore co-determined with the understanding of uncertainty as quantifiable risk. By allowing for uncertainty only in this sense, whether it is derived objectively or subjectively, a closed-system theoret-ical structure is both enabled and required. Variables have fixed meaning, the basic units are atomistic and their interrelations are deterministic, concepts are under-stood dualistically, and exogenous influences are either known (as in policy variables) or known to conform to a particular stochastic structure.

Open-system ontology and epistemology

Where instead real systems are understood to be open, requiring an open-system epistemology, there is also a parallel between the economist and the economic ac-tor. Methodological approach is the mechanism by which the economist attempts to build reliable (even if uncertain) knowledge.

The focus of a methodological approach based on an open-system ontology is then on how best to build knowledge of this system, even if its truth-value cannot be demonstrated. This was the purpose of Keynes's (1921) *Treatise on Probability*. He argued that, in the absence of certainty, we draw on a range of faculties and methods in order to establish belief as a basis for action. Not only do we draw on evidence and reason, as well as conventional judgement, but we also employ imagination and exercise sentiment in establishing our beliefs and applying them (or not) to action. Reason and evidence alone are inadequate as a basis for knowledge of an open system. Weight of argument tends to increase with the amount of supportive evidence, but each argument draws on a particular range of methods and none, in general, can be conclusive; beliefs are ultimately a matter of judgement.

Just as individuals need to form judgements about probabilities with respect to an open system using a range of methods, so do economists. Thus the methodological approach required by an open system is methodologically pluralist. This contrasts with the methodological monism of a closed-system approach which is identified with the formal deductive axiomatic systems which are compatible with certainty or quantifiable uncertainty. But, given that different groups of economists start from different open-system ontologies each will select methods to suit their understanding of the subject matter. Further, since for each the starting point is uncertainty in the sense of inconclusive knowledge, justification for each approach is a matter of persuasion rather than proof. In other words, an open-system approach is also methodologically pluralist.

Uncertainty in macroeconomics

We have seen that the position taken on uncertainty of knowledge underpins methodological approach. In this section we explore more explicitly what this means for uncertainty in macroeconomic theorising. We explore in turn a traditional mainstream closed-system approach to macroeconomics, a modified mainstream approach which aims to extend the macroeconomic role of uncertainty, and the Post-Keynesian approach as one exemplar of an open-system approach.[5]

Traditional mainstream macroeconomics

Rational expectations theory is an exemplar of closed-system ontology and epistemology, and has been the benchmark for mainstream macroeconomics since the 1980s. The subject matter and knowledge about it are both closed systems. This allows economics to consist solely of formal mathematical models as analogues of a closed-system reality (Lucas 1980). The focus of these models is equilibrium identified with the continual fulfilment of rational expectations even through economic fluctuations. Empirical testing and technical advance promote improvements to the models to be better analogues, just as observation and market competition induce economic agents to improve their own expectation formation in a manner consistent with economists' models.[6]

Indeed, ontological and epistemological uncertainty measured by statistical variance runs through all levels of rational expectations theory, from agents' expectations-formation to macroeconomic modelling. Further, the drive for consistency with respect to levels of rationality encouraged attention to the uncertainty that economists themselves face, not just in constructing models but also in deciding which is the best analogue model. But this 'model uncertainty' itself is represented by its own known complex stochastic structure (Dow 2004a).

The expression of the logical consequences of the rational expectations approach started to undermine it. Sargent (1984) pointed out that policy advice to a rational policy-maker was redundant. Indeed, only surprise monetary policy actions (inevitably within that framework random actions) could temporarily affect agents' behaviour. This conclusion followed from Lucas's (1976) critique that the expected consequences of economic policy are incorporated deterministically into rational agents' forecasts. But the possibility of multiple equilibria arising during the process of agents adjusting their beliefs raised particular concerns. We can see the methodological aversion to multiple equilibria in the way that they are addressed. Just two examples are Morris and Shin's (2000, p. 139) reference to 'our theoretical scruples against indeterminacy' and Farmer's (1991, p. 139) observation that 'many researchers have remained skeptical of studying models with multiple equilibria because it is widely believed that they do not lead to refutable predictions'.

Modified mainstream macroeconomics

We have seen that the absence of uncertainty other than quantifiable risk severely constrains what is admissible in macroeconomic theory. But mainstream macroeconomists have been grappling increasingly with the possibility of indeterminacy arising from the possibility of multiple rational expectations equilibria, a trend spurred on by the experience of the financial crisis. This experience put a clearer focus on the role of expectations in market fluctuations. Increasing attention has therefore been paid to how agents form and update their beliefs, including their beliefs about each other's beliefs.

While the earlier work on indeterminacy focused on temporary deviations from equilibrium due to diverse and/or mistaken beliefs, more recent work allows for the possibility that such deviations could have real consequences (Farmer 2019). In particular, incorporating learning into rational expectations models introduces the possibility that deviations from full employment equilibrium may persist. Thus, for example, Evans and Honkapojha (2013) consider how cognitive limitations and information asymmetries may require significant learning time for agents' beliefs to adjust to rational expectations. Successive shocks or structural changes could cause significant mis-specification such that beliefs may continue to diverge from rational expectations for a significant period of time, preventing real economic adjustment. The analysis conforms to the rational expectations convention of paralleling agents and economists as econometricians, required periodically to recalibrate their models.

The methodological constraints remain. For example, in addressing the experience of the crisis, Farmer (2013, p. 328) notes that 'a model of multiple equilibria is an incomplete model. It must be closed by specifying a belief function'. He then depicts beliefs as being subjected to an uncertainty shock, but this shock itself conforms to a known probability distribution.[7] The notion of uncertainty shock, introduced by Bloom (2009), was explored in more detail by Kozeniauskas et al. (2018). Preferring to analyse uncertainty as endogenous rather than an exogenous shock, they explore different types of uncertainty, with respect to macro expectations, firm-level and micro-informed expectations, and disparity of expectations respectively. All are measured by an indicator of expectation of variance (epistemological uncertainty) or by actual variance of one series or another (aleatory uncertainty).

The distinction between aleatory and epistemological uncertainty has spawned a confusing terminology in the adoption of the term 'fundamental uncertainty' which is more commonly associated with Keynesian uncertainty. In the mainstream literature, 'fundamental uncertainty' refers to real, quantifiable underlying risk while 'non-fundamental uncertainty' refers to deviations of beliefs from that measure. It is accepted that these deviations for individual agents may arise, not just from restricted private information, but also from additional private information; the latter poses problems for an econometric account of aleatory uncertainty which itself suffers from information asymmetry (Alessi et al. 2008).

Some analysts have in fact chosen to focus purely on epistemological uncertainty by direct measures of perceptions of uncertainty. Thus, for example, the frequency of the term 'uncertainty' in different texts, rather than variance in data series which are the object of uncertainty, is taken by some (see, e.g. Ahir et al. 2019) as an indicator of epistemological uncertainty. But of course, consistent with the mainstream methodological approach, this exercise implies that there is a fixed common meaning of 'uncertainty' for the users of the term (see further Dow et al. 2009).

Restrictions on information underpinning agents' beliefs has been the more common feature of mainstream analysis than additional micro-level information, providing a core explanation for the financial crisis (see, e.g. Beltran and Thomas 2010). Thus, for example, in initially refusing to prevent a bank failure in September 2007, the then Governor of the Bank of England identified relatively isolated mis-pricing of risk in the financial system as the source of the crisis (Giles and Daneshkhu 2007).

While beliefs conditioned on asymmetric information are often discussed in the mainstream literature in terms of 'ambiguity', the analysis fits squarely within the mainstream uncertainty framework (see further Dow 2016). Ambiguity refers to (quantifiable) epistemological uncertainty in the form of limited access to knowledge of risk; that risk is knowable, if not known, and thus refers to aleatory uncertainty. Camerer and Weber (1992: 330) define ambiguity as 'uncertainty about probability'. Orlik and Veldkamp (2004: Abstract) assume that agents, like 'Bayesian econometricians', measure it by the 'conditional standard deviation of GDP growth'. Since any such quantitative measure of ambiguity can vary in degree, there can be more or less ambiguity.

Mainstream macroeconomic analysis has thus evolved significantly to address the earlier inattention to the source, existence, and consequences of uncertainty. But it has done so in a way which is heavily constrained by the methodological approach whereby uncertainty refers only to quantifiable risk. For many analyses, also, uncertainty only plays an active role in crisis situations. While the analysis now addresses the degree of knowledge of quantifiable risk, and the possibility of real consequences of a low degree of knowledge, the framework itself pitches policy implications towards considerations of transparency to reduce information asymmetry. The goal is to use policy to encourage the swift return of the economy to a stable general equilibrium. Since theory is equated with models, the focus is on expectations of events rather than processes, and any institutional content is necessarily 'thin'. The analysis all follows from the presumption that uncertainty is (objectively and subjectively) quantifiable.

Post-Keynesian macroeconomics

All open-systems approaches to macroeconomics by definition accept the inconclusivity of argument, i.e. fundamental uncertainty (in the non-quantitative sense) as the general case. The common epistemology is therefore methodological-pluralist.

Each approach is identified by the particular form of openness that characterises its ontology (creative entrepreneurship in the case of neo-Austrian economics, evolution of institutions in the case of evolutionary economics, class struggle in the case of Marxist economics, and so on).[8]

Here we focus on Post-Keynesian macroeconomics, not least because it builds so directly on Keynes's thinking on uncertainty, as explained in Section 'Open systems' above. Post-Keynesian macroeconomic theory is conditioned by the realist acceptance of the openness of socio-economic systems, an ontology which encompasses both agency and structure, and a realist methodology where the range of methods employed reflects judgement as to the best way to build knowledge about those systems.

Post-Keynesian macroeconomics thus addresses an open-system ontology whereby indeterminacy is the norm, rather than restricted to times of crisis. Unlike in mainstream economics, indeterminacy in the economy is analysed in social and institutional, not just individualistic, terms. Thus uncertainty is seen to influence social conventions and the evolution of institutions rather than purely atomistic expectation formation and decision-making. In the general absence of quantifiable risk, conventional judgements emerge to aid decision-making. There is also room for agency at the level of the individual. Keynes (1936, p. 161) explains this with an explicit recognition of the absence in practice of quantifiable risk:

> our decisions to do something positive ... can only be taken as the result of animal spirits – a spontaneous urge to action rather than inaction, and not as the outcome of a weighted average of quantitative benefits multiplied by quantitative probabilities.

Over the long run, institutions have evolved to help mitigate the damaging effects of uncertainty: market regulation, the firm itself, money, and so on. Further practices have also evolved to reduce uncertainty, notably price stickiness. Post-Keynesian macroeconomics addresses processes rather than just events. The effects of uncertainty are embedded in the structures within which decisions are taken and markets operate.

Since the subject matter is not understood as a closed system, amenable to complete capture by a formal axiomatic model, the role of Post-Keynesian macroeconomics reflects the methodological approach to building knowledge under uncertainty. Mainstream macroeconomics has been driven by the need for consistency with microfoundations in order to construct a complete model. But, based on its ontology, Post-Keynesian macroeconomics incorporates influences in both directions between the micro level and the macro level without either being foundational (King 2012). Chick (2002) addresses head-on the methodological issues involved in not requiring micro-macro consistency in the mainstream sense when analysing the investment decision and its macro consequences. Pursuing provisionally separable lines of argument using different methods is a hallmark of an open-system methodology. It is therefore judged to be quite acceptable for separate macroeconomic and microeconomic models and theories to co-exist, informing each other, alongside other strands of argument, contributing to overall weight of argument. Further, since the aim is to address uncertainty in relation to real economic experience, which differs by time and place, and by such factors as specific institutional structure, the outcome is often context-specific. General principles are sought and applied where appropriate, but always recognising their provisionality in relation to context. Post-Keynesian analysis, in contrast to mainstream analysis, incorporates 'thick' institutions.

Post-Keynesian uncertainty means that conclusive pricing of risk is not feasible in real economic systems. So from a realist perspective the notion of a general equilibrium set of prices reflecting true risk is inapplicable; unlike mainstream models, there is no benchmark from which uncertainty can cause deviations. Of course in practice market prices are set, reflecting an assessment of risk. But, unlike with SEU theory, sometimes participants are too uncertain to be prepared to make bets (Runde 1995). Further, in the absence of 'true' prices, markets draw on conventional judgement and sentiment, as well as reason and evidence. Insurance companies generally exclude coverage of risks which cannot reasonably be quantified, and otherwise are forced to employ techniques to protect against losses when deciding on insurance premiums for risks they do insure against (Dow 2015).

Traditional Keynesian economics associated fundamental uncertainty, understood as the dual of certainty, particularly with the investment decision. Investment was thus the key exogenous variable in simple Keynesian models, its fluctuations explaining macro fluctuations. But, for all the (apparently exogenous) role of animal spirits in investment decisions, there was scope for a much richer analysis, not least in taking account of structures – the firm, specific sectors, and the economy. There was also scope for applying a non-dualistic understanding of uncertainty, as a matter of degree and also a matter of policy management. Post-Keynesian macroeconomics has thus built a body of theory further exploring the investment decision under a more full, non-dualistic, understanding of uncertainty. For example, Sawyer and Shapiro (2002) discuss the ways in which market structure influences investment decisions under uncertainty, with imperfect competition moderating uncertainty. Dow (2014) explores how government policy and institutional design can manage private sector investment by institutional measures to influence animal spirits and reduce uncertainty. A further strain of Post-Keynesian macroeconomics analyses the evolution of behaviour and institutions in terms of the relationship between real and financial capital. Echoing Keynes (1936: ch. 12), this research highlights increasing financialisation and its role in diverting attention and finance from real capital investment (see, e.g. Stockhammer 2004).

There has long been a Post-Keynesian focus on uncertainty in relation to money and finance, tied into analysis of investment. For Keynes (1936: ch. 12) the key problem was that investment by entrepreneurs was determined by comparing a projected return which was subject to a high degree of uncertainty with the cost of finance which reflected the more short-term perspective of financial markets, including the degree of their uncertainty. Liquidity preference, the defensive response to heightened levels of uncertainty, is exercised in different ways in different segments of the financial market, again requiring sector-specific analysis. Minsky's (1986) financial instability hypothesis is a prime example, analysing firms' investment and financing decisions in relation to their perceptions of risk, and the consequences for cash flow and capacity to borrow. At the same time the hypothesis draws on analysis of innovation in financial markets, market expectations of firms' risk, and the consequences for asset prices and the supply of credit. It is critical that, while markets implicitly price risk, this is understood to be based on perception of risk which is largely conventional and therefore vulnerable to discrete shifts as changes in the fragility of the financial system become apparent. Minsky (1996) makes explicit the foundational role of uncertainty.

Indeed Minsky's work highlights the positive role of a pluralist methodology to address an open-system reality. As Foley (2010) discusses, Minsky developed formal mathematical models, but held back from trying to encapsulate his theory of financial fragility fully in mathematical form. Minsky identified tendencies, for financial innovation, for cyclical patterns in debt and cash flow, etc.; these tendencies have been the subject of a range of mathematical models with empirical application (see Nikolaidi and Stockhammer, 2017, for a survey). This parallels Keynesian formal identification of the consumption function. The tendency for consumption to follow a stable relation with income was significant in that it tended to persist empirically *in spite of* changing underlying circumstances – a case of negative analogy (Carabelli 1988: ch. 4).

The indeterminacy which precludes fully formalising a Minskyan model is most evident in relation to the turning point of the asset price cycle at its peak. What is critical is the ever-increasing degree of financial fragility. What actually punctures expectations, sparking off a downward spiral, depends ultimately on the state of mind of markets and the timing of their recognition that views need to change as to the weight of argument behind expectations of a continuing boom. Mathematical models are a substantive feature of Post-Keynesian economics, but, in line with the methodological approach, constitute only one strand of argument (Dow 2019).

Conclusion

The purpose here has been to tease out the way in which uncertainty is understood within some different approaches to economics, how that corresponds to the character of these approaches, and how that in turn determines the character of macroeconomics within each approach. It has been argued specifically that a view as to whether or not real socio-economic systems are determinate or indeterminate, i.e. subject or not to some form of uncertainty, feeds directly into a view as to how to approach the task of building knowledge about those systems. Thus the view taken of uncertainty at the ontological and epistemological levels leads to the choice of methodological approach.

Traditional mainstream macroeconomics in the form of rational expectations theory conflates the epistemological and ontological levels, with uncertainty represented by quantified variance of macroeconomic data series. SEU theory focuses instead on estimated quantitative probability at the epistemological level, but with a working assumption that uncertainty at the ontological level is quantifiable. In the face of the undeniable volatility of the financial crisis, mainstream economics has been taking uncertainty more seriously, but has been heavily constrained by methodological approach. Uncertainty now plays a more active part in the macro economy, but only in the form of limited and/or differing information about the underlying variance of macroeconomic variables within a given structure. The methodological approach consistently requires complete argument to be expressed fully by deductivist mathematical models.

Post-Keynesian macroeconomics is considered here as representing an alternative, open-system, understanding of uncertainty. Since socio-economic systems are understood to be organic and evolving, the scope for conclusive argument is heavily limited. Rather the preference is to build (inevitably inconclusive) knowledge using a range of methods. One of these is mathematical modelling. But argument arising from such modelling is regarded as partial, requiring accompaniment by other forms of argument. Further, uncertainty understood as other than statistical variance is seen to play a key role, not only in influencing behaviour but also in influencing structure. Behaviour in the economy is based on a pluralist methodology, just like theory development, and draws on sentiment and convention as well as reason and evidence. This approach to uncertainty underpins the theory of investment and monetary theory. These theories in turn locate behaviour within an institutional environment, requiring analysis of institutional change, and how much of that is driven by the need to cope with uncertainty. A narrow understanding of uncertainty severely constrains mainstream macroeconomic theory. In contrast, a rich Post-Keynesian understanding of uncertainty has spawned a methodological approach which frees up macroeconomics to employ a range of methods and to adapt provisional theory to different circumstances.

Notes

1 A range of fruitful categorisations of uncertainty, for example, has been put forward (see, e.g. Vercelli 2002, Dequech 2011).
2 The various definitions offered separately for the term 'uncertain' do not add anything relevant for our purposes.
3 These correspond to Lawson's (1997) concepts of extrinsic and intrinsic closure.
4 See further Park and Kayatekin (2002) on Keynes's organicism and its implications.
5 See Dow (2016) for a more detailed discussion of how the concept of uncertainty is applied in different approaches to macroeconomics in their analysis of the recent crisis.
6 Sent (1998) provides an excellent account of the evolution of rational expectations thought on the part of Sargent.
7 Elsewhere he refers to animal spirit shocks (Farmer 2013) and sunspot shocks (Farmer 2015).
8 Lawson (2004) queries the ontological nature of these differences, focusing rather on openness in general; see also Dow (2004b).

References

Ahir, H., N. Bloom and D. Furceri (2019) 'New index tracks trade uncertainty across the globe', IMFBlog 9 September, https://blogs.imf.org/2019/09/09/new-index-tracks-trade-uncertainty-across-the-globe/, accessed 27 January 2019.

Alessi, L., A. Baridozzi and M. Capasso (2008) 'A review of Nonfundamentalness and identification in structural VAR models', ECB Working Paper No. 922, July.

Beltran, D. O. and C. P. Thomas (2010) 'Could asymmetric information alone have caused the collapse of private-label securitization?', Board of Governors of the Federal Reserve System, *International Finance Discussion Papers*.

Bloom, N. (2009) 'The impact of uncertainty shocks', *Econometrica* 77 (3), 623–85.

Camerer, C. and M. Weber (1992) 'Recent developments in modelling preferences: Uncertainty and ambiguity', *Journal of Risk and Uncertainty* 5, 325–70.

Carabelli, A. (1988) *On Keynes's Method*, London: Macmillan.

Chick, V. (2002) 'Keynes's theory of investment and necessary compromise', in S. C. Dow and J. Hillard, eds, *Keynes, Uncertainty and the Global Economy*, Cheltenham: Edward Elgar, pp. 55–67.

Chick, V. and S. C. Dow ([2005] 2012) 'The meaning of open systems', *Journal of Economic Methodology* 12 (3), 363–81, Reprinted in S C Dow, *Foundations for New Economic Thinking: A Collection of Essays*. London: Palgrave Macmillan, pp. 178–96.

Davidson, P. (1996) 'Reality and economic theory', *Journal of Post Keynesian Economics* 18 (4), 479–508.

Dequech, D. (2004) 'Uncertainty: Individuals, institutions and technology', *Cambridge Journal of Economics* 28 (3), 365–78.

Dequech, D. (2011) 'Uncertainty: A typology and refinements of existing concepts', *Journal of Economic Issues* 45 (3), 621–40.

Dow, S. C. (1995) 'Uncertainty about uncertainty', in S. C. Dow and J. Hillard, eds, *Keynes, Knowledge and Uncertainty*, Cheltenham: Edward Elgar, pp. 117–36.

Dow, S. C. (2002) 'Historical reference: Hume and critical realism', *Cambridge Journal of Economics* 26 (6), 683–97.

Dow, S. C. (2004a) 'Uncertainty and monetary policy', *Oxford Economic Papers* 56, 539–61.

Dow, S. C. (2004b) 'Reorienting economics: Some epistemological issues', *Journal of Economic Methodology* 11 (3), 307–12.

Dow, S. C. (2014) 'Animal spirits and organization', *Journal of Post Keynesian Economics* 37 (2), 211–32.

Dow, S. C. (2015) 'Addressing uncertainty in economics and in the economy', *Cambridge Journal of Economics* 39 (1), 33–48.

Dow, S. C. (2016) 'Uncertainty: A diagrammatic treatment', *Economics: The Open-Access, Open-Assessment E-Journal* 10 (2016-3), 1–25.

Dow, S. C. (2019) 'Opportunities and challenges for Post-Keynesian economics?', in J. Jespersen and F. Olesen, eds, *Progressive Post-Keynesian Economics: Dealing with Reality*, Cheltenham: Edward Elgar, pp. 1–15.

Dow, S. C., M. Klaes and A. Montagnoli (2009) 'Risk and uncertainty in central bank signals: An analysis of monetary policy committee minutes', *Metroeconomica* 60 (2), 584–618.

Evans, G. W. and S. Honkapojha (2013) 'Learning as a rational foundation for macroeconomics and finance', in R. Frydman and E. S. Phelps, eds, *Rethinking Expectations: The Way Forward for Macroeconomics and Finance*. Princeton: Princeton University Press, pp. 68–111.

Farmer, R. E. A. (1991) 'The Lucas Critique, policy invariance and multiple equilibria', *Review of Economic Studies* 58 (2), 321–32.

Farmer, R. E. A. (2013) 'Animal spirits, financial crises and persistent unemployment', *Economic Journal* 123, 317–40.

Farmer, R. E. A. (2015) 'Global sunspots and asset prices in a monetary economy', *NBER Working Paper* No. 20831, Cambridge, MA: National Bureau of Economic Research.

Farmer, R. E. A. (2019) 'The indeterminacy school in macroeconomics', NBER Working Paper 25879, Cambridge, MA: National Bureau of Economic Research.

Foley, D. K. (2010) 'Hyman Minsky and the dilemmas of contemporary economic method', in D. B. Papadimitriou and L. R. Wray, eds, *The Elgar Companion to Hyman Minsky*, Cheltenham: Edward Elgar, pp. 169–81.

Giles, C. and S. Daneshkhu (2007) 'No time for drastic measures, says King', *Financial Times*, 12 September.

Hume, D. ([1739–40] 1978) *A Treatise of Human Nature*, K. A. Selby-Bigge and P. H. Nedditch, eds, Second edition, Oxford: Clarendon.

Keynes, J. M. ([1921] 1973) *A Treatise on Probability, Collected Writings* vol. VIII, London: Macmillan, for the Royal Economic Society.

Keynes, J. M. ([1936] 1973) *The General Theory of Employment, Interest and Money, Collected Writings* vol. VII, London: Macmillan, for the Royal Economic Society.

King, J. E. (2012) *The Microfoundations Delusion: Metaphor and Dogma in the History of Macroeconomics*, Cheltenham: Edward Elgar.

Knight, F. (1921) *Risk, Uncertainty and Profit*, Boston and New York: Houghton.

Kozeniauskas, N., A. Orlik and L. Veldkamp (2018) 'What are uncertainty shocks?', *Journal of Monetary Economics* 100 (December), 1–15.

Lawson, T. (1997) *Economics and Reality*, London: Routledge.

Lawson, T. (1988) 'Probability and uncertainty in economic analysis', *Journal of Post Keynesian Economics* 11 (1), 38–65.

Lawson, T. (2004) '*Reorienting Economics*: On heterodox economics, themata and the use of mathematics in economics', *Journal of Economic Methodology* 11 (3), 329–40.

Lucas, R. E. Jr (1976) 'Econometric policy evaluation: A critique', *Carnegie-Rochester Conference Series on Public Policy* 1, 19–46.

Lucas, R. E. Jr (1980) 'Methods and problems in business cycle theory', *Journal of Money, Credit and Banking* 12 (4, part 2), 696–715.

Minsky, H. P. (1986) *Stabilizing an Unstable Economy*, New Haven: Yale University Press.

Minsky, H. P. (1996) 'Uncertainty and the institutional structure of capitalist economies', *Journal of Economic Issues* 30 (2), 357–68.

Morris, S. and H. S. Shin (2000) 'Rethinking multiple equilibria in macroeconomic modeling', in B. S. Bernanke and K. Rogoff (eds), *NBER Macroeconomics Annual*, 15, Cambridge, MA: MIT Press.

Nikolaidi, M. and E. Stockhammer (2017) 'Minsky models: A structured survey', *Journal of Economic Surveys* 31 (5), 1304–31.

Orlik, A. and L. Veldkamp (2014) 'Understanding uncertainty shocks and the role of black swans', New York University and Federal Reserve Board mimeo.

Park, M.-S. and S. Kayatekin (2002) 'Organicism, uncertainty and "societal interactionism": A Derridean perspective', in S. C. Dow and J. Hillard, eds, *Keynes, Uncertainty and the Global Economy*, Cheltenham: Edward Elgar, pp. 106–27.

Runde, J. (1990) 'Keynesian uncertainty and the weight of arguments', *Economics and Philosophy* 6, 275–92.

Runde, J. (1995) 'Risk, uncertainty and Bayesian decision theory: A Keynesian view', in S. C. Dow and J. Hillard, eds, *Keynes, Knowledge and Uncertainty*, Cheltenham: Edward Elgar, pp. 197–210.

Sargent, T. J. (1984) 'Autoregressions, expectations and advice', *American Economic Review* 74 (2), 408–15.

Savage, L. J. (1954) *The Foundations of Statistics*, New York: John Wiley & Sons, inc.

Sawyer, M. and N. Shapiro (2002) 'Market structure, uncertainty and employment', in S. C. Dow and J. Hillard, eds, *Keynes, Uncertainty and the Global Economy*, Cheltenham: Edward Elgar, pp. 45–54.

Sent, E.-M. (1998) *The Evolving Rationality of Rational Expectations: an assessment of Thomas Sargent's Achievements*, Cambridge, UK: Cambridge University Press.

Stockhammer, E. (2004) 'Financialisation and the slowdown of accumulation', *Cambridge Journal of Economics* 28 (5), 719–41.

Vercelli, A. (2002) 'Uncertainty, rationality and learning: A Keynesian perspective', in S. C. Dow and J. Hillard, eds, *Keynes, Uncertainty and the Global Economy*, Cheltenham: Edward Elgar, pp. 88–105.

9

PATH DEPENDENCY

Mark Setterfield

Path dependency: a general definition

A dynamical system displays path dependency if earlier states of the system affect later ones, including (but not limited to) anything that can be construed as a 'long run' or 'final' outcome of the system. As this definition makes clear, the essence of a path-dependent system is that 'history matters': outcomes – whether shorter term or longer lasting – are historically contingent. The obvious contrast is with an ordinary first-order autoregressive (AR1) process, in which history will appear to influence outcomes over *some* interval of time, only for this influence to disappear as the system eventually settles into a terminal outcome that reflects no influence of the adjustment path taken towards it.[1] Path dependency does not imply that all history matters, however. As will become clear, some concepts of path dependency allow for *selective history dependence* (only some events affect subsequent outcomes) and even *memory wiping* (whereby, under certain circumstances, the effects of previously influential events are forgotten).

Path dependency can be regarded as an 'organising concept' on the basis of which dynamical models of the economy can be constructed. In this sense, it is similar to the more familiar organising concept of equilibrium. In other respects, however, path dependency and equilibrium are conceptual opposites, at least as the latter is traditionally used in economic theory.

Concepts of path dependency

Various specific concepts of path dependency are consistent with the general definition provided above. Exactly how these concepts account for historical contingency differs, but the concepts themselves need not be considered mutually exclusive. More than one may be operative in a path-dependent system at any point in time, and different forms of path dependency may *interact* and, in so doing, contribute to the unfolding of a system's dynamics.

Cumulative causation (Veblen 1919; Young, 1928; Myrdal, 1957; Kaldor, 1970, 1972, 1981, 1985) is usually associated with the dynamics of wealth accumulation and growth. In this context, it describes self-reinforcing dynamics that give rise to

DOI: 10.4324/9781315745992-12

self-perpetuating virtuous or vicious circles of rapid or slow growth (respectively). The origins of cumulative causation are often traced to Adam Smith's dictum that 'the division of labour depends on the extent of the market' (and, following Allyn Young, *vice versa*). In other words, the expansion of product demand induces an expansion of productive capacity, while the expansion of productive capacity induces an expansion of product demand. In its modern Kaldorian variants, the Verdoorn law (linking the rate of growth of productivity to the rate of growth of real output) is understand to account for the first of these linkages, running from 'demand to supply'. The second, running from 'supply to demand', is understood to be incomplete in the sense that, in keeping with Keynes's principle of effective demand, an expansion of productive capacity will not induce an equivalent expansion in the demand for output. This creates a role for autonomous demand in determining the fate of a system subject to cumulative causation, thereby (and in traditional Keynesian fashion) privileging the demand side as the 'driver' of macroeconomic outcomes.

Lock-in, meanwhile, is the outcome of self-reinforcing dynamics that resolve into a particular outcome or state in which a system subsequently becomes 'stuck'. These states are often revealed as sub-optimal, but 'escape' from them requires non-marginal changes that are difficult to effect. The concept of lock-in has found widespread application in discussions of technology adoption, where it has been used to account for the rise to dominance and continued prevalence of technologies such as narrow-gauge railways, QWERTY keyboards, and VHS format video cassettes, even in the presence of seemingly superior competing technologies (David, 1985; Arthur, 1988, 1989).

Cumulative causation and lock-in together provide an example of how different concepts of path dependency may interact – and, in the process, how events at different *levels* of analysis (micro-, meso-, and macroeconomic) might interact in and contribute to the dynamics of a path-dependent system. Consider, for example, the growth model advanced by Setterfield (1997, 2002). According to this model, rapid growth in the past (resulting from a virtuous circle of cumulative causation) may cause an economy to get 'stuck' with certain industries and/or technologies inherited from its past history of development. This might occur if rapid growth promotes specialisation in production (in keeping with Verdoorn's law) while, at the same time, different components of the increasingly specialised production process (including plant, equipment, and human capital both within and between firms, industries, and the public sector) are *interrelated*, subject to common technical standards that create interconnections between them.[2] This interrelatedness makes it difficult to change one component of the production process without changing others, with the result that technical change may become prohibitively costly or, in an environment of private ownership and decentralised decision-making, excessively difficult to coordinate. In this way an economy can become 'locked in' to a particular technological base, inherited as a legacy of its past, from which it subsequently becomes difficult to deviate. This, in turn, may impair the future ability of the economy to realise the induced technological progress implicit in the Verdoorn law, if the type of technical change required is incompatible with the technical standards inherent in the technological base to which the economy is locked in. By fettering the cumulative growth dynamic of the economy in this manner, lock-in can transform a virtuous circle of rapid growth into a vicious circle of slow growth.

Although it is often treated as being synonymous with path dependency, *hysteresis* is, in fact, a third different specific concept of path dependency. Developed originally to describe the magnetic properties of ferric metals, hysteresis has been applied most often in macroeconomics in discussions of the equilibrium rate of unemployment and its potential variability in response to changes in the actual unemployment rate. Even then, use of the term hysteresis is contested because of the distinction between 'bastard' hysteresis (arising from the presence of unit or zero roots in linear dynamical systems) and 'true' hysteresis (Amable et al. 1993, 1994, 1995; Cross 1993, 1994, 1995). The latter results at the macroscopic level from compositional change at lower level(s) of a system, where the adjustment of heterogeneous 'parts' involves discontinuities (so that the resulting system is non-linear). The two key components of 'true' hysteresis are the non-ideal relay (Krasnosel'skii and Pokrovskii 1989) and the aggregation effects that result from heterogeneity at the micro level (Mayergoyz 1986). The workings of these components are demonstrated in Figure 9.1.

First, consider panel (a) of Figure 9.1, which depicts the relationship between the dependent variable x and the independent variable y for the ith agent. To make this relationship more concrete, we might think of y as the size of a regional market, and x as a binary measure of the ith firm's activity in this market, where x_{i0} denotes absence from the market and x_{i1} denotes the firm's presence. Suppose we begin at point A with $y = y_1$ and $x_i = x_{i0}$. Now suppose that a shock increases the size of the market to $y = y_2$. According to Figure 9.1(a) we will now arrive at point B, with $x_i = x_{i1}$. This is because the size of the market has crossed a critical threshold $\left(y = y_{iu}\right)$ sufficient to induce firm i to enter. Suppose, however, that the shock that triggered market entry is temporary and that the size of the market subsequently declines to $y = y_3 = y_1$. As indicated in Figure 9.1(a), we will nevertheless find ourselves at point C where it is still the case that $x_i = x_{i1}$. Technically, this is because of the non-linearity of the upper and lower 'arms' (denoted by the thick solid lines) of the non-ideal relay depicted in Figure 9.1(a), which govern the response of x_i to variations in y. In terms of the example of firm entry and exit used above to motivate Figure 9.1(a), this non-linearity might be explained by sunk costs, which result in firm i's continued participation in the regional market even after the factors that induced its initial entry have disappeared. The upshot of all this, as depicted in Figure 9.1(a), is that a temporary shock to y can have a permanent effect on x_i. More generally, we will observe that variations in y – even if transitory – that cross the upper or lower bounds y_{iu} and y_{il} will permanently alter x_i, while variations in y within these bounds will leave x_i unchanged. Note, then, that not *all* shocks change the outcomes of the system, which is thus said to have a *selective* memory.

In order to understand the importance of aggregation effects in systems of this type, consider now both panels (a) and (b) of Figure 9.1, which together illustrate the non-ideal relays characterising two different (heterogeneous) agents. The same transitory shock contemplated above (where y rises to y_2 before falling back to y_1) will result in the aggregate outcome $X = x_{i1} + x_{j1}$. Notice, however, that a subsequent transitory shock that sets $y = y_4$ before reverting to $y = y_1$ will result in the aggregate outcome $X = x_{i1} + x_{j0}$ (because $y_{il} < y_4 < y_{jl}$), whereas the result of this same shock would have been $X = x_{i1} + x_{j1}$ had it been the case that agents i and j were identical to one another (specifically, if we observed $y_{jl} = y_{il} < y_4$). The *aggregate* effect of a symmetric, transitory shock is therefore sensitive to the *composition* of the system – specifically, the way in which responses to shocks vary among heterogeneous agents.

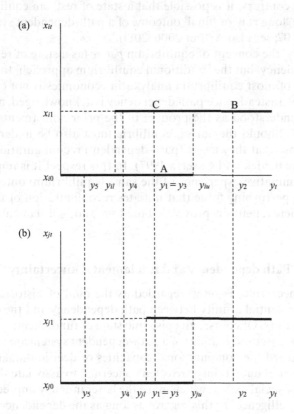

Figure 9.1 'True' hysteresis.

Finally, and starting again from $y = y_1$ in Figure 9.1, a transitory shock that sets $y = y_5$ before reverting to $y = y_1$ will result in the aggregate outcome $X = x_{i0} + x_{j0}$ (because $y_5 < y_{il} < y_{jl}$) *regardless* of the preceding sequence of events. This illustrates the importance of *non-dominated extrema* (such as $y = y_5$) in models of 'true' hysteresis. A transitory shock that sets $y = y_5$ will erase the effects of what are now the dominated extrema y_2 and y_4, rendering the latter irrelevant in the determination of current outcomes. This example also illustrates the capacity of certain types of shocks to 'wipe' the memory of systems displaying 'true' hysteresis. Put differently, while such systems can be said to display *irreversibility* (the effects of a transitory cause remain even after its removal) their outcomes are not *irrevocable*: they can, in principle, be undone by the subsequent application of an appropriate offsetting causal stimulus.

Path dependency and equilibrium

It is important to note that path-dependent macrodynamic models generally contrast with equilibrium theorising, because the latter is typically based on a path-independent 'traditional equilibrium' organising concept that is defined in terms of exogenous data and displays asymptotic stability (that is, it is a position to which the system will return following any arbitrary displacement). There is no necessary inconsistency between the concept of equilibrium *per se* and that of path dependency, however. On the contrary, it is possible that a state of rest –an equilibrium of some sort – will be the 'long run' or 'final' outcome of a path-dependent system (Lang and Setterfield 2006–07; see also Arthur 2006, 2013).[3]

Put differently, the concept of equilibrium *per se* (as a state of rest) is consistent with path dependency, but the 'traditional equilibrium approach' to theorising that is characteristic of most equilibrium analysis in economics is not compatible with path dependency. Instead, once path dependency is acknowledged, any equilibrium states must be understood as the product of the prior adjustments that preceded their attainment. Should they arise, equilibria must also be understood as *provisional*, in the sense that they await (path-dependent) reconfiguration in the course of historical time (Chick and Caserta 1997). In this respect it is important to note that even the cumulative experience of the same (equilibrium) outcome may eventually become a perturbing force that initiates reconfiguration of the system – as, for example, when repetition provokes boredom and, subsequently, behavioural change.

Path dependency and fundamental uncertainty

Fundamental uncertainty is often regarded as the dual of historical contingency. This suggests a potential affinity between path dependency and the concept of fundamental uncertainty. Of course, an epistemic state of fundamental uncertainty can always exist as long as the dynamics of a path-dependent system are sufficiently complicated as to exceed the computational capacities of decision-makers. But proponents of fundamental uncertainty are often concerned to associate the phenomenon with properties of social reality, which make the latter innately unpredictable by even an unbounded intelligence. In this regard, as long as the dependence of current outcomes on past states is not deterministic, a form of fundamental uncertainty will always exist in a path-dependent system because of the propensity for even random events to have permanent effects on the trajectory of a system (and so render even model-consistent expectations systematically incorrect). If the dynamics of path dependency are associated with *evolution*, moreover – defined here as a process of change involving novelty – then an affinity between path dependency and fundamental uncertainty is once again established, since novel outcomes cannot (by definition) be anticipated in advance.

A suggested typology of dynamical systems

The following typology of dynamical systems, based on the distinctions introduced by Kaldor (1934), helps to clarify the relationship between path dependency, equilibrium, and fundamental uncertainty:

- *determinate systems*: outcomes are defined and reached independently of the path taken towards them. Such systems are path independent, displaying 'strong' – that is, conventional asymptotic – stability, a hallmark of 'traditional equilibrium analysis'.
- *indeterminate systems*: outcomes are influenced by the adjustment paths taken towards them. Such systems are clearly path dependent but may be classified as either:

- *definite indeterminate*, if they eventually reach (historically contingent) equilibrium configurations (thus displaying what can be termed 'weak' stability); or
- *indefinite indeterminate*, if they never settle into a state of equilibrium. An indefinite-indeterminate system will remain in a continual state of path-dependent motion or flux: no concept of stability, weak or strong, applies to such systems.

Note that as defined above, determinate systems (even when they involve stochastic elements) are essentially 'pre-destined'. Their outcomes are therefore predictable in principle and fundamental uncertainty is not an innate feature of such systems: it can only arise as a result of computational limitations on the part of the decision-maker. Indeterminate systems, however, need not be 'pre-destined' as long as they involve stochastic elements or embody evolutionary path-dependent change. Fundamental uncertainty may therefore be an innate feature of indeterminate systems, regardless of the computational capacities of decision-makers.

A final concept that is useful in the categorisation of path-dependent systems is that of *resilience* (Holling 1973). Resilience calls attention to the 'durability' of a system (and hence its capacity for longevity), and can be thought of as the ability of a system to reproduce itself over time in a fashion that is sufficiently orderly as to avoid collapse. Resilience is seldom an issue in determinate systems, since automatic convergence towards a fixed point or trajectory that is (by definition) self-perpetuating in the absence of shocks would appear to remove all doubt as to whether or not the system has a capacity for longevity.[4] But it must always be taken seriously in an indeterminate system, particularly as the prospect of indefinite-indeterminacy means that the system has no identifiable final or end state. Hence consider an indefinite-indeterminate growth dynamic that involves debt accumulation. The variations in growth and hence the debt-to-income ratio and hence the debt-servicing demands placed on debtor units that will arise in such a system must remain within the bounds of feasibility (imposed by the debt-servicing capacities of debtor units) in order for the system to reproduce itself in an orderly fashion through time. As the occurrence of the 2007–2009 financial crisis and Great Recession suggests, however, such behaviour cannot be guaranteed: a seemingly orderly system can suddenly veer towards collapse, revealing in the process a marked lack of resilience. The potential ability to identify this problem in advance – and act so as to rectify it – can be thought of as motivating the search for appropriate 'macro-prudential' policies in the wake of the 2007–2009 crisis.

Notes

1 If the AR1 system has a unit root, or if its dynamics are explosive, then the influence of past events on the system's outcomes *will* be permanent. Unit roots are, however, an analytical special case. Explosive behaviour, meanwhile, is not generally thought to be characteristic of (and therefore of great value in portraying) economic dynamics, except when it is bounded and therefore strictly local (see, for example, Blecker and Setterfield, 2019, pp. 264–265).
2 Consider, for example, the way in which certain types of computer software work only on specific computer hardware and require a specific skill set in order to be operated.
3 Indeed, authors such as Hahn (1991, p. 73) argue that 'equilibrium economics in which neither initial conditions nor processes play a part … is neither credible nor indeed honest'. This suggests that what Lang and Setterfield (2006–07) identify as 'path-dependent equilibria' are, in fact, the only equilibria that merit attention.

4 Problems can of course arise as a result of large shocks ('tail events'), or even as a result of obstacles encountered in practice along a traverse path towards the system's end state that is otherwise guaranteed by asymptotic stability.

References

Amable, B., J. Henry, F. Lordon and R. Topol (1993) 'Unit-root in the wage-price spiral is not hysteresis in unemployment', *Journal of Economic Studies* 20, 123–35.

Amable, B., J. Henry, F. Lordon and R. Topol (1994) 'Strong hysteresis versus zero-root dynamics', *Economics Letters* 44, 43–7.

Amable, B., J. Henry, F. Lordon and R. Topol (1995) 'Hysteresis revisited: A methodological approach,' in R. Cross, ed., *The Natural Rate of Unemployment: Reflections on 25 Years of the Hypothesis*, Cambridge, UK: Cambridge University Press, pp. 153–180.

Arthur, W. B. (1988) 'Self-reinforcing mechanisms in economics', in P.W. Anderson, K. Arrow and D. Pines, eds, *The Economy as an Evolving Complex System*, Reading: Addison – Wesley, pp. 9–33.

Arthur, W. B. (1989) 'Competing technologies, increasing returns, and lock-in by historical events', *Economic Journal* 99, 116–31.

Arthur, W. B. (2006) 'Out-of-equilibrium economics and agent-based modelling', in L. Tesfatsion and K. Judd, eds, *Handbook of Computational Economics*, Volume 2, Amsterdam: North Holland, 1552–64.

Arthur, W. B. (2013) 'Complexity economics: A different framework for economic thought', INET Research Note #033.

Blecker, R. A. and M. Setterfield (2019) *Heterodox Macroeconomics: Models of Demand, Distribution, and Growth*, Cheltenham: Edward Elgar.

Chick, V. and M. Caserta (1997) 'Provisional equilibrium and macroeconomic theory', in P. Arestis, G. Palma, and M. Sawyer, eds, *Markets, Employment and Economic Policy: Essays in Honour of G. C. Harcourt*, London, Routledge, pp. 223–37.

Cross, R. (1993) 'On the foundations of hysteresis in economic systems', *Economics and Philosophy* 9, 53–74.

Cross, R. (1994) 'The macroeconomic consequences of discontinuous adjustment: Selective memory of non-dominated extrema', *Scottish Journal of Political Economy* 41, 212–21.

Cross, R. (1995) 'Is the natural rate hypothesis consistent with hysteresis?' in R. Cross, ed., *The Natural Rate of Unemployment: Reflections on 25 Years of the Hypothesis*, Cambridge, UK: Cambridge University Press, pp. 181–200.

David, P. A. (1985) 'Clio and the economics of QWERTY', *American Economic Review* 75, 332–7.

Hahn, F. (1991) 'History and economic theory', in K. J. Arrow, ed., *Issues in Contemporary Economics Volume 1: Markets and Welfare*, New York: New York University Press, pp. 67–74.

Holling, C. S. (1973) 'Resilience and stability of ecological systems', *Annual Review of Ecology and Systematics* 4, 1–23.

Kaldor, N. (1934) 'A classificatory note on the determinateness of equilibrium', *Review of Economic Studies* 2, 122–36.

Kaldor, N. (1970) 'The case for regional policies', *Scottish Journal of Political Economy* 18, 337–48. Reprinted in *Further Essays on Economic Theory*, New York, Holmes and Meier, 1978.

Kaldor, N. (1972) 'The irrelevance of equilibrium economics', *Economic Journal* 82, 1237–55.

Kaldor, N. (1981) 'The role of increasing returns, technical progress and cumulative causation in the theory of international trade and economic growth', *Économie Appliquée* 34, 593–617. Reprinted in *Further Essays on Economic Theory and Policy*, New York: Holmes and Meier, 1989.

Kaldor, N. (1985) *Economics Without Equilibrium*, Cardiff: University College Cardiff Press.

Krasnosel'skii, M. A. and A. V. Pokrovskii (1989) *Systems with Hysteresis*, Berlin: Springer-Verlag.

Lang, D. and M. Setterfield (2006–07) 'History *versus* equilibrium? On the possibility and realist basis of a general critique of traditional equilibrium analysis', *Journal of Post Keynesian Economics* 29, 191–209.

Mayergoyz, I. D. (1986) 'Mathematical models of hysteresis', *IEEE Transactions on Magnetics* 22, 603–08.

Myrdal, G. (1957) *Economic Theory and Underdeveloped Regions*, London: Duckworth.

Setterfield, M. (1997) 'History versus equilibrium and the theory of economic growth', *Cambridge Journal of Economics* 21, 365–78.

Setterfield, M. (2002) 'A model of Kaldorian traverse: Cumulative causation, structural change and evolutionary hysteresis', in M. Setterfield, ed., *The Economics of Demand-Led Growth: Challenging the Supply Side Vision of the Long Run*, Cheltenham: Edward Elgar, pp. 215–33.

Veblen, T. B. (1919) *The Place of Science in Modern Civilisation and Other Essays*, New York: Huebsch.

Young, A. (1928) 'Increasing returns and economic progress', *Economic Journal* 38, 527–42.

10

EQUILIBRIUM

Bert Tieben

The methodological assessment of equilibrium

The concept of equilibrium is generally seen as a dividing line between the schools of thought in economics (Milgate 1987; Dow 1996 [1985]). In this approach, mainstream economics is identified as 'equilibrium economics' and competing schools establish themselves as alternatives based on their critique on mainstream or neoclassical equilibrium. In a sense, their work represents 'anti-equilibrium', as in the title of Kornai's 1971 book.

The problem with the equilibrium/anti-equilibrium division is that it lacks clarity. The number of equilibrium concepts used in economic theory is large, so that it becomes virtually impossible to establish the precise objective of the attack on economic equilibrium. Is it general or partial equilibrium? Short-run or long-run equilibrium? Static or dynamic equilibrium? I concur with Backhouse (2004), who says that the critics generally fail to be explicit about the definition of the equilibrium theory which they are attacking. In heterodox circles, neoclassical equilibrium is mostly assumed to represent general equilibrium theory. But it may also represent a scientific research programme consisting of different equilibrium laws, as expounded by Hausman (1992). Thus the attack on 'equilibrium' may also involve the rejection of rationality, perfect competition, optimising behaviour or some other ingredient deemed vital to 'the' equilibrium model.

The problem of unclarity about the equilibrium concept is that criticism easily misses the mark. The critics attack a stylised form of general equilibrium theory, which the neoclassicals themselves do not even believe is true. The mainstream meets criticism by replacing one equilibrium model with the next. After all, one of the benefits of equilibrium is its purported modelling flexibility. In turn, the opponents do not even bother to evaluate the merit of such small adjustments and simply persevere in their criticism of what they perceive as the dominant mode of equilibrium theorising. The result is a kind of 'shadow fight', with schools of thought talking at cross purposes (Tieben 2012).

Underneath the confusion there is the broadly shared notion that equilibrium is indispensable to economic theory for both critics and proponents. Joan Robinson's

DOI: 10.4324/9781315745992-13

(1974) critique of equilibrium is well known, yet even Robinson stated that 'the concept of equilibrium, of course, is an indispensable tool of analysis' (Robinson 1962, p. 81). She referred to Marx's use of the case of simple reproduction to clear the ground for his analysis of accumulation. But the role for equilibrium should be exclusively analytical and even in a restricted sense 'in the preliminary stages of an analytical argument.' When it comes to the testing of hypotheses against the facts, one should ignore or reject the equilibrium concept as a guiding principle, given that 'we know perfectly well that we shall not find facts in a state of equilibrium' (ibid.).

In short, the equilibrium concept is pervasive but also elusive. This chapter will not attempt to present a structured review of what competing schools of thought define as the concept of equilibrium. Instead, it follows the thread provided by Robinson and studies the methodological role for equilibrium in macroeconomic theory. What is the method of equilibrium analysis? Robinson (1962) voiced a common methodological critique about equilibrium analysis: it does not correspond to empirical reality and should therefore be discarded. This line of thinking is imperative in Post-Keynesian economics, but it can also be found in the work of other schools of thought such as evolutionary economics, institutional economics and neo-Austrian economics.

But authors such as Backhouse (2004) argue that this line of attack is methodologically misguided. It ignores the fact that mainstream economics is much less centred on general equilibrium theory than is understood by competing schools of thought. Once general equilibrium theory was seen as the all-encompassing framework of analysis for mainstream economics, but according to Backhouse (2006) this situation has changed in the past 25 years. He observed a proliferation of applied theories based on a variety of assumptions related to uncertainty, limited information, bargaining, boundedly rational behaviour and other phenomena that do not fit the mould of general equilibrium theory. This has implications for how equilibrium should be seen.

According to Backhouse, equilibrium models are an instrument for solving problems. Hence, it is futile to make general statements about the relationship between 'the' equilibrium model and economic reality. Equilibrium is a characteristic of the model in question, not of economic reality. This interpretation has consequences for the methodological assessment of equilibrium in economics. It also has implications for the assessment of theories which are developed in opposition to what are considered 'dominant' equilibrium theories, which is the mainstay of several heterodox schools in economics.

This chapter investigates the opposition of these methodological assessments of equilibrium in macroeconomics. Is it true that the proliferation of equilibrium models invalidates the criticism of heterodox schools on equilibrium thinking? What use is the concept of equilibrium in macroeconomics if it is seen as a solution procedure, a characteristic of an economic model and nothing more?

What is equilibrium?

In spite of the proliferation of equilibrium models, there are a few basic definitions of the equilibrium concept that will aid the methodological assessment of its functions.

In an early contribution Robbins (1930) stressed the difference between equilibrium as a stationary position and as a balance of forces. The difference is that equilibrium in a stationary position exhibits no inherent tendency to change, whereas a balance of forces indicates the operation of forces pushing the system towards a position of rest in case of a disturbance. The system in question can be a market, an industry or the economy as a whole, the principle remains the same. Stationarity suggests that dated variables remain at their current values, assuming that given conditions likewise do not change. In a balance of forces, the focus is on changes in variables towards a position of rest, even though the system may never actually attain this position.

The notion of stationarity and balance of forces are often closely connected. Comparative statics in macroeconomic theory is good example. This modelling strategy studies dynamic changes by comparing two equilibria. The initial position of rest is disturbed by means of changes which are exogenous to the system. The system is then assumed to move to a new position of equilibrium where it remains, assuming that no further changes in the external environment occur. The comparison of the two equilibrium states is assumed to demonstrate the causal impact of the external factor, but this inference implicitly assumes that the process of gravitation itself does not alter the final equilibrium state. In other words, such mechanical notions of equilibrium exclude path dependency and other changes linked to the duration of time *per se*. They take place in logical time rather than in calendar time (Dow 1996).

The timing of Robbins's distinction is interesting, because exactly around this period economists started to include expectations in the framework of first and foremost business cycle theory. The works of Lindahl (1939 [1929]) and Hayek (1928 [1984]) are cases in point, with Keynes (1936, *CW* VII) and Hicks (1939) following suit. The inclusion of expectations required reformulation of the concept of equilibrium. This impact is most clearly seen in Hayek's definition of intertemporal equilibrium (Hayek 1928 [1984]). In this definition, economic variables change over time and simultaneously reside in equilibrium, as long as expectations turn out to be correct. The innovation of Hayek (1937) was to argue that in a multi-agent economy intertemporal equilibrium requires mutual compatibility of plans. Where people form expectations about each other's behaviour, the risk of infinite regress is imminent. If A expects B to call her, and B expects to receive a call from A, they both probably wind up waiting by the telephone. Equilibrium requires an additional condition to prevent a deadlock of this kind, which is that A and B beforehand know who is to make the call. Their plans must be mutually compatible in order to generate an equilibrium which stretches out over time and includes people's expectations about future events.

Backhouse (2004, 2006) stressed that the inclusion of expectations fundamentally altered the concept of equilibrium. Specifically, it invalidated the mechanistic metaphor as an adequate description of the nature of equilibrium. His argument was that plans of different agents are compatible or not. Hence, you are either in intertemporal equilibrium or you are not. There is no mechanism which is able to realign expectations once projections of different persons about future events have turned out to be incongruent. In other words, 'gravitating' and 'balancing' are not qualities for economies enveloping over time, with people holding expectations about the future.

This statement is not universally true. Böhm-Bawerk (1921) described the capital structure of production in Austrian capital theory as a 'pumping system', because price signals communicate changes in supply and demand throughout the different stages of the value chain. This allows timely realignment of saving and investment plans, as indicated by Hayek's triangles (Hayek 1931). For Austrian economics in-tertemporal equilibrium is guided by the price mechanism with all its purported economic benefits. Hommes (2013) forms a similar illustration from a different per-spective. He studied different forecasting heuristics and feedback loops using ex-perimental data to demonstrate how individual learning behaviour may converge upon coordinated aggregated outcomes. Nonetheless, to describe such processes as 'gravitating' is more problematic than in a simplified world where expectations are constant or of no importance. In the style of Walras, 'groping' is perhaps a more appropriate depiction.

From expectations it is a small step to strategic interaction. Equilibria involving strategic interaction can be seen as a subset of expectations-based equilibria, given that they focus on anticipations about other people's behaviour. This type of analysis is part and parcel of game theory.[1] Here equilibrium pertains when agents perceive no incentive to alter their behaviour. This occurs, for example, when each agent plays his optimal strategy, given the strategy played by his rivals, as in a Nash equilibrium. In co-operative games agents rest content with their current choices when they are unable to form a coalition to attain a better outcome. In both instances, the num-ber of specific equilibrium outcomes may be prolific, but the underlying concept of equilibrium is always the same: in equilibrium there is no incentive to alter current choices or behaviour.

In summary, we have four essential definitions of equilibrium with the first two based on a mechanical metaphor and the latter including elements of plan-formation and strategic interactions, i.e. explicitly behavioural elements:

• State of rest-1: No endogenous tendency to change
• Balance of forces
• Intertemporal equilibrium
• State of rest-2: No incentive for agents to change their behaviour

The first two definitions of equilibrium apply to both microeconomics and macroeco-nomics. The relationship between aggregate variables can be characterised by both a state of rest and a balance of forces. In these senses, equilibrium is a characteristic of macroeconomic systems. The other two notions can also apply to macroeconom-ics, but require an explicit microfoundation. For example, intertemporal equilibrium pertains in the context of intertemporal decision making. Overlapping generation models in macroeconomics are an obvious example. State of rest-2 may function as an explanation of why the macroeconomy stalls at sub-optimal levels of output and so grounds the first notion of equilibrium in behaviour at the level of individuals.

It is important to emphasise that equilibrium at the level of individuals is not a necessary condition for macroeconomic equilibrium. Keynes's unemployment equi-librium is an obvious example. It suggests that macroeconomic conditions form a constraint for workers to find a job. They are certainly not in equilibrium, while the economy as a whole finds itself in a state of rest. Similarly, Marshall discussed the no-tion of industrial equilibrium which implies that aggregate output is constant. In this situation, there are no profitable opportunities for general expansion or contraction. But as a result of differences in aptitude, luck and the maturity of capital, individual firms experience variations in profits. Thus, industry equilibrium does not imply that any one individual firm resides in equilibrium (Hart 2012).

This chapter focuses on macroeconomic equilibrium, but the examples provided above indicate that this analysis will also touch upon issues in microeconomics, given the importance of microfoundations to modern macroeconomic theory (Dow 1996).

The problem of general equilibrium

General equilibrium theory was once seen as the pinnacle of scientific achievement in economics. Deductive rigour made it 'the most prestigious economics of all and [it] set standards that all economists aspire to reach' (Blaug 1992, p. 169). Ackerman (2002, p. 126) claimed it continues to do so, counting more than thousand citations per year in an online search on 'general equilibrium' and 'with no evidence on declining interest in the subject'. He argued that general equilibrium models have become ubiquitous in such important areas as trade theory and environmental economics 'and are continuing to spread'. This makes his criticism of general equilibrium theory acute. Ackerman underlined the failure of general equilibrium theory to make progress in the proofs of uniqueness and stability of general equilibrium, as indicated by the Sonnenschein-Mantel-Debreu (SDM) theorem. Other complaints abound. In Blaug's view 'the leading characteristic [of GE theory] has been the endless formalisation of purely logical problems without the slightest regard for the production of falsifiable theorems about actual economic behaviour' (Blaug 1992, p. 192). In a similar vein, Morishima (1991, p. 70) warned that 'GET economists have sunk into excessive mental aestheticism' with potential disastrous consequences for economic science.

Ackerman (2002) argued that even from an analytical point of view the energy devoted to the continued development of general equilibrium theory is a wasted effort. According to him, general equilibrium theory will never overcome the flaws of the SDM theorem as a result of two fundamental problems. First, aggregation of individual behaviour endogenously generates instability, because groups of people display patterns of behaviour that are not present in the behaviour of individuals. Positive feedback loops such as the bandwagon effect mentioned by Keynes (1936, *CW* VII) are a case in point. This suggests that aggregate demand is not as well behaved as individual demand. Second, the underlying behavioural model of individual choice-making is a recipe for instability. In the general equilibrium model agents simply have too many choices. In the market arena they are constrained by nothing other than their income. This generates an incredible source of possible variation with other agents on their turn responding to altered choices, which cascades aggregate outcomes out of control. According to Ackerman, the root of the problem is too many degrees of freedom for individuals. In a social system people are interdependent and general equilibrium theory cannot handle any degree of interdependency: it treats individuals as atoms. Inclusion of social bonds and other forms of non-market coordination would take general equilibrium theory beyond the province of pure market exchange.

Equilibrium and problem solving

Backhouse's recent work on the methodology of equilibrium theory disagrees with Ackerman about the pervasiveness of general equilibrium theory. He argued that economists have left the ideal of a general equilibrium theory that encompasses all economic questions and forms the backbone of applied theories in the empirical stage of research. The development of theories is much more fragmented than it was 25 years ago, building on applied models with assumptions which do not fit the tight formal structure of general equilibrium theory. Empirical industrial organisation and new trade theory are cases in point. 'Different types of model[s] are constructed for different purposes, resulting in enormous variety' (Backhouse 2006, p. 155).

For Backhouse the turn of economics towards applied research indicates a methodological choice. Economists have become problem solvers. To understand the meaning of this term one has to observe that Backhouse takes economic modelling as a starting point for his methodological exegesis. 'Most economists, and certainly those who are criticised for their use of concepts of equilibrium, see themselves as concerned with building models, either theoretical ones or empirical ones' (ibid.). These models are simplified representations of the real world and in that sense do not adequately represent the real world. Backhouse sees economic models first and foremost as mathematical structures. This is important for the role of equilibrium, because in his view equilibrium is just a characteristic of the model in question (Backhouse 2004, p. 298). In this approach the search for equilibrium is primarily a modelling strategy. As an example, Backhouse refers to the plethora of equilibrium concepts in game theory, which in his view are better called 'solutions' to prevent terminological confusion (e.g. Backhouse 2006, p. 157).

Backhouse's analysis of the role of equilibrium as problem solver complies to the distinction in Hausman (1992) between equilibrium *models* and equilibrium *theories*. For Hausman models are definitions of predicates. They consist of sets of assumptions which make no claims about reality. As a result, they are trivially true and therefore untestable. In contrast, theories do make claims about reality. They consist of sets of connected lawlike assertions. The validity of these laws can be established in empirical tests. Accordingly, theories are true or false.

Obviously, there is a connection between equilibrium models and theories thus defined. Why engage in model building when explanation is the purpose of science? Hausman argued that conceptual exploration is one of the prime functions of economic models. Let's assume that we want to include expectations-formation in macroeconomics. Defining rationality in a formal model of the macroeconomy is a way to investigate the formal properties of this novel model without the claim that real people act in accordance with the rationality postulate. The model allows us to explore the conceptual, logical and mathematical consequences of rationality so defined (Hausman 1992, p. 77). In this role the model may also perform a pedagogical role. It demonstrates how economists include expectations in their formal models.[2]

If one is satisfied with the formal properties of the model, it can be used to develop theoretical explanations. For this step the relationship between the model and reality needs to be established. We add hypotheses to the model which state that the assumptions of the model are true of some part of the world. This results in a theory which can be verified or falsified to check its validity.

In the context of model-theory distinction, the logical corollary of Backhouse's argument about the role of equilibrium as a problem solver is that economists increasingly rest content with their formal models and do not bother to make the subsequent step and to use them to develop theories. Hausman (1992, p. 78) described an attitude of this kind as 'mysterious', because it would mean that economists are uninterested in explaining or predicting economic phenomena. Backhouse would also probably not accept this inference. He added that we can judge the success or failure of equilibrium models in economics, not in a general sense but on a case-by-case basis. He stated that 'equilibrium models should be evaluated not according to whether they conform to beliefs about what the world is like, but in terms of their problem-solving ability, where this refers to problems posed by our experience of the real world' (Backhouse 2006, p. 162). The relevant question for this evaluation is whether the equilibrium provides better solutions than other types of solutions. According to Backhouse, this judgement is a pragmatic one.

Pragmatic or not, the possibility of evaluation means that there must be a connection between the equilibrium model and economic reality after all and that we are dealing with equilibrium 'theories' rather than 'models'. What Backhouse probably means is that the collection of equilibrium models and theories in modern economics is more disorganised than it used to be. There is no single overarching paradigm – called neoclassical or otherwise – to guide the modelling exercise, or the influence of this paradigm is felt less than in the past. My inference would be that economists more quickly switch between paradigms. For example, New-Keynesians adopt neoclassical modelling techniques such as constrained optimisation, institutional economists apply the tools of evolutionary game theory and some Austrians even underpin the need to apply empirical tests to their theories. Economists have become pragmatists in the use of the equilibrium model, which offers certain advantages, and do not necessarily comply to an entire belief system which it is sometimes said to represent. As a result, the lines between the schools of thought in economics are less clearly drawn. The use of the equilibrium model is no longer taken as a defining characteristic of a specific school of thought or paradigm. Likewise in modern macroeconomics, there is no joint approach, common framework of research or even a shared belief about the functioning of the macroeconomic system that warrants us to speak of 'the' equilibrium paradigm.

Given the variety of equilibrium models, it becomes much harder to determine what counts as mainstream economics and what not.[3] This makes the methodological assault of heterodox schools on the mainstream a kind of shadow fight. They often define the properties of their own paradigm in opposition to the dominance of the equilibrium model in mainstream economics. But now it appears that they are combating a mythical opponent with potentially many heads like the Hydra. The result is confusion, because economists are often talking at cross purposes when they discuss the pros and cons of the equilibrium model. Their notions of equilibrium are sometimes exact opposites, as Backhouse (2004) argued. This unclarity does not aid theoretical progress. Backhouse stated that the greatest progress in developing new insights into the problems posed by heterodox economics has come from those who have applied formal techniques to specific problems. They used the equilibrium model to their advantage 'building up a new paradigm step by step' (Backhouse 2004, p. 302). As an example, he referred to the behavioural finance literature which has made significant progress in understanding some of Keyes's observations about financial markets such as the importance of investor sentiment.

What does not work is the rejection of orthodoxy wholesale, based on the notion that equilibrium is nothing but a blackboard exercise that fails to capture the essential qualities of economic reality. Backhouse (2004) called this approach a 'disaster'. It may have worked in the old days when monetarists confronted Keynesians and Post-Keynesians combatted new classicals. But that was then. In the world of problem solvers ontology is a word confined to the boundaries of a specific equilibrium model of which there are thousands. Today pragmatism reigns.

Critical realism

In Post-Keynesian circles the methodological assessment of equilibrium theory runs exactly counter to Backhouse's analysis of the equilibrium modelling strategy. For Jespersen (2009) the use of the general equilibrium method in macroeconomic modelling constituted the main methodological dividing line in macroeconomic theory. He identified two 'completely separate' methodologies in macroeconomic reasoning, one for neoclassical theory based on equilibrium models and another for Post-Keynesian theory based on causal relationships and path-dependent analysis. Moreover, he argued that it is only within the past 20–30 years that the methodological gulf separating these positions became apparent.

The methodology invoked by Post-Keynesians like Lawson and Jespersen is critical realism (Lawson 1997, 2003). This methodology distinguishes between the ontological level and the analytical level. According to critical realism, one of the purposes of theoretical development is to minimise the distance between theory and reality. This goal is furthered on different levels. First, there must be some kind of correspondence between explanatory variables and real economic behaviour such as consumer choice and investor decisions. Second, a series of tests must establish proximity between the analytical model and its explanandum, in the full knowledge that we are never able to close the gap between the real world and the theoretical model completely. In addition, language is of the essence in communicating results to those who should profit from the fruits of economic research like policy-makers and members of the general public. Mainstream economics adopts terms like rational expectations, which on closer inspection appear to be tautologies: these are so general that it is hard to conceive of someone acting irrationally. Models based on rational expectations may wrongly suggest that they were developed to increase the descriptive accuracy of economic theory and thereby create confusion about the goals of economics and its relationship to actual economic events (Jespersen 2009). Ultimately, the aim of critical realism is to create congruence between ontology and epistemology in an effort better to understand the complexities of reality.

By the standards of this approach neoclassical equilibrium analysis performs poorly. To begin with this branch of economics adopts logical deduction as the principal tool of inquiry. But deduction is not sufficient to penetrate into the essence of reality. In fact, deduction means that theory will never develop beyond the boundaries of the analytical level. The equilibrium solution to a model merely points the way to further refinements of the theoretical model, leading to further 'solutions'. The attraction of the equilibrium concept in this process is that it makes the model internally consistent. In logical analysis consistency is a cherished characteristic, which explains why so many economists build their theories on the edifice of some notion of equilibrium (Lawson 1997, p. 102).

More importantly, the ontology assumed by neoclassical equilibrium models is not that of economic reality (Lawson 2005, 2006). In other words, the assumptions underlying the equilibrium model are unrealistic. They assume, for example, perfectly competitive conditions, which are so demanding that no actual market can be found which satisfies these conditions. The same applies to other defining characteristics of the equilibrium model such as constant returns to scale, perfect foresight, neutral money, rationality, atomistic individuals etc. (Davidson 1972, 1991; Kaldor 1972; Eichner and Kregel 1975; Kregel 1976). On a higher level, neoclassical equilibrium theory adopts the mechanistic metaphor of equilibrium, which ignores the essential role performed by events taking place in historical time (Robinson 1974; Dow 1996).

The development of Post-Keynesian alternatives struggles with the inheritance of Keynes himself. His theory of effective demand builds on a static conception of equilibrium, allowing the macroeconomy to stagnate in far from optimal conditions, such as unemployment. Post-Keynesians do no cease to point out that the use of the word equilibrium for such positions is linguistically confusing, because the real economy is never actually at rest. They therefore sharply distinguish between short-period equilibrium, depicting the economy in a state of rest while expectations are assumed given, and the long-term process of economic development in historical time, which by definition cannot be captured by any equilibrium metaphor and is best described as path-dependent. In essence, the Post-Keynesian approach to macroeconomics implies the rejection of equilibrium in the long-run sense, while equilibrium in the short-period sense can be retained for pedagogical and theoretical purposes (Jespersen 2009).

However, it should be noted that Post-Keynesians are not unified in their approach to equilibrium theorising. Some Post-Keynesians adopt Shackle's (1972) dismissal of the equilibrium concept in any form. Shackle saw economics as a science of disorder. His 'kaleidic equilibrium' was deliberately internally inconsistent to emphasise that one cannot experience a position of rest in a world ruled by uncertainty. It merely functioned as a tool to investigate the dynamics of an economy which lacks equilibrium. On the other side of the Keynesian spectre, one finds the supporters of Sraffa, who are sympathetic to the Post-Keynesian cause but dismiss the adoption of equilibrium altogether. Their focus is on the analysis of long-term trends related to the production and distribution of surplus output (Sebastiani 1992; Caravale 1997). In the heated debates surrounding the capital controversies, the different camps collided with the Sraffians, who reproached Robinson for her unwillingness to reject all aspects of neoclassical theorising such as the supply and demand apparatus (King 2003, p. 99).

Equilibrium in an *a priori* setting

The Austrian school represents another tradition in macroeconomics which likes to criticise neoclassical equilibrium theory for its lack of realism.[4] However, the methodology of the Austrians is fundamentally different from the Keynesian approach, supporting a policy agenda which is even further removed from the Keynesian domain.

Given its focus on deduction, the methodology of Austrian macroeconomics is best compared to the modelling strategy of neoclassical economics. However, the Austrians approach economic theory as a strictly *a priori* framework, which ignores the relevance of empirical testing or other methods to check the correspondence between theoretical deductions and economic reality. Austrian economics builds on principles which are *a priori* true, because researchers know them to be true by means of introspection. Following the rules of logic then safeguards the veracity of the theoretical conclusions which are logically deduced from this system of first principles.

The strict *a priorism* of the Austrian school frequently causes misunderstanding of the Austrian stance on equilibrium modelling. After all, it was Hayek who developed the notion of intertemporal equilibrium and in the process applauded the progress made by the school of Lausanne. Cowen and Fink (1985) are a case in point, accusing Mises of inconsistency in his development of the Evenly Rotating Economy, which Cowen and Fink perceive as an instance of general equilibrium theorising, which the Austrians claim to reject.

I have argued elsewhere that criticism of this kind overlooks the crucial role played by equilibrium in the Austrian as an imaginary construction (Tieben 2012). It forms the locus of a thought experiment designed to study the essential properties of the market economy, such as entrepreneurship, money, coordination and uncertainty. The equilibrium concept describes an economy which lacks these essential properties. This allows it to function as a foil for the analysis of the 'real' market system. One of the best examples is Wieser's *Social Economics* (1927) which starts by addressing communism as an economic system, exactly because it lacks the properties which are critical to actual markets such as the right to private property. His benevolent dictator model, Hayek's notion of neutral money and Mises's Evenly Rotating Economy constitute other examples of Austrian argumentation in terms of imaginary constructions (Moss 1997).

Underlying these constructs is the fundamental notion that competitive markets always tend towards but never actually attain supply and demand equilibrium. This notion underpins Austrian market process theory which forms the core of the contemporary Austrian school (Koppl and Minniti 2010, Klein and Bylund 2014, Bowles et al. 2017). It has to be stressed that methodological assessment of this notion of economic order is only possible in the *a priori* framework. This means that empirical tests of any kind are ruled out. Austrians like Kirzner occasionally argue that history shows that actual markets comply to the image of economic order assumed by Austrian process theory, but these statements do not carry epistemological meaning. They are merely illustrations of the fact which Austrian economists assume to be true *a priori*, namely that under the force of competition markets always nudge closer to equilibrium.

Like the Post-Keynesians, Austrian economists do not unequivocally endorse the same view on the nature of equilibrium theory. Lachmann (1976) started a fierce controversy with his claim that market processes may tend towards either equilibrium or disequilibrium. In his view, the market process lacks a clear sense of direction, given that competitive forces may constitute a source of disruption as well as foster improved arbitrage. Which way the balance tips is *a priori* unknown. In a series of articles Kirzner (1994, 1997, 1999) strongly rejected this view on the nature of the market process for its nihilistic consequences. According to Kirzner, it would mean that Austrian economics loses its main organising principle. The argument that he uses sounds familiar: faced with a complex reality, economic theory needs to adopt simplifications in order to enable theory to develop and ultimately to improve understanding of the nature of actual markets. The counter claim of Lachmann was that his image of the market system in perpetual disarray is a better way to foster theoretical progress and improved understanding (Lachmann 1986).

Conclusion

In the end the equilibrium concept is indispensable to economic theorising. Even the harshest critics of 'equilibrium', however defined, adopt some kind of alternative equilibrium construct, which may not be called equilibrium but does provide a way for theories to deal with the complexities of actual economic systems.

This chapter focused on the methodological assessment of equilibrium theorising in a macroeconomic setting. It is refreshing to read Backhouse's analysis of the use of equilibrium models, which dispenses with the common critique that general equilibrium is unrealistic and that the neoclassical paradigm building on general equilibrium must for that reason be rejected. For Backhouse, the meaning of equilibrium is essentially that of a problem solver. This view makes it impossible to develop a methodological assessment of equilibrium theory in general. To say useful things about equilibrium requires study of the success of a specific equilibrium model in solving the problem it was designed for.

This methodological view on the nature of equilibrium theory is recommendable as it rightly acknowledges that macroeconomists have moved beyond abstract general equilibrium theory, which poses questions they cannot answer. But Backhouse's assessment does not cover the whole story. His claim that one cannot assess the validity of equilibrium theorising on the basis of its ontology is too strong. If one studies the actual modelling practice of equilibrium theorists, one encounters common elements which can be subjected to methodological scrutiny. At the very minimum equilibrium theorists share a joint outlook on how they perceive economic reality, a quality which Schumpeter (1949) has called a scientist's 'vision'. This vision is important to methodology, given that it structures the question of which problems are deemed relevant in the early stages of scientific development. After all, even problem solving starts with choosing a problem deemed worthy of scientific research. In later stages, 'vision' may still guide scientific practice in the form of specific assumptions explicitly or implicitly shared by the scientific community. It is the task of methodology to understand the nature and role of such guiding principles of which in the realm of macroeconomics equilibrium is an important part. It is at this point in particular that it is relevant to study the challenge of heterodox schools of thought to what they perceive as the orthodox or mainstream representation of equilibrium in macroeconomics.

Notes

1 See, for example, Hudik's (2020) reformulation of Hayek's notion of equilibrium as the compatibility of plans in terms of a game-theoretic framework.
2 Lindenberg (1990) used the theory of rationality in this sense as an example for other social sciences. In accordance with the view defended here, he stressed that the rationality postulate in economics should not be judged on the basis of its realism, but on its ability to provide 'theoretical guidance' for the analysis of the consequences of human decision making in different economic contexts.
3 This is the position I defend in the chapter on the methodology of the neoclassical school in this Handbook (Tieben 2023). In the past matters were different. For example, Dow (1996) treated equilibrium as the defining characteristic of mainstream economics.
4 The Austrian school fundamentally opposes the use of aggregate variables in economic theory. As a result, some may question whether we can speak of Austrian macroeconomics in a meaningful sense. Scott Scheall in this Handbook argues that the Austrian school does engage in macroeconomic analysis and he addresses their methodology in doing so. See Scheall (2023).

References

Ackerman, F. (2002) 'Still dead after all these years: Interpreting the failure of general equilibrium theory', *Journal of Economic Methodology* 9 (2), 119–39.

Backhouse, R. E. (2004) 'History and equilibrium: A partial defense of equilibrium economics', *Journal of Economic Methodology* 11 (3), 291–305.

Backhouse, R. E. (2006) 'Equilibrium and problem-solving in economics', in V. Mosini, ed., *Equilibrium in Economics: Scope and Limits*, London: Routledge, 150–65.

Blaug, M. (1992) *The Methodology of Economics, or How Economists Explain*, Second edition, Cambridge, UK: Cambridge University Press.

Böhm-Bawerk, E. von (1921) *Kapital und Kapitalzins. Zweite Abteilung: Positive Theorie des Kapitales*, Erster Band, Fourth edition, Jena: Gustav Fischer.

Bowles, S., A. Kirman and R. Sethi (2017) 'Retrospectives: Friedrich Hayek and the market algorithm', *Journal of Economic Perspectives* 31 (3), 215–30.

Caravale, G. (1997) 'The notion of equilibrium in economic theory', in G. Caravale, ed., *Equilibrium and Economic Theory*, London: Routledge, 11–35.

Cowen, T. and R. Fink (1985) 'Inconsistent equilibrium constructs: The evenly rotating economy of Mises and Rothbard', *American Economic Review* 75 (4), 866–9.

CW: see Keynes, J.M. (1971–1989).

Davidson, P. (1972) *Money and the Real World*, London: Macmillan.

Davidson, P. (1991) *Controversies in Post-Keynesian Economics*, Aldershot and Brookfield: Edward Elgar.

Dow, S. C. (1996 [1985]) *The Methodology of Macroeconomic Thought*, Second edition, Cheltenham and Brookfield: Edward Elgar.

Eichner, A. S. and J. A. Kregel (1975) 'An essay on post-Keynesian theory: A new paradigm in economics', *Journal of Economic Literature* 13 (4), 1293–314.

Hart, N. (2012) *Equilibrium and Evolution: Alfred Marshall and the Marshallians*, Basingstoke, Hampshire: Palgrave Macmillan.

Hausman, D. M. (1992) *The Inexact and Separate Science of Economics*, Cambridge, UK: Cambridge University Press.

Hayek, F. A. (1928) 'Intertemporal price equilibrium and movements in the value of money', in R. McCloughry, ed. (1984), *Money, Capital and Fluctuations*, London: Routledge & Kegan Paul, 71–117.

Hayek, F. A. (1931) *Prices and Production*, London: Routledge & Kegan Paul.

Hayek, F. A. (1937) 'Economics and knowledge', *Economica*, N.S. 4, 33–54.

Hicks, J. R. (1939) *Value and Capital*, Oxford: Clarendon.

Hommes, C. (2013) 'Reflexity, expectations feedback and almost self-fulfilling equilibria: Economic theory, empirical evidence and laboratory experiments', *Journal of Economic Methodology* 20 (4), 406–19.

Hudik, M. (2020) 'Equilibrium as compatibility of plans', *Theory and Decision*, 89 (3), 349–68.

Kaldor, N. (1972) 'The irrelevance of equilibrium economics', *Economic Journal* 82 (December), 1237–52.

Keynes, J. M. (1936) *General Theory of Employment, Interest and Money*, *CW* VII.

Keynes, J. M. (1971–1989) *The Collected Writings of John Maynard Keynes*, D. Moggridge, ed., 30 vols, London: Macmillan and New York: St Martin's Press.

King, J. E. (2003) *A History of Post-Keynesian Economics since 1936*, Cheltenham and Brookfield: Edward Elgar.

Kirzner, I. M. (1994) 'On the economics of time and ignorance', in P. J. Boettke and D. L. Prychitko, eds, *The Market Process: Essays in Contemporary Austrian Economics*, Aldershot and Brookfield: Edward Elgar, 38–44.

Kirzner, I.M. (1997) 'Entrepreneurial discovery and the competitive market process: An Austrian approach', *Journal of Economic Literature* 35 (1), 60–85.

Kirzner, I.M. (1999) 'Creativity and/or alertness: A reconsideration of the Schumpeterian Entrepreneur', *Review of Austrian Economics* 11 (1), 5–17.

Klein, P. G. and P. L. Bylund (2014) 'The place of Austrian economics in contemporary entrepreneurship research', *Review of Austrian Economics* 27 (3), 259–79.

Koppl, R. and M. Minniti (2010) 'Market processes and entrepreneurship studies', in Z. J. Acs and D. B. Audretsch, eds, *Handbook of Entrepreneurship Research*, New York: Springer-Verlag, 217–48.

Kornai, J. (1971) *Anti-Equilibrium: on Economic Systems Theory and the Tasks of Research*, Amsterdam: North-Holland.

Kregel, J. A. (1976) 'Economic modelling in the face of uncertainty', *Economic Journal* 86 (June), 209–25.

Jespersen, J. (2009) *Macroeconomic Methodology, a Post-Keynesian Perspective*, Cheltenham: Edward Elgar.

Lachmann, L. M. (1976) 'From Mises to Shackle: An essay on Austrian economics and the kaleidic society', *Journal of Economic Literature* 14 (1), 54–62.

Lachmann, L. M. (1986) *The Market as an Economic Process*, Oxford: Blackwell.

Lawson, T. (1997) *Economics and Reality*, London: Routledge.

Lawson, T. (2003) *Reorienting Economics*, London: Routledge.

Lawson, T. (2005) 'The (confused) state of equilibrium analysis in modern economics: An explanation', *Journal of Post-Keynesian Economics* 27 (3), 423–44.

Lawson, T. (2006) 'Tensions in modern economics. The case of equilibrium analysis', in V. Mosini, ed., *Equilibrium in Economics: Scope and Limits*, London: Routledge, pp. 133–49.

Lindahl, E. (1939 [1929]) 'The place of capital in the theory of price', in E. Lindahl, ed., *Studies in the Theory of Money and Capital*, New York: Augustus M. Kelley, pp. 271–350.

Lindenberg, S. (1990) 'Homo Socio-oeconomicus: The emergence of a general model of man in the social sciences', *Journal of Institutional and Theoretical Economics* 146 (4), 727–48.

Milgate, M. (1987) 'Equilibrium: Development of the concept', in J. Eatwell, M. Milgate and P. Newman, eds, *The New Palgrave: A Dictionary of Economics*, vol. 2, London: Macmillan, pp. 179–82.

Morishima, M. (1991) 'General equilibrium theory in the twenty-first century', *Economic Journal*, 101 (January), 69–74.

Moss, L. S. (1997) 'Austrian economics and the abandonment of the classic thought experiment', in W. Keizer, B. Tieben and R. van Zijp, eds, *Austrian Economics in Debate*, London: Routledge, pp. 151–71.

Robbins, L. C. (1930) 'On a certain ambiguity in the conception of stationary equilibrium', *Economic Journal* 40 (June), 194–214.

Robinson, J. (1962) *Economic Philosophy*, London: C.A Watts.

Robinson, J. (1974) 'History versus equilibrium', *Indian Economic Journal* 21 (3), 202–213.

Scheall, S. (2023) 'Complexity, policymaking, and the Austrian denial of macroeconomics', in V. Chick, J. Jespersen and B. Tieben, eds, *Handbook of Macroeconomic Methodology*, London: Routledge, pp. 208–219.

Schumpeter, J. A. (1949) 'Science and ideology', *American Economic Review*, 39(2), 346–59.

Sebastiani, M., ed. (1992) *The Notion of Equilibrium in the Keynesian Theory*, London: Macmillan.

Shackle, G. L. S. (1972) *Epistemics and Economics: A Critique of Economic Doctrines*, Cambridge, UK: Cambridge University Press.

Tieben, B. (2012) *The Concept of Equilibrium in Different Economic Traditions*, Cheltenham: Edward Elgar.

Tieben, B. (2023) 'The methodology of neoclassical macroeconomics', in V. Chick, J. Jespersen and B. Tieben, eds, *Handbook of Macroeconomic Methodology*, London: Routledge, pp. 172–186.

Wieser, F. von (1927) *Social Economics*, New York: Augustus M. Kelley.

11

CAUSALITY AND MACROECONOMICS

Alessandro Vercelli

Introduction

Causal assumptions and inferences played a crucial role in the genesis and evolution of macroeconomics. In particular, in macroeconomics we may observe a strict inter-action between the evolution of causality concepts, causal evidence, theoretical approaches and policy strategies (Vercelli 1991, Chapter. 7, pp. 106–23). I will restrict the analysis on six episodes that illustrate this process of coevolution since the Industrial Revolution: Hume causality and Classical Economics, Russell's criticism of causality and Neoclassical Economics, Cowles causality and New Classical Synthesis, Keynes causality and macroeconomic methodology, Granger causality and New Classical Economics, Pearl causality and pluralism in macroeconomics. These snapshots do not pretend to describe this co-evolutionary process in all its continuity and complexity but aim only to sketch some of its crucial features. In the first three episodes, the relevant concept of causality is deterministic, while it is probabilistic in the three following episodes, reflecting a change in the prevailing ontological perspective.

It is natural to start the investigation from David Hume, who was a seminal contributor to both the philosophy of causality and early macroeconomics (Hoover 2001). In Section "Hume and classical economics", I focus on the influence he exerted on Classical economists. After the Neoclassical revolution began in the 1870s, most economists abandoned the use of causal concepts, stressing the interdependence between economic variables, an attitude that had become widespread also in natural sciences and philosophy as witnessed, among others, by Bertrand Russell (see Section "Russell and neoclassical economics"). The Keynesian revolution in the 1930s revived the interest in causality within macroeconomics. Although it is now recognised that Keynes was a seminal forerunner of probabilistic causality, the Neo-classical Synthesis—namely the Keynesian school that became mainstream in the 1950s and 1960s—utilised sophisticated notions of deterministic causality for prediction and policy in the frame of large-scale econometric models worked out under the impulse of the Cowles Commission (Section "Cowles causality and the new classical synthesis"). After the downfall of the Neoclassical Synthesis, a few philosophers and economists revived the interest in probabilistic causality to cope with the growing uncertainty that characterises financialised capitalism. The deterministic

DOI: 10.4324/9781315745992-14

vision of causality that ruled from Aristotle to Neoclassical economics aimed to establish unshakeable foundations for knowledge, prediction and policy. Keynes rejected this view arguing that probabilistic causality assertions are dependent also on the cognitive paradigm entertained by decision-makers and the perceived weight of their arguments (Section "Keynes causality and macroeconomic methodology"). The New Classical revolution that occurred in the 1970s adopted a weak notion of uncertainty that could fit the rational expectations hypothesis and the stochastic general equilibrium approach. The search for unshakable foundations continued by working out forms of causal inference based on the so-called 'Granger causality', which was believed to be unconditional on *a priori* knowledge (Section "Granger causality and new classical economics"). The most recent contributions inspired by machine learning and artificial intelligence, as epitomised by Judea Pearl, confirm that any sort of causal inference is significant only within a well-specified scientific vision (Section "Pearl causality and macroeconomic pluralism"). In the concluding remarks, I discuss the relationship between different notions of causality and pluralism in macroeconomics.

Causality has to do with the basic structures of the real world, their link with our knowledge of it and of our action upon it. As Hume asserted many years ago, causal relations are the main 'ties of our thoughts; they are really to us the cement of the universe, and all the operations of the mind must, in a great measure, depend on them' (Hume 1739 [1888], p. 32). Scientists and philosophers have been particularly committed to defend and propagate their own views on causality, probably because the latter is profoundly entrenched in the epistemological and practical structures of adaptation to the real world. We need a thorough analysis of the meaning and implications of alternative notions of causality to improve the critical awareness and constructive robustness of macroeconomic arguments.

Hume and classical economics

David Hume is the fundamental root of the co-evolutionary process examined in this essay. He worked out a highly influential viewpoint on causality and a few fundamental contributions to early macroeconomics. In his philosophical works, Hume aimed to strip the concept of causality of its metaphysical overtones. He stressed in the end three characterising features of causality: spatial contiguity, temporal precedence and necessary connection between cause and effect. Hume argued that the latter is the fundamental condition and specified it as a counterfactual necessary condition: 'if the first [object] had not been, the second never had existed' (Hume 1777 [1902], p. 62). Hume provided empirical foundations to this condition by rooting it in the cognitive association between objects or events. This anti-metaphysical turning point reoriented the debate on causality in a more concrete direction that branched in many divergent research programmes. Nevertheless, Hume's ontological scepticism on causality did not impair his conviction that causal reasoning must play an important role in an empirical discipline such as macroeconomics, because:

> it is of consequence to know the principle whence any phenomenon arises, and to distinguish between a cause and a concomitant effect... nothing can be of more use than to improve, by practice, the method of reasoning on these subjects.
>
> *(Hume 1754 [1885]), p. 304)*

In his scanty but influential contributions to the genesis of modern macroeconomics, we easily detect the crucial role played by causal reasoning in the arguments. In particular, Hume emphasised that 'If we consider any one kingdom by itself, it is evident, that the greater or less plenty of money is of no consequence; since the prices of commodities are always proportioned to the plenty of money' (Hume 1754 [1885], p. 33). The only lasting effect of an increase or decrease in the quantity of money would be a change in prices in the same proportion. However, Hume did not deny that an increase in the quantity of money might exert temporary expansionary effects in the real economy:

> At first, no alteration is perceived; by degrees, the price rises, first of one commodity, then of another; till the whole at last reaches a just proportion with the new quantity of specie which is in the kingdom. In my opinion, it is only in this interval or intermediate situation, between the acquisition of money and the rise of prices, that the increasing quantity of gold and silver is favourable to industry.
>
> *(Hume 1754 [1885], p. 38)*

Hume conceives the gradual adjustment of prices and money wages to a change in the quantity of money as a disequilibrium process determined by the initial misperception of the reason underlying price increases and the slow adjustment of prices and wages to the new circumstances. Causality plays a crucial role that we can clarify with the help of the equation of exchanges ($MV = PT$) suggested much later by Irving Fisher (1920). Under the usual assumptions (constant velocity of circulation V and real income T), an increment in the quantity of money M increases the price index P in the same proportion. The variation of the exogenous variable M is the cause of a shift of the equilibrium level of the endogenous variable P. Causal arguments are involved also in the explanation of the propagation of the initial impulse within the system because of money illusion.

Hume's views influenced significantly the approach of the classical economists. Smith, Ricardo and Stuart Mill adopted versions of the Quantitative Theory of Money (QTM) based on long-run equilibrium, neutrality of money and reliance on market self-regulation. Adam Smith, who was a close friend and admirer of Hume, suggested in the title itself of his masterpiece that economists should seek to explain the causes of the wealth of nations. However, although Smith (1976 [1776]) relied on causal arguments, he did not discuss explicitly the meaning and methodological role of causality in economic theory. The same is true of Ricardo, though in the *Principles* (1817) he employed the word cause so often that he was reproached for his 'causalism' or 'successivism'. John Stuart Mill, the last eminent exponent of the classical school, emphasised that the point of view on causation adopted by Hume and the Classical economists requires the adoption of a postulate of invariance of nature (Mill 1843 [1874]). According to Mill's influential point of view on causality, the nexus between cause and effect is not a mere necessary condition as in Hume or a sufficient condition as in Ricardo's 'persistent' causes, but a more demanding necessary and sufficient condition. This fitted the approach pursued by Newtonian universal laws but did not say much on the case of economics if it is true, as Kalecki reportedly said, that 'Economics consists of theoretical laws which nobody has verified and of empirical laws which nobody can explain'.

As for macroeconomics, the early influence of Hume bifurcated into two main strands. The first one is represented among others by Smith, Ricardo and Mill whose causal arguments are significant but remain often implicit in their reasoning. However, the interplay of Classical theory with causal assumptions is easily detectable. Causal inferences crucially depend on how we describe the object of analysis. In particular, we find a strict dependence of causal arguments on where we put the boundaries of the system as well as on the nature of its dynamics. As for the boundaries, the crucial distinction between exogenous and endogenous variables identifies causes and effects. The QTM considers the quantity of money circulating in a country as the cause of domestic inflation because it assumes that the money stock is exogenous. However, according to Smith, the quantity of money is exogenous for the world economy as a whole but is partially endogenous in each country as it depends on the dynamics of its balance of payments (Dimand 2013). Ricardo took a controversial stance based on the sharp distinction between permanent (or deep) causes of inflation that are sufficient causes (not necessary as in Hume) of nominal prices variations, and temporary causes that are neither sufficient nor necessary causes of a change of prices (Marcuzzo and Rosselli 1994, p. 1258). The permanent causes are relevant for Ricardo's core theory concerning 'natural' values from which one can draw consequences that are virtually certain and thus predictable (ibidem). On the contrary, from the temporary causes one cannot derive reliable consequences, thus robust predictions, and general policy implications. However, Ricardo recognised that the temporary causes play a role in the analysis of transition periods triggered by policy measures such as change in taxes affecting relative prices, or institutional factors such as contracts fixed in money terms altering the distribution of income.

The second strand of classical monetary theory, represented among others by Thornton and Tooke, developed the short-period analysis of Hume without the theoretical rigour of the Ricardian analysis focusing on the temporary causes. Their analysis of the trade-off between some degree of monetary instability and higher economic activity anticipated to some extent the Phillips curve and the Keynesian policy strategy pursued after WWII. Hume himself provided an early hint in this direction by maintaining that, by iterating successive increments of money supply, wise policymakers could keep alive a beneficial stimulus to economic activity. Smith criticised this assertion as reminiscent of mercantilism, while Ricardo, Mill and later monetarists never supported this argument.

Russell and neoclassical economics

At the end of the 19th century, the debate on causality receded not only in philosophy but also in natural and social sciences. In physics, the systematic use of increasingly sophisticated mathematical methods convinced most practitioners that the formulation of physical laws relied on mathematical functions whose interpretation as causal relations seemed useless if not misleading. An obvious shortcoming of causality from this point of view is that most mathematical functions are in principle symmetric and invertible. At the end of the century, a new far-reaching interpretation of Hume's associative approach emerges, soon to become mainstream in empirical sciences. The crucial step towards the new point of view was the abandonment of determinism as a crucial requisite of rigorous theory. This turning point followed naturally from the emergence in physics of probabilistic theories, in particular statistical mechanics developed by Boltzmann in the 1870s. It was Galton, the cousin of Darwin, who in 1888 first suggested the concept of statistical correlation. He immediately realised that this new concept was far-reaching because it provided 'for the first time, an objective measure of how two variables are "related" to each other, based strictly on the data' (Pearl 2010, p. 409). However, it was his disciple Karl Pearson who understood all the potential of this new idea and started to build on it the foundations of modern statistics:

> I interpreted... Galton to mean that there was a category broader than causation, namely correlation, of which causation was only the limit, and that this new conception of correlation brought psychology, anthropology, medicine, and sociology in large parts into the field of mathematical treatment.
>
> *(quotation from Pearson in Pearl, ibidem)*

In this statement, Pearson did not mention economics but the use of modern statistics in economics and macroeconomics started soon after and spread rapidly with the development of econometrics from the 1930s. The adoption of this new approach contributed to a rapid decline of causality inference. For example, Russell maintained that

> all philosophers imagine that causation is one of the fundamental axioms of science, yet oddly enough, in advanced sciences, the word 'cause' never occurs ... The law of causality, I believe, is a relic of bygone age, surviving, like the monarchy, only because it is erroneously supposed to do no harm.
>
> *(Russell 1913, p. 1)*

Actually, at the turn of the 19th century causality declined not only in science but also in philosophy. The main critical argument was that the laws of physics are symmetrical, while causal relations are unidirectional, going from cause to effect. However, not all physical laws are symmetrical; on the contrary, some of them define an irreversible time arrow as in the case of the laws of thermodynamics developed in the 19th century. Moreover, the symmetric nature of mathematical functions and correlations used in many physical theories is not always an advantage over the asymmetric nature of causality. The knowledge of the causal direction 'makes a big difference in how we act. If the rooster's crow causes the sun to rise, we could make the night shorter by waking up our rooster earlier and making him crow' (Pearl 2010, p. 407). Notwithstanding the growing criticisms, the debate on causality never disappeared and eventually revived after WWII. The eminent philosopher Patrick Suppes noticed in 1970 that physicists were commonly using causality concepts and inferences in their most advanced contributions: 'There is scarcely an issue of "Physical Review" that does not contain at least one article using either "cause" or "causality" in its title' (Suppes 1970, p. 5).

According to a widespread criticism of causality, everything affects everything else. With the emergence of the neoclassical school in the 1870s, this criticism of causality became common in economics. In particular, the general equilibrium approach pioneered by Walras stressed the general interdependence between the economic variables in contrast to asymmetric causal dependence. The prevailing view became often explicitly anti-causal because, according to the influential opinion of

Robbins, the economists 'no longer enquire concerning the cause determining variations of production and distribution [but] enquire rather concerning the conditions of equilibrium of various economic "quantities"' (Robbins 1935, p. 67). Also in macroeconomics, the emergence and diffusion of the general equilibrium approach after WWII seemed to imply that all economic variables are mutually linked by a sort of general interdependence that cannot be accounted for by unidirectional causal relations (an early example of this view is Patinkin 1956).

However, the marginalist revolution did not altogether expunge causality concepts from economics. The causal tradition survived mainly in the Marshallian and Wicksellian schools because their interest in disequilibrium macroeconomic processes was inconsistent with a generic view of interdependence. Keynes innovated the Marshallian tradition, adopting an original causal approach (Section "Keynes causality and macroeconomic methodology"). The Wicksellian tradition was developed in a causal direction mainly by the advocates of period analysis (such as Myrdal, Lundberg and Lindahl). In the 1930s and 1940s, Scandinavian and Dutch scholars—such as Tinbergen, Haavelmo, and Wold—shaped the methodological approach of early econometrics. They aimed to combine the Wicksellian and Keynesian traditions following the conceptual framework of the Neoclassical Synthesis, reasoning in terms of causal relations, in spite of the disrepute into which causality had fallen in orthodox economic theory. Therefore, the rapid development of econometrics in the 1930s produced a revival of interest in causality in macroeconomics.

Cowles causality and the new classical synthesis

Hume's counterfactual conception of cause as a necessary condition implies that to change the unwanted features of the effects we have to change their causes. The counterfactual foundations of economic policy decisions are evident in the policy debates that raged in the period dominated by the Classical school. For example, according to the causal account of the QTM, if we want to avoid inflation we have to control the supply of money complying with strict rules. However, 'constant conjunction is too weak a reed to support a satisfactory account of the connection between causal knowledge and counterfactual analysis' (Hoover 2012). The Keynesian revolution advocated radical policy interventions requiring robust causal foundations (Keynes 1936 [1973], *CW* VIII). This prompted the elaboration of a more demanding conception of causality aiming to be fully operational. Simon and Wold provided the most important seminal contributions. Working independently, they developed a rigorous notion of causality for a class of models widely used in economic theory and econometrics, namely simultaneous-equations models involving the use of matrices. Simon's and Wold's concepts of causal order are very similar from the formal point of view, but differ significantly from the methodological point of view. Simon's approach focuses almost exclusively on the epistemic relationship between cause and effect as represented by the computation order of the solutions in a simultaneous-equations system. This order is completely determined when the system is recursive, while it is only partially determined when it is block-recursive (Simon 1957). However, Simon maintained that epistemic relations do not reveal by themselves anything about empirical causal relations unless we are able to detect some sort of correspondence between them and empirical relations (Vercelli 1992). Wold asserted that only a fully recursive model is able to describe the underlying causal structure, which is considered to be firmly rooted in the stimulus-response behaviour of economic agents. In this view, an interdependent model is the outcome of a mistaken specification. Wold's conception of causality is explicitly 'manipulative', as is apparent from the following definition worked out with Strotz in an influential contribution: 'z is a cause of y if, by hypothesis, it is or would be possible by controlling z indirectly to control y, at least stochastically' (Strotz and Wold 1960, p. 418).

In the 1950s and 1960s, the Cowles Commission adopted this conception of causality that provided the methodological foundations for classical econometrics that ruled until the early 1970s. In particular, they shared the view that no causal statement with an operational content may be consistently entertained without theoretical *a priori* assumptions:

> the decision that a partial correlation is or is not spurious (does not or does indicate a causal ordering) can in general only be reached if a priori assumptions are made that certain other causal relations do not hold among the variables.
>
> *(Simon 1957, p. 470)*

Therefore, according to this approach, an adequate econometric model must have two distinct but related sub-sets of assumptions specifying the probability distribution of the variables and their causal structure. Many critics of this conception of causality pointed out that the preference for recursive systems is unduly restrictive. However, there are many reasons for seeking recursiveness such as statistical and econometric convenience and intuitive appeal. In particular, according to this view, the ultimate foundations of economic causality are rooted in the nexus, existing at the level of individual agents, between a stimulus received by a decision-maker and his response. This approach claims to be based on a fundamental principle of intelligibility deriving from methodological individualism interpreted in a behaviourist perspective. However, it conflicts with another alleged principle of intelligibility held by most mainstream economists: the principle that only equilibrium configurations are fully intelligible as argued by Walras, and more recently by Lucas (1981). Equilibrium systems are typically characterised by symmetric relations among all the endogenous variables. The debate about recursive versus interdependent systems that raged in the 1950s and 1960s was very much the expression of the conflict between these two principles of intelligibility. A preference for recursive systems has often been the expression of a high level of attention paid to the role of partial equilibrium (as in the Marshallian school) or disequilibrium processes (as in the Wicksellian and Keynesian schools), or else to the role of bounded rationality (as in the case of Simon). On the other hand, a preference for interdependent systems has often been the expression of a deep belief in the predictive power of general equilibrium system based on the substantive rationality of decision-makers. This principle of intelligibility became dominant in the 1970s following the New Classical revolution in macroeconomics led by Lucas. This determined the temporary eclipse of Cowles macroeconomics based on large-scale structural models built on *a priori* causal assumptions. The new models adopted a different notion of causality believed to be unconditional on theoretical assumptions (namely, Granger causality discussed in Section "Granger causality and new classical economics"). However, after an eclipse of a couple of decades, the Cowles approach has been recently revived in updated forms (see Section "Pearl causality and macroeconomic pluralism").

Keynes causality and macroeconomic methodology

In the early 1970s, the attention turned towards probabilistic causality in both natural sciences and philosophy. Economics and econometrics were not exceptions. A few scholars pointed out that Keynes had discussed this issue in some detail in the *Treatise on Probability* (1921, *CW* VIII), where he worked out the foundations of his epistemological point of view. We find there an interesting outline of a theory of probabilistic causality that in many respects anticipates the recent theories. The interpreters of Keynesian thought have often underplayed the originality of Keynes's causality conception in his economic works, interpreting it as a version of deterministic causality close to that of Simon and Wold (an early insightful exception was Carabelli 1988). However, Keynes explicitly judged deterministic causality not very useful for social sciences (including macroeconomics) in which

> One is led, almost inevitably, to use 'cause' more widely than 'sufficient cause' or than 'necessary cause', because, the necessary causation of particulars by particulars being rarely apparent to us, the strict sense of the term has little utility.
>
> *(Keynes 1921 [1973], CW VIII, p. 306)*

Keynes felt the need for a much more comprehensive concept of causality than the traditional one: 'What is required is a concept of "probable cause", where there is no implication of necessity and where the antecedents will sometimes lead to particular consequents and sometimes will not' (ibidem, p. 306). He was fully aware of the novelty and difficulties of this task, because 'a partial or possible cause involves ideas which are still obscure' (ibidem, p. 182). The main problems arise from the conviction, then still rarely disputed, that the laws of nature are deterministic. Keynes manages to get round the obstacle by introducing a crucial distinction between 'causa essendi', namely the ontological cause that he conceives as deterministic, and 'causa cognoscendi', namely the epistemic cause that he conceives as probabilistic. He puts the main emphasis on the second concept, focusing on whether knowledge of one fact throws light of any kind upon the likelihood of another (Keynes 1921 [1973], *CW* VIII, p. 308).

According to Keynes, a deterministic ontological cause makes sense only whenever we have a complete knowledge of a certain set of phenomena that is accurate enough to be able to define a necessary or sufficient cause. This is possible only if we are able to determine the nomic conditions K (expressed by proposition k), both formal and theoretical, and the existential conditions, both general L (expressed by proposition l) and hypothetical H (expressed by proposition h), which make the causal influence of an event on another event sufficient and/or necessary condition for its occurrence. Keynes clarified the nexus between ontological and epistemic causality through a sequence of formal definitions of causality, definitions that progressively relax the hypothesis of complete relevant information. The starting point is the definition of sufficient cause:

Event B is a sufficient cause of event A in conditions kl, iff:

i   proposition b describes an event B prior to event A, described by proposition a

ii $a \, / \, bkl = 1$ and $a \, / \, kl \neq 1$.

This definition is progressively restricted in relation to further hypothetical existential knowledge, expressed by proposition *h*, leading to the definition of a possible cause under conditions *kl*. The final, and weakest, definition is that of causa cognoscendi, which Keynes conceives as an epistemic relation that does not necessarily imply a similar ontological relation. We may formulate the following definition:

> Event *B*, described by proposition *b*, is a causa cognoscendi of event *A*, described by proposition *a*, relative to the background knowledge *hkl*, if $a/bhkl \neq a/hkl$.

Keynes does not develop further his seminal investigation of probabilistic causality because the theory of epistemic causality ends up by overlapping with his theory of probability (see the Appendix to Vercelli 1992). Keynes's causality anticipates the more recent theories of probabilistic causality such as those of Suppes (1970) in philosophy and Granger (1969) in econometrics (see Vercelli 2001). However, behind the formal analogies, we may detect profound epistemological divergences between these theories. In particular, while Keynes insists that it is necessary to relate any causal statement to a well-defined theoretical background, the supporters of Granger causality claim that their conception of causality is superior to the alternative theories precisely because of its alleged independence of theoretical hypotheses. This different view on causality impinges on the lively debate between New Classical economists and different streams of Keynesian economists. We may understand better the nexus between Keynes's probabilistic causality and macroeconomics by utilising another original contribution of Keynes to probability theory: the weight of argument defined as 'the degree of completeness of the information upon which a probability is based' (Keynes 1921 [1973], *CW* VIII, p. 345). Given two sets of propositions, the set *h* of premises and the set *x* of conclusions, an argument *x/h* is, according to Keynes, a logical relation the knowledge of which permits one to infer *x* from *h* with a certain degree of rational belief *p* that defines the probability of *x* given *h*. The weight of argument $V(x/h)$ increases with the relevant knowledge *K* and decreases with the relevant ignorance and can thus be measured in the following way (as suggested in Vercelli 2010): $V(x/h) = K/(K + I)$.

When the weight of argument is equal to one, we are in a sort of Olympian world characterised by determinism and full 'rationality' where the agents have a complete knowledge of all the systematic causal factors and the residual uncertainty is nil. This extreme point of view has been abandoned long ago in macroeconomics. However, in the 1970s New Classical macroeconomics made fashionable a similar point of view characterised by rational expectations, implying that the residual uncertainty is restricted to the stochastic factors. Also in this case, the world to which the theory is applied is assumed to be closed and thus not subject to unexpected structural changes. In this world, the agents are fully 'rational', as they cannot learn more than they already know from the empirical evidence, apart from the necessary updating of the values assumed by the systematic factors. In the opposite case, when the weight of argument is zero, the uncertainty is radical and produces negative externalities that can be reduced only through appropriate policy instruments such as those advocated by Keynes himself. When the weight of argument is intermediate between one and zero, the uncertainty is strong and can be dealt with only by adopting a different decision rule fitting the hypothesis that the world is open (see Section "Concluding remarks"). Post-Keynesian macroeconomics struggled to build such a theory and is currently continuing to pursue this forward-looking goal.

Granger causality and new classical economics

The causality concept worked out by Granger (1969, 1980) for a few decades has been at the centre of a lively debate over the extent of its validity and its implications for macroeconomic theory. The debate was triggered by the publication of an influential article by Sims (1972), who used Granger causality to argue that, as asserted by Hume and later monetarists, the money stock exerts a causal influence on money prices and nominal income and not vice versa. Granger causality rapidly became very popular with New Classical economists (such as Lucas, Sargent and Barro), because it fitted well their equilibrium approach, and initially seemed to support the monetarist view. This conception of causality also became an important source of inspiration for the so-called new econometrics, a new approach founded on time-series analysis 'without pretending to have too much *a priori* economic theory', as its proponents usually claimed.

The basic idea of Granger causality is very simple. Correlation between two stochastic variables is neither a sufficient nor a necessary condition for causality but gives us a legitimate reason for believing that some sort of causal connection may exist between them, unless we can show that the correlation is spurious. Moreover, if we assume that the cause must precede the effect, we can ascertain empirically the direction of the causal nexus. The point of view that correlation plus a time lag pinpoints a causal relation is at first sight appealing because—differently from Cowles econometrics—it seems that we can demonstrate the existence and direction of a causal relation through statistical methods only, without any explicit intervention of specific subject-matter theoretical hypotheses. The causal relation so ascertained would be useful, at least for prediction purposes, under the assumption—very common in empirical sciences—that the regularities underlying the correlation and the direction of the temporal lag will not change in the period to which the prediction refers. In the 1960s, Milton Friedman used a simple inductive conception of causality based on a similar, though less sophisticated, Humean approach in order to support his argument that money causes nominal income and not the other way round. However, on that occasion, Tobin and other Keynesian economists were able to show, through appropriate counter-examples, that the causal relation so detected was likely to be spurious under reasonable assumptions. This debate convinced most economists that 'post hoc ergo propter hoc' (after this, therefore because of this), as Tobin dubbed the monetarist view of causality, is a fallacy, since we cannot prove the existence of empirical causal relations without referring to causal hypotheses specific to the subject matter. Tobin, who was the first president of the Cowles Commission (renamed Cowles Foundation after it moved from Chicago to Yale), confirmed in this debate one of the basic tenets of Cowles causality. Sims based his counterarguments on the more sophisticated version of Humean causality elaborated by Granger. Sims defended this method of identifying causal direction, saying that it 'does rest on a sophisticated version of the post hoc ergo propter hoc principle' (Sims 1972, p. 543) and that this theory-free approach is more reliable than that of Cowles causality. In particular, he claimed that his suggested tests are robust enough to overcome the objections raised by Tobin. Sims's arguments and tests made a significant contribution to the popularity of Granger causality, a popularity that increased in the subsequent years, owing to numerous lively interventions in the debate by supporters and detractors. The main issue at stake was, and still is, spuriousness. Granger, Sims and other supporters of this approach maintained that spuriousness is extremely unlikely with Granger causality and that, in any case, the likelihood of spuriousness may be settled empirically through appropriate tests, without the intervention of specific subject-matter hypotheses.

The existing Granger causality tests have in common a two-stage procedure of implementation (Sims 1972). In the first stage, researchers apply a sequence of statistical tests to data without making explicit their theoretical hypotheses, while in the second stage they interpret their results as if they were unconditional on theory. It could be objected that any procedure of selection and manipulation of data already presupposes a theoretical point of view, even if only implicitly. Whatever one may think of this preliminary objection, in the second stage insuperable difficulties emerge. The crucial problem is how to discriminate between genuine and spurious causes. We cannot do it without an explicit intervention of theoretical hypotheses. The supporters of Granger causality believe that they can get round this obstacle. They discuss a list of circumstances under which an apparent cause is likely to be spurious, in order to prove that these circumstances are extremely unlikely in the case of Granger causality. Unfortunately, this strategy fails (see Vercelli 1992 for more details). Moreover, the tests of Granger causality are subject to further limitations (ibidem). It seems unsafe to claim too much for these testing procedures in view of the long chain of restrictive assumptions marking each step of the procedure for the implementation of the tests and in view of the fact, fully recognised by Granger and Sims, that the list of sources of spuriousness cannot be exhaustive. They also admit that probabilistic causality is always defined in relation to a given background information. However, in other definitions (for example in Keynes and Suppes), the background information encompasses a theoretical framework while in this case it includes only the past and present values of the relevant stochastic variables. The inductivist approach of Granger causality leads to further limitations such as the exclusive reference to events that have actually occurred, and hence not to types of events and to dispositional variables.

Summing up, the alleged unconditional nature of Granger is groundless for two main reasons. First, a Granger cause cannot be more than an apparent cause unless we demonstrate the exhaustiveness of a list of circumstances that might induce spuriousness. Second, the counterfactual analysis underlying normative macroeconomics requires a structural approach to causality that implies the assumption of a specific theoretical framework. Therefore, we cannot rely on Granger causality tests to choose between alternative theoretical approaches (as recognised by Sims 1980, p. 30). However, within a specific theoretical framework, Granger causality tests might legitimately influence the choice of the model to be used in given circumstances and thus the consequent policy rule to be adopted. The evolution of New Classical economics is a case in point. In the early 1980s, the main causal factor of business cycle shifts from money shocks (Lucas 1981) to technology shocks (Kydland and Prescott 1982) following the results of Granger causality tests showed that the monetarist point of view was inconsistent with the empirical evidence (Sims 1980, p. 30). This causal U-turn modifies also the policy implications of mainstream theory from the strict monetarism of Volcker to the more permissive and discretionary policy inaugurated by Greenspan (the so-called 'Greenspan put' policy).

In the following period, the growing awareness of the shortcomings of the VAR approach to causality introduced by Granger and Sims forced the introduction of enough additional structure to permit a minimal counterfactual analysis. Structural VAR (SVAR) models have become the dominant approach of New Classical macro-econometrics. However, this approach is hardly consistent with the New Classical analysis. The structural coefficients that characterise the impulse-response functions of this approach are likely to change after a significant revision of the macroeconomic policy rules emphasised by the Lucas critique. The usual mainstream response, which maintains that the Lucas critique is correct but genuine changes in policy rules are rare, is not convincing and sounds *ad hoc* (Hoover 2012).

Pearl causality and macroeconomic pluralism

The most significant recent stream of the literature on causality takes inspiration from recent advances in Artificial Intelligence and Machine Learning. This approach synthesises contributions and empirical evidence emerging from many disciplines, such as engineering, biology and social sciences including macroeconomics. I refer in this section only to the most influential version of this stream, namely the Structural Causal Model (SCM) suggested by Judea Pearl (2009). A *leitmotif* of this approach is the constructive attitude borrowed by Cowles causality on the regression nature of all causal and counterfactual claims, and the methods that have been developed for the assessment of such claims (Pearl 2010, p. 1). The exponents of this school insist that there is no such thing as prior-free learning. In addition, while in Bayesian conditioning the sensitivity of priors tends to diminish with the size of the sample, in the SCM approach the sensitivity to prior causal assumptions remains substantial regardless of sample size.

The SCM provides updated mathematical and statistical foundations for a constructive analysis of causality, subsuming, unifying and extending other approaches to causation. The starting point of this research programme is a sharp distinction between associative and causality approaches to prediction and counterfactual action. The associative approach, foreshadowed by Hume and developed by traditional statistics since Galton and Pearce, builds on the concept of correlation and other kindred concepts such as dependence, likelihood and regression. This approach may be useful for prediction if all the underlying conditions are invariant but is unreliable in the common case of changing conditions. In particular, the associative approach does not work when the change in conditions occurs for pragmatic reasons, as in the case of policy interventions in economics or in the case of medical treatments. We cannot derive from the laws of probability theory how the properties of a distribution ought to change when we modify a relevant feature of the model. We can correctly implement this sort of inference only by adopting a causal approach based upon theoretical and judgemental assumptions. In principle, we cannot corroborate these assumptions with the sole exception of the rare cases in which we can resort to experimental control. Pearl introduces two main analytical innovations. First, he introduces an innovative use of graphical models where the arrows provide the causal directions. Graphical models, such as block diagrams and oriented graphs, have been used often in causal arguments, though mainly as pre-analytic devices having a heuristic or expositional value. Pearl believes that statisticians and empirical researchers should 'no longer ignore the mental representation in which scientists store experiential knowledge, since it is this representation, and the language used to access it, that determine the reliability of the judgments upon which the analysis so crucially depends' (Pearl 2010, p. 3).

Building on the vast and effervescent literature on Artificial Intelligence and Machine Learning, Pearl upgrades the role of causal graphical models as essential instrument of a thorough causal analysis by endowing this language with a rigorous syntactic and semantics. A causal graph is a way of encoding causal assumptions, while graphical models allow for the evaluation of their consequences. I limit myself to mentioning one important property of Pearl's causal diagrams:

> Causal assumptions are encoded not in the links but, rather, in the missing links. An arrow merely indicates the possibility of causal connection, the strength of which remains to be determined (from data); a missing arrow represents a claim of zero influence, while a missing double arrow represents a claim of zero covariance.
>
> *(Pearl 2010, p. 8)*

Pearl aims to integrate graphical models and statistical methods, since the latter provide the most powerful instruments of observation of the empirical evidence. The basic element of the latter is the notation $P(A \mid B = b)$ expressing the conditional probability of A being true given an observation of $B = b$. Causality goes beyond observation as it aims to guide our actions based on predictions conditional to manipulations of the system. Therefore, we need a further operator $P(A \mid \text{do}(B = b))$ expressing the probability of A given an intervention that sets B equal to b. The use of this operator can be easily generalised by taking into account multiple interventions, one or more observations and the change of the distribution of B. Pearl uses these causal diagrams to revive and update the Structural Equations Models (SEM) developed by Cowles econometrics. Diagrams of this sort allow the prediction of the system's behaviour not only under normal conditions but also under unusual conditions or new manipulations. In particular, the diagram tells us which equation we have to delete when we manipulate Y to understand its effects. Pearl extends the SEM approach from linear analysis to nonlinear and nonparametric models (namely, models in which the functional form of the equations is unknown). To do so, he redefines an effect as a general capacity to transmit changes among variables in consequence of hypothetical interventions in the model, as suggested earlier on by Strotz and Wold (1960). To develop further this approach, Pearl introduces the mathematical operator do(x) that represents physical interventions that delete certain functions from the model and replace them by a constant $X = x$, while keeping the rest of the model unchanged. Causal analysis in graphical models is based on the realisation that all causal effects are identifiable whenever the model is Markovian, that is, the graph is acyclic (containing no directed cycles) and all the error terms are jointly independent. Pearl's approach aims to be a constructive utilisation of the approach of traditional statistics. To this end, the researcher performs a sequence of modifications on $P(E \mid \text{do}(C))$ until do operators disappear. We can then estimate the relevant variables by using observational data, reducing the causal query to a probabilistic query.

Although the pathbreaking approach to causality suggested by Pearl is attracting the interest of a growing number of researchers in many disciplines, the empirical applications are still limited. Its potential in macroeconomics is promising and corroborates a theory-dependent pluralist vision of causality.

Concluding remarks

Since ancient Greece, many philosophers and scientists maintained that 'the true knowledge is causal knowledge'. This traditional motto remained unchallenged until the turn of the 19th century. The aspiration towards superior causal knowledge has often acted as a stimulus towards deeper and broader knowledge; however, this value judgement has also played the role of inducing many researchers to discredit different kinds of causal (or non-causal) approaches, repressing the necessary pluralism of critical knowledge. This sort of intolerant behaviour haunts many scientific disciplines, including macroeconomics, but is unjustified and dangerous. We should consider causality as a constructive way to coordinate knowledge, observation and action. In macroeconomics, different concepts of causality involve different approaches for implementing the best possible coordination between theory, evidence and policy strategy. Each of these approaches has different practical implications. We have thus to understand thoroughly the presuppositions and implications of alternative causal approaches to promote the necessary critical awareness in the interpretation of the empirical evidence and its use for policy choices.

The Keynesian concept of weight of argument suggests a classification of different causality approaches from the point of view of their utilisation for policy. To perform a fully reliable control of the economic system, causality should presuppose not only ontological determinism, as is widely recognised, but also a weight of argument equal to one, excluding any form of residual ignorance about the relevant causal factors. Under these assumptions, a rational decision-maker would be in a position of choosing the feasible option that maximises the objective function. This Olympian scenario is plausible only for a few well-established theories of physics but not for social sciences, including macroeconomics. Its inadequacy for social sciences emerges with clarity from Hume's contributions to causality. His conception of causality is a turning point because it defines causality in a way that is at first sight consistent with the traditional ontological determinism but provides epistemic foundations that are too weak to support counterfactual policy. In addition, the direction of causality remains pegged to the weak criterion of temporal succession that is highly vulnerable to spuriousness. The shortcomings of Hume's position stimulated the investigation of different approaches such as those summarised in the rest of this essay. Assuming, for the sake of simplicity, that the objective function is a standard utility function, we can investigate the impact of different measures of the weight of argument on the rational coordination of knowledge and action. The Cowles approach did not question the deterministic nature of ontological causality but strengthened the epistemic weight of causal arguments by presupposing a precise theoretical framework. This strategy endowed causality with the necessary robustness to support counterfactual policy making, although at the cost of recognising that the validity of causal arguments is conditional to the chosen theoretical assumptions. The New Classical approach is very close to the Olympian case assuming that the agents have rational expectations on the effects produced by a certain cause. In this case, the weight of argument is one by assumption as far as the systematic causes are concerned but less than one if we consider also the stochastic factors. The argument is thus affected by a certain amount of residual ignorance that, by definition, cannot be removed. In this case, according to the standard decision theory, the rational decision-maker should adopt the principle of maximisation of expected utility. However, the mainstream macroeconomists who have systematically adopted Granger causality within this approach did not succeed to avoid the conditionality of causality inference to the theoretical framework and had to introduce structural constraints to reduce the risk of spuriousness. Let us consider now the opposite case of weight of argument equal to zero, occurring when the decision-maker has to deal with radical uncertainty. In this case, the choice of policy actions cannot find any support in causal knowledge and must adopt a precautionary criterion of choice (such as the maximin). For intermediate values of the weight of argument, the rational decision-maker should adopt a decision criterion that combines the expected utility maximisation and the precautionary criterion with weights that depend on the distance from the extremes. In this case, causality may play a useful, though limited, role for the choice of the best possible action. This is the case of probabilistic causality as in Keynes, Suppes, Granger and Pearl. The lower the weight of argument, the more prudential should be the decision of rational agents. This makes explicit the limits of causality in macroeconomics, and clarifies the deep impact of epistemic conditions on rational decision making in macroeconomics. An increase in the weight of argument changes the behaviour of rational decision-makers in a direction that is less prudential and *vice versa*. Keynes and his followers have often emphasised this nexus. For example, Keynes underlined the nexus between weight of argument and liquidity preference, while Minsky focused on the role of the changes in the weight of argument in explaining business cycles.

Summing up, what we learn from causality inference depends on our *a priori* vision of the system to which we apply it. In particular, exogeneity is relative to the definition of the system's boundaries. Analogously, the dynamic path of disequilibrium processes depends on the definition of the dynamic behaviour of the system implying one or more equilibria and their stability or instability. However, given a vision of the macroeconomic system, causality may provide useful insights on how to solve the problem under study or—at least—on how to come to grips with it. This tentative conclusion would not satisfy a researcher who aims to discover the ultimate foundations of science but underlines the crucial role that pluralism plays, and must play, in any field of empirical science and in particular in macroeconomics.

References

Carabelli, A. (1988) *On Keynes's Method*, London: Macmillan.

CW: see Keynes (1971–1989).

Dimand, R. W. (2013) 'David Hume and Irving Fisher on the quantity theory of money in the long run and the short run', *The European Journal of the History of Economic Thought* 20 (2), 284–304.

Fisher, I. (1920) *The Purchasing Power of Money: Its Determination and Relation to Credit, Interest and Crises*, Second edition, New York: Macmillan Company.

Granger, C. W. J. (1969) 'Investigating causal relations by econometric models and cross-spectral methods', *Econometrica* 37 (3), 424–38.

Granger, C. W. J. (1980) 'Testing for causality: A personal viewpoint', *Journal of Economic Dynamics and Control* 2 (4), 329–52.

Hoover, K. D. (2001) *Causality in Macroeconomics*. Cambridge, UK: Cambridge University Press.

Hoover, K. D. (2012) Economic theory and causal inference, in U. Mäki, ed., *Philosophy of Economics*, San Diego: North Holland, pp. 89–113.

Hume, D. (1739 [1888]) *A Treatise of Human Nature*, L. A. Selby-Bigge, ed., Oxford: Clarendon Press.

Hume, D. (1754 [1885]) *Essays: Moral, Political, and Literary*, E. F. Miller, ed., Indianapolis: Liberty Classics.

Hume, D. (1777 [1902]) *Enquiries Concerning Human Understanding and Concerning the Principles of Morals*, Second edition. L.A. Selby-Bigge, ed., Oxford: Clarendon Press.

Keynes, J. M. (1921 [1973]) 'Treatise on probability', *CW* VIII.

Keynes, J. M. (1936 [1973]) 'The general theory of employment, interest and money', *CW* VII.

Keynes, J. M. (1971–1989) *Collected Writings*, (*CW*), D. E. Moggridge, ed., 30 vols, London: Macmillan and New York: St Martin's Press.

Lucas, R. E. (1981) *Studies in Business-Cycle Theory*, Cambridge, MA: The MIT Press.

Kydland, F. E. and E. C. Prescott (1982) 'Time to build and aggregate fluctuations', *Econometrica* 50 (6): 1345–70.

Marcuzzo, M. C. and A. Rosselli (1994) 'Ricardo's theory of money matters', *Revue Économique* 45 (5), 1251–1268.

Mill, J. S. (1843 [1874]) *A System of Logic*, New York: Harper & Brothers.

Patinkin, D. (1956) *Money, Interest, and Prices*, Evanston, IL: Row Peterson.

Pearl, J. (2009) *Causality: Models, Reasoning, and Inference*, Second edition, Cambridge, UK: Cambridge University Press.

Pearl, J. (2010) 'An introduction to causal inference', *The International Journal of Biostatistics* 6 (2), article 7, 1–52.

Ricardo, D. (1817) *On the Principles of Political Economy and Taxation*, London: John Murray.

Robbins, L. (1935) *An Essay on the Nature and Significance of Economic Science*, Second edition, London: Macmillan.

Russell, B. (1913) 'On the notion of cause', *Proceedings of the Aristotelian Society* 13 (1), 1–26.

Simon, H. A. (1957) *Models of Man*, New York: Wiley.

Sims, C. A. (1972) 'Money, income and causality', *The American Economic Review* 62 (4), 540–52.

Sims, C. A. (1980) 'Macroeconomics and reality', *Econometrica* 48 (1), 1–48.

Smith, A. (1776 [1976]) *An Inquiry into the Nature and Causes of the Wealth of Nations*, E. Cannan, ed., Chicago, IL: The University of Chicago Press.

Strotz, R. H. and H. O. A. Wold (1960) 'Recursive vs Nonrecursive systems', *Econometrica* 28 (2), 417–27.

Suppes, P. (1970) *A Probabilistic Theory of Causality*, Amsterdam: North-Holland Publishing Company.

Vercelli, A. (1991) *Methodological Foundations of Macroeconomics. Keynes and Lucas*, Cambridge, UK: Cambridge University Press. Chapter 7, pp. 106–23.

Vercelli, A. (1992) 'Probabilistic causality and economic models: A survey', in A. Vercelli and N. Dimitri, eds, *Macroeconomics: A Survey of Research Strategies*, Oxford: Oxford University Press.

Vercelli, A. (2001) 'Epistemic causality and hard uncertainty: A Keynesian approach', in M. C. Galavotti, P. Suppes, and D. Costantini, eds, *Stochastic Causality*, Stanford, CA: CSLI Publications, Chapter 8, pp. 141–156.

Vercelli, A. (2010) 'Weight of argument and economic decisions', in S. Marzetti and R. Scazzieri, eds, *Fundamental Uncertainty, Rationality and Plausible Reasoning*, Basingstoke and New York: Palgrave Macmillan, pp. 151–70.

12

MICROECONOMIC FOUNDATIONS OF MACROECONOMICS

Nuno Ornelas Martins

Introduction

Much contemporary debate on macroeconomics has been centred on its microeconomic foundations, that is, with finding ways of making macroeconomic theory consistent with the explanation of human agents provided by microeconomic theory (more specifically neoclassical microeconomic economic theory). This debate presupposes that macroeconomic theory, as developed by John Maynard Keynes (1936, *CW* VII), does not possess adequate microeconomic foundations. What is rarely noticed in these debates is that Keynes's own perspective also presupposed microfoundations, grounded on Keynes's own understanding of rationality and expectations. The difference is that rationality and expectations meant something different for Keynes (1936, *CW* VII) than what it means for Robert Lucas (1981), for example.

For Keynes (1936, *CW* VII), the state of long-term expectation is grounded on conventions, and rational (reasonable) behaviour in a context of uncertainty consists of following such conventions. This *conventionalist* approach to microfoundations stands in contrast to what may be seen as an *optimisation* approach, where the emphasis is on the optimisation of expected utility, which is the approach that is now dominant in New Classical Macroeconomics and also very influential in New Keynesianism. In this context, it is important to note that the use of the term 'classical' for designating the optimisation view, which is now widespread, is highly misleading, since the perspective of classical political economists like Adam Smith or David Ricardo was a conventional one, where human agents are essentially creatures of habit rather than utility optimisers.

The *optimisation* approach is usually operationalised through a utility function, which is used to represent the preference ordering of human agents, where preference orderings are assumed to be complete, reflexive, transitive and locally non-satiated. The *conventionalist* approach, in contrast, requires no utility function, nor even the idea of a preference, but solely that human agents act according to conventional rules of behaviour. Many subsequent debates within macroeconomics can be fruitfully interpreted in terms of a greater or lesser adherence to one of these two approaches to microfoundations: the conventionalist (often seen as the 'Keynesian') view, and

DOI: 10.4324/9781315745992-15

the optimisation (often seen as the 'New Classical') view. This helps shed light on the seemingly confusing debates on the methodology of macroeconomics since it first emerged after the contribution of Keynes.

In macroeconomics, the optimisation view is usually formulated using the model of the economy provided by Frank Ramsey (1928), which was concerned with optimising saving; it was extended in the 1960s by David Cass (1965) and Tjalling Koopmans (1965). As David Romer (2001, p. 173) argues, 'the Ramsey model is the natural Walrasian baseline model of the aggregate economy', in the sense that it excludes market imperfections and heterogeneities between agents. That is, the Ramsey model is the macroeconomic equivalent of the microeconomic Walrasian general equilibrium model. To a certain extent, one may say that the contrast between Keynes and Ramsey mimics, at the macroeconomic level, the differences between the microeconomics of Alfred Marshall's (1890) partial equilibrium theory (which allowed for a more conventionalist view taking historicity into account) and Léon Walras's general equilibrium theory, which focused on pure theory/perfect markets only.

The attempts to provide microeconomic foundations for macroeconomics based on an optimisation approach are not aimed so much at bringing consistency between microeconomics and macroeconomics; rather, the microfoundations project, as usually understood in macroeconomics, is driven by the attempt to fully replace a conventionalist approach by an optimisation approach. After having removed conventionalist elements from microeconomics, when moving from a Marshallian perspective towards a Walrasian perspective, the aim of contemporary mainstream economists centred on an optimisation approach is to remove the remaining conventionalist elements in Keynesian macroeconomics.

The extension of a Walrasian approach to macroeconomics started already with John Hicks's (1937) Investment/Saving – Liquidity preference/Money supply (IS-LM) model. As Hicks (1980–1981, pp. 141–2) himself writes, while noting the limitations of the IS-LM model, 'the idea of the *IS-LM* diagram came to me as a result of the work I had been doing on three-way exchange, conceived in a Walrasian manner'. The IS-LM model still contained, however, a balance between conventionalist and optimisation approaches, at least in comparison with the subsequent macroeconomic models building upon Ramsey's model. I will describe in more detail now the contrast between the optimisation view, which has been increasingly dominant, and the conventionalist view, which goes back to Keynes (Favereau 1988), and has been increasingly forgotten.

Keynes vs. Ramsey on microfoundation: savings and the rate of interest

The so-called Ramsey model, first presented in 1928 as a model where savings are determined endogenously, contains the basis of the dominant form of contemporary macroeconomics. Ramsey (1928) argues that saving is the result of an attempt to optimise consumption while taking into account the depreciation of capital that occurs as a result; the optimal rate of saving depends thus on how consumption influences both the individual's utility and the existing stock of capital. Preferences and capital are conceptualised using expected utility and the production function, respectively, notions that became central to contemporary economic theory. Ramsey's article was published in the *Economic Journal* following the encouragement of Keynes, who was the journal's editor, and who saw Ramsey's article as one of the most outstanding contributions to mathematical economics.

Ramsey's approach to saving stands in contrast to the one that was adopted by Keynes (1936, *CW* VII), in which saving depends upon the marginal propensity to save which, like the marginal propensity to consume, is exogenously given, rather than endogenously determined through a dynamic optimisation exercise as it is the case for Ramsey. For Keynes, the volume of saving is a result of the marginal propensity to save out of a given income, and income, in turn, depends upon effective demand, which is ultimately driven by the marginal propensity to consume out of a given income, and investment. Investment, in turn, depends upon the difference between what Keynes decided to call the marginal efficiency of capital (which is actually the internal rate of return of a given investment, that is, the rate that would make the various future cash-flows, or prospective yield as Keynes calls it, equal its replacement cost) and the interest rate.

For Keynes, the interest rate depends upon the supply of money, and liquidity preference. Liquidity preference, in turn, depends upon how uncertain human beings are of the future. It is uncertainty regarding the future that leads to the need of holding liquidity, which can be used under various possible scenarios. If we knew exactly the probability of each future scenario, we would not need liquidity, for we would simply decide all future options with the existing information on probabilities and scenarios.

Keynes's overall approach to human behaviour can be seen more clearly in Chapter 12 of his 1936 book *The General Theory of Employment, Interest and Money*, the book that establishes macroeconomics as a distinct field of analysis. But Keynes's views ultimately spring from his 1921 *Treatise on Probability*, an approach to probability that was criticised by Ramsey (1978) early on. Keynes (1921, *CW* VIII) believed that in situations of uncertainty there is no basis for attributing a numerical value to the probability of occurrence of a given scenario. Keynes's scepticism towards quantification appears also in his critique of econometrics when it was advanced by Jan Tinbergen (Lawson 1985b). Keynes believed that in econometric analysis, as in probability analysis under uncertainty, it is not possible to isolate the various outside disturbances in a sufficiently satisfactory way so as to achieve exact mathematical measurement. Exact mathematical measurement is possible only if the material under analysis were already constituted by isolated atoms (understood as isolated parts of a system) which are not subject to outside interference (Lawson 1985a). But since this is typically not the case in the material under analysis in economics, we are always subject to fundamental uncertainty, in which exact numerical analysis is not possible.

Since exact numerical analysis is not possible under uncertainty, what human beings do, Keynes (1936, *CW* VII, p. 152) argues, is to fall back on a convention, that is, to assume that the existing state of affairs will continue indefinitely. This does not mean that human beings believe this will be the case, and Keynes actually argues that such a possibility is most unlikely. But Keynes argues that doing so provides the most rational option when facing uncertainty, especially because it is likely that other human beings will also act according to conventions, and thus continuity and stability can be achieved in daily affairs. Furthermore, Keynes (1936, *CW* VII, p. 148) also argues that when taking decisions, it seems unreasonable 'to attach great weight to matters which are very uncertain'. Thus, conventional facts which are believed to be more stable will enter disproportionally in our long-term expectations, reinforcing conventional behaviour.

While Keynes saw human behaviour in terms of conventions, Ramsey's approach was more consistent with the idea that human beings optimise their expected utility. It becomes thus clearer why it is that Keynes assumes an exogenous marginal propensity to save which, like the equally exogenous marginal propensity to consume, is ultimately explained in terms of human conventions. But for Ramsey, whose conception pointed towards the possibility of optimisation given a certain expected utility, it was more natural to allow for the optimisation of the rate of saving as an endogenous feature of his model, taking into account expected utility and the depletion of capital, the impact of which is conceptualised through the production function.

It is not only the production function, but also the utility function that is essential to Ramsey's optimisation exercise. The use of an approach focused on optimisation in economics (rather than grounded on conventions) has been typically associated with whether a utility function is used. Those who focus on optimisation typically use a utility function in order to map the preference ordering of human agents and undertake an optimisation exercise. Those who focus exclusively on conventions tend to avoid using utility functions and simply describe human behaviour in terms of a rule of action, an approach which tends to be more favoured in social sciences other than economics today. In Keynes's day, a focus on conventions was more prominent in economics than today, not only in England, but especially in America through original Institutionalists like Thorstein Veblen and John Rogers Commons, before the emergence of New Institutionalism of authors such as Ronald Coase and Oliver Williamson, in which institutions are explained as optimisation exercises aimed at reducing transaction costs in a market.

The debate after the 1960s

The Ramsey model became more widely used after the 1960s, within New Classical Macroeconomics, and Keynesian ideas started to be included through the analysis of the process of price and wage formation by the New Keynesians, typically also using a version of Ramsey's model. Thus, while New Classical Macroeconomics assumes perfect competition regarding price formation, and thus assumes that economic agents are price-takers, New Keynesians include in their models rigidities regarding prices and wages due to menu costs and contracts.

The term 'New Keynesianism' is not an appropriate term for designating this approach. Firstly, the latter's underlying microfoundations are based on Ramsey's model. Secondly, the ways in which Keynesian elements are added to Ramsey's framework, through price rigidities, are actually something Keynes himself did not do. He allowed for situations of unemployment without price rigidities. It was the American Institutionalists and Post Keynesians who developed the idea of price rigidities, in line with their preference for mark-up pricing, which was also presupposed by Michal Kalecki (1971), who otherwise anticipated many of Keynes's ideas.

The microfoundations of New Classical Macroeconomics and Real Business Cycle theory imply that the choices individuals make are optimal reactions to economic fluctuations caused by exogenous technological shocks. But for optimal choices to be made, economic agents must know the rules of the game in advance, hence policy-makers must refrain from discretionary intervention, not only regarding fiscal policy but also monetary policy. While these microfoundations are usually associated with the Chicago school, the overall idea was already present at the

London School of Economics (LSE) at the time that Lionel Robbins (1938) and Friedrich Hayek (1948) developed a subjectivist approach against the Cambridge Marshallian and Keynesian approaches. And since human preferences are irreducibly subjective, they must be revealed in market exchange through prices, which become signals that allow for economic coordination, as Hayek (1948) and the Austrian school argued.

Hayek and the Austrian school were very critical of the mathematisation of economics, which they saw as an illegitimate transference of methods from the natural sciences to the social sciences. But the policy framework of setting clear rules while allowing for economic agents to engage in market exchange free from discretionary State intervention is the same policy framework we reach if we start from the microfoundations of New Classical Macroeconomics and Real Business Cycle theory.

The pure optimisation approach of New Classical Economics, despite its name, stands in contrast to the view of the classical political economists, for whom human agents are creatures of habit to a great extent, as behavioural economists have increasingly argued, while supporting the earlier approach of classical political economists like Smith (Ashraf et al. 2005). The history of the more recent debates in microeconomics and macroeconomics is still to be written, but it seems that the optimisation view and the conventionalist view remain very useful analytical categories for assessing these new debates as well, including those that scrutinise the behavioural foundations of economics (Sen 1987, 1997).

In a purely conventionalist view, human action is explained in terms of the weight of the past, that is, in terms of how habit and custom shape conventional rules of behaviour. In a purely optimisation view, human action is explained as a response to expected utility, which is supposed to be optimised. Hence, a purely conventionalist view will privilege a historically informed economics, while an optimisation view will favour a form of economics oriented towards mathematical methods of optimisation. The latter, of course, has been the main tendency of modern mainstream economics, contrarily to the more historically informed approach that prevailed in previous schools of economic thought.

Concluding remarks

In the early and mid-20th century, controversies in macroeconomic theory and method took place essentially between those who subscribed to a purely conventionalist view, such as Keynes and the Post-Keynesians together with the original American Institutionalists (not least when addressing business cycles, following Wesley Mitchell's lead), and those who adopted a mixture between conventionalist and an optimisation view, such as the Neoclassical Keynesians at Cambridge, Massachusetts (Harcourt 1972).

The centre of gravity of this controversy has, since the 1970s, moved from the conventionalist view towards the optimisation view, and until the 2007–2008 financial crisis the controversy related to the microfoundations of macroeconomics, at least within mainstream economics, was essentially between those who focus exclusively on an optimisation approach, as in the New Classical Macroeconomics, and those who endorse a mixture between the optimisation approach and the conventionalist approach, such as the New Keynesians, while neglecting the more historically informed approaches.

More recent debates, such as that surrounding Thomas Piketty's (2014) analysis of inequality, are also grounded on a similar distinction (Martins 2016). While Piketty emphasises conventional elements when explaining the roots of inequality in past history, critics of Piketty such as Gregory Mankiw (2013) focus on how inequality is a consequence of divergent degrees of marginal productivity of labour, which are a result of, and a precondition for, optimal choices by human agents with different endowments of human capital.

The debate concerning the fundamental distinction between a conventionalist perspective and an optimisation perspective has also important ideological undertones, because the policy implications are very different. If human beings are permanently optimising with full information, they might counterpose and react to macroeconomic policy, possibly undermining it, as argued in the Lucas (1981) critique, and policy-makers will be advised to refrain from State intervention. But if human beings are creatures of habit whose behaviour remains relatively stable even after policy changes, Keynesian policies of demand management can be implemented more effectively, and State intervention in general can be made effective when addressing social inequality, as argued by Piketty and many Keynesian economists more recently. So the distinction between a conventionalist and an optimisation approach also has important political implications, and can be analytically helpful not only regarding economic analysis but also regarding policy analysis.

References

Ashraf, N., C. F Camerer, and G. Loewenstein (2005) 'Adam Smith, behavioral economist', *Journal of Economic Perspectives* 19 (3), 131–45.

Cass, D. (1965) 'Optimum growth in an aggregate model of capital accumulation', *Review of Economic Studies* 32 (3), 233–40.

CW: see Keynes (1971–1989).

Favereau, O. (1988) 'La Theorie Généreale: de l'Economie Conventionnelle à l'Economie des conventions', *Cahiers d'économie politique*, 14–15, 197–220.

Harcourt, G. C. (1972) *Some Cambridge Controversies in the Theory of Capital*, Cambridge, UK: Cambridge University Press.

Hayek, F. A. (1948) *Individualism and Economic Order*, Chicago, IL: Chicago University Press.

Hicks, J. R. (1937) 'Mr Keynes and the classics: A suggested interpretation', *Econometrica* 5 (2), 146–59.

Hicks, J. R. (1980–1981) 'IS-LM: An explanation', *Journal of Post Keynesian Economics* 3 (2), 139–54.

Kalecki, M. (1971) *Selected Essays on the Dynamics of the Capitalist Economy*, Cambridge, UK: Cambridge University Press.

Keynes, J. M. (1921) *A Treatise on Probability*, *CW* VIII.

Keynes, J. M. (1936) *The General Theory of Employment, Interest and Money*, *CW* VII.

Keynes. J. M. (1971–1989) *Collected Writings*, (*CW*), D. E. Moggridge, ed., 30 vols, London: Macmillan and New York: St Martin's Press.

Koopmans, T.C. (1965) 'On the concept of optimal economic growth', in L. Johansen, ed., *The Econometric Approach to Development Planning*, North Holland: Amsterdam, 225–87.

Lawson, T. (1985a) 'Uncertainty and economic analysis', *Economic Journal* 95 (380), 909–27.

Lawson, T. (1985b) 'Keynes, prediction and econometrics', in T. Lawson and H. Pesaran, eds, *Keynes's Economics: Methodological Issues*, London: Croom Helm, pp. 116–33.

Lucas, R. (1981) *Studies in Business Cycle Theory*, Cambridge, MA: MIT Press.

Mankiw, G. N. (2013), 'Defending the one percent', *Journal of Economic Perspectives* 27 (3), 21–34.

Marshall, A. (1890) *Principles of Economics*, London: Macmillan.

Martins, N. O. (2016) 'Political aspects of the capital controversies and capitalist crises', *Journal of Post Keynesian Economics* 39 (4), 473–94.

Piketty, T. (2014) *Capital in the 21st Century*, Cambridge, MA: The Belknap Press of Harvard University Press.

Ramsey, F. P. (1928) 'A mathematical theory of saving', *Economic Journal* 38 (152), 543–59.

Ramsey, F. P. (1978) 'Truth and probability', in D. H. Mellor, ed., *Foundations: Essays in Philosophy, Logic, Mathematics and Economics*, London: Routledge, pp. 52–109.

Robbins, L. (1938) 'Interpersonal comparisons of utility: A comment', *Economic Journal* 48 (192), 635–41.

Romer, D. (2001 [1996]), *Advanced Macroeconomics*, Second edition, New York: McGraw Hill.

Sen, A. K. (1987) *On Ethics and Economics*, Oxford: Blackwell.

Sen, A. K. (1997), 'Maximisation and the act of choice', *Econometrica* 65 (4), 745–79.

13

OPEN AND CLOSED SYSTEMS

Victoria Chick

Introduction

Although economists use the word 'system' in everyday speech – an economic system, a banking system, a distribution system, for example – and Skinner (1979) has argued that Adam Smith thought in terms of systems, it was Boulding (1956) who introduced the formal concept into economics from systems theory. Systems *theory*, however, has not made much headway in economics, possibly because it is largely concerned with syntax rather than semantics, but the *concept* of a system is useful; it is particularly a hallmark of institutional economics: '[T]he idea of the economy as an open system [is] one of the defining characteristics of institutionalism' (Hodgson 2000, p. 319):

We need to define our terms. *The Oxford English Dictionary* offers many variants of the term 'system', of which the following are closest to what an economist usually means:

I An organized or connected group of objects. 1. A set or assemblage of things connected, associated, or interdependent, so as to form a complex unity; a whole composed of parts in orderly arrangement according to some scheme or plan; ...

II A set of principles, etc.; a scheme, method ... 8. The set of correlated principles, ideas, or statements belonging to some department of knowledge or belief; a department of knowledge or belief considered as an organized whole; ...

The defining characteristic is interconnections within a collection of things or ideas ('elements') that can be regarded as having a recognisable coherence or unity. Coherence or unity implies a boundary of some sort, within which the connections are rarely complete: the distinctive character of a system depends on the connections made.

Systems can be self-contained – they are called closed systems – or open, connected to or part of other systems. An open system has interactions with the

DOI: 10.4324/9781315745992-16

outside world, though to remain a system, it is still distinct. It is clear that all parts of the economic system interconnected to a greater or lesser degree and that the economic system as a whole is embedded in and connected to politics, philosophy, history, values – all the elements of social life. Ontologically, then, the economy is unequivocally an open system. National, and even local, economies are distinctive because of the social system in which they are embedded, which shapes the character of the elements and connections in each particular system.

In the real world, instances of perfect closure are rare. Scientists go to considerable trouble to approximate such systems in many experimental situations; this method is not available to macroeconomists, though of course they can be – and often are – a feature of economists' thought-experiments.

It is with these thought-experiments – theories and models – that this entry will be primarily concerned. We discuss the criteria that define closed and open systems and dimensions of openness, including the relation between the characteristics of the system studied and the systems used to analyse it, before introducing the different concept of open and closed system held by critical realists. A brief conclusion follows.

It is perhaps time to be a little more formal.

Open and closed systems

Let us again consult The Oxford English Dictionary:

> open system, a material system in which the total mass or energy fluctuates; an incomplete or alterable system (of ideas, doctrines, things, etc.).
> closed system, a complete and essentially unalterable system (of ideas, doctrines, things, etc.); a material system in which the total mass or energy remains constant; a self-contained realm, unaffected by external forces.

There is a general consensus that an actual economic system is open. No one can fail to notice its exchanges with the 'outside world': although it is never taken into account (because it is free), energy from the sun is fundamental; and we are now more conscious than earlier generations of openness at the other end of productive processes, namely waste. But at the level of theory there is choice: the thought-system may be open or closed.

The definitions refer to three characteristics, the degree of completeness, mutability and relation with 'the outside', and, as already mentioned, two levels, reality and ideas. These features are reflected in the criteria defining open and closed systems as they pertain to theories or models. These were originally derived by Dow (2002, pp. 139–40) and developed further in Chick and Dow (2005); they are reproduced here as Tables 13.1 and 13.2.

Conditions i–iv apply to characteristics of perceived reality (ontology) and v–viii to theories about reality (epistemology). The theoretical conditions follow from the conditions pertaining to reality. Satisfying any one of conditions i–iv is sufficient for openness in reality, and any one of conditions v–viii for openness of a theoretical system. This list should not be taken as exhaustive: open systems can always reveal new dimensions of openness.

Table 13.1 Conditions for open systems

Real-world systems

i   The system is not atomistic; therefore at least one of the following holds:
   a   outcomes of actions cannot be inferred from individual actions (because of interactions);
   b   agents and their interactions may change (for example, agents may learn).
ii   Structure and agency are interdependent.
iii Boundaries around and within the social or economic system are mutable for at least one
   of the following reasons: a. social structures may evolve; b. connections between structures
   may change; c. the structure-agent relation may change.
iv   Identifiable social structures are embedded in larger structures; these may mutually interact,
   for the boundaries of a social system are in general partial or semi-permeable.

Implications for theoretical systems

v   There may be important omitted variables or relations and/or their effects on the system
   may be uncertain.
vi   The classification into exogenous and endogenous variables may be neither fixed nor
   exhaustive.
vii Connections and/or boundaries between structures may be imperfectly known and/or may
   change.
viii There is imperfect knowledge of the relations between variables; relationships may not be
   stable.

Table 13.2 Conditions for *closed* theoretical systems

1. All relevant variables can be identified.
2. The boundaries of the system are definite and immutable; it follows that it is clear which
variables are exogenous and which are endogenous; these categories are fixed.
3. Only the specified exogenous variables affect the system, and they do this in a known way.
4. Relations between the included variables are either knowable or random.
5. Economic agents (whether individuals or aggregates) are treated atomistically.
6. The nature of economic agents is treated as if constant.
7. The structure of the relationships between the components (variables, subsystems, agents) is
treated as if it is either knowable or random.
8. The structural framework within which agents act is taken as given.

'Open' is not to be understood as the dual of 'closed'. Consider these criteria for a closed system (Table 13.2).

Whereas for open systems, the fulfilment of *any one* of the criteria marks the system as open, in the case of closed systems *all* the criteria must be met. Open systems are many and various, depending on which criterion obtains. Open systems lie on not just one but a variety of spectra (depending on which criterion applies), with closed systems at the extreme end (Mearman 2002, 2005). And so it might seem that open systems are far more likely, closed systems rare. But in the world of macroeconomic models, closed systems predominate. This has been partly a consequence of the widespread adoption of mathematical technique, where closure, if the model is specified correctly, gives demonstrable results. Just-determined, simultaneous-equation models, which can yield a unique solution, are the most obvious example. However, mathematical open-system models do exist (e.g. Skott 1989; Setterfield 2009) and closed models were popular before the subject relied so heavily on mathematics, so mathematics cannot bear the full burden of explanation.

There is another asymmetry: while closed systems must be completely closed, open systems cannot be completely open; they require some sort of boundary. That boundary might be vague and/or mutable, but a system must have limits of some sort to be a system at all.

Systems, theories and models

In macroeconomics, the thought-system may be represented by models or theories. In economics we often use the terms 'theory' and 'model' loosely; indeed, most mainstream economists do not differentiate: for them, models *are* theories, and theories take the form of models. But, for example, Leijonhufvud (1997) argues that they should be distinguished:

> He propose[d] to conceive of economic 'theories' as sets of beliefs about the economy and how it functions. They refer to the 'real world' – that curious expression that economists use when it occurs to them that there is one. 'Models' are formal but partial representations of theories. A model never encompasses the entire theory to which it refers.
>
> *(p. 193)*

While in broad agreement, we would put the matter slightly differently. Theories, we think, are more than 'beliefs': they are an interrelated set of ideas or hypotheses. Models are an interrelated set of formal propositions, often expressed as equations. They do both more and less than 'represent' theories: at best they explore part of the theory in which they are embedded, exploiting their ability to yield definitive results, but they fall short of the scope of the theory.

A model is a formal structure defined by its assumptions and definitions. Within the model these restrictions are complete and fixed. Such models are closed. Theories are broader than models. They may be either formal or informal and may encompass several models. A well-documented example of a macroeconomic theory encompassing models is that in Keynes's *General Theory* (1936, *CW* VII), within which Kregel (1976) found three models, each based on different assumptions about expectations. I have found several other models within it (Chick 1983, 2004).

Although models are systems, the conventional language attaching to them is tricky. Van der Lecq points out that in mainstream economics, 'openness' applied to models means something different from openness with respect to a system:

> Confusingly, in [mainstream] economics … [a] model which consists of only endogenous variables is called a closed model, whereas a model in which exogenous variables are included in order to solve it, is called an open model. The term open model reflects the idea that the model would be indeterminate without information from outside. … In the terminology [of systems], both closed and open models [in this sense] are examples of a closed system approach.
>
> *(Van der Lecq 1998, p. 161)*

She suggests the term 'isolated system' to cope with the fully endogenised model (such as a general-equilibrium model). This usage conforms to that in physics: a physical system is closed if the boundary is proof against the transfer of either matter or energy, while in an isolated system neither can cross the boundary.

Subsystems

An open system may be too complex and/or sprawling to be tractable. The remedy is to construct subsystems within the larger, open system. Think of almost any complicated system: your motor car manual is divided into the electrical system, the fuel system, steering, gears and transmission and so on. No one of these alone explains how your car works; but they are convenient subsystems. The human body is studied as separate fields: anatomy, physiology and so on. In terms of open systems, these are perfect examples of how to handle a complex subject without resorting to reductionism, through the device of taking first one element of the overall system, then another, as the object of analysis, using the method of *ceteris paribus* to provide a closure for each partial system and later removing it.

As in the passage from Leijonhufvud, these subsystems may be closed models or smaller, open theories. If the theorist remembers to keep the rest of the system 'at the back of his head' (Keynes 1936 *CW VII*, pp. 297–8), then the pieces should fit together when the additional conditions required to establish the borders of these subsystems are relaxed and the subsystems, modified as required, are re-integrated into the larger theory. Chick and Dow (2005) have called this the method of partial (in the sense of Marshall's partial equilibrium) and temporary closure. Setterfield (2001) calls it the open-system, *ceteris paribus* method. The procedure is safe if it ignores for the time being some aspects of reality in order to close the model. But it is possible to assume something which is false in terms of the larger system; that will preclude later relaxation and re-incorporation. Closure – or what to put in the pound of *ceteris paribus* – is a matter of judgement, and judgements can be misguided.

Consider, in that connection, the Classical Dichotomy: money is excluded from analysis until relative prices are determined and only brought in at the end to establish the absolute price level. By contrast, both Keynes and Hayek knew that the analysis is false for a money economy: Keynes expressed 'full agreement' with the following statement in Hayek's review of *A Treatise on Money*:

> [T]he task of monetary theory is ... nothing less than to cover a second time the whole field that is treated by pure theory under the assumption of barter.
>
> *(Quoted in Keynes 1931 CW XIII, p. 254)*

Indirect exchange, through the medium of money, is not neutral.

Or consider Walras's (1954 [1874]) decision to model first exchange, then production, capital formation and finally money. The last of these we have just covered. Walras constructed two layers of recontracting, one for production and one for exchange, in his production model. His followers were less careful, and simply extrapolated the theory of exchange to model production. But the basis of Walras's theory of exchange, the gross substitution theorem, is false in production, where labour and output are complements, not substitutes.

Dimensions of openness

The boundaries of economics

Macroeconomics is a system embedded in a social system, as argued earlier. We can even argue about the boundaries that define macroeconomics. The most obvious is that economics as currently practised by the majority deals with monetary transactions. Goods or services produced without reference to money, such as 'women's work' in the home, or volunteering, and work which is paid for indirectly, e.g. most government production, are not well accounted for in economics.

So economics is already a partial study of economic activity, though that partial sphere is influenced by what is going on in the larger economic system, let alone the rest of social life. Mainstream economics has made the focus of economics even narrower, rejecting the dimensions of ethics, morals or philosophy as unsuitable to the 'science' of economics.

On the other hand, subsets of economics are accepted, even entrenched: labour economics, money and banking, environmental economics, and so on – but typically, theories developed in these subsystems are not well integrated into a larger theory of the economy as a whole. Take by contrast the structure of Keynes's *General Theory*. The story opens with an explanation of the level of employment in terms of costs and the level of demand for goods and services that producers expect. Expected demand is not differentiated as between consumption and investment: that comes much later, after the theory of liquidity preference is proposed and the relationship between the rate of interest and the other determinants of investment are explained. In other words, Keynes starts with a very simplified theory and gradually relaxes the *ceteris paribus* assumptions on which it is based to move to a more complete, larger theory; but there is no contradiction.

Time

Perhaps the most interesting use of this nested technique has to do with time. (This has already been touched on in discussing Kregel's work, above.) Keynes had been taught by Marshall, and Marshall had 'cut up time' to produce a nested theory of markets. His example was the fish market. On the market day, fish are landed in early morning and should be sold by evening; in the short period, comprising several market days, there is time to put to sea again and work longer hours to increase the catch for the following days when demand is brisk; and in the long period, more boats could be built and fishermen recruited, further to expand supply. The price of fish would depend on the extent of possible adjustment in the length of time allowed. Note that variables that are exogenous in one time-frame are endogenous in another. In an open system these categories are not fixed.

Keynes adapted this scheme. The speculator has a short time horizon and his market moves quickly. The producer starts every 'day' (the period for which he takes production decisions) with the capital and labour force he has on hand but can increase output somewhat through overtime or by hiring more labour; this is the short period. The investor in capital equipment, however, must take quite a longer view. In an actual economy, all these activities are going on simultaneously, yet they provide another criterion, or another aspect of the earlier criterion, for leaving, say, investment in the pound of *ceteris paribus* while talking about output and employment, for example.

Keynes's system is open to the normal flow of time but involves a series of temporary closures, so that, although his formal apparatus is often static, what he is portraying is a sequence of decisions and actions through time. The system, being open to the future, can evolve, as of course the actual economy has done and will continue to do. Many business firms, already large in Keynes's time, are now huge and global in reach. The volume of transactions concerned with productive output in comparison to finance has shifted massively. Financial: markets for derivatives and shadow banks have appeared, and so on. Just as Keynes realised that the evolution of the economic structures from the time of Marshall necessitated new theory, so it is today. An open system alerts the reader to the possibility – indeed the certainty – that theories are bound to become obsolete, in whole or in part.

The relation between micro and macro

The charge that Keynesian macroeconomics has no microfoundations is well known and unresolved. (See for example Toporowski and Denis, 2016.) There are two senses in which this charge is absurd, but there is some truth in it, too. It is absurd on the part of the mainstream economists who lay this charge because what they mean is that the theory is not 'microfounded' on 'rational choice' theory. But rational choice theory is based on perfect (probabilistic) knowledge into the indefinite future, while Keynes's theory is based on an uncertain and unknown future.

The second absurdity is to ignore the rich discussion in *The General Theory* (especially Chapter 9) of motivation and decisions—to consume, to produce, how liquid to be, how much labour to hire, what wage to offer and to accept—which can only be taken by individuals on their own behalf or for an organisation.

The grain of truth is that the link between these decisions and the macrotheory is unclear. However, there are good reasons for this. The outcome of interactions between individual plans cannot be predicted unless we know the precise timing of all transactions – an impossible requirement. Generalising from micro decisions to macro outcomes founders on the fallacy of composition. This is ineradicable, and the rational response is to accept it. It follows that any attempt to make a connection between individual actions and macro outcomes necessarily involves a fudge of some kind. The mainstream economists have their fudge: the representative agent. (It should be recognised for the fudge it is.) Many Post-Keynesians have called for macrofoundations of microeconomics, but without the representative agent the link is no more definite that way round. Keynes leaves the matter unclear. What *is* clear is that each level of analysis is open to influences from the other, often in some unspecified way.

Critical realism

Tony Lawson has been responsible for importing the ideas of critical realism into economics. This school of thought is marked by the primacy accorded to ontology; critical realists argue that the focus on theory and lack of attention to ontology is a major flaw in economic theorising. As we have seen, it is easy to agree that real-world economic systems are open in many dimensions. Lawson and his followers further argue that theories should match the ontological characteristics: an open-system ontology demands open-system theorising. They argue, further, that the use of closed modes of theorising or modelling presupposes a closed-system ontology, and that since closed systems in actual economies are rare, most closed-system models are inappropriate. We explore the relation between theory and ontology below, but first there is an important difference of meaning to clear up.

What critical realists mean by open and closed systems is different from what we have been discussing up to now: they define a closed system as one in which there is a constant conjunction of events, such that if x occurs, y will follow, and an open system is one in which such a sequence cannot be relied upon. Whereas we have been talking up to now about the systemic structure of theories and models, their focus is on systems at all but on outcomes. Where we have concentrated on theory construction, their interest is in the validity or otherwise of attempts to find empirical regularities, whether to suggest new theories or to assess the credibility of old ones. This activity founders if the theories do not suggest a significant degree of event regularity, as, they argue, is usually the case.

It is very tempting to imagine that closed-system theories or models will result in event regularities and open-system theories will not, but Chick and Dow (2005) have demonstrated that there is no one-to-one relationship of this kind between structure and outcome. An event regularity may be found because the causal link has been correctly identified by a closed-system model in which all the relevant variables and other causal relationships are specified; but it could equally arise by chance or through a common causality. These latter two Lawson identifies as 'closures of concomitance'. By definition a chance correlation cannot be explained or predicted by modelling, and a common cause is also unlikely to be so revealed, as models are normally uni-causal in structure.

It needs to be stressed that the model must be *correct* if event regularities are to follow. If, for example, an important variable is omitted, the regularity may not manifest itself.

Open systems may also reveal event regularities – otherwise there would be no point in theorising in that way. But they need not do so. The choice between Dow's criteria and Lawson's is important here too. Consider, for example, the proposition that consumption will rise with income but less than equiproportionately. This proposition, with appropriate caveats concerning lags in adjustment to changed circumstances, survives the rise in investment which openness of the system allows.

Since there is no unique correlation between the critical realist definition of closed and open systems and that of the rest of economics and all of science, it is worth comparing Lawson's conditions for his concept of closure with Dow's. He specifies three conditions: extrinsic, intrinsic and 'aggregation'. The extrinsic condition is that external influences on the dependent variable(s) are uncorrelated with the explanatory variable(s). This corresponds to Dow's conditions 1 and 3.

The intrinsic condition is that relations within the system are known and predictable. This is given by Dow's conditions 4, 6, 7 and 8. The aggregation condition precludes interdependencies within the system. This is Dow's condition 5. That leaves condition 2: boundaries, which turns out to be quite a bone of contention.

151

Boundaries

At the beginning we described a system as a collection of elements and connections that had a certain coherence or unity. That definition implies a distinctive, recognisable quality, even though open. A cat is an open system, interacting with its environment in eating and breathing and excreting its waste. But it is distinct, even from other cats. It not only has its personal boundary but also a wider boundary of its territory, which other cats violate at their peril. Take away its personal boundary (skin it) and the cat ceases to be a cat. Boundaries, in the majority view, are an essential marker of a system.

Lawson (2004) has declared himself opposed to all boundaries as distortions of reality. I believe he is thinking of theoretical boundaries: I'm sure he knows a cat when he sees one, or can tell the difference between himself and me. But he sees economics, embedded in social life, as too interrelated to be 'cut up' by boundaries for analytical purposes without distorting that reality. This is, in effect, a distrust of abstraction, a technique on which theorising, and reasoning in general, has relied for centuries. A map is not the territory, but most of us find maps immensely useful, even revealing aspects of the territory obscured by its complexity in the absence of such a 'distortion'.

We are back to the question of judgement: what is a harmless abstraction and what is a distortion? Loasby (2003) has made a convincing case for the value of abstraction, in the form of closed systems: they have a sharp focus and give clear and demonstrable results. The problem of judgement, also dealt with above, remains. It is one of those problems in which, to paraphrase Keynes, you cannot convict your opponent, only convince him.

Conclusion

Economics is full of examples of talking at cross-purposes because the meaning of words is not clear. In this example, the words 'open system' have two meanings among heterodox economists, one referring to the structure of reality, models or theories and another to the conjunction of events generated in reality, models or theories. And an open model means something else again to a mainstream economist. Unfortunately, the meanings are not interchangeable: the choice is not neutral, for there is no simple mapping between them. This is not a comfortable situation, but it is one we can live with if we are clear what is meant. I have no intention of dictating what words mean, though I have my preferences.

Closed and open systems both have their uses, but creating a closure as an abstraction from reality is to be done with care: the chosen abstraction may be either apt or inappropriate and, if the latter, will yield misleading results. There are no rules to apply to this question: the choice is a matter of the theorist's judgement, and the evaluation of the suitability of that choice is, similarly, a matter of judgement. No objective criterion, such as internal consistency, is sufficient in making this judgement.

References

Boulding (1956) 'General system theory, the skeleton of a science', *Management Science* 2, 197–208. Reprinted in W. Buckley, ed., *Modern Systems Research for the Behavioral Scientist* (1968), W. Buckley (ed.), Chicago: Alaine.

CW: See Keynes, J. M. (1971–1989).

Chick, V. (1983) *Macroeconomics after Keynes: A Reconsideration of the General Theory*, Cambridge, MA: MIT Press.

Chick, V. (2004) 'On open systems', *Brazilian Journal of Political Economy* 24 (1) (93), January–March, 1–16.

Chick, V. and S. C. Dow (2005) 'The meaning of open systems', *Journal of Economic Methodology* 12 (3), 363–8.

Dow, S. C. (2002) *Economic Methodology: An Inquiry*, Oxford: Oxford University Press.

Hodgson, G. (2000) 'What is the essence of institutional economics?', *Journal of Economic Issues* 34 (2), June, 318–29.

Keynes, J. M. (1931) 'The pure theory of money: A reply to Dr Hayek', *Economica*, August, *CW* XIII, pp. 243–56.

Keynes, J. M. (1936) *The General Theory of Employment, Interest and Money, CW* VII.

Keynes. J. M. (1971–1989) *Collected Writings*, (*CW*), D. E. Moggridge, ed., 30 vols, London: Macmillan and New York: St Martin's Press and Cambridge, UK: Cambridge University Press.

Keynes, J. M. (1971–1989), *Collected Writings*, D.E. Moggridge, ed., 30 vols, London: Macmillan and New York: St Martin's Press.

Kregel, J. A. (1976) 'Economic methodology in the face of uncertainty: The modelling methods of Keynes and the Post-Keynesians', *Economic Journal* 86 (June), 209–25.

Leijonhufvud, A. (1997) 'Models and theories', *Journal of Economic Methodology* 4 (2), 193–8.

Loasby, B. J. (2003) 'Closed models and open systems', *Journal of Economic Methodology* 10, 285–306.

Mearman, A. (2002) 'A contribution to the methodology of post Keynesian economics', unpublished PhD thesis, University of Leeds.

Mearman, A. (2005) 'Sheila Dow's concept of dualism: Clarification, criticism and development', *Cambridge Journal of Economics* 29, 1–16.

Setterfield, M. (2001) 'Macrodynamics', in R. P. F. Holt and S. Pressman, eds, *A New Guide to Post Keynesian Economics*, London: Routledge, pp. 92–101.

Setterfield, M. (2009) 'Path dependency, hysteresis and macrodynamics', in P. Arestis and M. C. Sawyer (eds) *Path Dependency and Macroeconomics,* London: Palgrave Macmillan, pp. 37–79.

Skinner, A. S. (1979) 'Adam Smith: An aspect of modern economics', *Scottish Journal of Political Economy* 26, June, 109–25.

Skott, P. (1989) *Conflict and Effective Demand in Economic Growth*, Cambridge: Cambridge University Press.

Toporowski, J. and A. Denis (eds) (2016) 'Microfoundations; (five articles with introduction)', *Review of Political Economy* 28 (1), January, 90–167.

Van der Lecq, S. G. (1998) *Money, Co-Ordination and Prices*, Cheltenham: Edward Elgar.

Walras, L. (1954 [1874]) *Elements of Pure Economics*, trans. W. Jaffe, London: George Allen and Unwin.

14

MONEY AND MACROECONOMIC METHODOLOGY

Claude Gnos

Introduction

A traditional perspective, that is still predominant in modern textbooks and macroeconomic models, contends that money was invented and continues to be used to facilitate exchanges in a market economy. This perspective ranks money as a useful but normally neutral instrument in economic transactions. It notably supports the old quantity theory of money that Friedman and his followers have intended to revamp from the mid-20th century.

However, this view has been questioned for a long time by anthropological history (see Innes 1913). It is also inconsistent with the actual role of money in the capitalist economy. This is a point that Keynes, in his time, highlighted when opposing his analysis of the 'monetary economy of production' to the neoclassical model he labelled a 'real exchange economy' (Keynes 1933a, *CW* XIII).

This chapter is intended to inquire into the ins and outs of this opposition with reference to macroeconomic theory. First, we shall observe that breaking with the neoclassical/monetarist theory, which is explicitly micro-founded, allows us to formulate foundations for a true monetary macroeconomic theory, i.e. a macroeconomic analysis that transcends the microeconomic determinants of economic activity and attaches all due importance to money. This is an approach that Keynes initiated. Second, we will consider the theory of the monetary circuit that draws on Keynes's monetary macroeconomic theory. This theory provides an in-depth examination of the connection between money and the real and financial relationships inherent in the capitalist economy.

Keynes's 'monetary economy of production' in opposition to the neoclassical 'real exchange economy'

The neoclassical general equilibrium model is no doubt intended to represent the economy as a whole, which is usually considered as the mark of a macroeconomic theory. It describes an economy composed of interdependent markets that are

DOI: 10.4324/9781315745992-17

supposed to ensure equilibrium between supplies and demands throughout the economy. In this model, production amounts to exchanges between productive services and produced goods. Money intervenes as a medium of exchange and does not affect the determination of the real variables (see Walras 1954), hence the notion of 'real exchange economy' criticised by Keynes. Exogeneous variations of its quantity do not affect the determination of relative prices (i.e. the rate at which goods exchange for each other), they are just supposed to translate into variations in the general level of money prices. Variations in the quantity of money thus act in compliance with the classical quantity theory of money.

In a more elaborated version of the neoclassical model, money may play a complementary role. It is not only demanded for the purpose of exchanging goods and services. Friedman and his followers argued that money may be considered as an asset yielding a flow of services which, as such, are imbedded in a global process of wealth allocation. The methodology is unchanged, though.

A priori, the quantity theory of money may be seen as a means to introduce a macroeconomic dimension in an approach which is, otherwise, mainly interested in individual behaviours and market clearing (see Jespersen 2009, p. 21). On the traditional view, the quantity theory is concerned with the relationship between money supply and the general price level, both relating to the economy as a whole. On Friedman's view, it is mainly concerned with the demand for money, which may also be linked to the economy as a whole. It should be noted, however, that this way of dealing with money is in fact far from bringing the expected macroeconomic dimension to the neoclassical approach. This is so because the relationship between money supply or the demand for money and the general level of money prices is not determined on a specific macroeconomic basis but is fully determined by individual behaviours and market clearing.

Likewise we may observe with Jespersen that the macroeconomic theory of the interwar years, 'consisted ... of a number of mainly microeconomic ... analyses of the factors that influenced the development of the aggregated microeconomic variables' (ibid., p. 21). More recently, in keeping with the neoclassical approach, new classical economists have come to the conclusion that macroeconomics should be founded on microeconomics: 'New classicals believe that only when macroeconomic aggregates are explicable as consequences of well-formulated optimisation problems for individuals, i.e. only when complete micro-foundations are worked out, will macroeconomic reasoning be secure' (Hoover 1988, p. 87). The neoclassical approach to economics is clearly micro-founded: the aggregation of microeconomic variables does not change their very nature.

When writing his *Treatise on Money*, Keynes outlined a new approach to money and its role:

> I propose ... to break away from the traditional method of setting out from the total quantity of money irrespective of the purposes on which it is employed, and to start instead ... with the flow of the community's earnings of money income, and with its twofold division (1) into the parts which have been *earned* by the production of consumption goods and of investment goods respectively, and (2) into the parts which are *expended* on consumption goods and on savings respectively.
> *(Keynes 1930, CW V, p. 121)*

We may rightly argue that the determination of the community's earnings, that Keynes refers to, is dependent on individual behaviours, notably entrepreneurs' and consumers' behaviours and decisions with regard to what is to be produced and consumed. *A priori*, this is nothing new. One could think that, in this way, Keynes only put focus on a specific facet of the role of money and in no way dismisses the micro-founded approach to macroeconomics.

Truly, Keynes focuses on production and the ensuing formation and spending of money income. The divergence of both approaches is then clear. On Keynes's view, production is centre stage: besides its physical process, it originates the community's income that will be spent on the goods produced. Money plays a genuine role: it takes the form of the community's income successively formed and spent. These features, as such, are in no way dependent on microeconomic behaviours; they on the contrary form the framework under which the economic agents interact. The opposition between the two approaches is also confirmed by the role assigned to firms and entrepreneurs. On Walras's view, the entrepreneur, wearing his entrepreneur's hat (as a person he is a factor of production like other workers), is a mere intermediary between the market for productive services (including the productive services of the entrepreneur) and the market for manufactured goods. The volume of output and its distribution are determined by the interplay of supply and demand in markets depending on the productivity of each factor and on individual preferences. Keynes, for his part, puts entrepreneurs (as representatives of firms) and the investment of funds required to launch production to the fore. He refers to Marx's famous formula M-C-M', by which the investment of funds in production amounts to the transformation of a given sum of money (M) into goods (commodities) and then back into an increased sum of money (M'). As he puts it

> [t]he firm is dealing throughout in terms of sums of money. It has no object in the world except to end up with more money than it started with. That is the essential characteristic of an entrepreneur economy.
>
> *(Keynes 1933b, CW XXIX, p. 89)*

In this way, Keynes not only focuses on production and the ensuing formation and spending of the community's money income, he also emphasises the role and requirements of the finance involved in the production process. In other words, he considers the capitalist system and its logic which is not reduceable to the behaviour of individual economic agents. This system shapes the economy as a whole. It falls within a realist macroeconomic theory.

It is true that Keynes's *General Theory* has given rise to divergent interpretations and notably led to the so-called 'neoclassical synthesis' that intended to build a bridge between Keynes's way of thinking and the neoclassical theory. Even standard Keynesian economics has been intended to conciliate general equilibrium theory and Keynes's theory. Yet the principle of effective demand, which is central in the latter book, marked an indubitable continuity in Keynes's macroeconomic approach, putting to the fore the entrepreneur and the successive spending and proceeds the latter is expecting to incur and receive for a given volume of employment. As Keynes (1936, pp. 24–5) argues, 'entrepreneurs will endeavour to fix the amount of employment at the level which they expect to maximise the excess of the proceeds over the factor cost'. The excess of proceeds over factor cost is the profit or 'income of the entrepreneur', while the factor cost paid by firms constitutes the income of the factors of production (workers). Defined in this way, profit does not come in addition to factors' income, but is a redistributed part of it, transferred from purchasers to firms when revenue exceeds factor costs. On this view unemployment cannot result from a lack of income: production generates the income that is necessary and sufficient to pay for the goods produced. That is why Keynes pointed at a possible demand deficiency resulting from a deficiency of spending both on consumption and investment goods relative to current income, which he linked to consumers' propensity to consume and entrepreneurs' inducement to invest. This means that he clearly separates the macroeconomic analysis, that relates to the formation and spending of the community's income, from the microeconomic analysis that points to consumers' and entrepreneurs' behaviours.

The continuity of Keynes's analysis is as well confirmed by the 'finance motive' as defined in his 1937 articles on the interest rate (Keynes 1937a, 1937b). To start production, he argued, firms have to secure 'a provision of cash' provided by banks or the market, which 'does not absorb or exhaust any resources' but generates new net saving when spent on production: 'Each new net investment has new net saving attached to it' (Keynes 1937a, p. 247). The latter analysis is clearly in line with the analysis we just summed up. Entrepreneurs need money they will spend on production which, at least to the extent that it is not spent on production goods available but on factor cost, forms new incomes saved until they are spent on the goods newly produced.

The contribution of circuit theory

Keynes's genuinely macroeconomic approach, as we have just outlined it, has been disregarded by mainstream economists. It falls within the so-called Keynes heterodoxy. It has nonetheless inspired some economists, especially the Post-Keynesians, who predominantly endorse Keynes's emphasis on the role of uncertainty in the monetary production economy, and the circuitists, who insist on the flow of the community's monetary income successively formed and spent. The Post-Keynesian approach emerged in Anglo-Saxon academic circles while circuit theory flourished in France and Italy.

Truly, the concept of the circuit is not new. It was first promoted in economics by the Physiocrats of 18th-century France who viewed production as a cycle continually renewed, beginning with advances, that is, capital expenditures, and ending when the goods that had been produced were sold. This approach, although usually unsung, has in fact underpinned many approaches to economics from Marx to Wicksell and later by way of Schumpeter, Kalecki and J. Robinson. Today's French and Italian circuit schools mainly draw on Keynes's heterodoxy. Hence many affinities of circuitists with Post-Keynesians, notably with regard to the endogenous view of money, according to which money creation is credit-driven (Moore 1988). The French school has been founded by prominent academics: Bernard Schmitt (1960, 1966, 1984), Jacques Le Bourva (1962), Alain Barrère (1979, 1990) and Alain Parguez (1975). The Italian branch emerged in the 1980s on Graziani's (1989, 2003) initiative. French and Italian circuitist approaches have also inspired Post-Keynesians outside Europe, especially in Canada (Lavoie 1984; Seccareccia 1996; Rochon 1999).

On the neoclassical/monetarist view, money is an asset that acts as a neutral intermediary in exchanges of goods produced outside the monetary sphere. That is the so-called classical 'dichotomy'. Circuit theory, with its focus on the production process that is initiated by investment and is fully completed only after a lapse of time, entails a different conception of money and its role.

In an initial stage, circuitists argued that modern money is created by banks in response to demand for credit and consists in bank liabilities which are IOUs, that is, claims to sums of money that do not exist in any material form. Schmitt developed this argument in several publications in the 1960s and 1970s, which gave rise to what has become the common circuitist view that banks issue debts upon themselves *ex nihilo* which they lend to economic agents, especially firms, who spend them on goods and labour. Eventually, the argument goes, borrowers recover the money they spent, out of their own takings, and are thus able to reimburse the bank loans. This view has been notably endorsed by Parguez and Seccareccia (2000). However, Schmitt deepened his analysis and came to the conclusion that the definition of money may require some further thoughts (Schmitt 1984). He made his point with reference to bookkeeping, observing that, strictly speaking, banks do not issue liabilities which they lend to firms. They actually debit and credit accounts with purely nominal units of money and so build up assets and liabilities which simultaneously tie the banks themselves and their borrowers and depositors. This refinement has crucial implications for understanding the role of banks, the definition of money and the nature of the circuit (cf. Gnos 2003, 2006).

On the common circuitist view, banks' liabilities are counterparts to the produced goods and labour that borrowers (firms) employ during the production process. They are literally exchanged for goods and labour. In a sense, this view maintains the neoclassical approach by which economic transactions are exchanges achieved by means of a peculiar good or asset that is deemed to be money. Schmitt pointed out that the rigorous reference to bookkeeping delivers a more original view. Actually, the double-entry principle does not allow banks to extend credit to borrowers without gaining an equivalent credit from depositors. It is interesting to note that Keynes already made this argument in the *General Theory*:

> The prevalence of the idea that saving and investment, taken in their straightforward sense, can differ from one another, is to be explained, I think, by an optical illusion due to regarding an individual depositor's relation to his bank as being a one-sided transaction, instead of seeing it as the two-sided transaction which it actually is. It is supposed that a depositor and his bank can somehow contrive between them to perform an operation by which savings can disappear into the banking system so that they are lost to investment, or, contrariwise, that the banking system can make it possible for investment to occur, to which no saving corresponds.
>
> *(1936, CW VII, p. 81)*

On the Post-Keynesian side, this argument has been confirmed by Moore who notes that depositors are 'ultimately the creditors of bank borrowers' and concludes that banks are 'simply one type of financial intermediary' (1988, p. 20).

As a consequence, banks' liabilities, i.e. deposits, are the source of bank financing and match the credit they grant to borrowers. Depositors are creditors of banks and ultimately the creditors of bank borrowers. Banks, just as Moore emphasised, are but one type of financial intermediary; they are not the actual source of the credit granted to borrowers. Money creation has to be seen for what it really is: bookkeeping entries: debits and credits that banks record in their books in nominal units of account and that resolve into assets and liabilities denoting (indirect) financial relations between borrowers and depositors.

This analysis sheds new light on the payment of wages. The latter comes down to crediting workers' bank accounts with units of account and, in this way, defines assets and liabilities in banks' books that link workers (depositors) and firms (borrowers) through banks. There is no string of transmissions of deposits that the banks would issue on themselves, and then lent to firms which, in turn, would transfer them to workers. What then is the meaning of the financial relationship between firms and workers? The answer results from the asymmetrical relationship connecting firms and workers which underpins the circuit. Firms pay for labour having in view the output which that employment will generate and which they will subsequently sell at a profit, while workers accept to work for money wages having in view the share of output which they subsequently will buy. The output is thus the object of the commitment of both firms and workers in the production process and also of the financial relationships that are generated by this process. If production were an instantaneous process, firms would pay workers at once in kind (assuming that the nature of the goods produced would suit workers' needs). In reality, production takes time and consequently firms have to postpone delivering the goods being produced to workers, and so require credit from them. Monetary payments, that banks make by means of units of account, ratify the firms' commitment to deliver goods to their workers later on. Simultaneously, workers temporarily save their income in the form of bank deposits and thereby grant credit to firms. Furthermore, the homogeneity and convertibility of bank monies in domestic economies allow the development of a complex network of transactions allowing every worker and his dependants to buy whichever goods best meet their needs, regardless of the particular goods the worker actually produced.

Conclusion

The traditional view in economics is that money is somehow a good or a financial asset acting as a medium of exchange which is, at the macroeconomic level, subject to a quantitative relationship between supply of or demand for it (depending on whether we adopt the classical or the monetarist viewpoint) and the general price level. These views are widely shared within the academic circles. They involve the conception that macroeconomics has essentially to deal with aggregates determined by individual behaviours interacting in various markets, which means, in other words, that only microeconomics can make the foundation of macroeconomics.

It is the merit of Keynes's heterodoxy of allowing for another conception of macroeconomics. Ever since his *Treatise on Money* (1930) Keynes initiated what he later called, in his 'Preface' to his *General Theory*, 'a struggle to escape from habitual modes of thought and expression' (1936, p. viii), discarding *the quantity theory of money* and, instead, putting focus on the flow of incomes formed in production and spent on consumption and investment. On his view, production is at centre stage; it is a physical process taking place in a monetary and financial environment that links banks, firms and workers. These factors pertain to an economic system, capitalism, that enforces its logic and laws on the economy as a whole. Unfortunately, few schools of thought met this methodological challenge. The circuit school is one of them, exploring the way money makes macroeconomics analytically special.

Bibliography

Barrère, A. (1979) *Déséquilibres économiques et contre-révolution keynésienne*, Paris: Economica.

Barrère, A. (1990) 'Signification générale du circuit : une interprétation', *Economie et Sociétés*, série Monnaie et Production 2 (6), 9–34.

CW: see Keynes, J. M. (1971–1989).

Gnos, C. (2003) 'Circuit theory as an explanation of the complex real world', in L. P. Rochon and S. Rossi, eds, *Studies in Modern Theories of Money*, Cheltenham and Northampton: Edward Elgar, pp. 322–38.

Gnos, C. (2006) 'French circuit theory', in P. Arestis and M. Sawyer eds, *A Handbook of Alternative Monetary Economics*, Cheltenham and Northampton: Edward Elgar, pp. 87–104.

Graziani, A. (1989) *The Theory of the Monetary Circuit*, London: Thames Papers in Political Economy.

Graziani, A. (2003) *The Monetary Theory of Production*, Cambridge, UK: Cambridge University Press.

Hoover, K. D. (1988) *The New Classical Macroeconomics: A Sceptical Inquiry*, Oxford: Basil Blackwell.

Innes, A. M. (1913) 'What is money?', *The Banking Law Journal*, 30, May, 377–408.

Jespersen, J. (2009) *Macroeconomics Methodology, A Post-Keynesian Perspective*, Cheltenham and Northampton: Edward Elgar.

Keynes, J. M. (1930) *A Treatise on Money*, *CW* V and VI.

Keynes, J. M. (1933a) 'A monetary theory of production', *CW* XIII, pp. 408–11.

Keynes, J. M. (1933b) 'The distinction between a co-operative economy and an entrepreneur economy', *CW.* XXIX, pp. 76–106.

Keynes, J. M. (1936) *The General Theory of Employment, Interest and Money*, *CW* VII.

Keynes, J. M. (1937a) 'Alternative theories of the rate of interest', *Economic Journal* 47 (186), 241–52.

Keynes, J. M. (1937b) 'The 'ex ante' theory of the rate of interest', *Economic Journal* 47 (188), 663–9.

Keynes, J. M. (1971–1989) *Collected Writings*, D. E. Moggridge, ed., 30 vols, London: Macmillan and New York: St Martin's Press.

Lavoie, M. (1984) 'Un modèle post-Keynesien d'économie monétaire fondé sur la théorie du circuit', *Economies et Sociétés* 59 (1), 233–58.

Le Bourva, J. (1962) 'Création de la monnaie et multiplicateur du crédit', *Revue Economique* 13 (1), 29–56.

Moore, B. J. (1988) *Horizontalists and Verticalists: The Macroeconomics of Credit Money*, Cambridge, UK: Cambridge University Press.

Parguez, A. (1975) *Monnaie et macroéconomie*, Paris: Economica.

Parguez, A. and M. Seccareccia (2000) 'The credit theory of money: The monetary circuit approach', in J. Smithin ed, *What is Money?*, London and New York: Routledge, pp. 101–23.

Rochon, L.-P. (1999) 'The creation and circulation of endogenous money: A circuit dynamic approach', *Journal of Economic Issues* 33 (1), 1–21.

Schmitt, B. (1960) *La formation du pouvoir d'achat*, Paris: Sirey.

Schmitt, B. (1966) *Monnaie, salaires et profits*, Paris: Presse Universitaires de France.

Schmitt, B. (1984) *Inflation, chômage et malformations du capital*. Albeuve: Castella.

Schmitt, B. (1996) 'Unemployment. Is there a principal cause?', in A. Cencini and M. Barenzini, eds, *Inflation and Unemployment*, London and New York: Routledge, pp. 75–105.

Seccareccia, M. (1996) 'Post Keynesian fundism and monetary circulation', in G. Deleplace and E. Nell, eds, *Money in Motion: The Post Keynesian and Circulation Approaches*, London and New York: Macmillan and St. Martin's Press, pp. 400–16.

Walras, L. (1954) *Eléments d'Economie Politique Pure*, trans. W. Jaffé ed., *Elements of Pure Economics*, London: George Allen and Unwin.

PART III

Schools of thought

15

CLASSICAL POLITICAL ECONOMY

Nuno Ornelas Martins

Historical origins and development

Classical Political Economy is a term coined by Karl Marx (1999 [1867]) in order to designate an economic tradition ranging from William Petty to David Ricardo. Marx distinguished the 'classical' economists from the 'vulgar' economists. The vulgar economists were, according to Marx, a group of economists who appeared essentially after Ricardo and focused on superficial phenomena such as supply and demand, rather than on a scientific study of the underlying conditions of socio-economic reproduction as the classical authors had done. Adam Smith is seen as the key figure in classical political economy. However, Marx argues that Smith's thought contains not only valuable scientific insights but also vulgar elements. Hence, Marx distinguishes the exoteric elements in Smith's writings, which constitute its vulgar aspects developed by the vulgar economists, from the esoteric elements in Smith's writings, which contain valuable scientific insights developed by classical economists like Ricardo.

Marx's interpretation of classical political economy was abandoned after Alfred Marshall's (1920 [1890]) reinterpreted classical political economy in a radically different way. Marshall gave supply and demand analysis the central place in his theory, and reinterpreted the conception of Smith and Ricardo as one where supply and demand analysis is the central aspect too. Thus, rather than seeing a break in economic thought after Ricardo, Marshall instead saw continuity and wrote that his own work is in continuity with the contributions of Adam Smith, David Ricardo and John Stuart Mill. But such a reinterpretation means that, for Marshall, classical political economy consists of what Marx called vulgar political economy, that is, a study of supply and demand, rather than of the underlying conditions of socio-economic reproduction, as it should be the case according to Marx.

After Marshall, classical political economy starts to be identified with the set of writers ranging from Adam Smith to John Elliot Cairnes. This leads not only to the reinterpretation of Smith's and Ricardo's contribution in terms of supply and demand analysis, as noted above, but also to the inclusion in classical political economy of authors such as Thomas Robert Malthus, Jean-Baptiste Say, Nassau William

DOI: 10.4324/9781315745992-19

Senior and John Stuart Mill, who Marx saw as vulgar economists that developed a superficial explanation drawing upon supply and demand. Also, it leads to the exclusion from the classical category of authors like Richard Cantillon and François Quesnay, who are then seen as pre-classical authors. For Marx, in contrast, the *Tableau Economique* developed by Quesnay and used by the Physiocrats is essential for a proper understanding of the circular conception of socio-economic reproduction developed by the classical authors.

Value and distribution

To study the socio-economic process of reproduction, the classical authors structured their analysis in terms of the theory of value and distribution. The classical authors took land and labour as the original sources of value. The relative emphasis on land or labour varied across the classical authors. Petty and Cantillon found it useful to measure labour in terms of the quantity of land that is necessary to maintain a labourer for a given amount of time. Quesnay also focused on land and indeed took agriculture to be the source of the whole surplus produced in an economy.

Smith argues, however, that the surplus is produced not only in agriculture but also in other sectors of the economy. This is so because the origin of the surplus is not only land but also human labour. In fact, the division of labour throughout various sectors increases the surplus in various sectors, including in agriculture. Smith starts a new stage in classical analysis, where the emphasis is switched from land to labour. Smith refers to the labour that can be purchased using a given commodity (commanded labour) as the measure of value in exchange, while noting, however, that the source of value comes from the labour spent in the production of the commodity (embodied labour), a fact that, according to Smith, can be seen in a clearer way in primitive societies where virtually no capital is used and little division of labour exists.

But as Smith notes, as the division of labour leads to increasing specialisation it becomes difficult for a given labourer to produce all the commodities used by the labourer. Many commodities will have to be purchased in the market. Therefore, in a society where the division of labour reaches a higher stage, the labour that can be commanded becomes, according to Smith, the more appropriate measure of value, which reflects the power to purchase the labour of others, which is necessary for obtaining the needed commodities in such a society.

From this point onwards, we have an important difference between two different conceptions, with significant implications. Ricardo adopts a conception of value that finds its roots in the underlying conditions of socio-economic reproduction, as a classical political economist should do, according to Marx's conception. Hence, Ricardo takes value to be generated through the embodiment of labour in the (re)production process, and criticises Smith for his references to commanded labour. Malthus, in contrast, adopts a conception of value that finds its roots in market exchange, namely commanded labour, that is, how much labour can be purchased in the market using a given commodity, and argues that this is Smith's position too. In so doing, Malthus follows a route that falls within Marshall's conception of classical political economy, which is, as noted above, equivalent to what Marx called vulgar economy.

A central difference that emerges between Ricardo and Malthus (and the subsequent economic theory) in this process concerns the role of supply and demand.

This difference is, as noted above, the key to Marx's distinction between classical and vulgar political economy. For Ricardo (as for Smith), the natural price is determined by the conditions of production. Supply and demand, in contrast, influence only the variations of the market price around the natural price in an accidental, that is, non-systematic, way. It is for this reason that supply and demand are merely superficial phenomena, which disturb the systematic forces acting at the level of the conditions of production, which constitute the object of study of scientific economics.

For Malthus, in contrast, supply and demand influence not only the variations of the market price but also the underlying natural price. In fact, for Malthus the natural price is measured in commanded labour and thus must be found in market exchange, in a context where the forces of supply and demand play a systematic role. Thus, for Malthus a scientific economic study should be concerned primarily with supply and demand forces, rather than with the conditions of production.

From classical to neoclassical economics

Throughout the 19th century, the more influential branch of political economy followed essentially Malthus's approach. And as noted above, even Smith's and Ricardo's contributions were reinterpreted in terms of Malthus's approach, subsequently developed by Marshall. Hence, market exchange takes centre stage, rather than the (re)production process. Supply and demand start to be seen as the central aspect for an explanation of value.

For Smith and Ricardo, effectual demand is not an independent force, since it is defined with reference to a given natural price (it is the demand of those who can pay the natural price), and the natural price is, in turn, determined by the conditions of production. From Malthus onwards, in contrast, demand starts to be seen as an independent factor that, together with supply, is an ultimate and independent determinant of prices.

An important aspect that appears subsequently is the continuous introduction of subjective elements in the explanation of value. Indeed, once demand is seen as an independent factor, it starts to be seen, quite naturally, as a force which is greatly influenced by independent factors such as subjective preferences. Notions such as subjective desires start to play a central role in the explanation of demand through authors like Hermann Heinrich Gossen and Jules Dupuit, who anticipated many of the ideas that emerged subsequently with the marginal revolution. But subjective elements start also to be introduced in the explanation of the cost of production, especially through authors like John Stuart Mill and John Elliot Cairnes, who interpret the cost of production (labour and capital) in terms of subjective sacrifices.

Nassau William Senior emphasised the notion of abstinence, and also took the first postulate of political economy to be that each agent desires to obtain additional wealth with as little sacrifice as possible, leading to an emphasis on subjective desires as the cornerstone of economic analysis, in contrast to the classical emphasis on objective conditions of socio-economic reproduction. The emphasis on market exchange and subjective elements is further consolidated with the marginal revolution, brought about by William Stanley Jevons, Carl Menger and Léon Walras. After the marginal revolution, value is seen in terms of subjective preferences, and even the classical approach to the cost of production is reinterpreted in terms of subjective elements, most prominently by Marshall.

Thorstein Veblen (1900) coined the term 'neo-classical' in order to designate the contributions which were influenced both by the then 'new' developments in evolutionary theory brought about by Charles Darwin and Herbert Spencer, and by 'classical' economics construed according to Marshall's interpretation, and taking Mill and Cairnes as its key exponents. Veblen took Marshall's contribution to be representative of the best work done within the 'neo-classical' school. Marshall's *Principles of Economics* became indeed the key book used to teach economics and shaped what came to be called neoclassical economics.

The emphasis on market exchange and subjective elements that continued within neoclassical economics brings with it methodological individualism. Subjective preferences are always the preferences of a given individual. The classical emphasis on labour as a source of value, in contrast, pointed towards the labour process, which is a social activity. If we use the contemporary distinction between microeconomics and macroeconomics, we may say that the classical political economists placed emphasis on the macroeconomic process of reproduction, using aggregated quantities when studying the circular flow of income in terms of overall wages, profits and rent. After the marginal revolution, the emphasis is on microeconomic aspects, which are explained in terms of irreducibly subjective preferences. And even macroeconomics is seen by the neoclassical economists as being in need of microeconomic foundations, understood as a commitment to methodological individualism, in contrast to classical political economy, where macroeconomic analysis was undertaken by taking the social class, rather than the human individual, as the central unit of analysis.

Philosophy and methodology

The different conceptions of classical political economy adopted by Marx and Marshall spring from two different methodologies. Marx's methodology is centred on the macroeconomic conditions for socio-economic reproduction, while Marshall's methodology is centred on the microeconomic conditions for partial equilibrium in a given market. Marx and Marshall were both influenced by the philosophy of Friedrich Hegel and developed two different responses to a key problem posed by Hegel's philosophy, the *problem of internal relations*. It is the different responses of Marx and Marshall to the problem of internal relations that leads to their different methodologies and their different interpretations of classical political economy.

An *internal relation* is a relation which is constitutive of the related entities, making the whole more than the sum of its elements. As Tony Lawson (2003, p. 17) notes, 'Aspects or items are said to be internally related when they are what they are, or can do what they do, by virtue of the relations in which they stand'. According to Hegel's philosophy every aspect of reality is internally related to something else. This raises the problem of how we can study a reality which is deeply interconnected. Marx's solution to this problem is to focus on the conditions of socio-economic reproduction as a whole, rather than separating reality into supposedly independent components. In so doing, Marx also interprets classical political economy as a study of the process of socio-economic reproduction as a whole, which found its first systematic elaboration in Quesnay's *Tableau Economique*.

Marshall, in contrast, tries to focus on separate parts of the economic system, such as a concrete market, within what became known as Marshallian partial equilibrium analysis. But in so doing, Marshall struggled with one of the implications of internal relations: if everything is related to something else, how can we achieve knowledge of a given aspect of reality? By focusing only on one aspect, we will be missing its (internal) relations to the whole.

In *Industry and Trade*, Marshall (1923 [1919], pp. 677–8) argues that the differential calculus of Newton and Leibniz provides a solution to this problem: Marshall notes that by looking at infinitesimal changes, we can focus on the direct effects of X on Y, while assuming that the indirect effects of X on Y through Z can be ignored, since the effects of X on Y through Z will be the infinitesimal part of an infinitesimal change, that is, a very small thing of a very small thing (a second order of smalls), which can be ignored, for a time, in the pound of *ceteris paribus*, as Marshall (1920 [1890]) suggested. Marshall was much influenced by the use of differential calculus made in economics by Augustin Cournot and Johann Heinrich von Thünen. Drawing upon differential calculus, Marshall reinterprets previous analyses of supply and demand in terms of supply and demand curves that can be defined using differential calculus, while assuming everything else remains constant.

Piero Sraffa criticised Marshall's approach to internal relations and provided an alternative approach to the problem in line with Marx's original interpretation and development of classical political economy. Rather than focusing on the effects of a given change on another change as Marshall did, Sraffa focuses on the conditions for the reproduction of interconnected economic phenomena at a given moment (a given instant) in time. That is, we abstract from time and look at what Sraffa calls an 'instantaneous photograph' of the economy (see Martins 2013, Chapter 2, for a discussion). For if we allow for the passing of time, everything can change in an internally related world and there is no firm ground for a theory of value.

Sraffa believes that this is the classical method when addressing value: focusing on the conditions of reproduction of the economy as a whole, rather than on the (partial) equilibrium between different components, as Marshall did. But if we want to adopt this method in reality, we need the analogue of an 'instantaneous photograph' that persists through time. We can find this analogue in what Pierangelo Garegnani (1990) calls the 'normal position', which is a position in which certain core components of the economy persist through time, enabling the formation of human conventions, which regulate, for example, ordinary prices, and enable the coordination of socio-economic activity through habit and custom.

Gravitation and historical time

In order to apply the classical theory of value to the real world, we must provide an explanation of how a given normal position is reached. Time must be brought into the analysis. This is done through what Smith called 'gravitation'. However, by gravitation is meant only a vague reference to the process through which a given position is reached. In fact, given the existence of internal relations, it is not possible to provide an exact mathematical model of the process of adjustment of a part of the whole system. This is no problem under the classical conception, since the classical authors restrict the scope of mathematics (of which they use only simple arithmetic) to the study of the core elements for the reproduction of a given position, which Garegnani calls the 'normal' position.

Why 'normal'? Because if any position is to become a centre of gravitation to be reached through an internally related socio-economic process, it must be a reference point for human conventions to emerge, drawing upon (while reinforcing) the more persistent forces of the socio-economic system, which become manifest in the long period, as a normal, or conventional, position. As Garegnani (1990, p. 95) writes, 'The "normal position" may be taken as a typical instance of Pareto's "ideal phenomena" in economics, centred as it is on Adam Smith's "central price", to which "the prices of all commodities are continually gravitating" (1993 [1776], I, p. 51) and therefore providing what Pareto calls here a "general or average fact"'.

General or average facts provide the ground for the formation of human conventions. Gravitation, in turn, is described drawing upon a social analysis of human conventions (or, as the classical authors called it, habit and custom) that cannot be framed into exact mathematical terms, since everything is changing at the same time, and we cannot employ differential calculus to model changes while assuming everything else to remain constant, as if we were in a closed system. Closed systems exist typically in laboratory situations, or in some aspects of celestial mechanics (see Lawson 2003).

As Lawson (2003, Chapter 7) explains, Keynes identified the key methodological problems with the use of mathematical methods early on, noting how the application of mathematical techniques (that presuppose closed systems) outside the context of a controlled experiment presupposes that we are studying a world of independent atoms. Keynes (1936, *CW* VII, pp. 297–8) argued quite explicitly that the study of historical processes subject to uncertainty benefits more from a narrative description of human conventions than from the use of what he called 'symbolic pseudo-mathematical methods of formalising a system of economic analysis' which 'assume strict independence between the factors involved and lose all their cogency and authority if this hypothesis is disallowed'.

Joan Robinson's distinction between historical time and logical time is aimed at noting this methodological problem, related to the difficulties in describing mathematically a process through time. Thus, Joan Robinson (1980, p. 57) notes, while referring, like Sraffa, to instantaneous photographs, that we can take a number of still photographs of economies each in stationary equilibrium, but we cannot flip those photographs 'through a projector to obtain a moving picture of a process of accumulation'.

Robinson notes that it is the confusion between the study of equilibrium (emphasised by Marshall) and the study of a process of accumulation (emphasised by Marx) that leads to this methodological misunderstanding. Thus, Joan Robinson (1980) argues, when referring to the Cambridge Capital Theory Controversies (on which see Harcourt 1972) that reswitching and measuring capital are secondary questions, since, as Cohen and Harcourt (2003, p. 204) note, she believed that 'while reswitching and capital reversing were problematic for neoclassical capital theory, her methodological critique was far more important'.

The Cambridge Capital Theory Controversies led to a revival of classical political economy. According to Sraffa and Robinson the classical approach constitutes a more appropriate basis for macroeconomic theory given the methodological problems noted above. The problems Sraffa (1925, 1926) identified in Marshallian supply and demand analysis are also connected to these methodological issues. In particular, these problems are associated with the tendency to establish monotonic relations, which in neoclassical theory appear as supply and demand curves (for services, goods, labour or capital), so that processes of adjustment through time can be described in a mathematically exact way.

Limits of the use of mathematical analysis

Methodological problems associated with the attempt of subjecting historical processes to mathematical analysis reappeared again in general equilibrium analysis, which was seen, for a time at least, as a way to avoid the critique of Robinson (1953–1954) and Sraffa (1960), as Cohen and Harcourt (2003) argue. In an internally related world where everything can change at the same time, there is no reason to believe that supply and demand for capital, or for any good, can be described by monotonically decreasing demand curves combined with monotonically increasing supply curves. The various mathematical approaches to the process of adjustment towards equilibrium represented in terms of supply and demand curves were in fact found to be inconsistent.

There was never a satisfactory answer to the methodological critique raised by Sraffa and Robinson, which is the central issue at stake. No mathematical explanation of the process of adjustment towards a given price has proved more satisfactory than Adam Smith's vague reference to gravitation towards an ordinary ('normal') price that tends to persist through custom and habit, where this process is explained as an historical sequence grounded on human conventions and explained in terms of ordinary language, rather than resorting to the differential calculus of marginalist economics.

Concluding remarks

The Cambridge Keynesians recognised the methodological problems connected to internal relations and historical time, which underpin the critique raised by Sraffa and Robinson and their revival of classical political economy. But the implications of those methodological problems were never fully understood, not least the fact that a normal position that persists through historical time can be seen as an empirical analogue of an instantaneous photograph. Garegnani (1979) focused on the normal position, Robinson (1979) focused on the instantaneous photograph, and both failed to realise the connection between them, leading eventually to a split in the post-Keynesian camp. This split is an unnecessary one since, as Harcourt (1981) explains, a centre of gravity, taken as the possibility of a sustained rest-state (which is central to Garegnani's development of the Sraffian approach) is quite compatible with, and in fact essential to, the Kaleckian/Keynesian theory of unemployment.

In classical analysis prices are determined for a given set of quantities, in terms of the cost of production. Quantities, in turn, must be determined through another theory, such as the Kaleckian/Keynesian principle of effective demand. In Marshallian supply and demand analysis, in contrast, prices and quantities are determined simultaneously in a supply and demand diagram, and so there is no space for combining the Marshallian approach with a theory of effective demand such as Keynes's or Kalecki's (1971).

Keynes (1936, *CW* VII) adopted Marshall's definition of classical political economy and thus saw the Marshallian-Pigovian neoclassical framework as a continuation of the 'classical' school he criticised. Most economists nowadays also follow the Marshallian reinterpretation of classical political economy, which leads to an emphasis on a microeconomic study of supply and demand, in a market constituted by self-interest agents coordinated by an invisible hand, where there is an automatic tendency towards full employment.

But as Joan Robinson (1980, p. 48) noted, Keynes's *General Theory* had, like Kalecki's theory of employment and Sraffa's own approach, 'much more in common with the classical school of the first half of the nineteenth century than with the neoclassical doctrines in which Keynes himself was brought up'. This connection becomes much clearer once we follow Marx's original interpretation of classical political economy, according to which the classical conception consists of a study of the circular conception of macroeconomic reproduction, focusing on macroeconomic aggregate quantities such as wages, profits and rent.

Under such an interpretation, both classical political economy and Keynesian economics are complementary approaches to the study of the economy in terms of a circular macroeconomic conception. Although contemporary macroeconomics is often seen as a field where the two contending and dominant approaches are called New Classical Macroeconomics (NCM) and New Keynesian Macroeconomics (NKM), the fact is that neither is NCM classical if we take a methodologically informed view, nor is NKM Keynesian in any sense. Rather, both are a one-sided development of Walras' and Marshall's microeconomic approach (where both forget Marshall's concern with realistic analysis) which attempt to establish microeconomic foundations drawing upon a description of human agents which is radically different from the classical or the Keynesian (and also Marshall's, if properly interpreted) emphasis on habit, custom and conventions that cannot be reduced to the interaction of optimising agents.

References

Cohen, A. J. and G. C. Harcourt (2003) 'Whatever happened to the Cambridge capital theory controversies?', *Journal of Economic Perspectives*, 17(1), 199--214.

CW: see Keynes (1971–1989).

Garegnani, P. (1979) 'Notes on consumption, investment and effective demand: A reply to Joan Robinson', *Cambridge Journal of Economics* 3 (3), 181–7.

Garegnani, P. (1990) 'Sraffa: Classical versus marginalist analysis', in K. Bharadwaj and B. Schefold, eds, *Essays on Piero Sraffa Critical Perspectives on the Revival of Classical Theory*, London: Unwin Hyman, pp. 112–41.

Harcourt, G. C. (1972) *Some Cambridge Controversies in the Theory of Capital*, Cambridge, UK: Cambridge University Press.

Harcourt, G. C. (1981) 'Marshall, Sraffa, and Keynes: incompatible bedfellows?' *Eastern Economic Journal* 7, 39–50. Reprinted in P. Kerr (1982). ed., *The Social Science Imperialists: Selected Essays of G.C. Harcourt*, London: Routledge and Kegan Paul, pp. 250–64.

Kalecki, M. (1971) *Selected Essays on the Dynamics of the Capitalist Economy*, Cambridge, UK: Cambridge University Press.

Keynes, J. M. (1936) *The General Theory of Employment, Interest and Money*, CW VII.

Keynes. J. M. (1971–1989) *Collected Writings*, (*CW*), D. E. Moggridge, ed., 30 vols, London: Macmillan and New York: St Martin's Press.

Lawson, T. (2003) *Reorienting Economics*, London: Routledge.

Marshall, A. (1920 [1890]) *Principles of Economics*, London: Macmillan.

Marshall, A. (1923 [1919]) *Industry and Trade*, London: Macmillan.

Martins, N. O. (2013) *The Cambridge Revival of Political Economy*, London and New York: Routledge.

Marx, K. (1999 [1867]) *Capital*, Oxford: Oxford University Press.

Robinson, J. (1953–1954) 'The production function and the theory of capital', *Review of Economic Studies* 21 (2), 81–106.

Robinson, J. (1979) 'Garegnani on effective demand', *Cambridge Journal of Economics* 3 (2), 179–80.

Robinson, J. (1980 [1974]) 'History versus equilibrium', in *Collected Economic Papers* Volume 5. Cambridge, MA: MIT Press, pp. 48–58.

Smith, A. (1993 [1776]) *An Inquiry into the Nature and Causes of the Wealth of Nations*, Oxford: Oxford University Press.

Sraffa, P. (1925) 'Sulle relazioni fra costo e quantita prodotta', *Annali di economia* 2, 277–328.

Sraffa, P. (1926) 'The laws of returns under competitive conditions', *Economic Journal* 36 (144), 535–50.

Sraffa, P. (1960) *Production of Commodities by Means of Commodities: Prelude to a Critique of Economic Theory.* Cambridge, UK: Cambridge University Press.

Veblen, T. (1900) 'The preconceptions of economic science: III', *Quarterly Journal of Economics* 14 (2), 240–69.

16

NEOCLASSICAL MACROECONOMICS

Bert Tieben

Introduction

Macroeconomics is the branch of economic science which studies the operation of the economy as a whole (Chick 1983; Dow 1996). Neoclassical macroeconomics is generally seen as the school which studies macroeconomics through the lens of individual optimising behaviour. In other words, it applies the tools of microeconomics to the study of the economy as a whole and so aims to provide a proper microfoundation for macroeconomics (Weintraub 1979). The result is a focus on equilibrium outcomes; the situation where supply equals demand on all markets simultaneously or general equilibrium. Consequently, neoclassical macroeconomics is also often associated with the main characteristics of general equilibrium theory, such as the axiomatic method and the use of advanced mathematical tools.

Politically this has resulted in a school which was pro-market rather than pro-government in terms of economic policy. Since markets were assumed to clear always, there seemed little scope for fiscal policy or any other form of centralised intervention to steer the macroeconomy towards a higher level of welfare. This feature explained the traditional opposition between neoclassical and Keynesian macroeconomics with regard to economic policy.

This chapter studies the methodology of neoclassical macroeconomics. We shall argue that the methodology of neoclassical macroeconomics is best studied by looking at the history of the theories and schools within macroeconomics that used neoclassical as a label, such as the neoclassical synthesis or neoclassical growth theory in the 1950s. With regard to current approaches there is a growing awareness that neoclassical may not be an appropriate label for methodological inquiries. For example, Davis (2006) argued that modern theories have shifted in a direction which cannot be labelled neoclassical, because they use an empirical rather than a deductive method. Colander (2000) complained that the label neoclassical is often used inconsistently and therefore obfuscates rather than explains what economists do. According to him, especially heterodox schools in economics have a tendency to use the label neoclassical for what they perceive as the orthodoxy without a clear definition of what the orthodoxy is and why it should be called neoclassical.

DOI: 10.4324/9781315745992-20

It appears, then, that as a description of a particular school in modern economics the label neoclassical is adrift. To avoid confusion some even argue that it is best to drop the term neoclassical from our vocabulary altogether (Aspromourgos 1986; Lawson 2013).

In what follows I shall review these criticisms in more detail. They indicate that in our definition of neoclassical macroeconomics we should proceed with care. Without a proper definition, a methodological inquiry of the scope and content of neoclassical macroeconomics seems impossible. I therefore start with a brief analysis of the literature on the methodology of neoclassical economics in general. It is clear that neoclassical originally referred to developments in price theory based on novel concepts such as marginal utility and marginal productivity. I subsequently address the transition of the term neoclassical as a description of theories in the domain of macroeconomics. Lastly, I review the methodology of neoclassical macroeconomics to conclude that its common characteristics are methodological individualism based on the optimising techniques of microeconomics joined to an axiomatic programme which views theoretical equilibrium outcomes as representative of the actual economic situation.[1]

Neoclassical as a label for microeconomics

It is striking that even in the literature which explicitly deals with economic methodology unclarity abounds when it comes to the definition of neoclassical economics. A good example is Blaug (1980 [1992]) in his classic *Methodology of Economics*. In this book Blaug aimed for a methodological appraisal of neoclassical economics as a scientific research programme in the sense of Lakatos. This appraisal consisted of case studies such as the theory of consumer behaviour, the theory of the firm and general equilibrium theory. These theories are said to form 'satellite' programmes 'within a larger core program that is frequently called *neoclassical economics*' (Blaug 1980 [1992], p. 138). However, what constitutes this research programme is not defined and Blaug added that '"mainstream, orthodox" economics would be just as good a label'. In that light it is surprising that one of Blaug's case studies bears the title 'Keynesians versus Monetarists'. Should we infer from this that both Keynesian and monetarist macroeconomics should be seen as part of an all-encompassing neoclassical research programme? Without further explanation we simply do not know.

In other parts of the literature it is apparent that neoclassical is defined as a characteristic of microeconomics. Davis (2006) in an article on 'neoclassical dominance' argued that 'standard competitive marginalist thinking ... has been the mainstay of neoclassicism for many years' (Davis 2006, p. 3).[2] For Morgan and Rutherford (1998) post-war neoclassicism was 'full-fledged general-equilibrium mathematics', which complies to the definition of Rizvi (2003) who focused on constrained optimisation as the 'hallmark of neoclassical economics' (ibid., p. 378). According to Rizvi, this technique was most successfully applied in general equilibrium theory.

Hausman (1992) cast his nets wider. For him general equilibrium theory is just one of the augmentations of a more-encompassing 'equilibrium theory', which is defined in terms of seven laws such as the law of rationality, the law of consumerism, the law of profit maximisation, the law of diminishing rates of substitution and the law of diminishing returns in production. For Hausman (1992, p. 272) 'neoclassical economics is the articulation, elaboration and the application of equilibrium theory', which brings it firmly within the domain of microeconomics, given the nature of these laws of equilibrium theory. Moreover, he seemed to suggest that most modern economists adopt neoclassical economics as a paradigm. As he put it, equilibrium theory is 'absolutely central to the theoretical perspectives, problems and projects of contemporary "orthodox" economists' (ibid., p. 69).

Orthodoxy in this sense is often used as representation of mainstream economics, as Blaug pointed out above. For Colander, Holt and Rosser (2004) mainstream economics 'consists of the ideas that the elite of the profession finds acceptable, where by "elite" we mean the leading economists in the top-graduate schools' (Colander et al. 2004, p. 490). Orthodox is described as an 'intellectual category'. It is a 'backward looking term' which refers to what historians of economic thought have classified as 'the most recently dominant "school of thought" which today is "neoclassical economics"' (ibid.). The subject matter of this school was 'analysis that focuses on the optimising behavior of fully rational and well-informed individuals in a static context and the equilibria that result from that optimisation. It is particularly associated with the marginalist revolution and its aftermath' (ibid.).[3]

Based on this brief review we might infer that neoclassical economics is standard Marshallian price theory adjoined to some notion of Walrasian general equilibrium theory and their modern complements such as expected utility theory. Further, it is noteworthy that neoclassical is often used as a substitute for "mainstream" economics or the "orthodoxy". This practice is confusing when authors do not give a clear definition of neoclassical or mainstream economics. In the following I will discuss several examples of the mix-up between the two terms and try to avoid the term mainstream economics as much as possible. When the term is used, it will solely refer to what others have termed the "mainstream".

The origin of the term neoclassical

The definition of neoclassical economics in terms of several microeconomics theories or "laws" would comply to the historical origin of the term neoclassical, which was introduced by Veblen (1900). Veblen used the term to describe a group of marginalist writers like Jevons, J.B. Clark, Marshall, Cannan and the 'Austrian group'. Marshall was considered the key figure in this group for he best exemplified both the continuation of the classical tradition and the shift towards a new theory of price based on the 'subjectivisation of cost'. This was not seen as a radical departure but as a mere 'improvement upon the earlier doctrine' which is why the term *neo*classical seemed appropriate. Later he also suggested that the common ground with the classical tradition was the utilitarian approach and the assumption of a hedonistic psychology (Aspromourgos 1986, p. 266).

Aspromourgos (1986) argued that the label neoclassical persisted in the literature in the period after 1900, but also underwent change. He credited Hicks and Stigler to have widened the meaning of the term to include all marginalist founders and argued that most economists who used the term in the post-war period probably learnt it from Samuelson's textbook *Economics*, which was first published in 1948 and ran through 19 editions until 2010.

The paradox of neoclassical microeconomics

The paradox of the historical development is that from 1940 onwards the term neo-classical gained in importance, while its meaning became increasingly unclear, if not internally inconsistent. In particular the link with the classical ancestry was loosened to the extent that it can be doubted whether there is a meaningful strain of classical thinking in post-war price theory. Schumpeter (1954) was one of those who never accepted the classical pedigree of the marginalists in the first place. For him the the-oretical advance achieved by the marginalists took them to a different universe.[4] As a result, 'there is no more sense in calling the Jevons-Menger-Walras theory neo-clas-sic than there would be in calling the Einstein theory neo-Newtonian' (Schumpeter 1954, p. 919).

Aspromourgos (1986) followed a similar track when he argued that the theoretical progress in the theory of demand achieved by Hicks and Samuelson severed the link with the classics originally identified by Veblen: the utilitarian approach. Utility was no longer needed in the marginalist theory of value after the introduction of indif-ference curves and revealed preference. Additionally, Aspromourgos objected to the suggestion of doctrinal unity among the early marginalist writers that the notion of a neoclassical school suggests, which in his view was clearly not the case. As a result, his historical exegesis of the origin of the term neoclassical concluded that the term is really a misnomer, which is best entirely expunged from the language.

At this point the paradox emerges that the authors who are said to have built the canon of neoclassical economics in the traditional sense of marginalist microeco-nomic theory were not fond of using the term neoclassical, and in fact hardly used the term at all. From the start Stigler expressed doubt about the appropriateness of the term neoclassical and called it a 'nebulous description' because there was 'no unanimity regarding the term' (Stigler 1941, p. 8). Consequently, he used the term sparingly, and in his classic textbook *Theory of Price* not at all, in spite of its many historical digressions.[5]

Nonetheless his work is seen as that of the arch neoclassical. When Demsetz (1993) reviewed the lifetime achievements of his former colleague, he gave it the title *Mid-century Neoclassicist with a Passion to Quantify* and presented neoclassical theory as the binding element of Stigler's work:

> I shall make the case that his work was strongly guided by a penchant for defend-ing and extending neoclassical price theory. I do not know whether he knew how strong his predilection for neoclassical price theory was, or if he was aware of it all, but the pattern of his work is very consistent with a strong methodological preference of this sort.
>
> *(Demsetz 1993, p. 794)*

His choice of words suggests that Demsetz realised that he offered a reconstruction of Stigler's work in terms of neoclassical price theory. It is a pity that he used a term for this reconstruction which Stigler himself avoided. The latter simply referred to the post-war extensions of marginalist price theory as 'modern price theory'.[6]

Samuelson is likewise seen as an icon of neoclassical economics, especially as it concerns the spread of this doctrine for which his highly successful textbook *Eco-nomics* is deemed instrumental. Giraud (2011) analysed the first ten editions of

Economics and accused Samuelson of political and scientific bias 'in favour of neo-classical analysis' (ibid., p. 2). But in the first edition of *Economics* (Samuelson 1948) the term neoclassical is not used, while the explanation of marginal price theory is relegated to the last chapters of the book. In later editions Samuelson included a family tree of economics and it is here that the term neoclassical emerged in connection to the marginalist revolution of the 1870s. For Samuelson the key element of this revolution was the link between utility and the theory of demand in conjunction with Walras's mathematical analysis of general competitive equilibrium (Samuelson and Nordhaus 1985, p. 762).[7] In this short historical digression he also discussed the policy concerns of neoclassical economics and warned that neoclassical economists should not be seen as 'devotees of laissez-faire'. In contrast 'they want to find better ways for government to help (or stop hindering) economic progress' (ibid., p. 763).[8] In later editions this short historical digression was scrapped from the text, which left the reader with an unexplained family tree of economics on the final page of the book where the term neoclassical economics is attached to the box Walras, Marshall, Fisher, 1880–1910 and seems therefore of historical interest only. But what this history entails the reader was left to find out themselves.[9,10]

Neoclassical as a label for macroeconomics

If neoclassical is mostly seen as a (problematic) label for microeconomics, we need to ask what it means in the context of macroeconomics. Macroeconomics is here understood as the analysis of the economy as a whole, an endeavour which often requires argumentation in terms of economic aggregates like aggregate supply and demand (Chick 1983).

The most obvious connection between macroeconomics in this sense and neoclassical value theory would be the use of general equilibrium analysis which establishes equations for supply and demand in all markets and studies their interconnections. This is the approach of Dow (1996) in her *Methodology of Macroeconomic Thought*. Dow distinguished a broad category of Walrasian and non-Walrasian general equilibrium theory and disequilibrium theory as one of the four major schools in macroeconomics. The common factor of this broad class was 'the use of some kind of general equilibrium framework' (Dow 1996, p. 5). It has to be noted that Dow described this school as 'mainstream economics', not as neoclassical economics. This latter term is defined historically and refers to 'the English tradition emphasising utility theory' which was one of the currents of the marginalist revolution (ibid., p. 57).

But very often mainstream is taken as synonymous to neoclassical. Jespersen (2009) is a case in point. He distinguished two methodologies in macroeconomics: one based on the neoclassical general equilibrium model, the other on Post-Keynesian theory which relies on causal relationships and path-dependent analysis. The key to neoclassical macrotheory in this sense was a 'well-functioning and equilibrium-creating macroeconomic system ... the idealized basis model built on the assumption of rational expectations' (ibid., p. 14). This standard model was carried forward by different sub-schools, which according to Jespersen have dominated the post-war period at one time or another. This includes old-style Keynesianism based on the neoclassical synthesis (Hicks, Patinkin, Samuelson), monetarism (Friedman), new classical economics (Kydland, Lucas, Prescott) and New-Keynesian economics (Mankiw, Phelps).

The axiomatic approach as a defining characteristic

Such a broad category of neoclassical macroeconomics begs the question whether the theories it encompasses were actually bound by a common neoclassical methodology. Colander et al. (2004) described the methodological prescripts of the school as follows: Testing of theoretical results by means of 'conventional econometric techniques that are based upon a foundation of classical statistics [...] Perhaps the most important characteristic of the neoclassical orthodoxy is that axiomatic deduction is the preferred methodological approach' (Colander et al. 2004, p. 491).

Indeed, it was Lawson (2013) who most strongly argued that axiomatic deduction is the key characteristic of the neoclassical school, which for him represents a strategy of mathematical modelling. 'The defining feature of the mainstream is the *insistence* on methods of mathematical modelling' (ibid., p. 957, original emphasis). For Lawson this methodology is highly problematic, since it implicitly assumes an ontology of a closed system (or world) made up of isolated atomistic individuals.[11] This causes irreparable damage to the neoclassical programme, since Lawson claimed that the second defining characteristic is the general recognition that social reality portrays an open-processual nature (ibid., p. 976).[12] The ontology of neoclassical economics thus collides with the implicit assumptions of their methodology. This finding underpins his conclusion that neoclassicism has a 'debilitating' impact on the profession and should preferably be dropped (ibid., p. 951).[13]

There are solid reasons to argue that the axiomatic approach has been a main characteristic of post-war macroeconomics in several schools of thought. The neoclassical synthesis is a case in point, since it incorporated the Keynesian model into a general equilibrium framework (Patinkin 1956).[14] For Patinkin this was the logical way forward: 'For since monetary changes are assumed to affect all markets of the economy, their effects can be fully appreciated only by a simultaneous study of all these markets' (Patinkin 1956, p. 2). But he did not anticipate the loss of those aspects which later Post-Keynesians considered vital to Keynes's construction of the *General Theory*: fundamental uncertainty and the indeterminacy of macroeconomic outcomes.[15]

Later development of the Keynesian model merely worked to increase the degree of formalism in macroeconomics. Unemployment equilibrium requires that at least one market fails to clear, which collides with the idea of a general equilibrium. This point was taken up by Clower (1965) who added quantity constraints to the Keynesian model as a reflection of the fact that producers and consumers know that markets do not clear and incorporate this constraint into their decisions. The resulting fixed-price models introduced the representative agent into macroeconomics, a first step to provide microfoundations for macroeconomic theory. This project can be defined as the effort to reconcile macroeconomics and its analysis in terms of aggregates with microeconomics and its explanation of individual decision-making (Weintraub 1979).

New Classical economics responded to the challenge of Keynesian economics with models based on rational expectations. This assumption provided the next step in the microfoundations discussion. The effort to ground macroeconomics in microeconomic behaviour was considered so important that most theoretical developments in macroeconomics for some 30 years were aimed at solving this question (Dow 1996, p. 87). For example, New-Keynesians also started to use rational expectations in their models and developed theoretical arguments for the fixed-price assumption in terms of imperfect competition, strategic complementarities or menu-costs and the like (Mankiw and Romer 1991).

The point to stress here is the modelling strategy, which became increasingly mathematical and embedded in the axiomatic framework of general equilibrium analysis. As Weintraub (1979, p. 158) put it, 'any analysis which could even potentially serve as a piece of the microfoundations of macroeconomics story will involve a general equilibrium theoretic perspective'. The end result may have been logically consistent due to the general equilibrium framework and the use of the rational expectations hypothesis; it also came at a cost. Rational expectations presuppose equilibrium at the individual level so that the macroeconomic model can be built up from below. This secures consistency between the microeconomic basis and the macroeconomic outcome.

> In modern neoclassical analytical practice, "rational expectations formation" is an indispensable, model-based precondition for ensuring consistency between the sum of the rational, individually decided actions of the representative agents and the general equilibrium solution. In such models there is a predesigned coincidence between the micro-level and the aggregated macro-level.
>
> *(Jespersen 2009, p. 183)*

The cost of this success is the very factor which Keynes deemed the defining characteristic of macroeconomics: the fallacy of composition. This fallacy presents macroeconomic outcomes as the unintended result of decisions taken at the micro level. No one aims for a recession, but if individuals simultaneously increase their savings as a precaution in uncertain times, the result is a lack of effective demand which may push the economy into a state of recession. The general equilibrium framework precludes this kind of problems, since actual trading is suspended until a price vector is found to equate supply to demand in all sectors of the economy simultaneously. Based on rational expectations, individuals have adjusted their behaviour accordingly (they know the general equilibrium price vector), which precludes disappointment. Consequently, neoclassical macroeconomics requires an outside factor to generate meaningful short-run macroeconomic dynamics of the kind which causes inflation, unemployment etc. Such factors may be genuine surprises such as ad hoc and unforeseen policies or technology shocks, although even these can be endogenised in terms of a probability distribution as real business cycle theory has demonstrated.

The axiomatic approach in economics reached levels which Blaug (2003) called 'extreme'. This included several domains of macroeconomics. For Blaug the 'undisputed example' of formalism in the 1950s was growth theory of the Solow-Swan variety, generally described as neoclassical growth theory (Hoover 2003). In the Solow-Swan growth model firms adjust their inputs to reflect relative factor prices, which makes it neoclassical in comparison to earlier growth models of the Harrod-Domar type based on the assumption of fixed technology. The Solow-Swan growth model put the study of steady-state growth centre stage: equiproportionate increases in all the relevant economic variables into the indefinite feature. But where is steady-state growth in reality? There was now and then no empirical proof that actual economies are ever on a growth path characteristic of a steady state. Neoclassical growth theory dealt with a classroom exercise which is so abstract that even leading practitioners of growth theory have later questioned its validity. Blaug (2003, p. 405) cited Hicks on this matter, who said that 'they are shadows of real problems, dressed up in such a way that by pure logic we can find solutions for them'.

Empirical testing

Theoretical reasoning in neoclassical macroeconomics has a complement: empirical testing. Post-war macroeconomics developed econometric testing as a separate discipline. This discipline consisted of large structural macroeconometric models to a large extent developed in conjunction with the IS-LM model.[16] But such models were not intended as critical tests of macroeconomic theory. Economic theory was predominantly used to identify the estimated relationships. Time-series econometrics appealed even less to a priori theory. Since the 1980s structural VAR (vector autoregression) has become the key approach of macroeconomic research (Hoover 2003).[17]

There is a large measure of uncertainty about the exact role of empirical tests in post-war macroeconomics. The influence of Friedman's classic essay 'The Methodology of Positive Economics' (1953) has created an image that predictive power was key in empirical economics. This would imply a strong link between hypothesis formation on the basis of macroeconomic theory and the subsequent effort to either corroborate or dispel such hypotheses in terms of forecasting or backcasting. In part this notion is true. Blaug (1980 [1992], p. 205) argued that since the publication of the *General Theory* the driving force of macroeconomics was 'the pursuit of empirical validation'. The acceptance of Keynesian macroeconomics in the 1950s was a case in point. 'If Keynes's empirical predictions had been refuted, not once but again and again, they would soon have ceased to subscribe to Keynesianism despite all of its attractive trappings' (ibid.). But he remained nonetheless critical of the role of empirical testing in economics. According to Blaug, the main problem is that economists in general do not practice what they preach. Even when they claim that they are willing to abandon their theories in the face of conflicting empirical evidence, they seldom actually do so.[18] In general the empirical task is to corroborate rather than falsify the theory's predictions, a practice which Blaug described as 'playing tennis with the net down' (ibid., p. 241). Applied econometrics is flexible enough to allow researchers to select the best fit of a regression equation to the data and rationalise this finding in term of theory afterwards. In other words, finding empirical support for one's theory is easy, trying to dispel it very difficult.

There are many reasons why this strategy of what Blaug called 'innocuous falsificationism' persists. The first one is unwillingness to submit theories to critical empirical tests. In macroeconomics the capital debate is a typical example. This debate was a conflict between proponents of Post-Keynesian growth theory such as Robinson and Pasinetti and proponents of neoclassical growth theory (also known as the clash of the two Cambridges). The issue was about the possibility of capital-reversing and capital-reswitching which would invalidate the use of neoclassical aggregate production functions.[19] This debate was able to divide the ranks of economists for almost 20 years, because the proponents approached it as an exclusively theoretical controversy which needed a logical resolution. No one ever asked whether capital-reversal and -reswitching would ever actually occur and, if so, under what conditions. Blaug (1975) argued that it is well possible to treat capital-reversal and -reswitching as empirical propositions, but an empirical test to discriminate between the rival capital theories was never attempted. The battle ground remained strictly theorical which allowed the debate to drag on as ever more sophisticated arguments pro or con capital-reversal and -reswitching were being developed.[20]

The second reason why testing in macroeconomics remains undervalued is that the nature of economic data does not allow critical tests. Critical tests would allow economists to sharply distinguish between theories that are successful in terms of their predictive power and those that are not. We lack reliable data and powerful techniques to dispel unsuccessful theoretical propositions for once and all. It is not uncommon that different econometric studies reach conflicting conclusions. Consequently, conflicting theories may coexist for a long time, sometimes decades as we have seen.[21] This explains the survival of neoclassical macroeconomics, such as Solow-Swan growth theory and its successors, in spite of its poor empirical record.[22]

A third reason why empirical tests are not decisive in economics is the political aspect. Rosenberg (1992) interpreted general equilibrium theory as an implicit contractarian political philosophy, since it allows economists to argue that optimising individual decisions support welfare at the aggregated level, even though no single agent deliberately seeks to further this goal. In other words, by using general equilibrium theory, economists express their belief in the social contract as being essentially beneficial. According to Rosenberg, it is this implicit political philosophy which explains why economists insulate general equilibrium theory from economic data. He concluded that economics is best seen as applied mathematical politics, but not as science.

Rosenberg's conclusion applied to general equilibrium theory as the heart of microeconomics, but the microfoundations debate means it affects macroeconomics as well. Moreover, as Blaug (1980 [1992]) argued economic theory offers more than methods of scientific discovery. Especially in macroeconomics there is a close link between theoretical analysis and government policies. Emerging or sustained success in the policy arena may then motivate economists to ignore negative empirical results.

The methodology of neoclassical macroeconomics

What do these insights mean for the methodology of neoclassical macroeconomics? A first conclusion is that with regard to microeconomics the term neoclassical generally refers to the development of marginalist theories of price, but is found problematic as a common denominator of these theories. Thus Colander (2000) listed six methodological characteristics of neoclassical economics such as the focus on allocation as a research problem, the focus on marginal trade-offs, methodological individualism and the assumption of rationality as a behavioural postulate. He then concluded that these attributes do not adequately describe modern economics, which means that the neoclassical school does not exist. In fact he argued that the movement away from neoclassical economics already started in the 1930s.

Others like Davis (2006) support the analysis of Colander, but see the decline of neoclassical economics as a more recent event, spurred on by developments in game theory, behavioural economics and complexity theory. Although the difference with Colander may not be as large as it seems, given that the latter proposed the term 'new millennium economics' as a substitute for neoclassical.

Whatever the timing, the fact remains that there is a growing consensus in the economics profession that the dominant neoclassical school no longer exists, or at least should not be called neoclassical. Blaug represents a good example of this shift. In 1980 he focused his methodology of economics on what he called the mainstream, neoclassical school and did not even bother to define what it meant. In 2003 he found the use of the label neoclassical for both pre-war and post-war orthodox economics 'doubly confusing', because from an analytical point of view most of the post-war developments was incomparable to the achievements of earlier marginalist economists.[23] Hence he used the term 'formalist revolution' to indicate the clear break with the past that occurred after 1945. It is therefore not surprising that modern textbooks in the history of economic thought like Dupont (2017) do not use the label neoclassical economics at all.

If the use of the prefix neoclassical in microeconomics is open to criticism, then the situation in macroeconomics is even worse. The application of general equilibrium analysis and the search for the microfoundations of macroeconomics inspired commentators to label part of post-war macroeconomics as neoclassical. But the exact boundaries of neoclassical macroeconomics are impossible to draw. Jespersen (2009) subsumed a large part of post-war macroeconomics under this heading, including the neoclassical synthesis and modern extensions like new classical and New-Keynesian macroeconomics. But for Colander (2000) Keynesian economics was clearly outside the purview of what he saw as neoclassical. He stated that 'Keynesian macroeconomics has few of the characteristics attributed to neoclassical economics' (ibid., p. 133).[24] Weintraub (1979) in his review of the microfoundations literature used the term neo-Walrasian programme, since the general equilibrium framework had been the starting point of this branch of economics. It is unknow why we should organise schools of thought with very different and sometimes conflicting attributes under a general label called neoclassical.

The answer of Lawson (2013) to the last question would be method. The common element of methodological assessments of post-war macroeconomics is the axiomatic method and the focus on logical deduction. But the axiomatic method does not allow us to distinguish sharply between schools of thought in a historically meaningful way. Neo-Marxian analysis based on Sraffa (1960) is generally just as axiomatic in its approach as general equilibrium theory (Blaug 2003; 2008). Lawson's (2013) methodological exegesis of the neoclassical school likewise leads him to conclude that it encompasses a wide variety of theories and traditions including economists who will self-identify as heterodox, because they all apply mathematical modelling.[25]

Empirical methods will not help to draw a sharper line between the schools of thought in macroeconomics. Macroeconometric modelling has developed techniques which transcend the schools. Structural VARs are widely employed by new classicals, Keynesians and even heterodox macroeconomists (Hoover 2003, p. 425). Calibration was developed as a technique for real business cycle analysis, but can in principle be used for other fields where microeconometrics provides input for the numerical analysis of aggregate time series through model simulation (Hansen and Heckman 1996). There is no empirical method which separates neoclassical macroeconomics from the rest of the profession or it must be the unwillingness to critically test the theory's core assumptions like rationality and equilibrium, but even this attitude is shared by the profession at large as Blaug (1980 [1992]) has demonstrated.

This conclusion may lead us to ask why the term neoclassical gained popularity in the first place. It is very likely that the capital controversy greatly facilitated the spread of the label neoclassical economics. As Aspromourgos (1986) pointed out, Joan Robinson's *Collected Papers* are liberally peppered with the term. She added methodological critique to the theoretical debate on capital because of the reliance of neoclassical theory on the notion of static equilibrium, which contrasted with her perception of an ever-changing economic reality. According to Robinson (1962, 1974), this reality should be seen as an open and undetermined process. It was also the capital debate which may have inspired the use of the label neoclassical as the opponent for heterodox schools in economics. In this interpretation neoclassical represents what the heterodox schools are not: a science dominated by equilibrium models resting upon unrealistic assumptions, which merely serve the purpose of enabling a tractable mathematical solution and a host of other properties deemed undesirable. Dow (1996) is an example of this practice. She defined 'mainstream economics' as a broad group which is united by the fact that they use 'some kind of general equilibrium framework' (ibid., p. 5). She then added that there is 'another way of understanding mainstream economics in the negative sense of non-political economy' (ibid.). For Dow Neo-Austrian, Post-Keynesian and Marxian theory represent political economy. But she did not explain what political economy in this context means and in what sense mainstream economics does not comply with the criteria of political economy. The label merely served to draw a line between mainstream and thus orthodox economics and rival heterodox schools of thought.

From a methodological perspective the use of the label neoclassical by heterodox economists to describe "the opponent" is unwanted. If we accept Blaug's (1980 [1992]) definition of methodology as both a descriptive discipline – 'this is what most economists do' – and a prescriptive one, which addresses what economists should do (ibid., xii), then the orthodox/heterodox division does not promote methodological analysis. The definition of neoclassical economics in a negative sense leads economists to define it as what they believe that the rest of the profession is doing with the objective of carving out one's own research programme as the exact opposite. This too easily leads to a straw man representation of what the orthodoxy or neoclassical economics represents. In part Colander (2000) proposed to drop the label neoclassical economics from the vocabulary in order to prevent its use as the target for heterodox economists, which merely increases the confusion about what it actually means.

The end result is, therefore, that we have to be careful with a definition of the neoclassical school in macroeconomics and the methodology associated with it. There is sufficient ground to limit the scope of neoclassical macroeconomics to neoclassical growth theory of the Solow-Swan type. The work done in this field was consistent enough to be able to speak of a research programme in the sense of Lakatos (Cavusoglu and Tebaldi 2006). In addition, the pioneers of the theory self-identified as promoting a neoclassical approach to the study of economic growth (e.g. Solow 1956).[26] The publication of the model started a long period of debate in economics which critically compared the neoclassical theory of growth to the more classical-inspired alternatives developed in Cambridge, UK. In a sense the capital debate takes us back to the 1870s when the pioneers of neoclassical economics started to develop their marginalist alternative to classical value theory. As Cohen and Harcourt (2003, p. 208) summarised the debate:

While neoclassical economics envisions the lifetime utility-maximizing consumption decisions of individuals as the driving force of economic activity, with the allocation of given, scarce resources as the fundamental economic problem, the "English" Cantabrigians argue for a return to a classical political economy vision. There, profit-making decisions of capitalist firms are the driving force, with the fundamental economic problem being the allocation of surplus output to ensure reproduction and growth.

Lastly, neoclassical growth theory went hand in hand with an empirical programme to investigate the sources of economic growth called growth accounting. The characteristic of this programme was that the theoretical properties of the neoclassical growth model carried over to the interpretation of economic reality: observed growth paths were seen as equilibrium growth paths in line with the requirements of the neoclassical growth model. The theoretical model thus became a model of the actual capitalist world, as Solow (1988, p. 310) in his Nobel lecture acknowledged. This is the best example of the union between the axiomatic method and the perception of economic reality as a closed equilibrium system, which Lawson (2013) identified as the methodological characteristics of the neoclassical school.

Other branches of macroeconomics certainly share one or more of the attributes of neoclassical economics, but are better described via labels more closely linked to their intellectual ancestry like neo-Walrasian and New-Keynesian or are best represented by a label which indicates a time period like Post-Classical and New-Millennium economics.

Notes

1 The term 'equilibrium' requires an explicit definition, as is explained in the chapter on the notion of equilibrium in this handbook (Tieben 2023). In neoclassical economics equilibrium generally refers to the equality of supply and demand on all markets simultaneously or general equilibrium. When a different definition of equilibrium is used in this chapter, for example equilibrium seen as a steady state, I shall indicate this in the text.
2 It has to be noted that Davis explicitly denounced the task of discussing the meaning of neoclassical economics.
3 They referred to Leon Walras and Alfred Marshall as its 'early and great developers' and Hicks' *Value and Capital* and Samuelson's *Foundations of Economic Analysis* as its 'culmination'.
4 The word universe is used deliberately. Schumpeter (1954, p. 919) compared the replacement of the classic by the marginal utility system to the replacement of the geocentric by the heliocentric system. For Schumpeter, they were performances of the same kind: 'essentially simplifying and unifying reconstructions'.
5 I have checked the 1949 edition and the 1987 edition (Stigler 1987).
6 A good example is his description in his memoirs of the development of microeconomics at the Chicago school (Stigler 1988, p. 162).
7 This example is taken from the 12th edition of *Economics*.
8 Giraud (2011) argued that Samuelson deliberately developed a middle of the road stance with regard to government intervention to suit his readership and prevent political problems with both his own institution (MIT) and McCarthyist right-wing activists.
9 This example is taken from the 19th and last edition of *Economics* (Samuelson and Nordhaus 2010). The only other place where Samuelson uses the term neoclassical in this edition is when he discusses growth theory.
10 We could add Hicks as another example of the paradox of the neoclassical nomenclature. In his classic *Value and Capital* (1939) the word neoclassical is not used. Later he

expressed his dislike of the term. He considered using the title *Classics and Neo-Classics* for his collection of essays in economic theory, but argued that the term neo-classics had become blurred to the extent that it just caused confusion. He attributed this blurring to the overuse of the term by 'modern controversialists'. Since he wanted to use the term in its historical meaning, he substituted the term post-classical for neo-classical. See Hicks (1983, pp. xiii–xiv).

11 '[S]uccessful application of economists' mathematical tools requires event regularities or correlations. Systems in which such event regularities occur can be called *closed*' (Lawson 2013, p. 953, emphasis in the original).

12 This characterisation was partly based on the historical use of the term neoclassical by Veblen (1900). According to Lawson, Veblen identified especially Marshall as neoclassical for the fact that he could be seen as a midway figure between the classical school and their deductive method and the budding evolutionary approach. As Veblen himself put it, 'the work of the neo-classical economics might be compared ... with that of the early generation of Darwinians. [...] The prime postulate of evolutionary science ... is the notion of cumulative causative science' (Veblen 1900, pp. 265–266).

13 This historical reading is intriguing and amends the conclusions of Asproumorgos' historical exegesis of the origin of the term neoclassical.

14 It was Samuelson who gave this approach the name "neoclassical synthesis", see Blaug (2003), p. 407.

15 It has to be stressed that for Patinkin the neoclassical feature of his reconstruction of Keynesian macrotheory was the money demand function. He defined neoclassical as the shorthand designation for the cash-balance approach to monetary theory. See Patinkin (1956, p. 96).

16 Hoover (2003) reviewed post-war macroeconomics and concluded that nearly every post-war model was an elaboration of the IS-LM model, which reflected the mutual adaptation of the Keynesian model and the national accounting conventions that governed data collection.

17 Morgan (1990) has demonstrated that the early pioneers in econometric research such as Tinbergen were keenly aware of the theory-development and theory-testing roles of statistical research. She described the change in the notion of an econometric model in the post-war period as follows: 'Econometric models came to be regarded as the passive extensions of economic theory into the real world, as the statistical complements of pure economics' (ibid., p. 264).

18 Based on his interviews with the leading New-Classical macroeconomists in the 1980s and their counterparts, Klamer (1984) drew the same conclusion.

19 The Solow-Swan theory of economic growth treats the rate of interest as a function of the relative scarcity of capital in the economy. Capital is thus treated as a commodity like any other, which means that its allocation can be efficiently handled by the price mechanism. In contrast, the Keynesians would argue that capital is heterogenous and that the rate of interest is determined simultaneously with the value of the capital stock. The rate of interest can therefore not be used as an explanatory variable for the value of capital.

20 Looking back, Solow (1988, p. 309) said that he felt 'trapped' in the debate and that with hindsight the whole controversy had been 'a waste of time, a playing-out of ideological games in the language of analytical economics'. For reviews of the debate see Harcourt (1972), Blaug (1975) and Cohen and Harcourt (2003).

21 The increasing popularity of calibration techniques is testimony to the difficulty of designing decisive empirical tests in macroeconomics. Calibration is not a statistical test, but a simulation technique which involves the informal comparison of conclusions of model-based numerical simulation to actual data. See Hansen and Heckman (1996) for a description.

22 The Solow-Swan growth model inspired a specific empirical branch of research called growth accounting to decompose the drivers of economic growth. Looking back, Solow (1988) concluded that by and large this literature corroborated the main finding of his original studies of the 1950s, namely that technological progress explains circa 80%–90% of economic growth. This implies that growth is to a certain extent a black box, since technological progress is an external factor in Solow's model (the infamous 'residue').

Endogenous growth theory developed in the 1980s sought to remedy this defect, but does not command empirical support. See Cavusoglu and Tebaldi (2006).

23 He meant that pre-war economists would literally not understand works like Samuelson's *Foundations of Economic Analysis* (1947). See Blaug (2003), p. 396.

24 For him in the 1950s and 1960s macroeconomics was the essence of pragmatic eclectic modelling. These models lacked an explicit microfoundation. New-Keynesian models do incorporate rationality, but are seen by Colander as partial equilibrium models.

25 What matters most to Lawson is the conjunction of mathematical modelling and the belief that social reality is of an open-processual nature.

26 We should be careful not to conflate the person with the paradigm. When asked by Klamer whether he considered himself a Keynesian, Solow answered: 'That is true. I have no problem with that. Pretty clearly, I am also a neoclassical economist' (Klamer 1984, p. 131).

References

Aspromourgos, T. (1986) 'On the origin of the term "neoclassical"', *Cambridge Journal of Economics* 10 (3), 265–70.

Blaug, M. (1975) *The Cambridge Revolution: Success or Failure? A Critical Analysis of Cambridge Theories of Value and Distribution*, Revised Edition, London: Institute of Economic Affairs.

Blaug, M. (1980 [1992]) *The Methodology of Economics*, Second edition, Cambridge, UK: Cambridge University Press.

Blaug, M. (2003) 'The formalist revolution of the 1950s', in W. J. Samuels, J. E. Biddle and J. B. Davis, eds, *A Companion to the History of Economic Thought*, Oxford: Blackwell, pp. 395–410.

Blaug, M. (2008) 'The trade-off between rigour and relevance: Sraffian Economics as a case in point', *History of Political Economy* 41 (2), 219–47.

Cavusoglu, N. and E. Tebaldi (2006) 'Evaluating growth theories and their empirical support: An assessment of the convergence hypothesis', *Journal of Economic Methodology* 13 (1), 49–75.

Chick, V. (1983) *Macroeconomics after Keynes*, Cambridge, MA: MIT Press.

Clower, R. W. (1965) 'The Keynesian counter-revolution: A theoretical appraisal' in F. Hahn and F. Brechling, eds, *The Theory of the Interest Rate*, London: Macmillan, pp. 103–25.

Cohen, A. J. and G. C. Harcourt (2003) 'Retrospectives: Whatever happened to the Cambridge capital theory controversies?', *Journal of Economic Perspectives* 17 (1), 199–214.

Colander, D. (2000) 'The death of neoclassical economics', *Journal of the History of Economic Thought* 22 (2), 127–43.

Colander, D., R. Holt, and B. Rosser Jr. (2004) 'The changing face of mainstream economics', *Review of Political Economy* 16 (4), 485–99.

Davis, J. B. (2006) 'The turn in economics: Neoclassical dominance to mainstream pluralism', *Journal of Institutional Economics* 2 (1), 1–20.

Demsetz, H. (1993) 'George J. Stigler: Midcentury Neoclassicalist with a passion to quantify', *Journal of Political Economy* 101 (5), 793–808.

Dow, S. C. (1996) *The Methodology of Macroeconomic Thought, A Conceptual Analysis of Schools of Thought in Economics*, Cheltenham: Edward Elgar.

Dupont, B. (2017) *The History of Economic Ideas*, London: Routledge.

Friedman, M. (1953) *Essays in Positive Economics*, Chicago, IL: University of Chicago Press.

Giraud, Y. (2011) 'The political economy of textbook writing: Paul Samuelson and the making of the first ten editions of economics (1945–1976)', Thema Working Paper nr. 2011–18, Université de Cergy Pontoise.

Hansen, L. P. and J. J. Heckman (1996) 'The empirical foundations of calibration', *Journal of Economic Perspectives* 10 (1), 87–104.

Harcourt, G. C. (1972) *Some Cambridge Controversies in the Theory of Capital*, Cambridge, UK: Cambridge University Press.

Hausman, D. M. (1992) *The Inexact and Separate Science of Economics*, Cambridge, UK: Cambridge University Press.

Hicks, J. R. (1939) *Value and Capital*, Oxford: Clarendon.

Hicks, J. R. (1983) *Classics and Modern: Collected Essays on Economic Theory*, volume III, Cambridge, MA: Harvard University Press.

Hoover, K. (2003) 'A history of Postwar monetary economics and macroeconomics', in W. J. Samuels, J. E. Biddle and J. B. Davis, eds, *A Companion to the History of Economic Thought*, Oxford: Blackwell, pp. 411–27.

Jespersen, J. (2009) *Macroeconomic Methodology. A Post-Keynesian Perspective*, Cheltenham: Edward Elgar.

Klamer, A. (1984) *The New Classical Macroeconomics, Conversations with New Classical Economists and their Opponents*, Brighton: Wheatsheaf.

Lawson, T. (2013) 'What is this 'school' called neoclassical economics?' *Cambridge Journal of Economics* 37 (5), 947–83.

Mankiw, N. G. and D. Romer (1991) *New Keynesian Economics*, 2 vols., Cambridge, MA: MIT Press.

Morgan, M. S. (1990) *The History of Econometric Ideas*, Cambridge, UK: Cambridge University Press.

Morgan, M. and M. Rutherford, eds (1998) *From Interwar Pluralism to Postwar Neoclassicism*, annual supplement to *History of Political Economy*, vol. 30, Durham and London: Duke University Press.

Patinkin, D. (1956) *Money, Interest, and Prices*, Evanston, IL: Row, Petersen and Company.

Rizvi, S. A. (2003) 'Postwar neoclassical microeconomics', in W. J. Samuels, J. E. Biddle and J. B. Davis, eds, *A Companion to the History of Economic Thought*, Oxford: Blackwell, pp. 377–94.

Robinson, J. (1962) *Economic Philosophy*, London: C.A. Watts.

Robinson, J. (1974) 'History versus equilibrium', *Indian Economic Journal* 21 (3), 202–13.

Rosenberg, A. (1992) *Economics: Mathematical Politics or Science of Diminishing Returns*, Chicago, IL: University of Chicago Press.

Samuelson, P. A. (1948) *Economics*, first edition, New York: McGraw Hill.

Samuelson, P. A. and W. Nordhaus (1985) *Economics*, twelfth edition, New York: McGraw Hill.

Samuelson, P. A. and W. Nordhaus (2010) *Economics*, nineteenth edition, New York: McGraw Hill.

Schumpeter, J. (1954) *History of Economic Analysis*, London: Allen & Unwin.

Solow, R. M. (1956) 'A contribution to the theory of economic growth', *Quarterly Journal of Economics* 70 (1), 65–94.

Solow, R. M. (1988) 'Growth theory and after', *American Economic Review* 78 (3), 307–17.

Sraffa, P. (1960) *Production of Commodities by Means of Commodities: Prelude to a Critique of Economic Theory*, Cambridge, UK: Cambridge University Press.

Stigler, G. J. (1941) *Production and Distribution Theories: The Formative Period*, New York: Macmillan.

Stigler, G. J. (1987) *The Theory of Price*, Fourth edition, New York: Macmillan.

Stigler, G. J. (1988) *Memoirs of an Unregulated Economist*, New York: Basic Books.

Tieben, B. (2023) 'Equilibrium', in V. Chick, J. Jespersen and B. Tieben, eds, *Handbook of Macroeconomic Methodology*, London: Routledge, pp. 108–120.

Veblen, T. (1900) 'The preconceptions of economic science III', *Quarterly Journal of Economics* 14 (2), 240–69.

Weintraub, E. R. (1979) *Microfoundations: The compatibility of microeconomics and macroeconomics*, Cambridge, UK: Cambridge University Press.

17

KEYNES'S MACROECONOMIC METHOD

Victoria Chick and Jesper Jespersen

Keynes's lifelong struggle with macroeconomic method[1]

John Maynard Keynes (1883–1946) was born in Cambridge, England. He was enrolled in 1902 at King's College, Cambridge, where philosophy and ethics claimed his attention more than the subject he was reading: mathematics. Keynes was influenced by the philosophy of G.E. Moore, for whom the contemplation of beauty and the enjoyment of friendship were the true purposes of life. Under the influence of Moore, he developed an Ideal, which included not only Moore's concept of the good life, but also the acknowledgement that nothing in personal life or society can be considered as certain. This poses a challenge both to ethical conduct and to the meaning we are able to attach to knowledge about the future and, hence in the end to the meaning of Rationality.

In any case, Keynes took a first-class degree in mathematics in 1905 and then spent two years in the India Office. Here, he found the work boring and began to write a dissertation on *probability theory and rational beliefs*. Moore's answer to the ethical problem related to uncertainty had been an acceptance of social convention as the repository of accumulated wisdom. Keynes's critique of this position led him to develop a theory of rationality under uncertainty, which he first submitted to King's College as a fellowship dissertation in 1908. It was published in 1921 as *A Treatise on Probability* (hereafter *TP*).

While an undergraduate, Keynes developed the philosophical foundations on which his economic thinking stands, but went on through his academic life exploring its ramifications. It took a long time for the philosophical thinking of *TP* to become fully incorporated into his macroeconomic theory – not until *The General Theory*, presumably. His journey through economic analysis to this point, where at last his earliest work and his mature (but unfortunately) last book are united, is a long and tortuous one and documented in five books from 1913, *Indian Currency and Finance* to 1930, *A Treatise on Money* together with numerous academic and more popular papers reprinted in *CW*.[2]

DOI: 10.4324/9781315745992-21

Keynes's challenges: *uncertainty* and *persistent unemployment*

It is telling of the view among even established Keynes-scholars that the Collected Writings of John Maynard Keynes originally was planned, back in the early 1970s, not to include his fellow dissertation on 'probability theory', which Keynes, on his own initiative, published in 1921 as *Treatise on Probability*. In the 1970s, this book was considered as not relevant for scholars taking an interest into Keynes's economics.[3] Fortunately, this decision was challenged by among others Post-Keynesian scholars[4] who pointed out the close connection between Keynes's work on uncertainty/ probability and the new methodology to analyse the macroeconomics of reality as presented in *The General Theory of Employment, Interest and Money* (hereafter *GT*, Keynes 1936 [1973]).

In an uncertain world, all knowledge is at the best only probable. For Keynes, the fact that the future is uncertain takes us beyond the limited sphere to which classical probability (and rolling a die) applies. Fundamental uncertainty, where possible outcomes and their frequencies are unknown/unknowable, is simply a fact of reality; but a fact that should not paralyse human action, because life has to go on. So, one has to act as good as one can, given this lack of certain knowledge. A new approach to decision-making under uncertainty was to be established within economics. Keynes labelled it a theory of 'rational belief' where a proposition and its uncertain outcome is connected by scrutinising the available evidence and giving it a weight according to its (probable) reliability and relevance.

The logic of this process is not watertight, not demonstrable and somewhat subjective, contrary to classical logic. It belongs to human logic, and its rationality conforms better to the meaning of rationality in ordinary language. In the ever-changing world in which we live, it would be irrational to apply the concept of 'rationality' only to decision-making under certainty and perfect knowledge.

Rational belief, however, is an insufficient guide to ethical conduct since the consequences of our actions are at best only probable. Therefore, Keynes proposed that rational ethics should be based on motive rather than consequences. For instance, Keynes accepted behaviour guided by the profit motive, but decried the possession (or love) of money for its own sake. For him, 'being good' is the key ethical principle, rather than demonstratively 'doing good': an action is good to him if it is directed to something intrinsically worthwhile rather than towards some ulterior goal ('My Early Beliefs', Keynes 1949, *CW* X, p. 437). Accordingly, to Keynes, both economics and politics dealt only with means. They were facilitators of the good life, never ends in themselves.

Keynes, himself, mentioned at several instances that the theory and the new methodology, he was developing, while writing the *GT* could revolutionise economics, but it would appear so differently from the conventional approach that at the best it would take some time to be understood and accepted by the economic profession.[5] In fact, he anticipated in the foreword to the *GT* that his (older) colleagues would make a harsh judgement on his work and probably dismiss it, arguing that 'I am quite wrong … or saying nothing new' (Keynes 1936 [1973], p. v).

He was right, not only the older generation of economists struggled with Keynes's new macroeconomic method. This has been the case within the economic profession ever since: that the theoretical arguments within *GT* are building on a sea change in macroeconomic method caused by the introduction of uncertain knowledge and rational beliefs as guiding principles for economic actors in the macroeconomic market system, which therefore has to be analysed fundamentally different from neoclassical perfect information, general equilibrium economics.

Only after *A Treatise on Money* (Keynes 1930 [1972], *CW*, V and VI, hereafter *TM*) was published in 1930 did Keynes's loyalty to the neoclassical analytical framework of a self-adjusting, full employment market system slip. *TM* was developed alongside Keynes's work on the Macmillan Committee on Finance and Industry (1929–1931). But the Committee found his contribution less than convincing, because it could not explain the persistence of unemployment. Keynes had to accept this objection that there was a 'missing link' between his theory and the reality of employment.

Keynes's macroeconomic methodology of *The General Theory*

As soon as *TM* was out of his hands Keynes began to rethink the dynamics of the market system along an entirely new theoretical framework: could it be that the market system was not self-adjusting to full employment due to uncertainty and systemic openness? If actors do not possess perfect information about the future, market prices may go astray. Especially in financial markets there is no anchor. When the neoclassical *ceteris paribus* assumption is employed in macroeconomic analysis the systemic interdependence is missing.[6] These methodological challenges to conventional (neo) classical macroeconomics made Keynes draw a sharp dividing line among economists: On one side of the methodological gulf are those economists who presume from the very beginning that the entire macro-market system is self-adjusting, what today is called a general equilibrium framework. On the other side of this methodological dividing line we find those economists who doubt the self-adjusting mechanism exists in reality – at best, only consider it as a very, very special case without practical relevance.[7] A view Keynes reiterates on the very first page of *The General Theory*.

Keynes admitted in the preface to *GT* that the main problem with *TM* was that it followed the (neo)classical convention in taking for granted a 'long run', full employment equilibrium as its point of reference. This idea was dismissed in the *GT*. Accordingly, the use of the analytical concept of equilibrium in macroeconomics had to change as a consequence. This change of analytical framework was only the beginning of the radical shift in economic method from generalised market economics to macroeconomics that the *GT* presents. This shift is still not understood, nor is it accepted by today's mainstream economists employing the dynamic general equilibrium macro-models (see Jespersen, 2009).

Trend and cycles cannot be separated

In *The General Theory* the overarching analytical framework was changed fundamentally. Instead of a preconceived long-run outcome of (transitory) disturbances, Keynes adopted Marshall's three 'periods' analysis (*GT*, chapter 5): the market period (the 'day'), when output is fixed; the short period, when output could vary but capital is given (*GT*: most of the book); and the long period, when even real capital is variable (*GT*: mainly chapters 16 and 17). These are analytical constructs, allowing the theorist to separate factors which adjust quickly from those that move more slowly. Although artificial, the relevance of the separate periods is ensured by their strong correspondence with processes in actual time. Keynes made one modification to Marshall's short period: net new investment was a part of aggregate demand, but the resulting change in the capital stock was not allowed to affect the cost of producing output (aggregate supply) (Chick 1983).

Uncertainty and expectations

Immediately in *GT*, chapter 3 we see how an uncertain future shapes the determination of output and employment in the short period: the central concerns of the book. Output is decided by producers whose capital equipment is given: the decision takes place in the short period. Output takes time to produce, so the market for it lies in the future, which by argument is uncertain. Producers must form expectations of what the market will be like and set their output and employment accordingly. For the first time we have an explicit link to Keynes's earliest scholarly work, the *Treatise on Probability*; here is an exploration in the economics of rational decision-making in the face of uncertainty.

The expectations of producers are central, but Keynes carefully reflects also on what kind of expectations are important for other macroeconomic groups: households (GT, chapters 8 and 9), the investors in real capital (GT, chapter 11) and the financial speculators (GT, chapter 12). Economic activities with the shortest time horizons are in general the least uncertain; for instance, daily consumption is quite predictable, while real investment decisions are made in the light of longer-term, and therefore more uncertain, expectations. This is the opposite of the theory of *TM* and of neoclassical theory today, where unexpected events (for example, windfalls) can cause disturbance in the short run, but long-run equilibrium is certain and known.

The main analytical outcome of *GT* is a sequence of short-period equilibria adding up to a long period path-dependent system that Keynes also created in the *GT*. This is an example of an open-system analysis,[8] building on sequential semi-closed short-period analyses moving forward into an increasingly uncertain future, which cannot be predicted.

Equilibrium

With this new method comes a redefinition of macroeconomic equilibrium. It is not an end-point or a configuration existing out of time but a construction contingent on the analytical constraints imposed (for example, the short period) or the policy stance assumed (monetary policy is mentioned explicitly), where exogenous variables are held constant for the purpose of the analysis. Short-period equilibrium can pertain to a part of the system or to the whole: For example, 'the equilibrium level of employment [is] the level at which there is no inducement to employers as a whole either to expand or to contract employment' (*GT*, p. 27), and chapter 18 outlines the equilibrium of the system as a whole (*GT*, p. 249). There is no suggestion of labour market clearing; this is important, for unemployment had continued at a high level for 15 years when the *GT* was published. Keynes characterised persistent unemployment as unemployment equilibrium and in the *GT* provided a theory which could explain how such an equilibrium (as he defined it) could occur.

For large parts of the analysis Keynes takes expectations as given (Keynes 1937a). This allows him to get definite results. However, he relaxes this assumption to show where greater realism will lead. First he varies short-term expectations (output), then also long-term expectations (real investment). The latter is 'Keynes's model of shifting equilibrium, [which describes] an actual path of an economy over time chasing an ever changing equilibrium – it need never catch it' (Kregel 1976, p. 217).

The fallacy of composition[9]

Finally we must mention the importance of choosing the appropriate level of aggregation in macroeconomics, when analysing the economy as a whole.

> Though an individual whose transactions are small in relation to the market can safely neglect the fact that demand is not a one-sided transaction, it makes nonsense to neglect it when we come to aggregate demand. This is the vital difference between the theory of the economic behaviour of the aggregate and the theory of the behaviour of the individual unit ...
>
> *(GT, p. 85)*

Keynes indicated in the above passage that if one were to argue from an individual's behaviour by simple aggregation to the development in the economy as a whole, a wrong conclusion is likely to be obtained. This occurs because the economy as a whole is not the same as the sum of its parts, and to argue from the part to the whole in such a circumstance is likely to result in a methodological fallacy of composition.

The most famous example of such a fallacy between the individual and an aggregate outcome within the *GT* concerns individuals' saving behaviour. Increased marginal propensity to save (mps) of a single person has, as stated above, no impact on the system as a whole. But an increased mps of all people (perhaps due to unfavourable future prospects) would lead to lower consumption, smaller output and reduced employment, which might even reduce the total amount of savings. Collectively, aggregate savings must equal aggregate investments, so, the final macroeconomic outcome depends on what happens to real investments – most likely they will fall due to the reduced demand for consumption goods. Neither individually nor collectively do savers know this systemic interconnectedness, which is up to the macroeconomists to explain. But this little straightforward story of macroeconomics was called by neoclassical economist 'a paradox of thrift', because it runs counter to conventional full employment theory. Likewise, the 'multiplier' was considered as one of Keynes's mistaken conclusions: how could enlarged private or public investments increase output, when the economy was assumed to be either in full employment equilibrium or adjust to full employment by itself?

Another example concerns the labour market. Keynes's contemporaries reasoned that if the supply of labour exceeded demand (that is, there is unemployment), the price of labour – the wage level – must be 'too high', i.e. above its equilibrium level. This argument counts for a strawberry market. So, why not for the labour market employing the assumption of *ceteris paribus*. Once again Keynes pointed out (*GT*, chapter 19) that a reduced wage level might reduce production costs but would diminish *pari passu* wage-earners' income and therefore private consumption. The most likely outcome would rather be a smaller output and reduced employment.

One could summarise the above methodological arguments by saying 'The method is one of the messengers of macroeconomics'.

The principle of effective demand

Keynes's contemporaries were used to thinking that at the macroeconomic level aggregate demand could not be distinguished from aggregate supply: whatever was produced would generate an equal demand to absorb that output ('You will not find [effective demand] mentioned even once in the whole works of Marshall, Edgeworth and Professor Pigou'; *GT*, p. 32). But Keynes saw empirically that aggregate supply did not create its own demand and was in search of the theoretical justification for treating supply and demand as independent variables at the macro-level. He also saw that in real time producers must form expectations about the future level of demand to combine with their (known) cost structure to determine the profit-maximising level of output and thus employment.

If the result for the economy as a whole was less than full employment, there was nothing labour could do about it. This 'Principle of Effective Demand', as Keynes called it, was perhaps the most important theoretical contribution of the *GT*: it asserted the independence of demand from supply at the aggregate level, showed the importance of producers' uncertain expectations and established the systemic dependence of employment on producers' output decisions: the labour market should not and could not be analysed in isolation.

If expectations are not fulfilled, profits are larger or smaller than expected, and firms may alter their expectations, and their output decisions, but only in the future (*GT*, chapter 5). Current employment is determined by those earlier expectations, whether or not they are correct (*GT*, chapter 3). If expectations are fulfilled, the output and employment decisions are likely to be repeated unchanged. This result is called an equilibrium, whether full employment or not.

Aggregate demand

If the level of activity is stable, it is assumed that firms' expectations of demand will converge to the actual level of aggregate demand expressed in expenditure. Keynes continued the convention of dividing aggregate demand into consumption and investment. Consumption, he argued, was mainly responsive to changes in income and thus could not drive changes in income by itself. Consumption moved in the same direction as income but not to the full amount, because some income is saved: the marginal propensity to consume (mpc) is hypothesised to be less than one. This assumption gave Keynes powerful ammunition, for it put a stop to the automatic expansion of economic activity independently of (and most likely before) full employment, in contrast to the classical idea of the economic system as self-adjusting to full employment equilibrium.

Investment, the production of real productive capital, was, by contrast, not determined by current income, for two reasons: the purpose of investment is to expand the capacity to meet expected future, not current, increased demand; and (in Keynes's time) much investment was initially financed by bank loans. The first point is the source of Keynes's stress on long-term expectations as the main driving force of investment: expectations of future profits must be made for the entire life of the equipment. The second point overturns the classical causality between saving and investment. Bank loans are independent of current or prior saving; therefore, investment can take place without prior saving (Chick 1983: chapter 9).[10,11]

Liquidity preference

Along with long-term expectations, the other major factor influencing investment was the rate of interest. This represented the cost of obtaining funds to carry out the projects. Here, again, Keynes departed from conventional wisdom, which had treated interest and returns on real capital as synonymous. The rate of interest in *GT* is a purely monetary phenomenon, mainly determined by the degree of preference for liquid over illiquid financial assets. This preference will depend not only on the need for cash for routine transactions with a cushion for the unexpected expenditure but will also, sometimes largely, be determined by the expectations of future capital gains and losses on the part of speculators (*GT*, chapter 12), the bulls and bears introduced already in *TM*. The capital value of securities is inversely related to the rate of interest. Keynes framed liquidity preference in terms of expected interest rates and showed that an excessive preference for liquidity could keep rates too high to stimulate real investments sufficiently to provide full employment. The root cause of unemployment was not high wages but high rates of interest.

Liquidity preference and unemployment equilibrium gave Keynes the means finally to escape the quantity theory. He showed (*GT*, chapter 21) that only at full employment and with zero preference for liquidity would the quantity theory hold.

Both the speculators and those investing in real capital were subject to sudden changes in their expectations of an uncertain future. This made investment potentially volatile. However, real investment was also the economy's engine of growth. A rise in investment would cause consumption to rise as well, in accordance with the mpc, when the new factor income circulated around. If the process were to work its way out in full, the extent to which the change in income exceeded the rise in investment would be given by the 'multiplier', which depended on the mpc. With Keynes's new methodological perspective, such a boom was no longer seen as a deviation from long-run equilibrium, and thus deplored, but something to be welcomed as a means to reduce unemployment and, if needed, prolonged. Far from the classical economist's instinct to raise interest rates to choke off a boom, Keynes would rather keep interest rates low to facilitate the process as long as unemployment prevailed. Indeed, he favoured a general policy of low interest rates, as these would stimulate investment and, by making loans easier to pay off, prevent debt from accumulating. This is his characteristic policy conclusion (Tily 2009), far more than the policy usually associated with his name: fiscal stimulus. The latter policy might be the only instrument to take an economy out of a slump, but it was not a policy for all seasons.

The long run

The bulk of *GT* is occupied with short-period analysis, but the long-run effects of capital accumulation do claim Keynes's attention, mainly in chapters 16 and 17. Although he looked forward to the time when capital was no longer scarce, he saw that the existence of money as an alternative store of value presented a problem: that as capital accumulates, its diminishing scarcity value reduces the expected return on capital even to zero if scarcity ceases altogether. But the liquidity premium commanded by money, which is cheap to store and does not require any effort to generate the return that liquidity affords, will prevent the rate of interest from falling to zero. If the return on capital falls to zero, but the propensity to save is still positive at full employment, the only way to reduce saving to zero, to match the return on investment, is for income (and employment) to fall. A zero rate of new investment and saving at just full employment would be a fluke: the classical theorem that full employment characterises the long run was refuted.

The General Theory: A revolution in method and theory

The GT constitutes a sea change in macroeconomic analysis. Keynes demonstrated that unemployment equilibrium was a logical outcome of a macroeconomic system in which decisions are taken by many firms acting independently, all facing uncertain markets and future.

A revolution in economic method was needed to come to that conclusion, as the prevailing method ruled out any but temporary and self-correcting unemployment. In developing a path-dependent, open-system analysis, Keynes created a theory which reflected reality better than the theories of his predecessors (and most of his successors). There were many possible equilibria, depending on the constraints imposed and, more importantly, policies assumed, and there was no presumption that an actual economy would ever settle into any specific equilibrium, let alone one in which full employment prevailed.

Monetary factors were allowed their full economic impact, affecting all areas of 'real' economic life instead of being confined only to determining the price level. The 'classical dichotomy' between monetary and real factors was abolished and the quantity theory shown to characterise only a very special case.

The GT amounted to a revolution in both economic theory and method. It was an intellectually stunning achievement – so stunning that its path-breaking contributions have either not yet been understood by the majority of economists or have proved unpalatable and been transformed into something else. Whatever the cause, although mainstream textbooks in macroeconomics may claim that their short-run analysis is 'Keynesian' or 'New Keynesian', it is easily demonstrated that the theory presented is confined within a neoclassical analytical and methodological framework quite similar to that which Keynes intended to overturn.

Today, Keynes's macroeconomic thinking is mainly represented by the national income accounts, which on the other hand are in use worldwide.

Social philosophy supported by Keynes's macroeconomic method[12]

The development of Keynes's macroeconomic analysis, from the very first contribution in philosophy (see Fitzgibbons 1989) and in probability theory (published in 1921 as *Treatise in Probability*) leading up to the *GT* eventually provided the insight needed to realise his vision: to 'combine three things: economic efficiency, social justice, and individual liberty' ('Liberalism and Labour', Keynes (1926 [1931], *CW* IX, p. 311).

At the end of his life his view was still that individuals should have the possibility, but also the responsibility, to pursue their aspiration of a good life ('My Early Beliefs', Keynes 1949).[13] This presupposed an organisation by international, national and semi-official institutions of a reasonably stable and predictable structures, like for instance the Bretton Woods system, the regulation of private banks and of financial speculation to make the market system as a whole more stable, the experiences from the first half of the 20th century were terrifying. When Keynes in 1945 stepped down as editor of the *Economic Journal*, he summarised his view of the challenges to economists in the future the following way: 'I give you the toast to economists, who are the trustees not of civilisation, but of the possibilities of civilisation' (Harrod, 1953, pp. 193–4). The challenge was in some way to make the economists to apply a realistic method to macroeconomic analysis.

For a couple of decades after the war, parts of his social philosophy became accepted in mainstream thinking in Western economics and politics with regard to the organisation of the international monetary system and national commitments to full employment and a fairer distribution of income and wealth. But his methodological impact did not last. So, the challenge, mentioned by Keynes nearly 80 years ago, is still with us to be fulfilled.

Notes

1 In another paper, Chick and Jespersen (2016) give a more detailed presentation of the development in Keynes's economic analytical thinking. In this entry, the focus lies on his macroeconomic methodological novelties.
2 Keynes's life and theoretical development from early childhood until the publication of *The General Theory* are vividly and detailed presented in Skidelsky (1983, 1992).
3 In fact, this fate happened to all Keynes's philosophical papers from his undergraduate years as a student at King's College.
4 See Lawson and Pesaran (1985).
5 The revolutionary character of *GT* is apparent from Chapter 1 of the book. See also Skidelsky (1992), p. 439.
6 See 'Poverty in plenty: is the economic system self-adjusting?' (Keynes 1934).
7 Keynes called all previous economists 'classical', even his contemporary colleague in Cambridge, A.C. Pigou (who was only five years older than Keynes).
8 See, Chick, *Open/closed systems* and Setterfield, *Path dependency* in this Handbook.
9 This section is argued more extensively in the entry on 'Holism and the Fallacy of Composition' in this volume.
10 'The investment market can be congested through shortage of cash. It can never be congested through shortage of saving' (*GT*, p. 222).
11 Keynes made a reference to Wicksell on this point of saving and real investment diverting from each other due to financial intermediation (*GT*, p. 242).
12 With reference to the final chapter 24 in *GT*.
13 Presented to the Bloomsbury Group Memoir Club in 1938; but on Keynes's request not published until after his death.

References

Chick, V. (1983) *Macroeconomics after Keynes: A Reconsideration of the General Theory*, Cambridge, MA: MIT Press.
Chick, V. and J. Jespersen (2016) 'John Maynard Keynes' in G. Familo and H. G. Kurz, eds, *Handbook in Economic Analysis*, vol. 1, Cheltenham and Northampton: Edward Elgar.
CW: see Keynes (1971–1989).
Fitzgibbons, A. (1989) *Keynes's Vision: A New Political Economy*, Oxford: Clarendon Press.
Harrod, R. F. (1953) *The Life of John Maynard Keynes*, New York: Harcourt Brace & Co.
Jespersen, J. (2009) *Macroeconomic Methodology: A Post-Keynesian Perspective*, Cheltenham, and Northampton: Edward Elgar.
Keynes, J. M. (1913) *Indian Currency and Finance*, *CW* I.
Keynes, J. M. (1921) *A Treatise on Probability*, *CW* VIII.
Keynes, J. M. (1926) 'Liberalism and labour', in *CW* IX, pp. 307–11.

Keynes, J. M. (1930) *A Treatise on Money, CW* V and VI.

Keynes, J. M. (1931) *Essays in Persuasion, CW* IX.

Keynes, J. M. (1933) *Essays in Biography, CW* X.

Keynes, J. M. (1934) 'Poverty in plenty: Is the economic system self-adjusting?' in *CW* XIII, pp. 485–92.

Keynes, J. M. (1936) *The General Theory of Employment, Interest and Money, CW* VII.

Keynes, J. M. (1937a) 'The general theory of employment' in *CW* XIV, pp. 109–23.

Keynes, J. M. (1937b) 'The 'ex ante' theory of the rate of interest', in *CW* XIV, pp. 215–23.

Keynes, J. M. (1949) *My Early Beliefs*, in *CW* X, pp. 433–51.

Keynes. J. M. (1971–1989) *Collected Writings*, D. E. Moggridge, ed., 30 vols, London: Macmillan and New York: St Martin's Press.

Kregel, J. (1976) 'Economic methodology in the face of uncertainty: The modelling methods of Keynes and the post-Keynesians', *Economic Journal* 86, June, pp. 209–25.

Lawson, T. and M. H. Pesaran (1985) *Keynes' Economics: Methodological Issues*, London: Routledge.

Skidelsky, R. (1983) *John Maynard Keynes*, vol. 1: *Hopes Betrayed, 1883–1920*, London: Macmillan.

Skidelsky, R. (1992) *John Maynard Keynes*, vol. 2: *The Economist as Saviour, 1920–37*, London: Macmillan.

Tily, G. (2009) *The General Theory, the Rate of Interest and 'Keynesian' Economics: Keynes Betrayed*, London: Macmillan.

18

POST-KEYNESIAN METHODOLOGY

John E. King

Introduction

Post-Keynesian economics is a dissident school in macroeconomics based on a particular interpretation of John Maynard Keynes's *General Theory*, also involving some distinctive and controversial policy positions. It has several core propositions that distinguish it from both 'Old' and 'New Keynesian' theory (King 2015, Chapters 2–3). First, aggregate employment is determined in the product market, not the labour market, so that unemployment is essentially a macroeconomic problem that cannot be reduced to microeconomics. Second, involuntary unemployment exists, and it is caused by deficient effective demand; it would not be eliminated even if all labour market imperfections could be removed. Third, the relationship between aggregate investment and aggregate saving is fundamental to macroeconomic theory, and causation runs from investment to saving, and not vice versa. Fourth, a monetary economy is quite different from a barter economy, since money can be hoarded. It follows that money is not 'neutral', macroeconomic theory cannot be partitioned into separate 'real' and 'monetary' segments, and a monetary economy cannot be analysed 'as if' it were a barter economy, with money introduced at a later stage like the cheese course at a banquet. Fifth, the Quantity Theory of Money is seriously misleading, since it rests on the assumption that money is indeed neutral with respect to the determination of real output (and employment), and affects only the price level. Sixth, capitalist economies are driven by the 'animal spirits' of investors, which determine business investment decisions, rather than by precise calculations of future costs and revenues. In an uncertain world, decisions to invest depend on 'spontaneous optimism rather than a mathematical expectation' of profit (Keynes 1936, *CW* VII, p. 161).

The history of Post-Keynesian macroeconomics is documented by King (2002). As a distinct school of thought it originated in the 1950s and 1960s, more or less independently in Britain and the United States. By the early 1970s the term was being widely used to describe the ideas discussed above, and by the end of that decade a more or less clearly defined Post-Keynesian school had emerged. While there were some significant remaining disputes on theoretical questions, there was also substantial agreement on the fundamental issues of macroeconomic policy. The principle

DOI: 10.4324/9781315745992-22

of effective demand states that aggregate output and employment are normally demand-constrained rather than supply-constrained, so that the achievement and maintenance of full employment requires state intervention, in the form of fiscal and monetary policy, supplemented by an incomes policy to restrain inflation.

Post-Keynesian interest in methodology

Post-Keynesians have always taken a strong interest in macroeconomic methodology; two of the very few books devoted entirely to the subject have Post-Keynesian authors, one of them a co-editor of the present volume (Dow 1996; Jespersen 2009). In this they have taken their cue from Keynes, who began the *General Theory* with a call for greater realism in macroeconomic theory and a concern for the policy relevance of that theory:

> the characteristics of the special case assumed by the [neo]classical theory happen not to be those of the economic society in which we actually live, with the result that its teaching is misleading and disastrous if we attempt to apply it to the facts of experience.
>
> *(Keynes 1936, CW VII, p. 3)*

Much earlier, in his doctoral dissertation, published as *A Treatise on Probability*, Keynes had raised substantial issues of methodology: how to theorise, how to conduct empirical research and how to formulate sensible public policy, in a world in which fundamental uncertainty made the assignment of numerical probabilities to future outcomes distinctly problematic (Keynes 1921, *CW* VIII). He was convinced that the economic universe differed significantly from the natural world and that studying it posed serious problems that had defeated the great German physicist Max Planck, who had 'once remarked to me that in early life he had thought of studying economics, but had found it too difficult!' (Keynes 1951, *CW* X, p. 158n). This revealed that

> the amalgam of logic and intuition, and the wide knowledge of facts, most of which are not precise, which is required for economic interpretation in its highest form is, quite truly, overwhelming for those whose gift mainly consists in the power to imagine and pursue to their furthest points the implications and prior conditions of comparatively simple facts which are known with a high degree of precision.
>
> *(ibid., p. 158n)*

Edgeworth's approach to the subject, Keynes believed, was open to very similar objections:

> The atomic hypothesis which has worked so splendidly in Physics breaks down in Psychics. We are faced at every turn with the problems of Organic Unity, of Discreteness, of Discontinuity – the whole is not equal to the sum of the parts, comparisons of quantity fail us, small changes produce large effects, the assumption of a uniform and homogeneous continuum are not satisfied.
>
> *(ibid., pp. 232–3)*

Keynes repeated several of these themes in his widely read summary of the *General Theory* in the *Quarterly Journal of Economics* in the following year (Keynes 1937).

This continuing concern with methodology can also be seen in three generations of student textbooks. In 1973, in their very ambitious first-year undergraduate text, Joan Robinson and John Eatwell included index references to 'metaphysics', 'methods of economic analysis' and 'models', with additional relevant material in the discussions of 'political considerations' and 'technical relationships' (Robinson and Eatwell 1973); the senior author had already published a short book on *Economic Philosophy* (Robinson 1962). Almost 20 years later, Philip Arestis's more advanced undergraduate textbook contained extensive analysis of both the methodology of the 'Grand Neo-classical Synthesis' and of Post-Keynesian methodology, the latter including its emphasis on the need for realism in macroeconomic theorising (Arestis 1992, pp. 77–85, pp. 94–100). More recently, Marc Lavoie's graduate text devotes much of the early parts of a lengthy first chapter to such methodological themes as 'atomicism versus holism', 'ideology' and' 'instrumentalism versus realism', together with such related issues as formalism, microfoundations, rationality, realism and uncertainty (Lavoie 2014, Chapter 1). And the second volume of the authoritative *Oxford Handbook of Post-Keynesian Economics* has no less than nine of its 21 chapters on methodological topics (Harcourt and Kriesler 2013, pp. 45–201).

I myself have form in this area. The first edition of my *Elgar Companion to Post Keynesian Economics* had 80 entries, of which 13 were either devoted to methodological issues ('agency', 'Babylonian mode of thought', 'critical realism', 'non-ergodicity', 'open systems') or had a significant methodological component ('Austrian economics', 'econometrics', 'equilibrium and non-equilibrium', 'expectations', 'Fundamentalist Keynesians', 'Kaleckian economics', 'Keynes's *General Theory*', 'uncertainty'). No-one objected to the inclusion of any of these topics, and so when I prepared the expanded second edition ten years later, with an extra 32 entries, it contained another seven on methodology ('choice under uncertainty', 'conventions', 'Keynes's *Treatise on Probability*', 'macroeconomic methodology', 'pluralism', 'stock-flow consistent modelling', 'time-series econometrics') (King 2003, 2013). Many of these themes will recur in the present entry.

'Realism' in macroeconomics

How, then, should we approach the study of 'the economic society in which we actually live', drawing extensively on 'the facts of experience'? What, precisely, does the requirement that macroeconomic theory be 'realistic' actually involve? In order to answer these questions we need to raise questions of *ontology*, concerning the nature of the economic universe that is under scrutiny. As Keynes well knew, we cannot be sure that the future will be like the past. Economic events are not precisely predictable, like the times of high and low tides and the dates and times of solar and lunar eclipses. Short of major cosmic disasters (meteor impacts, for example), these happenings can be predicted today for centuries ahead. But it is not possible to make exact predictions of unemployment levels, exchange rates, wage levels or GDP growth a few months ahead, let alone for millennia.

Both the Post-Keynesian authors cited earlier have written on these questions. Sheila Dow has warned against 'dualistic' thinking, which imposes 'either/or', 'A or not-A', mutually exclusive categories of thought on a reality which is generally much more complicated than this. Instead the economic universe needs to be thought of as a continuum rather than a dichotomy. The principle of the excluded middle is a feature of Cartesian-Euclidian thought, which Dow rejects in favour of the more subtle and open-ended Babylonian mode of thinking that was espoused by the physicist Richard Feynman (Dow 1996, Chapter 2). All varieties of mainstream macroeconomics, from Old Keynesian theory to the New Neoclassical Synthesis, are Cartesian-Euclidian in their underlying methodology, not Babylonian. They rely on a single set of axioms that is supposed to be applicable to all forms of economic problems in all types of historical and social circumstances.

Dow suggests that the relationship between Cartesian-Euclidian and Babylonian thinking is related to another important distinction, between *closed-system* and *open-system* thinking, which is implicit in Keynes's *Treatise on Probability*:

> An open system is one where not all the constituent variables and structural relationships are known or knowable, and thus the boundaries of the system are not known or knowable. This is the province of fuzzy mathematics, with indeterminate boundaries of sets ... It is also the province of non-classical logic, where logical relations are applied to uncertain knowledge; this logic is variously known as ordinary logic or human logic.
>
> *(ibid., p. 14)*

If reality is understood in the Babylonian manner as an open system, Dow concludes, there is scope for free will, for individual and collective creativity, and for the evolution of individuals and institutions in ways that may be difficult to predict with any degree of precision. This implies that atomistic, reductionist ways of thinking will be less productive than a more organic approach that 'involves interdependencies which are complex and evolutionary, and thus not amenable to formalization with respect to separable elements within a single system of reasoning' (ibid., p. 15).

Jesper Jespersen arrives at similar conclusions by a slightly different route. He begins by rejecting the three fundamental axioms that underpin the models that are used by almost all mainstream macroeconomists:

1 The perfect functioning market economic system has a general equilibrium solution determined by macroeconomic structures.
2 It is a predetermined and, at least in the longer-run, self-adjusting system.
3 Dynamic general equilibrium models build upon neoclassical microeconomic first principles of individual rationality by using representative agent theory and assuming rational expectations and market clearing. (Jespersen 2013, p. 379)

However, Jespersen maintains, fundamental Keynesian uncertainty means that 'the relevance of models relying on representative (individual) agent theory and rational expectations collapses'. Such models need to be replaced by the analysis of 'a set of context-related and path-dependent trends leading into a (partly) unknown future' (ibid., p. 381). This leads Jespersen to concur with Dow on the need for open-system reasoning, in which the outcome is at least partially indeterminate. He notes the potential use of 'so-called "semi-closures", where parts of the system can be organized in a formalistic way'. For example, Keynesian income-expenditure models can be used to estimate the multiplier effects of changes in aggregate spending, 'given the specific and changeable conditions' and subject to the persistence of 'reasonable stable structures and unchanged expectations' (ibid., p. 382).

Both Dow (1996, Chapter 3) and Jespersen (2009, Chapter 2) are attracted by the principles of *critical realism* that were developed by the philosopher Roy Bhaskar and advocated by the Cambridge economic methodologist Tony Lawson (2003). There are six underlying principles. First, objects of social inquiry exist independently of their investigation, and are not constructed by the inquirer (thus the more extreme versions of postmodernism are inconsistent with critical realism). Second, relations of cause and effect are involved, with causality attributed to the structures, powers, mechanisms and tendencies that generate specific events. Third, the object of science is to explain observed events or data; prediction is never primary or sufficient. Fourth, social and economic systems are presumed to be open rather than closed. Fifth, economic theories are historically and socially specific, and often need to change when the context changes. Finally, social institutions are not exogenous to human agency (Jefferson and King 2011, pp. 960–1).

These principles cannot be reconciled with the fundamental axioms of mainstream macroeconomics identified by Jespersen, or with the Euclidian-Cartesian mode of thought that was criticised by Dow. Do they rule out *any* form of mathematical theorising, statistical research or policy prescription? Fortunately not. Lawson acknowledges that a case can be made for the recognition of *partial* event regularities, or 'demi-regs', which do allow for some prediction (and hence some assessment of the likely consequences of alternative macroeconomic policy decisions, which would be impossible if no event regularities could ever be established). Similarly, Sheila Dow concedes that *partial* closure of open systems is sometimes possible, so that the use of formal mathematical and statistical methods is not entirely excluded, but cautions that such partial closures are 'always open organically to influences from other parts of the overall system', and should not be used dogmatically (Dow 1996, p. 14). This leads us to the next important methodological issue for Post-Keynesian macroeconomists, the validity (or otherwise) of mathematical models and econometric estimation.

Formalism: for and against

Most Post-Keynesians would agree that some degree of formalism is indeed essential for a proper understanding of the business cycle, of the process of economic growth and of the relationship between cycles and growth. Two of the three textbooks discussed earlier include substantial mathematical modelling and make detailed reference to econometric evidence. Even Robinson and Eatwell's *Introduction to Modern Economics* contains a surprising number of equations (mainly but not exclusively in chapter appendices), given Joan Robinson's proud – one might almost say defiant – ignorance of mathematical techniques. Philip Arestis's *Post-Keynesian Approach to Economics* has no fewer than 222 numbered equations, while the admittedly very much longer *Post-Keynesian Economics* by Marc Lavoie has 374 equations and a 'notation list' of mathematical symbols that covers more than six pages (Lavoie 2004, pp. vii–xiii). All these texts also contain many diagrams, some of them very complex.

Similarly, Michał Kalecki's (unwritten and possibly largely unconscious) ideas on methodology bear a close resemblance to the six fundamental principles of critical realism. It can be taken for granted that he assumed the capitalist economy to exist independently of his observation of it (principle one). In trying to discern cause and effect, he was implicitly trying to understand causal processes and explain observed events and data (principles two and three). His use of advanced mathematical modelling was motivated by the need to understand the real world, which he understood as a set of open systems characterised by some degree of event regularity (principle four). He took the principle of historical specificity directly from his reading of Marx (principle five), and saw the endogenous nature of social institutions (principle six) as a necessary consequence of his position on issues relevant to the third and fifth principles (Jefferson and King 2011, pp. 962–70). And yet, as early as the mid-1930s, his pioneering work in macroeconomics placed him in the top 1% of mathematical economists of the time (see especially Kalecki 1935).

Kalecki was also a pioneer in the careful use of econometric methods, and later generations of Post-Keynesians have made widespread use of these techniques. In the 1980s, for example, Alfred Eichner estimated structural equations for a short-period macroeconometric model of the United States economy and Philip Arestis performed similar estimations for the United Kingdom (Downward 2013, p. 132). A significant proportion (perhaps the majority) of papers published in the principal Post-Keynesian journals in the 21st century continue to use either cross-sectional or time-series econometrics, in addition to descriptive statistics and other types of informal empirical evidence. There are no strong grounds for objecting to these practices. If 'the assumptions involved in estimating coefficients are shared with all (even descriptive) empirical analysis ... then logically any empirical analysis advocated by Post Keynesians can embrace econometric *estimation*' (ibid., p. 136; original stress). Indeed, it could be argued that their strong concern with policy issues means that Post-Keynesian must embrace econometric estimation of the signs and approximate magnitudes of such critical variables as fiscal policy multipliers. How else could they mount any convincing opposition to the austerity measures that have inflicted so much damage on so many European economies?

A suitably nuanced conclusion to these controversies was provided by another of the co-editors of the present volume. In a paper entitled 'On the importance of knowing one's place', Victoria Chick argues that formal methods should indeed be used in economics, but they should be confined to appropriate areas. 'Formal techniques are powerful tools, but they can also be dangerous; the problem is to identify applications where they can be used safely' (Chick 1998, p. 1859). There is a serious risk that economic theorists are led by their use of precise axiomatic modelling to neglect the irreducibly limited and imperfect nature of human knowledge. Moreover, technical advances in economics are not theoretically or politically neutral. When neoclassical Keynesians applied these techniques to the *General Theory*, the consequence was a radical and undesirable change in the way in which Keynes's analysis was understood (ibid., p. 1865). 'Formalism is fine', Chick concludes, 'but it must know its place. Economists need to debate further the boundaries of that place' (ibid., p. 1868).

What, then, is ruled out by these dangers posed by formalism? There is no simple or universally applicable answer to this question. Post-Keynesians are economic *theorists*, after all. Just as some degree of abstraction is unavoidable in any attempt to theorise about the economy, so some degree of formalism is also necessary and helpful. Precisely how much formalism is justified in any particular case remains, always and inevitably, a matter of judgement. Post-Keynesians claim that this rather imprecise conclusion is superior to that which prevails in mainstream macroeconomics, where there is almost no discussion, and hence almost no questioning, of the limits to formal modelling.

The microfoundations delusion

With the publication of *General Theory* macroeconomics came to be regarded as a separate, semi-autonomous sub-discipline within economics, on a par with microeconomics and every bit as important. Post-Keynesians regard the mainstream dogma that we must provide *microfoundations* for macroeconomics as fundamentally misguided, since it would involve the reduction of macroeconomics to microeconomics (King 2012). If this were to be accepted, macroeconomics would become nothing more than an application of microeconomic theory, like industrial organisation or environmental economics. And there would be some very dangerous implications for macroeconomic policy. Treating the government's finances in the same way as the finances of an individual or a household seems to provide a strong argument for fiscal austerity. The case for wage cuts to reduce unemployment also seems to be straightforward, since, in any individual market (for labour or for goods), the existence of excess supply proves that the price (or wage) is too high, and needs to be reduced.

One argument used in defence of this microfoundations dogma is ontological. The economy is, after all, made up of individuals, who must therefore be the starting point for any analysis of the ways in which they interact. A second case relies on the supposed success of *economics imperialism* in its assault on the other social sciences: microeconomic models have been used successfully to deal with all manner of social and political questions, like voting behaviour, crime, discrimination and the family, it is suggested, and so they should be applied also to macroeconomics. Finally, this argument is extended to the physical world: micro-reduction has succeeded in the natural sciences, most obviously in biology with the triumph of modern genetics, and the principle should therefore be extended to economics.

The first of these three propositions involves a rather elementary confusion between *ontological reduction* and *explanatory reduction*. To say that *A* (the economy) is made up of *B*s (individual human beings) is to say something about ontology – what exists. It is rather obviously true. But it does not follow from this that *A* can and must be *explained* in terms of statements about *B*s, and only in terms of statements about *B*s. If *A* is the banking system, for example, and *B* represents the tellers (and other employees) who work for the banks, it would be foolish to maintain that knowledge about the tellers is all that we need to understand the behaviour of the system in which they work.

The second argument is no stronger. It is simply not true that mainstream microeconomic models and econometric techniques have been applied to problems that were previously the preserve of political scientists, sociologists and anthropologists with such great success that these academic failures have been forced to give up much of their intellectual territory to the economists. The third argument, that hierarchical reduction has succeeded in the natural sciences (above all in biology) and should therefore be applied to economics, is also weak. The relationship between an organism and its environment is actually very complex, and involves mutual influence and two-directional causation (Lewontin et al. 1984).

In fact there are two insuperable difficulties with this third argument, and hence with the microfoundations dogma as a whole: downward causation and the fallacy of composition. The difficulties posed by *downward causation* can be seen very clearly from an example used by the biologist Richard Dawkins, a strong supporter of micro-reduction, for whom 'the behaviour of a motor car' is to be fully explained in terms of its component parts, 'cylinders, carburettors and sparking plugs' (Dawkins 1976, p. 12). But this, of course, is nonsense. Changes in the social, political, economic and cultural context in which cars are driven frequently affect not just the car as a whole machine, but also some or all of its parts. Thus causation runs downwards, from the larger to the smaller units, and not just upwards from the smaller to the larger, as Dawkins maintains. To understand the causes of changes in car components over time, we need to know about society, politics, psychology and the economy.

The second problem with micro-reduction stems from the fact that 'the whole is not equal to the sum of the parts' (Keynes 1951, *CW* X, p. 233). To deny this is to fall into the fallacy of composition (Jespersen 2009, Chapter 7). One example is the *paradox of thrift*: any individual who decides to save a larger proportion of her income can indeed increase her savings but, unless there is an increase in investment (or government spending, or net exports) this will *not* be true of an increase in everyone's savings propensity, which will simply reduce aggregate income and leave the volume of aggregate saving unchanged. Second, there is a *paradox of liquidity*: any individual bank or other financial company wishes to increase its liquidity, it can always do so (at a price). But if all financial companies attempt to do so, the consequence will be a reduction in aggregate liquidity and (in the absence of government intervention) the real possibility that the whole system will collapse. Third, there is the Kaleckian *paradox of costs*: a wage rise is very bad news for any individual capitalist, but it may be good news for them all, taken together, if the consequent rise in consumption expenditure raises the level of economic activity and thereby increases aggregate profits. Other examples of the fallacy of composition are discussed by Lavoie (2014, pp. 16–22). All this suggests that economists need to be very careful in their use of language: 'microfoundations' is a particularly poor choice of metaphor.

The case(s) for pluralism in economics

Implicit in much of the previous discussion has been an argument – really a number of overlapping arguments – for pluralism in macroeconomics. One case for the 'analysis and advocacy of "many-ness"' in economic theory (Garnett 2013, p. 446) comes from a recognition that we live in a very complicated world, so that it is inherently implausible that one single theoretical approach will be able to capture its full economic complexity. A second argument derives from the fact that we also live in a constantly changing world, so that no single economic theory can adequately explain every stage of its continuing transformation. Third, the evident failure of economics imperialism relieves us from the threat of subservience to a single, monolithic neoclassical theoretical apparatus and offers the opportunity of improved relations with our neighbours in the other social sciences and a better understanding of our own history. It also raises two further questions. Should Post-Keynesianism itself be a broad or a narrow church? What are its intellectual relations with other schools of dissident economic thought? On the first question, opinions are divided. There have always been distinct branches of Post-Keynesian macroeconomics, and the relationships between them have generated considerable controversy (King 2002, Chapter 10).

Whether the Post-Keynesian school would be better as a broad church or a narrow church involves questions of methodology, no less than disagreements over theoretical analysis and economic policy. To mix the metaphors even further, Marc Lavoie declares that he 'tend[s] to favour a "broad-tent" approach. I am a "lumper" more than a "splitter"', believing as he does that 'a synthesis of the various strains of post-Keynesian economics is possible' (Lavoie 2014, p. 44). Others, most notably the leading 'Fundamentalist Keynesian' authority Paul Davidson, would strongly disagree.

On the second question, the Post-Keynesian microeconomist Fred Lee argued that a single, coherent and more or less united heterodoxy is emerging in economics, bringing together six heterodox traditions – Post-Keynesian-Sraffian, Marxist-radical, Institutional-evolutionary, social, feminist and ecological economics – to constitute a single coherent alternative to mainstream economics (Lee 2013). I do not find this story very convincing, since it exaggerates the points of agreement and underestimates the elements of disagreement between the rival non-mainstream schools of thought. Perhaps it should be seen as a manifesto for the future development of heterodox economics; but it is not an accurate description of the status quo.

Consider the cases of Sraffian and institutional economists. Sraffians appear to their many Post-Keynesian critics to be engaged in closed-system theorising, ignoring fundamental uncertainty, money and the principle of effective demand; there are no agents, no entrepreneurs, no profit expectations, no financial constraints or financial instability (Hart and Kriesler 2014). Institutionalists, in contrast, tend to be much less well-disposed towards any formalism in theory or research methods. As we have seen, however, few Post-Keynesians are opposed in principle to formal modelling, so long as it is of the right type, or to the use of econometric methods, providing that they are employed with the appropriate care and restraint.

There are also serious methodological issues concerning the relationship between Post-Keynesian macroeconomists and two other heterodox (or quasi-heterodox) schools, behavioural macroeconomics and complexity theory (see King 2015, Chapter 4). There is rather more common ground with Austrian economics, including a shared hostility to general equilibrium, and to neoclassical theorising more generally, and an acceptance of fundamental uncertainty and the role of historical time. But differences in political philosophy, and in attitudes to macroeconomic policy, have made cooperation between Post-Keynesians and Austrians very difficult to achieve.

A rather less extreme position than that advanced by Fred Lee has been proposed by Edward Fulbrook, the founding editor of *Real-World Economics Review*, one of the e-journals published by the World Economics Association (www.worldeconomicsassociation.org). Fulbrook has identified some important shared principles of an emerging 'New Political Economy' that is being developed in opposition to the 'Old Political Economy' which all heterodox economists reject (Rosenberg 2014). They are (i) acceptance of the need for pluralism; (ii) the ontology of much economic phenomena does not lend itself to formal modelling and mathematical deduction; (iii) economic analysis should be reality-based, not model-based; (iv) non-equilibrium rather than equilibrium thinking; (v) non-market clearing rather than market clearing; (vi) denial of stable preferences and rational, maximising behaviour; (vii) emergent properties, which make micro-reduction impossible and the microfoundations metaphor inapplicable; (viii) non-ergodicity; (ix) the economy is a subset of the planet, and not *vice versa*; and (x) a sharp distinction between positive and normative statements cannot be maintained. Fulbrook argues that these principles inspired a 'pluralist revolution' in the natural sciences almost a century ago. A similar revolution in economics is long overdue.

Conclusion

As with several other heterodox schools, Post-Keynesians have always taken a strong interest in questions of methodology. Indeed, some friendly critics argue that they have taken too much interest, their excessive concern with the philosophy of science serving to distract their attention from more pressing matters of economic theory and public policy (Fontana and Gerrard 2006). While this may have been true for a while in the 1980s, it is almost certainly not justified criticism today. Indeed, a strong case can be made that 'macroeconomic disagreement is based on methodological differences' (Jespersen 2009, p. 231), so that there are very substantial benefits in terms of theory and policy to be derived from the study of these differences.

References

Arestis, P. (1992) *The Post-Keynesian Approach to Economics*, Aldershot: Edward Elgar.

Chick, V. (1998) 'On the importance of knowing one's place: The role of formalism in economics', *Economic Journal* 108 (451), November, pp. 1059–69.

CW: see Keynes (1971–1989).

Dawkins, R. (1976) *The Selfish Gene*, Oxford: Oxford University Press.

Dow, S. C. (1996) *The Methodology of Macroeconomic Thought*, Cheltenham: Edward Elgar.

Downward, P. (2013) 'Econometrics', in J. E. King, ed, *The Elgar Companion to Post Keynesian Economics*, Second edition, Cheltenham: Edward Elgar, pp. 132–8.

Fontana, G. and B. Gerard (2006), 'The future of Post Keynesian economics', *Banca Nazionale del Lavoro Quarterly Review* 59 (236), pp. 49–80.

Garnett, R. (2013) 'Pluralism in economics', in J. E. King, ed, *The Elgar Companion to Post Keynesian Economics*, Second edition, Cheltenham: Edward Elgar., pp. 446–52.

Harcourt, G. C. and P. Kriesler (2013) *The Oxford Handbook of Post-Keynesian Economics. Volume 2: Critiques and Methodology*, Oxford: Oxford University Press.

Hart, N. and P. Kriesler (2014) 'Keynes, Kalecki, Sraffa: Coherence?', University of New South Wales, mimeo.

Jefferson, T. and J. E. King (2011) 'Michał Kalecki and critical realism', *Cambridge Journal of Economics* 35 (5), September, pp. 957–72.

Jespersen, J. (2009) *Macroeconomic Methodology: A Post Keynesian Perspective*, Cheltenham: Edward Elgar.

Jespersen, J. (2013) 'Macroeconomic methodology', in J. E. King, ed, *The Elgar Companion to Post Keynesian Economics*, Second edition, Cheltenham: Edward Elgar, pp. 379–83.

Kalecki, M. (1935) 'A macro-dynamic theory of business cycles', *Econometrica* 3 (3), July, pp. 327–44, reprinted in J. Osiatýnski, ed, *Collected Works of Michał Kalecki. Volume 1. Capitalism, Business Cycles and Full Employment*, Oxford: Clarendon Press, pp. 120–38.

Keynes, J. M. (1921) *A Treatise on Probability*, *CW* VIII.

Keynes, J. M. (1936) *The General Theory of Employment, Interest and Money*, *CW* VII.

Keynes, J. M. (1937) 'The general theory of employment', *Quarterly Journal of Economics* 51 (2), February, pp. 109–23.

Keynes, J. M. (1951) *Essays in Biography*, *CW* X.

Keynes, J. M. (1971–1989), *The Collected Writings of John Maynard Keynes*, D. Moggridge, ed., London: Macmillan and New York: St Martin's Press.

King, J. E. (2002) *A History of Post Keynesian Economics Since 1936*, Cheltenham: Edward Elgar.

King, J. E. (ed.) (2003) *The Elgar Companion to Post Keynesian Economics*, Cheltenham: Edward Elgar.

King, J. E. (2012) *The Microfoundations Delusion: Metaphor and Dogma in the History of Macroeconomics*, Cheltenham: Edward Elgar.

King, J. E. (ed.) (2013) *The Elgar Companion to Post Keynesian Economics*, Second edition, Cheltenham: Edward Elgar.

King, J. E. (2015) *Advanced Introduction to Post Keynesian Economics*, Cheltenham: Edward Elgar.

Lavoie, M. (2014) *Post-Keynesian Economics: New Foundations*, Cheltenham: Edward Elgar.

Lawson, T. (2003) *Reorienting Economics*, London and New York: Routledge.

Lee, F. S. (2013) 'Heterodox economics and its critics', in F. S. Lee and M. Lavoie, eds, *In Defense of Post-Keynesian and Heterodox Economics: Response to Their Critics*, London and New York: Routledge, pp. 104–32.

Lewontin, R. C., S. Rose, and L. J. Kam (1984) *Not in Our Genes: Biology, Ideology, and Human Nature*, Harmondsworth: Penguin.

Robinson, J. (1962) *Economic Philosophy*, London: Watts, reprinted Harmondsworth: Pelican Books, 1964.

Robinson, J. and J. Eatwell (1973) *An Introduction to Modern Economics*, Maidenhead: McGraw-Hill.

Rosenberg, P. (2014) 'New paradigm economics versus old paradigm economics. Interview with Edward Fulbrook', *Real-World Economics Review* 66, 13 January, pp. 131–43 (http://rwer.paecon.net/PAEReview/issue66/Fulbrook66.pdf) (consulted 22 December 2014).

19

COMPLEXITY, POLICYMAKING, AND THE AUSTRIAN DENIAL OF MACROECONOMICS

Scott Scheall

Introduction

On a common, if rather narrow, definition of the field, Austrian economists deny that macroeconomics has any positive scientific value. If macroeconomics is conceived not in terms of a broad analytical concern for the general functioning of the economy, but as a kind of theorising that uses the aggregative concepts and analytical framework developed by John Maynard Keynes and his various descendants, then Austrians do not do macroeconomics. On this definition, there is no uniquely Austrian method of macroeconomics and my task here is entirely negative: explain the Austrian denial of macroeconomics. On a more generous definition, however, Austrian economists are famous purveyors of macroeconomics. If macroeconomics encompasses more than Keynes and his methodological (if not necessarily theoretical or ideological) descendants – if it includes, in particular, the business-cycle theorising that dominated so much of economic science throughout the 19th and early 20th centuries – then there is an Austrian method of macroeconomics to explain. Part of my task, therefore, must be to distinguish the methodological aspects of business-cycle theorising, as Austrians do it, from those of macroeconomics proper, sufficiently well to explain why Austrians happily engage in the former, while angrily denying the value of the latter. From an Austrian perspective, what makes the sort of business-cycle theorising that they do legitimate, but macroeconomic methods as descended from Keynes impermissible?

A purely methodological explanation of the Austrian rejection of macroeconomics

It is possible to answer this question in a strictly methodological way. Several of the central precepts of modern macroeconomics are direct opposites of the methodological rules that Austrians have followed since Carl Menger (1883) first sparked the *Methodenstreit* against the younger branch of the German Historical School in the 1880s.

Austrians are methodological *individualists* (see Chapter 4 of Hayek 2010 [1952]). They contend that, as economic phenomena emerge from the actions of and

DOI: 10.4324/9781315745992-23

interactions among individuals situated in particular social contexts, the only legitimate units of economic analysis are individuals. Austrians are also methodological
subjectivists (see Chapter 3 of Hayek 2010 [1952]). Human action is not decided by
objective considerations. Individual human actors do not have epistemic access to
the objective truth concerning circumstances relevant to their actions. Rather, they
have subjective beliefs about these circumstances that, though they may be (and often
are) mistaken, are in any case the ultimate wellspring of human action. Humans act,
not because the world *is* a particular way, but because they *believe* it to be a particular
way (Hayek 2014 [1943]).[1]

Macroeconomic method, on the other hand, is collectivist and objectivist (Hayek
2010 [1952], Chapters 5 and 6). Macroeconomics deals in aggregated measures and
means, like a nation's Gross Domestic Product (GDP) and its average price level,
that purport to express and explain objective economic reality. Austrian economists
argue, however, that such aggregated figures are causally irrelevant to economic phenomena (Hayek 2014 [1975], pp. 363–4). They are not causally efficacious: they give
rise to no interesting economic phenomena. True, their subjective reflections in the
minds of individual actors may figure in these actors' decision-making: what people
subjectively believe about GDP or the Consumer Price Index (CPI) might enter into
their respective plans of action, but the purportedly objective measures themselves
are not the kind of things that can give rise to economic effects (Hayek 2012 [1931,
1935], p. 195). It is always people, never any aggregate or average, who labour and leisure, purchase and sell, produce and consume, and borrow and loan. Neither do the
mathematical figures of macroeconomics necessarily express the economic effects of
human action (Hayek 2014 [1975], p. 363). They are mere theoretical constructions
and, like all such constructions, reflect the preferences of their designers. In order to
construct a measure of, say, production in a national economy, choices must be made
as to what to include and exclude. Different designers will make different choices.
Thus, different measures, though perhaps called by the same name, will express different phenomena, none of which need be of economic interest. The supposedly objective measures of macroeconomics are, in the final analysis, products of the minds
of social scientists (Hayek 2010 [1952], Chapter 5). '[I]n the social sciences often that
is treated as important which happens to be accessible to measurement' (Hayek 2014
[1975], p. 363). Like the proverbial drunk searching for the house keys he misplaced
in an entirely different location, macroeconomists always look under the streetlamp
because that's where the light is best, even though the phenomena of interest – the
keys! – are not to be discovered there.

From an Austrian perspective, the economist's task is to trace the emergence of
economic phenomena from the actions of and interactions among individuals that
are prompted by these individuals' subjective beliefs about relevant circumstances.
Unless grounded in a micro analysis that accounts for the emergence of economic
phenomena from the actions of and interactions among individuals (and, thus, from
individuals' subjective beliefs), the aggregated and, by pretence, objective measures
of macroeconomics have no place in economic analysis.

This purely methodological explanation of the Austrians' rejection of macroeconomics might be best summarised in the terms that Hayek developed in his later
methodological writings (see esp. Hayek 2014 [1955], 2014 [1964] and 2014 [1975]). According to Hayek (2014 [1964], 260–2), *complex phenomena* are those that require a
complex model consisting of many variables open to the effects of the environment.

Naturally, as the number of variables required to adequately explain some phenomena increases, our ability both to cognitively trace in theoretical terms the interrelations among the phenomena these variables represent and to discover their empirical values at any given time – in other words, our ability to explain the phenomena – becomes more limited. Complex phenomena require models that respect this complexity and avoid the temptation to oversimplify the phenomena, i.e. to treat in terms of a few variables what can be adequately explained only in terms of many variables and their interrelations with each other, and the environment (Scheall 2019). In particular, scientists of complex phenomena must be less ambitious in their explanatory aims than scientists of simpler phenomena explicable in terms of comparatively few variables in a closed system can afford to be (Hayek 2014 [1975], pp. 371–2). *Explanations of the principle* that account for the mechanism whereby the phenomena of interest emerge from their individual causal factors, even if this means that specific manifestations of the phenomena cannot be fully explained (Hayek 2014 [1955], p. 203), and *pattern predictions* that describe broad patterns to be observed in the phenomena but not specific events (Hayek 2014 [1964], pp. 259–60) are the just-practicable objectives of the sciences of complex phenomena. From this perspective, individualism and subjectivism are methods for frankly dealing with the complexity of economic phenomena, while collectivism and objectivism are methods for pretending this complexity does not matter to economic analysis.

The pretence of macroeconomic knowledge: practical/political and psychological aspects of the Austrian denial of macroeconomics

Austrians insist that respecting the complexity of economic phenomena, acknowledging the explanatory and predictive limits of economic analysis matters a great deal; and the reasons why it matters extend beyond purely methodological concerns (Hayek 2014 [1975]).

Social science has rarely, if ever, been done purely for its own sake. Political economists have always been interested in the practical significance of their theories for improving social conditions. Indeed, modern macroeconomics was born in the wake of the Great Depression (Keynes 1936, *CW* VII); its original *raison d'être* was practical. Austrians reject macroeconomic method less for any specifically scientific reasons than because they see it as ill-adapted to the practical – *political* – ends for which it is supposed to be a means, namely, the goal of maintaining and, in times of economic distress, improving the health of the economy. Yet, even more troubling for Austrians than the deficiencies of macroeconomics as a countercyclical policymaking instrument *per se* is the way that these shortcomings are obscured by macroeconomics' false façade of scientific respectability and the effects of this obfuscation on the psychologies of economic policymakers (Hayek 2014 [1975]).

By oversimplifying the complex phenomena of economics – that is, by treating phenomena the explanation of which requires a model of many variables open to the environment in terms of a closed model consisting of a few variables – macroeconomic method imparts to the results of macroeconomic analysis an unmerited sheen of scientific virtue (Hayek 2014 [1975], p. 367). Together with the relative ease of measuring their variables, the oversimplified models of macroeconomics appear to place the economic policymaker in an epistemic position adequate to the tasks of effective countercyclical macroeconomic management. But, if there is anything to the

Austrians' methodological arguments, this is *mere* appearance; macroeconomic method manages no such epistemic feat (Hayek 2014 [1975], pp. 362–3).

In other words, the methods of macroeconomics, founded on a mistaken *scientistic* conception of scientific practice, deceive the economic policymaker into thinking they can manage the economy on the basis of their macroeconomic knowledge. Macroeconomics is founded on 'a false belief that the scientific method consists in the application of a ready-made technique, or in imitating the form rather than the substance of scientific procedure, as if one needed only to follow some cooking recipes to solve all social problems' (Hayek 2014 [1975], p. 368).

Austrians contend that when policymakers act on this epistemic basis despite its manifest inadequacy, the consequences tend to be not merely benign but cancerous to economic health. Austrians deny macroeconomics not merely because it is scientifically inadequate and practically ineffective, but because it warps the psychology of policymakers in a way that facilitates rather than forestalls economic distress.

> If man is not to do more harm than good in his efforts to improve the social order, he will have to learn that in this, as in all other fields where essential complexity of an organised kind prevails [i.e., in all those fields that study phenomena the explanation of which require a model of many variables open to the environment], he cannot acquire the full knowledge which would make mastery of the events possible.
>
> *(Hayek 2014 [1975], p. 371)*

If economic policymakers are not to create more economic suffering than they mitigate, then they must learn that macroeconomics is not a cooking recipe for the mitigation of economic suffering.

A primer on Austrian business cycle theory

Austrian Business Cycle Theory (ABCT) is built upon the foundations of Carl Menger's (1871) capital theory as extended by Eugen Böhm-Bawerk (1959 [1888]) and Swedish economist Knut Wicksell (1959 [1893], 1934), and later elaborated by Ludwig von Mises (1981 [1912]) and F. A. Hayek (2012 [1929], 2012 [1931, 1935], 2007 [1941]). According to the Austrian theory of capital, producing goods for final consumption proceeds over several time-consuming stages, from the initial input of original factors of production (labour and land), to the production and application of various intermediate capital goods, to the penultimate emergence of consumables and their ultimate consumption. At the beginning of this process (or intertemporal 'production structure') are stages of production remote in time from final consumption, e.g. research and development, mineral extraction and production of the most durable capital goods, like plant equipment and commercial buildings. At the end of this structure of production are those stages near in time to the consumer, e.g. wholesale and retail operations. Goods pass through several stages before emerging from the process ready for consumption.

Importantly, Austrians conceive of capital goods as heterogeneous and of varying degrees of specificity, a conception that methodologically rules out any treatment of capital as an aggregate of homogeneous stuff (Hayek 2012 [1937]; 2012 [1939], pp. 223–6). Capital is not some lump of undifferentiated goods all uniformly applicable come what may to whatever production process. Some capital goods are relatively non-specific and can be used in many stages across the production structure. A Phillips-head screwdriver, for example, might be used both in mineral extraction and in retail operations. Other capital goods, however, are highly specific and applicable only to a unique stage of a particular production process. A computer program required to fabricate a kind of fastener specific to a particular model of earth-moving equipment might find no alternative use should the equipment manufacturer go out of business.

The temporal duration or 'roundaboutness' of the production structure is directly related to its value productivity (Hayek 2012 [1931, 1935], p. 219), more value being producible in a longer than in a shorter length of time, other things equal. Of course, consumers prefer more value to less, but also prefer to wait a shorter to a longer time to consume. Thus, consumers face a trade-off, i.e. whether to sacrifice time for more valuable consumption goods or valuable consumption goods for more time.

On the Austrian conception, the interest rate on bank loans plays an important part in coordinating economic decision-making across time (Hayek 1995c [1931]; 1999 [1928]). It is an indicator of the state of supply and demand in the market for loanable funds (Hayek 2012 [1931, 1935], p. 211). On the assumption that the supply of loans is the sum of that portion of their respective incomes that individual consumers have saved for future consumption, the bank rate of interest is a marker of the manner in which consumers are making the above trade-off – it is an indication of their preferences for time over value, value over time – at any given moment. Other things equal, when the bank rate falls, it is a signal to producers that consumers have made relatively more of their savings available for future consumption, i.e. that consumers are prepared to wait longer for more value and, therefore, that producers can profitably extend the production structure further into the future by engaging in more roundabout and more productive production processes. Conversely, when the bank rate rises, it is an indicator that consumers have made relatively less of their savings available for consumption in a future period, i.e. that the trade-off between value and time has shifted in favour of time and, thus, that producers will find more profit in less productive shorter-duration production processes.

On the demand side of the loanable funds market, investors prefer longer-term investments, other things equal, a simple implication of the standard model of cash-flow discounting. A lower interest rate increases the comparative value of any future cash flow; it indicates to investors that future cash flow will cover their immediate expenses and so, ceteris paribus, a lower interest rate encourages greater investment in stages on the remote end of the structure of production. Thus, on the Austrians' (Wicksell 1898) interest theory, the bank rate serves to coordinate the savings and consumption decisions of wage-earners with the decisions of producers with regard to the production of goods in 'higher-order' stages temporally remote from consumption versus the production of goods in 'lower-order' stages near to consumption. The interest rate on loans

> governs not only the level of investment but also the allocation of resources within the investment sector. [...] As implied by standard calculations of discounted factor values, interest rate sensitivity increases with the temporal distance of the [...] stage of production from final consumption.
>
> *(Garrison 1996, p. 101)*

Where the connection is intact between the bank rate, expectations concerning the profitability of investments in different stages of the production structure and consumer's decisions to consume in the present rather than save for the future, the loanable funds market functions relatively smoothly, according to the theory. Consumers increase (decrease) their savings, meaning that they are prepared to wait longer (shorter) for more (less) value. The interest rate falls (rises), signalling producers that there is profit to be had in lengthening (shortening) the structure of production and, since the interest rate is an effective signal of future consumer demand in this scenario, the supply of consumption goods that eventually reaches market meets a commensurate demand.

Of course, individual producers are not omniscient. Profit expectations for particular investments sometimes disappoint. However, without some intervening factor that breaks the connection between the loan rate, profit expectations and consumers' decisions to consume in the present rather than save for the future, Austrians argue that there is no reason why many producers should all make such errors *en masse*, as they do when boom turns to bust during a typical business cycle.

ABCT holds that, in modern industrial economies, in fact, there is an intervening factor that disrupts the bank rate's signalling function, namely, the elasticity of the money supply. On Wicksell's (1898) theory, the rate of interest that equilibrates the supply of consumers' voluntary savings with the demand for loans is the *natural rate of interest*. Other things equal, when the supply of loanable funds exceeds voluntary savings, as can happen only where the currency is elastic, the bank rate falls below the natural rate.

There is some disagreement within the Austrian camp whether exogenous interference on the part of bankers, typically, central bankers, to deliberately expand the money supply beyond available savings is necessary (it is undoubtedly sufficient) to force the bank rate below the natural rate – the view defended by Mises (1981 [1912]) – or whether the expansion of the supply of loans beyond the extent of voluntary savings is an endogenous consequence of modern banking practices in economies with elastic currencies – the view defended by Hayek (2012 [1929], 2012 [1931, 1935]). On Hayek's view, an autonomous increase in the natural rate due to either improved profit expectations or a drop in voluntary savings, *if uncompensated by a commensurate increase in the bank rate*, bears the same effects as a deliberate lowering of the bank rate below the natural rate. This case is important, according to Hayek (2012 [1929], p. 123), not merely because it is 'probably the commonest in practice, but [due] to the fact that it must inevitably recur under the existing credit organization'. Expansion of the money supply can occur 'automatically under certain conditions – without the necessity for any special assumption of the inadequate functioning of any part of the system' (Hayek 2012 [1929], p. 124). In particular, it is not possible for bankers to know at any given moment whether their lending activities constitute the creation of new credit or the distribution of accumulated savings:

> As credit created on the basis of additional deposits does not normally appear in the accounts of the same bank that granted the credit, it is fundamentally impossible to distinguish, in individual cases, between deposits based on savings and those that result from the extension of credit.
>
> *(Hayek 2012 [1929], p. 131)*

It is well to note the distinct implications of these competing Austrian visions for the complexity of both the postulated causes of the cycle and countercyclical policymaking. On Mises's (1981 [1912]) view, at least in a world where a true gold standard is in effect, the cycle cannot be set in motion without a deliberate decision by (central) bankers to make loans available at rates below the natural rate. In order to avoid the cycle, consequently, central bankers need only enforce the gold standard and resist any political pressure to abrogate it; and private bankers need only resist any incentives to profit at the expense of their competitors by expanding their lending activities beyond the extent of voluntary savings. According to Hayek's vision, on the other hand, there is no possibility of effective countercyclical policy (see especially the Fourth Lecture of 2012 [1931, 1935]). The impossibility of distinguishing bank deposits due to savings from those due to the credit activities of competing banks means that the natural rate of interest is a mere theoretical figure that is not discernible in practice. Even if this problem could somehow be solved (and all of the other assumptions underlying ABCT realised), however, it is not obvious that we would want to eliminate bank credit, which makes possible 'a speed of development exceeding that which people would voluntarily make possible through their savings' (Hayek 2012 [1929], p. 143). A policy that will effectively annihilate economic fluctuations can be bought only at the price of slower economic growth. More to the present point, there is some tension even within the Austrian camp concerning the degree of simplification appropriate to models of the complex phenomena of business cycles.

In any case, in both its relatively simple Misesian and comparatively complex Hayekian forms, when the supply of loans extends beyond the amount of savings made available by consumers for the purposes of future consumption, the rate of interest on loans no longer serves as a reliable signal to producers of consumers' preferences for present versus future consumption. As in the case where all loans are financed by savings, when the interest rate falls, in keeping with the implications of cash-flow discounting, producers face a (ceteris paribus) greater incentive to invest in more remote stages of production; the structure of production is extended further into the future. As a consequence, land and labour are bid away from those stages near consumption and the owners of these resources receive an income fillip that other landowners and labourers do not receive. Indeed, as the prices of consumption goods rise as a result of supply restrictions due to the bidding away of resources from the near stages of production, everyone but the lucky owners of those resources bid away towards the remote end of the production structure is forced to consume less than they prefer. In other words, the owners of the factors of production receive an income boost financed out of the *forced savings* of everyone else (Hayek 2012 [1931, 1935]; 2012 [1932]).

As those who initially receive the new money spend it in various ways (and those who earn their incomes in related fields spend their newly increased incomes etc), the effects spread across the entire economy – eventually, everyone earns back some of their forced savings. However, importantly, there is no reason to think that, in this process of first losing and then recovering some of the income they would have preferred to consume in the first place, consumers have altered their preferred mix of consumption and savings in favour of more valuable consumption goods and less time. There is every reason to think they still prefer consumption goods in the relative near-term. Unfortunately, as it is following a shortfall of the loan rate below the natural rate, the extended production structure is set to deliver consumables at a more distant time in the future. The economic crisis has struck: If consumer demand is to be satisfied, many of these longer-term investments will have to be shut down and their non-specific capital goods re-distributed – a time-consuming process – to near stages of production.

ABCT explains economic disequilibrium in terms of the discombobulating effect that credit expansion has on the delicate links between the interest rate, the supply of and demand for loanable funds, and consumers' preferences and producers' decisions. Unless the relevant connections are re-established via some other equally effective knowledge-coordinating mechanism, producers will be led to make investments in various stages of the structure of production – that is, to either lengthen it or shorten it by engaging in more or less roundabout, and, therefore, more or less productive, production processes – that, unless preternaturally lucky, will not find a commensurate demand when the relevant consumption goods reach market and, thus, will turn out unprofitable.

Austrian methodology and Austrian business cycle theory

We understand, I hope, the methodological, practical and psychological reasons why Austrians reject macroeconomics, narrowly construed. It remains to explain why, despite this rejection, Austrians engage in the historically and, to some degree, conceptually related practice of theorising about the business cycle. In what ways and to what extent does Austrian Business Cycle Theory exemplify the methodological precepts of theoreticism, individualism and subjectivism that Austrians have always followed? How and how far does ABCT respect the complexity of business-cycle phenomena? Finally, what is the significance of ABCT for countercyclical policymaking and the psychology of economic policymakers?

As noted in the first footnote above, the Austrians' theoreticism is more pertinent to their denial of econometrics than to their rejection of macroeconomic methods as such. However, there is a concern somewhat related to theoreticism that figures in the Austrians' rejection of the macroeconomic theory specifically developed by Keynes (1930a, *CW* V, 1930b, *CW* VI, 1936, *CW* VII). Recall that, from an Austrian perspective, economic explanation requires not just a theory but a theory adequate to the complexity of the phenomena. In their famous debate, Hayek's (1995a [1931]; 1995b [1931]; 1995 [1932]) main complaint against Keynes's *Treatise on Money* (1930a *CW* V, 1930b, *CW* VI) was the inadequacy of the latter's theoretical conception of *capital*, a conception not remedied in Keynes's (1936 *CW* VII) later *General Theory*. Hayek argued that marrying Austrian capital theory to the other elements of Keynes's system resulted in an account of industrial fluctuations that looked much like ABCT.[2] In fact, however, capital figured in Keynes's economic thinking hardly at all. From Hayek's perspective, the crucial scientific difference between the two theories was that his theory incorporated capital, while Keynes's theory did not.

Hayek (1995b [1931], pp. 162–3) acknowledged that Austrian capital theory was incomplete and deficient in various respects, but, surely, he thought, some conception of capital – especially one that, whatever its other faults, was realistic in the sense of emphasising the time-consuming nature of production and the heterogeneity of capital goods – was better than altogether ignoring whatever part capital played in the promulgation of cycles. If capital figured in causing economic fluctuations, Keynes's theory would systematically neglect its significance. If capital theory had problems that needed to be resolved before it could effectively figure in an adequate explanation of the cycle, the proper response was to try to resolve these problems – which is precisely what Hayek attempted to do over the course of the next decade (see Hayek 2007 [1941]) – not to ignore them and proceed immediately to a concomitantly inadequate explanation of the cycle. Simply put, from an Austrian perspective, the proper response to the inadequacies of capital theory, such as it was in the early 1930s, was to further complexify the theory to better accord with the very complicated nature of the phenomena. Keynes, on the other hand, moved in the opposite direction, (over) simplifying his theory by removing capital from consideration.

At first glance, it might seem that ABCT fails to live up to the standards of the Austrians' avowed commitment to methodological individualism. After all, the theory proceeds not from the subjective perspectives of flesh-and-blood individuals but from the (ex hypothesi) shared subjective beliefs and attitudes of abstract classes of persons, e.g. consumers, savers, producers in various stages of the production process, entrepreneurs, borrowers, lenders, bankers, etc. As methodological individualists, Austrians are typically portrayed as rejecting the aggregative methods of macroeconomics: 'Mr. Keynes's aggregates conceal the most fundamental mechanisms of change' (Hayek 1995a [1931], p. 128). However, we can now see that, in fact, Austrians do not reject aggregation *per se*, but rather, aggregation at a level so high that the relevant causal factors are obscured. For Hayek and the Austrians, the important phenomena regarding the cycle – which Hayek (2012 [1929], p. 80) thought modern statistical methods had established conclusively – were *changes in relative prices (and, thus, profits) among different industrial sectors of the economy*. An appropriate theory of industrial fluctuations did not necessarily need to be fully disaggregated to the level of real flesh-and-blood individuals; rather, it needed to be sufficiently disaggregated to illustrate these changes in relative prices and profits, their causes and their consequences. For this, it sufficed to proceed from classes of individuals hypothesised to share many relevant subjective beliefs and attitudes in common, which – in keeping with the Austrians' methodological subjectivism – give rise to their actions in the economy. Put another way, there are rational limits to the need to complexify one's theory in order to account for economic phenomena that are determined by the nature of the problem under analysis.

The difficulties of economic policymaking are part and parcel of ABCT (see esp. the Fourth Lecture of Hayek's (1931 [2012]) *Prices and Production*). Indeed, the natural rate of interest – the rate that would equilibrate the supply of voluntary savings and the demand for loans in a counterfactual world in which the currency is inelastic – is not a measurable figure. Under prevailing credit institutions, we do not know how to prevent the cycle. Much of the knowledge that the economic policymaker would need in order to use ABCT as an effective policy tool is not available. However, even if the natural rate of interest were a known variable, this knowledge would hardly ease the policymaker's task. ABCT (at least, Hayek's version) implies that eradicating the cycle would require putting an end to bank credit. However, bank credit allows for more rapid economic growth. Thus, the policymaker confronts a difficult trade-off that ABCT is impotent to decide: controlling the cycle means limiting the prospects for rapid economic growth, while promoting these prospects implies a relative inability to control the cycle (Hayek 2012 [1929], p. 143). Even if all of these difficulties could be resolved, however, it would not suffice for policymakers to maintain the bank rate of interest at the natural rate. The effectiveness of a policy of monetary neutrality requires that all of the conditions assumed by ABCT obtain, including the premises of the general equilibrium theory at its core, i.e. full price and wage flexibility, correct foresight, etc (Hayek 2012 [1931, 1935], p. 282). Where these conditions do not hold, frictions will impede the smooth and rapid adaptation of the price system to changes in the economic data that is assumed by equilibrium theory and which is necessary for a policy of monetary neutrality to be an effective tool of countercyclical economic policymaking (Hayek 2012 [1931, 1935], p. 283).

As an attempt to come to grips with some massively complex phenomena, ABCT explains the principle that gives rise to, and predicts patterns to be observed in, business-cycle phenomena, but it does not aspire to a full explanation or a precise prediction of particular instances of the trade cycle. Indeed, an implication of the theory and the methodological principles upon which it is built is that such explanations and predictions are beyond the ken of cognitively limited human beings. Built upon the methodological principles of theoreticism, individualism and subjectivism, as well as a profound appreciation of the limitations that complexity places on the possibilities for explaining and predicting, and, therefore, controlling via political means, business-cycle phenomena, there is little prospect that Austrian Business Cycle Theory could ever serve as a tool of political mischief, unlike the oversimplified methods of macroeconomics that encourage economic policymakers to pretend to knowledge they do not possess.

Notes

1 Though it is only indirectly relevant in the context of a discussion of macroeconomic method, the Austrians' emphasis on the importance of *theory* to economic explanation should also be noted (Hayek 2010 [1952], p. 134). Austrians insist – indeed, they were early defenders of the view, which later became commonplace in the wake of Thomas Kuhn's (1962) *Structure of Scientific Revolutions* – that there is no such thing as brute, atheoretical, empirical observation. All sensory experience is mediated by theoretical considerations. Even the simplest, say, visual experience of a patch of red involves interpretation in terms of a theory that distinguishes red from other colours (and colours from other properties). Related to this, Austrians also deny that theories can be logically inferred from experience in any straightforward way (Menger 1883).

   The practical significance of their *theoreticism* is opposition to historicist and inductive methods. Thus, this theoreticism is less apparent in Austrian attitudes to macroeconomics *per se* than in their rejection of econometrics.
2 For an interesting effort at synthesizing the Austrian and Keynesian theoretical frameworks while remaining mostly true to the methodological precepts of the Austrian School, see Garrison (2001).

References

Böhm-Bawerk, E. (1959 [1888]) *Positive Theory of Capital*, translated by George D. Hunke, South Holland: Libertarian Press.
Garrison, R. W. (1996) 'The Austrian theory: A summary', in R. Ebeling, ed., *The Austrian Theory of the Trade Cycle and Other Essays*, Auburn: Ludwig von Mises Institute, pp. 98–106.
Garrison, R. W. (2001) *Time and Money: The Macroeconomics of Capital Structure*, London and New York: Routledge.
Hayek, F. A. (1999 [1928]) 'Intertemporal price equilibrium and movements in the value of money', in S. Kresge, ed., *The Collected Works of F.A. Hayek, Volume V, Good Money, Part I: The New World*, Chicago, IL: The University of Chicago Press, pp. 186–227.

Hayek, F. A. (2012 [1929]) 'Monetary Theory and the Trade Cycle', in H. Klausinger, ed., *The Collected Works of F.A. Hayek, Volume VII, Business Cycles, Part I*, Chicago, IL: The University of Chicago Press, pp. 49–165.

Hayek, F. A. (2012 [1931, 1935]) *Prices and Production*, in H. Klausinger, ed., *The Collected Works of F.A. Hayek, Volume VII, Business Cycles, Part I*, Chicago, IL: The University of Chicago Press, pp. 169–283.

Hayek, F. A. (1995a [1931]) 'Reflections on the pure theory of money of Mr. J.M. Keynes', in B. Caldwell, ed., *The Collected Works of F.A. Hayek, Volume IX: Contra Keynes and Cambridge*, Chicago, IL: University of Chicago Press, pp. 121–46.

Hayek, F. A. (1995b [1931]) 'A rejoinder to Mr. Keynes', in B. Caldwell, ed., *The Collected Works of F.A. Hayek, Volume IX: Contra Keynes and Cambridge*, Chicago, IL: University of Chicago Press, pp. 159–64.

Hayek, F. A. (1995c [1931]) 'The "Paradox" of saving', in B. Caldwell, ed., *The Collected Works of F.A. Hayek, Volume IX: Contra Keynes and Cambridge*, Chicago, IL: University of Chicago Press, pp. 74–120.

Hayek, F. A. (1995 [1932]) 'Reflections on the pure theory of money of Mr. J.M. Keynes (Continued)', in B. Caldwell, ed., *The Collected Works of F.A. Hayek, Volume IX: Contra Keynes and Cambridge*, Chicago, IL: University of Chicago Press, pp. 174–97.

Hayek, F. A. (2012 [1932]) 'A Note on the Development of the Doctrine of "Forced Saving"', in H. Klausinger, ed., *The Collected Works of F.A. Hayek, Volume VIII, Business Cycles, Part II*, Chicago, IL: University of Chicago Press, pp. 156–70.

Hayek, F. A. (2012 [1937]) 'Investment that raises the demand for capital' in H. Klausinger, ed., *The Collected Works of F.A. Hayek, Volume VIII, Business Cycles, Part II*, Chicago, IL: University of Chicago Press, pp. 206–11.

Hayek, F. A. (2012 [1939]) 'Profits, Interest, and Investment' in H. Klausinger, ed., *The Collected Works of F.A. Hayek, Volume VIII, Business Cycles, Part II*, Chicago, IL: University of Chicago Press, pp. 212–55.

Hayek, F. A. (2007 [1941]) *The Pure Theory of Capital*, in L. H. White, ed., *The Collected Works of F.A. Hayek, Volume XII, The Pure Theory of Capital*, Chicago, IL: The University of Chicago Press.

Hayek, F. A. (2010 [1952]) 'Scientism and the study of society', in B. Caldwell, ed., *The Collected Works of F.A. Hayek, Volume XIII, Studies on the Abuse and Decline of Reason: Text and Documents*, Chicago, IL: The University of Chicago Press, pp. 75–166.

Hayek, F. A. (2014 [1943]) 'The Facts of the Social Sciences', in B. Caldwell, ed., *The Collected Works of F.A. Hayek, Volume XV, The Market and Other Orders*, Chicago, IL: The University of Chicago Press, pp. 78–92.

Hayek, F. A. (2014 [1955]) 'Degrees of explanation', in B. Caldwell, ed., *The Collected Works of F.A. Hayek, Volume XV, The Market and Other Orders*, Chicago, IL: University of Chicago Press, pp. 195–212.

Hayek, F. A. (2014 [1964]) 'The Theory of Complex Phenomena', in B. Caldwell, ed., *The Collected Works of F.A. Hayek, Volume XV, The Market and Other Orders*, Chicago, IL: University of Chicago Press, pp. 257–77.

Hayek, F. A. (2014 [1975]) 'The pretence of knowledge', in B. Caldwell, ed., *The Collected Works of F.A. Hayek, Volume XV, The Market and Other Orders*, Chicago, IL: University of Chicago Press, pp. 362–72.

Keynes, J. M. (1930a) *A Treatise on Money. Part I: The Pure Theory of Money*, in D.E. Moggridge, ed., Keynes (1971–1989) *The Collected Writings of John Maynard Keynes*, Volume V, London: Macmillan and New York: St Martin's Press.

Keynes, J. M. (1930b) *A Treatise on Money, Part II: The applied theory of money*, in D.E. Moggridge, ed., Keynes (1971–1989) *The Collected Writings of John Maynard Keynes*, Volume VI, London: Macmillan and New York: St Martin's Press.

Keynes, J. M. (1936) *The General Theory of Employment, Interest, and Money,* in D.E. Moggridge, ed., Keynes (1971–1989) *The Collected Writings of John Maynard Keynes,* Volume VII, London: Macmillan and New York: St Martin's Press.

Kuhn, T. (1962) *The Structure of Scientific Revolutions,* Chicago, IL: University of Chicago Press.

Menger, C. (1871) *Grundsätze der Volkswirtschaftslehre.* Wien: Wilhelm Braumüller.

Menger, C. (1883) *Untersuchungen über die Methode der Sozialwissenschaften, und der politischen Oekonomie insbesondere,* Leipzig: Duncker & Humblot.

Mises, L. von (1981 [1912]) *Theory of Money and Credit,* Indianapolis: Liberty Fund.

Scheall, S. (2019) 'On the Method Appropriate to Hayek Studies' Œconomia– History / Methodology / Philosophy 9 (1), pp. 29–35.

Wicksell, K. (1959 [1893]) *Value, Capital, and Rent,* London: George Allen and Unwin.

Wicksell, K. (1898) *Geldzins und Güterpreise,* Jena: Fischer.

Wicksell, K. (1934) *Lectures on Political Economy, Vol. 1.* London: George Routledge and Sons.

20

WHAT WAS MARX'S METHOD, ACTUALLY?

Alan Freeman

Introduction[1]

To the unreflecting mind, it is a simple matter to discover a 'Marxist Macroeconomic Methodology'; we need only summarise what Marxist economists do or, even better, get an eminent Marxist to. There is, however, a catch: Marxists have no common method. There is no canonical body of work, as in neoclassical economics, which scholars of Marxist approaches to macroeconomic phenomena can refer to.

Yet, disconcertingly, the notion of a single, monotheoretic Marxism is embedded not only in mainstream but in heterodox writings. Dow (1985, p. 77) lists ten 'Historical and Methodological Development of Schools of Thought in Macroeconomics', summarising 'Marxian theory' thus: 'Modern Marxian Theory is derived directly from the works of Marx'. Tellingly, she does not specify a similarly defined 'Keynesian' economics: the ten schools include three flavours of Keynesianism, and Keynesians themselves recognise that their views are marked as much by disagreements as commonalities.

True, *mainstream* economics regales us with 'Keynesian' economics, commanding all to accept the imposed views of the dominant current as representative of the whole. It is however a cause for reflection that Keynesians can view 'Marxism' as they themselves are viewed by the mainstream. Clearly some superior engagement, cognisant of differences within 'schools', is called for.

Beginning in the 1980s, alternative interpretations of Marx's value theory (Freeman and Carchedi 1996, Freeman et al. 2001, Kliman 2007) challenged the claim that the 'Marxist Economics' of Western academia (Samuelson 1971) is 'derived directly from the works of Marx'. They showed (Kliman 2007; Kliman and McGlone 1988) that it is derived from a different theoretical system proposed by Ladislaw von Bortkiewicz (1984) as a *correction* to Marx, whose methodological basis is the requirement that society should reproduce itself perfectly in every period.

Scholars from the Temporal Single System Interpretation (TSSI) of Marx describe the resulting system as 'Marxism Without Marx' (MWM) (Freeman 2010). Twenty-five years of study, including fruitful encounters with Post-Keynesians and Austrians (Freeman et al. 2014), have yielded recognition, be it patchy and grudging, that

DOI: 10.4324/9781315745992-24

this constitutes a bastardisation—with important similarities to Robinson's Bastard Keynesianism. It is a General Equilibrium (GE) system, imposing on history's most consistently equilibrium-free thinker the supposition that the magnitudes of all endogenous variables, be they prices, values, employment, quantities produced and consumed, or the profit rate, must all be deduced from the assumption that the economy does not change while they are formed. In this Say's Law system, attributed to Say's fiercest critic, no goods remain unsold, money has no place, and endogenous crisis is theoretically impossible.

Post-Keynesians will recognise the symptoms. Here, however, the similarity ends. Bastard Keynesianism is dedicated to *sanitising* Keynes: MWM is dedicated to *disproving* Marx. This provides its practitioners with the justification for *alternative* theories which, they claim, reproduce Marx's conclusions without recourse to his theories. MWM is thus neither derived from Marx, nor a macroeconomic theory. MWM writings make no attempt to explain how a real economy behaves: their sole preoccupation is to prove Marx could not. To be sure, their literature draws on the Sraffa-inspired Linear Production Systems expounded by Pasinetti (1979) or Kurz and Salvadori (1995). But no serious contemporary claims that these systems are derived 'directly from Marx', and since Steedman (1977), it is generally accepted that they cannot be.

A wider tradition does derive from Marx, but names like Kautsky, Lenin, Hilferding, Luxemburg, Trotsky, Bukharin, Preobrazhensky, Grossman, or Rosdolsky, with the possible exception of the unignorable Mandel (1974), figure neither in economics curricula nor, tellingly, in the MWM literature.

There is, therefore, no 'Marxist' macroeconomic methodology as conventionally understood. I will therefore present 'Marxist Economics' as I think Marx would have: as an attempt not to understand the capitalist economic system, but to excuse it: in short, as a waste product of history.

Origins and structure of Western Marxist economic theory

I start by formalising Marx's views as a number of propositions.

Proposition 1: labour, engaged in the production of commodities, is the sole source of value;

Proposition 2: the owners of the means of production appropriate what remains of this value, after deducting the value consumed in producing it.

From these Marx deduces several conclusions, most notably in Volume III where prices depart from values. This is done for the special case where commodities are sold at their price of production but applies to any set of market prices. We can express this generally with two further propositions:

Proposition 3: The value transferred to the product by those commodities consumed in producing it (constant capital) is proportional to their price.[2]

Proposition 4: The value deducted from the living labour engaged in making that product (variable capital) is proportional to the price of the goods consumed by the labourers.

These are completely compatible with propositions 1 and 2, so we can treat 1–4, together with conclusions 1–3 below, as a coherent formalisation of Marx's theory of value. The proof of this assertion having been given by many TSSI scholars, we will not repeat it. Marx's three most contested conclusions follow:

Conclusion 1: the total value of the commodities produced in any period does not differ from the total value realised.

Conclusion 2: the total value appropriated by the owners of the means of production is unaffected by the divergence of realised value from produced value.

Conclusion 3: the ratio between profit and accumulated privately owned value decreases as long as accumulation proceeds.

In class terms 1 and 2 state that labour remains the sole source of value when prices diverge from values, and that the distribution of value between classes is determined by production relations alone. Conclusion 3, commonly called the Law of the Tendency of the Rate of Profit to Fall (LTRPF), covers many issues, not least that it corresponds to reality: the list includes financial crashes, cyclic recessions, the course of technological change, and population dynamics.[3]

The best account of Marx's transmogrification at the hands of Marxist economists is Kliman and McGlone's (1988) seminal exegesis of Bortkiewicz (1952, p. 9), who did *not* claim, as alleged by Samuelson (1971), Steedman (1977), and MWM writers, that Marx fails to transform input prices. To the contrary, Bortkiewicz *accepts that Marx does so*. His objection is Marx does not make input prices *equal* to output prices.

His grounds are that unless this is so, goods remain unsold (ibid., p. 12):

> What happens now, when price-calculation … replaces value-calculation? … The workers thus must go short, or, put in another way, *some of the goods made in I and V find no outlet*. In this regard, therefore, the price model *breaks down.* (my emphases)

The price calculation 'breaks down' not because inputs are untransformed but because if transformed as Marx proposes, there is insufficient monetary demand to pay for the outputs at their modified prices. In short, Marx's transformation violates Say's Law.

Bortkiewicz then develops a 'correction' by imposing perfect reproduction, yielding an entirely different system which can be formalised in three further propositions:

Proposition 5: The amount of every commodity produced each year is completely consumed in that year.

Proposition 6: Prices and values remain constant throughout production.

Proposition 7: The rate of profit is uniform, that is, everywhere equal.

Propositions 5–7 are equilibrium assumptions. Yet equilibrium is conspicuously absent from Marx's analysis: consider only his account of equalisation (Marx 1894, p. 169). Profits tend to equalise, not because prices confirm to an ideal equilibrium but because they don't; actual, real-life capitals always seek a surplus profit, a profit different from the average, causing capital to migrate from spheres where profit is below average to those where it is above:

> Within each individual sphere of production, there take place changes, i.e., deviations from the general rate of profit … Since the general rate of profit is not only determined by the average rate of profit in each sphere, but also by the distribution of the total social capital among the different individual spheres, and since this distribution is continually changing, it becomes another constant cause of change in the general rate of profit.

Marx's profit rate, unlike Bortkiewicz's, is never actually equalised. It is an average, an ideal around which individual profit rates fluctuate chaotically.

It's about time

Equilibrium propositions 5–7 are normally presented in discrete time; it is doubtful that GE can even be formalised in continuous time. Marx's temporalism does indeed lend itself to a continuous formalisation, which we omit since his critics only consider discrete time.[4]

Discrete time leads to period analysis, for which Schumpeter credits Sismondi, and can be formalised in either temporal or equilibrium systems. The latter were introduced by Walras (Bridel 1997), popularised by Marshall (Dobb 1973, pp. 184–5), and adapted to Marx by Bortkiewicz, a devout Walrasian (Gattei 1982), who explains his motives (1952 [1906], pp. 23–4) as follows:[5]

> Alfred Marshall said once of Ricardo: 'He does not state clearly, and in some cases he perhaps did not fully and clearly perceive how, in the problem of normal value, the various elements govern one another mutually, not successively, in a long chain of causation.' This description applies even more to Marx…[who] held firmly to the view that the elements concerned must be regarded as a kind of causal chain, in which each link is determined, in its composition and its magnitude, only by the preceding links…Modern economics is beginning to free itself gradually from the successivist prejudice, the chief merit being due to the mathematical school led by Leon Walras.

Bortkiewicz's system can be solved for values, prices, and the uniform profit rate by writing down a simultaneous equation system derived from 6 and 7; TSSI scholars call this 'simultaneism'. The result ensures that Say's Law proposition (5) holds. In contrast, if Bortkiewicz's numerical example is analysed temporally, stocks of unsold goods are carried over from period 1 to period 2.

Bortkiewicz's system being static, MWM writers fall back on the Walrasian stratagem known as comparative statics. As a last refuge they rechristen this 'long-run' or 'structural' analysis (Kurz and Salvadori 1995), adding the claim that equilibrium prices constitute a 'centre of gravity' around which market prices fluctuate.[6] The key notion remains, however, that *the endogenous variables are wholly determined in each period in isolation from all other periods.* To illustrate, suppose an evolving set of variables is given by

$$Z^t = \left\{ z_1^t, z_2^t, \ldots z_n^t \right\} \qquad (1)$$

and that A^t is a set of parameters changing independently of Z^t, say

$$A^t = \left\{ a_1^t, a_2^t, \ldots a_n^t \right\} \qquad (2)$$

Z in general is determined by the difference equation system

$$Z^{t+1} = f\left(A^t; Z^t \right) \qquad (3)$$

223

The A^t, typically technical coefficients or consumer preferences, evolve under their own laws, independently of Z^t. Following the general usage of dynamic analysis (Dore 1993), we term A^t the exogenous and Z^t the endogenous determinants of the motion of the system.

Under general conditions, (3) has a unique solution depending on f and the values of A^0, Z^0 at some time in the past, usually termed the 'initial conditions' (Spiegel 1994). This is the temporal formalisation. However, a particular instance of this general case is a hypothetical stationary state in which S stays fixed. Equation (14) then becomes the simultaneous equation system

$$Z^{*t} = f\left(A^t; Z^{*t}\right) \qquad (4)$$

whose solution Z^{*t} also exists under general conditions given by the Brouwer fixed-point theorem (Istratescu 2001).

Now, the temporal solution Z^t registers genuinely dynamic endogenous effects. In contrast, though Z^{*t} also varies over time it does so only because of changes in A, giving a flicker-book impression of dynamism. To put it rigorously, Z^{t+1} is *functionally independent* of Z^t. It is therefore not true, outwith the exceptional case of an economy that really is static (that is to say, in which neither Z nor A is changing over time) that

$$Z^t = Z^{*t} \qquad (5)$$

the difference being especially marked for endogenous effects that produce long-term changes such as the falling rate of profit or unequal exchange. In particular, Marx's much-disputed conclusion 3 applies to equation (3) but not (4). The MWM claim that Okishio's (1961) celebrated theorem refutes Marx's proof of the LTRPF thus applies only to GE interpretations of Marx, not to any temporal interpretation.

A further complication makes it clear where these differences arise. Prices in system (4) are supposed to be the same at the end of the current period as at the start of this same period. They therefore differ from prices at the start of the next period: but the end of the current period and the start of the next are the same notional point in time. The fiction leads to *exchange-inconsistency* (Freeman 2020b), a form of stock-flow inconsistency. Buyers would have to pay a sum of money different from what sellers receive. In consequence value is created out of nothing, the root error in Okishio's theorem.

The two-system fallacy

How do Bortkiewicz's assumptions account for the contradictions he finds in Marx's theory? Surely, a theory valid out of equilibrium must also hold in equilibrium, which is merely a specific case? Indeed, Bortkiewicz himself advances this argument. The answer arises from a *further* assumption: the 'two-system' definition of value (Sweezy 1984 [1949], pp. 199–200):

Proposition 8: Commodity values are given not by the sum of direct labour and consumed constant capital in the price system, but by the solution to a different system, the 'value system' in which the profit rate is not equalised. These 'two systems' are the bedrock of the MWM critique of Marx and the origin of the entire fiction that he failed to transform values. This critique rests not directly on equilibrium but on this further 'correction', which Bortkiewicz uses to restate the problem in an entirely different manner from Marx. He identifies two 'equalities' which must both be satisfied, if Marx is to be deemed consistent:

Conclusion B1: Total outputs in the value system must equal total outputs in the price system.

Conclusion B2: Total profit in the value system must equal total profit in the price system.

These conclusions do not follow from propositions 5–7 because they refer to two different economies. They are hence incompatible with propositions 1 and 2. Either value can be created without labour (if conclusion B1 is dropped) or profit can arise without exploitation, if conclusion B2 is dropped. The end result is a theory of value comprising propositions 1, 2, and 5–8 but not 3 and 4. It produces *different numbers* from Marx's theory, comprising propositions 1–4 but not 5–8.

Bortkiewicz's system, in short, is not Marx's. Not until Steedman (1977) finally concluded that this system could not be defended as a theory of value did critical scholars re-examine Marx's own theories, realising two *interpretative* points:

Interpretative Point 1 (Temporal): In Marx, both prices and values are equal, at the start of any period, to their magnitudes at the end of the *preceding* period, not to their future magnitudes at the end of the *same* period.

Interpretative Point 2 (Single System):[7] value is determined from price by the living labour added to the value transmitted to the product by constant capital in a *single* economy, not by its magnitude in a hypothetical *different* economy.

Under this interpretation, conclusions 1–3 *all* follow from propositions 1–4. TSSI scholars argue, applying the Barkai-Stigler criterion (Kliman 2007, p. 63), that it best expresses Marx's actual theory. On this basis Marx's theory is moreover *inductively scientific*: compatible with observation. His prices are those observed in the market, not the ideal Say's Law prices of the MWM interpretation. Money exists and can be accumulated; it is not, as in MWM and indeed all Linear Production Systems, a mere *numéraire*. The primary elements of crisis—that circulation is interrupted when money is hoarded, and that capital retreats into its money form when the rate of return on productive investment is driven down by accumulation—are easily represented theoretically. Not least, the driving force of the capitalist economy—the pursuit of an above average profit—is transparent to view.

Political economy and the theory of class

So much for the method of the Marxists: does it help us clarify, if asked, what Marx's own 'macroeconomic methodology' was? In a book on methodology, it would be remiss not to try, but the question is not unproblematic.

The first problem is *purpose*. Morticians and physicians both study the human organism, using different methods, but evisceration is not the basis of a methodological school in the Health Sciences. Marx's purpose was so different from conventional economists that even treating him as one easily leads to confusion: as Desai (2016) notes, the divorce of 'economics' from the other social sciences is the outcome of a Weberian reconstruction which prevents any single discipline reaching politically dangerous conclusions.

This is illustrated by the question 'What is Volume III of *Capital* for?' Economists invariably focus on its 'pure economic' content, notably the so-called 'transformation problem' and the LTRPF. But only 16 chapters of this volume deal with such issues. The remaining 36 (Freeman 2019) provide an analysis of *classes*, each defined by the relation between its revenue and its property (the famous 'property relations'): merchants, bankers, landowners, industrialists, and so on.

These 36 chapters do not stand apart from the rest of *Capital:* they are a major part of what Marx's majestic account of the capitalist economy is *for*. He starts where Ricardo (1817, p. 1) leaves off:

> The produce of the earth—all that is derived from its surface by the united application of labour, machinery, and capital, is divided among three classes of the community; namely, the proprietor of the land, the owner of the stock or capital necessary for its cultivation, and the labourers by whose industry it is cultivated...
>
> To determine the laws which regulate this distribution, is the *principal problem in Political Economy.* (my emphasis)

The difference between Ricardo, whose focus was the distribution of value, and Smith, whose interest was its source, is passed over in the standard view of a uniform pre-Marginal Classical tradition united by the Labour Theory of Value. Marx's objective was to understand *how classes behaved*, by asking where their revenue came from. Crucially, their 'behaviour' includes the ideas they champion. The quest for an adequate theory of distribution thus drives his search for an adequate theory of value, since we cannot speak of distributing any produced substance without saying what that substance is.

The economic foundation of classes appears in no other 'economic methodology' except tangentially in Institutionalism, yet is a mere introduction to an even wider divergence of purpose. Marx was a revolutionary, a product of 1789 and 1848, who, in common with his contemporaries, sought the emancipation of humanity. Like them, he saw classes as the primary instrument of human oppression. Humans lacked freedom, not as some vague existential consequence of their general condition, but because other humans deprived them of it.

Unlike his contemporaries he predicted that the overthrow of the old aristocratic order would lead not to a society of universal rights, as proclaimed by French and American insurgents, but to a *new* class society: capitalism. This too would pass, but how destructively, and with what result, would be the outcome of conscious human action. The reason to study classes is, therefore, to prepare humanity to create a new order founded on genuinely universal freedom.

Marx studied economics, therefore, to understand the new classes springing from a commodity economy. This is not a 'different way of doing economics': it is a way of doing something economists do not.

Doctrine versus science: Marx, Engels, and historical materialism

The next problem is the nature of methodological enquiry itself. Economists tend to understand method *prescriptively*, a means of producing or using theory. Indeed, the standard UK economics curriculum (Freeman 2008) is organised on this basis. Prescriptive methodology is responsible for the *deductivist* view (Freeman 2020a) that we can reach correct conclusions about the world through a mechanical sequence of deductions from a single set of *doctrinal* first principles. Since only one deduction can be so made, this leads to *monotheoreticism* (Freeman 2016), causing economics to behave as a religion, not a science.

Equilibrium is archetypal: its first principle being that the market is perfect, any proposition that the market can fail is not deducible from a GE system and appears illogical or absurd, which is why Marx's conclusions appear 'inconsistent' to MWM writers.

Nevertheless, we cannot reach a 'correct' Marx, much less a correct theory, by simply abolishing equilibrium. A positive conclusion cannot come from a negative assumption: saying the world is 'not in equilibrium' does not found a theory. Had Copernicus merely said 'the Sun does not orbit the Earth', omitting that the Earth rotates and orbits the Sun, he would have simply been a nihilist.

Did Marx, then, enunciate some *alternative* set of prime principles? This attractive conception is open to equally widespread abuse. Attempts to codify Marx's ideas as a deductive system frequently result in new doctrines, because his process of enquiry is inductive. *Capital* volume I thus opens with a *fact*: capitalist society comprises a 'gigantic heap of commodities', and the investigator's job is to interrogate various theories until they explain this fact—in contrast with the standard method, which is to lay out a set of assumptions and torture the facts until they comply with them.

Misunderstandings multiply when writers ignore Marx's (1973, p. 101) distinction between the order of investigation and the order of exposition. An investigator tests a variety of theories against observation and, having done so, presents the conclusions in some structured way. But *an exposition is not a proof*: a theory is proven when it *explains what we see*, which is why Marx's writings are filled with countless references to empirical reality. A structured exposition *lays a theory open* to inductive scrutiny: if any step in the chain of reasoning contradicts any fact, nothing beyond that step can be accepted as valid without further study. If we ignore the function of induction in this process, exposition morphs into doctrine.

For this reason, there are many possible expositions of the same conclusion, of which Marx's is only one. So what does Marx's achieve? Precisely in laying out the hidden presuppositions of the various theories assessed. Marx uses logic to *uncover the structure of ideas*: in studying the relation of proposition B and C to a proposition A on which they depend logically, he asks not 'Which follows from A?' but 'What must we suppose about A if we think we can deduce B or C from it?'

The controversy around the LTRPF provides a clear example of the mistakes which arise from a doctrinal reading of Marx. All his critics, not least Robinson (1942), many interpreters (Heinrich 2013), and no few defenders (Carchedi and Roberts 2013) treat Marx's exposition as a *proof* that the rate of profit falls, a deductivist statement about the inevitable fate of capitalism. But as Kliman et al. (2014) explain, Marx provides an *explanation* of the observed fact that, for long periods and in many countries, it falls over time.

This is a very different thing. Marx's LTRPF establishes that the observed fall is caused by capitalism, arising endogenously from accumulation. Of course, if capitalism stops accumulating, the rate of profit ceases falling, which has happened at least three times in history, most recently World War II. But the cause of these reversals was exogenous: under war and fascism, much accumulation is taken out of the hands of private capital and organised by the state.

The 'law', in short, expresses the relation between concealed, autonomous accumulation driven by the search for surplus profit, and conscious human intervention. This is completely coherent with Marx's emancipatory purpose: it tells us which free choices will escape the domination of the alienated results of our own class society. It also offers a rational ethics: War being destructive, Communism is preferable.

In summary, if the notion of 'methodology' is to be useful in understanding Marx, it should be descriptive, not prescriptive, and clearly distinguish Marx's mode of exposition from his method of enquiry.

Marx's method of enquiry

As far as Marx was concerned, he simply practised science and, indeed, invited Charles Darwin to write a preface to *Capital*. Nevertheless in the novel context of studying the capitalist economy, his own scientific praxis was distinctive.

His meticulous pluralism, while not differentiating him from other scientists, sheds light on this issue. He studied the entire field of economic theory, polishing the seats of the British Library in the process. Why? Because in order to select between a variety of explanations of the facts, one must be familiar with the candidates. This takes us to the threshold of a quite profound issue of method. To interrogate an idea, as noted, we must know its presuppositions; but to understand these, we must also know *where economic ideas come from*. In Skidelsky's (2020) language, this could be called a *contextual* approach. Marx at one and the same time attempts to explain reality by means of theoretical ideas *and* how that reality could give rise to those ideas. This principle contrasts with the idealist neoclassical tradition in which theory is timeless, ahistorical, Platonic, and generates itself out of itself.

He and Engels described the principle as 'Historical Materialism' in a justly famous passage (Marx 1979 [1859], p. 20):

> The mode of production of material life conditions the general process of social, political and intellectual life. It is not the consciousness of men that determines their existence, but their social existence that determines their consciousness. At a certain stage of development, the material productive forces of society come into conflict with the existing relations of production or—this merely expresses the same thing in legal terms—with the property relations within the framework of which they have operated hitherto. From forms of development of the productive forces these relations turn into their fetters. Then begins an era of social revolution. The changes in the economic foundation lead sooner or later to the transformation of the whole immense superstructure.

A key question is then 'what leads to a theory being adopted?' which is just another way of asking what determines consciousness. A simplistic positivist answer is that theories are adopted when people see they are true. However the basic distinction between appearance and essence means that things are not, in general, what they seem. Marx further held that in capitalism, social relations are disguised by commodity fetishism, leading to the persistent belief that they are relations between things, and believed this to be one of his major discoveries.

In consequence, however, *ideas arise from the material circumstances of classes and their adoption is an outcome of class struggle*. This is the capstone of a methodology as relevant today as in its Victorian heyday, explaining why MWM is so pervasive, and why false theories *in general* predominate in economics.

Theoretical counter-revolutions and the history of economic theory

Bourgeois intellectual society, from the earliest days of political economy, has treated its honest economists as carriers of some kind of virus: ideas so dangerous that they threaten the very fabric of civilisation. This obliges it to seek 'safe' economics: approaches that permit tinkering but under no circumstance the conclusion that anything is fundamentally wrong.

The earliest exemplar is James Mill's reaction to the Ricardian Socialist Hodgskin: 'if [Hodgskin's ideas] were to spread they would be subversive of civilised society' (Dobb 1973, p. 98). Hodgskin (1825), when Marx was seven, had drawn a natural conclusion from Ricardo's finding that rent was a deduction from profit, not (as in Smith) the reward to a factor of production. In that case, argued Hodgskin, why stop at rent? Why not recognise all revenues of property, notably profit, as a simple deduction from the value created by the labourer?

The anti-Ricardian reaction, led by John Stuart Mill, was described thus by Marx (1906[1867], pp. 17–18):

> Let us take England. Its Political Economy belongs to the period in which the class struggle was as yet undeveloped. Its last great representative, Ricardo, in the end, consciously makes the antagonism of class interests, of wages and profits, of profits and rent, the starting point of his investigations, naively taking this antagonism for a social law of Nature. But by this start the science of bourgeois economy had reached the limits beyond which it could not pass...

What prevented, and still prevents society 'passing beyond' these limits is, precisely, the material circumstances of its new and now dominant classes, for whom an economic theory that explained the real source of their wealth and power was anathema.

The role of material interest is absent from both modern economics and its methodology, in which theory arises from theory. *Cui Bono* plays no part in evaluating the results; it was not until its hundredth year (DeMartino and McCloskey 2016) that the American Economic Association even required authors to disclose sources of funding. In all Keynes's insightful discussion of Say's Law, we find no hint of why Say thought as he did, or why his ideas became popular. For Marx this is the key question: it is impossible and wrong to detach, in searching for a superior theory, the material interests at stake.[8] Whereas Keynes complains at politicians enslaved by scribblers, for Marx the scribblers are imprisoned by their classes.

Mill's refusal to accept the logically undeniable deduction of the Ricardian socialists, *not* on the grounds of their empirical validity, but their social acceptability, ushered in the age of religious economics, in which theories are judged not by their exoteric ability to explain observed reality but by their *esoteric* suitability for preserving the social order. This age is marked, mirroring the high and low tides of capitalist accumulation sometimes referred to as 'Kondratieff waves', by waves of economic thought.[9]

The boom times such as 1848–1870, 1893–1928, or 1942–1974 are marked by theoretical regression: anti-Ricardian reaction in the British capitalism's mid-Victorian heyday; Marginalism in the age of 'concrete, steel, electricity and imperialism' (Freeman 1995); and General Equilibrium in the post-war Long Boom. Amidst a general rise in prosperity—at least in the colonial nations, things being otherwise in countries impoverished by their enrichment—and propelled by a cornucopia of technological marvels, properties approaching divinity are assigned to the market system, a phenomenon I term 'Capital Worship' (Freeman 2014, p. 100). The economy is *naturalised*, presented as the product of 'human nature' which we disobey at our peril. It is *eternalised*; market relations, we are told, have always existed and always will. The capitalist is *deified*: the bold entrepreneur and the beneficent financier stalk the textbooks. The working class is *dehumanised*, reviled for Luddite obstruction of progress manifested in evil demands like safe working conditions or decent pay, and not infrequently *racialised*, characterised as unfit for any other social station. The peasantry is dismissed as a backward fetter on progress, surplus to requirements and fit only for slaughter like the Irish or export to the colonies like the Scots.

Nevertheless, in the golden ages, and in the ideologically dominant countries, the subject of contention is the share of a growing pie. A Labour Aristocracy either emerges or regains control, 'safe' parties of opposition are moulded with carrots and sticks, and the intellectual classes are reduced to their primary function of proselytising. Alternative or critical ideas are found in subjected countries, in 'loser' capitalist nations, in the ranks of the oppressed, and in the works of the exiled and marginalised—like Karl Marx.

Advances in economic thought appear during Depressions, when reality rudely intrudes on the comfortable fictions of the golden periods. As Tucholsky (1994 [1929]) perceptively remarks, 'Political Economy is when people wonder why they have no money'. Or, indeed, no jobs. It was during the first Great Depression, from 1870 until modern imperialism in the early 1890s, that Marx's ideas really began to take hold. Böhm-Bawerk (1949[1896], p. 3) thus laments:

> As an author Karl Marx was enviably fortunate. No one will affirm that his work can be classed among the books which are easy to read or easy to understand. Most other books would have found their way to popularity hopelessly barred if they had laboured under an even lighter ballast of hard dialectic and wearisome mathematical deduction. But Marx, in spite of all this, has become the apostle of wide circles of readers, including many who are not as a rule given to the reading of difficult books.

The agency of theoretical change is, thus, a material force: the working class. This is why the adoption of Marx's knowledge by the mass workers' movement after 1870 arose for profoundly scientific reasons: it made sense of their experience. The economists could ignore and suppress it, but the world did not—the most extreme expression being the Russian revolution. Veblen's success in America can be traced to a similar process, though with less explosive results.

An analogous process took place in the second Great Depression but with a new twist. Keynes saw through Say's Law and knew that goods circulated only so long as people spend money and do not hold on to it. He also understood that the working class was a fact of life: its livelihood could not be entrusted to the market. As World War II drew to its close, with millions of war-scarred young men and women expecting a better life and Russia's sphere of influence extending into Europe's Eastern hinterland, Welfare and Demand Management came to be recognised as compromises necessary to capitalist survival, provoking Friedman's famous remark that 'we are all Keynesians now'.

The twist is this: while Keynes certainly added to the general body of economic knowledge, actually he *re*discovered what Marx long insisted on. His theory of investment (Freeman 2016) is closer to Marx's than generally realised, although his formulation adds a genuinely new element to economic knowledge.

The *re*-discovery of past known truths in Great Depressions is hence central to the way economic thought evolves. If we recognise it as integral to the acquisition of economic and social knowledge, we must equally recognise the vital importance of accuracy in interpretation and honesty in citation. Keynes's account of what he terms the 'classical tradition'—Say's Law economics—would be a masterpiece of historical and economic investigation but for one absence—Marx, who gets one mention, in the company of two virtual unknowns, Silvio Gesell and Major Douglas (Keynes 1936, p. 33).

Had Keynes drawn the conclusion, from this offhand acknowledgement of Marx's contribution, that most of what he sought required the *recovery* of Marx's *discoveries* as a whole, instead of inventing a fictitious alternative history, the current state of economic thinking may well have been different. Instead, knowledge of Marx has come down to successive generations of Western post-war economists not as Keynes's mighty precursor but the progenitor of an obscure and self-contradictory algebraic system for calculating non-existent prices.

Two further facts now emerge. First, Golden-Age theories cannot be reduced to mere 'discoveries', even religious ones. We cannot understand them even as the invention of better and better ways to glorify Mammon. They are best described as *theoretical counter-revolutions*. Their function is to suppress, isolate, and eliminate the contagion of scientific understanding that takes root in times of trouble. In the case of marginalism this is now fairly clear. Böhm-Bawerk, Finance Minister of Austria-Hungary charged with imposing austerity on the seething masses of its sprawling territories, is explicit, as our quote above illustrates, that the reason for a new theory of value is to put paid to Marx's.

Second, the contest is not a simple knock-down fight between marginalism in the blue corner and value theory in the red. The strategy is Jesuitical; it sows confusion and disarray in the ranks of its opponents by means of rhetoric disguised as logic, rewards those who see 'sense', and isolates those who do not. *Isolation* and *internal confusion* are the combined weapons of this offensive. MWM is hence not just a 'failed' Marxism but entirely antithetical to it, one of the principal means by which conventional economics quarantines Marx's infectious ideas.

The material origins of simultaneist Marxism

MWM's 'success' poses a general question facing all economics: why does it adopt, as adequate descriptions of reality, algebraic systems from which the most important feature of reality—movement—has been removed?

Marx's historical materialist method offers an answer. 'Marxist Economics' is a product of definite material circumstances. Notwithstanding its 19th-century origins, it took firm root as the 'received view' of Marx during the most profound period of regression in economic thought yet seen, in that it *perfected* all previous counter-revolutions in the all-encompassing paradigm of General Equilibrium. The GE paradigm is *itself a* methodology—whose purpose is to rule all others.

With GE's triumph, this world has changed forever. It is not just 'Marxism' and 'Keynesianism' that deserve better than to be designated 'schools'. The equilibrium paradigm cross-cuttingly polarises the whole of economics, and this rift is now the *principal* methodological divide of economics. A GE variant appears in *every* 'School' of thought, whereon it becomes the dominant method: 'Bastard Keynesianism', Marxism Without Marx, General Equilibrium Marginalism (as opposed to Austrian Marginalism), Rational Expectations, and so on. It becomes the General Method of Economics, and all schools lose their identity to become simple variants of a single method.

Why? Again, materialism comes to our aid. GE vaccinates the subject against the virus of science. It seals any new discovery in a Black Box which not even Pandora can open, outside which no trace can be found of imperfection. Within *each* 'school' we find two opposed methods: the GE Method in vermiculate variants, and a minority temporal current, shouting to get out of the shrinking space allowed it. Respectability is accorded those who sign the pact, and reframe their heretical temporal theory in equilibrium form; all others are denied prizes, publication, funding, promotion, recognition, and jobs. This is not some casual accident but an institution, arising from the integration of the profession into the banking industry on the one hand, and the world's Treasuries on the other.

MWM thus emerged as a 'safe' Marxism. Sweezy (1942)—the first genuine Marxist to do so—openly endorsed the idea of Marx's theory as variant of GE, cementing in place the hopeful belief that Marx's economics could be in some way 'integrated' into a standard economics curriculum. The price seemed acceptable: sacrificing the ability to explain the contradictions that ripped capitalism apart in the Great Depression seemed of little consequence in a 25-year post-war Golden Age.

Only when the 1974 Slump shattered the illusion that capitalism had entered a permanent new age of expansion and stability, as interest in Marx's politics rose sharply in the wake of the Vietnam War and 1968, did the true extent of the price paid became clear, as writer after writer began repeating the monotonous Bawerkian mantra that 'Marx's method contains insoluble logical contradictions'.

MWM was caught in a trap of its own making. It faced three choices: with Steedman and Roemer, renounce Marx's legacy and set out to reproduce selected 'conclusions' by other means;[10] obstinately declare the legacy sound; or return to the study of Marx's own ideas, not as a dogmatic gospel, but to find out what they really were.

Results and prospects

The above analysis presents a final empirical difficulty. Why, in the wake of a depression that, truth be told, started in 1974 and is now the longest in history, has economics not 'rediscovered' Marx or, for that matter, Keynes? Surely we should expect a new Keynes or a new Marx?

Again, materialism comes to our aid. Marx's and Keynes's discoveries became *widespread* not just in depressions but with the rise of mass popular movements of discontent. They took root when popular radicalisation transgressed the boundaries of peaceful bourgeois life, erupting in the Russian revolution in 1917, the Chinese in 1949, and the mass revival of Communism in Western Europe in the wake of Liberation. Economics did not save itself; it had to be saved from itself, by huge class forces.

Perhaps the most critical element of Marx's method is voiced in the famous Eleventh Thesis on *Feuerbach*: reason lives in action. I think that, if alive today, Marx, his family, and his old friends Fred and Mary would be on the streets or online fighting racism, climate change, the barbaric sanctions imposed on the people of Venezuela, Cuba, and Iran, and the growing war drive against China; and using the experience thus gained lay bare the economic causes of these phenomena, knowing as a true child of the enlightenment that the most effective basis for ending evil is understanding, and the best way to understand evil is to stand up to it. That, in my own understanding, was Marx's Method.

Notes

1 I dedicate this article to Victoria Chick, whose passing I learned of on the day of submitting the final version of this text, without whose patient advice and unremitting criticism it would never have appeared, and to Paolo Giussani, whose sad passing ends a chapter in the history of Marxist thinking. It owes much to Radhika Desai, Andrew Kliman, many TSSI scholars, and Ernest Mandel without whom Marxist Political Economy would be poorer beyond imagining. All errors are my own.
2 The proportion is the *Monetary Expression of Labour Time* or MELT, due to Ramos (1995). It is the money price that expresses a given number of hours, and is constant throughout the economy at any given time.
3 See Heinrich (2013) and the response from Kliman et al. (2014).
4 Freeman (1996, 2020a) provides a continuous time analysis. Marx, following the Physiocrats especially Sismondi, analyses reproduction in discrete time but tellingly, not transformation. MWM conflates the two, attributing to Marx the idea that values form an orderly queue until December 31st before reincarnating as prices on January 1st— miraculously, one year earlier.
5 I am indebted to Michele Naples for pointing out this passage.
6 Freeman (2020b) comprehensively refutes this claim.
7 'Simultaneous Single System' theories (Kliman 2007, p. 33) accept 1–6 but not 8. The transformation 'problem' is absent from such theories, but the LTRPF (conclusion 3) does not hold.
8 This is remote from the crude reading that Marx chose theories that served the cause of the working class. To the contrary, he sought to purge theory of everything constructed to serve the cause of the bourgeois class. What best served the working class was truth.
9 I am indebted to Ingo Schmidt (2018) for this insight.
10 With scant success: see Kliman and Potts (2015).

References

Böhm-Bawerk, E. von (1949 [1896]) 'Karl Marx and the close of his system,' in P. Sweezy, ed. 1984 [1949]. *Karl Marx and the Close of His System: Böhm-Bawerk's Criticism of Marx*, New York: Augustus M. Kelley and London: Merlin, pp. 1–118

Bortkiewicz, L. von (1984) 'On the correction of Marx's fundamental theoretical construction in the third volume of *Capital*', in P. Sweezy, ed. 1984 [1949] *Karl Marx and the Close of His System: Böhm-Bawerk's Criticism of Marx*, New York: Augustus M. Kelley and London: Merlin, pp. 197–221.

Bridel, P. (1997) *Money and General Equilibrium Theory: From Walras to Pareto, 1870–1923*, Aldershot: Edward Elgar.

Carchedi, G. and M. Roberts (2013) 'A critique of Heinrich's, "Crisis Theory, the Law of the Tendency of the Profit Rate to Fall, and Marx's Studies in the 1870s"'. Monthly Review Commentary section, December 1, 2013.

DeMartino, G, and D. McCloskey, eds., (2016) *The Oxford Handbook of Professional Economic Ethics*, Oxford: OUP.

Desai, R. (2016) 'The value of history and the history of value', in T. Subasat, ed., *The Great Meltdown of 2008: Systemic, Conjunctural or Policy-created*? Cheltenham: Edward Elgar, pp 136–56.

Dobb, M. (1973) *Theories of Value and Distribution Since Adam Smith*, Cambridge: CUP.

Dow. S. (1985) *Macroeconomic Thought: A Methodological Approach*, Oxford: Blackwell.

Freeman, A. (2008) 'Submission from the association for heterodox economics to the international benchmarking review on research assessment', in F. Lee and W. Elsner, eds., *Publishing, Refereeing, Ranking, and the Future of Heterodox Economics*, Special issue of *On the Horizon*, vol. 16 (4), pp. 279–85.

Freeman, A. (2010) 'Marxism without Marx', *Capital and Class* 34 (1), 84–97.

Freeman, A. (2014) 'What causes booms', in A. K. Bagchi and A. C. Chaterjee, eds, *Marxism: with and Beyond Marx*, London: Routledge, pp. 92–114.

Freeman, A. (2016) 'First tell no untruth', in G. DeMartino, and D. McCloskey, eds, *The Oxford Handbook of Professional Economic Ethics*, Oxford: Oxford University Press, pp. 651–69.

Freeman, A. (2016) 'Self-imposed division, overlooked continuity: Marx, Keynes and the rate of profit'. https://www.academia.edu/22259154/Self-imposed_division_overlooked_continuity_Marx_Keynes_and_the_Rate_of_Profit

Freeman, A. (2019) 'Value and class', in M. Vidal, T. Rotta, T. Smith, and P. Prew, eds., *The Oxford Handbook of Karl Marx*, Oxford: Oxford University Press, pp. 151–72.

Freeman, A. (2020a) 'A general theory of value and money part 1: Foundations of an axiomatic theory', *World Review of Political Economy* 11 (1), pp. 28–75.

Freeman, A. (2020b) 'Unidentified gravitational objects: Equilibrium, price fluctuations, and the centre of gravity fallacy', Unpublished paper.

Freeman, A., A. Kliman and J. Wells (2001) *The New Value Controversy in Economics*: Cheltenham: Edward Elgar.

Freeman, A. and G. Carchedi (1996) *Marx and non-Equilibrium Economics*, Cheltenham: Edward Elgar.

Freeman, A., V. Chick and S. Kayatekin (2014) 'Samuelson's ghosts: Whig history and the reinterpretation of economic history', special edition of the *Cambridge Journal of Economics* 38 (3), pp. 519–29.

Freeman, C. (1995) 'The third Kondratieff wave: The age of steel, electrification and imperialism.' Sussex: SPRU.

Gattei, G. (1982) 'Les chaires 'Ratées' de Ladislaus von Bortkiewicz,' *Revue Européenne des Sciences Sociales* 20, p. 62.

Heinrich, M. (2013). 'Crisis theory, the law of the tendency of the profit rate to fall, and Marx's studies in the 1870s', *Monthly Review* 64(11).

Hodgskin, T. (1825) *Labour Defended against the Claims of Capital*. https://www.marxists.org/reference/subject/economics/hodgskin/labour-defended.htm, accessed 3 March 2023

Istratescu, V. I. (2001) *Fixed Point Theory. An Introduction*, Dordrecht: Reidel Publishing Company.

Keynes, J. M. (1936) *The General Theory of Employment Interest and Money*, London: Macmillan.

Kliman, A. J. (2007) *Reclaiming Marx's Capital: A Refutation of the Myth of Inconsistency*, Lanham, MD.

Kliman, A. J. and N. Potts (2015) *'Is Marx's Theory of Profit Right? The Simultaneist-Temporalist Debate*, Maryland: Lexington.

Kliman, A., A. Freeman, A. Gusev and N. Potts (2014) 'The unmaking of Marx's capital: Heinrich's attempt to eliminate Marx's crisis theory'. www.ideas.repec.org/p/pra/mprapa/48535.html

Kliman, A. and T. McGlone (1988) 'The transformation nonproblem and the nontransformation problem', *Capital & Class* 35, Summer, 56–83.

Kurz, H. and N. Salvadori (1995) *Theory of Production: A Long-Period Analysis*, Cambridge, UK: Cambridge University Press.

Mandel, E. (1974) *Late Capitalism*, London: Verso.

Marx, K. (1906 [1867]) *Capital*, volume I, F. Engels, ed., New York: Modern Library.

Marx, K. (1973) *Grundrisse*, London: Penguin.

Marx, K. (1979 [1859]) *A Contribution to the Critique of Political Economy*, New York: International Publishers.

Marx, K. (1894) *Capital*, volume III, F. Engels, ed, New York: Modern Library.

Okishio, N. (1961) 'Technical changes and the rate of profit', *Kobe University Economic Review* 7, 85–99.

Pasinetti, L. L. (1979) *Lectures on the Theory of Production*, London: Palgrave Macmillan.

Ramos, A. (1995) 'The monetary expression of labour: Marx's twofold measure of value', Mini-conference of the International Working Group on Value Theory (IWGVT) at the Eastern Economic Association. http://copejournal.com/wp-content/uploads/2017/02/Ramos-The-Monetary-Expression-of-Labour-Marxs-Twofold-Measure-of-Value.pdf

Ricardo, D. (1817) *The Principles of Political Economy and Taxation*, London: John Murray.

Robinson, J. (1942 [1960]) *An Essay on Marxian Economics*, London: Macmillan.

Samuelson, P. (1971) 'Understanding the Marxian notion of exploitation: A summary of the so-called "transformation problem" between Marxian values and competitive prices', *Journal of Economic Literature* 9 (2), 399–431.

Schmidt, I. (2018) 'Are there long waves of economic thought?', presented to conference of the Society for Socialist Studies, unpublished.

Skidelsky, R. (2020) *What's Wrong with Economics?: A Guide for the Perplexed*, New Haven: Yale University Press.

Steedman, I. (1977) *Marx After Sraffa*, London: New Left Books.

Sweezy, P. (1942 [1970]) *The Theory of Capitalist Development: Principles of Marxian Political Economy*, New York: Modern Reader Paperbacks.

Sweezy, P. (ed.) (1984 [1949]) *Karl Marx and the Close of His System: Böhm-Bawerk's Criticism of Marx*, New York: Augustus M. Kelley and London: Merlin

Tucholsky, K. (1994 [1929]) *Schnipsel*, Rohwolt.

21

METHODOLOGICAL PLURALISM IN MACROECONOMICS

Alessandro Vercelli and Ioana Negru

Introduction

In contemporary macroeconomics, there is plenty of heterogeneity between and within schools, but very little engagement amongst different streams of thought, particularly between the dominant paradigm and the heterodox approaches (see e.g. Dow 1996 [1982]). Many disagreements between economists and schools of thought stem from deep-seated theoretical, methodological and ideological differences that prevent a constructive dialogue between them. We advocate instead methodological pluralism, namely a standpoint, grounded in epistemic pluralism, which affirms the existence and legitimacy of various methodological positions and seeks to reject general aprioristic methodological prescriptions. From the normative point of view, we define pluralism in terms of tolerance (Vercelli 1991; Negru 2007). Normative pluralism advocates an attitude of active tolerance towards different macroeconomic visions and methods and rejects active intolerance, especially when it leads to hostile words or acts that may assume different degrees of opposition from prejudice to persecution. In science, as elsewhere, an attitude of active tolerance can be built only through a constructive dialogue between different schools of thought. Unfortunately, in recent times, it is difficult to find an attitude of active tolerance within macroeconomics. Notwithstanding a widespread lip-service to pluralism, the prevailing attitude is usually one of active intolerance or, in the best cases, of passive tolerance. What follows aims to reconstruct the genesis of this awkward situation and to discuss whether there is a viable way out.

Scientific revolutions in mainstream macroeconomics

The birth of macroeconomics as a distinct sub-discipline of economics is the outcome of a methodological revolution. In *The General Theory*, Keynes laid the foundations of macroeconomics as distinct and autonomous from microeconomics (Keynes 1973 [1936]). This paradigmatic shift is the inevitable consequence of his rejection of the methodological approach of Classical Economics:

DOI: 10.4324/9781315745992-25

> I am chiefly concerned with the behaviour of the economic system as a whole ...
> And I argue that important mistakes have been made through extending to the
> system as a whole conclusions which have been correctly arrived at in respect of
> a part of it taken in isolation.
>
> *(Keynes 1973 [1936], CW VII, p. xxxii)*

The new methodological approach rejects not only the 'fallacy of composition' but
also other fundamental postulates of classical microeconomics that Keynes argues to
be counterfactual in the economy as a whole. In particular, he rejected the belief that,
in the absence of external interferences, a market economy is capable of keeping, or
rapidly recovering, a state of full-employment equilibrium. This new methodological approach has far-reaching implications for the real world. From this interpretive
point of view, the persistent involuntary unemployment that has characterised the
slumps of business cycles and, in a much more dramatic measure, the Great Depression are mainly the consequence of a macroscopic market failure that shows the inability of the market, left to itself, to self-regulate. From the policy point of view, the
stabilisation of the business cycle and the implementation of full-employment equilibrium require the adoption of counter-cyclical policies and fiscal policies meant
to keep the economic system as close as possible to full-employment equilibrium.
A particular version of Keynesian macroeconomics usually called Neoclassical Synthesis, based on a questionable understanding of Keynes's approach and its policy
implications, became mainstream in the Bretton Woods era (1944–71) supporting a
period of unprecedented stability and prosperity.

In this period, the classical approach tried hard to challenge the academic and
political hegemony of the Keynesian approach by resorting to an updating of the
time-honoured monetarism based upon the Quantity Theory of Money, as refur-
bished by Milton Friedman (1969). This alternative approach sees the State not as a
potential solution of the economic problems but as their ultimate source because its
intervention in the economy is bound to impair the autoregulation process implemented by free markets. In particular, the government succumbs to the temptation
of manipulating the money supply in a way inconsistent with market stability. In
this view, we may overcome monetary instability only by constraining monetary
policy within fixed rules. The stagflation of the 1970s seemed to confirm the monetarist thesis undermining the hegemony of Keynesianism. This eventually shifted
the academic and political consensus towards monetarism until a full-fledged anti-
Keynesian counter-revolution broke out and shifted the hegemonic view towards a
new version of the classical paradigm based on a radically innovative methodological approach. The New Classical Economists led by Lucas carried on a far-reaching
counter-revolution that took macroeconomics by storm, rapidly becoming mainstream (Lucas 1981). A methodological revolution played a crucial role, also in this
case, in the justification, legitimation and diffusion of this radical change of paradigm. The crucial innovation was a new view of equilibrium that started to be
seen not as a possible state that can or cannot be reached according to the dynamic
properties of the system, but as the only possible object of analysis on the part of
economics, at least if we take the latter as a genuine scientific discipline. This state
of affairs is the only one consistent with the alleged substantive rationality of the
agents that, in this view, have full information on the systematic factors underlying

the empirical evidence in economics. Their expectations are thus bound to be rational, implying that their errors observed ex post are the inevitable consequence of the stochastic factors acting in the market. Disequilibrium is considered as unintelligible and, consequently, unemployment cannot be involuntary because of structural factors such as the insufficient effective demand in Keynes. The business cycles are not endogenous oscillations around an equilibrium trend but exogenous displacements of the equilibrium itself. The core of the theory is the so-called 'equilibrium business cycle' approach, which excludes by definition the Keynesian proposition that counter-cyclical policies can contribute to stabilise economic fluctuations. This sort of interventionist policy would only increase the variance of the stochastic determinants of economic behaviour, reducing the efficiency of the market. In the influential monetary business cycle model of Lucas, the exogenous shocks that trigger and sustain the fluctuations derive from an active, and thus not fully predictable, monetary policy. This approach recovers the policy prescriptions of Friedman, providing more robust microfoundations to his anti-Keynesian stance. The empirical evidence soon questioned the causal relation from money to the real economy and induced the exponents of the New Classical approach to reverse the direction of causality. The new view of the equilibrium business cycle approach, soon dubbed the 'real business cycle' approach, identifies the exogenous impulses with technological shocks (Kydland and Prescott 1982). However, also in this case, the uncritical adoption of the New Classical assumptions implies that the Keynesian policies cannot improve on unfettered markets, because any sort of policy intervention would only increase the confusion between change of absolute and relative prices, reducing the efficiency of markets. The opposite conclusions drawn from Keynesian models are rejected. It is argued that they are derived from an approach that relies on shallow behavioural evidence without providing adequate microeconomic foundations in terms of deep parameters that are invariant to the policy rules adopted. According to this rejection, often called the 'Lucas critique', the agents would react to the new policy environment by changing their behaviour in such a way as to reach the previously established goals.

The extraordinary academic success obtained by the New Classical paradigm did not stop the evolution of the Keynesian paradigm. The exponents of mainstream Keynesianism soon elaborated a new version of their view, dubbed New Keynesian Economics, to respond to the criticisms of New Classical Economics. They accepted a great part of the new methodological approach worked out by Lucas. In particular, they accepted the methodological requirement of microfoundations in terms of the Arrow-Debreu model of stochastic general equilibrium. They adopted also the Rational Expectations Hypothesis abandoning the adaptive expectations approach utilised by the Keynesian exponents of the Neoclassical Synthesis and the Classical macroeconomists relying on Friedman's version of Monetarism. In addition, they forsook the dynamic foundations of equilibrium that had provided until then the main justification of Keynesian policies as the only way to conquer the instability (or weak stability) of full-employment equilibrium. However, the New Keynesian Economists worked out a new compelling argument to justify the active regulation of the economy, claiming that within the New Classical methodological context it is sufficient to allow for the existence of at least one market imperfection to justify the adoption of Keynesian short-run policies. In this view, the equilibrium realised by unfettered markets is not optimal because it is constrained by market imperfections. These constraints can be re-laxed through apt policies that update those suggested by Keynes. The list of mar-ket imperfections considered by the New Keynesian Economics is very long. The early contributions focused on price rigidity, mainly because of staggered con-tracts (Fisher), wages (Taylor) and prices (Calvo). In the 1980s, the New Keynesian economists modelled further kinds of market imperfection, focusing on the exis-tence of efficiency wages (Shapiro and Stiglitz), menu costs (Mankiw), bounded rationality (Akerlof and Yellen), monopolistic competition (Blanchard and Kiy-otaki), coordination failures (Cooper and John) and so on. The New Keynesian models analysed the consequences of one or more of these imperfections that may have a different impact in different countries and historical periods. Models that considered more than one imperfection show that their co-existence and possi-ble interactions make a significant difference in analysis and policy that become both much more complex and context-dependent. Though the methodological ap-proach of New Keynesian Economics is similar to that of New Classical Econom-ics, the policy implications are quite different. The basic idea is that it is possible to improve the welfare of citizens by eliminating, or at least mitigating, the existing market imperfections, and/or counteracting their negative consequences. While New Classical economists assumed that prices and wages flexibility succeed to maintain the full-employment equilibrium also within a short-term time horizon, New Keynesian economists assume that the market's optimal equilibrium may be reached only in the longer run through policies succeeding to counteract market imperfections. For example, in the case of nominal wages stickiness, fiscal and monetary policies may aim to affect price inflation to implement variations in real wages consistent with full employment.

In the 1990s, a few leading macroeconomists started to combine the intertem-poral optimisation approach of Real Business Cycle models with the assumption of market imperfections as analysed by New Keynesian models based, in particu-lar, on nominal rigidities and imperfect competition. The resulting fusion between the two main streams of macroeconomics, dubbed New Neoclassical Synthesis or New Consensus, provided the theoretical foundations for much of contempo-rary macroeconomic analysis and policy (Woodford 2009). The approach of the new synthesis adopts methodological foundations in terms of the intertemporal stochastic general equilibrium model first advocated by the New Classical econ-omists as providing the necessary microfoundations to macroeconomic models (Lucas 1981). However, the policy implications of this sort of consensus macro-economic models crucially depend on the market imperfections emphasised by the New Keynesian economists. For example, these models adopt the Keynesian distinction between short and long run because market imperfections have differ-ent consequences according to the time horizon. This implies that the pillars of classical monetary economy, namely the classical dichotomy between monetary and real economy and money neutrality, hold only in the long run. Therefore, this approach recovers a role for monetary policy and counter-cyclical policies, though limited to the short run. In this view, business cycles do not depend only on money shocks, as in the monetarist approach of Friedman and Lucas, but also on other kinds of shocks, including the technological shocks emphasised by the exponents of the Real Business Cycle approach, as well as on output gaps as in the traditional Keynesian models. As it had already happened in the past with other forms of eclecticism, this alleged consensus was fragile and was destabilised by the financial crisis of 2007–2009 and the ensuing Great Recession. This led to a renewed polarisation between the Classical and the Keynesian sides. After a short-lived swing in 2007–2009 towards the Keynesian polarity, most policymakers reverted towards the rigid new classical orthodoxy based on *laissez faire* and financial austerity.

This bird's-eye view of the evolution of macroeconomics since its inception clearly shows that we cannot ignore methodological pluralism neither from the descriptive nor from the normative point of view. Periods of scientific revolution characterised by a harsh conflict between competing macroeconomic paradigms alternate with periods of normal science where the confrontation between competing paradigms is typically repressed by the mainstream school of thought.

Methodological pluralism in heterodox macroeconomics: The case of the Austrian and Post-Keynesian schools

So far, we have limited the historical reconstruction of the evolution of macroeconomics to the dialectics and co-evolution between the most successful alternative paradigms that struggled to acquire and maintain hegemony in the Academia and policy-making, namely the Classical and the Keynesian paradigms. In the same period, we find in macroeconomics a wide plurality of heterodox paradigms supported by methodological approaches having radically different interpretive and policy implications, including the Post-Keynesian, Austrian, Marxian, Institutionalist and Evolutionary schools. The heterodox schools challenge the mainstream approaches, emphasising their theoretical, methodological and policy shortcomings while providing a crucial stimulus for a healthy evolution of macroeconomics. How can we take account of this extensive pluralism in research, teaching and policy-making?

Before trying to answer this question we briefly consider in this section two heterodox schools that managed to exert a significant influence on the co-evolution of mainstream macroeconomics: the Post-Keynesian school and the Austrian school. The Post-Keynesian school contributed in particular to a growing awareness of the crucial role of macroeconomic instability propagated by bounded rationality decision-making, while mainstream macroeconomics struggled to confine its relevance to the periods of crisis as a special case within a completely different methodological approach based on rational expectations. Austrian economics, mainly through Hayek, had a deep impact on the pre-analytic vision of New Classical economics based on methodological individualism and the optimality of free markets, but they never accepted the analytic approach based on the Arrow-Debreu stochastic general equilibrium model. These two examples confirm the importance of methodological paradigms in demarcating different schools of macroeconomics and their epistemic and policy implications. Other heterodox schools of thought played an important role in the evolution of macroeconomic theory and policy. However, the critical investigation of their methodological foundations and policy implications would require an extensive and complex analysis that goes beyond the constraints of this essay.

Contemporary Post-Keynesian economics

The origin of Post-Keynesian Economics is rooted in the writings of Keynes's 'apostles' (close collaborators and pupils such as Joan Robinson, Kahn, Kaldor and Kalecki). After Keynes's death, they tried to extend his theory to new fields (such as growth theory) and to defend the genuine interpretation of the master's theory from hostile interpretations by neoclassical economists and 'revisionist' interpretations by the exponents of the Neoclassical Synthesis. This Cambridge tradition interacted with the Neo-Ricardian School pioneered by another eminent collaborator of Keynes (Sraffa) and catalysed other streams of research from the UK (Chick and Thirlwall), the US (Weintraub, Davidson and Minsky), Italy (Pasinetti, Garegnani and Graziani), Austria (Steindl and Rothschild) and many more. The common radical criticisms against the neoclassical approach produced a growing convergence that gave birth in the 1970s to an autonomous school of thought. This school managed to exert a significant influence amongst academic economists and practitioners but not a continuous and systematic impact on policymakers and regulators.

The Post-Keynesian school remained articulated in many streams that retained a few common points. First, it argued that the macroeconomic equilibrium implemented by unfettered markets is often characterised by a certain degree of involuntary unemployment. What causes this suboptimal state is a deficient amount of effective demand that depends mainly on the product market and the financial system. In this view, contrary to mainstream opinion, the causation goes from investment to saving and not *vice versa*. This implies that the crucial physiological role of the financial system is not the intermediation between saving and investment but the financing of real investment. According to Post-Keynesians, a monetary economy is quite different from a barter economy. In particular, the classical dichotomy between the real and monetary sides of the economy does not hold, money is not neutral and finance plays a crucial role. This implies a rejection of the Quantity Theory of Money for three basic reasons: (i) the creation of money is mainly endogenous, so that causation goes from income to money; (ii) the velocity of money circulation is endogenous and thus highly variable, as it depends on money demand and liquidity preference; (iii) inflation may be affected also by a cost-push induced by increases in wages or in the price of primary products.

Most Post-Keynesians share these points but combine and articulate them in different ways and with different weight. A case in point is uncertainty, with its far-reaching implications for pluralism of methods. Minsky argued that analysis of capitalism without (strong or radical) uncertainty is like Hamlet without the Prince (Minsky 2008 [1975], p. 57). In particular, a sophisticated financial system is characterised by strong or radical uncertainty that is cause and effect of its instability, while the equilibrium approach of mainstream macroeconomics crucially depends on the assumption of weak uncertainty, or mere risk deriving from known probability distributions. In a capitalist economy, even if we assume that the economy is in a state of equilibrium, financial tranquillity cannot persist for a long time because the growing confidence in the stability of the system validated by persisting equilibrium induces the economic units to increase their indebtedness, starting a sequence of financial fluctuations that eventually degenerate into a great crisis. Most Post-Keynesians reject the mainstream concept of uncertainty as simple and measurable risk, namely mere stochastic variance that does not affect the equilibrium value of systematic variables. This common trait of Post-Keynesian scholars confirms the deep affinity with Keynes's epistemology and its pluralistic implications in an open world (Chick 2013, pp. 56–72). In an uncertain world, the weight of macroeconomic arguments is bound to be limited and controversial (Vercelli 1991, pp. 220–4). As Keynes argues, in empirical sciences such as macroeconomics, 'arguments are rational and claim some weight without pretending to be certain ... most of the arguments, upon which we habitually base our rational beliefs, are admitted to be inconclusive in a greater or less degree ...' (Keynes 1990[1921], *CW* VIII, p. 3). We can thus avoid systematic mistakes only by learning from a frank dialogue with dissenting interlocutors in the light of the available empirical evidence.

The Austrian school's macroeconomic approach[1]

The origins of the Austrian approach are usually traced back to the ideas of Carl Menger (1950 [1871]). His approach to economics exerted a considerable influence on the research agenda of eminent Austrian economists (such as von Mises and Hayek) and their followers (such as Rothbard, Kirzner and Rizzo) establishing what is today called the 'Austrian school'. The Austrian economists rejected a number of crucial classical and neoclassical core principles and established their school of thought as an alternative to mainstream economics. Despite a pronounced heterogeneity, we can identify in Austrian economics three fundamental features: methodological individualism (Negru 2013), subjectivism as a foundation of knowledge (Shand 1984) and a mistrust of mathematical and econometric models (Backhouse 2000).

First, the most important unit of analysis is the individual and its choices within economic processes. The market is the fundamental human institution of economic activity, as it coordinates individual decisions and choices and assumes liberty as a necessary precondition for its efficient functioning. In particular, Hayek's appreciation of markets rests on their epistemic role in transmitting relevant knowledge to individuals at a low cost for society. Hayek (1948) recognised the so-called 'information problem', stressing that knowledge is scattered amongst individuals and cannot be totally transferred from one individual to another (Negru 2007, p. 67). Markets are thus the most efficient means of coordinating resources, being superior to a planned, socialist system.

Second, individual knowledge is subjective in nature. Hayek revised an argument advanced by Mises in 1920 about the limitations of human knowledge known as the 'calculational argument': the processes of exchange and the coordination of prices that rely on demands, scarcities and signals about individual needs would not be possible in the absence of markets. This argument has far-reaching implications regarding the limitations of governmental macroeconomic policies that should be kept at a minimum. In other words, Austrians see the economy as a complex and evolutionary system opposing the practice of most macroeconomic policies that over-simplify its functioning.

Third, the Austrian approach has been entirely based on qualitative methods such as specific descriptions, logical or graphical analyses, and understanding (verstehen) of individual choices. According to Mises (1999 [1949]), mathematical methods cannot explain market processes that are the outcomes of a myriad of human actions and subjective choices. For Mises, quantitative economics is not possible given that all 'quantities' are subjective and the observations should be contextualised, making forecasting extremely difficult and unreliable. Although milder in his criticism of mathematics, Hayek opposed the false pretence of objectivity of data implied by quantitative economics, calling 'scientism' the uncritical application of methods developed in natural sciences to social sciences, including economics. Hayek contends that an acceptance of the core Austrian principles and methodology implies a rejection of the econometric approach in economics. Austrians also question statistical aggregation, as most continuous changes on the markets are unquantifiable so that this approach favours statistical control and social engineering that threatens individual freedom (Hayek 1952). Finally, Austrians criticise the concept of equilibrium and advance instead a theory of market and dynamic processes whereby creative entrepreneurs promote change. One criticism is that equilibrium is an abstract notion, a pure construct, isolated from reality, which facilitates rigour at the expense of deep explanation (see Denis 2004). Most Austrian economists, including Hayek (1948), question also the assumptions underlying the equilibrium model, namely perfect competition, perfect knowledge and economic rationality.

In what follows, we focus on the implications of the Austrian approach for system-wide economics referring almost exclusively to the arguments put forward by Hayek, its most influential representative. The apparent paradox to be explained is that, notwithstanding the Austrian denial of any scientific value to macroeconomics (at least as usually defined), the Austrian paradigm exerted a significant influence on the recent evolution of macroeconomics, playing a momentous, though often overvalued, role in the New Classical revolution. Lucas (1981, pp. 215–9) fully recognised the influence of Hayek in inspiring his own denial of Keynesian macroeconomics. He accepted and developed the argument that Keynes-style macroeconomics is inconsistent with the methodological individualism that is the hallmark of 'serious economics'. Therefore, in this view borrowed from Hayek, system-wide economics has to return to the traditional approach of business cycle theory and does not need a specific sub-discipline, autonomous from microeconomics. However, the analytical implementation by Lucas of this common vision is in sheer opposition to the epistemic and methodological tenets of Austrian economics. Lucas pretends to have solved the contradiction emphasised by Hayek between business cycle theory and the General Equilibrium approach by inserting the Rational Expectations hypothesis. However, this hypothesis contravenes Austrian subjectivism by assuming that subjective expectations equate their objectively true value. In addition, the analytic foundations of New Classical models, based upon the Arrow-Debreu general equilibrium model, contradict the Austrian rejection of mathematical models in economics. Finally, while New Classical policy suggestions are based on the systematic use of econometric models, Hayek rejects this approach because the empirical evidence is theory-dependent and the econometric methods cannot cope with the complexity of individual interactions. The strong Austrian requirement of methodological individualism does not leave much space for theoretical and methodological pluralism. However, the New Classical demarcation criterion between good and bad economics based on its analytic version of the required microfoundations further restricts the scope of admissible theories excluding the Austrian school itself (Vercelli 2016).

A deficit of pluralism in macroeconomics?

While the classical approach focused on the self-regulating full-employment equilibrium as represented by a general equilibrium method, Keynes forged a more general methodology capable of dealing also with a different sort of equilibrium positions inconsistent with full employment and liable to instability, taking into account the behaviour of boundedly rational agents under conditions of strong uncertainty. According to Keynes, these and other systemic features, considered at best secondary anomalies by classical macroeconomics, imply what he calls the *fallacy of composition*, that may heavily distort the results obtained through methodological individualism. In the era ruled by mainstream Keynesian macroeconomics, the dialogue between alternative paradigms was quite lively. The confrontation between different schools of thought occasionally betrayed forms of intolerance between interlocutors, but almost always a certain degree of mutual respect was maintained. In that period the Neoclassical Synthesis, namely the mainstream Keynesian school, argued in favour of its superiority over the classical school and other non-classical schools, but did not adopt a strict demarcation criterion implying the exclusion of the alternative paradigms, such as the influential monetarism of Milton Friedman, from the Academia or policy-advising.

After the New Classical Revolution, mainstream macroeconomics adopted a very strict demarcation criterion prescribing that sound macroeconomics requires proper microfoundations as a necessary hallmark of scientific rigour (see, e.g. Vercelli 2016). The absence of this requisite in a research programme was deemed a sufficient condition for excluding its research fruits from publication and for excluding its members from selections and promotions, at least in the departments of economics. The prevailing attitude of mainstream macroeconomics amounted to strict methodological monism from different points of view, which has several aspects:

i Ontological monism. In this view, the central object of macroeconomics is the market conceived as a self-regulating system based on the interaction of free individuals capable of maintaining, or promptly recovering, the full-employment equilibrium state. This sort of free-competition market equilibrium is believed to be an optimal state in a pregnant sense (the usual one is Pareto optimality). In this view, the equilibrium state of the real system is not affected, at least in the long period, by money and finance (classical dichotomy).
ii Epistemological monism. The assumption of rational expectations implies that the representative agent does not make systematic predictive errors. Errors of prediction are thus merely stochastic and, by definition, cannot be avoided.
iii Policy monism. The ontological and epistemological monism imposes narrow constraints on the choice of policy strategy. These assumptions imply that, in principle, that *laissez faire* is the best policy strategy, while any deviation from financial orthodoxy is assumed to disturb the optimal results of unfettered markets.

These forms of monism lead mainstream economists to embrace the Tina fallacy ('there is no alternative'). If there is no alternative, by definition, there is nothing one can learn from researchers entertaining different ontological and epistemological assumptions that could lead to diverging policy strategies. There is thus no way for dissenting macroeconomists to convince mainstream interlocutors of the possible existence of a better paradigm to direct our choices in a more satisfactory direction.

Of course, in mainstream macroeconomics monism is not without exceptions. Mainstream researchers may entertain different variants of the theoretical and methodological assumptions. However, a significant dialogue between alternative points of view is mainly confined to the interpretation of the empirical evidence and the understanding of its implications for macroeconomic policy. The application of different methods to available data sets may easily produce divergent conclusions that usually do not affect the basic tenets of the mainstream paradigm or the general outlines of policy strategy but only the precise modalities of its implementation. Is this all the pluralism we need? We do not think so. The interpretation of the empirical evidence and its policy implications strictly depend on the methodological assumptions and their underlying ontological and epistemological postulates. A serious and constructive appraisal of alternative paradigms and methodologies requires a genuinely pluralist attitude. This is not easy. The lack of pluralism also affects most heterodox schools that often entertain an ambiguous attitude towards pluralism. These schools have often fought the risk of marginalisation by appealing to pluralism. However, the willingness to entertain a constructive dialogue with other schools of thought, including alternative heterodox schools, has been limited.

Concluding remarks

We have argued in this essay that macroeconomics suffers from a serious deficit of pluralism that impairs its critical awareness and its ability to respond to emerging problems. We advocate a rapid shift towards a workable form of pluralism, namely the adoption under reciprocity of an attitude of active tolerance towards different scientific visions and methodologies. As is well known, if people are tolerant towards the intolerant, this may increase the power of intolerance. The process in principle ends only when the tolerance is completely defeated, even if some tolerance for circumscribed minorities could be retained for cosmetic reasons. Karl Popper (1945) called this contradiction the 'paradox of tolerance'. This is also the paradox of pluralism in macroeconomics: an aprioristic dismissal of minority scientific visions could further strengthen the hegemony of an intolerant mainstream vision. Tolerance can emerge and stay alive only if the dialogue between alternative schools is robust and characterised by a disposition to learn from arguments advanced by alternative schools. This presupposes the common adoption of a sufficiently tolerant demarcation criterion. One could have the temptation of advocating the rejection of any sort of demarcation line within science to avoid any sort of exclusion (Feyerabend 2010). However, a position of methodological 'anarchism' could be counterproductive in the longer period, giving too much space, if not encouragement, to low-quality research, damaging especially the most serious alternatives to the mainstream approach that could become more easily assimilated to what Popper calls pseudoscientific doctrines

(Popper 1963). However, the demarcation criterion should be inclusive of all schools of thought that have some recognised relevance for macroeconomic research and policy.

The awareness that different visions lead to different descriptions, explanations and predictions of the empirical evidence, as well as to different policy strategies, does not lead to relativism. The recognition of advantages and disadvantages of existing macroeconomic visions does not exclude a motivated ranking between them according to principles and values that we have to make fully explicit. Moreover, an open-minded disposition to dialogue does not imply eclecticism, as many critics contend and stigmatise. In most cases the new knowledge acquired through dialogue is accommodated within the existing paradigm, contributing to its evolution. Only in exceptional cases may learning through dialogue lead to a change of paradigm. And even more rarely the new paradigm amounts to a mere combination between elements of different paradigms. In any case, eclecticism is not necessarily a bad thing. In the Section 'Scientific revolutions in mainstream macroeconomics' we mentioned a few influential examples of eclecticism. The eclectic nature of the Neoclassical Synthesis, of the New Keynesian Economics and of the New Consensus did not prevent these schools of thought producing interesting and influential contributions. However, often the heterogeneous parts of an attempted eclectic synthesis are not fully congruent, making the latter highly fragile to new historical problems or environments.

We believe that the roots of the existing intolerance towards alternative schools of thought are to be found in the pedagogical strategy pursued by most mainstream macroeconomists. Very often, what is taught as macroeconomics is limited to the mainstream paradigm, without soliciting the necessary awareness of the cognitive and policy implications of rival heterodox schools. Furthermore, there is a dominance of econometrics and mathematics courses on the economics curriculum to the detriment of courses on the critical use of mixed and qualitative methods in macroeconomics. This bias was signalled as a cause of the 2008 financial crisis, in the context of dogmatic mathematical teaching in (macro) economics (see Hodgson 2008; Krugman 2009). Analogously, many critical economists stigmatised the absence of economic history and history of economic thought from the economics curricula, which has deprived students of learning about the context and origin of macroeconomic ideas (Keen 2009) and their consequences. In addition, macroeconomics should be taught in a richer empirical way than it is done currently, and macroeconomists should debate more often the shortcomings of alternative economic models in order to encourage the introduction of new elements of economic thinking to the benefit of the discipline (Jespersen and Madsen 2013). Teachers should become the students' critical interlocutors, who avoid sharing their 'idiosyncratic' views in teaching macroeconomics, but encourage the students to develop their own critical abilities of understanding how the economy works and its implications for public policy.

Summing up, to react to the deficit of pluralism in contemporary macroeconomics we suggest adopting a very broad demarcation criterion checking the consistency and originality of a paper or individual research programme within their own assumptions and methodologies. This orientation towards dialogue and reciprocal tolerance requires a radical change in the teaching of economics as well as in the rules of its utilisation by mass media and policymakers. Anyone should understand that there are always one or more alternatives in theory, methodology and policy. A wise selection of the best one is never a trivial issue and requires the scrutiny of a plurality of viewpoints.

Note

1 We are aware that certain authors (e.g. Lewis, 2017, in Review of Austrian Economics) distinguish between Old Austrian Macroeconomics and New Austrian Macroeconomics, but for the purpose of this paper, we will not address this debate here.

References

Backhouse, R. (2000) 'Austrian economics and the mainstream: View from the boundary', *The Quarterly Journal of Austrian Economics* 3 (2), 31–43.

Chick, V. (2013) 'The future is open: On open-system theorising in economics', in J. Jespersen and M. O. Madsen, eds, *Teaching Post Keynesian Economics*, Cheltenham and Northampton: Edward Elgar, pp. 56--72.

CW: see Keynes, J. M. (1971–89).

Denis, A. (2004) *The Hypostatisation of the Concept of Equilibrium in Neoclassical Economics*, paper presented at the 6th Annual Conference of the Association of Heterodox Economics, July, University of Leeds.

Dow, S. (1996 [1982]) *The Methodology of Macroeconomic Thought: A Conceptual Analysis of Schools of Thought in Economics*, Cheltenham and Brookfield: Edward Elgar.

Feyerabend, P. (2010 [1975]) *Against Method*, Fourth edition, New York: Verso Books.

Friedman, M. (1969) *The Optimum Quantity of Money*, London: Macmillan.

Hayek, von F. (1948) *Individualism and Economic Order*, London: Routledge.

Hayek, von F. (1952) *The Sensory Order*, London: Routledge and Kegan Paul.

Hodgson, G. (2008) 'After 1929 economics changed: Will economists wake up in 2009?', *Post-Autistic Review* 48, 273–9.

Jespersen, J. and M. O. Madsen, eds, (2013) *Teaching Post-Keynesian Economics*, Cheltenham and Northampton: Edward Elgar.

Keen, S. (2009) 'Mad, bad and dangerous to know', *Real-World Economics Review* 49, 2–7.

Keynes, J. M. (1990 [1921]) *A Treatise on Probability*, *CW* VIII.

Keynes, J. M. (1973 [1936]) '*The General Theory of Employment, Interest and Money*', *CW* VII.

Keynes, J. M. (1971–89) *Collected Writings*, D. E. Moggridge, ed., 30 vols, London: Macmillan and New York: St Martin's Press.

Krugman, P. (2009) 'How did economists get it so wrong?', *The New York Times*, September 2, available at: https://www.nytimes.com/2009/09/06/magazine/06Economic-t.html, accessed on 20th August 2020.

Kydland, F. E. and E. C. Prescott (1982) 'Time to build and aggregate fluctuations', *Econometrica* 50 (6), 1345–70.

Lewis, P. and R.E.Wagner (2017) 'New Austrian Macro Theory: A Call for Inquiry', *Review of Austrian Economics*, vol. 30 (1), March, pp. 1-18.

Lucas, R. E. Jr. (1981) *Studies in Business-Cycle Theory*, Boston: MIT Press.

Menger, C. (1950 [1871]) *Principles of Economics*, Glencoe: Free Press.

Minsky, H. (2008 [1975]) *John Maynard Keynes*, New York: McGraw-Hill.

Mises, von L. (1999 [1949]) *Human Action*, Auburn: Ludwig von Mises Institute. Available on-line at www.mises.org, accessed on-line on 10th of August 2020

Negru, I. (2007) *Institutions, Markets and Gift: Neoclassical, Institutionalist and Austrian Perspectives*, PhD Thesis, Nottingham Trent University, July 2007.

Negru, I. (2013) 'Revisiting the concept of schools of thought in economics: The example of the Austrian school', *American Journal of Economics and Sociology* 72 (4), 983–1008.

Popper, K. (1945) *The Open Society and Its Enemies* (2 Volumes), London: Routledge.

Popper, K. (1963) *Conjectures and Refutations: The Growth of Scientific Knowledge*, London: Routledge.

Shand, A. (1984) *The Capitalist Alternative: An Introduction to Neo-Austrian Economics*, Great Britain: Wheatsheaf.

Vercelli, A. (1991) *Methodological Foundations of Macroeconomics. Keynes and Lucas*, Cambridge, UK: Cambridge University Press.

Vercelli, A. (2016) 'Microfoundations, methodological individualism and alternative economic visions', in *Microfoundations*, J. Toporowski and A. Denis, eds, *Review of Political Economy* 28 (1), 153–67.

Woodford, M. (2009) 'Convergence in macroeconomics: Elements of the new synthesis', *American Economic Journal* 1 (1), 267–79.

PART IV

Models, econometrics and measurement

22

USE OF MATHEMATICS IN MACROECONOMIC ANALYSIS

Lars W. Josephsen

Introduction

Mathematics and mathematical models are ubiquitous in macroeconomic theory building. One reason is that mathematics for many researchers is linked to analyses characterised by internal consistency, precision and objectivity. However, it is contested what role mathematics and mathematical models in practice play – and should play – as a scientific language and an analytical tool in doing economics.

This chapter is an attempt to draw attention to a rather broad field of methodological themes related to the use of mathematics in macroeconomic analyses and the question of the use and misuse of mathematical modelling in macroeconomic theory.

The overall layout is this: This introduction presents strayed quotations from well-merited economists demonstrating a broad spectrum of positions, reflects on the concept of 'model' and sketches some generic aspects of mathematical modelling. Some further examples of modelling issues are briefly mentioned. The next section: *Mathematics – a language and a tool* contains general reflections on potentials and limitations associated with the use of mathematics in relation to macroeconomic analyses. Some of the virtues of mathematics in this context are well-defined concepts, rigorously formulated arguments and relations between variables, precise descriptions of presupposed assumptions and internal consistency. Concerning the limitations of mathematics as a tool, attention is given to *programming, delicacy or coarseness* and *non-completeness*. Section 3: *Issues related to formalising macroeconomic models* takes a closer look at the exemplary issues mentioned in the Introduction. The issues are *system closure; stable/unstable structures; uncertainty;* and *blind spots*. The aim is to contribute to methodological reflection on the possible use of mathematics. Section 4: *Concluding remarks* closes the chapter.

There are many conflicting positions across the entire field.[1] The economist Michael Hudson puts the key question whether disagreement on the application of mathematics in economics is due to factors 'inherent in the mathematisation of economics, or does it follow from the particular way in which mathematics has been applied?' (Hudson 2015, p. 100).

DOI: 10.4324/9781315745992-27

In the 1930s the economist John Maynard Keynes expressed a critical view on the application of mathematics in economic analysis:

> Economics is a science of thinking in terms of models joined to the art of choosing models which are relevant to the contemporary world. It is compelled to be this, because, unlike the typical natural science, the material to which it is applied is, in too many respects, not homogeneous through time.
>
> *(Keynes 1938, CW XIV, p. 300)*

and

> It is a great fault of symbolic pseudo-mathematical methods of formalising a system of economic analysis ... that they expressly assume strict independence between the factors involved and lose their cogency and authority if this hypothesis is disallowed; whereas, in ordinary discourse, where we are not blindly manipulating and know all the time what we are doing and what the words mean, we can keep 'at the back of our heads' the necessary reserves and qualifications and the adjustments which we shall have to make later on, in a way in which we cannot keep complicated partial differentials 'at the back' of several pages of algebra which assume they all vanish. Too large a proportion of recent 'mathematical' economics are merely concoctions, as imprecise as the initial assumptions they rest on, which allow the author to lose sight of the complexities and interdependencies of the real world in a maze of pretentious and unhelpful symbols.
>
> *(Keynes 1936, CW VII, p. 297)*

The discourse on appropriate use of mathematics and mathematical models in macroeconomics has intensified during the last decades and has prompted vigorous and sometimes bitter disputes.[2] Disagreements unfold in parallel with expansion of modelling practice in macroeconomic analysis and increased use of models in preparation of policy advice. The disputes are not only of academic interest but signify broader perspectives since they in many cases influence choices of preferred macroeconomic strategies and policies.[3]

Many decades after Keynes, economists wonder 'can we say that mathematics provides the key to understanding the major economic problems to our time?' (Hudson 2015, p. 99).

The Nobel laureate economist Robert Lucas expressed a radical position when concluding:

> mathematical analysis is not one of many ways of doing economic theory: It is the only way. Economic theory is mathematical analysis. Everything else is just pictures and talk. ... why I think we value mathematical modeling: It is a method to help us get to new levels of understanding of the ways things work.
>
> *(Lucas 2001, pp. 26, 9)*

In contrast, Hudson states:

> If today's economics has become less relevant to the social problems that formed the subject matter of classical political economy a century ago, its scope has narrowed in large part because of the technocratic role played by mathematics.
>
> *(Hudson 2015, p. 100)*

Other renowned scholars in economics express more moderate views, as for example

> Economic models dress common sense in mathematical formalism. ... In truth, simple models of the type that economists construct are absolutely essential to understanding the workings of society. ... When models are selected judiciously, they are a source of illumination. When used dogmatically, they lead to hubris and errors in policy.
>
> *(Rodrik 2015, p. 11)*

Similarly, the economist Steve Keen, a critic of mainstream economics, states:

> Though mathematics has definite limitations, properly used it is a logical tool that should illuminate, rather than obscure. Economists have obscured reality using mathematics because they have practiced mathematics badly, and because they have not realized the limits of mathematics.
>
> *(Keen 2011, p. 402)*

These different quotations illustrate that it is obviously relevant to try to disentangle the sketched spectrum of viewpoints concerning use of mathematics in macroeconomics, the more so as the dispute indirectly reflects the fact that macroeconomic models have become gradually more technically (read: *mathematically*) advanced, due to rapid expansion in computer power and a continuously growing flow of available economic data. Virtues like transparency and accessibility of applied macroeconomic models to interested non-specialists (including economists and policymakers) have become correspondingly poorer, and this reinforces challenges related also to educating economists, as highlighted by Streeten (2002, pp. 18–20). An information gap between economic model-builders and people solving practical economic problems at the societal level is ascending to worrisome levels.

Why are mathematical models used in macroeconomic analysis?

When you address mathematics as an analytical tool in macroeconomics you will often meet expressions like *mathematical models, mathematical economics, mathematical modelling* and *economic models in mathematical formalism* (cf. the above-mentioned quotes by Keynes, Lucas and Rodrik).

Such expressions all refer to the important subject *mathematical formalism*, which in this context is the relevant keyword, since it points towards the decisive criterion that *all arguments* must be expressed in mathematics. This understanding is highlighted by Chick and Dow (2012, p. 141): 'Formalism is taken ... to mean mathematical formalism, that is, a methodology which requires all arguments be expressed, or at last be expressible in mathematics'. Adopting this position implies that application of mathematical formalism in macroeconomic analysis presumes relevance, validity and acceptance of these rather strong methodological requirements.

According to the economist and social scientist Asad Zaman models of various character (including mathematical models) inevitably are applied in modern macroeconomic analyses because of the complexity and interactivity of economic systems:

> it is important to understand that modern economics is entirely based on models. There is a lot of merit to the idea that economic knowledge must be encapsulated

in models. This is because economic systems are complex and interactive. ...
This also explains the central importance of mathematics in modern economics.
When we want to piece together parts of a complex system into a whole, mathematics is necessarily and inevitably involved, because the required integration
cannot be done intuitively and qualitatively.

(Zaman 2020, p. 1)

What is 'a model'?

This chapter applies deliberately a broad and spacious model definition (usable for
all types of models, including macroeconomic models): a model is a kind of *imitation*
or *picture* of a target system or phenomenon in the real world, often created as an
abstraction with an analytical purpose. The concept of a 'model' should not be confused with a 'theory', which is a broader concept; a specific model might thus belong
to a 'theory' that may accommodate several distinct models.

We draw upon the philosopher Uskali Mäki when we distinguish between 'model'
and 'model description'. The latter includes 'mathematical equations, verbal charac-
terisations or boxes and arrows on a black board' (Mäki 2018, p. 6). Mäki qualifies
the point by suggesting: 'Nothing is a model in itself. Modelhood requires a larger
structure within which an object becomes a model. This larger structure embodies many of the dimensions that are characteristic of scientific disciplines' (Mäki
2018, p. 5). Mäki denotes such structures 'modelling endeavour frameworks'. These
frameworks include *inter alia* model purpose, target, audiences, diverse types of axioms and assumptions, and proper domain of application. In turn this approach
requires a focus on the model *description*, which appears as the outcome of a transformation of an implicit model to an explicit model (cf. the subsection on mental
models below).

Mäki's approach provides a kind of warning against a too simplistic use of the
concept of 'a model': a model always comes with a specific conceptual framework –
often tacitly concomitant.[4]

The model definition above may form the backdrop for several diverse *model ty-
pologies*. I shall not go deeply into this topic but just make some remarks concerning
a few general types of models (analytical models, mental models, and descriptive and
prescriptive models), and present some preliminary reflections on 'modelling issues'.

Analytical models

The term *analytical model* indicates a model developed with the specific purpose of
exploring an actual target system. An analytical model is constituted by a hypothesis
(a set of hypotheses) or a theory concerning the target system in question: its nature,
its internal structure and components, and its possible relations to and interactions
with other real-world phenomena. When it comes to analytical *economic* models, the
hypotheses/theories are often, but not always, formulated in mathematical terms.[5]

Mental models

The term 'mental model' denotes a brain-internal image of a real-world phenomenon, sometimes conceived as a 'preunderstanding' of the target system in question.

The user of an actual model may or may not be fully aware of the existence of this preunderstanding. Although mental models are *implicit*, they will often influence the model-user's conception of the target system. In this way our mental models may shape or affect how we think and act. Mental models become *explicit* when they are *transformed*. The transformation process is illustrated in the figure, showing that a mental model can be either *articulated* in the form of a *verbal model description* or *formalised* in the form of a mathematical model, consisting of a set of mathematical equations supplemented by some assumptions and axioms, articulated verbally and/or mathematically if possible. The key point here is that through the transformation process mental models are 'brought into the open' (cf. Senge 2006 p. 166). *Verbalised* as well as *formalised* models can be systematically explored – not only by the model-user herself but also by other investigators. It is worthwhile to mention that an explicit model will include far more details than its mental origin (Figure 22.1).[6,7]

Descriptive and prescriptive models

Models are in the first-place *descriptive* tools, designed to describe and analyse *observations of behaviour* of real-world phenomena, aiming at improving the understanding of the phenomena under study ('how the world may work'). However, models may also serve *prescriptive* aims ('how we envisage the world may or ought to evolve'). Prescriptive models prevail in policy advice but are not always declared as such. In this connection it is important to distinguish between *prediction of the future behaviour* of a target system and *deduction* of *implications* of a model of that system (Davies 2019, p. 161).

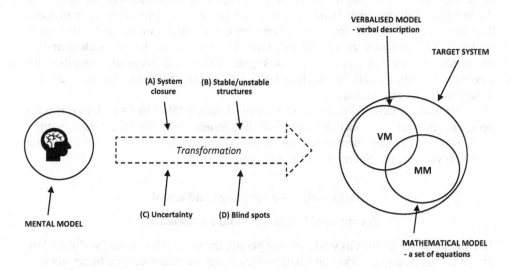

From mental model to verbalised or mathematical models
Four modelling challenges: (A), (B), (C) and (D)

Figure 22.1 From mental model to verbalised or mathematical models: four challenges.
Source: Made by author.

Modelling issues

All types of models are born with issues or challenges related to *discrepancies or differences* between a given real-world target system on the one side and chosen models or model descriptions of the target on the other. Real-world systems and their theoretical counterpart-models belong to two different 'worlds' or conceptual levels, therefore such differences will always exist. Real-world systems refer to ontological reflections, whereas theoretical systems are part of an epistemological endeavour. Whether a mathematical approach in a given situation is useful or not depends on the character of this discrepancy/difference. Appraisal of the relevance and the truth value of specific models cannot be based on mathematical argumentation but must rest on 'non-mathematical' experience and conceptions. This general statement applies of course also for mathematical macroeconomic models.

Certain issues represent challenges for mathematical models in the sense that mathematics and mathematical methods are not (necessarily) always useful as tools for solving macroeconomic problems due to characteristics of the highly abstract formalism as such. The mathematical set-up will often take the form of a set of coupled differential equations. Actual models will require specification of system boundaries and other presupposed assumptions, expressed mathematically – if possible. Examples of such specifications could be selected variables, adopted axioms, equations describing interdependence between some (endogenous) variables, possible decision-rules such as optimisation and equilibrium principles, time span of available historical data of key variables, purpose of the modelling work and neglected but potentially influential circumstances or factors.

We suggest that the very *transformation* of an (implicit) mental model of a real-world target system into a mathematical model is inevitably escorted by *issues* or *challenges* that may or may not be formulated explicitly in actual model descriptions. As mentioned above such issues are inherent in the very transformation process. The modelling issues/challenges represent potential pitfalls or obstacles in model-building, and they may imply seriously flawed or useless (irrelevant) understanding of the target system. Consequently, we suggest that it is a necessary condition for developing useful models that such modelling issues are 'brought into the open' and described and treated adequately.

To be more concrete we unfold in Section 'Issues related to formalising macroeconomic models' some examples of modelling issues under the following headings: *system closure*; *stable/unstable structures*; *uncertainty*; and *blind spots*. These issues will be reviewed and illustrated (cf. the figure).

Mathematics – a language and a tool

The natural language – and mathematics

In daily parlance laymen as well as scientists use the *natural* language ('ordinary language'). This language serves (at least) two purposes: communication, understood as transmission of knowledge, propositions, statements, ideas, etc., and analysis aiming at increasing knowledge. In addition to the natural language most scientists apply specially developed vocabularies and formalisms adapted to their particular field of interest, in other words, they use their specialised 'lingo', that often – but not always – includes mathematics.

According to the economist and philosopher Kenneth E. Boulding (1910–1993), it is commonplace to regard applied mathematics as a language *and* a tool. As a *language* mathematics serves communicative purposes by the transmission of knowledge, and in so far as mathematics is used as an analytical tool, it serves the purpose of increasing knowledge (Boulding 1955, p. 1). However, mathematics possesses potentials as well as limitations in relation to both aspects when applied to macroeconomic analyses.

Potentials

Application of mathematics as a formalised language is attractive as a tool in scientific inquiry since the discipline offers an array of advantages: univocal procedures for logical reasoning; methods for ensuring well-defined concepts and terms; rigorous formulation of arguments and envisaged functional relations between variables and their changes; options for precisely describing presupposed assumptions and for ensuring internal consistency between calculated model outcomes and the presupposed assumptions; and finally (a certain degree of) objectivity. In addition, mathematically formulated information is apt when it comes to management and analysis of large amounts of data.

These virtues form a backdrop for valuing applied mathematics as a means for provision of forceful methods in many fields of knowledge development and management. Especially, in relation to a large group of studies of natural systems, mathematics and mathematical modelling have been indispensable and have been characterised as 'unreasonably effective' (Wigner 1960). In studies of macroeconomic phenomena applied mathematical methods and techniques have under certain conditions elicited useful instruments for handling problem analysis and systems modelling. Having stated this it should be kept in mind that mathematics as a tool has limitations. Some of these will be outlined below.

The scientist Geoff Davies states: 'Mathematics makes no direct reference to the observable world, even though mathematical problems are often motivated by questions about the world'. 'Mathematics is also a very useful and frequently used tool in the *deductive* stage of the scientific process' and 'In scientific inquiry mathematics is only a tool, and it is not itself science' (Davies 2019, pp. 159, 169). In other words: mathematics should not *as such* be regarded as part of science, and mathematical formalism can by no means replace the hard work of creating useful (and 'non-mathematical') ideas by which scientists try to connect and align observations and models in ways that facilitate and improve the understanding of the real-world systems under study – which is at the centre of the very scientific endeavour.[8]

Limitations

I will focus here on three general types of limitations in relation to mathematical analyses in social sciences, drawing on Boulding (1955, pp. 1–2).[9] Overall headlines of the three types are: 1. Programming/rigidity, 2. Delicacy or coarseness and 3. Non-completeness. They are unfolded below.

1 **Programming/rigidity.** The concrete mathematical *operations* must be distinguished from the *programming* of these operations. 'Programming', however, is

the real art of the mathematician, and paradoxically enough, programming itself cannot be done wholly by mathematical operations. The creative act in mathematics itself involves a great deal of 'not-mathematics' (Boulding 1955, p. 1). This activity requires intuition and experience concerning matters outside the mathematical universe.

Search for new knowledge within a discipline by mathematical means may include exploring the limits of the discipline in question. 'The rounded growth of knowledge ... requires both mathematics and something that is not mathematics. By inquiring into the limitations of mathematics we may become clearer as to what is not-mathematics' (Boulding 1955, p. 1). The category 'not-mathematics' is important, since mathematical expression of macroeconomic problems pre-supposes supplementary linguistic components, rendering description of selected real-world phenomena outside mathematics. Formulation of these components is not necessarily constricted by rules of classical logic or by high precision but has merits of offering options for diverse interpretations. In this context ordinary language is an appropriate tool. A frequently quoted aphorism hits this point spot-on: 'It is better to be vaguely right than exactly wrong'.[10] An important comment to that statement is suggested by Syll (2015): '[economic] epistemology has to be founded on ontology' (p. 52).[11]

2. **Delicacy or coarseness.** Some mathematical approaches may be inappropriate in relation to given tasks of analysis. The choice of specific mathematical subdisciplines requires careful (ontological) considerations concerning the nature of the phenomenon in question and on efforts to ensure aligning of tool and task. 'The delicacy or coarseness of a tool has an important effect on the task which can be done with it; we don't cut out cataracts with a buzz-saw or cut down trees with a scalpel.' ...

    > This is a problem of considerable importance for the social sciences, where the empirical universe itself is frequently 'coarse' in texture. A good example of this difficulty is the theory of 'rational behavior' in economics. The calculus is too fine, since relationships in the empirical world are not continuous, and the theory of uncertainty is largely an attempt to discuss vagueness by means of clear concepts!'
    >
    > (Boulding 1955, p. 1)

3. An additional aspect of the 'delicacy/ coarseness' limitation is *the time scale* related to the actual phenomenon. This implies a necessity of efforts to ensure aligning the time scale(s) of the system in question and the time conditions of the observational endeavour.

4. **Non-completeness.** It is obvious that most real-world phenomena are too complex to be encapsulated within simplistic mathematical formalism. Think of happiness, anger, friendship, well-being and so on. 'Mathematics is not a complete language, but is a device for talking about some things, not about all things, and it is further abstracted from the empirical world than ordinary language'. 'All language involves abstraction (orderly loss of information) ... Mathematics is an abstraction from ordinary language, an abstraction which again involves loss of richness of information' (Boulding 1955, pp. 1–2).[12]

In this context it is worthwhile to mention a semantic problem that may cause confusion in the public debate: Certain words/concepts are ingrained in ordinary language, carrying diverse contents and connotations (referring to, for example, cultural, historical, national or ideological understandings), and simultaneously the very same words/concepts are established as well-defined terms in the special vocabulary of a particular professional discipline (a specific *lingo*), and as such they can more easily than otherwise be expressed as mathematical quantities. A well-known example is the concept of 'growth'. Generally, this word means a positive change or an increment of some specified entity, whereas growth in the *lingo* of economics clearly represents increasing gross domestic product, GDP. In this context growth always implies increased material flows through the economic system. This ambiguity of 'growth' lies often behind futile disputes on macroeconomic policy.

Winding up, we think it is worthwhile to regard mathematics as a highly abstract *sub-language*, embedded in ordinary language with no direct connection to the real world, and provided with its own rules of reasoning and a specific type of logic.

Issues related to formalising macroeconomic models

The previous section outlined three types of general limitations connected to mathematical analysis in social sciences, originally highlighted by Boulding (1955). The present section puts focus on issues that represent other potential challenges to the application of mathematical approaches in relation to macroeconomic analysis and therefore should be explored. The selected issues do not represent genuine principal limitations, but they nevertheless deserve special attention in relation to considering mathematics as a tool in this context. Thus, the aim of the present section is to offer some further methodological reflections related to cases where economists address macroeconomic problems through mathematical modelling. The starting point is here the very formalisation, i.e. the process by which an informal (mental) macroeconomic model or theory is transformed to a verbalised model or a mathematised version/a mathematical model. This approach was sketched in the Introduction and illustrated by the figure.

From a methodological point of view, it is interesting whether it is possible to define precise criteria to guide selection of appropriate mathematical tools for specified macroeconomic problems. However, there is no univocal answer to this question. Keynes's reflections support this view (cf. his quotes in the 'Introduction' above).

The scope of the section is limited since it does not provide a general, systematic investigation of macro-economic modelling issues, but is restricted to displaying four selected *illustrative* examples of such issues/challenges, namely *system closure*; *stable/unstable structures*; *uncertainty*; and *blind spots* (cf. the figure).

The account below tries to throw light on some characteristics connected to especially the application of mathematics.[13]

Ideally, the first three issues should be included and explicitly addressed in model descriptions, whereas the last issue concerns factors that are model-invisible or silenced or unknown and therefore by definition are absent in model descriptions. Unanswered questions related to this issue may show up in pursuing lessons in connection to model evaluation.

System closure

A model-builder's primary focus is, understandably, placed on the target system itself – its nature, structure, internal constituents and other properties. Observation of these factors in connection with an actual macroeconomic system provides the basis for description of mathematical models of that system. Cases where awareness of a precise delineation of the target system (that is, specification of system *boundaries*) is given a relatively low priority may leave it undecided whether applied variables are endogenous or exogenous. Ontologically, economic systems are open systems, but in practice they are treated as (partially and provisionally) closed systems.[14] The boundary of a given system represents the outcome of a choice made by the model-builder, and this choice defines the distinction between endogenous and exogenous variables.[15]

Thus, the choice made by the model-builder of the boundaries of an economic system under study should imply an explicit and precise separation between endogenous and exogeneous variables. In turn this introduces restrictions on the mathematical space within which the dynamics of the system can evolve. Disputes on selection of models should not focus on whether the systems are regarded as open or closed, but instead explore the concrete choice of partial closure.

The lesson is that insufficient attention to target system boundaries in macroeconomic modelling may invoke models that at best will create confusion in economic debates. It may also lead to flawed understanding of the dynamics of the target systems.

Stable/unstable structures

A mathematical model consists of a certain structure, presumed to be immutable in theory. The structure is often taking form of a system of equations describing a real-world system under study by a fixed set of variables and their changes in time, internally connected through specified functional relations (which often are assumed to be linear). Altogether such a model will depict the economic system as a dynamic system subject to certain exogenous factors. The system variables represent monetary consequences of economic transactions made by households, firms and other economic actors, and their mutual interactions. The equations may also contain reference to (some of the) external conditions under which the economic processes are evolving.

However, target systems in the real world do rarely live up to all assumptions that are embedded in the mathematical model, such as those outlined above. Households may change their preferences over time, corporations may alter their business model, institutions may change their policy strategies and so on. Aiming at making the mathematical model-descriptions tractable in practice, basic presupposed assumptions integrated in the model are often expressed as *time-invariant* functional relations. In addition to the mentioned challenges, mathematical descriptions may be dependent on several other assumptions as, for example, actors' access to perfect market information, neglect of transaction costs or non-existence of bankruptcy of firms.

Model-users are not always aware of all assumptions made by 'model-owners' and/or model-builders, and sometimes not every assumption is brought explicitly 'into the open'. It seems obvious that a systematic screening of such mathematical models is needed with a focus on whether the set of the actually chosen structures is complete and relevant.

Uncertainty

Uncertainty[16] refers to situations where the future evolution of a target system is profoundly unknown (Dow 2012). Model-builders nevertheless sometimes try to overcome this difficulty: Uncertainty of specific factors may be treated through introduction of *quantitative, subjective risk estimates* and/or stochastic elements in actual model variables, as observed by Boulding.[17] However, application of mathematical analysis of macroeconomic problems under uncertainty conditions will not always be able to deliver successful outcomes. Some examples: the macro-economic consequences of a not-foreseen crisis in the financial system, of a rapidly expanding pandemic or of a natural disaster as, e.g. an earthquake.

In cases of this character, the outcome of model-based scenarios may presumably be seriously flawed or useless. A closely related situation is represented by mathematical analysis of macroeconomic problems, built on assumptions that imply that the very mathematical set-up deliberately *a priori* excludes catastrophic system developments.[18] (The background might be model-builder's ignorance of such potential events.) Here mathematical analysis will not be able to deduce implications that are likely to be interpreted as catastrophic outcomes, that is, mathematical exploration cannot adequately reflect future real-world changes even if disasters are possible in the real world, however rare they might be.

Blind spots

Blind spots are model-invisible factors, that is, real-world phenomena, that are excluded from the model universe, whether they are deliberately ignored (motivated by diverse reasons) or they are not recognised or acknowledged. Examples: macroeconomic models that simply ignore the existence of a financial sector and/or debt (Bezemer and Hudson 2016, p. 475), or models without integrated feed-back mechanisms from environmental change to the economic system (Davies 2019, pp. 66–84).

Macroeconomic models that do not explicitly include potentially significant variables will obviously not be able to adequately reflect the full spectrum of future real-world outcomes. The impact of very rare and/or extreme events like, e.g. financial system meltdown and climate catastrophes, that are neglected by certain models, are examples of methodological blind spots. No mathematical analysis within the framework of such macroeconomic models will be able to remedy this situation.

Concluding remarks

Macroeconomic models face challenges of being caught in some *model pitfalls*, and they are subject to the risk of producing flawed conclusions and eventually flawed economic policy guidance. The application of mathematics does not *per se* solve such analytical challenges, but 'non-mathematical' experience and reflections are undeniably required.

Any application of mathematical modelling in macroeconomic analyses should aim at providing *fully disclosed descriptions* of the actual models. This includes clarification of potentially unsolved questions associated with generic modelling issues. We have looked at four such issues: *system closure*; *stable/unstable structures*; *profound uncertainty*; and *blind spots*.

Focus on such challenges will obviously strengthen methodological reflections and improve modelling endeavours.

Usefulness of mathematical models in macroeconomic analysis is not an either/or question. Mathematics and mathematical models play a central role in macroeconomic problem analysis. Macroeconomic themes represent a broad array of issues, and examination of these involves a correspondingly broad spectrum of models that extend from easy-to-understand models to highly elaborated and complex models. The actual choice of model type will often involve dilemmas of conflicting overall goals.

Mathematical models in macroeconomics may serve two diverse purposes: The first is to improve understanding of the dynamics of macroeconomic phenomena. The second is to prepare political-economic strategies and/or to formulate possible policy guidelines for decision makers. The former may contribute to inform debates of political-economic issues at large, whereas the latter entails inherent risks of implying misleading and flawed decisions, even if these are formed in accordance with the best intentions.

Rigour and precision of mathematical concepts and approaches imply a propensity by analysts to regard logical deduction as the only reasoning tool and to value internal consistency and objectivity as the real merits of mathematical macroeconomic models. Analysts might at the same time be subject to the risk of paying less or no attention to appraisal of the relevance of model outcomes, based on the decisive similarity between target and model systems.

Macroeconomic predictions come with considerable *uncertainties* due to profound lack of knowledge concerning future socio-economic development and many other factors. Uncertainty problems are amplified with the increasing time horizon of calculations.

Economies in the real world are open systems, which underlines the importance of careful delineation of target systems made by analysts and defined through their choice of mathematical models. If the target system includes natural systems, the actual problem description is even more important. In the case of combined climate-economy models, there are substantial uncertainties, not the least on the climate side (such as irreversible processes and tipping points). This may generate blind spots that are or could be crucial for the relevance of the corresponding models.

Notes

1 A vast majority of economists in academia and in policy institutions who are engaged in theoretical and practical analyses of economic problems feel seemingly comfortable in general when applying mathematical methods and models at macro as well as micro levels. However, there is a growing minority of scholars from economics and other disciplines, who express major reservations in these matters by addressing critique to a series of specific limitations of mathematics as language and tool when applied in economics. During a period of several decades the overall question has been raised repeatedly on the proper role mathematics plays in economics. A provisional list of critical voices includes Keynes (1936), Boulding (1955), Morgenstern (1963), Quddus and Rashid (1994), Streeten (2002), Keen (2011), Lawson (2010, 2012), Rodrik (2015), Hudson (2015), Bezemer and Hudson (2016), Syll (2015, 2016), Mäki (2018) and Zaman (2020).
2 An important example is the thought-provoking debate on climate-economy models, where Nordhaus (2008, 2018) and Tol (2017, 2018) represent one side of the dispute, whereas Pindyck (2013a, 2013b, 2017) and Keen (2020) represent the other.
3 Although the context of this chapter is macroeconomic methodology, some of the presented considerations address general issues concerning models in science, including issues common for macro- and microeconomic methodology.
4 Yet another critical approach to the very concept of 'a model' is suggested by the economist Lars P. Syll: "Using formal mathematical modeling, mainstream economists like

Rodrik sure can guarantee that the conclusion holds given the assumptions. However, there is no warrant that the validity we get in abstract model worlds automatically transfer to real world economies. Validity and consistency may be good, but it isn't enough. From a realist perspective both relevance and soundness are *sine qua non*" (Syll 2016, p. 147).

5 The application of statistical methods in macroeconomic analyses *as such* represents a specific class of mathematical issues, related to, for example, the validity of data in time series, regression analysis and statistical inference. However, this field of topics is not explicitly addressed in this chapter.

6 Due to the focus on mathematics in this chapter we exclusively regard *formalised* models in the following (cf. the figure). It should be noted that a mental model and its corresponding formalised version are not identical, due to 'the non-neutrality of formalism', an important aspect examined by Chick and Dow (2012, pp. 140–61).

7 The concept of 'mental model' is further explored in a trichotomy of models presented by Zaman (2020).

8 Parenthetically it could be mentioned that Boulding has contributed to introduction of 'General systems theory' as a meta-discipline that describes a level of theoretical modelbuilding which lies somewhere between the highly generalized constructions of pure mathematics and the specific theories of specialized disciplines such as physics, biology, ecology, social sciences (Boulding 1956). An additional reference to this important issue, cf. Morin (2008).

9 Boulding also labels 'limitation' as 'bias'.

10 Carveth Read (1898) *Logic: Deductive and Inductive*. Retrieved 9.8.2021 at https://www. goodreads.com/author/quotes/3242545.

11 The significant relevance of epistemology and ontology in the context of macroeconomic methodology is not further pursued in the present text.

12 There are other possible limitations connected to application of mathematics in macroeconomic analyses, related to themes as, e.g. implications of a marginalist approach, the profound uncertainty of the future, the axiomatic foundation and challenges in learning processes. However, a comprehensive discussion of these and other relevant themes lies outside the scope of this chapter.

13 Methodologically, the chosen approach is not perfect, since the mentioned four modelling issues not necessarily are mutually independent.

14 A thorough account of system closure, including definitions of open and closed systems, is presented in Chick and Dow (2005). These authors apply a terminology that presupposes distinction between 'system', 'theory' and 'model'. Alternatively, Mäki (2018) underlines an approach to system closure, where the 'modelling endeavour framework' is key (cf. the subsection 'What is a model?'). The two approaches are obviously not methodologically identical, but there are seemingly some similarities connected to their attention to the concept of 'system boundary'.

15 Many endogenous variables may be mutually interdependent, whereas exogenous variables represent envisaged impact on the system driven by circumstances that are independent of the internal dynamics of the target system.

16 We distinguish between uncertainty and risk. The former is perceived as the result of cognitive limitations or inaccessibility of information and cannot be formalised in any univocal way, whereas the latter refers to quantifiable risk describable by use of stochastic methods.

17 'The theory of uncertainty is largely an attempt to discuss vagueness by means of clear concepts', cf. Section 'Mathematics – a language and a tool', Subsection 'Limitations', item 2.

18 A catastrophic outcome for a society may be defined as a dramatic drop in welfare that eventually might imply serious breakdown of physical infrastructure, social security, energy and food and water supply, etc. Models that exclude such potential options and solely address potential marginal impact to the entire economy might (indirectly) support a reasoning that assumes no need for expecting true catastrophes. An example could be eventual ecological collapse related to seemingly 'modest' climate changes (e.g. global temperature increase by 2°C) (cf. IPCC 2018 and 2021; Gills and Morgan 2020).

References

Bezemer, D. and M. Hudson (2016) 'Finance is not the economy: Reviving the conceptual distinction', *Journal of Economic Issues* L (3), 745–68. doi: 10.1080/00213624.2016.1210384

Boulding, K. E. (1955) *The Limitations of Mathematics: An Epistemological Critique*, [Boulding's contribution to a seminar in the application of mathematics to the social sciences, summarised by Harold Slater]. http://www.compilerpress.ca/Competitiveness/Anno/Anno%20Boulding%20Limitations%20of%20Mathematics%201955.htm. accessed 16 August 2020

Boulding, K. E. (1956) 'General systems theory: The skeleton of science', *Management Science* 2 (3), 128–39.

Chick, V. and S. C. Dow (2005) 'The meaning of open systems', *Journal of Economic Methodology* 12 (3), 363–81.

Chick, V. and S. C. Dow (2012) 'The Non-neutrality of Formalism', in S. C. Dow, ed., *Foundations for New Economic Thinking: A Collection of Essays*, Basingstoke Hampshire and New York: Palgrave Macmillan, pp. 140–61.

CW: see Keynes, J.M. (1971–1989).

Davies, G. (2019) *Economy, Society, Nature: An Introduction to the New Systems-Based, Life-Friendly Economics*, Bristol: World Economics Association Books.

Dow, S. C. (2012) 'The issue of uncertainty in economics', in S. Dow, ed., *Foundations for New Economic Thinking: A Collection of Essay*, Basingstoke Hampshire and New York: Palgrave Macmillan, pp. 197–209.

Hudson, M. (2015) 'The use and abuse of mathematical economics', in M. Hudson, ed., *Finance as warfare*, Bristol: World Economics Association Book series, pp. 99–132.

Gills, B. and J. Morgan (2020) 'Global climate emergency: After COP24, climate science, urgency, and the threat to humanity', *Globalizations* 17 (6), 885–902. doi: 10.1080/14747731.2019.1669915

Intergovernmental Panel on Climate Change, IPCC (2018) 'Global warming of 1.5°C: Summary for policy makers', UN IPCC: Geneva.

Intergovernmental Panel on Climate Change, IPCC (2021) 'Climate change 2021: The physical science basis, summary for policy makers', Assessment Report 6 (AR6), UN: Geneva. https://www.ipcc.ch/report/ar6/wg1/downloads/report/IPCC_AR6_WGI_SPM.pdf, accessed 16 August 2021.

Keen, S. (2011) *Debunking Economics*-Revised and Expanded Edition, London and New York: Zed Books.

Keen, S. (2020) 'The appallingly bad neoclassical economics of climate change', *Globalizations* 18 (7), 1149–77, http://dx.doi.org/10.1080/14747731.2020.1807856, accessed 3 January 2021.

Keynes, J. M. (1936) *The General Theory of Employment, Interest and Money, CW VII.*

Keynes, J. M. (1938) Letter from Keynes to Harrod, 4 July 1938, *CW*, XIV.

Keynes, J. M. (1971–1989) *Collected Writings*, (*CW*), D. E. Moggridge, ed., 30 vols, London: Macmillan and New York: St Martin's Press.

Lawson, T. (2010) *Really Reorienting Modern Economy*. https://www.ineteconomics.org/uploads/papers/INET-C@K-Paper-Session-6-Lawson.pdf, accessed 1 July 2020.

Lawson, T. (2012) 'Mathematical modelling and ideology in the economics academy: Competing explanations of the failings of the modern discipline?' *Economic Thought* 1 (1), 3–22.

Lucas, R. E. (2001) 'Professional Memoir', published in W. Breit and B. T. Hirsh eds., (2004), *Lives of the Laureates*, Fourth edition, Cambridge: MIT Press, pp. 279–94.

Mäki, U. (2018) 'Rights and wrongs of economic modelling: Refining Rodrik', *Journal of Economic Methodology* 25 (3), 218–36.

Morgenstern, O. (1963) 'Limits to the uses of mathematics in economics', *Econometric Research Program*, Memorandum no. 49, Princeton University.

Morin, E. (2008) *On complexity*, Cresskill: Hampton Press, Inc.

Nordhaus, W. D. (2008) *A Question of Balance. Weighing the Options on Global Warming Policies*, New Haven: Yale University Press.

Nordhaus, W. D. (2018) 'Projections and uncertainties about climate change in an Era of minimal climate policies', *American Economic Journal: Economic Policy* 10 (3), 330–60.

Pindyck, R. S. (2013a) 'The climate policy dilemma', *NBER Working Paper Series*, Working Paper 18205, National Bureau of Economic Research: Cambridge.

Pindyck, R. S. (2013b) 'Climate change policy: What do the models tell us?' *Journal of Economic Literature* 51 (3), 860–72. http://dx.doi.org/10.1257/jel.51.3.860, accessed 7 July 2020.

Pindyck, R. S. (2017) 'The use and misuse of models for climate policy', *Review of Environmental Economics and Policy* 11 (1), 100–14.

Quddus, M. and S. Rashid (1994) 'The overuse of mathematics in economics: Nobel resistance', *Eastern Economic Journal* 20 (3), 251–65.

Read, C. (1898) *Logic: Deductive and Inductive*, https://www.goodreads.com/author/quotes/3242545, accessed 9 August 2021.

Rodrik, D. (2015) *Economic Rules. The Rights and Wrongs of the Dismal Science*, New York and London: W. W. Norton & Company.

Senge, P. M. (2006) *The Fifth Discipline. The Art & Practice of the Learning Organisation.* Random House: Business Books.

Streeten, P. (2002) 'What's wrong with contemporary economics?' *Interdisciplinary Science Reviews* 27 (1), 13–24.

Syll, L. P. (2015) 'On the use and misuse of theories and models in mainstream economics', Bristol: *World Economic Association Book series.*

Syll, L. P. (2016) 'When the model becomes the message – a critique of Rodrik', *Real-World Economics Review* 74, 139–55. http://www.paecon.net/PAEReview/Issue74/Syll74.pdf

Tol, R. S. J. (2017) 'The structure of the climate debate', *Energy Policy* 104, 431–38.

Tol, R. S. J. (2018) 'The economic impacts of climate change', *Review of Environmental Economics and Policy* 12 (1), 4–25.

Wigner, E. (1960) 'The unreasonable effectiveness of mathematics in the natural sciences', *Communications in Pure and Applied Mathematics* 13 (I), 1–14.

Zaman, A. (2020) 'Models and reality: How did models divorced from reality become epistemological acceptable?', *Real-World Economics Review* (91), 20–44. http://www.paecon.net/PAEReview/issue91/Zaman91.pdf

23

EXPLANATION AND FORECASTING

Marcel Boumans

Introduction

An explanation is an answer to a *why* question. Finding such a kind of answer is generally considered to be the core activity of science. But not every answer to a *why* question is scientific. Therefore it needs to meet certain requirements. The most dominant requirement in science is that a scientific explanation should show some event or some regularity to be an instance of a fundamental law. Carl Hempel (Hempel and Oppenheim 1948) developed this view into what is called the deductive-nomological model of explanation or covering-law model.

In a deductive-nomological explanation, a statement of what is to be explained (the *explanandum*) is deduced from a set of true statements that includes at least one law (*nomos*). This latter set of statements is called the *explanans*. Schematically, this can be expressed as follows:

Explanans:
Laws: $L_1, ..., L_m$
True statements of initial conditions: $c_1, ..., c_n$

Explanandum: E

where the solid line represents a deductive inference.

According to this model of explanation, laws are essential to scientific explanations. Moreover, they are also essential to predictions. Because laws are universal with respect to time, they comprehend the future as well as the past, so they are equally able to offer an explanation of what has happened and to predict what will happen. Explanation and prediction are two sides of the same coin which can be demonstrated with the deductive-nomological model. This is known as the symmetry thesis. On the one hand, scientific explanation involves filling in what is missing above the inference line:

DOI: 10.4324/9781315745992-28

	laws
?	?
initial conditions	
―――― or	――――
explanandum	explanandum

On the other hand, prediction involves filling in what is missing below the inference line:

laws
initial conditions
―――――
?

Hempel's model, however, is problematic when it is applied to macroeconomics for two reasons. The first problem is whether economic laws exist. If not, then there is no scientific explanation and no scientific prediction possible in macroeconomics. Macroeconomics can then only be a descriptive science, a position Paul Samuelson (1963, 1964, 1965) maintained for a short period in the 1960s (see Boumans and Davis 2016, pp. 55–9). The other problem is that the model induces a symmetry between explanation and prediction. A consequence of this symmetry is that the explanatory power can be assessed by investigating whether it also provides accurate predictions. When it appears that the predictive performance in economics is bad does this mean that economic explanations are bad too?

Because of these two problems this chapter explores a methodology of explanation and prediction for a lawless science such as macroeconomics. Explanation and prediction in macroeconomics have a different model than Hempel's and are not symmetrical with respect to each other. The next section discusses the methodology of explanation in macroeconomics. As will be shown, one needs, however, to make a distinction between prediction as forecasting and prediction as policy analysis. The methodology of both will be discussed in subsequent sections.

Explanation

Philosophers have employed various standard criteria to distinguish laws from other types of generalisations. These criteria take the forms of laws that are said to be exceptionless generalisations and to make no reference to particular objects or spatio-temporal locations and to have a very wide scope – in other words they are universal. James Woodward (2000) shows that these criteria are not helpful for understanding the features that characterise explanatory generalisations in, for example, economics. 'In general, it is the range of interventions and changes over which a generalisation is invariant and not the traditional criteria that are crucial both to whether or not it is a law and to its explanatory status' (Woodward 2000, p. 222).

Woodward's idea of invariance is that a generalisation describing a relationship between two or more variables is invariant if it would continue to hold – would remain stable or unchanged – as various other conditions change. The set or range of changes over which a relationship or generalisation is invariant is its domain of invariance. So, invariance is a relative matter: a relationship is invariant with respect to a certain domain. It is this notion of invariance that is useful for understanding explanatory practice in macroeconomics and not the concept of a law of nature fulfilling the above-mentioned criteria of universality.

Two sorts of changes can be distinguished that are relevant to the assessment of invariance. First, there are changes in the background conditions to a generalisation, that is, changes that affect other variables besides those that figure in the generalisation itself. Second, there are changes in those variables that figure explicitly in the generalisation itself. In his discussion of invariance, Woodward emphasises that only a subclass of this latter sort of changes is important, namely changes that result from an intervention, that is, changes that result from a causal process having specific causal characteristics. The reason he gives for this is that some background conditions are causally independent of the factors related by the generalisation in question and therefore of no importance. However, other background conditions might be causally connected to some of the factors related by the generalisation, and changes in these conditions might disrupt the relationship. A relationship that holds in certain specific background conditions and for a restricted range of interventions might break down outside of these.

In Woodward's account of explanation in relation to invariance, the difference between laws and invariant generalisations is considered as a matter of degree: laws are generalisations that are invariant under a very large and very important set of changes. The interesting questions for macroeconomists, therefore, are not only whether a relationship is invariant under certain specific kinds of changes and interventions but also under which changes it remains invariant; they want to know the domain of changes for which it holds. Macroeconomists are faced with constantly changing background conditions and they would like to know whether the relationships on which they base their policy advices still hold tomorrow.

Woodward's (2000) account of invariance is based on Haavelmo's (1944) account of autonomy, which had an enormous influence on the methodology of macro-econometric modelling through the Cowles Commission. To clarify Haavelmo's account, the next exposition is based on Boumans's (2005) interpretation of Haavelmo's discussion of autonomous relationships.

Let y be an economic variable whose behaviour is explained by a function, F, of independent causal factors $x_1, x_2, \ldots$: $y = F(x_1, x_2, \ldots)$. The way in which the factors x_i might influence y can be represented by the following equation:

$$\Delta y = \Delta F(x_1, x_2, \cdots) = \frac{\partial F}{\partial x_1} \Delta x_1 + \frac{\partial F}{\partial x_2} \Delta x_2 + \cdots \tag{1}$$

where the deltas, Δ, indicate a change in magnitude. The terms $\frac{\partial F}{\partial x_i}$ indicate how much F will proportionally change due to a change in the magnitude of factor x_i.

Suppose we are trying to discover an invariant relationship (in the sense of Woodward) that could explain the phenomenon y. In principle, there are an infinite number of factors, $x_1, x_2, \ldots$, that could influence the behaviour of y, but we hope that it may be possible to establish a constant and relatively simple relation between y and a relatively small number of explanatory factors, x.

Based on the statistics available, a specific set of observations S, we find a limited number of factors (n) that actually have influence:

$$\Delta y_S = \frac{\partial F}{\partial x_1} \Delta x_1 + \cdots + \frac{\partial F}{\partial x_n} \Delta x_n \tag{2}$$

The causal factors that appear in this explanation have shown actual influence on y based on the data set S, that means: $\frac{\partial F}{\partial x_i} \Delta x_i \neq 0$ ($i = 1, ..., n$). Thus, the relationship $y = F(x_1, ..., x_n)$ explains the actual observed values of y.

The fundamental problem, however, is that it is not possible to identify the reason for a factor – say x_{n+1} – not being taken into our explanation, that is to say, the reason why its influence was negligible, $\frac{\partial F}{\partial x_{n+1}} \Delta x_{n+1} \approx 0$. We cannot know whether this is because its potential influence is very small, that is to say, $\frac{\partial F}{\partial x_{n+1}} \approx 0$, or whether the variation of this factor in this specific data set S was too small, $\Delta x_{n+1} \approx 0$. We only would like not to account for factors in the explanation whose influence was not observed because their potential influence was negligible. At the same time, we want to include those factors whose potential influence is sufficiently large enough but were not observed because they varied so little that their potential influence was veiled.

The variation of x_{n+1} is determined by other relationships within the economic system. In some cases a virtually dormant factor may become active because of changes in the economic structure elsewhere. However, deciding whether a factor should be included in the explanation of y should not depend on such changes. The explaining relationship should be invariant ('autonomous' as Haavelmo called it) with respect to structural changes elsewhere. Only its potential influence (whether $\frac{\partial F}{\partial x_{n+1}} \approx 0$ or not) should be decisive.

The main problem then becomes: how do we know which potential influences should be included in the explanation of y? One solution is to extend the number of data sets, and to explore whether some of them show sufficient variation in x_{n+1}. If so, these data sets could then be used to determine whether the potential influence of x_{n+1} on y is significant.

This approach depends considerably on the availability of statistics. These days of 'big data' this is perhaps not such a problem, but in the 1950s it was. The Cowles Commission chose therefore another solution by building models as comprehensive as possible, based on *a priori* theoretical specifications. Theory will tell which factors should be included.

An important critique of the Cowles Commission approach of macro-econometric modelling came from Milton Friedman. He opposed the approach in which models are aimed as 'photographic reproductions', that is, models that aim at realisticness in the sense that they provide a description of reality as comprehensively as possible. For Friedman the relevant question to ask about the assumptions of a theory is not whether they are descriptively realistic, 'for they never are', but whether they are 'sufficiently good approximations for the purpose in hand' (Friedman 1953, p. 15).

To clarify Friedman's position we will analyse with Haavelmo's framework an example Friedman (1953) discusses in some detail, namely a Galilean fall experiment. Galileo had designed his experiments such that although carried out in the open air with specific objects, the law he found applies to all bodies in vacuum. The empirical regularity he found by his fall experiments is a very simple one: distance is proportional to time squared. From this empirical finding Galileo inferred a law of falling bodies that states that the acceleration of a body dropped in a vacuum is a constant and is independent of the mass, composition and shape of the body, etc.

The question is, to what extent the law of falling bodies can be applied outside a vacuum. According to Friedman, to answer this question one has to take into account the kind of object that is to be dropped. Galileo's law works well if applied on compact balls. 'The application of this formula to a compact ball dropped from a roof of a building is equivalent to saying that a ball so dropped behaves *as if* it were falling in vacuum' (Friedman 1953, p. 16). Air resistance is negligible for compact balls falling relatively short distances, so they behave approximately as described by Galileo's law.

The problem, now, is to decide for which objects the air resistance is negligible. Apparently, this is the case for a compact ball falling from a roof of a building, but what if the object is a feather or the object is dropped from an airplane at an altitude of 30,000 feet? One of the traditional criteria on laws is that they must contain no essential reference to particular objects or systems: they are universal. In contrast to this traditional view, Friedman argues that a specification of the scope of objects and systems for which a generalisation applies should be attached to the generalisation, a view similar to Woodward (2000).

To deal with this problem of specification, two options are possible. One is to use the most comprehensive theory – the Cowles Commission approach. However, the extra accuracy it yields may not justify the extra costs of achieving it. The second option is to select the phenomena for which the theory works. That is to say, to indicate the scope for which the 'law' works, for example, the law of falling bodies (outside a vacuum) holds for compact balls and not for feathers. This means that one should specify the scope for which a generalisation holds, but this should be stated independently of this generalisation. Thus, one should not incorporate this specification into the generalisation itself, for example, by adding a relevant variable to the model, as the Cowles Commission aimed at. Having a generalisation that has been successfully used to model and explain certain phenomena, it is a separate empirical question what the full range of phenomena is that can be explained by it and of which answer should not have been built into this generalisation.

To clarify Friedman's position within Haavelmo's framework, a comprehensive explanation of the motion of a falling body can be represented by equation (1) above:

$$\Delta y = \Delta F\left(x_1, x_2, \cdots\right) = \frac{\partial F}{\partial x_1}\Delta x_1 + \frac{\partial F}{\partial x_2}\Delta x_2 + \cdots$$

Suppose that y is the motion of a body, x_1 is gravity, x_2 air resistance, and $x_3, x_4, \ldots$ are other specification of the circumstances (e.g. temperature, magnetic forces). The law of falling bodies says that in a vacuum ($x_2 = 0$, but the notion of 'vacuum' in this law in fact also supposes that inference by other disturbing causes is absent: $x_3 = x_4 = \ldots = 0$) all bodies fall with the same acceleration regardless of mass, shape or composition: $\frac{\partial F}{\partial x_1}$ is equal for all bodies. However, in the open air, the shape and the substance of the falling body determine which of the other-than-gravity interfering factors can be considered as having a negligible influence (i.e. $\frac{\partial F}{\partial x_i} \approx 0$). For example, air resistance is negligible for compact balls falling relatively short distances, so they behave as if they are falling in vacuum. However, for feathers the air resistance does interfere. Similarly, magnetic forces act on steel balls and not on wooden balls, etc. To conclude, one has to specify the class of phenomena for which a specific model is an adequate representation.

Prediction as forecasting

While Friedman was not traditional in his interpretation of laws, he, however, maintained the symmetry thesis: the validity of an explanation should be assessed by its predictive performance. In his view, the validity of the model equations should not be determined by high correlation coefficients.

> The fact that the equations fit the data from which they are derived is a test primarily of the skill and patience of the analyst; it is not a test of the validity of the equation for any broader body of data. Such a test is provided solely by the consistency of the equations with data not used in the derivation, such as data for periods subsequent to the period analysed.
>
> *(Friedman 1951, p. 108)*

Because predictions are never exact, they should be evaluated by determining whether they fall within a certain range of acceptable outcomes. A model's prediction therefore should be compared with a standard of comparison, a null hypothesis, against which to test the hypothesis that the econometric model makes good predictions. Friedman proposed these null models to be what he called 'naive models'. The first – naive model I – predicts that next year's value of any variable will equal this year's value plus some white noise, that is, a random normal disturbance ε_t^I with zero mean and constant variance. The second – naive model II – predicts that next year's value of any variable will equal this year's value plus the change from last year to this year plus a random normal disturbance ε_t^{II} with zero mean and constant variance.

Naive model I: $\quad y_{t+1} = y_t + \varepsilon_t^I$

Naive model II: $\quad y_{t+1} = y_t + \left(y_t - y_{t-1}\right) + \varepsilon_t^{II}$

While the naive model tests became one of the many diagnostic tests to improve decision-making for building larger models (see, for example, Christ 1966, pp. 571–5) and Friedman's involvement with the origination of these tests forgotten (Boumans 2016), Friedman's emphasis on testing models by assessing their predictive performance came to be seen as a ratification among economists who generally shared an instrumentalist position with respect to models.

This commonly shared instrumentalism is based on a confusion of anti-realism with anti-realisticness and was partly due to Friedman's own imprecise phrasing of his position, as in his famous dictum: 'Truly important and significant hypotheses will be found to have "assumptions" that are wildly inaccurate descriptive representations of reality, and, in general, the more significant the theory, the more unrealistic the assumptions (in this sense)' (Friedman 1953, p. 14). In the discussions with respect to whether Friedman's methodology is instrumentalist, realism was understood to refer to a specific view of how a theory is related to truth, namely that the theoretical assumptions are true. Some philosophers and economists came to interpret Friedman's methodology as instrumentalist, because they understood the expression 'an unrealistic assumption' to mean an untrue assumption. A different reading of this dictum is that unrealistic means not accurate in all the details of the assumption, which applies not only to any approximation, like a 'non-photographic reproduction', but also to any abstraction or idealisation.

But this had, and still has, also to do with the omission of many economists to see the difference between models and theories. Theories are expected to tell the truth about certain phenomena, but models have a different epistemological function. Exemplary for this view on models is the following claim, which comes also rather close to Friedman's: 'Remember that all models are wrong; the practical question is how wrong do they have to be to be useful' (Box and Draper 1987, p. 78).

Generally, models are built to answer specific questions. The assessment of the reliability of an answer depends on the kind of question investigated. As we saw above, the answer to a 'why' question is an explanation. The premises of an explanation have to include invariant relationships and thus the reliability of such an answer depends on whether the domain of invariance of the relevant relationships covers the domain of the question. The answer to a 'what will happen' question is a prediction. The assessment of a prediction could be to evaluate how the model has performed with respect to the predictions made in the past.

The problem of evaluating models built for forecasting is that one cannot get around invariance. There must be a stable bridge that connects the past and present with the future. As discussed above, to evaluate invariance its domain should be considered. In other words, one has to investigate what the list of all relevant non-negligible potential influences is. To ensure invariance, this list should be complete. This latter point was also emphasised by John Maynard Keynes when he was criticising Tinbergen's econometric method: 'Am I right in thinking that the method multiple correlation analysis essentially depends on the economist having furnished, not merely a list of significant causes, which is correct so far as it goes, but a complete list?' (Keynes 1939, p. 560).

But these considerations are not sufficient for the evaluation of the predictive performance of a non-natural science such as economics. Predictive power also implies that both the domain of invariance as well as the magnitudes of the potential influences should be invariant. This point, too, was raised by Keynes in his critique on Tinbergen's method:

> [T]he environment in all relevant respects, other than the fluctuations in those factors of which we take particular account, should be uniform and homogeneous over a period of time. We cannot be sure that such conditions will persist in the future, even if we find them in the past.
>
> *(Keynes 1939, pp. 566–67)*

This latter point was discussed extensively in Keynes's *Treatise on Probability* (1921, *CW* VIII) under the heading of the theory of statistical inference: 'It seeks to extend its description of certain characteristics of observed events to the corresponding characteristics of other events which have not been observed' (Keynes 1921, *CW* VIII, p. 358). For inductive inference based on statistical analysis it is of relevance to show whether the statistical series shows some 'stability'. The verification of whether a statistical series has some stability is required because the condition for economic statistical series to be applicable for inductive inference is that it shows sufficient 'homogeneity' or 'uniformity'. By uniformity, Keynes (1921, *CW* VIII, p. 252) meant that 'mere differences of position in time and space are treated as irrelevant'.

Predictions as policy analysis

This all shows why economists perform so badly when it concerns forecasting. But should they be good forecasters, in a similar role as weather forecasters? Or does this view miss the point for which macroeconomic models are built? Macroeconomists, in particular the ones we have mentioned so far, are interested in economic policy. They are not so much interested in answering 'what will happen' questions but more in 'what-if' questions. Most if not all macroeconomic models are not built to predict, but are supposed to addresses questions related to policy design and analysis.

The main difference between 'what will happen' and 'what-if' questions is that the answers to the latter include a kind of uniformity clause, that is to say, they include ceteris paribus assumptions which define the domain for which the design and analysis can be applied. Because we do not know the complete list of all potential influences and we also do not know whether and how they will change in the future, we assume that ceteris paribus conditions apply to them. To clarify this, we will use the same framework (equation 1) as above. For example, when macroeconomists want to know how a change in the interest rate, say x_1, may influence the purchasing power for a specific country, say y, they assume that all other factors do not change: $\Delta x_i \approx 0$ for $i > 1$. Alternatively, they assume that these other factors are absent, that is, $x_i \approx 0$ for $i > 1$ (ceteris absentibus) and that $\dfrac{\partial F}{\partial x_1}$ is stable for the intervention that is being investigated, such that for policy design the following model can be used:

$$\Delta y = \frac{\partial F}{\partial x_1} \Delta x_1$$

The next step in the policy analysis is to include some other factors that may be relevant too, by lifting the ceteris paribus assumptions for them. Knowledge about the potential influence of these factors remains, however, essential. They should remain invariant with respect to variations in the factors, that is, invariant for all kinds of policy interventions, Δx_i. This issue was put again on the macroeconomic modelling agenda in the late 1970s by Robert Lucas (1976) in his critique on econometric policy evaluations. Policy evaluations require invariance of the structure of the model under policy variations. The underlying idea, known as the Lucas critique, is that estimated parameters that were previously regarded as 'structural' in econometric analysis of economic policy actually depend on the economic policy pursued during the estimation period. Hence, the parameters may change with shifts in the policy regime.

Lucas's critique was not new, see discussions above related to Haavelmo and Keynes, but in the 1980s a third way to deal with the issue of the invariance of potential influences was offered. Besides looking for a solution in theory or the enlargement of data sets, Fynn Kydland and Edward Prescott (1982) proposed calibration. They characterised calibration in two different ways. First, as 'specifications of preferences and technology [...] close to those used in many applied studies', which they considered to be stable across these studies, and secondly as 'the selection of parameter values for which the model steady states values are near average values for the American economy during the period being explained' (Kydland and Prescott 1982, p. 1360). Later, these second values came to be replaced by 'stylised facts'. Thomas Cooley and Prescott (1995, p. 3) describe calibration as choosing the model parameters 'so that [the model] mimics the actual economy on dimensions associated with long term growth' by setting parameter values equal to certain 'more or less constant' ratios. These ratios were the stylised facts of economic growth, 'striking empirical regularities both over time and across countries'. Stylised facts illustrate 'economic laws at work'. They hoped that by the calibration methodology the magnitudes of the potential influences, $\frac{\partial F}{\partial x_i}$, represent stable facts of an economy.

Conclusions

> In practice we have tacitly agreed, as a rule, to fall back on what is, in truth, a *convention*. The essence of this convention – though it does not, of course, work out quite so simple – lies in assuming that the existing state of affairs will continue indefinitely, except in so far we have specific reasons to expect a change.
>
> *(Keynes 1921, CW VII, p. 152)*

According to Hempel's deductive-nomological model we need universal laws to make explanations and predictions scientific. Woodward, however, argues that whether or not a generalisation can be used to explain and predict has to do with whether it is invariant rather than whether it is universal. A generalisation is invariant if it is stable or robust in the sense that it would continue to hold within a certain domain. Unlike universality, invariance comes in graduations or degrees. A generalisation can be invariant even if it has exceptions outside its domain or holds only over a limited spatio-temporal interval. An invariant generalisation can also be more limited in scope than a law, as it holds for a smaller range of different kinds of systems or phenomena. As long as we clearly indicate the domain and scope of an invariant relationship we do not need universal laws in our scientific explanations and predictions.

Woodward's account is rather similar to, and is actually built upon Haavelmo's account of potential influences. To know the invariance domain of a generalisation one needs to know which of the potential influences are non-negligible. The problem however is that this kind of knowledge is only revealed if the causal factor in question has varied. But for an explanation or prediction we need a complete list of all the non-negligible causal factors. To solve this problem the Cowles Commission suggested to give theory the responsibility of completing this list.

Friedman, doubting whether it ever would be possible to arrive at such comprehensive models, suggested an alternative methodology: investigate the scope of the model to determine for which economic systems, time period or phenomena the model applies. He also proposed that the evaluation of a model should be determined by its predictive performance.

While the predictive performance is useful to determine the scope of the model in question, one will never be sure whether the future will fall outside this scope. For prediction one also needs to know whether the magnitudes of the potential influences are stable across time. They could be influenced by policy interventions. To deal with the problem Prescott suggested to use for the determination of these magnitudes the stable facts of an economy, that is to say, stable across a very long period.

Whether economics models are built for explanatory, predictive or policy purposes, invariance is the key issue on which the success of these models depends. As a consequence, the existence of invariant macro-relationships determines the success of macroeconomics as a separate field. This is most clearly illustrated by the discussions in the 1970s about the alleged stability of the Phillips curve and the Lucas critique that followed it, resulting in a call for microfoundations, and the end of macroeconomics as a separate field.

References

Boumans, M. (2005) *How Economists Model the World into Numbers*, London and New York: Routledge.

Boumans, M. (2016) 'Friedman and the Cowles Commission', in R. A. Cord and J. D. Hammond, eds., *Milton Friedman: Contributions to Economics and Public Policy*, Oxford: Oxford University Press, pp. 585–604.

Boumans, M. and J. B. Davis (2016) *Economic Methodology: Understanding Economics as a Science*, Second edition, London: Palgrave Macmillan.

Box, G. E. P. and N. R. Draper (1987) *Empirical Model-Building and Response Surfaces*, New York: Wiley.

Christ, C. F. (1966) *Econometric Models and Methods*, New York: John Wiley and Sons.

Cooley, T. F. and E. C. Prescott (1995) 'Economic growth and business cycles', in T. F. Cooley, ed., *Frontiers of Business Cycle Research*, Princeton: Princeton University Press, pp. 1–38.

CW: see Keynes (1971–1989).

Friedman, M. (1951) 'Comment', in *Conference on Business Cycles*, New York: National Bureau of Economic Research, pp. 107–14.

Friedman, M. (1953) 'The methodology of positive economics', in *Essays in Positive Economics*, Chicago and London: University of Chicago Press, pp. 3–43.

Haavelmo, T. (1944) 'The probability approach in econometrics', supplement to *Econometrica* 12, July, pp. iii–vi, 1–115.

Hempel, C. G. and P. Oppenheim (1948), 'Studies in the logic of explanation', *Philosophy of Science* 15 (2), 135–75.

Keynes, J. M. (1921) *A Treatise on Probability*, *CW* VIII.

Keynes, J. M. (1936) *The General Theory of Employment, Interest and Money*, CW VII.

Keynes, J. M. (1939) 'Professor Tinbergen's method', *The Economic Journal* 49, 558–68.

Keynes, J. M. (1971–1989) *The Collected Writings of John Maynard Keynes (CW)*, D. E. Moggridge, ed., 30 vols, London: Macmillan and New York: St Martin's Press.

Kydland, F. E. and E. C. Prescott (1982) 'Time to build and aggregate fluctuations', *Econometrica* 50 (6), 1345–70.

Lucas, R. E. (1976), 'Econometric policy evaluations: A critique', in K. Brunner and A. H. Meltzer, eds, *The Phillips Curve and Labor Markets*, Amsterdam: North-Holland, pp. 19–46.

Samuelson, P. (1963) 'Problems of methodology: Discussion', *American Economic Review* 53 (2), 231–6.

Samuelson, P. (1964) 'Theory and realism: A reply', *American Economic Review* 54 (5), 736–9.

Samuelson, P. (1965) 'Professor Samuelson on theory and realism: Reply', *American Economic Review* 55 (5), 1164–72.

Woodward, J. (2000) 'Explanation and invariance in the special sciences', *British Journal for the Philosophy of Science* 51 (2), 197–254.

24

USING MACROECONOMIC MODELS IN POLICY PRACTICE

The relationship between models and reality

Frank A. G. den Butter

Introduction

There are three ways to use economic models in practical policy analysis. A first way is through theoretical models which describe and interrelate the individual choice behaviour of economic subjects on the basis of the rationality postulate. This yields qualitative statements about how policy measures may affect the choice behaviour and therefore about the welfare effects of the policy. A second way is quantitatively to examine the choice behaviour at the individual level. Methods used here range from a simple descriptive-static analysis of data to advanced econometric estimates of micro-economic models. This path is often followed when evaluating individual policy measures. The disadvantage, however, is that the policy analysis always has a partial character and does not take into account the economic interactions and complexities at the macro level. Thus, it neglects the repercussions (or externalities) that individual behaviour has on other economic subjects. The macro behaviour is not equal to the sum of the behaviour at micro level: this is called 'the fallacy of composition' (see Caballero 1992).

A third way for policy analysis is to use empirical macroeconomic models. These models provide a quantitative interpretation of the economic theories and models that describe the mechanisms at work at the macro level. Thus, these macro models are, as it were, a synthesis between qualitative theoretical considerations and the empirical analysis of individual behaviour. This chapter centres on this third way of using models for practical policy analysis. It addresses the methodology of these macroeconomic models and uses the Netherlands as a case study, since these models have traditionally played an important role in economic policy analysis in the Netherlands, but also elsewhere.

The contents of the chapter are as follows. The next section describes the history of the use of empirical macroeconomic models in policy analysis. First, it summarises how in the Netherlands changes in the focus of economic policy and shifts in economic thinking gave rise to using different generations of macroeconomic models in policy analysis. Next, uses of models in other countries are discussed. Section 'Art and science of model use' argues how there should always be interaction between the

DOI: 10.4324/9781315745992-29

outcomes of model calculations from the computer and the interpretation of these outcomes by experts in order to come to a good narrative in the policy debate on the effectiveness of proposed and evaluated measures. In a way it combines art and science. Here various methods of using models in policy analysis come to the fore. Finally, 'Conclusion' ends the chapter.

History of economic model building for policy practice

The Netherlands

In building and using empirical macroeconomic policy models, the link with demands from policy practice has always been leading. That was already the case when Tinbergen (1936) constructed his first empirical macro model for the Netherlands in 1936. It is regarded as the first of its kind. At the time, there was a lively discussion among economists in the Netherlands about whether the gold standard should be maintained or whether it would be better to abandon and to devalue the guilder and let it float. Tinbergen used his macro model to demonstrate the benefits of devaluation for employment in the so-called 'Preadvies' (advisory report) for the annual meeting of the Netherlands Association of Economics and Statistics (today Royal Netherlands Economic Association).

After the Second World War, the model-based macroeconomic analysis of the Central Planning Bureau (CPB, today: Netherlands Bureau for Economic Policy Analysis), of which Tinbergen was a founder and the first director, played an important role in the design of economic policy in the Netherlands. Until the mid-1980s, three generations of models can be distinguished (see Den Butter 1991). In the 1950s and 1960s, with prosperous economic growth and almost full employment, the CPB used demand-driven models with a Keynesian signature for short-term economic analysis. The main aim of these models was, in addition to the preparation of forecasts, to underpin an anticyclical demand policy. The models showed, in full compliance with the Keynesian policy formulation, that in times of economic boom a spending restriction was the best policy measure, while during a cyclical downturn a demand impulse was appropriate.

In the beginning of the 1970s, this first generation was replaced by a second generation of models. Now the supply side of the economy became better portrayed, using a clay-clay vintage approach as the core of the model (Den Hartog and Tjan 1976). A third generation came into use at the beginning of the 1980s. Here a detailed description of the monetary sector was integrated in the models of the previous generation. During this period, the CPB lost its monopoly position and macroeconomic models were also applied elsewhere in the Netherlands in policy analysis. An example was the MORKMON model at the Dutch Central Bank.

The link between the science of model building and policy practice is neatly shown by the fact that the change of the model generations coincided with major changes in the government's view on economic policy. The first change in thinking was related to the effects of the policy of wage moderation. From the Keynesian perspective, wage moderation is not warranted in a period of stagnation, because this only slows down spending. In the 1970s, however, the Keynesian recipe appeared unhelpful in combatting persistent stagflation. In the vintage approach scrapping of old vintages, including employment connected with those vintages, is determined by real wage costs. Higher wages did lead, according to the model, to more scrapping and to less employment. So the model contributed to the arguments for wage moderation as an adequate policy response to unemployment and inflation. Thanks to wage restraint, the life of capital goods was extended and the profitability of the business sector and thus the competitive position increased. According to the model calculations, this positive effect of wage moderation far exceeded the negative effect on spending. A lively discussion, both among Dutch economists and policy-makers resulted in (some kind of) a consensus on the usefulness of the wage moderation policy. It took further shape in the Wassenaar Agreement of 1982, which is commonly regarded as the start of the 'Dutch miracle' of unemployment reduction and enhanced economic growth.

The transition from the second to the third generation of models also ran parallel with a major policy change. The end of the 1970s and the beginning of the 1980s were characterised by large monetary fluctuations (exchange rates, international capital flows, interest rates) and a sharp increase in both the size of the public sector and the government budget deficit. The addition of a monetary sector to the models revealed the adverse effects of these turbulences, and in particular of a budget deficit which was too high. The model outcomes suggested that a fall in the government deficit and a stop on the growth of the public sector would, in the somewhat longer term, have a favourable effect on economic activity and employment. This provided the arguments for the government to focus on austerity measures in order to reduce the government's budget.

This history of the use of macroeconomic models in the Netherlands sheds light on the interaction between economic thinking and the design of policy measures. The mechanisms described in the models are more or less based on the mainstream economics of the period. So the models of the first generation in the 1950s and 1960s were traditional short-run Keynesian demand models. The second generation of models of the 1970s incorporated concepts from supply-side economics and included medium-term structural developments. The third generation of models paid much attention to monetary and fiscal policy and to the activist role of the government. Naturally, new theoretical ideas are not always immediately incorporated in the models. On the other hand, theory formation in economics is much inspired by developments and problems that occur in practice. The history of model building in the Netherlands in the 1950s to the 1980s provides a good illustration of this interaction between theory, policy and the building of macro models for policy advice. Of course, there is always some lagged response of model builders to new needs from policy practice and the relevant theory formation.

The question now arises, in this historical review of model building, what the fourth generation of policy models looks like and with what policy change this generation can be associated. A major reason from policy practice that wishes to avail itself of another generation of models is that more and more doubts have arisen about how 'makeable' the society is: can policy measures be implemented without fundamentally affecting the behaviour, on which the models are based? The models of the first three generations, in accordance with Tinbergen's theory of economic policy, gave a rather control-technical view of society. By turning the buttons of the policy instruments, policy-makers were able, as it were, to generate effects through the existing mechanisms that would steer the economy in the right direction. The objection of, among others, Robert Lucas (1976) to this control-technical use of the policy models is that the policy measures are anticipated and therefore give rise to different behaviour and thus to other mechanisms (the so-called 'Lucas-critique').

In order to account for such effects, other types of models are needed than the usual macroeconomic models according to Tinbergen's theory of economic policy (1952, 1956). As a result, much more attention has been paid to the underlying micro-economic behaviour and theoretical underpinning of the models. The policy has shifted attention to the promotion of market forces, to flexibilisation and to the prevention of asymmetric information. The elimination of inefficiencies in the field of taxation has also become an important point of attention in economic policy. In addition, much attention has been paid to measures aimed at specific sectors and income groups. The result is that partial and general applied equilibrium models have started to play an increasingly important role in the analysis. These models consistently describe how, and with what speed, the economy moves to a structural equilibrium and how policy measures can affect both the structural equilibrium itself and the road towards that equilibrium. They also allow modelling of the propagation of shocks through markets and the spill-over effects to other markets (see, e.g. Borges 1986; Bovenberg 1987). In this context, the applied general equilibrium model of the CPB, 'MIMIC', played a central role in policy analysis in the Netherlands at the end of the last century and in the beginning of this century (see Gelauff and Graafland 1994).

Model used elsewhere

Tinbergen's method of model-based policy analysis soon obtained international fame in the profession. As a commissioned research project for the League of Nations, Tinbergen (1939) published a macroeconomic policy model for the United States which was meant to test the policy relevance of various business cycle theories collected by Von Haberler (1937). Other early policy models in the United States are those of Klein (1950) and Klein and Goldberger (1955) which were mainly used for cyclical policy analysis. Boumans (2005) discusses how these early model-based cyclical analyses can be placed in the history of economic thought. Just after the Second World War Tinbergen (1951) also constructed a macroeconometric policy model for the United Kingdom.

Model-based policy analysis seems to be subject to more competition in the Anglo-Saxon world (United States, United Kingdom) than in the Netherlands, where CPB still holds a dominant position. In the American institutional setting the preparation of budgetary and monetary policy is quite separated. Donihue and Kitchen (2000) describe how the 'Troika' in the US Administration, which comprises senior officials of the President's Council of Economic Advisors, the Department of the Treasury and the Office of Management and Budget, comes to some kind of consensus about the forecast for the economy which acts as input to policy-making of the US Government. Meanwhile, the staff of the Federal Reserve Board uses its own models and has its own philosophy on model-based policy analysis. Edison and Marquez (1998) provide a unique insight in the models-policy interaction in the decision-making process at the Federal Reserve System. Brayton et al. (2014) give a more recent overview of the use of the macroeconomic model at the Federal Reserve Board.

In a number of other industrialised countries, macroeconomic modelling and model-based policy analysis started to be most actively practised at central banks:

prominent examples are Italy and Canada (Banca d' Italia 1970; Fazio et al. 1970; Helliwell et al. 1971). After the innovative work at Banca d'Italia, the role of models in Italian economic policy seems to have become less pronounced (see Siviero et al. 1997). Today Banca d'Italia uses a DSGE model (see later) for policy analysis in the Euro area (see, e.g. Bartocci et al. 2017) and a dynamic quarterly econometric policy model (BIQM) (see, e.g. Miani et al. 2012, Bulligan et al. 2017) for short-run analysis and forecasting. On the other hand, as witnessed by Duguay and Longworth (1998), the Bank of Canada has for a long period retained a prominent role in the models-policy interaction and in the preparation of Canadian economic policy. Its governor, Poloz (2017), gives a recent overview of the history of model building and its use at the Bank of Canada, and prospects for new developments.

In Norway, economic planning in the first post-war years was dominated by the ideas of Ragnar Frisch, with Tinbergen the first Nobel laureate in economics. The planning in Norway had a strong administrative and directive character: it was integrated throughout the bureaucracy (Bjerkholt 1998). A difference as compared to the Netherlands was that the modelling and policy preparation in Norway was not executed at an independent bureau but was located within the Central Statistical Bureau. However, the policy-making was in fact the outcome of a close interactive cooperation between the Department of Economics at the Central Bureau of Statistics, the Ministry of Finance and the econometricians of the Institute of Economics at the University of Oslo. The models used in Norway for policy preparation were large input/output models closely connected to the system of National Accounts. Besides also sectoral and purposed-oriented models were used depending on the political needs and preferences for policy change (Dupont-Kieffer 2003).

In this respect there existed a difference in orientation and philosophy of model building between Frisch and Tinbergen as first winners of the Nobel Prize in Economics. Whereas Tinbergen, in his first modelling exercise for the Netherlands in 1936, was already very concerned with the analysis of policy measures, Frisch focused more on the help of models in optimal decision-making. According to Frisch, this planning had to be done on the basis of decision models in which the goals of economic policy were reached as good as possible with the aid of mathematical programming. In fact, the way in which policy preparation was organised in Norway has been the subject of a dispute between Tinbergen and Van Cleeff in the early days of the Dutch CPB. The latter advocated an approach in line with the business planning methodology of Frisch (see Van den Bogaard 1999). In the end, the separation of responsibilities between policy-makers and policy analysts proposed by Tinbergen became the leading philosophy (even in Norway). Yet this idea of planning the economy like planning a business is still present in the name of the CPB: Central Planning Bureau. That is why the CPB likes to call itself in English Netherlands Bureau for Economic Policy Analysis in order not to be regarded as a genuine 'planning bureau'.

In a more general sense, there has been a lively debate on the (political) neutrality of economic modelling, which culminated in a conference organised by the Pontifical Academy of Sciences in the Vatican in 1963 on 'the role of econometrics in formulating development plans' (Dupont-Kieffer 2019). There were two key contributions, namely by Richard Stone on econometric models and by Ragnar Frisch on the role of econometrics in designing and implementing economic policies.

The crucial question was how to combine the positive aspects of modelling the economy – to understand how the economy works and what mechanisms play a role – with normative aspects. From that perspective, Frisch seems aware that the modelling of economic phenomena cannot be done in isolation of the social and political context, especially when dealing with political actions. Including personal elements, from both the expert and the politician, relies, according to Frisch, on two major working stages: the selection and the implementation stages. Selection consists in setting specific economic objectives and implementation involves creating institutions in charge of the realisation (Dupont-Kieffer 2019).

In this respect there are some parallels between the plan-based policy analysis by Frisch and the policy model-based methodology of Tinbergen. In both cases political preferences, which are given to the economist, are crucial for selection and implementation of policy measures. However, in Tinbergen's methodology, only the effects of policy measures are calculated whereas implementation is left to political decision-making.

New developments

Good stewardship with respect to the environment, with combatting pollution, reducing emissions of greenhouse gases so as to prevent further global warming, promoting a transition to the use of renewable energy and enhancing environmental quality, became a major policy concern. Therefore, macroeconomic models that include the effects of environmental policy would classify for a fifth generation of policy models. However, these various aspects of environmental policy are so diverse that it is difficult to incorporate them in one encompassing model, which also comprises a full-fledged analysis of other macroeconomic policy concerns. Therefore, up to now, models used to analyse the effects of various kinds of environmental policy mostly focus on one specific effect of such policy. Three examples of such model-based analyses are discussed below.

Firstly, there is the question whether national income accounting provides a correct picture of the state of the economy as it does not take the costs of the use of the environment and hence environmental degradation (sufficiently) into account. Depending on the perspective, national income is incomplete, misleading or both. Many attempts have been made to improve and/or supplement this central statistic of national accounts. In the Netherlands such correction of national income was advocated by Hueting (e.g. 1974, 1992). In his methodology, the environment is a welfare-generating economic good, where, beyond some limits, there is an absolute preference for conservation of the natural environment. Hueting's methodology to come to a Sustainable National Income (SNI) indicator has been applied by Gerlagh et al. (2002) using the SNI-AGE model which is an Applied General Equilibrium (AGE) model. Two equilibrium simulations with the model are made: one that represents an unrestricted equilibrium which mimics as good as possible the actual national income in the year of observation, and one simulation where the environmental restrictions are included. The difference between the two simulations gives the correction for the national income in the year of observation, so that the SNI can be calculated. These model exercises show that national income is much overvalued when irreversible loss of the environment is not taken into account.

However, such calculations do not sufficiently take into account that technological progress can be directed towards reducing the use of the environment in production. This observation resulted in many model-based theories on the relationship between sustainability and economic growth, the so-called green growth models. Hallegatte et al. (2012) and Smulders and Withagen (2012) provide extensive surveys of these models and theories, whereas Den Butter (1998) describes early modelling attempts in the Netherlands. A major point of debate in these models is whether economic growth is essential for innovations which enhance the efficiency of the use of the environment (or energy) in production or whether there is always a trade-off between economic growth and environmental quality. Recently, the avoidance of waste and reuse of materials – circularity as it is called – has received ample attention in environmental policy. McCarthy et al. (2018) present a critical survey of recently developed macro models of circularity.

The credit crisis of the late 2000s and the resulting 'Great Recession' evoked renewed attention in policy modelling to the impact and propagation of different types of shocks through the economy. From that perspective the use of dynamic stochastic general equilibrium (DSGE) models is advocated, especially for monetary policy (Walsh 2010). Kremer et al. (2006) endorse the use of these models in monetary policy analysis as estimated DSGE models can be used to tackle normative issues concerning monetary policy. That is because the models provide an integrated approach to the study of the business cycle and the study of the optimal response of policy-makers to shocks. In that sense the models may include a kind of Taylor rule for monetary policy, albeit with more sophistication and with more shocks that policy has to react upon. These DSGE models are related to Vector Autoregressive (VAR) models in time series analysis. VAR models provide a general class of models to measure empirical relationships between time series and to separate induced effects (endogenous) from autonomous or unexpected shocks which are in front of the causality chain. The problem with VAR models is that it is very much the data which determine the dynamic specification of the model. So it is difficult to tell the story behind the outcomes of such models. For that reason restrictions are imposed to the specification of VAR models, which yield structured VAR models (SVAR). In DSGE models it is welfare optimising theory, which accounts for these restrictions. A problem is that identifying restrictions on shocks to the model are needed where these shocks are supposed to be orthogonal, i.e. independent of each other. However, Den Butter and Koopman (2001) show, using Kalman filter identification techniques in structural time series modelling, that the cyclical and structural shocks may not be independent, and that the orthogonality condition is too restrictive.

Another major policy question with respect to the credit crisis and Great Recession was whether the measures of austerity and reduction of public spending were too restrictive and therefore had a procyclical effect intensifying the crisis. This question evoked research on new types of Keynesian models which describe the propagation of demand shocks in the economy. An example is Beaudry and Portier (2018) who empirically investigate whether a New Keynesian model where demand shocks have expansionary effects regardless of the degree of sticky prices, or a Real Keynesian model as they call it, provides the best representation of reality. The authors find that the data point to model parameters that fall within the Real Keynesian model, which also allows for sticky prices, rather than within a New Keynesian model. It implies that there is a trade-off between anticyclical demand policy to obtain employment stability and the objectives of monetary authorities to obtain price stability. In that case there is a challenge for monetary policy if authorities want both to achieve price stability and favour employment stability.

The corona crisis provided another major challenge for model-based economic policy analysis. The problem here is that the source of the crisis lies outside the field of economics, whereas previous crises often were caused by a specific economic shock. It implies that, although in some policy discussions (and countries) the suggestion of a trade-off between economic costs and costs in terms of public health came about, the major argument and policy goal was to restrict the spread of the virus as much as possible at lowest economic costs. Hence, the analysis became normative with respect to public health (deaths, restrictions on hospital capacity), whereas, in terms of the Tinbergen theory, policy was instrumental at reaching these goals.

Art and science of model use

This section surveys various methodologies of using empirical macroeconomic models in the practice of policy preparation (see also Maas 2014, Chapter 9). It requires a combination of using the computer for model calculations and of tacit knowledge and intuition on the actual working of the economy. In order to be relevant and effective for political decision-making the computer output of the model calculations should be accompanied by a narrative which explains in a trustworthy fashion why policy proposals based on the calculations are welfare-enhancing or not and should be implemented or not. In other words, it requires a combination of science and art to translate model-based analyses to policy plans.

Making the model fit for policy analysis

After the empirical model has been set up and the parameters of the individual model equations have been estimated or determined using other empirical evidence, the model is not yet fit for use in policy analysis. Now it is necessary to gain more insight in the full working of the model. A first exercise is to see whether the model in a dynamic simulation mimics reality to a sufficient degree. For dynamic time series models a criterion is whether the difference between realised and simulated values in the within sample extrapolation does not become too large. In an equilibrium model the criterion is whether the equilibrium calculated by the model more or less represents the actual equilibrium of the economy. The result of this exercise is that the structure of the model is to be changed or that parameters are to be recalibrated. It may require several rounds of improving the model. Then, in order to make the model fit for use in actual policy analysis, some pilot exercises are to be made using the model for investigating actual policy problems. In case a sufficiently convincing narrative can be derived from the model calculations, the model seems ready for use in practice.

Forecasting: combining model-based outcome with tacit knowledge

Forecasts on the economy, made by institutes like the CPB, the EU, the OECD, the World Bank or the IMF, which have large professional staff, do not fully depend on the model results. Here the combination of art and science, as noted above, is well illustrated by the way forecasts are produced. In the final analysis, the making of forecasts is primarily an art in which human intuition plays an important role, but the scientific forecasting method, in this case the use of models, is an essential tool in this art of forecasting.

In a sense the macroeconomic forecaster can be seen as a fortune teller. The model, or more generally the economic and statistical methodology, is used as a crystal ball. The crystal ball on itself does not provide a good forecast: the fortune teller is needed to interpret the reflections in the ball. The same applies to macroeconomic forecasts. The consensus forecasts used in policy practice, as mentioned, never come straight from the computer. The professional forecaster always needs a trustworthy story on the forecast and should explain how the forecast came about. That is why the publications of the forecasting industry do not contain tables with forecasts only, but are mainly filled with reflections on future economic development. These reflections explain the assumptions on which the forecasts are based and discuss the conditions for these future developments to occur.

Much more so than using time series models (e.g. VAR models) for forecasting, the use of causal macroeconomic policy models provides insight into the economic mechanisms on which the forecast is based. Moreover, it offers the possibility of adding judgemental elements to the forecast. As a matter of fact, such judgemental elements have already been included in the design of the model, in particular when selecting the theoretical basis of the model and specifying behaviour. In the forecasting phase, additional judgemental information is introduced into the model via autonomous terms in the behavioural equations. They are called 'constant adjustment' or 'add-factors'. With the help of this additional information, the forecaster indicates to what extent it is anticipated that the future path of a specific macroeconomic variable will deviate from the normal path as described by the model. In this way informal and intuitive knowledge, but also practical knowledge about events that the model does not take into account, can be introduced in the model forecast in a way which is consistent with the behavioural description given by the model. Such additional information may, for example, relate to the additional demand for television sets during the Olympics, to wage increases settled in collective agreements or to the intuitive feeling that the positive wealth effects of a cyclical upturn will, in the short run, not lead to the additional consumption that the model predicts based on experiences from the past.

The use of add-factors forces the forecaster to quantify the insights about future developments that deviate from the normal pattern. It implies that, inherent in the behavioural description of the structure of the economy by these models, these factors may not be added to definition equations, but exclusively to behavioural equations. If, for example, the forecaster believes that the model yields too low a prediction of the national income, it should be indicated to which behavioural equation the add-factor is to be added in order to improve the national income forecast. The forecaster must be aware that the structured economic model consists of a number of simultaneous equations and that the addition of information to one behavioural equation spills over to the forecasts of all other endogenous variables of the model. This is one of the main advantages of using a macroeconomic model for forecasting: the forecasts are consistent with each other and the assumptions underlying the forecasts are made explicit. This makes the narrative more transparent.

Impact analysis of policy measures

Using empirical macro models for computing the effects of policy measures (impulse-response analysis or what-if analysis) is at least as important as the help that the models offer in the making of forecasts. Actually, the models are also better equipped for policy analysis than for forecasting. Effects of policy measures (or other autonomous impulses) are calculated as the difference between the central projection (e.g. the forecast) without policy or impulse and the alternative projection *cum* policy or impulse. The quality of the forecast is less relevant in this case as the difference between both projections is not much affected by the way the central projection describes future developments. Too high expectations about the quality of model forecasts may sometimes even threaten to discredit the use of macro models in policy analysis. It is interesting to note that Tinbergen did not make any forecasts with his first model for the Netherlands, but that he only used the model to calculate the consequences of a devaluation. Especially in the Netherlands, therefore, this type of model-based measurement of policy effects has played a central role in the link between science and policy analysis. Examples include calculations of the consequences of wage moderation, regulatory energy taxes, various ways to cut government spending, budgetary neutral tax shifts, the macroeconomic importance of major infrastructure projects etc. The tables with impulse effects are called, following Tinbergen's 1936 wording, 'railroad time tables'.

Economic models are needed to estimate the influence of policy measures, because in economics a controlled experiment is not possible such as in the natural sciences and in the medical sciences. After all, it is usually impossible to put together a group of citizens who are confronted with a tax increase, whereas a control group does not experience this tax increase. Such an experiment could be used to examine how the tax increase affects economic behaviour. Yet, in some specific cases regulations for a certain group were adjusted while remaining unchanged for another group. Empirical economists are currently very interested in these so-called natural experiments. In situations where experiments of this kind have occurred, consciously or unconsciously, the behaviour of the affected group of citizens should be compared with that of the control group, like in a real experiment. A well-known early example is the study of Card and Krueger (1994, 1995) on the impact of the minimum wage on employment (and unemployment) in the United States. In doing so, they use the fact that the minimum wage is changed in one state and not in the neighbouring state. They deduce from the differences that an increase in the minimum wage has little or no negative consequences for employment – an outcome which has, by the way, been much challenged.

Another way economists have tried to mimic the experiments from natural and medical sciences is through laboratory experiments. Here participants in the experiments are to make choices in a specific experimental set-up, where the (monetary) reward is linked to the choice they make. In this way rational behaviour with respect to specific choice problems is simulated. Svorenčík and Maas (2016) report on a witness seminar, where all pioneers involved in these economic laboratory experiments discuss how this field has evolved and became a well-respected part of economic methodology. An example in macroeconomics is an experiment commissioned by the Dutch Ministry of Social Affairs and Employment to investigate the effects of a capital market-based financing of social security (see Van Winden et al. 1999).

Sensitivity analysis

Sensitivity analyses indicate to what extent forecasts and calculated impulse effects depend upon the input of exogenous variables and/or of the parameter values and specification of the model. A first type of sensitivity analysis is a so-called uncertainty analysis. Here alternatives to a central projection or baseline forecast are made with changed values of exogenous variables. It may give a feel for the influence of uncertain future developments on model outcomes, such as oil price or world trade shocks. Another type of sensitivity analysis relates to the uncertainty about whether the model of the central projection adequately describes the economic situation in the period under review. In this case, for instance, two impulse-response analyses can be conducted: one which compares the central projection with the impulse projection in the base specification of the model and another which compares the central projection with the impulse projection in an alternative specification of the model. The difference between these two impulse-response effects provides an indication of the importance of behavioural changes in, for instance, the elasticities representing the effects of a tax increase. When the analysis shows that the sensitivity is high, an attempt can be made to determine the relevant parameter values better using more data and advanced econometric methodology.

Scenario analysis

Finally, setting up various scenarios is a well-tried way of exploring the future. In its simple form, a scenario is nothing more than a coherent extrapolation of the past under certain assumptions about exogenous developments. In case the scenario is based on one specific empirical model, the central scenario is the extrapolation with the most likely values of the exogenous developments. In fact, it could be seen as the central projection in a forecasting exercise. Other assumptions about the exogenous developments then provide other scenarios and can be used to explore the impact of uncertainty.

Yet, it is too simple to regard a scenario analysis just as a kind of forecasting exercise. A main purpose of scenario analysis is to map a wide range of possible future developments. The scenarios show the consequences of those possible futures and may indicate how unwarranted developments can be avoided by appropriate policy measures. However, which of the possible futures is regarded as most probable is up to the policy-makers. The CPB occasionally used scenarios for the exploration of the developments in the long term (see, e.g. CPB 1992, 2010), for instance on future developments in Europe and on Europe's place in the rest of the world. Although in the CPB the scenario analysis is set up from the tradition of model use for policy analysis, these scenarios are only loosely based on models: empirical relationship based on data from the past plays a less prominent role than in the short- and medium-term analyses.

Organisation of policy analysis

The use of model-based policy analysis is a good example to illustrate the interaction between economic science and policy. Such interaction requires comprehensive organisation of channels of mutual knowledge spill-overs between academic economists and policy-makers who are confronted with the actual economic problems – the implementation stage as coined by Frisch. The institutional embedding of the scientific input in policy preparation and policy-making is decisive for such spill-overs.

This industrial organisation of policy preparation is different in every country (see Van den Bogaart 1999, for the Netherlands, Norway and France, and Den Butter 2011, for the Netherlands).

Conclusions

In practising the use of macroeconomic models for policy purposes there is a mutual relationship between economic methodology and policy practice. Den Butter and Morgan (1998) show that the design of models and methods is much influenced by the actual political need for policy analysis and by the specific economic circumstances. In principle, the calculations aim at separating the debate on the functioning of the economy from the negotiations on the trade-off between the policy objectives on the basis of the different political preferences. In practice, however, the model calculations are also used to separate the matters on which one agrees in the policy debate from the matters on which one disagrees. Yet this may pose the problem that policy proposals which cannot be firmly underpinned by model-based analysis may receive less attention or are even disregarded.

This review of macro model-based economic policy analysis demonstrates that good forecasts of future developments and a good assessment of appropriate policy measures will always require a combination of model and man, of science and art. We do not have to fear that man will not be needed anymore to forecast and plan the future, even with ever more advanced artificial intelligence. In other words, the emotions and intuition of Captain Kirk will always be necessary to decide about the new adventurous journeys of Spaceship Enterprise. However, also the rational help of Dr. Spock, based on detailed information about risks and challenges, remains indispensable.

References

Banca d'Italia (1970) *Un Modello Econometrico dell' Economia Italiana* (M1B1), Centro Stampa, Banca d'Italia, Roma.

Bartocci, A., L. Burlon, A. Notarpietro and M. Pisani (2017) Macroeconomic effects of non-standard monetary policy measures in the euro area: The role of corporate bond purchases, *Bank of Italy Working Paper* no 1136.

Beaudry, P. and F. Portier (2018), Real Keynesian models and sticky prices, *NBER Working Paper* 24233, Cambridge: National Bureau of Economic Research.

Bjerkholt, O. (1998) 'Interaction between model builders and policy makers in the Norwegian tradition', *Economic Modelling* 15, 317–39.

Bogaard, A. A. van den (1999) *Configuring the Economy. The Emergence of a Modelling Practice in the Netherlands, 1920–1955*, Amsterdam: Thela Thesis.

Borges, A. M. (1986) 'Applied general equilibrium models: An assessment of their usefulness for policy analysis', *OECD Economic Studies* 7, 7–43.

Boumans, M. (2005) *How Economists Model the World into Numbers*, London and New York: Routledge.

Bovenberg, A. L. (1987) The general equilibrium approached: Relevant for public policy? in *The Relevance of Public Finance for PolicyMaking*, Proceedings of the 41st Congress of the International Institute of Public Finance, Madrid, pp. 33–43.

Brayton, F., T. Laubach, and D. L. Reifschneider (2014) *The FRB/US Model: A Tool for Macroeconomic Policy Analysis*, FEDS Notes, Washington: Board of Governors of the Federal Reserve System.

Bulligan, G., F. Busetti, M. Caivano, P. Cova, D. Fantino, A. Locarno, and L. Rodano (2017) The Bank of Italy econometric model: An update of the main equations and model elasticities, *Working Paper* no. 1130, Bank of Italy.

Butter, F. A. G. den (1991) 'Macroeconomic modelling and the policy of restraint in the Netherlands', *Economic Modelling* 8, 16–33.

Butter, F. A. G. den (1998) 'Macroeconomic modelling for sustainable development: The Dutch experience', in J. C. J. M. van den Bergh and M. W. Hofkes, eds, *Theory and Implementation of Economic Models for Sustainable Development*, Dordrecht: Kluwer Academic Publishers, pp. 235–54.

Butter, F. A. G. den (2011) 'The industrial organisation of economic policy preparation in The Netherlands', in J. Lentsch and P. Weingart, eds, *The Politics of Scientific Advice; Institutional Design for Quality Assurance*, Cambridge, UK: Cambridge University Press, pp. 177–214.

Butter, F. A. G. den and M. S. Morgan (1998) 'What makes the models-policy interaction successful?', *Economic Modelling* 15, 443–75.

Butter, F. A. G. den and S. J. Koopman (2001) 'Interaction between structural and cyclical shocks in production and employment', *Weltwirtschaftliches Archiv* 137 (2), 273–96.

Caballero, R. J. (1992) 'A fallacy of composition', *American Economic Review* 82, 1279–92.

Card, D. and A. B. Krueger (1994) 'Minimum wages and employment: A case study of the fast-food industry in New Jersey and Pennsylvania', *American Economic Review* 84, 772–93.

Card, D. and A. B. Krueger (1995) *Myth and Measurement; The New Economics of the Minimum Wage*, Princeton: Princeton University Press.

Centraal Planbureau (CPB) (1992) *Scanning the Future; A Long-term Scenario Study of the World Economy, 1990–2015*, The Hague: Sdu Publishers.

Centraal Planbureau (CPB) (2010) *The Netherlands in 2040*, The Hague: Sdu Publishers.

Donihue, M. R. and J. Kitchen (2000) 'The Trioka process, economic models and macroeconomic policy in the USA', in F.A.G. den Butter and M. S. Morgan, eds, *Empirical Models and Policy Making: Interactions and Institutions*, London: Routledge, pp. 229–43.

Duguay, P. and D. Longworth (1998) 'Macroeconomic models and policymaking at the Bank of Canada', *Economic Modelling* 15, 357–75.

Dupont-Kieffer, A. (2003) *Ragnar Frisch et l'économétrie: l'invention de modèles et d'instruments à des fins normatives*, Paris: Thèse de doctorat.

Dupont-Kieffer, A. (2019) 'The Vatican conferences of October 7–13, 1963: Controversies over the neutrality of econometric modeling', *History of Political Economy* 51, 515–34.

Edison, H. J. and J. Marquez (1998) 'US monetary policy and econometric modelling: Tales from the FOMC transcripts 1984–1991', *Economic Modelling* 15, 411–28.

Fazio, A., G. Caligiuri, F. Cotula and P. Savona (1970) *A Model of the Financial Sector of the Italian Economy*, Paper presented at the Second World Congress of the Econometric Society, Cambridge.

Gelauff, G. G. M. and J. J. Graafland (1994) *Modelling Welfare State Reform*, Amsterdam North-Holland.

Gerlagh, R., R. B. Dellink, M. W. Hofkes, and H. Verbruggen (2002) 'A measure of sustainable national income for the Netherlands', *Ecological Economics* 41, 157–74.

Hallegatte, S., G. Heal, M. Fay, and D Treguer (2012) From growth to green growth: A framework. *NBER Working Paper* 17841, Cambridge: National Bureau of Economic Research.

Hartog, H. den and H. S. Tjan (1976) 'Investment, wages, prices and demand for labour (a clay-clay vintage model for the Netherlands)', *De Economist* 124, 32–55.

Haberler, G. von (1937) *Prosperity and Depression: A Theoretical Analysis of Cyclical Movements*, Geneva: League of Nations.

Helliwell, J. F., H. T. Shapiro, G. R. Sparks, I. A. Steward, F. W. Gorbet, and D. R. Stephenson (1971) *The Structure of RDX2*, Part 1 and Part 2, Ottawa: Bank of Canada.

Hueting, R. (1974) *New Scarcity and Economic Growth*, Amsterdam: North Holland.

Hueting, R. (1992) 'Correcting national income for environmental losses: A practical solution for a theoretical dilemma', in J. J. Krabbe and W. J. M. Heijman, eds, *National Income and Nature: Externalities, Growth and Steady State*, Dordrecht: Kluwer, pp. 23–47.

Klein, L. R. (1950) *Economic Fluctuations in the United States, 1921–1941*, New York: Wiley.

Klein, L. R. and A. S. Goldberger (1955) *An Econometric Model of the United States, 1929–1952*, Amsterdam: North Holland.

Kremer, J., G. Lombardo, L. von Thadden, and Th. Werner (2006) 'Dynamic stochastic general equilibrium models as a tool for policy analysis', *CESifo Economic Studies* 52 (4), 640–65.

Lucas, R. E. (1976) 'Econometric policy evaluation', in K. Brunner end A. H. Meltzer, eds, *The Phillips Curve and Labor Markets*, Amsterdam: North Holland, pp. 19–46.

Maas, H. (2014) *Economic Methodology: A Historical Introduction*, London: Routledge.

McCarthy, A., R. Dellink, and R. Bibas (2018) 'The macroeconomics of the circular economy transition: A critical review of modelling approaches', *OECD Environment Working Papers*, No. 130, Paris: OECD Publishing.

Miani, C, G. Nicoletti, A. Notarpietro, and M. Pisani (2012) 'Banks' balance sheets and the macroeconomy in the Bank of Italy Quarterly Model', *Bank of Italy Occasional Paper* No. 135.

Poloz, S. S. (2017) *Models and the Art and Science of Making Monetary Policy*, Princeton Developments Ltd Distinguished Lecture in Finance, University of Alberta School of Business.

Siviero, S., D. Terlizze, and I. Visco (1997) 'Are model based inflation forecasts used in monetary policy making? A case Study', *Tinbergen Institute Conference Paper*.

Smulders, S. and C. Withagen (2012) Green growth. Lessons from growth theory, *World Bank Policy Research Working Paper*, WPS6230, Washington: World Bank.

Svorenčík, A. and H. Maas (2016) *The Making of Experimental Economics; Witness Seminar on the Emergence of a Field*, Cham, Heidelberg, New York: Springer.

Tinbergen, J. (1936) 'Kan hier te lande, al dan niet na overheidsingrijpen een verbetering van de binnenlandse conjunctuur intreden, ook zonder verbetering van onze exportpositie? Welke lering kan ten aanzien van dit vraagstuk worden getrokken uit de ervaringen van andere landen?', in *Praeadviezen voor de Vereeniging voor de Staathuishoudkunde en de Statistiek*, Den Haag: Nijhoff, pp. 62–108.

Tinbergen, J. (1939) *Statistical Testing of Business-Cycle Theories 2: Business Cycles in the United States of America 1919–1932*, Geneva: League of Nations.

Tinbergen, J. (1951) *Business Cycles in the United Kingdom 1870–1914*, Amsterdam: North Holland.

Tinbergen, J. (1952) *On the Theory of Economic Policy*, Amsterdam: North-Holland.

Tinbergen, J. (1956) *Economic Policy: Principles and Design*, Amsterdam: North-Holland.

Walsh, C. E. (2010) 'Using models for monetary policy analysis', *International Journal of Central Banking* 6, 259–70.

Winden, F. A. A. M. van, A. Riedl, J. Wit, and F. van Dijk (1999) *Experimenteel Economisch Onderzoek naar het Plan Van Elswijk*, CREED Research Paper.

25

TRADITIONAL METHODS OF MACROECONOMETRICS

Henning Bunzel

Early macroeconometric models at the Cowles Commission

Macroeconomic models are designed to describe the operations of the entire economy, such as growth in national production, unemployment, wage changes and inflation.

The macroeconometric approach was developed by the Cowles Commission, inspired by the debate between Keynes and Tinbergen about the use of estimated macroeconomic models. Tinbergen (1937) estimated the first macroeconometric model to explain the business cycle. The work used economic theory to design stochastic, behaviourally dynamic equations, which could be estimated and tested against the data. The work was assigned by the League of Nations and the purpose was to design an economic policy to combat the high unemployment resulting from the Great Depression. Tinbergen wanted to replace the current vague, descriptive analyses of business cycles with an empirical analysis based on an economic macromodel. The model consisted of 22 equations in 31 variables. Major components of the model were national product, investment and consumption expenditures. The model exercise resulted in a strong policy recommendation: devaluation of the Dutch Guilder to tackle unemployment.

Some of the relations in Tinbergen's model had similarities with the new economic theory in Keynes' *General Theory* (1973 [1936]). But Keynes was very critical of Tinbergen's quantitative process, see Keynes (1939) and the responses, Tinbergen (1940) and Keynes (1940). These were some of Keynes's criticisms:

- Economics does not gain anything by putting economic theory into mathematics and testing hypotheses.
- It is not possible to establish a connection between theory and empirical evidence.
- Data has large measurement errors and does not correspond to the concepts of the theory.
- Analysis requires a complete list of all the relevant factors.
- Relations and parameters are not invariant over time and across regimes.
- Functional form and dynamics are not correctly specified.
- Estimated relations are just correlations and not causal relations.

DOI: 10.4324/9781315745992-30

Today it is agreed that a mathematical model can be used together with data to make generalisations, but the assumptions of the model must be discussed and it must be explained how the model relates to the real world. Tinbergen and modern econometricians maintain that testing indeed can prove a theory to be incorrect or at least incomplete. To establish the connection between theory and empirical evidence the model must be identified, see below.

The failures of macroeconometric models in the 1970s resurrected the debate, see Patinkin (1976) and Hendry (1980). Patinkin argued that the models of the 1970s still suffered from the same problems as in the 1940s; Hendry argued that one reason for this is that practice lagged strongly after econometric theory and demonstrated that it is a myth that correlations cannot be used because they may be nonsense correlations. A careful econometric analysis will show that the nonsense correlation is not a stable correlation with innovation errors.

The Cowles Commission approach

The early development of macromodels up to the 1960s was strongly influenced by the Cowles Commission approach. The Cowles Commission was chaired by Jacob Marchak (1943–1948) and followed by T.C. Koopmans (1948–1955).[1]

The research programme included specifying Simultaneous Structural Equation Models, which determined necessary and sufficient conditions for identifying the parameters of interest. This generated consistent estimators and methods to test the complete models, see Christ (1994). Following Wren-Lewis (2018) this type of models is named traditional Structural Econometric Models [SEM].

The motto of the Cowles Foundation is *Theory and Measurement* which implies that their approach focuses on linking economic theory to mathematics and statistics. The 'measurement without theory' was regarded with great contempt. It was models of the theory that should be estimated; anything else was *'ad hoc'*, and in his Nobel lecture Frisch is very critical of the purely empirical schools:

> The schools, however, had an unfortunate and rather naive belief in something like a 'theory-free' observation. 'Let the facts speak for themselves.' The impact of these schools on the development of economic thought was therefore not very great, at least not directly. Facts that speak for themselves talk in a very naive language.
>
> *(Frisch June 17, 1970)*

It was important that the model could be used to evaluate how economic policy could improve the performance of the economy.

Simultaneous Structural Equations. The Cowles Commission approach assumed economic behaviour to be the result of the simultaneous interaction of different agents, hence a system of simultaneous equations was needed.

The variables in macroeconometric models most often represent macroeconomic aggregates rather than individual choice variables. The behavioural equations intend to describe economic decisions, but they are not aggregated individual choices described by microeconomic models (see the consumption function (0.4) below); rather, they are approximations to individual choices as influenced by aggregation, heterogeneity in the population, macro restrictions and feedback, interactions and expectations of agents.

The Cowles Commission approach assumes that a complete economic theory supplies a functional form and variables for a structural equation.

Joint Distribution. Haavelmo (1944) presents the *joint distribution* of all observable variables for the sample period as the most general statistical model allowing estimation and inference of a macroeconometric model. The variables explained by the model are named *endogenous* variables; the other variables are named *exogenous* and *predetermined* variables.

Morgan (1990) presents evidence that most pre-1940 economists like Keynes did not believe that probability theory could be applied to economic data, because the data could not be considered a random sample (independent observations); the exogenous variables were stochastic, and the parameters of the distributions were changing over time.

Haavelmo's introduction of the concept of the joint distribution for all relevant economic variables was an important breakthrough in econometric theory.

Consistent Estimators. An estimator is consistent if the estimates get close in probability to the unknown, true parameters as the sample size increases. It was proved that Ordinary Least Squares (OLS) with endogenous variables as explanatory variables are inconsistent estimators. Using the joint probability function (0.5) they developed consistent estimators like Full Information Maximum Likelihood (FIML) and several Limited Information Maximum Likelihood (LIML) estimators. FIML uses all equations and data requiring large computer capacity. Notice that experience has shown that the numerical differences between OLS and FIML are small and often not statistically significant, justifying the common use of OLS.

Identification Problem. If you have a model with more than one equation the equations must be identified; otherwise, a mixture of the parameters in the model is estimated and hence the estimated parameters cannot be associated with the structural parameters. The well-known example is a model with a demand and supply function.

Demand: $y_{1t} = \alpha_{11} + \beta_{11} y_{21} + \alpha_{12} z_{2t} + \alpha_{13} z_{3t} + u_{1t}$

Supply: $y_{1t} = \alpha_{21} + \beta_{21} y_{2t} + \alpha_{22} z_{2t} + \alpha_{23} z_{3t} + u_{2t}$

We have T observations on the endogenous variables y_1 and y_2 (quantity and price).

Except for the arbitrary naming of the parameters the two equations are similar. Therefore, we obtain the same estimates in the two equations and $\hat{\beta}_{11}$ cannot be interpreted as a demand elasticity.

The demand equation can only be identified if one or more exogenous variables are excluded compared to the supply equation.

The problem was well known but the Cowles Commission derived sufficient and necessary conditions for the linear structural model to be underidentified, just identified or overidentified, (Koopmans 1949), based on the prior belief that certain parameters in the equation are zero, i.e. variables are excluded from the equation. It does not matter if the excluded variables are endogenous, exogenous or predetermined. In practice, several exogenous variables are needed for a model to be identified.

For a non-linear model, explicit conditions for identification do not exist, but it is still very important to prove that the parameters are identified. The question is whether the data-generating process has sufficient information about the parameters of the model.

The parameter vector Θ_0 is globally identified in Θ if $\Theta_1 \in \Theta$ and $\Theta_0 \neq \Theta_1$ imply that there is a positive probability that values of the density function are different, $f(y | \Theta_0) \neq f(y | \Theta_1)$, such that data can choose between different models.

Assume that the mean function is linear.

Then the *structural form* is

$$\mathbf{B}\mathbf{x}_t = \Sigma_{i=1}^m \mathbf{C}_i \mathbf{x}_{t-i} = \varepsilon_t \tag{1}$$

The *reduced form* is

$$\mathbf{x}_t = \Sigma_{i=1}^m \Pi_i \mathbf{x}_{t-i} + \varepsilon_t \tag{2}$$

where $v_t = \mathbf{B}^{-1}\varepsilon_t$ and $\Pi_i = -\mathbf{B}^{-1}\mathbf{C}_i$

The reduced model, (2), can be considered a linear combination $(-\mathbf{B}^{-1}, \mathbf{C}_i)$ of the structural equations. The parameters in the structural model $(\mathbf{B}, \mathbf{C})$ can only be obtained from the parameters in the reduced model (Π) if all parameters in the structural model are identified.

Testing Models. It is important to test the specification of the complete model and not just the single equation. The Cowles Commission did not design such tests, but Christ (1951) tested the model developed by Klein and Goldberg (1955) by comparing forecasts with new data. The models were used for forecasting the endogenous variables. Forecasts were done using the reduced model or solving a non-linear simultaneous equation model for the endogenous variables. This will require externally generated forecasts of the exogenous variables.

The first model constructed using the Cowles Commission approach was a small model for the United States, Klein (1950) using consistent estimators. Later Klein and Goldberg (1955) built a larger model for the United States, which was continued as the Wharton model and Project Link.

Frisch and Tinbergen shared the first Nobel Prize in 1969. Klein received the Nobel Prize in 1980.

Introducing a structural equation

Haavelmo (1944) defined a structural equation as a behavioural equation that would not change the functional form, parameters or variables if another structural equation would change. It is named a *structural* equation because the functional form and the involved variables are derived from economic theory and the parameters have an economic interpretation.

The private, aggregate consumption function (3) is an example of a *structural equation* where α_2 is interpreted as the marginal propensity to consume.

The equation contains endogenous y_t and exogenous z_t variables. The exogenous variables are uncorrelated with the error term ε_t.

$$c_t = a_1 + \alpha_2 y_{t2} + \beta_1 z_{1t} + \varepsilon_t$$

An early example of an aggregate consumption function is

$$c_t = \alpha_1 + \alpha_2 Y_t^d, \alpha_1 > 0, 0 < \alpha_2 < 1 \qquad (3)$$

c_t real private consumption during period t

Y_t^d real disposable income during period t

The derivation of (0.3) from economic theory can be a verbal story as in Keynes's *General Theory of Employment, Interest and Money* (1973 [1936]). He wrote

> the propensity to consume is a fairly stable function so that, as a rule, the amount of aggregate consumption mainly depends on aggregate income...
>
> The fundamental psychological law upon which we are entitled to depend with great confidence both *a priori* from our knowledge of human nature and from the detailed facts of experience, is that men are disposed, as a rule and on the average, to increase their consumption as income increases, but not by as much as the increase in their income.
>
> *(Keynes 1973[1936], CW VII, p. 96)*

Hence, Keynes argued that

$$C_t = C\left(Y_t^d\right) \text{ and } \frac{dC_t}{dY_t} = \alpha_2, \ 0 < \alpha_2 < 1$$

In a subsequent section (p. 97), he asserted that

> it is also obvious that a higher absolute level of income will tend, as a rule, to widen the gap between income and consumption. For the satisfaction of the immediate primary needs of a man and his family [there] is usually a stronger motive than the motives towards accumulation, which only acquire effective sway when a margin of comfort has been attained. These reasons will lead, as a rule, to a greater proportion of income being saved as real income increases.[2]

This assertion requires $\alpha_1 > 0$ and as a result, $\frac{dC_t}{dY_t}$, will decrease with the level of income.

The linear function form of (0.3) is determined from data. It may only be a good approximation around the current value of $\left(C_t, \ Y_t\right)$. (4) is specified for a single household but the aggregate consumption function summed over all households may be different, i.e. $\frac{C_t}{Y_t^d}$ tends to be constant, requiring $\alpha_1 = 0$.

An example of deriving a consumption function of non-durables for a family from micro theory using a constant intertemporal elasticity of substitution utility function is Sørensen and Whitta-Jacobsen (2005).

In summary, this aggregate consumption function depends on current disposable income, Y^d, the expected rate of income growth g, the real rate of interest r and the market value of private wealth V

$$C = C\left(\underset{(+)}{Y^d}, \ \underset{(+)}{g}, \ \underset{(?)}{r}, \ \underset{(+)}{V}\right)[[Tab]] \qquad (4)$$

The signs below the variables in (4) indicate the sign of the partial derivations implied by the theory.

If consumers are optimistic about the future they will expect a high value of g, resulting in an increase in C. Indirectly, a higher g implies higher equity and house prices, which again imply higher V, and indirectly higher C. If C increases, it implies higher Y^d through higher production and employment. C and Y^d are determined simultaneously.

Sørensen and Whitta-Jacobsen illustrate how this consumption function can explain the observed cross-section relationship between income and consumption, the short- and long-run changes in consumption, and the effect of temporary and permanent tax cuts.

1960s macroeconometric models

In the 1960s, the flagship for econometrics clearly was SEM. It was one- or multi-sectoral macromodels with a flavour of the Keynesian theory, estimated using national accounting data and mathematical-statistical methods.

In 1984 Richard Stone (1913–1991) was awarded the Nobel Prize for his work within the development of national accounts. Input-output tables are of crucial importance to national accounts and the link between input and output in macromodels. Wassily Leontief (1905–1999) was awarded the Nobel Prize in 1973 for the input-output models.

Later models often had more than 1,000 equations. Many of the equations were technical equations defining tax and the public budget system. They were mainly used for forecasting, see Bodkin et al. (1991). By the end of the 1960s, most OECD countries and Central Banks were using such macroeconometric models. The data used for these macroeconometric models always includes national accounts for the post-war period, i.e. only 20–25 years, and the computational power was very limited. Therefore, the equations to be estimated had to be simple, i.e. linear, and most of the exogenous variables must be excluded from the equation. Only estimators estimating each equation sequentially could be applied, like Limited Information Maximum Likelihood (LIML) and Two-Stage Least Squares (TSLS).

1970s challenges of macroeconometric models

In the middle of the 1970s, several changes in economies and developments in econometric methods resulted in heavy criticism of the standard macroeconometric model. The criticism included both the economic theory used in the models and the econometric methods used. Most models failed to forecast the effects on the industrial economies and their recovery from the oil price shocks in 1973 and 1979. These failures caused macroeconometric models to lose general acceptance.

The identification of models requires *a priori* restrictions to zero values for many parameters in an equation. Liu (1960) and Sims (1980) argue that the simultaneous interaction of economic variables includes almost all economic variables; therefore no equations are identified. Sims proposes the use of a Vector Autoregressive model (VAR), see (0.9), which is a data-driven method without *a priori* restrictions. As more data is available, it is possible to estimate larger VAR models but still with few variables compared to macroeconometric models.

From the start of the Cowles Commission work Friedman (1953) had been critical of the Keynesian economic theory used in their models, and in the 1970s, monetarism became a serious competitor to Keynesian Macro Theory. There was no longer a common understanding of an economic theory that could be used as a basis for the empirical models. It became more natural instead to use empiricism to test which theory was correct and to a greater extent 'Allowing Data to Speak Freely', see Hoover et al. (2009).

The Lucas critique, Lucas (1976), claimed that the current macromodels could not be used to predict the effects of future changes in economic policy, because the relation is not invariant to policy changes. It was argued that parameters had to be deep parameters for the relation to be invariant to policy changes. A parameter was believed to be deep if it was a parameter in a microeconomic function, for example, a utility function, and the utility function was estimated directly. A new group of macromodels was created. These models were based on microeconomic functions and rational agents. The expectations of the rational agents should be equal to future values of the macroeconometric model (model-consistent expectations). They claimed that the aggregation problem was solved by introducing the Representative Agent, which represented all persons, firms, etc. in the economy. One large group of such models are Dynamic Stochastic General Equilibrium (DSGE) models.

Sonnenschein (1972) and others showed that the behaviour implied by the model at the micro-level, for example, the negatively sloped compensated demand curve, is not implied at the macro-level. These models are most likely weakly identified, see Romer (2016). There is no reason to expect these estimates to be stable across policy changes. In general, the issue of identification is not discussed in the papers. In practice, they are most likely identified by strong priors about the parameters.

Many of the new concepts like the Representative Agent, rational expectations, and Non-Accelerating Inflation Rate of Unemployment (NAIRU) are rejected on empirical grounds (Bårdsen et al. 2005, Fair 2018, 2019, Hendry 2017).

Juselius (2023) argued that the Cointegrated Vector Autoregressive Model (CVAR), see (10), can be used to check the assumptions of the DSGE model. Moreover this check leads to the conclusion that all assumptions of the model lack empirical support. Juselius also concludes that CVAR results are more supportive of traditional Keynesian models.

It is obvious that better economic theory is needed in areas like aggregation, heterogeneity of populations, interactions of agents, forming of expectations, linking of real and financial economics and growth.

In summary, there seems to be no econometric-theoretical argument in favour of these new microfounded models (Wren-Lewis 2018). The next section shows how new econometric methods can solve many of the problems raised in the 1970s. The best research strategy seems to be to continue improving the Haavelmo approach to macroeconometric model-building.

Model discovery, test for exogeneity and other developments in macroeconometric methods

Causality is not a well-defined concept, see Zellner (1988), Heckman (2020) and Vercelli (2022). Correlation does not imply causation. The Cowles Commission realised that causal interpretation requires a well-specified model representing the causalities.

If it is accepted that it is possible to construct such a model, then comparative statistic exercises with ceteris paribus changes are what economists mean by causal effects.

Many different theoretical models may be consistent with the same data. In economics, this is called the problem of identification.

Identification specifies the conditions under which structural parameters can be identified from data.

However, a maintained structural model does not prove these causalities, just that they cannot be rejected by data.

It is therefore important to include as many restrictions as possible in the model, to discuss how the model can explain past data and potential, new data values; to discuss how the restrictions can predict values that can be verified by data; and subject the model to extensive empirical verification. In this respect, VAR models are often 'too broad'.

David F. Hendry (1995) played a crucial role in the new development of the econometric technique after the 1970s. In the early period, he was a promotor of the LSE methodology, see also Mizon (1995).

In the Cowles Commission approach, the macromodel delivered by the economic theory was considered a maintained hypothesis tested against available data, and no method of model selection was proposed.

Hendry and Johansen (2015, p. 94) argue that to ensure that the maintained macromodel is *complete and correct*

> it seems essential to nest 'theory-driven' and 'data-driven' approaches in order to retain theory insights when exploring empirical interrelations, while also evaluating both the theory and the data evidence

and

> guiding empirical discovery by the best available theoretical ideas, but always being prepared to have those ideas rejected by sufficiently strong counter-evidence.

Hendry and Johansen defined a model to be complete and correct if

> there are no omitted variables that are relevant in the data generating process (DGP), [see (0.5)], and no included variables that are irrelevant in the DGP, and all included variables enter with the same functional forms as in the DGP.
>
> *(ibid, p. 95)*

In addition it is postulated that the error term added to the theoretical model is uncorrelated with all included variables and independently and identically distributed.

It is suggested to extend the Haavelmo approach by preceding the specification of the macromodel with one or more data analyses, for example, using CVAR, see Juselius (2023), to include all possible relevant variables as part of the 'from general to specific' procedure, and to test all the stochastic assumptions.

Let the stochastic variables relevant for the macroeconometric model be denoted as

X_0 initial conditions

$X_T^1 = [x_1, ..., x_T]$ are the set of stochastic variables to be analysed

$Q_T^1 = [q_1,..., q_T]$ are the deterministic terms

$\Theta_T^1 = (\theta_1,..., \theta_T)$ are the parameters

Then the DGP is defined by the joint data density $f_X(\cdot)$ conditional on the past and the parameters can always be factorised as

$$f_X(\mathbf{X}_T^1 \mid \mathbf{X}_0, Q_1^T, \Theta_T^1) = \Pi_{t=1}^T f_{x_t}(\mathbf{x}_t \mid \mathbf{X}_{t-1}^1, \mathbf{X}_0, \mathbf{q}_t, \Theta_t) \tag{5}$$

This sequential factorisation does not assume random sampling, constant parameters and non-stochastic exogenous variables. In practice, this general model must be reduced and the validity of each reduction must be tested to make sure that (5) still is a good approximation to the data-generating process. (8) can be used to exclude irrelevant variables, and it is only necessary to focus on submodels (6) where the regressors are weakly exogenous variables.

Even after this reduction in variables the macroeconometric model may be too large for the new time-series methods. No final solution has been found but Bårdsen et al. (2005) and Garratt et al. (2006) have designed a working method with core and subsystems being analysed separately using a decomposition into conditional and marginal models. There is a risk of ignoring possible influence across the subsystems in which case the conditioning is invalid, i.e. the weak exogeneity assumption is not satisfied, see below. But for the time being this method may do.

Granger non-causality. Granger (1969) developed a testable concept, *Granger non-causality.*

Granger non-causality assumes that a cause must appear before the effect in time. The variable y does not Granger-cause the variables z if the distribution of z at time t, f_{z_t} does not change if the history of y_{t-1}, is removed from the universe of information at time t.

In other words, y_{t-1} is irrelevant to the behaviour of z_t, y_{t-1} cannot help in forecasting z_t, and if z_t has an effect on y_t there is no feedback from y_{t-1} to z_t.

There are several difficulties with the definition. Which variables must be included in the universe of information, how long a lag should be used, how should parameter constancy, homoscedasticity and linearity be treated in an empirical test?

The Granger non-causality test cannot be used to test for a causal effect. It does not have the structural model and the parameter specification needed for weak exogeneity, and if the variables involve forward-looking behaviour the direction of Granger causality may be opposite the direction of causation. The financial 'efficient market hypothesis' is such an example. In that theory stock prices incorporate the markets' best forecast of the present value of future dividends. If this forecast is based on more information than previous dividends, then stock prices will Granger-cause dividends, but in reality future dividends cause stock prices.

It is common to explain exogeneous variables as variables determined outside the structural model, or to assume that the variables are independent of the error term in the equation $E(\varepsilon_t \mid Z_t) = 0$. But these may not establish the relevant concepts of exogeneity for estimation (weak), forecasts (strong) and policy analysis (super exogeneity), see Hendry (1995) chapters 5 and 9.

Granger non-causality is not a necessary or sufficient condition for weak exogeneity.

Exogeneity. It is important to test the assumptions of exogeneity.

The stochastic variables z_t are *weakly exogeneous* for the parameters of interest φ, if φ is only a function of the parameters $\Theta_{y/z}$ in the conditional distribution $f_{y|z}$ and the parameters in the marginal and conditional distribution are variation free. It may require detailed analysis to determine if z_t is weakly exogeneous for the parameters of interest, especially if the model is non-linear, contains expectations or time-dependent error terms.

If z_t are *weakly exogeneous* for φ we can concentrate on the conditional distribution

$$f_{y|z}\left(y_t \middle| z_t, Y_{t-1}, \Theta_{y|z} \right) \tag{6}$$

for *estimation* and *inference*, and ignore the marginal distribution.

If Z_t is weakly exogeneous with regard to the parameters φ and Y_{t-1} does not Granger-cause Z_t conditional on $[Y_{t-1}, Z_{t-1}]$ then Z_t is *strongly exogeneous* for φ.

If Z_t is strongly exogeneous for the parameters of interest, then $f_{y|z}()$ can be used for *forecasting*.

Assume that

$$f_{y|z}\left(y_t \middle| z_t, Y_{t-1}, Z_{t-1}, \Theta_{y|z} \right) \tag{7}$$

does not change with z or $f_z\left(z_t \mid Y_{t-1}, Z_{t-1} \right)$ and z_t is weakly exogeneous for ω then z_t is *super exogeneous* for ω.

Given *super exogeneity*, we can use the model to evaluate changes in the economic policy and the Lucas critique does not apply to this model.

To test for super exogeneity we need an event that affects Θ_z or $f_z\left(z_t \mid Y_{t-1}, Z_{t-1}, \Theta_z \right)$ then test that $f_{y/z}(y_t / z_t, Y_{t-1}, Z_{t-1}, \Theta_{y/z})$ is stable across that event.

Searching for all relevant variables. Often the failure of a model is caused by structural shifts, which may occur because all relevant variables are not included. Including all possible variables may cause the variables included by theory in the structural equation to be excluded in the reduction process. You can make sure that the structural variables are not excluded in the reduction process due to correlation with the extra variables by using the specification suggested by Hendry and Johansen (2015).

The structural equation is

$$y_t = \beta' x_t + \epsilon_t$$

After inclusion of all possible relevant variables the equation is

$$y_t = \beta' x_t + \gamma' w_t + \epsilon_t$$

w_t are exogenous or predetermined variables that may be part of the DGP, but *a priori* theory suggests $\gamma_0 = 0$

w_t and x_t are orthogonalised by regressing w_t on x_t with the residuals $\hat{u}_t$.

The extended structural equation is reformulated to

$$y_t = \beta^{+'} x_t + \gamma \hat{u}_t + \varepsilon_t^+$$

According to Frisch and Waugh (1933), the estimators $\hat{\beta}$ in the structural equation and $\hat{\beta}^+$ and the residuals $\hat{e}$ and $\hat{\varepsilon}^+$ are equal.

Before this analysis, you may be able to remove a lot of the w_t variables by testing if w_t does not Granger-cause y_t and x_t.

Let y_t be endogenous, z_t exogenous and w_t nuisance variables, then we are analysing

$$f_y\left(y_t \mid \mathbf{Y}_{t-1}, \mathbf{Z}_t, \mathbf{W}_t, \phi_1\right)$$

Assume that $\mathbf{W}_{t-1}$ does not Granger-cause $y_t, \mathbf{Z}_t$ conditional on $\mathbf{Y}_{t-1}, \mathbf{Z}_{t-1}$ then

$$f_y\left(y_t \mid \mathbf{Y}_{t-1}, \mathbf{Z}_t, \mathbf{W}_t, \phi_1\right) \equiv f_y\left(y_t \mid \mathbf{Y}_{t-1}, \mathbf{Z}_t, \phi_2\right) \tag{8}$$

$\mathbf{W}_t$ disappears completely and we can concentrate on the interaction between y_t and z_t.

Nonstationarity. Two forms of nonstationarity have been studied a lot since Haavelmo introduced the joint density function. One is changes in the distribution, like shifts in means, unconditional variances and other parameters, the other is stochastic trends (integrated data).

The problem with integrated data has received much attention since the beginning of 1990. This type of nonstationarity is treated via unit roots and cointegration, see, for example, Engle and Granger (1987) and Johansen (1988).

A popular time-series model is the VAR model

$$x_t = \mu + \Sigma_{i=1}^k \Pi_i x_{t-i} + \varepsilon_t \tag{9}$$

If x_t are non-stationary $I(1)$ variables and there are one or more cointegrating relations, then Granger has shown that VAR can be written as a vector equilibrium-correcting model (CVAR):

$$\Delta x_t = \Sigma_{(i=1)}^{(k-1)} A_i \Delta x_{(t-i)} + \alpha(\beta' x_{(t-1)}) + \varepsilon_t \tag{10}$$

where α, β are $n x r$ matrices of rank $r < n$ and $\beta' x_{t-1}$ are r cointegrating $I(0)$ relationship (stochastic long-run equilibria).

These stochastic long-run equilibria can often be related to economic theory. If the economy is out of long-run equilibria, the coefficients A_i determine the short-term dynamics towards equilibria. Therefore, (10) includes all short- and long-term dynamics. Clive W.J. Granger and Robert F. Engle shared the Nobel Prize in 2003.

CVAR is used to determine cointegrated relations, and the corresponding equilibrium correction models can just be included as equations in Haavelmo's framework.

It is evident that any econometric model is unlikely to coincide with the DGP, but according to LSE methodology, see Mizon (1995) and Hendry (1995), the model should be an *encompassing, congruent model*. Congruency and encompassing can be tested using available information. If the encompassing approach is followed, a further benefit is that a forecast failure is a potential improvement of the model.

Bårdsen et al. (2005) is a good example of a model-building project, which uses many of the approaches mentioned in this section.

The location shifts are very damaging to forecasts, see Clements and Hendry (1995). The location shifts lead to systematic forecast failure for models with CVAR equations, because such equations correct back to the previous location, and not the new mean. Hence forecasting is no longer just solving the macromodel for forecasted predetermined variables.

Concluding remarks

Haavelmo's approach from 1944 with one joint distribution for all variables relevant for a macroeconometric model and the use of structural equations 'derived' from economic theory is still the best approach for a macroeconometric modelling project, which uses new econometric methods. The LSE approach followed by many of Hendry's articles on how to do econometric modelling has had a major influence on applied work. It is essential to nest 'theory-driven' and 'data-driven' approaches and to guide the empirical discovery by the best available theoretical ideas but always to be prepared to have these ideas rejected by sufficiently strong counter-evidence. It is important to include all relevant variables and test the stochastic assumptions of the model. Many of these approaches can be included in the Haavelmo approach, so Haavelmo's articles from the 1940s are still relevant more than 50 years later.

Notes

1 The Cowles Commission had many other research programs than Simultaneous Structural Equation Models, and this method has been used for many other applications than macroeconomic models covered in this chapter.
2 The quotation and the two previous ones can be found on pp. 96–97, Keynes (1936). These brief quotations do not fully justify Keynes's theory of consumption. He did in fact discuss a host of other factors likely to influence private consumption. Still, it is fair to say that as a first approximation he believed that current consumption depends mainly on current real disposable income.

References

Bårdsen, G., Ø. Eitrheim, E. Jansen, and R. Nymoen (2005) *The Econometrics of Macroeconomic Modelling*, Oxford: Oxford University Press.

Bodkin, R., L. Klein, and K. Marwah (1991) *A History of Macroeconometric Model-Building*, Aldershot: Edgar Elgar.

Christ, C. (1951) 'A test of an econometric model for the United States 1921–1947', *NBER Working Paper*.

Christ, C. (1994) 'The Cowles Commission's contributions to econometrics at Chicago, 1939–1955', *Journal of Economic Literature* (XXXII), 30–59. *Cowles Foundation Discussion Paper no 2165.*

Clements, M. and D. Hendry (1995) 'Forecasting in cointegrating systems', *Journal of Applied Econometrics* 10 (2), 127–46.

CW: see Keynes, J. M. (1971–1989).

Engle, R. and C. W. J. Granger (1987) 'Co-integration and error-correction: Representation, estimation and testing', *Econometrica* 55 (2), 251–76.

Fair, R. (2018) 'Macroeconometric Modeling', (fairmodel.econ.yale.edu/mmm2/mm2018.pdf)

Fair, R. (2019) 'Some Important Macro Points', *Cowles Foundation Discussion Paper No. 2165.*

Friedman, M. (1953) *The Methodology of Positive Economics*, Chicago, IL: Chicago University Press.

Frisch, R. (June 1970) *Prize Lecture Nobel Prize.* (www.nobelprize.org, 16).

Frisch, R. and F. Waugh (1933) 'Partial time regression as compared with individual trends', *Econometrica* 1 (4), 387–401.

Garratt, A., K. Lee, M. H. Pesaran, and Y. Shin (2006) *Global and National Macroeconometric Modelling: A Long-run Structural Approach*, Oxford: Oxford University Press.

Granger, C. (1969) 'Investing causal relations by econometric models and cross-spectral methods', *Econometrica* 37 (3), 424–38.

Heckman, J. J. (2020) 'Causal parameters and policy analysis in economics: A twentieth retrospective', *The Quarterly Journal of Economics* 11 5(1), 45–97.

Hendry, D. (1980) 'Econometrics-alchemy of sciences', *Economica* 47 (188), 387–406.

Hendry, D. (1995) *Dynamic Econometrics*, Oxford: Oxford University Press.

Hendry, D. (2017) 'Imperfect knowledge, unpredictability and the failures of modern macroeconomics', *Technical Report*, Oxford University.

Hendry, D. and S. Johansen (2015) 'Model discovery and Trygve Haavelmo's legacy', *Econometric Theory* 31 (1), 93–114.

Hoover, K., S. Johansen, and K. Juselius (2009) 'Allowing the data to speak freely: The macroeconometrics of the cointegrated vector autoregression', *American Economic Review* 98 (2), 251–5.

Haavelmo, T. (1944) 'The probability approach in econometrics', *Econometrica* 12, July, iii–vi+1–115.

Johansen, S. (1988) 'Statistical analysis of cointegration vectors', *Journal of Economic Dynamics and Control* 12 (2–3), 231–54.

Juselius, K. (2023) 'Macroeconometrics linking theory with evidence using cointegrated VAR', in J. Jespersen, V. Chick and B. Tieben, eds, *Handbook of Macroeconomic Methodology*, Oxon: Routledge.

Keynes, J. M. (1939) 'The league of nations. Professor Tinbergen's method', *The Economic Journal* 50 (190), 154–6.

Keynes, J. M. (1940) 'On a method of statistical business-cycle research. A comment', *The Economic Journal* 49 (195), 558–77.

Keynes, J. M. (1971–1989) *The Collected Writings of John Maynard Keynes*, D. E. Moggridge, ed., 30 vols, London: Macmillan and New York: St Martin's Press.

Keynes, J. M. (1973 [1936]) *The General Theory of Employment, Interest and Money*, CW VII.

Klein, L. (1950) 'Economic fluctuations in the United States 1921–1941', *Technical Report*.

Klein, L. and A. Goldberger (1955) 'An econometric model of the United States 1929–52', *Contributions to Economic Analysis*, Amsterdam: North-Holland.

Koopmans, T. (1949) 'Identification problems in economic model construction', *Econometrica* 17 (2), 125–44.

Liu T. (1960) 'Underidentification, structural estimation, and forecasting', *Econometrica* 20 (4), 855–65.

Lucas, R. (1976) 'Econometric policy evaluation: A critique', *Carnegie-Rochester Conference Series on Public Policy* 1, 19–46.

Mizon, G. (1995) 'The LSE methodology', *Progressive Modelling of Macroeconomic Time Series*, Dordrecht: Kluwer Academic Publishers, pp. 107–70.

Morgan, M. (1990) *The History of Econometric Ideas*, Cambridge, UK: Cambridge University Press.

Patinkin, D. (1976) 'Keynes and econometrics: On the interaction between macroeconomic revolutions of the interwar period', *Econometrica* 44 (6), 1091–123.

Romer, P. (2016) 'The trouble with macroeconomics', *The American Economist* 20, 1–20.

Sims, C. (1980) 'Macroeconomics and reality', *Econometrica* 48 (1), 1–48.

Sonnenschein, H. (1972) 'Market excess demand functions', *Econometrica* 40 (3), 549–63.

Sørensen, P. and H. Whitta-Jacobsen (2005) *Introducing Advanced Macroeconimcs: Growth and Business Cycles*, New York: McGraw-Hill Education.

Tinbergen, J. (1937) 'An economic approach to business cycle problems', *Technical Paper*.

Tinbergen, J. (1940) 'On a method of statistical business-cycle research. A reply', *The Economic Journal* 50 (197), 141–54.

Vercelli, A. (2022) 'Causality and macroeconomics', Entry in this Handbook.

Wren-Lewis, S. (2018) 'Ending the microfoundations hegemony', *Oxford Review of Economic Policy* 34 (1–2), 55–69.

Zellner, A. (1988) 'Causality and causal laws in economics', *Journal of Econometrics* 39 (1–2), 7–21.

26

MACROECONOMETRICS

The cointegrated VAR methodology

Katarina Juselius

Introducing the cointegrated VAR (CVAR) method

A theory-based economic model is often taken to the data by adding a stochastic error to a mathematically well-defined model and then applying statistical methods to get estimates of its structural parameters. In contrast, a well-defined probability-based statistical model for the same data uses likelihood inference to answer the economic questions of interest. In the first case, statistics are used passively as a tool to get desired estimates. In the second case, they are used actively as a means to analyse the underlying data-generating process. In the first case statistics is primarily used to illustrate prior beliefs, in the second case to make correct inference about the complex economic reality.

The vector autoregressive (VAR) process based on normally distributed errors has frequently been used as a statistical description of macroeconomic time-series data. This is because the VAR model is flexible, easy to estimate, and it usually gives a good fit to macroeconomic data. But, because the unrestricted VAR model is difficult to interpret in terms of economically meaningful parameters, it has mostly played a subordinate role in economic modelling.

When Clive Granger in 1981 introduced the concept of cointegration among non-stationary variables as a means to distinguish between long-run and short-run information in the data, the potential usefulness of the VAR for economic modelling increased significantly. As a result, he was rewarded the Nobel Prize in Economics in 2002. Subsequently, when Johansen (1988, 1996) developed the basic mathematical theory for likelihood-based inference in nonstationary processes, the necessary tools for CVAR modelling as a methodology for valid inference in economic models based on nonstationary data became more widely available (Johansen and Juselius 1990, 1992, 1994, Juselius 2006). It facilitated likelihood-based inference on long-run and short-run structures, on dynamic adjustment in the short and the long run, on complex multiplier effects, and many more issues of economic interest.

My own research on the methodology of macroeconomic applications was strongly influenced by two early pioneers in this field, Ragnar Frisch and Trygve Haavelmo, both of them Nobel Prize winners. In particular, the probability approach to

DOI: 10.4324/9781315745992-31

macroeconomics as outlined in Trygve Haavelmo's famous monograph (Haavelmo 1944) stands out as a major source of inspiration and guideline. The monograph makes an important distinction between statistical inference in economic models based on (i) experimental design data artificially isolated from other influences so that the validity of the *ceteris paribus* clause is satisfied; (ii) non-experimental data obtained by 'passive' observations for which there is no control of how the data have been generated. In the first case, inference is valid provided the experimental design is valid. In the second case, the validity of inference on economic parameters is not granted simply because observed macro variables do not correspond sufficiently closely to the 'true' measurements of the theoretical variables. One might even ask whether it is at all possible to confront stylised economic models with the complex macroeconomic reality without compromising high scientific standards. Haavelmo's answer was to introduce the concept of a 'design of experiment' for data obtained by 'passive observations' and discuss the validity of inference in a probability framework.

Haavelmo's probability approach requires a statistically well-specified model where basic underlying assumptions have been checked against the data. But, macroeconomic data are difficult because there is just one realisation for each period. We know what the unemployment rate was at a certain time period, but not what it would have been had the economy experienced different shocks. Economic time-series data are also difficult because they are typically strongly time-dependent. Where we are today is very much dependent on where we were yesterday and before. Therefore, the analysis of macroeconomic data is typically associated with problems such as multicollinearity, spurious correlation and regression, time-dependent residuals, normalisation, reduced rank, simultaneity, autonomy, and identification. While these problems were acknowledged by Haavelmo and Frisch, they were not satisfactorily solved at that time. Juselius (2015) argues that it was because they would have needed the theory of nonstationary processes which was only developed many decades later (Johansen 1988, 1996; Phillips, 2001).

Since all of the above problems can be addressed within the CVAR model, Hoover and Juselius (2015) and Juselius (2015) argue that the CVAR model is a potential candidate for Haavelmo's 'design of experiment for data by passive observations'. Because the CVAR represents a likelihood-based approach to economics, it satisfies Haavelmo's vision of a joint probability formulation of the observable data (Juselius 2006, 2015). To illustrate, Juselius (2015) translates one of Haavelmo's own economic models (Haavelmo 1954) into a set of testable hypotheses on the CVAR model.

The consequence of having just one realisation from the underlying stochastic process is that the econometrician is forced to make simplifying assumptions about this process, assumptions which are testable, but generally require data over a fairly long time period. The problem is that macroeconomic data are typically short, definitions may change, and the data-generating process is typically non-constant in mean and variance due to changing regimes, political reforms, and interventions. With these caveats in mind, I shall discuss the CVAR approach as a scientifically sound empirical methodology for the analysis of nonstationary economic data (Juselius 2006).

The rest of the chapter is organised as follows: Section 'The CVAR model' introduces briefly the CVAR model and argues that it is basically a broad description of dominant features of economic data, such as dynamics, interactions, pronounced persistence, and structural breaks. Thus it offers a practical and well-worked-out methodology for the analysis of macroeconomic data. Section 'Five common misconceptions' discusses five frequent misconceptions on CVAR modelling in practice and Section 'Theoretical assumptions that are problematic in a nonstationary world' outlines three standard assumptions in economic models that are crucially important when data are nonstationary. Section 'Linking theory with evidence: a bridging principle' suggests a bridging principle for how to link an economic model with the data so that all basic assumptions can be tested based on scientifically valid principles. Section 'Concluding remarks' concludes.

The CVAR model

The CVAR approach is Popperian in the sense that the fundamental principle builds on the ability to falsify a hypothesis. By so doing, it offers a framework within which data are allowed to speak freely without being silenced by prior restriction.

In the unrestricted form the CVAR describes the data vector $x_t' = \left[x_{1,t}, x_{2,t}, ..., x_{p,t} \right]$ as an autoregressive vector process of order k augmented with some deterministic terms:

$$\Delta x_t = \Pi x_{t-1} + \Gamma_1 \Delta x_{t-1} + ... + \Gamma_k \Delta x_{t-k} + \mu_0 + \mu_1 t + \Phi_1 D_t + \varepsilon_t, \tag{1}$$
$$t = 1,..., T$$

where Π, Γ_1,..., Γ_k are unrestricted coefficient matrices of dimension $p \times p$, μ_0 is a $p \times 1$ vector of constant terms, μ_1 a $p \times 1$ vector of trend coefficients, and D_t a $p \times m$ vector of suitably defined dummy variables accounting for political reforms and interventions, Φ_1 a $p \times m$ matrix of unrestricted dummy coefficients, and ε_t a $p \times 1$ vector of normally distributed uncorrelated random shocks. While (1) is essentially just a broad description of the variation of the data, it allows the data to speak as freely as possible about the underlying empirical regularities.[1] In line with Juselius (2021a), I argue that the VAR model represents a set of possible economic models. Its usefulness comes from the possibility to test relevant hypotheses based on scientifically valid principles. Hypotheses not rejected by the tests are sequentially imposed on the model, thereby narrowing down the search for the most empirically relevant model among the possible set. If a theoretical model is empirically relevant, its major features would become increasingly visible during the testing-down process. Since the 'final' model satisfies the probabilistic assumptions it is, therefore, consistent with Haavelmo's vision of a probability approach to economics. But, since the VAR is a broader description of the economic reality than postulated by the simplified theory, the analysis often produces new results not formulated before. Such hypotheses have to be tested on new data. In this sense, the CVAR approach resembles a progressive research programme.

The statistical analysis starts with testing the number of stationary cointegration relations, r, in the VAR system. The hypothesis that there are r irreducible cointegration relations (Davidson, 1998) is formulated as a reduced rank hypothesis:

$$\Pi = \alpha \beta' \tag{2}$$

where α, β are $p \times r$ and $r \leq p$. Eq. (2) tells us that there are r stationary relations among nonstationary variables, $\beta' x_t$, and $p - r$ exogenous forces driving the system. If $r = 0$, there are no long-run equilibrium relationships in the data, if $r = p$, x_t is stationary.

In the remaining cases, x_t is cointegrated with r cointegrating relations $\beta'x_t$. They can – after being economically identified – be interpreted as stationary equilibrium errors, i.e. stationary deviations from long-run static equilibrium relations.

When the reduced rank has been determined, a large number of additional hypotheses can be tested, such as exogeneity, endogeneity, long-run homogeneity, identifying restrictions, zero restrictions, etc. When no more restrictions can be validly imposed, the CVAR has been simplified as much as possible but no more. If the economic model is empirically relevant it should become visible in the parsimonious CVAR.

Inverting (1) with $\Pi = \alpha\beta'$ allows us to express the vector, x_t, as a function of the shocks, ε_t, and the deterministic terms – constant, trend, and dummies:

$$x_t = \beta_\perp \alpha'_\perp \Sigma^t_{i=1}\left(\varepsilon_i + \mu_0 + \mu_1 t\right) + C^*(L)\left(\Phi_1 D_t + \varepsilon_t\right) + X_0 \tag{3}$$

Where $\beta_\perp$, $\alpha_\perp$ are the orthogonal complement of β, α with $\alpha'_\perp \Sigma^t_{i=1}\varepsilon_i$ being a measure of the $p-r$ stochastic trends and $\beta_\perp$ the loadings of the stochastic trends onto the variables and $C^*(L)\left(\Phi_1 D_t + \varepsilon_t\right)$ is a measure of the stationary movements around the trends. The common stochastic trends, $ct_t = \alpha'_\perp \Sigma^t_{i=0}\varepsilon_i$, correspond to the exogenous forces that have pushed the system out of equilibrium, and the α coefficients describe how the system pulls back towards equilibrium after the system has been pushed away by exogenous shocks. The formulation (3) allows us to calculate impulse response functions and long-run dynamical effects of exogenous shocks to the system, the so-called long-run multiplier effects.

Economic data frequently exhibit too much persistence to be tenable with the $I(1)$ assumption. The hypothesis that x_t is an $I(2)$ process, i.e. nonstationary of second order, is also formulated as a reduced rank hypothesis, $\alpha_\perp \Gamma \beta'_\perp = \xi\eta'$, where ξ, η are $p-r \times s$, $\Gamma = I - \Gamma_1 - ... - \Gamma_k$, and $\alpha_\perp$, $\beta_\perp$ are the orthogonal complements of α, β. While the $I(2)$ model offers a richer structure than the $I(1)$ model, it is also technically more complex and will not be further discussed here. The interested reader is referred to detailed discussions in, for example, Johansen (1997, 2006) and Juselius (2006, 2018).

To summarise, the CVAR is inherently consistent with a world where unanticipated shocks accumulate over time to generate stochastic trends that move economic equilibria – the pushing forces – and where deviations from these equilibria are corrected by the dynamics of the adjustment mechanisms – the pulling forces. Thus, the CVAR model has a good chance of nesting a multivariate, path-dependent data-generating process and relevant dynamic macroeconomic theories (see Hoover et al. 2008).

Five common misconceptions

CVAR modelling is widely used in empirical macro modelling, but it is unfortunately also widely misused and, hence, has often been brought into disrepute by the profession. As this is likely to stand in the way for well-argued and useful CVAR applications, I will start by briefly discussing five of the most frequent misconceptions.

Misconception 1: *CVAR models provide nonsensical results.* While I agree that there are numerous published papers that report nonsensical CVAR results, most of them give the impression of being done by statistical non-experts. Data have been read in and the VAR button has been pushed. But, a correct CVAR analysis has nothing to do with pressing the VAR button. It is not a method that can be applied mechanically, it depends upon the researcher's judgement and expertise and requires interaction between the analyst and the data. For example, it does not make sense to work with a VAR model until you have checked whether (1) the sample period is representative for your research questions, (2) the chosen information set is sufficiently broad to adequately answer the questions of interest, (3) the most important institutional changes have been controlled for, (4) the parameters of interest are reasonably stable over time, (5) the residual mis-specification tests are acceptable, just to mention some of the important steps. If you sidestep them, you will likely get nonsense. For a more detailed discussion, see Juselius (2006, 2021a).

Misconception 2: *CVAR models are so general that they can show anything.*[2] *Without the mathematical logic of the economic model, one opens up for the possibility of quackery.* On the contrary, scientific objectivity requires that data are not constrained from the outset in a theoretically pre-specified direction. Otherwise it is not possible to know which results are due to the assumptions made and which are true empirical findings. This point is amply illustrated in Juselius and Franchi (2007) where the results of a Real Business Cycle (RBC) theory model reported in Ireland (2004) were empirically checked. In the Ireland paper, the RBC theory was taken to the data using a Dynamic Stochastic General Equilibrium model. The CVAR check of the same data showed that essentially all RBC assumptions lacked empirical support and that the conclusions became reversed. Hence, Ireland's empirical findings reflected the assumptions made rather than the empirical reality.

Misconception 3: *The quality and the informational content of macroeconomic data are too low. Hence, it is not possible to make sense of the results unless the empirical model is constrained by theory from the outset.* No doubt, macroeconomic data seldom represent the true measurements of the theoretical variables. For example, the representative agent's income, consumption, and hours worked in a DSGE model have little in common with the various measurements of aggregate income, private consumption, and total hours worked that can be found in the publications of the Statistical Office. But, while macro data are contaminated with measurement errors, such errors may not be of great concern for the more important long-run analyses unless the errors are systematic and accumulate to a nonstationary process. Whatever the case, theoretically correct measurements do not exist and, hence, cannot be used by politicians and decision makers to react on. The forecasts, plans, and expectations that agents make are based on the observed data and we better understand them, however imperfect they are. Besides, macroeconomic data are surprisingly informative provided you let them tell the story they want to tell. Juselius (2021a) provides a comprehensive illustration.

Misconception 4: *Economic variables cannot be unit root nonstationary, because they do not drift away forever from their equilibrium values like true $I(1)$ or $I(2)$ processes do. In particular, economic variables cannot be $I(2)$ because static equilibrium errors cannot not be truly $I(1)$ as is typical in the $I(2)$ model.* While this is obviously correct, it does not exclude the possibility that variables over finite samples may exhibit a persistency profile that is *empirically* indistinguishable from a unit root/double unit root process (Juselius, 2013). Also, economic relationships seldom remain unchanged over long periods of time, so the infinity argument may not be highly relevant. Rather than a structural parameter, it is more useful to consider an empirical unit root to be a useful statistical approximation that allows economic variables/relations to be classified as stationary, near $I(1)$, or near $I(2)$. Such a classification of data into more homogeneous groups is often fundamental for a successful empirical specification of the economic model. For example, an $I(1)$ variable cannot be significantly related to an $I(0)$ variable, neither can an $I(2)$ variable to an $I(1)$ variable, but the statistical analysis can tell us how to combine them in stationary cointegrated relationships which then can be given a more meaningful interpretation. By exploiting the information in the data given by the integration/cointegration property of the variables, one can obtain robust estimates of long-run, medium-run, and short-run causal structures in the data. In the words of Hoover et al. (2008), the CVAR allows the data to speak freely about the mechanisms that have generated them. For a more detailed discussion, see Juselius (2006, 2013).

Misconception 5: *Crisis periods are aberrations – black swans – outside the range of empirical modelling.* Contrary to this, our experience demonstrates that crisis periods are not outside the range of serious CVAR analyses. For example, Juselius and Juselius (2013) demonstrate that the Finnish crisis at the beginning of the 1990s could be properly analysed and understood using the CVAR model, Juselius and Dimelis (2019) demonstrate that the utterly harmful mechanisms behind the recent Greek crisis could be unveiled using an $I(2)$ CVAR analysis, and Juselius (2021a) shows that US unemployment could be adequately modelled from 1985 to 2020, a period that includes the financial crisis. Data covering crises periods are typically consistent with complex adjustment dynamics towards long-run equilibria and nonstandard expectations formations. Such features can easily be modelled with the $I(2)$ CVAR model. Besides, crisis periods tend to occur too frequently to be treated as aberrations – black swans. The seed to an economic crisis is sown long before its outbreak. Therefore, if crisis mechanisms are not properly understood, then many extant models will fail to predict, explain, and prevent the next economic crisis.

Theoretical assumptions that are problematic in a nonstationary world

Applications of the CVAR to numerous macroeconomic problems in different sectors of the economy, in different historical periods, and in a wide variety of countries have shown that the empirical support for basic hypotheses underlying mainstream macroeconomic models is systematically weak. This may seem puzzling considering the profession's trust in the same models. Some assumptions often routinely made in standard economic models might explain why.

The stationarity assumption

Traditionally, most macroeconomic models were not formulated with an explicit distinction between stationary and nonstationary processes in mind. The idea of a stochastic trend pushing the system out of equilibrium and the adjustment dynamics pulling the system back to equilibrium was essentially first introduced in economics in the framework of the dynamic stochastic general equilibrium (DSGE) model. This model is taken to the data as if the assumed theoretical model is a true representation of the empirical reality. For example, the exogenous (and endogenous) forces are assumed known and the model is estimated subject to this assumption.

In contrast, the exogenous forces in the CVAR model are defined in terms of the statistical properties of the model and, hence, testable. Numerous empirical CVAR applications have shown that both the number and the source of the exogenous shocks pushing the system tend to deviate from what is theoretically assumed. Also, the nonstationary exogenous trends in standard economic models are assumed to be purely exogenous. If they become stationary, then the system would also become stationary.

In contrast, our CVAR results suggest that the nonstationarity of the variables can often be associated with self-reinforcing feed-back dynamics, i.e. the nonstationarity is often generated by the dynamics within the economic system.

The inherent nonstationarity of economic variables/relations has fundamental implications for the use of the *ceteris paribus* assumption, the role of expectations, and the aggregation problem in economic models, all of which are to be discussed next.

The ceteris paribus assumption

In a theoretical model the *ceteris paribus* assumption allows us to keep certain variables fixed and, therefore, to focus on those of specific interest. In an empirical model the *ceteris paribus* variables, rather than constant, are generally stochastic processes. In a probability-based approach, such as the CVAR, relevant *ceteris paribus* variables need, therefore, to be brought into the empirical analysis by conditioning. If the *ceteris paribus* variables are nonstationary (as they mostly are), then they often are highly influential for the empirical conclusions. For example, if a macroeconomic model is derived under the *ceteris paribus* assumption, 'the real exchange rate is constant or at least stationary', the probability is high that the economic model disregards features which are essential for a good empirical understanding of the economic problem. As the real exchange rate tends to fluctuate in very persistent long swings around its equilibrium value, this is a fundamental problem with many 'closed-economy' models. But it is not just the real exchange rate which is a crucial *ceteris paribus* variable due to its nonstationarity. Also the real interest rates, the term spread, and the domestic-foreign interest differential are enormously important variables, all of which are typically assumed to be stationary, albeit empirically indistinguishable from a nonstationary process. The habit of routinely using the *ceteris paribus* assumption has probably prevented us from learning about some of the most fundamental causes of persistent macroeconomic fluctuations in the real economy.

To summarise: the classification of variables into endogenous, exogenous, and *ceteris paribus* prior to estimation can be hazardous for learning what is empirically correct and relevant in macroeconomics.

The expectations assumption

While few economists question the crucial role that expectations play for economic behaviour, many disagree about how to handle them in economic models. For empirical econometricians, the main problem is that expectations are generally unobservable. The so-called rational expectations hypothesis (REH) solves this problem by assuming that (rational) economic agents are predicting future outcomes based on the chosen theoretical model assumed to be a true representation of the economic reality. Many macroeconomic models are estimated subject to such REH restrictions without first testing their validity. When tested they are typically rejected. Johansen and Swensen (1999, 2004) are two examples. In a nonstationary world with breaks and unit root trends, this may not be very surprising as the assumption that economic agents are then able to forecast future outcomes without making systematic errors seems *a priori* implausible. Proponents of REH argue that its role is only to secure internal model consistency. Against this argument stands the empirical result that the internal feed-back dynamics of the model look totally different under imperfect knowledge expectations as compared to REH expectations and that the former seems to fit the data much better (Juselius 2017, 2021b).

But, although expectations by and large are unobservable, this is not the case with the so-called consensus forecasts that record the actual expectations of professional forecasters. These are now available for sufficiently long periods to allow a systematic study of how they are formed and how they affect the economy. For example, Juselius and Stillwagon (2018) studied the role of consensus forecasts of the three-month interest rates for the US dollar–UK pound market, and find that unanticipated shocks to the consensus forecasts are a major cause of the long persistent swings typical of this market. The results show that it is interest rate expectations – measured by the consensus forecasts – that push the interest rates and the exchange rate away from long-run equilibrium values, whereas in the medium run it is the changes in the nominal exchange rate that push the foreign currency market. Such an autonomous role for interest rate expectations is congruent with models emphasising imperfect knowledge, but against the REH. How to treat unobserved expectations without relying on implausible assumptions is an important and challenging problem.

The aggregation problem

Economists are frequently divided on the question whether macroeconomic models should be micro-based or macro-based, that is, whether or not it is meaningful to analyse macroeconomic behaviour based directly on microeconomic units, such as individuals, households, and enterprises. Those advocating for a more traditional Keynesian approach – not the New Keynesian approach – typically argue that macroeconomic behaviour cannot be derived directly from the corresponding microeconomic behaviour, the link is too weak and sometimes even non-existing. For example, many important macro variables, such as inflation and GDP growth, have no direct correspondence to individual behaviour on the micro level. In other cases, rather than addressing the difficult problem of aggregating heterogeneous agents, many mainstream models assume away the aggregation problem by assuming a representative agent. While it facilitates a mathematical formulation of the economic problem, the simplicity comes at a cost of empirical relevance. This is probably why empirical CVAR results tend to deviate so strongly from those of mainstream models.

As a result of this critique, the profession has increasingly turned to microeconometric analyses based on panel data on individuals, households, and businesses to obtain estimates of behavioural parameters in macroeconomic models. But, while such analyses are valuable, they are not substitutes for a serious macroeconometric analysis based on aggregated data. This is because microeconometric analyses cannot say much about how a political reform is likely to affect, say, the inflation rate, the unemployment rate, the interest rate, and the foreign exchange rate, and they can rarely say anything about the magnitude, nor the dynamics, of multiplier effects. On the other hand, microeconometric analyses may provide valuable information on how different groups in the economy react on political reforms, something the macroeconomic analysis cannot do due to the lack of suitably aggregated group data. Hence, the obvious solution is to combine the two approaches.

But, the aggregation problem is not just about the macro aggregation of micro units, it is also about spatial aggregation of macro variables, such as EU-wide data, which are constructed by aggregating the macro variables of the individual member states. That this can be a surprisingly complex task when data are nonstationary is shown in Juselius and Beyer (2009), where the sensitivity of outcomes for different aggregation methods was studied using a large simulation study. While there were useful lessons to be learned, the results also demonstrated the difficulties of selecting a viable aggregation procedure that works well for different types of data, in particular when these data exhibit breaks and unit roots.

Thus, the aggregation problem is theoretically difficult and cannot be assumed away without compromising valid inference in macroeconomic models. Against this rather pessimistic view stands the fact that CVAR analyses as a rule tend to find plausible macroeconomic relationships – of a more traditional Keynesian flavour – in aggregated macroeconomic data. Considering that macro variables are aggregates of millions of idiosyncratic micro units, this may seem highly surprising. An often overlooked paper by Clive Granger (1981) suggests a plausible explanation: if each micro unit contains a small common component and a large idiosyncratic component, then – as the number of micro units grow – the common component will become more and more visible in the aggregate. At the same time the idiosyncratic component will shrink.

Linking theory with evidence: a bridging principle

Many empirical models focus on a few specific assumptions of the theoretical model which are then tested. But as forcefully argued by Spanos (2009) such econometric tests are valid *only* to the extent that the probabilistic assumptions underlying the fully specified model are satisfied vis-à-vis the data in question. In practice the economist is faced with the problem that a statistically well-specified empirical model and a theoretically well-specified economic model represent two different entities without any direct link between the two. A so-called theory-consistent CVAR scenario (Juselius 2006, Juselius and Franchi 2007, Juselius 2017, 2021a) offers a bridging principle. The main idea is to translate all basic assumptions about the shock structure and the steady-state behaviour of the theoretical model into testable hypotheses on the pulling and pushing forces of a CVAR model.

Such a CVAR scenario describes a set of testable empirical regularities one should find in the data when the basic assumptions of the theoretical model are empirically valid. For example, most economic models are inherently consistent with a given number of endogenous variables and exogenous driving trends. This can be translated into a testable hypothesis on the reduced rank of the CVAR. The assumptions of which variables are exogenous and which are endogenous can be translated into testable hypotheses on the adjustment coefficients. Most models also assume certain equilibrium relationships to be stationary. This can be formulated as testable hypotheses on the pulling forces of the CVAR model. An economic model that passes the first check of such basic hypotheses is potentially a candidate for an empirically relevant economic model. In practice, the modelling takes place in two steps: the first step tests hypotheses on the model's long-run structure and, if they are not rejected, then the second step tests hypotheses on the short-run structure conditional on the estimated long-run structure. The econometric justification for such a two-step procedure is that the long-run parameter estimates are super t consistent when data are unit root nonstationary, whereas the short-run ones are only $\sqrt{t}$ consistent.

This idea is the guiding principle in Juselius (2006) which demonstrates that essentially all the basic assumptions underlying Romer's theoretical model on monetary inflation (Romer 1996) are strongly rejected by the data. Similarly Juselius (2009) formulates a theory-consistent CVAR scenario for an international monetary model and shows that a stationary Purchasing Power Parity (PPP) is logically inconsistent given the integration properties of the data. Frydman and Goldberg (2007, 2011) show theoretically that a nonstationary PPP needs a nonstationary Uncovered Interest Parity (UIP) to become stationary. Empirical support for the combined hypotheses has been found in Juselius (1995, 2006, Chapter 21), Johansen et al. (2010), Juselius and Assenmacher (2017), Juselius (2021b, 2022), and Juselius and Stillwagon (2018). Another example already mentioned is the real business cycle (RBC) theory model in Ireland (2004) which was tested using a theory-consistent CVAR scenario in Juselius and Franchi (2007). The RBC assumptions were tested, essentially all of them rejected, and the main conclusions reversed.

That the profession has lacked a bridging principle linking the theoretical assumptions of the economic model with the empirical reality of the observed data might explain why so many mainstream macroeconomic models continue to be in use in spite of their dismal empirical performance. It may also explain why Haavelmo's probability approach to economics has not caught on among the majority of today's economists.

Concluding remarks

The basic idea of the macro-econometrics of the CVAR model is to offer a scientifically viable procedure for how to check the empirical validity of theoretical assumptions and at the same time to learn more about important issues/problems in the economy. This could, for example, involve detecting changes in structure, estimating and comparing structures before and after a regime shift, observing similarities and dissimilarities between different economies, and relating these to institutional changes. Using the CVAR as a magnifying glass has revealed dominant features in economic data such as a pronounced persistence (i.e. slow adjustment back to equilibrium states), structural breaks, non-constant parameters, and strong feed-back dynamics. These are frequently inconsistent with basic assumptions underlying mainstream macroeconomic models and suggest that a change in the research paradigm for empirical macroeconomics is much needed (Juselius 2010, 2011).

Because the CVAR model is tailor-made to study long-run, medium-run, and short-run structures in the same model, a proper CVAR analysis allows the complexity of the empirical reality to be analysed and fully comprehended at the background of not just one but preferably all potentially relevant economic models. Thus, it allows us to adequately test the assumptions underlying economic models – bringing those assumptions to the data. In this sense, the CVAR model can be thought of as providing a broad confidence interval within which empirically relevant economic models should fall. If the outcome of the empirical testing is that a particular assumption isn't in the data and that the economic conclusion is not robust to this assumption, then the economic model should be revised. Following this simple rule could mean a big step forward towards an improved understanding of our macro economy.

Until now, our CVAR results have consistently rejected mainstream macroeconomic models – also the New Keynesian ones – but have been supportive of more traditional Keynesian models. My best guess for an empirically relevant theory in macroeconomics would be Keynesian macroeconomics with a fully incorporated financial sector and with expectations based on uncertainty, loss aversion, and imperfect/incomplete knowledge.

These theoretically puzzling, but empirically and econometrically well-founded results signal the need for new theory and deserve to be taken seriously. There is little doubt that empirically unfounded economic policy has exacerbated some of the defining problems of our time, such as recurring crises, increasing inequality, and growing populism.

Notes

1 Note, however, that this is NOT a call to let data speak by themselves without theory, nor to let data speak without rigour. A statistical VAR analysis, to be valid, has to obey equally strict rules as a mathematical analysis of an economic model.
2 A sure proof that the person in question has never performed a proper CVAR analysis.

Bibliography

Engle, R. F. and C. W. J. Granger (1987) 'Cointegration and error correction: Representation, estimation and testing', *Econometrica* 55 (2), 251–76.

Frydman, R. and M. Goldberg (2007) *Imperfect Knowledge Economics: Exchange Rates and Risk*, Princeton: Princeton University Press.

Frydman, R. and M. Goldberg (2011) *Beyond Mechanical Markets: Risk and the Role of Asset Price Swings*, Princeton: Princeton University Press.

Granger, C. W. J. (1981) 'Some properties of time series data and their use in econometric model specification', *Journal of Econometrics* 16, 121–30.

Haavelmo, T. (1944) 'The probability approach to econometrics', *Econometrica* 12 (Supplement), 1–118.

Haavelmo, T. (1954) 'Structural models and econometrics', Unpublished paper presented at the Econometric Society Meeting 1954 in Stockholm. http://www.sv.uio.no/econ/english/research/networks/haavelmo-network/ publications/files/th1955b-es-1954-uppsala.pdf

Hoover, K. D., S. Johansen, and K. Juselius (2009) 'Allowing the data to speak freely: The macroeconometrics of the cointegrated vector autoregression', *American Economic Review* 98, 251–5.

Hoover, K. D. and K. Juselius (2015) 'Trygve Haavelmo's experimental methodology and scenario analysis in a cointegrated vector autoregression', *Econometric Theory* 31 (2), 249–74.

Ireland, P. N. (2004) 'A method for taking models to the data', *Journal of Economic Dynamics and Control* 28 (6), 1205–26.

Johansen, S. (1988) 'Statistical analysis of cointegration vectors', *Journal of Economic Dynamics and Control* 12 (2–3), 231–54.

Johansen, S. (1996) *Likelihood-Based Inference in Cointegrated Vector Autoregressive Models*, Oxford: Oxford University Press.

Johansen, S. (1997) 'Likelihood analysis of the $I(2)$ model', *Scandinavian Journal of Statistics* 24 (4), 433–62.

Johansen, S. and K. Juselius (1990) 'Maximum likelihood estimation and inference on cointegration — with applications to the demand for money', *Oxford Bulletin of Economics and Statistics* 52 (2), 169–210.

Johansen, S. and K. Juselius (1992) 'Testing structural hypotheses in a multivariate cointegration analysis of the PPP and the UIP for UK', *Journal of Econometrics* 53 (1–3), 211–44.

Johansen, S. and K. Juselius (1994) 'Identification of the long-run and short-run structure: An application to the ISLM model', *Journal of Econometrics* 63 (2), 7–36.

Johansen, S., K. Juselius, R. Frydman and M. D. Goldberg (2010) 'Testing hypotheses in an $I(2)$ model with piecewise linear trends. An analysis of the persistent long swings in the Dmk/$Rate', *Journal of Econometrics* 158 (1), 117–29.

Johansen, S. and A. R. Swensen (1999) 'Testing exact rational expectations in cointegrated vector autoregressive models', *Journal of Econometrics* 93 (1), 73–91.

Johansen, S. and A. R. Swensen (2004) 'More on testing exact rational expectations in cointegrated vector autoregressive models: Restricted constant and linear term', *The Econometrics Journal* 7 (2), 389–97.

Juselius, K. (1995) 'Do purchasing power parity and uncovered interest rate parity hold in the long run? An example of likelihood inference in a multivariate time-series model', *Journal of Econometrics* 69 (1), 211–40.

Juselius, K. (2006) *The Cointegrated VAR Model: Methodology and Applications*, Oxford: Oxford University Press.

Juselius, K. (2009) 'The long swings puzzle: What the data tell when allowed to speak freely', in K. Patterson and T. C. Mills, eds, *Palgrave Handbook of Econometrics: Vol. 2: Applied Econometrics*, London: Palgrave MacMillan, pp. 349–84.

Juselius, K. (2010) 'Time to reject the privileging of economic theory over empirical evidence? A reply to Lawson', *Cambridge Journal of Economics* 35 (2), 423–36.

Juselius, K. (2011) 'On the role of theory and evidence in macroeconomics', in W. Hands and J. Davis, eds, *The Elgar Companion to Recent Economic Methodology*, Chapter 17, Cheltenham: Edward Elgar Publishing, pp. 404–26.

Juselius, K. (2013) 'Imperfect knowledge, asset price swings and structural slumps: A cointegrated VAR analysis of their interdependence', in E. Phelps and R. Frydman, eds, *Rethinking Expectations: The Way Forward for Macroeconomics*, Princeton: Princeton University Press, pp. 328–50.

Juselius, K. (2015) 'Haavelmo's probability approach and the cointegrated VAR', *Econometric Theory* 31, 213–32.

Juselius, K. (2017) 'Using a theory-consistent CVAR scenario to test an exchange rate model based on imperfect knowledge', *Econometrics* 5 (3), 30. https://doi.org/10.3390/econometrics5030030

Juselius, K. (2021a) 'Searching for a theory that fits the data: A personal research odyssey', *Econometrics* 9 (1), 5. https://doi.org/10.3390/econometrics9010005

Juselius, K. (2021b) 'Disequilibrium macroeconometrics', *Industrial and Corporate Change* 30 (2), 357–76. https://doi.org/10.1093/icc/dtab029

Juselius, K. (2022) 'A theory-consistent CVAR scenario: Testing a rational expectations based monetary model', forthcoming in *Econometrics*.

Juselius, K. and K. Assenmacher (2017) 'Real exchange rate persistence and the excess return puzzle: The case of Switzerland versus the US', *Journal of Applied Econometrics* 32 (6), 1145–55. https://doi.org/10.1002/jae.2562

Juselius, K. and A. Beyer (2009) 'Does it matter how to measure aggregates? Monetary transmission mechanisms in the Euro area', in J. Castle and N. Shephard, eds, *The Methodology and Practice of Econometrics: A Festschrift in Honour of David Hendry*, Oxford: Oxford University Press, pp. 365–85.

Juselius, K. and S. Dimelis (2019) 'The Greek crisis: A story of self-reinforcing feed-back mechanisms', *Economics: The Open-Access, Open-Assessment E-Journal* 13 (2019-11), 1–22. http://dx.doi.org/10.5018/economics-ejournal.ja.2019-11

Juselius, K. and M. Franchi (2007) 'Taking a DSGE model to the data meaningfully', *Economics, The Open-Access, Open Assessment E-Journal* 1, 4, http://dx.doi.org/10.5018/economics-ejournal.ja.2007-4.

Juselius, K. and M. Juselius (2013) 'Balance sheet recessions and time-varying coefficients in a Phillips curve relationship: An application to Finnish data', in N. Haldrup, M. Meitz, and P. Saikkonen, eds, *Essays in Nonlinear Time Series Econometrics*, Oxford: Oxford University Press, pp. 118–38.

Juselius, K. and J. Stillwagon (2018) 'Are outcomes driving expectations or the other way around? An $I(2)$ CVAR analysis of interest rate expectations in the dollar/pound market', *Journal of International Money and Finance* 83 (May), 93–105.

Phillips, P. C. B. (2001) 'Optimal inference in cointegrated systems', *Econometrica* 59 (2), 283–306.

Romer, D. (1996) *Advanced Macroeconomics*, New York: McGraw Hill.

Spanos, A. (2009) 'The pre-eminence of theory versus the European CVAR perspective in macroeconometric modeling', *Economics: The Open-Access, Open-Assessment E-Journal* 3, 10, 1–14. http://dx.doi.org/10.5018/economics-ejournal.ja.2009-10

27

NATIONAL ACCOUNTS AND MACROECONOMIC METHODOLOGY

Geoff Tily

Introduction[1]

"While the GDP and the rest of the national income accounts may seem to be arcane concepts, they are truly among the great inventions of the twentieth century."

(Paul A. Samuelson and William D. Nordhaus cited in Landefeld 2000, p. 6)

If anything, this remark – from a US Department of Commerce commemoration – is an under-exaggeration. The National Accounts are essential to the management and operation of a monetary economy. With money understood properly as a book entry, the accounts are a tangible record of the macroeconomic outcomes of monetary interactions. Like money, the Accounts are a social technology – inherent to economic and social advance. Alongside wider statistics on the economy and society, National Accounts also support democratic processes – with the economy important in voting decisions.

However, there is – rightly – disquiet about whether this infrastructure, and specifically whether Gross Domestic Product (GDP), has set society on a wrong course. And it is arguably true that real GDP growth has come to define – dictate, maybe – the possibilities of the economy and even society. Long before the pandemic, many authors were very pessimistic about these possibilities. But an emerging literature is wrong to blame measurement, when the fault is more with how measurement has been used. There is a need to stand back and separate the role and theory of *economic statistics* and the role and theory of *economics*. Economic statistics are now understood according to the present policy and methodological approach, but the most important steps in their development came under a different methodological approach. Under this approach GDP is still important, but as part of a wider National Accounting framework.

The structure and definitions of contemporary National Accounts emerged as part of a wider theoretical and policy infrastructure motivated and developed above all by Keynes. A leading figure in economic debate, he also played a vital role in parallel measurement initiatives up until the end of the Second World War. However, the subsequent defining role for real GDP *growth* reflected a *rival* methodological

DOI: 10.4324/9781315745992-32

approach that emerged into the public domain after the war, an approach fundamentally at odds with Keynes's own.

The second section provides a brief and informal overview of the National Accounts and GDP in theory and practice, from GDP as an entry in a sequence of accounts to its place in the output-gap framework. In the middle two sections the history of accounts is briefly reviewed, with emphasis on the interplay with wider economic and policy methodology. Wartime and post-war initiatives aimed at full employment gave way around the time of the Marshall Plan to targeting growth and productivity. In the penultimate section a conventional narrative of post-war economic outcomes according to the output-gap framework is outlined, ending recent calls for a more welfare-oriented approach. A conclusion argues we should be careful about shooting the messenger.

The National Accounts and GDP in theory and practice

The National Accounts are a set of accounts, with structures and rules partly overlapping with commercial accounting practices. Each account includes a balancing item to ensure total resources match total uses. Table 27.1 shows UK GDP of £2.1 trillion in 2018 as the balancing item on the 'production account', with the relevant coding from the System of National Accounts.[2]

Ahead of the production account (coded: I.) comes the goods and services account (0.) where supply (output plus imports) is matched to demand (intermediate consumption, final consumption, gross capital formation and exports). After the production account comes a sequence of income (II.), capital (III.1) and financial accounts (III.2), and balance sheets (IV.).

The rules for allocating transactions within the accounts evolve over time and are set out as part of the (periodically updated) System of National Accounts (SNA). 'Output' captures all transactions within the production boundary, so for example government services are included as 'non-market services', but 'non-traded output' such as domestic cooking and cleaning is excluded. In the 1990s certain financial services were switched from intermediate to final consumption. In the latest SNA, research and development expenditures were capitalised (i.e. switched from intermediate consumption). These allocations are the subject of intense debate among national accountants and a matter of some controversy among commentators (both before and after the event).

The output (or production), expenditure and income measures of GDP – usually denoted GDP(O), (E) and (I) – follow from these accounts and the supplementary detail on the supply-and-use tables. (The latter tables match supply and demand by product on the horizontal dimension according to industries on the vertical dimension.) The three measures of GDP also familiarly arise from the sum of value added by

Table 27.1 UK Production account for 2018, £ trillion

Resources		Uses	
Output (P.1)	3.6	Intermediate consumption (P.2)	1.7
– taxes on products (D.21)	0.2	GDP (B.1)	2.1
– subsidies on products (D.31)	0.1		
Total resources	3.9	Total uses	3.9

Source: Office for National Statistics, Blue Book 2020 and author calculations

industry (output), the sum of final consumption and investment expenditures and net trade (expenditure) and the sum of payments to the factors of production (income).

Fundamental to national accounting is the allocation of economic activity into sectors (hence 'sector' as well as 'national' accounts):

- Households and non-profit institutions serving households
- Corporations – financial and non-financial/public and private[3]
- Government (local and central = general)
- Rest of the world

Familiar from macroeconomics textbooks, the expenditure measure of GDP sums demand across all sectors and corresponds (broadly) to the familiar identity $Y = C + I + G + X - M$ (where C and G are household and government consumption, I is investment – strictly, gross fixed capital formation – across all sectors, X is exports and M is imports). Figure 27.1 shows annual figures for UK GDP(E) growth from the year before the global recession allocated into the contributions from each component.[4] The figures show the composition of recent changes in aggregate demand: the recession of 2008–2009 was driven initially by negative investment; austerity has meant the contribution from government expenditure (in black) has been mostly imperceptible ever since.

As far as trade unions are concerned a vital use of GDP(I) figures is to assess changes in the labour share over time, measured by compensation of employees (wages and salaries plus employers' pension contributions) as a share of GDP.

Confronting income and expenditure by sector (and adjusting for 'transfers' such as flows of interest and tax) is the point of departure to the fuller sequence of accounts. Many of the balancing items are of interest in their own right, like households' gross disposable income and public sector net borrowing/lending. The (financial) balance sheets underpin measures of aggregate indebtedness, not less importantly for the private as well as public sector.[5]

But, in practice, the reading of economic conditions today is still dominated by real GDP growth. In both finance ministries and central banks, this is done in the context of the output-gap framework (Section 'From full employment to productivity and real growth'). 'Conjunctural' readings of demand/outcomes are set against a preconceived trajectory for supply potential, with the latter often based on moving averages of preceding outcomes (though a fuller production-function approach is also used).

The output-gap framework is set in real terms, and so analysis is mainly based on GDP adjusted for price change ('deflated'; strictly, valued in the prices of a given reference year). GDP estimates tend to be published on a quarterly basis. Annual measures are derived as the sum of quarterly figures but can also be assessed separately from annual benchmarking surveys (which form the basis for the full articulation of National Accounts). The various survey and methodological processes mean that estimates are continuously revised, with the revision performance of interest in its own right. Growth tends to be understood in annual terms, so standard comparisons are of year with previous year, or quarter with the same quarter a year ago.[6]

Plainly there is a wide range of other economic statistics, not least for prices and the labour market. But the National Accounts have a special central role, with most data compiled according to or influenced by national accounting standards. Outside practicalities, the system is sophisticated, rich and, for many, a construction of great elegance.

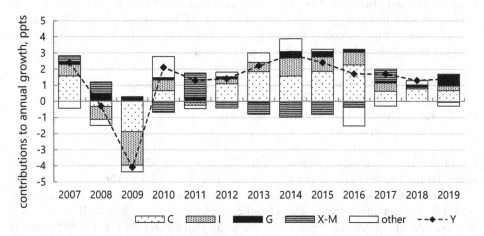

Figure 27.1   Contributions to UK GDP(E) growth, percentage points (ppts).
Source: ONS Quarterly National Accounts and author calculations.

National accounting and economic methodology

There is an extensive literature on the history of National Accounts and GDP, and the field has become very active in recent years as authors seek to make sense of wider economic failures on both sides of the 2007–2009 global recession. This section offers a brief review, with emphasis on both US and UK contributions and related methodological factors.

While many trace national income estimation back to at least William Petty in the second half of the 17th century, for most the critical phase of development comes over the inter-war years. Studenski's (1958) canonical account of the 'extraordinary flourishing' from 1918 to 1939 gives most prominence to US developments, in particular at the Brookings Institute and the NBER. The literature is nearly unanimous in celebrating above all the contribution of Simon Kuznets. Tily (2009) gave more prominence to UK developments, above all the role of Keynes but also the earlier contributions from Alfred Flux, Arthur Bowley, Josiah Stamp and, in particular, Colin Clark, all coming ahead of the better-known contributions from James Meade and Richard Stone.

A number of recent contributions are preoccupied with the limitations of GDP as a measure of social progress (e.g. Coyle 2014; Pilling 2018). Others have examined the broader context of both US and UK developments. In the course of his study of globalisation and neoliberalism, Slododian (2017) reckons the world economy came into being 'on paper and in numbers' in the 1930s. He traces investigations on business cycles (and associated 'barometers') from the US across business cycle institutes 'established throughout Europe and the Soviet Union' (ibid., p. 60), with the League of Nations in Geneva becoming the 'hub' for all such efforts. Most recently Fright (2021) has emphasised the important role across these institutions of funding from the Rockefeller Foundation, and how the Foundation was instrumental in a wider 'zeitgeist' of a 'data-driven, "realistic" approach to economics' (p. ii.). This institutional landscape and mindset meant that even when Keynes wrote his *Economic Consequence of the Peace* in 1919, he was able to draw on relatively rich empirical information.

Fright also warns that existing histories give too much emphasis on GDP, 'focus[ing] only on one aspect of the national accounts to the exclusion of others' (ibid., p. 1). He 'argues that national accounts were part of a broader shift in economics which sought to use economic statistics to inform government decision making' (ibid.). While his work concentrates on the inter-war period, the subsequent shift of emphasis away from the broader accounts can be clarified by addressing parallel shifts in policy and methodology.

In the period of most rapid development, while all were concerned to understand the economy better, Keynes's approach led to specific measurement needs. These were motivated in general by his macroeconomic approach and more specifically by his emphasis on the *demand* side of the economy. As part of the theoretical scheme of the *Treatise on Money* (1930) he set out 'fundamental equations', likely the first articulation of macroeconomic identities and closely related to the variables and relations underlying estimates of national income. Colin Clark's (1932) key innovation was then to begin to elaborate the expenditure approach to the measurement of national income. The separate identification of household expenditure allows the estimation of the marginal propensity to consume and so the (national income) multiplier.

The decisive innovations in national accounting came when Keynes applied his *General Theory* to the financial conduct of the Second World War. In his February 1940 *How to Pay for the War* (*CW* IX, pp. 367-439), Keynes made the case for a scheme deferring part of individuals' earnings until after the end of the war. Greatly increased wartime production would be concentrated in the apparatus of war rather than in consumer goods and services; with wartime employment and earnings increasing in parallel to production, more money would be chasing fewer consumer goods and services. Deferring earnings would reduce the chance of inflation during the war, and releasing the earnings would bolster demand and reduce the chance of deflation after the war.

In order to estimate the necessary withdrawal from private incomes to restrain consumption expenditures, Keynes (with the support of Erwin Rothbarth of the Cambridge University Statistical Department) refined the approach to the aggregate measure of national income and devised a rudimentary set of sector accounts. Mitra-Kahn (2011) shows Keynes's measure for the first time separately identifying government final consumption expenditure, and also regards this as the fundamental distinction between Kuznets's and Keynes's approach (see next section). The sector accounts included 'income and outlay' accounts for the government and household sectors, with incomes equal to outlays and balancing items carried through the accounts. In parallel contributions, Keynes also devised the conception of a 'gap' to capture the difference between increased income and reduced production of consumer goods and services, a precursor to the later theory of the output gap. The critical difference was that Keynes was concerned with the consequences of a higher *level* of employment and activity, not with *rates of growth* (see, e.g. The Theory of the 'Gap', 1941, *CW* XXII, pp. 289–94).

Keynes's and Rothbarth's estimates were published in 1941 as a UK Government White Paper: *An Analysis of the Sources of War Finance and an Estimate of the National Income and Expenditure in 1938 and 1940* (Cmd. 6261, 1940). Shortly afterwards (at Keynes's suggestion) James Meade and Richard Stone (1941) published in the *Economic Journal* a technical article presenting a fuller framework of accounts for a national economy. In his massive history of National Accounting, Andre Vanoli (2005, p. 20) commends the system: 'the set of tables published in 1941 represents indeed a system of national accounts in the form of a linkage among a coherent set of macroeconomic totals'.

Richard Stone subsequently led work on developing international standards at the United Nations. The opening section of the first of these reports warned:

> It has come to be realised in recent years that national income studies which had their origin in an attempt to measure certain broad totals have a much more general interest and usefulness if they provide information on the structure of the constituent transactions and on the mutual independence of these transactions. This is particularly true where national income studies are used in connection with the formulation of economic policy since, in this case, it is the interrelationship of transactions that is important rather than individual totals, such as the national income or gross national product.

From full employment to productivity and real growth

Under the UK Labour government from 1945 to 1951 the economic lessons of war were applied to policymaking under conditions of peace. Full employment was maintained and the provision of social services greatly extended. But in parallel there was a growing shift of emphasis to the supply side of the economy and, as a result, towards aggregate measures of real GDP growth. This shift of emphasis, and associated measurement initiatives, originated in the US.

Initially US national accountants had followed the UK lead. While for example Diane Coyle (2018) argues this meant moving away from 'economic-welfare conception', Mitra-Kahn (2011) shows the debate at the time concerned the inclusion of government consumption expenditures in the aggregate measure. Both Simon Kuznets in the US and Colin Clark in the UK operated as if value is only created by market activity, so government activity cannot be the final output/production: 'the more the government spent, the less was available for private consumption and investment, thereby reducing national income' (Mitra-Kahn 2011, p. 213). Unsurprisingly Keynes's 'intuition was so much revolted' by this approach as he wrote to Nicholas Kaldor (ibid., p. 212). Mitra-Kahn (ibid., pp. 243–4) goes on to recount how the US was won over: Keynes met US national accountants on a visit to Washington D.C. over May to July 1941; though the decisive moment was seemingly when Kuznets's assistant Robert Nathan retired as Chief of the National Income Division at the US Department of Commerce to be replaced by Milton Gilbert. When in May 1942 Gilbert and Robert B. Bangs (1942) produced estimates on this basis, they introduced for the first time the terminology 'gross national product' (ibid., p. 246).[7]

The subsequent US lead followed from parallel initiatives around productivity. Once more motivated by wartime conditions, Wasser and Dolfman (2005, p. 8) report that Congress in June 1940 authorised the BLS 'to make continuing studies of labor productivity and appropriated funds for the establishment of a Productivity and Technological Development Division'. These initiatives initially concerned industry-level efficiency, but post-war attention shifted to whole-economy performance. According to US historian Charles S. Maier, the foundation of the US approach to global economic policy after the Second World War was the 'politics of productivity': 'American blueprints for international monetary order, policy towards trade unions, and the intervention of occupation authorities in West Germany and Japan sought to transform political issues into problems of output, to adjourn class conflict for a consensus on growth' (Maier 1977, p. 607).

This approach set the National Accounts as part of the infrastructure of international politics and led to the dominance of real GDP growth. Maier regards the Organisation for Economic Cooperation and Development (OECD) as critical to the US strategy of 'ensur[ing] the primacy of economics over politics, to de-ideologize issues of political economy into questions of output and efficiency' (Maier 1977, p. 629).

Ahead of the OECD and alongside the Economic Cooperation Administration (ECA) in the US, the Organisation for European Economic Cooperation (OEEC) was set up as the European end of the infrastructure for the implementation of the Marshall Plan. In early discussions the supply and demand perspectives emerged into the open. Initially the European countries argued:

> before World War II, the sixteen participating nations were ... highly efficient in trade, industry, and agriculture and derived a substantial income from international trade ... Trade, industry and agriculture had been twisted out of shape by the forces of war.

Under the European Recovery Act James Silberman and Kenneth Van Auken of the BLS were sent to investigate industrial production in England and France, and begged to differ.

> Countering claims by Europeans that the major problem was the war's destruction, Silberman pointed out that in the pre-War period, Europe had fallen so far behind the United States in output per person that trade relations had been seriously disrupted. His analysis prompted the rallying cry of 'productivity' that swept over Europe.
>
> *(Wasser and Dolfman 2005, p. 48)*

European countries were effectively obliged to address economic performance on this view (see below discussion of the UK). Lequiller and Blades (2014, p. 439) recognise Richard Stone's work on developing an international standard originated in the associated monitoring arrangements. Published by the United Nations (1947), the work would underpin the first (1953) System of National Accounts. Still rooted in the accounting perspective, the Preface to the latter document indicated the future direction of travel:

> This report is confined to national accounts expressed in current money terms. For many purposes it is necessary to make comparisons over time in terms of constant prices. The many conceptual and statistical problems involved in obtaining the information for such comparisons are not examined in this report.
>
> *(SNA 1953, p. vii)*

At the aggregate level, productivity statistics were, and remain, based on comparing constant price or real GDP with various measures of labour input.

The decisive shift towards the routine use of the real terms/supply-side infrastructure was the introduction of growth targets. Matthias Schmelzer (2016) organises his acclaimed *The Hegemony of Growth* around the three OEEC/OECD growth targets. Later labelled 'The European Manifesto', Ministers agreed in August 1951 'that the broad objective of their policies will be to expand total production in Western

Europe by 25% over the next five years' (ibid., p. 123). The second (and likely least unfamiliar) came when the OEEC became the OECD on 30 September 1961; on 17 November the OECD issued a 50% growth target for 1960–1970. The third was a 65% target for 1970–1980.

The vital technical initiative came alongside the second target: Arthur Okun's 1962 Cowles Foundation paper, 'Potential GDP: Its measurement and significance', outlined (and illustrated) for the first time the framework based on the output gap – the difference over time between potential and actual output. The paper reinforced the notion of a 'constant growth rate (r) of potential output'; and Okun observed 'The trend growth rate, fitted to 1947-60 quarterly data, was 3.9 per cent' (perhaps not coincidentally corresponding to the second target). At this point the infrastructure of contemporary economic policy and debate was complete.

The agenda very quickly impacted on the UK. The original concern of post-war policy was maintaining full employment and preventing excess inflation, as Christopher Dow (1964, p. 27) recognises in his authoritative assessment. The post-war Labour Government was naturally wary that the productivity agenda was aimed at undermining their employment goals. Indicatively, Gottwald (1999, p. 109) finds of the origins of the Anglo-American Council on Productivity: 'The British government's compelling need for such a council arose from the concerns that any lack of cooperation with the ECA might result in congressional critics forcing reduction or even discontinuation of Marshall Plan aid'. In office from October 1951, the Conservative party were more enthusiastic. From 1947, the Treasury had published an annual economic survey; from 1952 it was based primarily on measures in real terms (Dow 1964, p. 34). In a 1956 White Paper on 'The Economic Implications of Full Employment', the Government was 'pledged to foster conditions in which the nation can, if it so wills, realize its full potentialities for growth in terms of production and living standards' (Hutchison 1968, p. 123).

But the decisive change followed the second growth target. In May 1962 the National Economic Development Council was established by the Conservative Government to 'explore implications of four per cent growth rate' (Brittan 1964, p. 141). 'Growthmanship' became a new orthodoxy. In his own contribution to the debate, F. T. Blackaby (1963, p. 489) cites a leader column, 'The Pulse of Britain', and a 'crop' of letters to The Times in July 1962 – as evidence of 'a tendency – rather more marked than usual, I think – to accept without demur that Britain's economic performance has been poor and to put it down to some social malaise'. In contrast to post-war objectives, Blackaby claimed 'economic growth ... as the single most important objective of economic policy and consequently the most important criterion of economic performance', with, moreover, 'price stability as a less important objective' (ibid., pp. 490–1). His paper offered evidence of the British malaise on his preferred measure, with a comparison of real GNP growth and productivity over episodes from 1922 to 1961. In February 1963, the NEDC confirmed the 4% growth target for 1961–1966, equivalent to the annual rate implied by the OECD target.

Post-war outcomes according to the growth framework

More than half a century later the framework is still not dislodged, but growthmanship has become stagnationism and some want to give up on growth altogether. Diane Coyle's GDP: a Brief but Affectionate History offers an account of this trajectory. In general terms outcomes depend on both supply and demand, but the supply side is dominant. At best demand can only ensure that supply-side possibilities are realised, but demand management has been bedevilled with dangers and misjudgement becomes the norm.

The post-war golden age is portrayed as the economy reverting to its pre-1914 trend, with Coyle deferring to a 1969 assessment by Ferenc Janossy.[8] On the supply side: 'Particularly important was the continuously improving level of education among the workforce. In addition, a succession of new technologies became available and entered into wider use … Perhaps as important was the steadily improving availability of consumer goods'. 'Keynesian' demand management policies and the Marshall Plan (both in the context of the need to repair and replace assets destroyed in the war) ensured that demand was adequate to permit the economy to operate at full potential.

'A Crisis of Capitalism' (the title of Coyle's Chapter 3) puts paid to the post-war era. Policymakers (and the wage-earning public) mistake the high growth of potential output over the post-war era as permanent. The inflation of the 1970s is therefore the result of expanding demand (including wage bargaining) to sustain post-war growth, when potential output growth has contracted. Coyle attributes this to 'Human nature and politics being what they are' (p. 64); the role of the US, 'growthmen' economists, the British media and the OECD are not mentioned.

An appeal to the veracity of monetarism (ibid., p. 78) implies that the traumas of the 1980s reflected the costs of containing demand to restore an appropriately downgraded perspective on potential output. In the 1990s comes 'The New Paradigm', as technological gains 'gave way to the longest period of expansion in GDP the United States had seen since the dawn of capitalism' (p. 82). But once more 'the New Economy hype looks almost delusional' (p. 83). Again, the surge in potential output was not sustained; but, again, policymakers operated on the basis that it would be sustained (and were encouraged in this by many commentators).

From this point forward, Coyle argues that national accountants exacerbated the confusion by bad accounting decisions. First, the implementation of quality adjustment for high-tech items and the capitalisation of own-account software 'may well have given the impression of a greater acceleration in growth than was the case' (ibid., p. 90). Second, in the run-up to the global financial crisis, readings were distorted by the evolving international rules for the treatment of the financial sector. (Labelled 'financial intermediation services indirectly measured', unsecured lending to households was deemed final rather than intermediate output. Incorporated into the accounts when credit was growing rapidly, the change meant higher GDP growth.) David Pilling, first in the *Financial Times*, made the charge explicit: 'If banking had been subtracted from GDP, rather than added to it, as Kuznets had proposed, it is plausible to speculate that the financial crisis would never have happened' (Pilling 2014).

Arriving in the present, Coyle and Mitra-Kahn (2017) argue:

> changes in the economy, being restructured by digital technology and paying the price for unsustainable growth, make the case for a new measurement framework more pressing than ever. GDP was never an ideal measure of economic welfare and its suitability has been decreasing.

They consider that the latest supply-side developments (digital technology) and the past misrepresentations that led to unsustainable growth have finally made GDP redundant. A two-stage reform is proposed, addressing long-standing and widely shared concerns with GDP. First, obtaining 'a better measure of welfare' through additions to (e.g. intangibles) and subtractions from (e.g. finance) GDP, and also 'adjusting for income distribution'. Second, and more substantially, 'replacement of GDP' with a 'dashboard' recording stocks of key assets: physical assets, natural capital, human capital, intellectual property, social and institutional capital, and net financial capital.

In the meantime, GDP and productivity growth across the world is grinding to a halt (even before the pandemic struck). Looking ahead many commentators see no grounds to expect any change for the better. Sixty years of chasing growth has led to what is known as stagnationism.

Conclusion

There is a need for a sharper dividing line between measurement and the framework within which measurement has been operated. Underpinned by supply-side thinking, the growth framework has been disastrous since its inception.

As Coyle's account illustrates, repeated misreading of economic conditions has been endemic to policy. Inflation, repeated recession, financial disarray and austerity have throughout been set against the background of a building environmental disaster.

But the relevance of the Accounts is a separate matter from the relevance of the supply-side framework. It is likely that a demand orientation might better explain recent outcomes, including a deeper understanding of ongoing financial imbalances. Furthermore, a demand orientation might provide the best means to resolve the crises facing society. The National Accounts remain essential to any such assessment. The Accounts were originally devised to support demand-side initiatives to resolve the crisis of the 1930s, to support the full utilisation of resources for the war effort and to maintain full employment into the peace.

Ahead of the steadily intensified emphasis on growth and the output-gap framework, in Britain over the 1940s and across much of Europe over the 1950s record lows in unemployment and significant gains in the standard of living were secured and sustained. These unprecedented outcomes were the result of aiming policy at aggregate demand, across domestic and international monetary architecture and policies, as well as fiscal policy (Tily 2006 [2010]). The idea that this was not good enough may have become mainstream opinion, but it had nothing to do with Keynes. As Roy Harrod (1974, p. 17) observed: 'I don't see how Keynes can have been expected to have systematic ideas on growth; his systematic ideas related to full employment'. Ultimately, the vindication of these ideas has been inhibited by the growth framework. Here Schmelzer's (2016, p. 6) 'underlying interests that are served and at the same time concealed by the dominance of the growth framework' might be in play.

Moreover there is evidence that – even as soon as 1941 – Keynes saw where things were headed. Replying to concerns of a US colleague, he wrote: 'There is a great danger in quantitative forecasts which are based exclusively on statistics relating to conditions by no means parallel. I have tried to persuade Gilbert and Humphrey that they should be more cautious' (*CW* XXIII, pp. 191–2).

Really the place of measurement in society is extraordinary. Ahead of the war, measuring the economy was very much in its infancy. After the war, the possibilities for economic activity (and by association for society as a whole) have been understood according to imagined projections of a specific (occasionally modified) measure of national income in real terms. It is right that this dangerous charade be brought to an end, but it is wrong to shoot the messenger.

Notes

1 The views are the author's own, not those of the TUC. Thanks once more to Fenella Maitland-Smith for National Accounts discipline and helping me to get the story straight, and to Stewart Kingaby at the (then) Central Statistical Office for setting it all off so well (the usual disclaimers apply).
2 *UK National Accounts* [the Blue Book]*: 2020*, Office for National Statistics, https://www.ons.gov.uk/economy/grossdomesticproductgdp/compendium/united kingdomnationalaccountsthebluebook/2020.
3 The financial sector is further sub-divided into 'monetary and financial institutions', 'insurance companies and pension funds', 'other financial intermediaries' and the central bank.
4 Contributions follow from deriving the growth of $Y = C + I$; $r = 100\ (Y - Y_0)/Y_0 = 100\ (C - C_0)/Y_0 + 100\ (I - I_0)/Y_0$.
5 See Thomas and Nolan (2016) for a valuable account of the history of the UK position.
6 The most-timely comparisons are quarter on previous quarter – though timeliness is set against increased volatility (in part given complexities with adjusting for seasonal patterns) – which can be annualised (roughly) by multiplying by four. On the latter point, analyses of growth are rooted in the standard compound interest formula $y_{t+n} = y_t\ (1 + r/100)^n$. So, in this case of converting a quarterly into an annual growth rate, strictly: $(1 + r_Q/100)^4 = (1 + r_A/100)$; $r_A = 100((1 + r_Q/100)^4 - 1)$.
7 They include the footnote: 'Thus, the concept of gross national product used here is inclusive of government operations financed by business taxes. This is one of the important respects in which it differs from the concept made familiar by the notable work of Professor Kuznets'.
8 The Bank of England (2018) historic data for the UK show average annual GDP growth of 2% in the 20 years ahead of the First World War (1894–2014) and 2.7% in the 20 years after the Second World War (1948–1968). This is a material difference in the context of long-run growth.

References

Bank of England (2018) 'A millennium of macroeconomic data' (version 3.1). https://www.bankofengland.co.uk/statistics/research-datasets

Blackaby, F. T. (1963) 'The recent performance of the British economy', *The Advancement of Science*, London: British Association for the Advancement of Science, 1939–1976, 489–98.

Brittan, S. (1964) *The Treasury under the Tories, 1951–1964*, Harmondsworth: Penguin.

Cmd. 6261 (1941) *An Analysis of the Sources of War Finance and an Estimate of the National Income and Expenditure in 1938 and 1940*, London: Her Majesty's Stationary Office.

Coyle, D. (2014) *GDP: A Brief but Affectionate History*, Princeton: Princeton University Press.

Coyle, D. (2018) 'It's all in Kuznets…', The Enlightened Economist blog, 17 November. http://www.enlightenmenteconomics.com/blog/index.php/2018/11/its-all-in-kuznets/

Coyle, D. and B. Mitra-Kahn (2017) 'Making the future count', Indigo prize essay, 14 September. http://global-perspectives.org.uk/wp-content/uploads/2017/10/making-the-future-count.pdf

CW: see Keynes, J. M. (1971–1989).

Dow, J. C. R. (1964) *The Management of the British Economy*, 1945–60, Cambridge, UK: Cambridge University Press.

Fright, M. (2021) 'The moments of, and movements for, national accounts: Contextualising changes to British national accounting during the 1930s to 1950s', PhD dissertation, Cambridge University.

Gilbert, M. and R. B. Bangs (1942) 'Preliminary estimates of Gross National Product, 1929–41', *Survey of Current Business* 22 (5), 9–13. https://fraser.stlouisfed.org/files/docs/publications/SCB/pages/1940-1944/3387_1940-1944.pdf

Gottwald, C. H. (1999) 'The Anglo-American council on productivity: 1948–1952, British productivity and the Marshall Plan', PhD dissertation, University of North Texas. https://digital.library.unt.edu/ark:/67531/metadc279256/?q=order%20books%20were%20full#top

Harrod, R. F. (1974) 'Keynes's theory and its applications', in D. E. Moggridge, ed., *Keynes: Aspects of the Man and His Work*, London and Basingstoke: Macmillan, pp. 1–12.

Hutchison, T. W. (1968) *Economics and Economic Policy in Britain, 1946–1966: Some Aspects of Their Inter-Relations*, London: George Allen and Unwin Ltd.

Keynes, J. M. (1971–1989) *Collected Writings*, D. E. Moggridge, ed., 30 vols. London: Macmillan and New York: St Martin's Press.

Landefeld, J. S. (2000) 'GDP: One of the great inventions of the 20th century', Bureau of Economic Analysis, *Survey of Current Business* 80 (1), (January), 6–9. https://apps.bea.gov/scb/pdf/BEAWIDE/2000/0100od.pdf

Lequiller, F. and D. Blades (2014) *Understanding National Accounts: Second Edition*, OECD Publishing. http://www.oecd.org/sdd/UNA-2014.pdf

Maier, C. S. (1977) 'The politics of productivity: Foundations of American international economic policy after World War II', *International Organisation* 31 (4), (Autumn), 607–33. https://www.imf.org/external/datamapper/datasets/GDD

Meade, J. E. and R. Stone (1941) 'The construction of tables of national income, expenditure, savings and investment', *Economic Journal* 51, (June–September), 216–33.

Mitra-Kahn, B. (2012) *Redefining the Economy: How the 'Economy' was Invented*, 1620, PhD dissertation, University of London.

Okun, A. M. (1962) 'Potential GNP: Its measurement and significance', Cowles Foundation Paper 190. https://milescorak.files.wordpress.com/2016/01/okun-potential-gnp-its-measurement-and-significance-p0190.pdf

Pilling, D. (2014) 'Has GDP outgrown its use?', *Financial Times*, 4 July. https://www.ft.com/content/dd2ec158-023d-11e4-ab5b-00144feab7de

Pilling, D. (2018) *The Growth Delusion: The Wealth and Well-Being of Nations*, London: Bloomsbury.

Schmelzer, M. (2016) *The Hegemony of Growth: The OECD and the Making of the Economic Growth Paradigm*, Cambridge, UK: Cambridge University Press.

Tily, G. (2006 [2010]) *Keynes's General Theory, the Rate of Interest and 'Keynesian Economics': Keynes Betrayed*, Basingstoke: Palgrave Macmillan.

Tily, G. (2009) 'John Maynard Keynes and the development of National Accounts in Britain, 1895 to 1941', *Review of Income and Wealth* 55 (2), (June), 331–59.

Thomas, R. and L. Nolan (2016) 'Historical estimates of financial accounts and balance sheets', Part of National Accounts articles, Historical estimates of financial accounts and balance sheets Release, 12 January 2016. https://webarchive.nationalarchives.gov.uk/20160131203146/http://www.ons.gov.uk/ons/rel/naa1-rd/national-accounts-articles/historical-estimates-of-financial-accounts-and-balance-sheets-by-institutional-sector—a-first-step-towards-reconstructing-the-data-for-the-uk/rpt—historical-estimates.html

United Nations (1947) 'Measurement of national income and the construction of social accounts', a report of the Sub-Committee on National Income Statistics of the League of Nations Committee of Statistical Experts.

Vanoli, A. (2005) *A History of National Accounting*, Amsterdam: IOS Press.

Wasser, S. F. and M. L. Dolfman (2005) 'BLS and the Marshall Plan: the forgotten story', *Monthly Labor Review*, June. https://www.bls.gov/opub/mlr/2005/06/art4full.pdf

PART V

Communicating macroeconomics

28

THE RHETORICAL PERSPECTIVE ON MACROECONOMICS

Macroeconomics is good for making sense of the macroeconomy

Arjo Klamer

The purpose of macroeconomics

'What is economics good for?'
 Nothing. I think it is fun. I am actually amazed that I am getting paid for doing it.'

Whenever I speak with economists, I try to ask them what economics is good for. Quite often I receive an answer like this, or a variation thereof. The cynicism that speaks through such a response contrasts with the idealism that I hear so now and then in answers like:

'Economics is good for a better world. I do it because I hope to influence policies, to get them better and so contribute to a more just, sustainable or free world.'
 'Economics provides rationales for policy.'
 'With economics we can address major issues like climate control, inequality, economic instability, unemployment.'
 'What if economics has not succeeded in any of those goals?'
 'We have to keep striving for them. Without them to strive for, doing economics does not make sense.'

Idealists envision a purpose, something to strive for.

 During my growing up as an economist, I identified with the idealism of macroeconomists like Jan Tinbergen, Jan Pen (another Dutch economist), and John Maynard Keynes and I was impressed with the influence that economists like Milton Friedman and Friedrich Hayek were having. All these economists had a better world in mind and tried to contribute to it with their economics. We were all Keynesians at

DOI: 10.4324/9781315745992-34

first; then the tide turned. Economists began to warm up to the free market vision of Friedman and Hayek. At the same time a greater part of the world still appeared to practice the economics that Karl Marx had been preaching. The idealists owned the world, at least so it seemed up till the mid-1980s.[1]

Then doubts took over the world of macroeconomists. New-classical economists paralysed the macroeconomic discussion with their claim that activist Keynesian policies is of no real consequence for significant macroeconomic variables, not even in the short run. The argument was that with rational expectations agents would anticipate the effects of policy interventions and with their actions undo those effects (Klamer 1984). New-Keynesians were challenged to offer new theoretical justifications for activist policies consistent with microeconomic foundations. Possibly because of the stalemate that followed, the optimism with which economists had entered the policy field turned into scepticism if not outright pessimism. The surveys that I conducted with David Colander among graduate students at the end of the 1980s displayed the scepticism (Klamer and Colander 1990). These students considered problem-solving and mathematical competencies a great deal more important than knowledge of the real economy or doing policy-relevant work for a successful career as an academic economist. Most of them were frustrated by that.

In the late 20th century the influence of macroeconomics appeared to wane in a serious way feeding the cynicism among economists. Politicians conducted far-reaching economic policies like the introduction of the euro, stringent measures for debt-ridden countries like Portugal and Greece, and trade interventions against the advice of economists. There was no macroeconomic study that concluded that the introduction of the euro would promote economic growth. And yet that was the argument that European politicians made to motivate the euro; in reality the demise of the German mark was the price that Germany had to pay for its re-unification. The argument, therefore, was political rather than economical (see Szasz 2001). To justify the debt reductions for countries like Greece and Portugal during the crisis in the euro area European politicians cited a study by the MIT macroeconomists Reinhart and Rogoff (2010) who had calculated that a debt/GDP ratio of over 90% would be detrimental for economic growth. Unfortunately, graduate students found serious errors in their calculations with the consequence that politicians have become even more wary citing scientific research (see for an account Yalcintas and Kosel 2021, chapter 7). During the Corona crisis debt ratios were suddenly of no consequence anymore. Politicians were unanimous in their eagerness to finance massive support programmes with public debt. Macroeconomists were left wondering when they have to pay the price, for example, in the form of inflation, or serious financial imbalances.

In an analysis of the impact of academic economists on the NAFTA negotiations, I concluded that they were crowded out, to the point that they were even ridiculed by politicians (see Klamer 2007). The US under the presidency of Trump started trade wars with China and Europe against the advice of most macroeconomists. Its council of economic advisers played an undetectable role. What macroeconomists had envisaged as the rationale, the purpose, of their research – rationalising macroeconomic policies – appeared to have come to nothing much. Politicians appeared not to care for the outcomes of macroeconomic research.

Might it be, then, that idealists have overstated the importance of economics? Should macroeconomists be more modest? Do they still have a purpose or are the cynics right?

Keynes mused in 1931 that he expected that the economic problem would be resolved in hundred years hence and economics 'should be a matter for specialists – like dentistry' (Keynes 1931, *CW* IX, 373). Economics would be a toolbox with the equipment that we need to address mundane problems. But we are almost there, in 2030, and the future that Keynes imagines appears as far off as ever, the dramatic increase in wealth notwithstanding. The economy continues to dominate the news, political agendas, and quite a few dinner conversations. The preoccupation with wealth appears even stronger than at the time of Keynes. All that would point at an important role of economists. After all, they are the ones who can explain economic events and predict what is going to happen in the economy.

But it is the claim of explanation and prediction that is undermining idealistic macroeconomists. Politicians and the general public begin to see what most economists already know: macroeconomics is not very good in explaining what is happening in the economy and is especially disappointing when it comes to predictions. The science of economics has not lived up to the expectation that idealist economists like Jan Tinbergen, Robert Solow, and Paul Samuelson evoked by claiming that economics was growing into a real science, like physics, with a clear method and reliable results. With robust explanations economists would generate reliable predictions, if not about future interest rates, then about the effects of policies. When politicians want to do know *what* the unemployment rate will be *when* they increase taxes on CO_2 emissions, economists should be able to tell with their models. In practice it did not quite work that way. Economic reality proved to be too complex – too many factors weigh in on any such causal connection – to produce sturdy predictions. Chicago economists rubbed salt in the wound with their claim that economic policy can have no systematic effect on the economy for if it did economists would be able to anticipate the effects and get rich in the stock market, an outcome that is ostensibly not the case. This conclusion rendered much policy work of economists futile. At least so it seemed. The current state of affairs, therefore, seems to favour a cynical attitude.

Neither the cynics nor the idealists are right, so I will argue. Following the lines of earlier work (Klamer 2007), I will show that both positions imply a mistaken picture of what a science like economics is about, and how it 'works' within and without academia. The cynics are right in their dismissal of the idealist position, but the idealists rightly believe in the relevance of economics although that relevance is different from what they claim. At issue is the often implicit and sometimes explicit methodological framework in which economists think.

My argument is that that framework is misguiding economists and makes them overlook what is really happening.

Conventional methodological wisdom

The methodological framework shows in what Joan Robinson called the toolbox of standard economics (Robinson 1964 [1962]). This tool box consists of modelling techniques, a great variety of heuristics – like 'when modelling economic behaviour use constrained maximization set-ups' – and all kinds of empirical methods. All this constitutes what Kant would call theoretical reason and what economists may call the theory or the analytics of economics. Underlying these heuristics are values, that is, qualities that standard economists consider to be important when practising their science, such as 'being systematic', 'being able to quantify theoretical notions', 'being positive', or, as non-economists would say, 'being objective'.

The premise of standard economists is that their theoretical reasoning has consequences for policymakers. Especially when they write the conclusions of their research, they tend to articulate policy consequences, suggesting that policymakers are the addressees. The dominant perspective is still that of an engineer, just as Jan Tinbergen conceived it (Tinbergen 1956). The economist builds a model with knobs or instruments that the policymaker can use to get the desired outcomes. The economist is presumed to be disinterested, like a real nerd, to get the model right regardless of the consequences. It should be obvious that quantification is crucial as policymakers want to know 'how much': how much to decrease taxes to get how much decrease in the unemployment rate.

When operating with this methodological framework you are made to think in terms of propositions, claims, findings, results, explanations, and predictions. The metaphor is that of a complicated machinery that is modelled by economists and incomprehensible to others, that takes inputs in the form of all kinds of data and produces propositions about the real world. As if the science of economics is about making claims about the economy. As if economics provides predictions and results. As if tested propositions and true predictions are the criteria of truthful theories. As if the truth of economic models is what matters.

Even if this methodological conception of economics is still conventional wisdom among economists – my bet it is –, it is highly problematic. Karl Popper announced in the 1930s that scientists cannot verify, that is, prove their empirical propositions. They can only falsify, that is, disprove them (Popper 1956 [1934]). Later philosophers of science pointed out that scientists cannot even do that. Theories are composed of all kinds of propositions and techniques. Facts are constructs. Accordingly, when constructed facts disprove a composed theory, it is impossible to tell what the problem is, which part of the theory is wrong, or whether the facts are wrong (see Klamer 2007).

These philosophical insights undermined the faith in the objectivity of economics as a science and may account for the cynicism that is now rampant among economists. The cynics practice economics without the expectation to find the truth, serve policies, or enlighten anyone. The pragmatics will hold on to the conviction that economics, even if not the harbinger of truths, has sufficient validity to support one policy or another.

The point is that those who are aware of the limitations of economics as a science end up more likely as cynics than romantics or idealists. It is hard to maintain the ideal of economics as a science dedicated to good and sensible policy when we realise that economists are unable to provide clear and quantifiable causal relations and that politicians seeking the advice of economists only have to look for the economists with a favourable perspective. It is just not the case that economists provide 'objective' knowledge for policymaking.

Practising economists appear to be aware of their incapability to produce truths and of their limited impact on policy. They will never appeal to the truth, at least not among each other as in 'hey, this theory, this model is true, ye know'. They also do not seem to be interested in the impact of economics. There is no attempt made, as far as I know, to determine the impact of economics on the economy, on policy. That is strange as you would expect that the efforts of thousands and thousands of economists worldwide would be good for better economies and if not that, better policies. The knowledge of economists is not considered to be part of the production function. It is not that investment in economic research has an economic pay-off, at least that has never been determined. How strange that is, especially given the inclination of economists to claim almost any subject for their domain. Sex, death, suicide, the climate – you name it – and it has been subject to economic modelling. The big exception is the economic impact of economics itself. There have been some economic analyses of what economists do – with attention to their incentives and such – but there is no calculation of the impact. On that economists remain nearly silent.

Even if economic ideas were to have an impact, as the idealists would like to see, that poses a problem from the conventional methodological standpoint. When a theory affects the reality it intends to explain, it ceases to be right. This possibility is not accounted for in the conventional methodology as it tries to evoke the science of physics as its exemplar. Phil Mirowski speaks of the physics envy of economists: they would like to see their science on a par with physics (Mirowksi 1989). If it would be, objectivity requires that the researchers do not influence the reality that they are studying. The problem for economists is that their reality includes themselves, among other humans. Without taking into account the effect of an economic theory on agents, the theory would be incomplete.

All this feeds the cynical perspective. If the impact of economics does not make logical sense, why do economics at all?

Not only the dominant methodological framework clouds the view on what makes economics relevant, so does the metaphor of rational choice. Ever since the famous essay by Lionel Robbins entitled *An Essay on the Nature and Significance of Economic Science* (1932), economists seem wedded to the idea that agents make rational choices in conditions of scarcity. Many an economist defines his or her subject thus. This idea has dictated the method of economic theorising and modelling. Surely, many economists have taken exception, among whom Keynes, Hicks (see Klamer 1989), the Austrians, and more recently behavioural economists. Being the exception, they deviate from the standard and that remains rational choice or constrained maximisation constructions. It has proven to be a fertile heuristic for economic theorising giving space for endless variations and mathematical specifications.

However, as the distractors are eager to point out, the metaphor of rational choice has serious shortcomings. One of those is that it has been resistant to account for learning and with that for the role that knowledge has in rational choice. When we allow for learning, we have to acknowledge that the knowledge of rational agents will differ. If agents know that, they have an incentive to acquire the better knowledge of others. Systematic differences would not be able to persist, as is maintained in the efficient market thesis of, among others, Fama (1970). The rational expectations hypothesis was postulated, therefore, to assume that rational agents incorporate the best knowledge available and that would be the economic model in which they are assumed to operate. That move would make sense considering the heuristic of rational choice. But does it?

Realising how our students have the greatest difficulties comprehending the models and take years to master them and knowing how terrible everyone else scores on the most basic economic tests, it is hard to accept that agents are as knowledgeable as the model assumes. Again, learning is not part of the model. And how to account for the fact that models of economists differ and often reach different conclusions?

Which model should a rational agent adopt? What if rational agents have limited access or have to deal with the uncertainties that economists face themselves? What would be the rational thing to do?

Apart from all these objections, a consistent application of rational choice makes the entire exercise of economics irrelevant, at least for the purpose of policy. The argument is more or less the argument on the logical inconsistency of truthful theories that have an impact on the reality that they explain. If economists were to agree on the very best, most truthful model, its predictions would be mute, as rational agents will anticipate them. Rational choice, strictly interpreted, renders predictions of economic theories irrelevant, and makes sure that they have no impact on economic outcomes and are of no use for policymakers.

Just as awkward are the models that fail to account for the behaviour of policymakers, certainly if their actions impact economic outcomes. When the assumption is that economic agents are rational, agents in politics should be assumed to be rational as well. When I hear economic model builders complain about the stupidity of policymakers who do not heed their advice, my question is how they account for such behaviour. Why don't they build in the stupidity to increase the explanatory and predictive power of their model? I know that the proposal is not decent, for stupidities are not part of the repertoire of human agency in economic theory. In all fairness, James Buchanan and Gordon Tullock (1962) developed an economics of political agency and even received a Nobel Prize for their work, yet the internalisation of policymakers has not become standard. Far from it. Accordingly, we get stuck with an anomaly in economic theory.

The rhetorical/discursive move

The reasoning thus far gives the cynics more reasons to gloat than the idealists. It appears that the practice of economists serves that very practice, and not much more. A well-founded impact on policy or on economic processes, for that matter, is illusory.

In the meantime, the idealist position appears to be based on faith. However, their fate will change with a change of perspective. At least that is what I want to show.

The rhetorical or discursive move shifts the attention away from the propositional logic that informs the conventional methodological perspective to the rhetorical and discursive characteristics of economics. This move was set in by (now) Deirdre McCloskey with her article and book *The Rhetoric of Economics* (1983, 1985), Phil Mirowski (1989), Klamer (1984, 2007), Klamer et al. (1988), and others. This move makes us think of economics as a bunch of conversations – among which conversations on econometrics, game theory, Post-Keynesian economics, behavioural economics, general equilibrium theory, industrial organisation – each of which has distinct rhetorical characteristics in the metaphors, narratives, themes, plots, protagonists, exemplars, and the like that they employ. The casting of individuals as rational choice makers is an example of a metaphor. Following Milton Friedman economists recognise a metaphor with the notion of 'as ... if' reasoning: the claim is not literally true but is fertile in its analytical possibilities. The price mechanism is another example: as if constant adjusting prices are a mechanical process.

Another rhetorical device is narrative – the telling of stories. As McCloskey (1990) has pointed out story telling is very much part of what economists communicate. The way economists tell about the impossibility of predicting future interests, or share prices for that matter, evokes the American narrative: 'If you're so smart, why aren't you rich?' Economists who suggest that they can predict the future are selling snake oil. The story evokes advertisements promising innocent onlookers richness, a fast buck. Why would anyone tell you how to get rich? If we economists would know, we would not be teaching and driving an old Toyota. In *Tenured Professor* the economist John Kenneth Galbraith is playing with the theme in fiction, to show that economists have even the ability to tell a real story (Galbraith 1990).

In my own study of narrative in economics I reach the conclusion that the main narrative that academic economists tell is a narrative about themselves, about the finding of solutions to anomalies, to reach policy conclusions, about other economists being mistaken, and about the superiority of their own approach (Klamer, 2007). These are stories internal to academia, and therefore only of interest to people operating in academia. Rare are the attempts to tell stories of economic research to outsiders. They appear mainly in biographies[2] and in the writings about the history of economic thought.

The rhetorical perspective highlights what is going on in the communication of ideas. Whereas the main issue in the standard methodology is the relationship between the theory and reality and with that the truth value of the theory, when communication is the subject the truth of what is communicated is not what counts, but its meanings are and the interest that is addressed turn out to count most. The receiver must find the message interesting and of interest to be persuaded or to pay some attention. That's why economists will rather say that a paper they like is interesting or relevant rather than calling the argument true. In general, participants in academic conversations rarely appeal to the truth among each other. They only will do so when challenged by outsiders.

For McCloskey the main reason to highlight the rhetorical devices of modern economics is to point out that the conversation of economics has much in common with the human conversation in general and the conversation on poetry and then humanities in particular. By speaking in metaphors and narratives economists are like poets. She pursues this rhetorical characterisation to apply it to market behaviour to observe that agents in markets use rhetoric as well in their communication. In her recent work she makes the link with virtue ethics to argue that bourgeois virtues operate in markets and render them effective (McCloskey 2007). It is a way to colour the picture of the economy with 'real' humans. The impact of this move remains to be seen.

I rather see the benefits of the rhetorical perspective to observe differences among the economic conversations and between the academic conversation and the everyday and political conversations. Behavioural economics is different from neoclassical economics because it uses a different metaphor for decision making, one that pictures people with cognitive limitations and even some emotions whereas the neoclassical metaphor of Max U pictures people as agents maximising a utility function under some constraints. And where academic economists like to minimise narrative and prefer mechanical metaphors and mathematical symbols, policymakers prefer narratives with winners and losers, about trade wars, of emerging powers, of exploitation, all notions that economists avoid as the pest.

What follows is that different conversations may communicate different meanings. Behavioural economics gets us to attach different meanings to human behaviour than a standard neoclassical conversation does. We are made to think of endowment effects, cognitive dissonance, and nudging. The latter concept is also what contributes to the putative relevance of behavioural economics as it makes politicians aware of the superior effects of positive stimuli over punishing measures. Yet, nudging also evokes the meanings of paternalism and manipulation. This shows that the proliferation of meanings is hard to control. That is precisely the rhetorical problem that anyone faces who wants to communicate an idea, no matter how truthful or evidence based the idea is.

Highlighting the meanings that economists communicate brings out another purpose of economics. Rather than providing true or at least plausible explanations and predictions, and with those truthful propositions, economists provide metaphors, narratives, concepts, and a perspective that enables people to make sense of the complex and quite incomprehensible beast that we call the economy.

Take the notion of markets. The standard economic perspective focuses on markets in the aggregate, on the labour market, on the market for good and services, on international markets. When economists speak of consumption, they do not think of people cooking and eating meals, driving their car, and typing on a keyboard but of the buying of goods and services. When macroeconomists speak about money, they do not refer to the amount of money people make or the amount of money people own – the common meanings that 'money' has – but to the money supply and the demand for the means of exchange. When macroeconomists think about trade in terms of transactions that cross borders, they think of markets, of mutually beneficial exchange, and the tendency towards equilibrium if only prices are allowed to change whereas most other people think in terms of power, of countries that overpower other countries, of warlike situations, and therefore of the need for protection.

This goes to show that economists try to convey ideas that go counter to ideas commonly held. They make sense of the world in a particular way, not easily understood unless people have taken some economic classes at school or at university.

Neo-liberalism is the way economists make sense of all kinds of situations in terms that economics dictates. I call this process 'sense-making'. It is to see markets where there may be none. It is because of economists that people will now see markets anywhere, including a labour market, a market for beer or whatever, or even a marriage market. Because of sense-making by economists, managers in the health care sector began to see health care as a market and officials at universities now see education as a market. Neo-liberalism is the embracement of economic sense-making by managers, civil servants, and politicians (Zuidhof 2012). It is not that neo-liberals (who by the way do not refer to themselves with this term) apply the explanations and predictions of economists but use their sense-making or at least their interpretation of the terms that economists use.

An anecdote may clarify the claim. When I took on the position of governor of my town (a political position similar to an alderman, or deputy major), I noticed that my civil servants were using all kinds of economic terms. They spoke, for example, about their customers. When I asked, they turned out to be the recipients of welfare and unemployment benefits. They also claimed to work demand oriented. Does that mean that a homeless man gets what he asks? Does he get drugs, for example? No, if he asks what we have determined he can get, he gets just that. Of course, they worked result-oriented and when we needed a service, like consultants for people into debt, we would issue a tender. Why? 'Because competition is good for our customers.' It was as if my civil servants had taken an introductory economics class. I am not sure they would pass the exam though, as they did not have a clear understanding of all those terms. My first measure was that I disallowed the term 'customer', and suggested they use 'inhabitant' or 'candidate' if someone was trying to find work. That did not make me popular at first. But for me it was a matter of principle that the sphere of the government and of health care and education is not a market but rather a sphere of relationships and human interactions (Klamer 2017).

With this experience I realised that civil servants, and so does basically everybody, have to make sense of the beast that we call the economy. They have to interpret what they hear and read in the news, they have to understand what it means when economists say that the economy is in crisis or why a government that runs a deficit is not necessarily evil and what it means that China is about to become the dominant economy. They need to make sense of low interest rates, of the high prices of houses. They need some notions, a language to talk about all these things at the kitchen table in the corridors of the office and in the café. And that is how Keynes's famous remark at the end of *The General Theory* comes to mind:

> Is the fulfilment of these ideas a visionary hope? [...] the ideas of economists and political philosophers, both when they are right and when they are wrong, are more powerful than is commonly understood. Indeed, the world is ruled by little else. Practical men, who believe themselves to be quite exempt from any intellectual influences, are usually the slaves from some defunct economist. Madmen in authority, who hear voices in the air, are distilling their frenzy from some academic scribbler of a few years back.
>
> *(Keynes 1936, CW VII, 383)*

However, practical men and women may also embrace ideas that have been proven false. Quite popular, for example, is a mercantilist reading of the economy. When European politicians are arguing that we are in a trade war with the Chinese and that we need to make ourselves strong by protecting out interest in order to win this war, they fall back to the mercantilist creed that Adam Smith had tackled and destroyed intellectually. It is the implied narrative that appeals in the political arena. Its drama apparently plays out so much better than the narrative of contemporary economics that is about general equilibrium, mutual gains, comparative advantage, and such. It is hard to make sense of the situation with such terms, at least when people like to hear dramatic stories.

Furthermore, the meanings that people attach to economic terms differ from how economists would define them. 'The market' is for an economist quite a specific situation with a product, demand and supply forces, and a (flexible) price. Everyday people may rather think of (big) business, greed, commercialism, profit seeking. Money for them means all kinds of things that economists name differently. In common understanding, things that cost a lot of money have a high price and people with little money are poor. But economists would say that an economy that revolves around money is an economy with a strong pricing mechanism or a developed financial sector.

Those differences in meanings frustrate many an academic economist trying to tell his or her story in the public sphere. Only a few are skilled at this. They understand the rhetorical gap between academic and everyday discourse.

It is about the meanings, stupid

Now we are ready to see that both the cynics and the idealists are mistaken and right at the same time. When caught up with a conventional methodological perspective the cynics are right in the sense that economics does not have impact with its truth claims, its explanations, and its predictions. The idealists overstate their case when they hold on to their belief that economic truths hold sway. Yet the idealists are right in their conviction that economics has serious impact and the cynics are mistaken in denying that impact, as soon as we interpret impact bearing on the sense-making.

We may call the intermediate position pragmatic. Economics as science works and it works well.

Notes

1 See, for example, *Conversations with Economists* in which all economists portrayed confess to idealistic motives for doing economics (Klamer 1984).
2 See, for example, the ones by Kindleberger (1991) and Milton and Rose Friedman (1980) about their own lives, by Skidelsky on John Maynard Keynes (1983, 1992, 2000), and Erwin Dekker (2021) on Jan Tinbergen.

References

Buchanan, J. and G. Tullock (1962) *The Calculus of Consent*, Michigan: The University of Michigan Press.

CW: see Keynes, J.M. (1971–1989).

Dekker, E. (2021) *The Life and Work of Jan Tinbergen: Model Economist*, Cambridge, UK: University of Cambridge Press.

Fama, E. (1970) 'Efficient capital markets: A review of theory and empirical work', *The Journal of Finance* 25 (2), 383–417.

Friedman, M. and R. Friedman (1980) *Free to Choose*, New York: Harcourt.

Galbraith, J. K. (1990) *A Tenured Professor*, New York: Houghton Mifflin Harcourt.

Keynes, J. M. (1931) *Essays in Persuasion*, *CW* IX.

Keynes, J. M. (1936) *The General Theory of Employment, Interest and Money*, *CW* VII.

Keynes, J. M. (1971–1989), *The Collected Writings of John Maynard Keynes*, D. E. Moggridge, ed., 30 vols, London: Macmillan and New York: St Martin's Press.

Kindleberger, C. (1991) *The Life of an Economist*, Oxford: Basil Blackwell.

Klamer, A. (1984) *Conversations with Economists*, Littlefield: Rowman and Allanheld.

Klamer, A., D. McCloskey and R. M. Solow (eds) (1988) *The Consequences of Economic Rhetoric*, Cambridge, UK: Cambridge University Press.

Klamer, A. (1989) 'An accountant among economists: Conservations with Sir John R. Hicks', *Journal of Economic Perspectives* 3 (4), 167–180.

Klamer, A. (2007) *Speaking of Economics: How to be in the Conversation*, London: Routledge.

Klamer, A. (2017) *Doing the Right Thing: A Value Based Economy*, London: Ubiquity Press.

Klamer, A. and D. C. Colander (1990) *The Making of an Economist*, Totoma: Westview Press.

McCloskey, D. N. (1983) 'The rhetoric of economics', *Journal of Economic Literature* 21 (2), 481–517.

McCloskey, D. N. (1985) *The Rhetoric of Economics*, Madison: University of Wisconsin Press.

McCloskey, D. N. (1990) *If You're So Smart: The Narrative of Economic Expertise*, Chicago, IL: University of Chicago Press.

McCloskey, D. N. (2007) *The Bourgeois Virtues: Ethics for an Age of Commerce*, Chicago, IL: Chicago University Press.

Mirowski, P. (1989) *More Heat than Light*, Cambridge, UK: Cambridge University Press.

Popper, K. (1956 [1934]) *The Logic of Scientific Discovery*, London: Julius Springer.

Reinhart, C. M. and K. Rogoff (2010) 'Growth in a time of debt', *American Economic Review: Papers and Proceedings* 100 (2), 573–8.

Robbins, L. (1932) *An Essay on the Nature and Significance of Economic Science*, London: MacMillan.

Robinson, J. (1964 [1962]) *Economic Philosophy*, Harmondsworth: Pelican Books.

Skidelsky, R. (1983) *John Maynard Keynes: Hopes Betrayed 1883–1920*, Volume I., London: MacMillan.

Skidelsky, R. (1992) *John Maynard Keynes: The Economist as Savior 1920–1937*, Volume II, New York: The Penguin Press.

Skidelsky, R. (2000) *John Maynard Keynes: Fighting for Britain 1937–1946*, Volume III, New York: MacMillan.

Szasz, A. (2001) *De Euro*, Amsterdam: Schilt Publishing.

Tinbergen, J. (1956) *Economic Policy: Principles and Design*, Amsterdam: North Holland.

Yalcintas, A. and E. S. Kosel (2021) *Word, Objects and Events in Economics: The Making of Economic Theory*, New York City: Springer.

Zuidhof, P. W. (2012) *Imagining Markets: The Discursive Politics of Neoliberalism*, Rotterdam: Erasmus Universiteit.

29

TEACHING MACROECONOMIC METHODOLOGY

Jan Holm Ingemann

Introduction

As a point of departure for this chapter, it is claimed that, in teaching macroeconomics, methodology should not be considered a theoretical, demarcated and abstract issue detached from macroeconomics and social context. The methodology should rather be considered on an integrated basis when macroeconomic problems are identified, described and understood.

Consequently, it is also claimed that it is meaningless just to implant macroeconomic methodology into the students. Reflection is a process, and our task as teachers is to assist the students in establishing and evolving a methodological space of reflection as a cumulative process nourished by open-minded analysis of real-life problems.

It is a general observation that one always has to start somewhere, and that 'somewhere' in this case is where the students find themselves. This trivial observation can easily be neglected when it comes to teaching macroeconomic methodology. In such a case, the initial situation is a student with no or at the best very limited knowledge concerning macroeconomics in general and macroeconomic methodology in particular.

From the claims above it also follows that we as teachers have to motivate the students to start a learning process where the need for methodological tools, insights and reflections is realised. Related to that challenge, it is argued here that the principles from problem-based learning (PBL) are tailor-made for this purpose. According to these principles, we should take our starting point in real, social problems and let them act as the pivot of academic learning. As a part of that process, students gradually realise the need for explicit methodological knowledge and reflection.

Hence, the teaching subsequently will have three beginnings related to the learning process of macroeconomic methodology: (1) a real problem in social surroundings that can be described, conceptualised and interpreted by means of macroeconomic theory; (2) the introduction of macroeconomic theory at a basic level; and (3) the introduction of macroeconomic methodology. These three beginnings should be serial more than parallel in time.

DOI: 10.4324/9781315745992-35

In the following paragraphs, the points above will be unfolded, first by providing a few fundamental characteristics of PBL and then by using some reflections and experience with teaching macroeconomics and macroeconomic methodology.

Problem-based learning (PBL)

PBL is a pedagogical model for learning at the university level (Kolmos et al. 2004, Krogh and Jensen 2013). In this model, the approach to learning is based on the following characteristics:

* *Exemplary*: learning by a hands-on analysis of real-life problems.
* *Realistic*: explaining and understanding real-life problems.
* *Critical*: being open to the fact that different perspectives and approaches have different capabilities and constraints.

Whatever society we are citizens in, our social surroundings are filled with real-life problems. We are confronted with these problems when we consult all kinds of media and when we discuss current life and social challenges with family, friends, neighbours, people at the pub and so forth. These real-life problems are examples of social problems or issues, and, amongst fellow citizens, they are discussed and conceptualised in everyday language and interpreted from citizens' different perspectives and notions. However, they are also examples reflecting functions, mechanisms, structures and institutions within the actual social context (Mills 2001). That is the exemplary part.

In the university context, the examples urge scholars to find social-scientific, including macroeconomic, interpretations. However, the everyday formulation of the problem will first have to be substituted with a scientific one that employs concepts from a relevant theory. This enables the use of scientific tools and methods. That is the realistic part, where the need for theory and the relevance of academic skills to be able to search for scientific interpretation are realised.

The final characteristic principle relates to the fact that a well-selected macroeconomic case or example could be used as an eye-opener for the students to see how important the choice of analytical principle (i.e. 'methodology') is for the outcome. Such an example could be the substantial element in a learning process as a movement from the immediately ascertainable facts to a deeper understanding of macroeconomics. In that process, different perspectives and heuristics will be offered, and amongst these some might be more relevant than others. The task then is to find the most satisfying and relevant method for the chosen example (Negt 1974). That is the critical part.

Bringing the three principles together in interplay, teachers create an educational experience where real-world problems guide the learning process and set a standard for pertinence within the cumulative process of building knowledge of the chosen subject and the methods used to analyse it. The problem should be a formulation of some phenomenon, development or challenge in the real world, such as the financial crisis, Brexit, the working poor, lockdown. The problem then structures the learning process, encouraging the student to ask the question: Which evidence, theoretical concepts, methods and so forth can support my efforts to reach better descriptions and deeper interpretations than the immediate observations? The proof of the pudding is that substantial elements and methods are experienced as pertinent when they contribute to a better explanation and/or understanding of the exemplary problem (Ingemann and Madsen 2019).

With these principles in mind, we shall now turn to more specific considerations related to macroeconomics and methodology.

Methodology and macroeconomics

According to this Handbook, methodology comprises (1) knowledge of different methods, (2) principles for the choice of method and (3) the consequences of this choice for the analytical outcome. This is a very clear and straightforward definition. However, from a teaching perspective – and considering the specific focus on macroeconomic methodology – this knowledge of methods and so forth is here seen as being closely related to a specific field of research, in this case macroeconomy, and also related to real-world problems, as Fullbrook (2007) has argued.

Macroeconomic methodology enables us to identify, describe and interpret macroeconomic problems in our social surroundings and subsequently to realise and learn. It is thus stated – in accordance with the PBL principles described above – those macroeconomic problems are not, in this teaching perspective, perceived as theoretical problems but as problems identifiable in reality. It is, for instance, *not* financial crisis *per se* (i.e. an abstract phenomenon) that we are aiming to analyse – that is what proper theory can help us do. Instead, it is *a* financial crisis in some specific area in the world at a specific actual or historical time that is our subject. Thus, macroeconomic methodology is knowledge assisting us in answering the question: How is it possible to understand the specific macroeconomic problem that has been chosen and hence contribute to a process of learning about reality?

However, while learning by means of real-world problems is stressed, it is not implied that we should neglect theory. Understanding the real world is the aim, while methodology, theory and empirical evidence are analytical prerequisites. In fact, macroeconomic methodology tells us how to perform analysis by allowing the real-world problem, theory and empirical evidence to interact. In other words, methodology implies epistemological assumptions (the understanding of how we can explain and/or understand the field of research). In addition, macroeconomic theory and the use of it imply certain ontological assumptions, that is, assumptions regarding the field of research (economics of society in a macroeconomic perspective, how we can conceptualise the elements, actors and relations). Therefore, epistemology and ontology will inevitably enter the picture.

However, this understanding of the epistemological basis as well as its relation to ontological assumptions does not necessarily need to be taught to the students in the initial phase. Contrary to conventional teaching, it is the assumption in PBL that the students should first grapple with problems they actually do not know how to grasp. This attempt will expose the need to learn and assimilate adequate tools, including theories and methodology (Ingemann and Madsen 2019).

It is also an implicit purpose of PBL to motivate the students by means of their immediate interest in their social surroundings as citizens (Mills 2001). The problem presents itself to the student as it occurs in an immediate form. The student is then encouraged to explore the available theories and methods in an open-minded and critical spirit. Thus, we are aiming to avoid putting the student into a methodological straitjacket, closing their eyes to new understandings (Feyerabend 1993) and limiting their efforts by a paradigmatic protective belt where crucial questions are abandoned (Lakatos 1978).

To sum up, we should in our teaching be aware of the need for macroeconomic methodology and the proper and adequate use of it. However, we should do so without teaching it to the students *ex ante*. Instead, we should invite them to do their own methodological reflections as possibilities emerge in general and *ex post* in particular.

Macroeconomic methodology on its own

The reflections *ex ante* and *ex post* during the explorative learning process will ideally impose a gradual recognition amongst the students of how important the choice of analytical method is. The *Methodenstreit* (Fusfeld 2008) is a very useful case for highlighting the importance of such choices. In brief, the debate was the first fundamental and explicit one on methodology in economics. The dispute is still very important and vivid as it involves fundamental disagreements and contrasting concepts related to the philosophy of science and their implications for macroeconomic methodology (e.g. fundamental differences in the use of micro and macro perspectives). Furthermore, the story concerning the battle is itself exciting, which helps to make the students engage in methodological thinking. Investigation into *Methodenstreit* exemplifies a fundamental introduction to the meaning and potential of methodology, as it represents the battle between two ideal-typical positions in economic methodology, outlined below.

The two positions represented a very radical conflict between Gustav von Schmoller and Carl Menger (Hodgson 2001; Milonakis and Fine 2009). The former was an advocate of the German Historical School, at that time the dominant paradigm, while the latter represented a new Austrian paradigm that subsequently initiated what was later baptised as the marginal revolution. The ontological, epistemological and methodological assumptions of the two positions were highly conflicting, and it is precisely in that conflict that we are able to illustrate the importance of avoiding the methodological straitjacket: A closed and narrow methodology implies a closed and narrow perspective on reality, closing your eyes to fruitful interpretation of your social surroundings. We should instead aim for open methodology (Lawson 1998; Chick 2004).

The German Historical School's ontology implied a conception of society in which the economy was considered an integrated part of a social governance and allocation system – that is, in a context which should embrace both time and space (in a geographical sense). This again implied an epistemology which emphasised the need to study the economy in context and employ a macro perspective. In this perspective, the state was included as an institution where various policy options are open and where the evolution can take different paths due to different decisions followed by different actions. Hence, policy-learning would make sense (Campbell et al. 2006).

In contrast, the (new) Austrian position was built upon an ontology advocating pure economy, where the latter was demarcated to a narrow field of economic allocation in a micro perspective, that is, the position was based on assumptions concerning isolated individuals striving to maximise individual utility. General social elements were excluded and looked upon as exogenous, and the maximisation was looked upon as an individual activity in an institutional vacuum where time and space did not matter. The epistemology accordingly focused on the isolated activity of individuals and was subsequently reduced to armchair economics built upon axiomatic assumptions and logical chains of reasoning *ceteris paribus*. According to this position, the state and, consequently, political action were irrelevant to the maximisation process of individual utility and should be delimited to actions without disturbance of the atomistic process.

The neoclassical impact on the evolution of economics as part of the social sciences was fortified during the 20th century (Lawson 1998). In this process, the change in the field of research was strengthened by Lionel Robbins (1932), who named the neoclassical ontology *pure economics* and epistemology *pure theory* in his definition of economics: economics is about allocation of scarce resources. Thus, the aim was rather seen to evolve techniques tailor-made to solve puzzles about allocation in various fields (Hodgson 2001; Milonakis and Fine 2009) based on closed-system thinking.

As pointed out above, the *Methodenstreit* illuminates two fundamentally different research procedures and demonstrates how essential the choice of methodological standpoint is. From the point of view of macroeconomics, the aim should be recognition of real-world problems, and, consequently, economics should be a crucial and open part of the social sciences rather than a laboratory for techniques to solve utility puzzles. In this connection, it is fortunate that the marginal revolution was met by the Keynesian counterrevolution (cf. Keynes 1936), which clarified the importance of the macro perspective, the context of time and space and in particular the importance of policy decisions. Thus, we can relate to a series of enlightening debates such as Keynes versus Tinbergen (on econometrics and models) and later Post-Keynesianism versus Monetarism, where it is obvious to state the importance of (1) methodological reflection and (2) context and reality. Similarly, the methodological basis has been further clarified by means of insights from critical realism that strengthen and explicate more implicit and unfinished solutions launched by the German Historical School. We will return to the latter milestone at the end of the chapter.

Methodology and real-life analysis

Above, the *Methodenstreit* was presented as a crucial example of the fundamental implications of methodological choices. In addition, real-world problems were emphasised as a key – in combination with adequate methodological choices – to enable students '*to see the world in a grain of sand*' (cf. the famous poem by William Blake) or, in this case, to enable students to understand macroeconomics at a deeper level with reality as the starting point. Thus, it is useful to be more specific about how we can understand the concept of reality and where it fits in our efforts to teach students about macroeconomic methodology.

In everyday understanding, reality is often regarded as being in contrast to theory. Menger saw reality as coincidental and confusing, while he instead pointed towards theory as pure and in line with a rationalist philosophy of science. Other paradigms point to empirical evidence as a reflection of reality and ask what can be measured, described and explained by means of quantitative methods, while reflection and conceptualisation tend to be seen as theory and in some ways in opposition to this empirical reality.

However, such understanding is here rejected as misleading from a realistic point of view. Meaningful theory cannot be without some kind of empirical substance – in the case of such absence, the concepts can only be used to categorise 'empty boxes', as noted in Joan Robinson's critique of neoclassical economists up to the 1929 crisis (Robinson 1971). On the other hand, meaningful empirical data cannot be thrown out in favour of theory; we need concepts to categorise reality and choose appropriate data as a foundation for interpretation. Hence, it is necessary to adopt a more dialectic understanding of the relationship between theory and empirical evidence. Of course, macroeconomic methodology – and the teaching of it – should be in accordance with this dual perspective.

The acceptance of the need for dialectics between theory and empirical evidence implies a methodological understanding of the process of creating knowledge and obtaining insight. But how do we tell the students to identify reality? Students will immediately tend to generalise from their own, individual, everyday perspective and thus be blind to the social perspective and the 'economy as a whole' – in other words they will tend to exclude the importance of context and hence of the structure of the actual society.

The German Historical School is once again useful as it can assist us in relating our immediate, individual experience to the general social context. It was the starting point for the paradigm that German capitalism was substantially different from British capitalism. The initial research problem was understanding the poor growth and lack of development of the German economy while the British economy was marked by growth in continuation of industrialisation. However, in realising substantial differences between the two economies, the Germans acknowledged that it would not be adequate just to copy the British path. Here, Schmoller and his predecessors as well as inheritors pointed towards context as the fundamental concept to characterise reality. In line with American institutionalists like Veblen and Commons (Hodgson 2001), context was seen as the key to understanding economies and how they differ, evolve and can be managed – an insight that Keynes (1936) so groundbreakingly formulated in his own way with his emphasis on macroeconomy.

Context is located in historical time and geographical space. Economies in Northern and Southern Europe differ as much as Northern economies now differ from Northern economies 50 years ago.

Context consists of the various aims and systems of interpretation on which institutions are based and which constitute the framework within which social interactions take place. We can use macroeconomic methodology (as outlined below) to help us identify the salient features of the context and its implications. We can then construct theory based on empirical evidence. The evidence must be based upon meaningful concepts and relations between the concepts (that is, theory), and theory must contain concepts and relations that conform to the reality that we are able, directly or indirectly, to identify and perceive. This establishes the dialectical relationship between perception and conception mentioned above.

By means of the *Methodenstreit*, we have been able to answer questions concerning what macroeconomic methodology is about and why it is so crucial to make proper methodological choices. The obvious next step is to answer the question concerning how to use proper methodology in practice. It is here that it is most useful to draw upon insights from critical realism.

How to choose macroeconomic method? A general answer

Critical realism has helped social scientists in general and macroeconomists in particular to be aware of methodological challenges that exist; it is also fruitful, as it reveals possibilities for overcoming these challenges. Critical realism is a philosophy of science based on a realistic ontological basis, and then widens that basis to better encompass the complexity of human activity in a specific context.

The epistemological basis is widened as well, taking into consideration that observation and empirical data are necessary prerequisites for understanding reality. But they are not sufficient. Fundamental causes, mechanisms, institutions, structures and so forth do not meet the eye and cannot be registered by other human senses. To use the analogy of an iceberg, you can see the tip, but you cannot (at least not immediately) use your senses to realise what is beneath the surface of the water.

Thus, methodology – and the mix of methods we need to employ in our epistemic efforts – must be wide-ranging. We cannot delimit our efforts to observing and taking measures of the world in the form of quantitative and qualitative evidence, nor can we just sit in an armchair speculating over abstract puzzles. We need to find the modus to put the methods in synergetic interplay, taking our starting point in reality and referring to that (only partly observable) reality in our efforts gradually to reach better descriptions, explanations and understandings.

The critical realist epistemology, based upon the ontology of our complex world, is made operational in three strata, as follows:

- Empirical observation and description
- Search for incidents and patterns
- Interpretation: Explanation and understanding of underlying mechanisms and context

This process may serve as a useful description of the main elements of the organising pattern for both analytical application and teaching macroeconomic methodology.

In the upper stratum, we search for empirical evidence, e.g. some kind of data that in an immediate sense is able to describe our case or problem in a real-world context. The middle stratum opens up an explorative analysis in search of incidents and patterns in the social reality described by means of our empirical observations and the context in which our case or problem is embedded. The underlying, deep stratum represents the final interpretation of what we explored in the two upper strata with the aim of enabling us to explain and understand what we have discovered and described by means of the two upper strata.

The two upper strata are observable by means of our human senses. Thus, we can make use of data and induction when we investigate them. On the other hand, the lower stratum is not observable by means of our senses – at least not in any immediate sense. In the latter, we thus need to make use of various kinds of rationalisation and imagination and, consequently, be more deductive in our methods. In addition, it is worth mentioning that the former paragraphs depict an ideal-typical description of the epistemic process: for teaching reasons it is always necessary to idealise and exaggerate to be clear. Carried out in praxis, the strata will have more blurred boundaries, and the process will have an iterative nature.

Finally, it is necessary to further elaborate on context. The three strata provide an excellent structure for understanding the process by which we are able to reach a deeper understanding of real-life problems. However, for teaching purposes we need to be specific and explicit in revealing how the concept of context should be

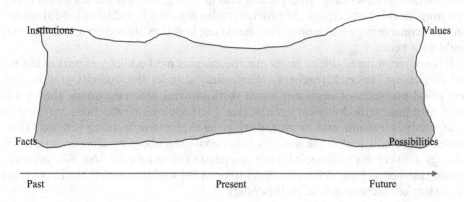

Figure 29.1 Reality and context.
Source: Based on Ingemann (2019).

understood and, thus, what kind of substance we should include in the research and learning process. A possible specification is presented in Figure 29.1.

The figure should be interpreted so that we assume a case or problem in reality. The context of this case can be described by means of horizontal and vertical axes where reality is stretched between four corners. The horizontal axis represents time or history: past, present and future. The bottom part of the vertical axis refers to context that you are able to relate to in an objective manner. In the past it is facts, and consequently it represents dimensions that we are able to observe; in the future it is possibility where these facts can evolve, limited by objective constraints. In the upper part of the vertical axis, social values are considered. In the past, social decisions have been made and actions taken based upon institutions that gave meaning to social groups. Pointing to the future, the institutions can evolve according to values underlying and directing future decisions and actions. The future is seen in the critical realist perspective; it '*offers the possibility of human* emancipation *through* structural transformation' (Lawson 1998, p. 277).

The process of recognition as described above implies that analytical considerations are deeply rooted in real-life problems. In this process, theory should provide heuristic tools enabling scholars to conceptualise real-life macroeconomic problems and to suggest further solutions.

Summary

Macroeconomics is about real-world economics, and macroeconomics should consequently be aimed at describing and interpreting the real world and thereby enable us as well as our fellow citizens to understand it better in order to influence it politically in a struggle for the common good. Macroeconomic methodology, thus, should enable us to describe, interpret and affect that which takes place around us.

When we are teaching macroeconomic methodology, we should know where we are going. We have a mission, and that is to help the students learn how to apply macroeconomic analysis to real-world settings. The mission is not about macroeconomic methodology in its own right but to enable us as economists to improve our contribution to describing, interpreting and affecting the real-life social economy. Teaching, in this respect, should provide students with a foundation for current reflections concerning what economists should do, how they should do it and how they could do it better.

It is not recommendable to teach macroeconomic methodology as part of the initial curriculum. Instead, teachers are encouraged to let the students grapple with real-world problems or cases and assist them in using macroeconomic theory and tools, avoiding methodological straitjackets. Methodological reflections are inherent to an analysis, *ex ante* and *ex post*, during the explorative learning process. Thus, students gradually realise the need for being conscious about macroeconomic methodology. During this process, it is recommended to introduce the *Methodenstreit* and ensuing methodological debates in order to open the students' eyes to the importance and extent of macroeconomic methodology.

References

Campbell, J. L., J. A. Hall and O. K. Pedersen (2006) *National Identity and the Varieties of Capitalism: The Danish Case*, Copenhagen: DJØF Publishing.

Chick, V. (2004) 'On open systems', *Brazilian Journal of Political Economy* 24 (1), 3–16.

Feyerabend, P. (1993) *Against Method*, London: Verso.

Fullbrook, E. (2007), 'Introduction', in E. Fullbrook, ed., *Real World Economics: A Post-Autistic Economics Reader*, London: Anthem Press, pp. 1–10.

Fusfeld, D. R. (2008) 'Methodenstreit', in S. N. Durlauf and L. E. Blume, eds., *The New Palgrave Dictionary of Economics*, Second edition, London: Palgrave Macmillan, pp. 4179–80.

Hodgson, G. M. (2001), *How Economics Forgot History: The Problem of Historical Specificity in Social Science*, London: Routledge.

Ingemann, J. H. (2019), 'Lost and Found – om virkelighed og samfundsøkonomisk videnskab', in P. Nielsen, T. B. Dyhrberg and A. B. Hansen, eds, *Økonomi på tværs – festskrift til Jesper Jespersen*, Frederiksberg: Frydenlund Academic, pp. 113–27.

Ingemann, J. H. and P. T. Madsen (2019) 'Problem-based learning and mainstream economics – post-Keynesian economics to the rescue?', in J. Jespersen and F. Olesen, eds, *Progressive Post-Keynesian Economics: Dealing with Reality*, Cheltenham: Edward Elgar, pp. 143–54.

Keynes, J. M. (1936) *The General Theory of Employment, Interest and Money*. London: Macmillan.

Kolmos, A., F. K. Fink and L. Krogh (2004) *The Aalborg PBL Model: Progress, Diversity and Challenges*, Aalborg: Aalborg Universitetsforlag.

Krogh, L. and A. A. Jensen (eds) (2013) *Visions, Challenges, and Strategies: PBL Principles and Methodologies in a Danish and Global Perspective*, Aalborg: Aalborg University Press.

Lakatos, I. (1978) *The Methodology of Scientific Research Programmes*, Cambridge, UK: Cambridge University Press.

Lawson, T. (1998) *Economics and Reality*, London: Routledge.

Mills, C. W. (2001) *Sociological Imagination*, Oxford: Oxford University Press.

Milonakis, D. and B. Fine (2009) *From Political Economy to Economics Method, the Social and the Historical in the Evolution of Economic Theory*, London: Routledge.

Negt, O. (1974) *Soziologisches Phantasie und Exemplarisches Lernen*, Frankfurt Am Main: Europäisches Verlagsanstalt.

Robbins, L. (1932) *An Essay on the Nature and Significance of Economic Science*. London: Macmillan.

Robinson, J. (1971) *Economic Heresies: Some Old-Fashioned Questions in Economic Theory*, London: Macmillan.

NAME INDEX

Note: Page numbers followed by "n" denote endnotes.

349

INDEX

Note: **Bold** page numbers refer to tables; *italic* page numbers refer to figures and page numbers followed by "n" denote endnotes.

Printed in the United States
by Baker & Taylor Publisher Services

Printed in the United States
by Baker & Taylor Publisher Services